Handbook of
MEDIA ECONOMICS

Handbook of
MEDIA ECONOMICS

Volume 1A

Edited by

SIMON P. ANDERSON
Commonwealth Professor of Economics,
University of Virginia,
Charlottesville, VA, USA

JOEL WALDFOGEL
Frederick R. Kappel Chair in Applied Economics,
Carlson School of Management,
University of Minnesota, Minneapolis, MN, USA

DAVID STRÖMBERG
IIES, Stockholm University, Stockholm, Sweden

ELSEVIER

Amsterdam • Boston • Heidelberg • London • New York • Oxford
Paris • San Diego • San Francisco • Singapore • Sydney • Tokyo
North-Holland is an imprint of Elsevier

North-Holland is an imprint of Elsevier

Radarweg 29, PO Box 211, 1000 AE Amsterdam, The Netherlands
The Boulevard, Langford Lane, Kidlington, Oxford OX5 1GB, UK

British Library Cataloguing-in-Publication Data
A catalogue record for this book is available from the British Library

Library of Congress Cataloging-in-Publication Data
A catalog record for this book is available from the Library of Congress

ISBN: 978-0-444-62721-6 (Vol. 1A)
ISBN: 978-0-444-63685-0 (Vol. 1B)

For information on all North-Holland publications
visit our website at http://store.elsevier.com/

ELSEVIER • Book Aid International

Working together
to grow libraries in
developing countries

www.elsevier.com • www.bookaid.org

Publisher: Nikki Levy
Acquisition Editor: J. Scott Bentley
Editorial Project Manager: Joslyn Chaiprasert-Paguio
Production Project Manager: Nicky Carter
Designer: Alan Studholme

Typeset by SPi Global, India
Printed and bound in the UK

INTRODUCTION TO THE SERIES

The aim of the *Handbooks in Economics* series is to produce Handbooks for various branches of economics, each of which is a definitive source, reference, and teaching supplement for use by professional researchers and advanced graduate students. Each Handbook provides self-contained surveys of the current state of a branch of economics in the form of chapters prepared by leading specialists on various aspects of this branch of economics. These surveys summarize not only received results but also newer developments, from recent journal articles and discussion papers. Some original material is also included, but the main goal is to provide comprehensive and accessible surveys. The Handbooks are intended to provide not only useful reference volumes for professional collections but also possible supplementary readings for advanced courses for graduate students in economics.

Kenneth J. Arrow and Michael D. Intriligator

CONTENTS

Volume 1B

INTRODUCTION

Media markets are special in many ways, and they take on an importance that is much larger than their accounting contribution to GDP. First, on the consumer side, is the astonishingly large fraction of leisure time devoted to them. Second, on the advertiser side, they provide a conduit for firms to get consumers to buy goods, which supports employment in the advertising industries and may foster economic growth by enabling innovations to be brought quickly and profitably to market and rewarding risk-taking. Third, the media plays a very special role in providing information on current events and politics. However, the media by necessity systematically filters and biases this information. How much and which information is transmitted is likely to affect wide range of political, economic, and social outcomes, including political accountability, corporate accountability, financial market performance, and educational and family choices. Because of these effects, the media is a particular industry that is specifically regulated in the constitutions of most democratic (and nondemocratic) countries.

Foremost, perhaps is the paramount role of informing the electorate, arising largely as an externality to news consumption. In terms of market performance, media markets may embody several key features that give rise to specific types of market failure. Many media have relatively high fixed costs and low marginal costs, and hence a paucity of equilibrium product offerings, leading to preference externalities in content provision whereby majority groups' tastes tend to be catered at the expense of minorities. This news bias also alters the trade-off in political competition and therefore introduces a bias in public policy against the interest of minority groups. Moreover, the business model of advertising finance is that of a two-sided market with media outlets (platforms) delivering eyeballs to sell to advertisers, which is a quite different market structure from traditional market interactions.

This volume (1A and 1B) contains 19 chapters on the state of the art on the economics of media. These chapters are divided broadly into three parts.

Part I. Media market structure and performance, covering theory and methodology.

Chapter 1 explores the implications of the high fixed costs and heterogeneous consumer preferences endemic to media markets and the ensuing preference externalities in media markets. Both the positive and the normative economics are developed through a suite of theoretical models that are then illuminated empirically.

Chapter 2 covers the theory of two-sided markets as it relates to media markets. Platforms realize a two-sided balance between the two sides, and in competition with each other. The extent of consumer (viewer) multihoming is a key driver of positive predictions. Advertising revenues ultimately underwrite programming content, and this feature impacts performance measures from static market efficiency through genre choice and equilibrium variety.

Chapter 3 reviews the techniques of empirical industrial economics most helpful for the study of media markets. The chapter includes an extensive discussion of demand modeling, as well as entry modeling. The chapter takes a more methodological approach than others in the volume.

Much of the media sector is dependent on advertising for revenue. Chapter 4 takes a detailed look (primarily theoretical) at the background to the economics of advertising. It develops various conceptual roles that advertising may take, and it draws out the consequences for evaluating the surplus associated to advertising. This is a key ingredient to evaluating the performance of ad-financed media.

Chapter 5 takes a primarily marketing perspective to describe audience behavior and consumer response to ads. It discusses recent innovations such as advertising avoidance, advertising targeting and personalization, and reviews how the landscape has changed over the last decade.

Chapter 6 explores merger policy and regulation of media industries. These industries require a dedicated analysis distinct from standard markets because of their two-sided nature and because of their pivotal place in providing information. The chapter exposits the extant theory, delivers some empirical evidence on the consequences of mergers, and discusses recent cases.

Part II. Industry sectors, covering the economics of particular media industries. The first three chapters of this part give historical background and empirical results on various pertinent aspects, with special emphasis on the US landscape. The last three chapters of this part address various facets of the economics of the Internet.

Chapter 7 surveys the economics of television, the dominant entertainment medium for most consumers. The chapter describes incentives for production and consumption of content, recent trends in television and online video markets, and the state of economic research on these industries. Topics emphasized include pay television, vertical relations, the role of public television, and growing online video.

Chapter 8 on radio pays special attention to the effects of recent consolidation in the United States. It also addresses the impact of the public sector and findings on the extent of overentry in the sector. Another contribution is to depict the interaction between the music and radio industries.

Chapter 9 on newspaper and magazines describes the history and structure of print markets in the United States. The chapter discusses these sectors in the context of two-sided markets. It includes discussions of whether or not advertising is a net nuisance to print media consumers, antitrust issues in print markets, and the effect of the Internet on these sectors.

Chapter 10 on media economics of the Internet is a primarily theoretical synthesis of recent key advances as applied to this emergent sector. The chapter includes discussion of such pertinent aspects as aggregators, search engines, and Internet service providers.

Chapter 11 covers the topic of privacy and the Internet, which has been an issue of much public concern and debate. A conceptual framework is developed and related to empirical estimates. Further topics include advertising, social networks, data security, and government surveillance.

Chapter 12 addresses user-generated content and social media. It covers an eclectic set of applications in a fast-moving sector, and pays particular attention to determining the quality of the content.

Part III: The political economy of mass media, covering the effects of media on political, economic, and social outcomes. Chapters 13–17 discuss the media's political coverage, bias and capture, and the resulting effects on political accountability. Chapter 18 covers effects in finance and Chapter 19 covers effects on social outcomes.

Chapter 13 presents a baseline model of how the information filtering caused by media coverage affects political accountability. It discusses the welfare consequences of private provision of news as well as regulation to solve the problem of underprovision of news. The model also supplies an array of testable implications, used to organize the existing empirical work. The key questions are: what drives media coverage of politics; how does this coverage influence government policy, the actions and selection of politicians, and the information levels and voting behavior of the public?

Chapter 14 discusses how bias may reduce the informativeness of media, undermining its positive role for political accountability. It surveys the theoretical literature on the market forces that determine media bias. A simple model is used to organize the literature on the determinants of bias, focusing first on supply-side forces such as political preferences of media owners, and then turning to demand-side forces working through consumer beliefs and preferences. The chapter defines bias, analyzes its welfare consequences and how these are affected by, for example, competition.

Chapter 15 surveys empirical studies of media bias, with a focus on partisan and ideological biases. The chapter discusses the methods used to measure media bias, the main factors found to be correlated with media bias and measures of the persuasive impact of media bias on citizens' attitudes and behavior.

Chapter 16 surveys models of media capture and media power. In both cases, media sources deliberately deviate from truthful reporting in order to affect electoral outcomes. The chapter speaks of media capture when the government has an active role in capturing the media, and media power when media organizations distort news reporting for political ends. The chapter discusses theories of when news manipulation is more likely to succeed and electoral outcomes are more likely to be distorted. It discusses how media regulation can reduce the extent of these two phenomena.

Chapter 17 surveys the empirical literature on the determinants and the consequences of media capture. It reviews the literature on the determinants of media capture. It discusses the methods used to control media, and examines the evidence on the effect of media capture on media content. Next, it presents evidence on the effects of captured media on the behavior of people, as well as the effects of independent media in captured environment. It concludes by discussing the factors that limit the effect of propaganda.

Chapter 18 reviews and synthesizes a rapidly growing subfield that analyzes the relation between media and financial markets. The chapter discusses theories of the role of information provided by media in financial markets. It describes new data and methods that have enabled powerful tests of theories and have the potential to address longstanding puzzles in finance, such as why trading volume and stock price volatility are so high. The chapter presents evidence on, for example, the effect of the volume and content of media coverage on market activity and stock prices.

Chapter 19 reviews the literature on the impact of media exposure on a wide net of social and economic outcomes: education, family choices, labor and migration decisions, environmental choices, health, crime, public economics, attitudes, consumption and savings, and development economics. It stresses five themes: (i) the key role of the demand for entertainment; (ii) the importance of crowding out of alternative activities (substitution effect); (iii) identification of causal effects—credible estimates are available for some topics and media but not for others; (iv) effects may differ by type of media; and (v) both the substitution effect and the demand for entertainment play an important role for the policy impacts.

Simon P. Anderson
Joel Waldfogel
David Strömberg

CONTRIBUTORS

Simon P. Anderson
Commonwealth Professor of Economics, University of Virginia, Charlottesville, VA, USA

Steven T. Berry
David Swensen Professor of Economics, Yale University, New Haven, CT, USA

Ambarish Chandra
Department of Management, University of Toronto at Scarborough and
Rotman School of Management, University of Toronto, Toronto, Ontario, Canada

Gregory S. Crawford
Department of Economics, University of Zürich, and CEPR, Zurich, Switzerland

Stefano DellaVigna
University of California, Berkeley and NBER, Cambridge, MA, USA

Ruben Enikolopov
Icrea-Barcelona Institute of Political Economy and Governance; Universitat Pompeu Fabra,
Barcelona, Spain; Barcelona Graduate School of Economics, Barcelona, Spain, and The New
Economic School, Moscow, Russia

Øystein Foros
NHH Norwegian School of Economics, Bergen, Norway

Matthew Gentzkow
Department of Economics, Stanford University, Palo Alto, CA, USA, and NBER, Cambridge,
MA, USA

Bruno Jullien
Toulouse School of Economics, Toulouse, France

Ulrich Kaiser
Department of Business Administration, Chair for Entrepreneurship, University of Zurich,
Zurich, Switzerland; Centre for European Economic Research, Mannheim, Germany; Centre
for Industrial Economics at the University of Copenhagen, Copenhagen, Denmark, and Institute
for the Study of Labor, Bonn, Germany

Hans Jarle Kind
NHH Norwegian School of Economics, Bergen, Norway

Eliana La Ferrara
Bocconi University and IGIER, Milan, Italy

Michael Luca
Harvard Business School, Boston, MA, USA

Martin Peitz
Department of Economics, University of Mannheim, Mannheim, Germany

Maria Petrova
Icrea-Barcelona Institute of Political Economy and Governance; Universitat Pompeu Fabra, Barcelona, Spain; Barcelona Graduate School of Economics, Barcelona, Spain, and The New Economic School, Moscow, Russia

Andrea Prat
Columbia University, New York, NY, USA

Riccardo Puglisi
Department of Political and Social Sciences, Università degli Studi di Pavia, Pavia, Italy

Markus Reisinger
Department of Economics, Frankfurt School of Finance & Management, Frankfurt, Germany

Régis Renault
PSL, Université Paris Dauphine, LEDa, Paris, France

Jesse M. Shapiro
NBER, Cambridge, MA, USA, and Department of Economics, Brown University, Providence, RI, USA

James M. Snyder Jr.
Department of Government, Harvard University, and NBER, Cambridge, MA, USA

Lars Sørgard
NHH Norwegian School of Economics, Bergen, Norway

Daniel F. Stone
Department of Economics, Bowdoin College, Brunswick, ME, USA

David Strömberg
IIES, Stockholm University, Stockholm, Sweden

Andrew Sweeting
Department of Economics, University of Maryland, College Park, MD, USA

Paul C. Tetlock
Columbia University, New York, NY, USA

Catherine E. Tucker
MIT Sloan School of Management and NBER, Cambridge, MA, USA

Joel Waldfogel
Frederick R. Kappel Chair in Applied Economics, Carlson School of Management, University of Minnesota, Minneapolis, MN, USA

Kenneth C. Wilbur
Rady School of Management, University of California, San Diego, CA, USA

ACKNOWLEDGMENT

Simon Anderson gratefully acknowledges the NSF for their support.

DEDICATION

We dedicate this Volume to our respective wives, children, and parents.

PART I

Media Market Structure and Performance

CHAPTER 1

Preference Externalities in Media Markets

Simon P. Anderson*, Joel Waldfogel[†]

*Commonwealth Professor of Economics, University of Virginia, Charlottesville, VA, USA
[†]Frederick R. Kappel Chair in Applied Economics, Carlson School of Management, University of Minnesota, Minneapolis, MN, USA

Contents

Handbook of Media Economics, Volume 1A
ISSN 2213-6630, http://dx.doi.org/10.1016/B978-0-444-62721-6.00001-9

Abstract

Media industries typically exhibit two fundamental features, high fixed costs and heterogeneity of consumer preferences. Daily newspaper markets, for example, tend to support a single product. In other examples, such as radio broadcasting, markets often support multiple differentiated offerings. Both contexts can deliver preference externalities, when the options and well-being for consumers depend on the number and mix of consumers according to their content preferences. This chapter presents evidence on these fundamental features of media markets. We then incorporate these features into a suite of theoretical models to obtain both a description of media markets as well as predictions for how they would be expected to function. In Section 1.3, we turn to "results," i.e., empirical evidence on the questions illuminated by the theoretical models. We then explore the effects of technological change, and we suggest directions for future work.

Keywords

Preference externalities, Media markets, Differentiation, Entry, Broadcasting

JEL Codes

D43, L13, L82

1.1. INTRODUCTION

One of the basic intuitions about markets implicit in many elementary discussions—and explicit in the work of Friedman (1962)—is that markets, unlike political decision processes, avoid the tyranny of the majority. "Each man can vote, as it were, for the color of tie he wants and get it; he does not have to see what color the majority wants and then, if he is in the minority, submit" (p. 15). To say this another way, the products that a consumer gets from the market depend only on his own preferences and means, but they do not depend on the preferences of others. Yet, when fixed costs are substantial, this intuition is not correct. Consumers get products that they find appealing only to the extent that others share their preferences, giving rise to a phenomenon one might term "preference externalities" and which we define more precisely below.

Preference externalities are common in media markets for three reasons. First, media products tend to have high—and almost exclusively—fixed costs. In the absence of fixed costs then the market could provide a continuum of products catering to diverse preferences. That is, every taste type could have its own tailored service, provided at marginal cost (Mussa and Rosen, 1978, deliver a "quality" model along these lines). Then there is no preference externality problem, and no worry about product selection distortion. Of course, fixed costs are not zero, and whether a market is served at all depends on whether a firm or firms can extract sufficient net revenues to cover entry costs. A second important feature of media markets is that the structure of preferences differs substantially across groups of consumers. Men and women tend to prefer different types of media products, as do young and older people, as do blacks and whites, as well as Hispanics versus non-Hispanics. Preference cleavages are not by any means limited to the distinctions among

US consumer groups. The different linguistic groups within Europe, for example, provide excellent additional examples. The more that preferences differ across groups, the less that entry targeting one group will benefit members of another group. The more heterogeneous is the population in terms of tastes for different varieties, and the more intense the willingness to pay for different variants (and the less substitutable are the variants for consumers), the more types will be produced.[1]

Finally, in many media markets advertising finance is the sole, or at least a major, source of revenues. This means that if advertising demand is weak, then the market may not be served. This could be a major problem in market provision (and hence a role for government intervention, for example, with a public broadcaster) in less developed nations, or in other contexts in which audiences have insufficient commercial value to advertisers to cover costs with revenue. When the market is served, markets provide content appealing to consumers whom advertisers covet rather than content appealing to consumers themselves, giving rise to another reason why the content one faces might depend on the preferences of others.

Prominent examples of media markets with preference externalities are newspapers, radio and television stations, magazines, and various kinds of web properties. The way that preference externalities operate depends largely on the magnitude of fixed costs in relation to market size and, consequently, the number of products in the market. At one extreme are daily local newspaper markets, many of which are literal monopolies. If consumers affect each other in daily newspaper markets, it will be through the quality and positioning of the sole product. Local radio markets, with about 20 products per market across large US metropolitan areas, provide a contrasting example. With multiple products in the market, groups of consumers with heterogeneous tastes can affect each other by bringing forth additional products that may, or may not, appeal across groups.

This chapter lays out a framework for thinking about media products embodying fixed costs, heterogeneity of consumer preferences and product differentiation, and advertiser finance. First, we present some evidence on a few primitives: that making products available has significant fixed costs, how preferences differ across groups, and the important role of advertiser rather than user finance of products. We then incorporate these features into a suite of theoretical models to obtain both a description of media markets as well as predictions for how they would be expected to function. For example, how does the mix of consumers, by preference groups, affect the targeting of the product or products, as well as the well-being of market participants? How does market size affect entry and welfare? How do market outcomes relate to optimal configurations? We use these models both to illuminate how preference externalities operate in media markets as well as how ongoing changes in technology—reducing entry costs relative to market

---

[1] Preference externalities are not specific to media markets and can arise whenever fixed costs are high and preferences differ across groups of consumers. See, for example, Bhattacharya and Packalen (2008, 2011) and Chevalier et al. (2008). Related issues arise in Handbury (2011), Haurin and Rosenthal (2009), Rosenthal and Strange (2004), Choi and Bell (2011), as well as Cutler et al. (2008).

size—would be expected to change media markets. In Section 1.3 we turn to "results," i.e., empirical evidence on the questions illuminated by the theoretical models. We discuss empirical results on entry and preference externalities that speak to the predictions, we discuss the effects of technological change, and we suggest directions for future work.

1.2. FIXED COSTS AND HETEROGENEOUS PREFERENCES

1.2.1 Fixed Costs

Media outlets, such as newspapers and radio and television stations, have cost structures that are predominantly fixed. The cost of putting together a daily newspaper is based mostly on the staff of reporters and editors, and this cost does not vary directly with the number of copies produced (although a newspaper with more content might attract more readers). To a varying degree across different sorts of media products, these fixed costs are large, in the sense that markets can support few, or sometimes only one, product(s). In the late 1990s the *Columbus Dispatch*, the major newspaper serving a metropolitan area of roughly 3 million people, had 69 reporters and editors. At the same time, the *New York Times*, serving the 22 million person metro area around New York, had about 300 reporters and editors.[2] According to the Bureau of Labor Statistics, reporters and editors earn an average of $44,000 per year.[3] Hence, the annual fixed cost of putting together content at these two papers was roughly $3 million and $13 million respectively. Radio stations have a similar cost structure, although their absolute level of fixed costs is much lower than for newspapers. One cost estimate for a rudimentary religious radio station puts the annual cost of operation at $142,000 per year.[4] Typical radio stations have more employees, including at least six on-air personalities, as well as other managers, sales staff, and engineers, bringing their costs of operation to about $650,000 per year according to one estimate (without interest service on a license).[5] The budget of a public radio station serving Garden City, Kansas (population 26,000) was reportedly $1 million in 2014.[6] The marginal cost of serving an additional listener to a radio station is, of course, zero.

These estimates are of course rough, but they provide clear substantiation of high fixed costs: it's clear that the availability of these media products depends on many others also wanting them.

---

[2] See http://www.census.gov/population/cen2000/phc-t3/tab03.txt for 2000 population and Burrelle's Media Directory for information on newspaper staff size.

[3] See http://www.bls.gov/oes/current/oes273022.htm.

[4] http://www.christianradiohome.com/operating_costs.asp.

[5] http://en.allexperts.com/q/Radio-Industry-2499/2008/10/radio-station-budget.htm.

[6] Brad Cooper. "State Subsidy to Kansas Public Broadcasting Could Disappear." *Kansas City Star*, April 29, 2014   http://www.kansascity.com/news/government-politics/article347706/State-subsidy-to-Kansas-public-broadcasting-could-disappear.html.

1.2.2 Preference Heterogeneity

Theoretical characterizations of preferences commonly represent them as smooth distributions, such as consumers whose preference for some one-dimensional characteristic (such as the sweetness of cider) is distributed uniformly between, say, a and b. Such characterizations are of course useful for the development of tractable models, but they seem to miss much of the nature of preference heterogeneity in reality, particularly for media products.

For example, in the US, blacks and whites have starkly different preferences over most sorts of media products. The broadcasting industry tends to divide its radio stations into about 30 station types targeting different sorts of consumers. These formats include categories like "top 40" (or "contemporary hit radio"), "album-oriented rock," "adult alternative," "country," and so on. Some formats, such as those with "urban" or "black" in their names, are targeted explicitly at African American listeners. Racial differences in listening by format are stark. The most popular format overall is country music, which attracts 12% of listening among non-blacks. Yet, country music attracts only 1.5% of black listeners, so that the audience for country music is 97% non-black (see Waldfogel, 2003). At the other end of the spectrum, stations whose format names include the word "black" (such as "black/adult contemporary" or "black/oldies") attract less than 3% of non-black listening and almost 60% of black listening, producing audiences that are about 90% black. Blacks and whites have starkly different preferences in radio programming.[7]

Hispanics and non-Hispanics, too, have starkly different preferences in radio programming. Stations broadcasting in Spanish attract roughly 50% of Hispanic listeners in the US markets with substantial Hispanic populations. These same stations attract only trace amounts of non-Hispanic listening.

Preference differences are not limited to radio. Newspaper and television preferences also differ by race. In markets with two daily papers—typically a broadsheet and a tabloid—the market share of the broadsheet is generally much larger in heavily white neighborhoods, which is suggestive of preferences that differ by race. While black and white television viewers both rank some television programming highly—such as football—many television shows that are top-rated among whites are often bottom-rated among blacks. For example, in 1998 when *Seinfeld* was the top-rated show among whites, it was ranked 50th among black viewers, while the comedy *"Between Brothers"* was ranked first among blacks and 112th among whites.[8]

Preferences also differ by gender and age. In 1993 less than 1% of listeners below age 45 listened to stations in the big band/nostalgia format, while these stations attracted 14% of listeners over age 65. By contrast, top 40 stations attracted 38% of under-18 listening,

---

[7] See also Aldrich et al. (2005).
[8] See James Sterngold. "A Racial Divide Widens on Network TV." *New York Times*, December 29, 1998.

while such stations attracted less than 2% of over-65 listening. Album-oriented rock stations attracted 20% of male listening but only 10% of female listening.[9] Two points bear emphasis, however. First, these preference differences tend not to be as stark as those differences by race and Hispanic status. Second, while preferences differ across groups, the share of population does not differ much across markets according to age or gender, while the black and Hispanic shares vary greatly. This is important because the mechanisms we'll study—entry and consumption in response to population—are visible only by way of comparisons across markets.

While the shares of population by gender and age are quite similar across metropolitan areas, the shares of population in minority groups with different preferences for media content vary substantially. Across the top 100 US metro areas in 1993, the median black share was 6.3%, while the median Hispanic share was 2.1%. The metro area at the 90th percentile of the black share distribution was just under a quarter black, while the metro area at the 10th percentile was just under 1% black. The 90th percentile Hispanic share was 21%, while the 10th percentile Hispanic share was under 1%. These magnitudes of variation in the mix of consumers with different media product preferences raise the possibility of detecting impacts of preference group sizes on product targeting and consumption.

Just as preferences vary across demographic and ethnic groups within the United States, preferences for some kinds of media products vary across national groups. While German, French, and American consumers have access to almost all of the same music and movies, their consumption patterns are starkly different. Music consumption in each country exhibits a substantial amount of home bias: 29% of French consumption is domestic, while only 3% of German consumption is French; 21% of German consumption is domestic music, while less than 2% of French consumption is German. Much of the difference in consumption patterns stems from language: Austrians consume German music at elevated rates, Belgians listen to French music, and vice versa. Two repertoires that all destinations consume at elevated rates are those of Great Britain and the United States, which make up 10–30% of consumption and 30–60% of consumption outside of their home markets.[10] We see very similar patterns in cross-national tastes for movies.[11]

It is a widespread phenomenon in media markets that preferences differ, sometimes starkly, across groups. And the mix of different preference groups differs across place, raising the possibility of both the operation and detection of preference externalities.

---

[9] See table 5, p. 40, Joel Waldfogel, 1999. "Preference Externalities: An Empirical Study of Who Benefits Whom in Differentiated Product Markets." NBER Working Papers 7391, National Bureau of Economic Research, Inc.

[10] See Aguiar and Waldfogel (2014) and Ferreira and Waldfogel (2013).

[11] See Ferreira et al. (2013).

1.2.3 Willingness to Consume Second-Choice Products

While consumers from many groups prefer one sort of media product to another, there is also fairly clear evidence that consumers are, in many cases, willing to consume a second-choice product—rather than forgoing consumption in the category altogether—when a more desired product is not available. Consider again the example of race and radio in the US. Waldfogel (1999) documents that while black listeners clearly prefer black-targeted programming, blacks continue to listen to the radio nearly as much in markets that lack black-targeted programming. While 18.4% of blacks listened to radio (for at least 5 min during an average quarter-hour in 1997) in markets with four or more black-targeted stations, 17.3% of blacks listened to the radio in markets with 0 or 1 stations in black-targeted formats. Patterns were similar for Hispanics. This strongly suggests that blacks and Hispanics are willing to consume second-choice alternatives when most preferred alternatives are unavailable.[12]

1.2.4 Advertiser Finance

Some media products are financed by users directly; others are financed by advertisers. Television and radio have traditionally been financed entirely by advertisers. Newspapers and many magazines have been predominantly advertiser-financed. In 1999, for example, roughly 80% of newspaper revenue was derived from advertisers. Magazines populate a spectrum from those that are predominantly financed by advertisers—such as bridal and photography magazines—and those that are mainly financed with subscription revenue, such as *US Weekly* or *Scientific American*.[13]

Since the advent of cable television in the 1970s, user finance has grown in prominence. Many channels—such as HBO and Showtime—are financed entirely by users and carry no advertising. The financial model for radio has also changed over time. While radio programming was user-financed at the dawn of the industry in the 1920s, it was entirely advertiser-financed for most of the twentieth century. Satellite radio, which emerged in the US in 2001, is user-financed and carries no ads.[14] Internet radio is financed with a mix of advertiser and user finance.

When newspapers placed their content online, most initially relied only on revenue from advertisers. While the *Wall Street Journal* instituted a paywall in 1997, most newspapers did not immediately follow. Beginning around 2010, many newspapers began to put their content behind paywalls, shifting back toward a mix of user and advertiser finance.[15]

---

[12] See Waldfogel (1999), table 7.
[13] Authors' calculation using data from the Publisher's Information Bureau for 2000.
[14] http://en.wikipedia.org/wiki/Satellite_radio.
[15] See Chiou and Tucker (2013).

Reliance on advertiser finance also allows advertisers' potentially different valuation of audience demographic to influence the mix of available programming. See Napoli (2002, 2003).

1.2.5 Change in Costs over Time

Because of technological change—mostly due to digitization—fixed costs have been shrinking in relation to market size for many media products. Moreover, marginal costs for physical media products such as newspapers and magazines have fallen to zero. Fixed costs for media products fall in relation to market size, in turn, for two reasons. First, fixed costs may fall absolutely, as when new digital technology makes it less expensive to produce and publish a text product. A newspaper or magazine does not, in principle, need printing or distribution capabilities. Second, digitization enables broad geographic distribution, so that products that were once local can instead be available nationally or internationally.

The marginal cost of serving a household view newspaper has traditionally been the cost of printing and delivering a physical paper. More recently, as newspapers have moved toward digital distribution, the marginal cost has fallen toward zero.

New technologies have changed "radio" in a few important ways. First, US satellite radio has as its market footprint the entire country. Given the large market size, it is possible to offer a large number of program options, 151 on Sirius in the US.[16] This is far more varieties than are available over the air in even the largest markets. Second, satellite radio is user-financed, with monthly fees of $10–15.[17] Third, the Internet has enabled distribution of audio programming online, with three features that differ from terrestrial radio: (a) As with satellite, the market size is enlarged (an entire country rather than a metropolitan area). (b) Programming is customized to the user's taste. Services such as Pandora and Spotify allow users to listen to individualized "stations" that are customized to the users' preferences. (c) These services have both ad-supported and user-supported versions.

Many media markets—newspapers, radio, television (outside of prime time)—have traditionally been local. The arrival of the Internet is in some ways like the dawn of free trade. Providers can make their text, audio, and video available to consumers anywhere, which creates opportunities to reach more consumers. But at the same time, products everywhere now face greater competition.

1.3. THEORY

Preference externalities are part of the broader economic problem of product selection. We do not attempt to review that vast literature. One stream has followed from

---

[16] See http://en.wikipedia.org/wiki/List_of_Sirius_Satellite_Radio_stations.
[17] See http://www.siriusxm.com/ourmostpopularpackages-xm, accessed June 17, 2014.

Hotelling's (1929) model of spatial competition, which provides a template for viewing the product specification as a choice variable. A second stream follows Chamberlin's (1933) work on monopolistic competition, and focussed on the number of product variants. This vein was resurgent after Spence (1976) and Dixit and Stiglitz (1977) revisited it using representative consumer models (most centrally the CES), and it is currently employed in international trade research following Melitz (2003). Meanwhile, structural empirical work in industrial organization is based on discrete choice models, and frequently on the logit model (following the seminal work of Berry et al., 1995) that is closely related to the CES.

Below, in Section 1.3.3, we elaborate upon models in these veins in order to concentrate on preference externalities in the context of media. First though, we describe (and extend) the classic contributions to media economics of Steiner (1952) and Beebe (1977). These authors, providing precursors to preference externalities, explicitly addressed market failures in ad-financed markets, and it is with them that we begin the narrative. Steiner's principle of duplication stressed excessive attention to majority preferences to the exclusion of minorities, while Beebe's lowest common denominator (LCD) programming type stressed a tendency to cater to base levels of tastes.

Questions we seek to address through the models include the determinants of the number of products in the market, as well as their positioning, and the operation of positive and negative externalities. What determines when more media consumers make other media consumers better or worse off? How do different business-finance models (subscription/ads/mixed) affect predictions? What are the effects of mergers on product positioning and other outcomes? What can we say about the efficiency of the market outcomes?

We then describe some evidence in Section 1.4.

1.3.1 Classic Models

1.3.1.1 Preference Externalities with Spectrum Constraints: Steiner and Beebe Models

Steiner's (1952) model was explicitly directed at media markets with advertising finance. It assumes that each viewer is worth the same amount to advertisers, and that viewers' single-home, media platforms strive to deliver the maximal number of viewers to advertisers. Each viewer has one preferred genre choice, and will not watch/listen to another choice. If several platforms serve the same genre, viewers are split equally, so there is no interaction among the platforms (for example, they do not compete by restricting ad nuisance in order to be more attractive than rivals in the same genre).[18] There is a spectrum

---

[18] See Chapter 2 for extensive analysis of platform competition when ads are a nuisance to media consumers. The Steiner and Beebe models are also discussed in Chapter 6.

constraint on the number of channels that can be broadcast into the market: we shall see in the logit analysis that similar forces are at play without this.

The setup gives rise to duplication of popular channels at the expense of those with fewer adherents. An ensuing preference externality is thus that a more popular genre attracts too many platforms. There thus can be a negative preference externality on small groups that cease to be served when numbers of viewers in a larger channel rise and platforms switch format. There is, though, a positive externality on own-group members by having more variety (although Steiner suppressed this possible welfare benefit by assuming that more choice within a genre is purely duplicative).[19] The social cost is expressed through wasteful copying, although if there are many channels (low fixed costs), preference externalities disappear because each preference type will get what it wants.

Suppose that were just two groups of viewers in a TV market. Each viewer is worth the same amount to advertisers. Seventy percent will watch only a game show and 30% will watch only a reality show. With one market slot available, only the majority will be served. With two market slots, two private firms will both air game shows. This is Steiner's *Principle of Duplication* that the market solution doubles up on the more lucrative niche (as long as this is large enough).[20] Sharing a 70% market is more profitable than airing a reality show.[21] This wasteful competition is the simplest form of the *Tyranny of the Market* (Waldfogel, 2007): majority tastes override minority ones in a marketplace of few alternatives. Notice that the market failure can be resolved in several ways. One is to set one channel aside for a public firm that would cater to those who want drama. Another resolution, surprisingly, is to allow the market to be served by a two-channel monopoly.[22] Such a situation, where the platform would not cannibalize its own

---

[19] Notice that when there are no channel number restrictions (for example, in magazines), then a group's preferences are served only if fixed costs can be covered. In that sense, there remains only the traditional monopoly underserving problem that firms cannot extract the full social surplus from their creations, and so may not serve when they ought to. However, preference externalities might still arise if platform costs depend on the number (and scale) of other platforms. For example, input prices (journalists, say) might rise with the number of platforms. Then the preference externality problem might work in a manner similar to the spectrum restriction case: popular genres crowd out less popular ones, and more people in the popular genre may attract more platforms there and raise costs across the board and so strand less popular offerings.

[20] This duplication (and an unserved minority) prevails as long as $v_A/2 > v_B$, where v_i is the viewership in segment $i = A, B$.

[21] If we had a subscriber price system, with subscribers all with the same willingness to pay, then we have very different outcomes: because of Bertrand competition, two media firms would never select the same channel. Instead, they differentiate to relax price competition, entailing a monopoly in each segment. Nuisance costs of advertising would also mitigate the tendency to duplicate.

[22] Yet another is by stipulating that the bidding process factor is not just which franchise would pay more for the slot, but also broadening the competition to require that other factors than pure profitability be decisive in awarding the franchise. For example, the fourth ITV slot in the UK also asked participants bidding for the prize to describe the program content they would provide.

reality show, was one of Steiner's chief findings: monopoly can outperform (wasteful) competition.

Now modify the numbers so that 78% will listen only to rock and the other 22% only to classical radio. With three slots (or indeed with fixed costs between 22% and 26% of total possible revenues), all will air rock programming, leaving the classicists unserved. With four stations and beyond, the classical listeners will be served (providing, of course, that fixed costs can be covered with a 20% market share). More generally: *minorities will be served providing there are enough stations*, but resources will still be wasted through excessive duplication of the most popular genres. Notice that the assumption of a fixed number of slots was not important to generating the outcomes. For example, if fixed costs lay between 30% and 35% of the total possible market revenue in the first case, then the outcome is the duplication, with drama unserved.

1.3.1.2 The Tyranny of the Yuppies

In the advertising-financed business model, media firms aim to deliver bundles of consumers to advertisers. Firms then are paid by advertisers according to the dollar desirability of the audience delivered—different audiences involve different demographics of heterogeneous desirability to advertisers. Competition among platforms in providing genres is then governed by the tastes of advertisers for the audience composition. Consumer sovereignty is consequently *indirect*—the consumer's preferences are not counted directly, but rather it is the preferences of the advertisers that count. Consumer preferences only count to the extent that consumers are wanted by advertisers. Thus, some consumer groups can be disenfranchised in the market system for the twin reasons of fixed costs (or limited spectrum availability in the central examples below) and the desire to deliver consumers attractive to advertisers. Even with traditional market systems, we can have a majority tyranny, but the ad-finance system exacerbates this. A pay system (pay-per-view on TV, Internet paywalls, or subscription to satellite radio) removes the latter distortion, but many media remain ad-financed, or with a mixed system (newspapers and magazines that carry ads and charge a subscriber price too).

We can illustrate the indirect sovereignty of the ad-financed system in the context of the Steiner model. Suppose that in the original example the watchers of reality are worth to advertisers five times as much as game-show watchers. This could be because viewing preferences are correlated with willingness to pay for advertisers' wares: yuppies are particularly attractive to broadcasters because they are attractive to advertisers. They are just coming into incomes, and their early choices (e.g., Ford or Bank of America) will likely persevere. Influencing their choices early on will likely have a high present value. Because they are worth five times as much, they are now the prime desired real estate. Accordingly, two private firms will now air reality shows. The simple mapping from dollar values and market shares to viewer attractiveness is to multiply each viewer segment by its economic weight. Thus, normalizing the game-show watchers to 1, the game-show segment is worth 70 points in total, while the reality show segment is worth 150, thus flipping the pattern of duplication. The example is extreme, but it underscores the importance of the advertisers, and it shows the algorithm of converting viewer numbers into dollar terms and then performing the Steiner analysis with the economic weights.

Here then the tyranny is that of the economic majority, which may well be the numerical minority. Arguably, this is why we see sitcoms with 20-something yuppies living in New York lofts.[23]

1.3.1.3 Lowest Common Denominator

Steiner's setup is extreme because he supposes that viewers will only watch one genre. Beebe (1977) extended Steiner's preference setup to allow viewers to have taste rankings over program types. Second choices will be watched if first choices are not available. A second choice that is shared by several viewer groups is a LCD programming type. As we show, with few possible channels, LCD programming might prevail, even to the extent of being duplicated.

To illustrate, suppose 60% of the audience will listen to folk music, and country if folk is unavailable. The other 40% have bluegrass as first preference, and country as second. Here country is the LCD taste, the one people will listen to if their first preferences are not available. Now, a monopoly channel need air only country to get the whole market, and has no desire to set up a second channel. By contrast, competition with two slots will yield first preferences being aired. Then, in contrast to Steiner's setup, the monopoly performs worse than competition, by aiming just for the minimum acceptable.

The LCD is not just a monopoly phenomenon. Suppose now that first tastes are drama, news, and sport for each third of the population. If the first choice is unavailable, viewers will all watch sitcoms. Now the equilibrium for two private stations is to both provide sitcoms. Doing so gives each half the market, while choosing any other genre gives a third. As with the Steiner analysis, the same points apply if it is fixed costs that determine the number of platforms. Also, if there are enough slots, then first preferences are satisfied by the market outcome, although duplication remains. Furthermore, LCD programming is supplanted in favor of first preferences. This suggests the pattern of how the market is catered as a function of overall market size: small markets get LCD programming, while the largest ones get programming catering to quite specialized tastes.

The framework above suggests a general tendency of offerings that get finer as the market expands, and positive externalities within own-group size, with possible positive spillovers to similar groups (and such spillovers less likely for more dissimilar groups).

[23] Again, a public broadcaster's role may be to provide nature programs that might have a high consumption benefit that potential watchers cannot express through the ad-financed market system, especially if these watchers are older and perhaps less prone to altering their purchase behavior in response to ads.

These results come from an "inverted pyramid" structure of preferences. On each level are genres, these getting finer from the bottom (the LCD) to the top (where each taste type is represented). The idea is that most people will tune in if their most preferred option is available, fewer if a broader-based option is all that is available. For illustration, suppose that 80% of the population will listen to the lowest-level (LCD) program. If two middle-level programs are available, 45% of the population will listen to each. At the top level, all listen and the split is equal. So, let us trace how the market develops as we decrease fixed costs (equivalently, as we increase the number of consumers across the board). This is the market size effect. With a small market, just the LCD programming is provided. Then, as the market expands, the two mid-level ones are offered. This arises because, rather than sharing the smaller LCD base, stations do better going higher for a base-extension effect as they offer better-matched content. And, if the rival is doing so, it is better for a second station too, since the LCD loses half its potential audience when the rival "upgrades." A further market size rise will double the number of offerings again, for similar reasons. Notice though that the "doubling" at the last stage here was an artifact of the assumed symmetry in the preference divisions. If instead the middle level were split say 55% to 40%, then the first market expansion effect above the LCD is to offer the two more specialty genres, but then a further across-the-board increase will impact first the 55% who will get upgrades, and the 40% will be temporarily left behind until a further expansion makes them worth dividing.

The important take-aways from these models are therefore mainly for markets served by few platforms. A market served only by a single platform will tend to serve up an LCD offering. With two platforms, the LCD type might be duplicated, or a second popular genre (or another LCD) might be broached. As the number of platforms rises, more diverse preference types will be served, and pure LCD types will tend to be surpassed (although they may indeed represent the first preferences of some viewers, in which case they will prevail). However, duplication will pile up in the most popular formats. Moreover, there is bias toward those viewers whom the advertisers most want to reach. Notice finally the positive preference externalities in the examples above. As own-group size expands, it becomes more likely one's higher preferences get catered to. Moreover, by taking away some of the clientele of the erstwhile LCD, there is a greater likelihood that the other clients on the LCD base get an upgrade. Thus, we expect positive preference externalities with respect to own types, with weaker spillovers to similar types.

While the principles described above in the Beebe and Steiner analyses resonate, the models are too sparse. To gain more depth, we apply their insights into first a spatial model and then into a logit model. In both cases we explicitly introduce different consumer types so as to be able to track the effects of population composition on product selection (positioning and variety). The former approach is well configured to deal with markets with very few firms, while the latter deals better with markets with larger numbers.

Our objectives in this section are to incorporate the fundamental features of media markets discussed above—fixed costs, product differentiation, tastes that vary across groups, and advertiser finance—into models of product differentiation. We discuss the ensuing empirical implications for the relationship between the size and mix of the number of potential consumers and the number and targeting of products, as well as the ensuing welfare of various kinds of consumers (i.e., the within-group and across-group preference externalities).

1.3.2 Spatial Models

1.3.2.1 Negative Preference Externalities Under Monopoly

We begin with a monopoly model with two types of consumers, illustrated by reference to daily newspaper markets. The two groups, whom we term "whites" and "blacks," have different product preferences, with their ideal products represented along a one-dimensional spectrum. Assume there is a continuum of W-type agents uniformly distributed on $[0,1]$ with density f_w and a continuum of B-type agents uniformly distributed on $[z,1+z]$ with density $f_b < f_w$. Let $z \in [0,1]$ so that the degree of overlap is $1-z$. The probability of any type buying the newspaper, and hence getting exposed to any ads in the paper, is $d(p + t|x - x_n|)$, which is decreasing in its argument. Here p is the price of the newspaper (if any), x_n is its location in the content space, x is the "ideal" content location of an agent of type x, and t is the "transport" cost rate from not getting the ideal newspaper content. Furthermore, assume there is a mass A of advertisers. Each is willing to pay w to contact a W-type reader and b to contact a B-type one. Let $w > b$ so that the W-types are more attractive to advertisers. Therefore, we have a majority group which is also worth more to advertisers, and its preferences overlap with the minority one: apart from the assumption that the majority is worth more, there is no loss in generality assuming they are on the left of the spectrum. The assumptions are illustrated in Figure 1.1.

We consider in turn the preference externalities under pure advertising finance, pure subscription pricing, and the mixed business model: see Chapter 2 for more details, along with a consideration of ad nuisance to consumers, which has here been suppressed. Loosely, the first case transpires if advertiser demand is strong enough.

The equilibrium has the (profit-maximizing) newspaper choose its content location, and price where appropriate. Each consumer is therefore worth p plus either w or b (depending on its type) times A, the mass of advertisers (and A ads will be placed in the paper, charging advertisers the full value of their surplus). In what follows, we eschew

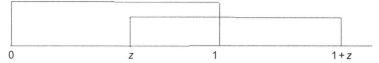

| 0 | z | 1 | 1 + z |

Figure 1.1 Preference structure (consumer densities) producing a negative preference externality with monopoly.

a full equilibrium description because the factors on which we focus are quite immediate in their impact on the price/location solution: the properties claimed are readily derived. Notice first that if all consumers are equally valuable to the advertisers, and their densities are the same, then the monopolist's profit-maximizing location (under each of the three business models) is the center of the full market, i.e., at $(1 + z)/2$. This benchmark allows us to compare the externalities exerted under asymmetric advertiser preference to contacting the two types, or different densities of them.

Under pure advertising finance (e.g., commercial TV or terrestrial radio), the B-types are less valuable. If indeed $b = 0$, then they have no commercial value and their preferences are irrelevant. The content format chosen is then $x_n = \frac{1}{2}$, which is the mean of the W-type consumer distribution. As b rises, the chosen content location rises, reaching the benchmark point $(1 + z)/2$ only when b gets as high as w and even then only when $f_b < f_w$. Equivalently, we can say that the larger is f_w or w, then the more is the content tilted toward the W-types, so that the preference externality of catering to the type of greater mass or greater value is detrimental to the other type (but is advantageous to the majority). The impact of the preference externality to the B-types is more severe the greater is z, corresponding to a greater preference divergence.

For pure subscription pricing, the difference in advertiser valuations is taken off the table, and the preference externality depends solely on the single source of differentiation between the two types, their different densities. The preference externality effect is therefore weaker. But still, the more W-types there are, the closer is the content location to their mean at $\frac{1}{2}$, and the further away from the B-types' desiderata.[24]

With a mixed-finance model, the solution for the content location choice lies between the two cases noted above. Again, more W-types move the location away from the B-types, as does a higher advertiser preference for contacting the W-types. Moreover, the larger is A, the more reliance on advertising finance, and the lower the copy-price so as to attract more consumers to deliver to the advertisers. Then again, the closer is the location to the mean of the W-types. The problem is more severe the more tastes differ across groups.

To summarize, the bias against the B-types is greater the more W-types there are, the larger the discrepancy in their values to advertisers, the more different their tastes from the mainstream, and the greater the weight given to advertisers in the business model.

1.3.2.2 Preference Externalities Under Duopoly

When demand is sufficiently strong, there will be more than one product. There remain some markets in the US with more than one paper, though this was quite common some decades ago. Accordingly, we next allow for two competing media outlets. To do so, we

---

[24] Another possible driver impinging on locations would be differential purchase probabilities. They have been suppressed here but are readily introduced.

assume that subscription prices are fixed, or indeed zero (as per commercial TV or radio), so we take price competition off the table.[25] We continue to assume there is no ad nuisance impinging on reader choices. These missing features are analyzed in detail in Chapter 2, but our emphasis here is on preference externalities between different groups.

We simplify the spatial model above slightly by assuming that $z=1$, so that the B-types "start" where the W-types end. The total market length is now 2. Denote the media firms' locations as $x_1 < x_2$, so that Firm 1 serves predominantly the W-types. We first characterize these via the first-order conditions for equilibrium locations. The key condition is that a move in of δ by Firm 1 (located at x_1) expands its loyal base by δ, while picking up only an extra base of $\delta/2$ from the rival's consumers. The change in profits is thus the value gained on the LHS minus the value lost on the RHS (where its market length has decreased by $\delta/2$). Thus, its profit increases by corresponding values of the consumers gained and lost. In equilibrium, the marginal consumer is a W-type. Thus, the local profit increment from moving in for Firm 1 is

$$[\delta d(p + t(x_1)) - (\delta/2)d(p + 1/2t(x_1 + x_2))]wf_w,$$

which is the value of demand gained on its LHS minus the loss on the RHS.

The corresponding effect for the other firm from moving left is analogously

$$\delta bf_b d(p + t(2 - x_2)) - (\delta/2)wf_w d(p + 1/2t(x_1 + x_2)).$$

For this firm, each gained consumer is worth less because they are B-types.

Setting both of these first derivatives to zero yields the equilibrium solution when firms are not back-to-back. Because the left sides of these expressions are the same (these are transfers at the interior margin), the equilibrium conditions imply that wf_w $d(p + t(x_1)) = bf_b d(p + t(2 - x_2))$. Then, because $wf_w > bf_b$ (by the assumption that Ws are worth more than Bs) the implication is that $x_1 < 2 - x_2$. That is, Firm 1 is closer to the median W-type than Firm 2 is to the median B-type. Moreover, both are closer to the market center (here set to 1) than to the edges. The reason is that each firm picks

---

[25] There is a voluminous literature on equilibrium existence in prices and locations. Anderson et al. (1992, Ch. 8) summarize the state of the art two decades back, and the field has not developed much more in the interim, at least as relates to the current application. In particular, Hotelling's (1929) claimed "minimum differentiation" result was shown to be incorrect by d'Aspremont et al. (1979). Osborne and Pitchik (1987) solve his original two-stage location-then-price model with linear transport costs, by analyzing the mixed strategy equilibrium to the price sub-game and engaging this to the location stage. They find (pure strategy) equilibrium duopoly locations just inside the quartiles, at which locations the price equilibrium is in (non-degenerate) mixed strategies. d'Aspremont et al. (1979) propose the "fix" used by most subsequent authors, by replacing linear transport costs with quadratic ones. This ensures tractable price sub-game solutions in pure strategies, but with a radical change in the equilibrium locations. Instead of "minimum differentiation," the locations are at the extremes. Therefore, fixing prices as we do here is hardly innocuous.

up more demand on the interior boundary between them, and that demand is worth relatively more to the firm with the predominantly minority readership.

The implication is that the Ws are better served than the Bs, although each group would be better off in aggregate if the other were not there.[26] Note too that the presence of the B-types draws Firm 1's location inward even if few B-types actually read it. The induced bias toward middle-of-the-road coverage is greater for the minority paper than for the majority one.

The bias toward the center—and the minimum differentiation result associated with Hotelling (1929)—is tempered by the elasticity of demand in the model above. The more inelastic is demand, then the closer together will the firms locate.[27]

We can now describe preference externalities at the differentiated outcome. The mechanism is quite interesting. Suppose the population of Ws rises across the board (an increase in f_w) or, equivalently, if the value of the Ws rises to advertisers (an increase in w). Then the first-order condition of outlet 1 remains unchanged, because the relative value of readers at each margin is unchanged. However, the other outlet's profit is now higher when it moves in because of the increased value of serving the marginal W-type. Thus, outlet 2 moves left; this in turn causes the first outlet to cut left too. So the upshot is that both outlets are further left in the new equilibrium. The implication for the well-being of the two groups (in aggregate) is that the Bs are worse off on average. The Ws are better off for two reasons (although those just right of the erstwhile location of outlet 1 are worse off). First, those served by outlet 1 are better off on average because 1's location is more central to them. Second, those Ws whose preferences are more extreme so that they chose before the outlet catering predominantly to B-types (the B-leaning Ws) are also better off because their outlet now delivers content closer to their ideal.

Now consider the effects on locations of a merger (here to monopoly), and assume that the two-outlet firm keeps publishing both media. Then we can view the location choice for each outlet as internalizing the effect of its location choice on the demand of the other. The upshot is that equilibrium locations are further apart because they avoid cannibalization of the sibling outlet's readers. Therefore, the prediction is that mergers lead to more diversification, moving away from the excessive tendency to centralize that is epitomized in the Hotelling model.

---

[26] Modulo the possibility that the B-types might not be served at all if they were alone: the existence of the W-types raises the profitability of the B-type paper and may thus enable the fixed costs to be covered. This form of "cross-subsidization" is discussed further below when we explicitly consider the model with entry.

[27] The term "Principle of Minimum Differentiation" is due to Boulding (1966). In the setup above, there is back-to-back location if demands are too inelastic, i.e., (from the location derivatives) if firms do not want to move outward from a common location x_m satisfying $d(p + tx_m) > \frac{1}{2}d(p)$ and $bf_b d(p + t(2 - x_m)) > \frac{1}{2}wf_w d(p))$. Note that x_m should further satisfy the condition that firms' profits are equal, so that neither firm wishes to flip its position with its rival.

The model with two firms delivers two key results. First, we see an across-group preference externality: having more W-type consumers delivers such consumers better choices in the aggregate but makes the others worse off. Second, merger tends to spread the two products apart. Adding more firms to the linear depiction of preferences rapidly encumbers the structure, so we eschew further development of this model in order to elaborate more subtle and intricate patterns of preference structures (albeit with significant simplifications).

1.3.3 Market Size and Equilibrium Media Diversity

Above we considered product positioning, consumption, and the well-being of market participants in contexts with small and fixed numbers (1 or 2) of products. Here we shift the analysis to the number of firms or products operating. The first question to address is the determination of the number of entering products which, as we have suggested above, has an important impact on the way that preference externalities operate.

The logit model gives us a simple setup for illustrating this relationship. We begin with one category of products targeting the single group of consumers. Products are differentiated but symmetrically so. Hence, additional products will expand the market, but all varieties attract identical shares. Suppose the group has "economic mass" M, which is the product of the number of consumers and their economic weight to advertisers. Each product has entry cost F, and we define n as the number of products that enter. The share of the population consuming any particular product i is then

$$\mathbb{P}_i = \frac{e^s}{1 + ne^s}.$$

This is the classic symmetric logit with an outside option, and s represents the attractiveness of listening.

Under free entry, products enter until profit opportunities are dissipated. Ignoring integer constraints, the free entry condition is $M\mathbb{P}_i = F$, or $M\frac{1}{n + e^{-s}} = F$, which determines the number of products as:

$$n = \frac{M}{F} - e^{-s}.$$

The resulting equilibrium number of firms is the integer component of n. Hence, we have monopoly if $\frac{M}{F} - e^{-s} \in (1, 2)$, etc.

This simple setup yields a number of predictions relevant to preference externalities. For a given positive value of potential consumers to advertisers, a larger population gives rise to a larger economic mass M. So, first, as M rises, the number of products that can profitably operate (modulo integer constraints) rises as well. Second, consumption also rises with M (and with n). Note that overall revenue is $\frac{Mne^s}{1 + ne^s}$. Finally, given that *per capita* consumer surplus is proportional to $\log(1 + ne^s)$, then consumer welfare also rises with the population size. That is, this simple entry model delivers a positive within-group preference externality: consumers benefit one another by bringing forth additional products which, in turn, attract a larger share of consumers to consume.

The equation $n = \frac{M}{F} - e^{-s}$ delivers another set of insights. As written it implies a particular relationship between market size (M) and entry. If the fixed costs associated with entry are constant across markets of different sizes, then for markets with many entrants, the relationship between M and n is nearly linear. On the other hand, if the fixed costs are higher in larger markets, then the number of products available will rise more slowly. Fixed costs may be higher in larger markets for two broad reasons. First, input prices may be higher in larger markets for cost-of-living reasons. Second, if quality is produced with fixed costs—as is plausible for media products—then firms in larger markets may have incentives to spend more in an attempt to attract a larger share of a larger market (see Sutton, 1991). The general point is that while entry grows in market size across a range of plausible models, the positive relationship may be tempered by other factors affecting the determinants of fixed costs.

1.3.4 Optimum Media Diversity

The (first-best) optimum problem is to choose the set of products to maximize social surplus. As long as private and social marginal benefits coincide, this is the sum of all agents' surpluses. In particular, we shall assume for the present argument that social and private benefits from advertising coincide (the analysis is readily amended if there are advertising spillovers). Hence social surplus is equal to the sum of consumer surplus, advertiser net surplus, and firm profits. We can in general write the last two terms as advertiser gross surplus minus total fixed costs, because the price paid for advertising is a transfer from advertisers to firms. Moreover, for simplicity we assume that the advertiser willingness to pay is fixed at w per listener reached (and so advertiser net surplus is zero).

Then, given a mass of M listeners worth w each to advertisers, the social surplus (SS) is

$$SS = M \ln(1 + n \exp s) + wM(1 - \mathbb{P}_0) - nF.$$

Here the middle term is the advertiser revenue (all those listening times w) and $\mathbb{P}_0$ is the non-listening probability, and so for the logit model we use

$$1 - \mathbb{P}_0 = \frac{n \exp s}{1 + n \exp s}.$$

Differentiating with respect to n to find the optimal variety yields a quadratic function of the form

$$Mw \exp s + ZM \exp s - Z^2 F = 0,$$

where we have set $Z = (1 + n \exp s)$. The relevant root is the positive one.

It is readily shown that the optimal number is increasing in w, which makes sense because then it is more important to ensure more communication from advertisers to listeners. Moreover, we can draw some pointers by comparison with the equilibrium solution we derived above, namely $n = \frac{wM}{F} - \exp(-s)$. First notice that if w is too low, then the market solution is zero, while the optimum can have positive numbers. This feature is just the point that an ad-financed system needs a strong enough ad demand to be viable, but the optimum also figures in the consumer benefits.

Indeed, the current example always involves under-entry in the equilibrium (this can be seen by inserting the equilibrium number into the expression for the optimum above). We should note that this is one theoretical solution to the question of whether free entry delivers the right amount of entry. Other models, e.g., Mankiw and Whinston (1986), with homogeneous products and Cournot competition, deliver excess entry; their model with differentiated products delivers ambiguous results. In the end whether entry is excessive is an empirical question, but it is one that can only be addressed using some explicit modeling framework.

1.3.5 Cross-Group Externalities

Individual consumers may consume the content targeted mainly at others, and may benefit correspondingly, but not as much as if the content were targeted at their own type. Indeed, it may be that more individuals of the other type—even if there is some chance that the stations provided would be consumed—actually cause own-side welfare to fall. That is, there may be negative preference externalities from other-side participation. This would stem from crowd out of own-side media offerings. We now make these claims precise by showing them in a rigorous model (although it is clearly highly specific and parametric).

To this end, suppose that there are two types of individual (i.e., two groups) and two basic program types. Let the economic masses of the W- and B-types be M_W and M_B, respectively. Stations/firms take one of two basic types. Listening to an "own-side" station is associated with an attractivity measure $s > 0$; listening to an "other-side" station garners attractivity $-s$. This symmetry assumption will be clear in the choice probability formulae below and is a sort of normalization: negative values are not negative utilities, and still have positive choice probabilities, although lower than own-side stations. The formulation will generate "cross-over" across programming. The larger s (and hence the smaller is $-s$), the fewer people listen to other-side stations. Notice too that the formulation implies that the chance of listening to one's own side increases in the number of own-side stations available, and decreases in the number of other-side ones.

Specifically, suppose that n_w denotes the number of w-type stations available, and similarly for n_b. The logit formulation gives us the chance that a W-type listens to a particular w station as:

$$\mathbb{P}_w^W = \frac{\exp s}{1 + n_w \exp s + n_b \exp(-s)},$$

and the chance a W listens to a given b station is

$$\mathbb{P}_b^W = \frac{\exp(-s)}{1 + n_w \exp s + n_b \exp(-s)}.$$

From these we can calculate various statistics of interest. For example, the ratio of W's listening to b stations to those listening to w stations is

$$\frac{n_b \exp(-s)}{n_w \exp s} = \frac{n_b}{n_w} \exp(-2s),$$

which is small if s is large, but increases in the number of opposite-side stations, and decreases in own-side ones. Indeed, here the number of cross-overs is proportional to the relative number of stations on the "other" side. The more variety there is, the more likely the listener finds something that resonates.

The next key step is to find out how many stations of each type there are in the market, and how this depends on the numbers of listeners of each type. That is, we take the analysis of the single type we had earlier, and now we use the central ideas to find the breakdown of numbers of each station stripe.

1.3.6 Variety

Before getting to "thick" markets with many stations of each type, we first look at "small" markets that can support one or two stations, and we ask what determines whether and when the market gets a station for each type, or if only one type is represented (so that here we are paying special attention to integer numbers of stations). Then we draw out the implications for the preference externalities.

To trace out a coherent picture, we shall fix M_B and vary M_W up from nothing to see how market provision changes. We concentrate on endogenously small station numbers, and this will ensue if fixed costs are quite high. Accordingly, assume that the entry cost, $F \in \left(M_B \frac{\exp s}{1 + \exp s}, M_B \right)$. This will ensure that there is no station at all without at least some W's, and that there is at least one station when W's and B's have equal market weight. The lower bound condition already makes a useful point. In weak markets, even if they are preponderantly of one type, sometimes enough of the other type is needed to support a single station for the majority. Of course, some part of the minority needs to be willing to listen to an other-side station (i.e., s should not be too large). But here is an elementary preference externality. If enough own-side listeners are not available, then the other side can exert a positive influence by enabling service when none would be forthcoming in their absence. As one might expect, we cannot have too much of a good thing: if the minority gets too powerful, it may cause the market to tip to the other station type. Or indeed, in the benign case, it may simply lead to a station of its own type being added.

There are thus two cases of interest. As we show, which one holds depends on whether F is larger or smaller than $M_B \frac{\exp s + \exp(-s)}{1 + \exp s \exp(-s)}$ (note that this expression is larger than $M_B \frac{\exp s}{1 + \exp s}$, which is the stand-alone profit from the B's). Even if the s taste parameter were the same across markets, the numbers of each type are not, and so we can see various different patterns in a cross-sectional analysis.

Consider first the case $F \in \left(M_B \frac{\exp s}{1 + \exp s}, M_B \frac{\exp s + \exp(-s)}{1 + \exp s \exp(-s)} \right)$. For low enough M_W there is no station at all, because there are not enough B's to cover the fixed cost on their own. As M_W rises, it becomes profitable to have a single station, and it is a b type (because the B's carry more economic weight). As M_W rises further, but still below M_B, there is enough profit in the market for a station of each type to survive.[28] To summarize, the progression as M_W rises is no firm, then a b –type, then a w –type too.[29]

The preference externalities for this case are all positive (at the switch-point between regimes—and zero elsewhere) for both types. The B's need enough W's to float a first station. Adding further W's enables another station to enter. It is a w-type, and this benefits both groups, though the W's benefit more than the B's for the addition. The next (complementary) case highlights the possibility of negative preference externalities.

Now consider the case $F \in \left(M_B \frac{\exp s + \exp(-s)}{1 + \exp s \exp(-s)}, M_B \right)$. Again, think of raising M_W; the first threshold crossed is again the market's ability to support a firm, and it is a b-type. However, now as M_W rises further, the fixed cost is quite large, and indeed (from the condition given) there is no room for two firms for $M_W < M_B$ (and for M_W at least a bit above M_B). However, once M_W passes M_B, a w-type is more profitable than a b-type. Thus, the b-type is displaced. The equilibrium sequence (as a function of increasing M_W) is then no firm, b-type only, w-type only.

The preference externality is clearly beneficial to both types as M_W rises above the first threshold, and the market is served. However, the second threshold is where the b-type gets replaced by a w-type, and the market retains a single firm. This favors the W-types,

---

[28] To see that both survive, note indeed that the market can support one firm of each type (but no more) at $M_W = M_B$, where profit of each firm (by symmetry) is then $M_B \frac{\exp s + \exp(-s)}{1 + \exp s \exp(-s)}$, which is below the entry cost by assumption in this case.

[29] What happens if M_W increases further? More and more ws enter, and at some point (depending on parameter values) the b actually switches type. This is the pattern suggested in the analysis below of the continuous case. In the next case considered, the type-switching occurs immediately (in the sense that there is no intervening regime where both types coexist).

but it is a negative externality on the B's. The subsequent analysis picks up the narrative with the simplification of neglecting integer constraints in the number of firms, but the broad story is coherent with that just outlined, and extends it to more firms.

1.3.7 Multiple Stations

To analyze preference externalities in larger markets with two taste groups and with multiple stations of each type, we ignore the integer constraint, and first determine the equilibrium numbers of firms of each type. There are two equations in two unknowns (n_w and n_b):

$$M_W \mathbb{P}_b^W + M_B \mathbb{P}_b^B = F$$

$$M_W \mathbb{P}_w^W + M_B \mathbb{P}_w^B = F,$$

which are the zero profit conditions for b and w stations respectively.

These equations define two entry reaction functions for the two station types in terms of numbers of each type. We solve for the numbers via a more indirect method. That is, we write the second equation above in terms of the variables in the first one, which enables us to solve for the equilibrium market shares of each station. We then use the share expressions to solve for the equilibrium numbers, and with this information we can find the equilibrium consumer surplus for each viewer type.

First note that $\mathbb{P}_w^W = \mathbb{P}_b^W \exp 2s$ and $\mathbb{P}_w^B = \mathbb{P}_b^B \exp(-2s)$ (using the odds ratios of the different types),[30] and thus we can rewrite the two equations to be solved simultaneously as

$$M_W \mathbb{P}_b^W + M_B \mathbb{P}_b^B = F$$

$$M_w \mathbb{P}_b^W \exp 2s + M_B \mathbb{P}_b^B \exp(-2s) = F.$$

The solution yields the two choice probabilities as $\mathbb{P}_b^W = \frac{F}{M_W} \frac{1}{\exp(2s)+1}$ and $\mathbb{P}_b^B = \frac{F}{M_B} \frac{\exp(2s)}{\exp(2s)+1}$ (with analogous expressions for the w stations). These expressions already give us the breakdown of listeners as $\frac{\mathbb{P}_b^B}{\mathbb{P}_b^W} = \frac{M_W}{M_B} \exp(2s)$. In equilibrium then, the ratio of own-side to other-side listening of any given station is proportional to the ratio of other-side to own-side populations! The fraction of listeners to a b station is slanted more toward B-types when there are more W's around because then there are a lot of w stations so the W's are much more likely to find what they want among the w stations, and few will listen to the b station. So, while it may seem that the listenership is quite segregated by this metric of relative listenership, it is rather that the majority group has a lot of choices. Conversely, a population with a large B representation will have a more even listenership for each b station.

---

[30] Hence own type is preferred by the factor exp(2s).

Now we can find the equilibrium numbers from the conditions

$$\mathbb{P}_b^B = \frac{\exp s}{1 + n_b \exp s + n_w \exp(-s)}$$

$$\mathbb{P}_b^B = \frac{\exp(-s)}{1 + n_w \exp s + n_b \exp(-s)}.$$

These imply that

$$1 + n_b \exp s + n_w \exp(-s) = \frac{M_B}{F}(\exp s + \exp(-s))$$

$$1 + n_w \exp s + n_b \exp(-s) = \frac{M_W}{F}(\exp s + \exp(-s)),$$

and from there we can solve out for the equilibrium number of w- stations as

$$n_w = \left(\frac{-\exp s}{\exp 2s + 1} + \frac{M_W}{F} \frac{\exp 2s}{(\exp 2s - 1)} - \frac{M_B}{F} \frac{1}{(\exp 2s - 1)} \right).$$

The equilibrium n_b expression just transposes M_W and M_B.

Before we turn to the precise preference externality that we get from analyzing the equilibrium welfare of the two groups, there are several take-aways from these numbers. First of all, clearly the number of stations increases in own-side market presence, and decreases (linearly) in other-side market presence. That is, B presence crowds out w stations, *ceteris paribus*. This effect was already apparent in the monopoly analysis above. Below we look at the ratio of the two types of station as a function of the group populations. Second, if market presence is the same for both groups ($M_W = M_B$), then the total number of station is $\frac{-2\exp s}{\exp(2s)+1} + \frac{M}{F}$, where M is total population. Recalling the single market case had $n = \frac{M}{F} - \exp(-s)$, this implies that there are more stations in a homogeneous market.[31] The reason is that the population's tastes as a whole are better matched on average. Of course, there are several caveats to such conclusions: for example, the analysis has assumed that stations are symmetric. In many instances stations differ substantially in their profitability and listener base sizes.

Third, the equilibrium ratio of firms is

$$\frac{n_w}{n_b} = \frac{\left(\exp s(1 - \exp 2s) + (\exp 2s + 1)\left(\dfrac{M_W}{F} \exp 2s - \dfrac{M_B}{F} \right) \right)}{\left(\exp s(1 - \exp 2s) + (\exp 2s + 1)\left(\dfrac{M_B}{F} \exp 2s - \dfrac{M_W}{F} \right) \right)}.$$

To get some traction on how this depends on the total population make-up, if the M's are large then this is approximately $\dfrac{\left(\dfrac{M_W}{F} \exp 2s - \dfrac{M_B}{F} \right)}{\left(\dfrac{M_B}{F} \exp 2s - \dfrac{M_W}{F} \right)} = \dfrac{k \exp 2s - 1}{\exp 2s - k}$, where we have set $M_W = k M_B$.

---

[31] Comparing numbers, the statement holds if $\exp(-s) < \dfrac{2 \exp s}{\exp 2s + 1}$, which is true for $s > 0$.

In the relevant range (for positive numbers of each station type), this is an increasing and convex function of k. Hence, the fraction of w-type stations increases with the fraction of W-types, and does so at an increasing rate. As with the monopoly analysis earlier, the b-stations get increasingly crowded out by w-types, which nonetheless attract B-type listeners as they provide more and more alternatives. The majority tastes increasingly dominate the market's offerings. However, this market tyranny is perhaps somewhat more benign than it might appear because in the model the B's do benefit from the increased variety of w stations.

To analyze this effect in more detail, we now turn to the groups' welfare. From the Log-Sum formula for consumer surplus in the logit model, the expected welfare of an arbitrary W-type is $\ln(n_w \exp s + n_b \exp(-s) + 1)$. Using the equilibrium values for station numbers, this welfare is an increasing function of the expression

$$\left(\frac{-\exp s}{\exp 2s + 1} + \frac{M_W}{F} \frac{\exp 2s}{\exp 2s - 1} - \frac{M_B}{F} \frac{1}{\exp 2s - 1} \right) \exp s$$
$$+ \left(\frac{-\exp s}{\exp 2s + 1} + \frac{M_B}{F} \frac{\exp 2s}{\exp 2s - 1} - \frac{M_W}{F} \frac{1}{\exp 2s - 1} \right) \exp(-s).$$

Clearly per W welfare increases in W market presence, so there are positive own-side preference externalities. But the other striking feature of the expression is that it is independent of M_B. This says that there are zero preference externalities from the other side. Given the empirical findings in this regard (none or mildly negative cross effects), this is quite a compelling benchmark. Here two effects are canceling out. First, a larger B presence would mean more b stations, which has a beneficial effect on W welfare through more choice. And indeed the total number of stations is higher. But more B's also implies some crowding out of more highly valued w stations, which depresses welfare.

To put this last point in a wider perspective, recall that the model has simplified by assuming strong symmetry in station valuations, namely that the other-side attractiveness is $-s$. If instead the other-side valuation were higher, then the preference externality would be positive: the first effect would dominate.[32] However, if the other-side valuation were lower, then the crowd-out effect would dominate, and the preference externality would be negative.

Finally, with the welfare analysis in hand, we can look at the equilibrium mix of listeners in the market, which is another empirically measurable statistic that can be tracked as a function of population composition. The fraction of W's listening is $\frac{n_w \exp s + n_b \exp(-s)}{1 + n_w \exp s + n_b \exp(-s)}$ while the B fraction is analogous. We already effectively determined the behavior of this expression in the welfare analysis. In particular, the numerator is independent of M_B and so therefore is the denominator. This means that the fraction

---

[32] To see this, suppose both station types had the same attractiveness, s. Then more of the "other" type is good, because they are equally valued, and more other-side presence just increases variety.

of W's who listen to radio is independent of the number of B's. This is not because the W's do not listen to b stations. Rather, it is because the extra b stations crowd out w ones at exactly the rate that keeps overall W listening the same. As noted above, this is an artifact of assuming valuation symmetry. If instead other-side valuations were less than $-s$, then there would be fewer W listeners as M_B rose. The reason is the dominant crowd-out effect. Put another way, negative cross preference externalities go hand-in-hand with decreasing listener shares. Regardless, the prediction for own-side presence is that more listen: the presence of more W's increases the equilibrium fraction of W's who listen.

1.4. EMPIRICAL RESULTS: FACTS RELEVANT TO PREDICTIONS FROM THEORY

We now turn to assessing the state of empirical knowledge on the predictions arising from the theoretical models articulated above. There are both positive implications and normative implications. Among the positive predictions are the following.

First, the positive within-group preference externality: more valuable audiences—either because they are larger or more valued by advertisers—attract more entry and deliver group members more surplus. Second, as is implied above, ad prices matter. Third, there is an inverted pyramid of variety—larger markets have more variety, allowing consumers to trade up from lower second to higher choices. Fourth, when markets support few products (and most clearly with literally one product), positioning depends on the relative economic mass of the underlying demand groups. A single product locates nearer the larger mass of consumers, delivering them greater surplus. Fifth, as a result, there is a positive own-group effect and the possibility of a negative across-group effect; with $N=1$, the negative across-group effect is immediate; it can also arise with small numbers of products as a group grows large enough to attract targeted entry and consumers withdraw from second-choice products to newly available first choices. Finally, when markets support many products, own-group effects tend to be positive while across-group effects tend to be zero. In addition to these positive predictions, we can also explore normative statements. Free entry can deliver a sub-optimal number of products as well as a sub-optimal mix of products.

This section of the paper proceeds via the following sections. First we review what is known about the basic own-group preference externality. This is the relationships between market size and entry, between market size and variety, and between market size and consumption.

Second, we review what is known about analogous mechanisms in contexts with multiple groups. This, in turn, differs according to whether there are few (one or two) or many products. We discuss product positioning by monopolists as well as the ensuing own-group and cross-group preference externalities. We then review the evidence on how group sizes affect targeted entry and group consumption in contexts that can support multiple entrants. Third, we discuss the available evidence on ownership and product positioning. We then apply the empirical evidence to normative questions with a review of the empirical literature on the efficiency of entry into media markets.

1.4.1 The Own-Group Preference Externality

1.4.1.1 Market Size and Entry

One stark prediction emerging from both the models reviewed above (as well as common sense) is that, just as market size tends to promote entry in markets generally, this is also true in media markets. And this is indeed true for a variety of media. A variety of studies document that larger markets have more radio stations (Berry and Waldfogel, 2001; Rogers and Woodbury, 1996; Sweeting, 2010; Wang and Waterman, 2011). Larger markets also have more daily newspapers (Berry and Waldfogel, 2010; George, 2007; George and Waldfogel, 2003), weekly newspapers, and local television stations (Waldfogel, 2004).

While all positive, the relationships between market size and entry differ substantially across media products; and these relationships reveal something about the relative size of fixed costs in relation to market size across products. The average number of daily newspapers per market in the top 283 markets was 3.23 in 2001.[33] Around the same time, the average number of radio stations, including only those broadcasting from inside the metropolitan area, was 24.5 across 246 US markets in 1997.[34]

1.4.1.2 Market Size and Variety

Larger markets can support more products. In general, entry might affect consumers through two mechanisms: prices might fall, or the appeal of the most appealing varieties might increase with entry. Both are possible with entry in media markets, although we focus on the second, in part because ad prices are often set outside of local media markets that are the focus of this chapter.

If entry delivers satisfaction through the variety channel, then it must be the case that large markets have not only more but more varied products. Radio markets provide an illustrative example. Using the 1997 data, while the elasticity of the number of stations with respect to population is 0.31, the elasticity of the number of varieties is 0.27. Hence, most of the growth in the number of products available in larger markets arises from growth in variety as opposed to duplication.[35]

The relationship between market size and variety is related to the willingness of consumers to accept second-choice alternatives. The willingness to accept second-choice

---

[33] Berry and Waldfogel (2010).

[34] Waldfogel (1999).

[35] The evidence that the number of varieties increases in market size rests on the idea that differently named broadcast formats are meaningfully different. There is some question about this (see DiCola, 2006).

programming means that a relatively small number of varieties can attract consumption from a large share of the market. Hence, a small market with few product options can have a high share of population consuming. As a market becomes large enough to support more varieties, some consumers formerly choosing the least common denominator will switch over to a more preferred variety. This has two possible consequences.

The first is that generalist (LCD) programming may lose support as a market becomes large enough to support specialist programming. It is possible that some generalist programming would be withdrawn as consumers with specialized tastes withdraw their support from generalist programming. This is a potential variant on a negative across-group preference externality.

A second set of consequences is that larger markets will have more varied programming and, moreover, that share of population listening to generalist format should fall in market size. Various studies confirm that larger markets have more formats as well as more stations. The most commonly available format, country music, garners a smaller share of listening in larger markets. The same is true for other generalist formats, such as "full service/variety" and oldies. The opposite is true for formats such as jazz and classical music, which are only supplied by the market in large markets.

1.4.1.3 Market Size and Quality

A feature of the relationship between market size and entry is the nonlinearity in the relationship between market size and entry. For example, a regression of the log of the number of daily newspapers in a US metropolitan area on the log of population yields an elasticity of entry with respect to population of 0.5 (Berry and Waldfogel, 2010). An analogous regression using 1997 US data across 260 US markets yields an elasticity of 0.3.[36] By contrast, Berry and Waldfogel (2010) show that the relationship between entry and population is nearly linear for the restaurant industry.

The deviation from linearity arising in media industries could arise for a variety of reasons, including price competition in the advertising market. Yet radio ads have close substitutes in newspaper, television, and outdoor ads, suggesting a limited role for ad price competition to explain the nonlinearity. A second possibility is that the fixed costs themselves rise in market size, and indeed they do. We see strong direct evidence of this in daily newspaper markets. Berry and Waldfogel (2010) show that the number of pages and staff per daily newspaper rise across markets with market size: the elasticities of pages and staff with respect to population are 0.2 and 0.5 respectively.

Direct evidence on how the costs of radio station operation vary with market size are not systematically available, but we do have two pieces of evidence indicating higher costs in larger markets. First, Duncan (1994) reports some data on annual pay of on-air talent across about 100 US radio markets in 1993, including the highest reported

---

[36] Authors' calculation for this chapter, using the data in Waldfogel (2003).

salary per market and a typical range. A regression of the log of the top salary on log of population yields an elasticity of 0.87 (with a standard error of 0.04). Using the midpoint of the typical salary range, the elasticity of salary with respect to market size is 0.26 (0.02). These size differences in salary dwarf the cost-of-living differences across markets and therefore clearly indicate higher costs in larger markets. Using the 16 markets for which a metro area CPI exists, the elasticity of the cost of living with respect to population is about 0.03. The pay–market size relationship also suggests that higher-quality talent gravitates to larger markets and that the stations in larger markets have higher quality.

Second, there is related indirect evidence: the relationship between the number of listeners per station and market size is strongly suggestive that costs are higher in larger markets. A regression on the average number of listeners per local US radio station on metro area population, using 1997 data, yields an elasticity of 0.8. Unless ad revenue per listener fell sharply with market size—and there is no evidence that it does—this would indicate that radio stations in larger markets have higher average revenue. With free entry, revenues tend to provide reasonable approximations for costs, so the fact that larger-market stations have more revenue indicates that their costs are higher as well.[37]

That larger markets have more media products provides a mechanism by which additional entry might deliver more valuable choices to consumers. That is, entry is a mechanism for the delivery of the basic own-group preference externality. Costs that rise with market size seem on the face of it to mitigate the positive effect of market size on the desirability of options for media consumers, but that depends on what gives rise to higher costs in larger markets. For example, if larger markets had higher costs simply because of higher input prices (land, etc.), then the deviation from linearity of entry in market size would inhibit the welfare benefit of fellow consumers. On the other hand, if the higher costs in larger markets reflect higher investment—and associated higher-quality products—then the interpretation would be different.

There is a variety of reasons to see the higher costs in larger markets to be reflective of greater investment in quality and, moreover, that media markets provide good examples of Sutton's (1991) prediction that market structure need not grow fragmented as markets get large when quality is produced through investments in fixed costs. In newspapers, some of the direct input cost measures—page length and staff size—are directly suggestive of quality. Moreover, some other measures of quality, such as the number of Pulitzer Prizes per newspaper, are also higher in larger markets (Berry and Waldfogel, 2010).

That quality rises in market size provides a second mechanism, in addition to variety itself, whereby consumers might deliver more surplus to one another.

---

[37] One might worry that this is driven by large markets where spectrum scarcity delivers rents to stations that can enter, but this seems not to be the case. The elasticity is 0.65 even for markets with fewer than 1 million residents.

1.4.1.4 Market Size and Consumption

Larger markets have more—and higher-cost—products. If these products are more attractive relative to the outside good, then markets with more and/or better products should also have higher consumption. Such evidence would close the loop on the basic own-group preference externality.

A number of papers on radio broadcasting document that a higher share of the population is drawn to consumption in markets with more products. For example, Waldfogel (1999) shows that AQH listening, which averaged 14.8% of population across 246 US metro areas in 1997, was 0.3 percentage points higher in markets with 1 million more persons (or 0.2 if allowing for various controls such as region and the percent driving to work). OLS estimates show that listening is 0.07 percentage points higher in markets with one additional station and 0.12 percentage points higher in markets with one additional format. When stations and formats are instrumented with the level of population, the station and format coefficients rise to 0.10 and 0.18 respectively. This provides evidence that additional stations attract listeners through the greater product variety. George and Waldfogel (2000) provide direct evidence of this mechanism in daily newspaper markets. In a regression of the share of population subscribing to a local daily on MSA population and controls, they find a modest positive effect of about 2% per additional million population.[38]

1.4.2 Preference Externalities with Multiple Consumer Types

The evidence thus far presented concerned one group of consumer. Given the rather stark differences in preferences across groups outlined in Section 1.1—for example, between blacks and whites and between Hispanics and non-Hispanics—it is useful to group consumers with similar preferences together, then to ask how preference externalities function both within and across groups. As the theoretical discussion of Section 1.2 highlights, however, preference externalities work differently depending on the number of products in the market. Here, we begin with the evidence on monopoly (or near-monopoly) markets.

1.4.2.1 Preference Externalities in Markets with Few Products

Daily newspaper markets have few products per market. Most US metropolitan areas have only one. In such markets—as the Hotelling-style positioning model above indicated—the mechanism for preference externalities is the positioning of products, rather than entry.

George and Waldfogel (2000, 2003) examine daily newspaper markets in the US. They take the view that a local newspaper makes its targeting decision at the metropolitan area level. Thus, product characteristics should be a function of the distribution of consumer types in the metropolitan area. Their consumption data, by contrast, are at

---

[38] George and Waldfogel (2000).

the zip-code level. If zip codes differ substantially in their composition by preference group, then they can determine which groups find the local paper's targeting appealing.

They present direct evidence on the relationship between the distribution of consumer types in the metropolitan area and the positioning of the newspapers. In particular, they characterize the local product according to the percentage local coverage that is "hard" news (news, business, government, etc.) as a function of local demographics. They find that metropolitan areas with a higher black population share have a lower hard news share.

To measure own-group and cross-group effects, they regress the share of a zip code's population purchasing the local paper on consuming at the zip-code level. To see their approach, imagine that they had group-specific consumption data (e.g., the share of a zip code's white or black consumers choosing the local paper). Then they could regress

$$s_z^w = \alpha_0 + \alpha_1 W_M + \alpha_2 B_M + \epsilon_z^w, \tag{1.1}$$

$$s_z^B = \beta_0 + \beta_1 W_M + \beta_2 B_M + \epsilon_z^B, \tag{1.2}$$

where s_z^w shows the fraction of white population in zip code z consuming the paper, W_M is metro area white population, B_M is metro area black population, the αs and βs are coefficients, and the ϵ terms are errors. If targeting follows group preferences, then we would see positive own-group effects through $\alpha_1 > 0$ and $\beta_2 > 0$: e.g., whites would purchase the paper more in markets with larger white population, all else constant. Negative cross effects would emerge if, say, blacks purchased the paper less in markets with more whites, all else constant ($\alpha_2 < 0$ and $\beta_1 < 0$).

Extant data, which show total sales by zip code (s_z), do not allow this approach. However, if we note that the share of a zip code consuming the paper is the weighted sum of the unobserved shares of blacks consuming and the unobserved share of whites consuming:

$$s_z = b_z s_z^B + (1 - b_z) s_z^W, \tag{1.3}$$

then we can plug (1.1) and (1.2) into (1.3) to yield

$$s_z = \alpha_0 + \alpha_1 W_M + \alpha_2 B_M + (\beta_0 - \alpha_0) b_z + (\beta_1 - \alpha_1) W_M b_z + (\beta_2 - \alpha_2) B_M b_z + \nu_z.$$

That is, they estimate the coefficients of interest by regressing the zip-code consumption share on the metro black and white population, as well as interactions of the metro area group populations on the zip-code black share.

Using this approach George and Waldfogel (2003) find positive own effects, particularly for blacks. That is, in markets with larger white populations, all else constant, a higher share of whites are attracted to the newspaper, by about 5% per additional million whites. In markets with more blacks, a higher share of blacks are attracted to consumption, by about 40% per additional million blacks. Cross effects, by contrast, are negative. Adding a million whites reduces black circulation by about 15%. Adding a million whites has a statistically insignificant impact on white newspaper consumption. Evidence on Hispanics and non-Hispanics is quite similar in direction and relative magnitudes. Higher non-Hispanic population raises non-Hispanic reading by a small amount. Higher Hispanic population raises Hispanic circulation substantially (by a substantial amount). The cross effect running from non-Hispanics to Hispanics is negative: an additional million non-Hispanics reduces Hispanic circulation by about 20%. The cross effect operating in the other direction is not significant.

The negative cross effects running from majority population to minority consumption tendencies are stark and constitute the fairly direct evidence of the tyranny of the majority in a market context. A single product courting the widest possible audience is driven by metropolitan area composition in a way such that larger population of one group reduces the other group's consumption.

Gentzkow and Shapiro (2010), while aiming at a different question, provide complementary evidence of an analogous tyranny of the majority (see Chapter 14). They show that local newspapers are positioned politically according to the preferences of consumers in the metropolitan area. Zip-code level demand, by contrast, depends on more local preferences. Evidence for preference externalities operating through positioning is, for example, that newspaper circulation is high in heavily Republican zip codes of metropolitan areas that are also highly Republican.

1.4.2.2 Preference Externalities with Heterogeneous Consumers in Markets with Many Products

We documented above that larger markets have more and more varied radio stations. When we divide consumers into different groups according to their radio programming preferences we see more specific evidence of targeting. A regression reported in Waldfogel (1999) of the number of black-targeted radio stations in a metropolitan area on black population and white population shows that markets with a million more blacks have 7 more black-targeted stations, while an additional million whites reduces black entry by 0.6 stations. Similarly, white-targeted entry is 4.6 stations higher in a market with an additional million white consumers but 12.8 lower in a market with an additional million black consumers. That is, own effects on entry are positive, while cross effects on entry are negative. Similar own and cross effects appear among Hispanic and non-Hispanic stations. Positive own effect is larger for the minority group. Negative cross effects are larger for the impact of minority population on majority-targeted programming.

Group-targeted entry is particularly valuable to consumers. In a regression of white AQH listening on the numbers of white- and black-targeted stations and controls (instrumenting entry with the levels of group population), an additional white station raises listening by 0.15 percentage points while an additional black station raises white listening by only 0.12 percentage points. An additional black station raised black listening by 0.78 percentage points while an additional white station raised white listening only 0.19

percentage points. Patterns were similar for effects of Hispanic and non-Hispanic stations on group listening.

The direct relationship between group listening and the populations of the respective groups summarizes the preference externality. Using data on 100 US metro areas with separate data on black and overall listening in 1997, Waldfogel (1999) documents that own-group listening is higher in markets with more members of the own group. White listening is 0.4 percentage points higher in metro areas with an additional million whites, and black listening is 2.7 percentage points higher in markets with an additional million blacks. Cross effects are insignificant, although the point estimate of black population on white listening is negative. These estimates confirm the prediction of the two-group logit model, of positive own-group and zero cross-group preference externalities.

1.4.3 Efficient Entry and Preference Externalities

Models of the efficiency of entry patterns, such as the logit model articulated above and that of Mankiw and Whinston (1986), have implications related to preference externalities. With fixed costs, with one group of consumers and one type of symmetrically differentiated product, marginal entry reveals the market's implicit welfare weight on the marginal consumer. That is, suppose that the last entrant costs $1 million and raises overall consumption by 10 units. For the sake of discussion, assume that marginal entry has no effect on prices. This reveals that the market values consumers at $100,000. This characterization is a slight over-simplification in that, while marginal entry raises consumption by 10 on net, the gross consumption of the marginal entrant will typically exceed 10. Say it's 50. Then while 10 consumers are now getting some product rather than no product, the other 40 are getting a product better than a product they were already consuming.

Berry and Waldfogel (1999) study the efficiency of entry into US radio broadcasting, treating welfare as the value of advertising produced, less the fixed costs of station operation. That is, they examine the efficiency of the market from the standpoint of direct market participants, the buyers and sellers of advertising. They find that US radio markets had about three times too many stations than the number that would maximize the welfare of market participants. Understanding that radio programming has value to listeners, they also inferred the value that a marginal listener would need to have attached to programming to render observed entry patterns efficient. They found this to be $893 per year, while the ad revenue was $277 (both in 1993 dollars). Note that the implicit value is larger in larger markets, as they have more entry and a smaller net impact of the marginal station on total listening, as well as higher costs of station operation.

The market's welfare weight arises from a mechanism related to the preference externality: it shows how much firms in the market expend to deliver consumption to one additional individual (again, putting aside the benefit experienced by consumers finding a better product). One of the themes we have explored in this chapter is the potentially different treatment that media product markets can deliver to different groups.

Berry et al. (2014) explore this question in a two-group extension of Berry and Waldfogel (1999). BEW develop an empirical model of entry into radio broadcasting with two groups of consumers and two groups of stations, where the groups considered are (a) blacks and whites and (b) Hispanics and non-Hispanics. In the black–white model, BEW estimate group-specific nested logit models of radio listening, where blacks and whites have potentially different preferences for black- and white-targeted programming respectively. Given data on ad prices by type of listener, the observed entry patterns can be used along with the listening model to estimate the revenue of the marginal station— and therefore the fixed costs—of each station type. Estimated fixed costs, along with the listening demand functions, can be used to infer the welfare weights that the market attaches to listeners of the two types. They find that the market attaches two to three times higher welfare weight to white relative to black listeners. Weights are slightly higher for non-Hispanic than Hispanic listeners.

1.5. TECHNOLOGICAL CHANGE, FIXED COSTS, AND PREFERENCE EXTERNALITIES

The dependence of one's consumption options on the preferences of others has its starkest impact on isolated consumers. A lone black consumer in an otherwise white metropolitan area will face no options targeted to his or her group and will be delivered little satisfaction by the product market. Media products at their economic core are digitizable audio, video, and text. Given technological change of the past few decades, including the Internet, satellite radio, and even the earlier innovation of cable television, media products are easily transportable (easily communicated) across space.

This has important consequences for the operation of preference externalities. The basic idea of preference externalities is that consumers' options and ultimate satisfaction (in their capacity as product consumers) are limited by the economic mass and preference mix of the fellow consumers with whom they share the market. With the development of contemporary communication technologies, one's fellow consumers need not be geographically local.

Beginning in the late 1990s newspapers and radio programming began to be distributed online and therefore in non-local markets. For example, the *New York Times* and the *Wall Street Journal* began online distribution in 1996, while *USA Today* appeared online even earlier, in 1995.[39] Many local newspapers, ostensibly targeted to local consumers, also appeared online in the mid to late 1990s. With this development, consumers around the country (and the world) could get access to many products not specifically targeted to their local populations.

---

[39] See http://en.wikipedia.org/wiki/The_New_York_Times#Web_presence, http://en.wikipedia.org/wiki/The_Wall_Street_Journal#Internet_expansion, http://en.wikipedia.org/wiki/USA_Today.

While Internet distribution was a radical departure from local physical distribution, it had a precursor in national physical distribution of papers such as the *New York Times* and the *Wall Street Journal*. The *New York Times*, a paper targeted at upscale New York residents as well as educated and cosmopolitan readers outside of the New York metropolitan area, launched a national edition in 1980 and expanded national distribution to 100 cities between 1996 and 2000.

George and Waldfogel (2006) document that as the *Times* became available—and purchased—across the US, the circulation of local papers declined among targeted readers. That is, the highly educated readers turned their attention away from local papers. At the same time, the local papers, ceding the readers lost to the *Times*, shifted their targeting toward more local issues. These changes increased circulation among less educated readers. With the national distribution of the *Times*, educated consumers in locales around the country had access to a more appealing product than could profitably have been made available by a product targeting one local community at a time.[40]

Effects need not have been unambiguously positive. While educated consumers gained access to a product with more extensive national and global coverage, those among them forgoing the local product for the *Times* would lose ready access to local news. Similarly, those consumers continuing to purchase the now-more-locally-targeted local newspapers would have less ready access to non-local information.

The spread of the Internet, a conduit giving consumers access to both local and distant products and information, holds the promise of "liberating" consumers from the tastes of their neighbors. Sinai and Waldfogel (2004) provide some evidence of liberation along these lines. Despite the well-known "digital divide," that blacks are less Internet-connected than whites, Sinai and Waldfogel (2004) document that blacks are more likely to connect as they are more geographically isolated. That is, blacks living in metropolitan areas with fewer fellow black consumers were more likely to connect than blacks in areas with larger local black populations, conditional on individual characteristics. Two mechanisms may have accounted for this result. First, the local within-group preference externality would tend to provide more products more appealing to blacks in local markets with large black populations. Second, those consumers lacking local preference compatriots would be more likely to find products of interest online, whose economic constituency was drawn from around the country. These examples show that technological change that links consumers and products across space have changed the way that preference externalities function.

---

[40] George (2008) and George and Hogendorn (2013) provided related evidence that the spread of the Internet has drawn younger and more educated readers away from traditional newspapers. Mooney (2010) documents the role of new technology in changing the distribution of listeners among programming formats in radio.

The availability of non-local products in competition with products that had previously faced only local competition has had major effects. For example, according to the Newspaper Association of America, combined subscription and advertising revenue fell by over 50% from 2000 to 2010.[41] According to Arbitron, radio listening fell 15% between 1998 and 2007.[42]

Many local products have languished in the face of non-local competition. For example, many newspapers have folded in the past decade. Some have raised concerns that the decline of local newspapers will make it difficult for consumers and citizens to remain well informed. Yet it should be noted that the Internet has also given consumers ready access to information that is not disintermediated. Whether consumers would grow less well informed is an open question.

Technological change has reduced the costs of producing media products and has increased market size by linking consumers together via the Internet. Together, of course, these developments reinforce the reduction in fixed costs relative to market size and may mitigate the occurrence of preference externalities. While new technology reduces the cost of delivering basic products, access to many consumers can give rise to costs that are endogenously large as firms vie for enlarged—and potentially global—audiences. Preference externalities are likely to be with us for some time, although the specific contexts where they arise may change.

ACKNOWLEDGMENTS

We thank Lisa George for useful comments, and Alison Oldham for research assistance. The first author gratefully acknowledges the NSF for support.

REFERENCES

Aguiar, L., Waldfogel, J., 2014. Digitization, Copyright, and the Welfare Effects of Music Trade. IPTS, Seville. Mimeo.

Aldrich, E.M., Arcidiacono, P.S., Vigdor, J.L., 2005. Do people value racial diversity? Evidence from Nielsen ratings. Top. Econ. Anal. Policy 5, 1396; B.E. J. Econ. Anal. Policy 5 (1), ISSN (Online) 1935-1682, ISSN (Print) 2194-6108, doi: 10.1515/1538-0653.1396, February 2005.

Anderson, S.P., De Palma, A., Thisse, J.F., 1992. Discrete Choice Theory of Product Differentiation. MIT Press, Cambridge, MA.

Beebe, J.H., 1977. Institutional structure and program choices in television markets. Q. J. Econ. 91, 15–37.

Berry, S.T., Waldfogel, J., 1999. Free entry and social inefficiency in radio broadcasting. RAND J. Econ. 30, 397–420.

Berry, S.T., Waldfogel, J., 2001. Do mergers increase product variety? Evidence from radio broadcasting. Q. J. Econ. 116, 1009–1025.

Berry, S.T., Waldfogel, J., 2010. Product quality and market size. J. Ind. Econ. 58, 1–31.

Berry, S.T., Levinsohn, J., Pakes, A., 1995. Automobile prices in market equilibrium. Econometrica 63, 841–890.

[41] http://www.naa.org/Trends-and-Numbers/Newspaper-Revenue.aspx.
[42] http://wargod.arbitron.com/scripts/ndb/ndbradio2.asp.

Berry, S.T., Eizenberg, A., Waldfogel, J., 2014. Fixed Costs and the Product Market Treatment of Preference Minorities. NBER Working Paper 20488.

Bhattacharya, J., Packalen, M., 2008. Is Medicine an Ivory Tower? Induced Innovation, Technological Opportunity, and For-Profit vs. Non-profit Innovation. National Bureau of Economic Research. No. w13862.

Bhattacharya, J., Packalen, M., 2011. Opportunities and benefits as determinants of the direction of scientific research. J. Health Econ. 30, 603–615.

Boulding, K.E., 1966. Economic Analysis, Microeconomics, vol. I, fourth ed. Harper & Row, New York.

Chamberlin, E., 1933. The Theory of Monopolistic Competition: A Re-orientation of the Theory of Value. Harvard University Press, Cambridge, MA.

Chevalier, J., Harrington, D.E., Scott Morton, F., 2008. Differentiated to Death? Yale University. Manuscript.

Chiou, L., Tucker, C., 2013. Paywalls and the demand for news. Inf. Econ. Policy 25, 61–69.

Choi, J., Bell, D.R., 2011. Preference minorities and the Internet. J. Mark. Res. 48, 670–682.

Cutler, D.M., Glaeser, E.L., Vigdor, J.L., 2008. When are ghettos bad? Lessons from immigrant segregation in the United States. J. Urban Econ. 63, 759–774.

d'Aspremont, C., Gabszewicz, J.J., Thisse, J.F., 1979. On Hotelling's "stability in competition" Econometrica 47, 1145–1150.

DiCola, P., 2006. False Premises, False Promises: A Quantitative History of Ownership Consolidation in the Radio Industry. Future of Music Coalition, Washington, DC. http://www.futureofmusic.org/sites/default/files/FMCradiostudy06.pdf.

Dixit, A.K., Stiglitz, J.E., 1977. Monopolistic competition and optimum product diversity. Am. Econ. Rev. 67, 297–308.

Duncan, L., 1994. Duncan's Radio Market Guide.

Ferreira, F., Waldfogel, J., 2013. Pop internationalism: has half a century of world music trade displaced local culture? Econ. J. 123, 634–664.

Ferreira, F., Petrin, A., Waldfogel, J., 2013. Trade and Welfare in Motion Pictures. University of Minnesota. Unpublished Paper.

Friedman, M., 1962. Capitalism and Freedom. University of Chicago Press, Chicago.

Gentzkow, M., Shapiro, J.M., 2010. What drives media slant? Evidence from U.S. daily newspapers. Econometrica 78, 35–71.

George, L.M., 2007. What's fit to print: the effect of ownership concentration on product variety in daily newspaper markets. Inf. Econ. Policy 19, 285–303.

George, L.M., 2008. The Internet and the market for daily newspapers. B.E. J. Econ. Anal. Policy 8. No. 1 (Advances), Article 26.

George, L.M., Hogendorn, C., 2013. Local News Online: Aggregators, Geo-Targeting and the Market for Local News. Available at SSRN. http://ssrn.com/abstract=2357586 or http://dx.doi.org/10.2139/ssrn.2357586.

George, L.M., Waldfogel, J., 2000. Who Benefits Whom in Daily Newspaper Markets? NBER Working Paper 7944.

George, L.M., Waldfogel, J., 2003. Who affects whom in daily newspaper markets? J. Polit. Econ. 111, 765–784.

George, L.M., Waldfogel, J., 2006. The New York Times and the market for local newspapers. Am. Econ. Rev. 96, 435–447.

Handbury, J., 2011. Are Poor Cities Cheap for Everyone? Non-homotheticity and the Cost of Living Across US Cities.

Haurin, D.R., Rosenthal, S.S., 2009. Language, agglomeration and Hispanic homeownership. Real Estate Econ. 37, 155–183.

Hotelling, H., 1929. Stability in competition. Econ. J. 39, 41–57.

Mankiw, N.G., Whinston, M.D., 1986. Free entry and social inefficiency. RAND J. Econ. 17, 48–58.

Melitz, M., 2003. The impact of trade on aggregate industry productivity and intra-industry reallocations. Econometrica 71, 1695–1725.

Mooney, C.T., 2010. Turn on, tune in, drop out: radio listening, ownership policy, and technology. J. Media Econ. 23, 231–248.

Mussa, M., Rosen, S., 1978. Monopoly and product quality. J. Econ. Theory 18, 301–317.

Napoli, P.M., 2002. Audience valuation and minority media: an analysis of the determinants of the value of radio audiences. J. Broadcast. Electron. Media 46, 169–184.

Napoli, P.M., 2003. Audience Economics: Media Institutions and the Audience Marketplace. Columbia University Press, New York.

Osborne, M.C., Pitchik, C., 1987. Equilibrium in Hotelling's model of spatial competition. Econometrica 55, 911–922.

Rogers, R.P., Woodbury, J.R., 1996. Market structure, program diversity, and radio audience size. Contemp. Econ. Policy 14, 81–91.

Rosenthal, S.S., Strange, W.C., 2004. Evidence on the nature and sources of agglomeration economies. In: Duranton, G., Henderson, V., Strange, W. (Eds.), Handbook of Regional and Urban Economics Chapter 49, vol. 4. pp. 2119–2171. ISSN 1574-0080, ISBN 9780444509673, http://dx.doi.org/10.1016/S1574-0080(04)80006-3.   http://www.sciencedirect.com/science/article/pii/S1574008004800063.

Sinai, T.M., Waldfogel, J., 2004. Geography and the Internet: Is the Internet a substitute or a complement for cities? J. Urban Econ. 56, 1–24.

Spence, M., 1976. Product selection, fixed costs and monopolistic competition. Rev. Econ. Stud. 43 (2), 217–235.

Steiner, P.O., 1952. Program patterns and preferences, and the workability of competition in radio broadcasting. Q. J. Econ. 66, 194–223.

Sutton, J., 1991. Sunk Costs and Market Structure: Price Competition, Advertising, and the Evolution of Concentration. MIT Press Books, The MIT Press, Cambridge, MA.

Sweeting, A., 2010. The effects of mergers on product positioning: Evidence from the music radio industry. RAND J. Econ. 41, 372–397.

Waldfogel, J., 2003. Preference externalities: an empirical study of who benefits whom in differentiated-product markets. RAND J. Econ. 34, 557–568.

Waldfogel, J., 2004. Who benefits whom in local television markets? In: Brookings-Wharton Papers on Urban Affairs, 2004, pp. 257–305.

Waldfogel, J., 2007. The Tyranny of the Market: Why You Can't Always Get What You Want. Harvard University Press, Cambridge, MA.

Wang, X., Waterman, D., 2011. Market size, preference externalities, and the availability of foreign language radio programming in the United States. J. Media Econ. 24, 111–131.

CHAPTER 2

The Advertising-Financed Business Model in Two-Sided Media Markets

Simon P. Anderson*, Bruno Jullien[†]
*Commonwealth Professor of Economics, University of Virginia, Charlottesville, VA, USA
[†]Toulouse School of Economics, Toulouse, France

Contents

Abstract

This chapter focuses on the economic mechanisms at work in recent models of advertising finance in media markets developed around the concept of two-sided markets. The objective is to highlight new and original insights from this approach, and to clarify the conceptual aspects. The chapter first develops a canonical model of two-sided markets for advertising, where platforms deliver content to consumers and resell their "attention" to advertisers. A key distinction is drawn between free media and pay media, where the former result from the combination of valuable consumer attention and low ad-nuisance cost. The first part discusses various conceptual issues such as equilibrium concepts and the nature of inefficiencies in advertising markets, and concrete issues such as congestion and second-degree discrimination. The second part is devoted to recent contributions on issues arising when consumers patronize multiple platforms. In this case, platforms can only charge incremental values to advertisers, which reduce their market power and affect their price strategies and advertising levels. The last part discusses the implications of the two-sided nature of the media markets for the choice of content and diversity.

Keywords

Two-sided markets, Ad-financed business model, Single-homing consumers, Competitive bottlenecks, Multi-homing consumers, Media see-saws, Advertising congestion, Genre choice, Equilibrium platform variety

JEL Codes

D43, L11, L13, L82, L86, M37

2.1. INTRODUCTION

Media markets are important for their consumption value to consumers, their conduit of potential consumers to advertisers in generating product sales, communication of political information to voters, and the ongoing transformational impact of the Internet. Most media markets are financed all or in part by advertising. This aspect renders them substantially different from standard product markets, requiring a dedicated analysis of their performance. Such analysis has (surprisingly) only developed in detail over the last decade or so, with the recognition that they are two-sided markets. A two-sided market is one where two groups of agents, here media consumers and advertisers, interact through intermediaries (platforms).

The consequences for market performance are quite profound. Platforms face a two-sided equilibrium balance calculus to extract revenues from (potentially) both sides interacting on them. In doing so, they must account for the consequences for the participation on each side from attracting more participants on the other side. In the media context, this means that the business model is to deliver potential consumers to advertisers while advertiser's presence is typically a turn-off for consumers. Surplus and merger analysis must account for the impacts on three groups of agents. Consumer sovereignty can be indirect in such markets because consumers are valuable only insofar as they are desired by advertisers.

In the sequel, we first describe the preferences and objectives of the agents interacting through the platforms. We then set out (in Section 2.3) the equilibrium analysis of two-sided market balance when media consumers choose only one platform (single-homing consumers—SHCs). The competitive bottleneck induced from single-homing begets several puzzles for the positive analysis and strong conclusions for the normative analysis. These are addressed through considering the possibility that (some) consumers multi-home (Section 2.4). Multi-homing gives rise to incremental pricing of ads whereby platforms can only charge for the extra value they deliver to (multi-homing) advertisers. This leads to reluctance for platforms to deliver multi-homing consumers (MHCs) due to their lower value. Section 2.5 draws some implications for platform content choice in both product specifications (short run) and overall product diversity (long run). Section 2.6 concludes with some outstanding research directions.

2.2. CAST OF CHARACTERS

The essence of two-sided markets is that the interaction between two groups of actors is mediated by platforms. In media markets, the two groups are advertisers and consumers, and the platforms are the media themselves. The general theory of such markets was first propounded by Caillaud and Jullien (2001, 2003) and Rochet and Tirole (2003), and has been further elaborated in a voluminous literature. Key milestones and surveys are Armstrong (2006) and Rochet and Tirole (2006).

This literature traditionally distinguishes between usage externalities and participation externalities. Usage externalities arise (for example) for credit cards or click-through advertising, where the platform charges its members per interaction, so that individual interaction behavior matters. Participation externalities arise (for instance) for club membership, where platforms charge their members for access, so that potential members care about the level of participation on the other side. The distinction, although a useful operational tool, is somewhat artificial as it depends as much on tariff structure choices as on technologies (see Rochet and Tirole, 2006).[1] As with many two-sided markets, typical media markets (and models thereof) involve elements of both.

The theoretical literature on platform economics has traditionally concentrated on cases where there are no own-side network effects—participation has no direct effect on the well-being of other members on one's own side of the market—but there are cross-side network effects, which can be either positive or negative.[2] In the media context, consumers typically do not care about how many other consumers are engaged on a medium (modulo fashion and water-cooler effects), but advertisers might well care whether competitors are also airing ads. Advertisers want an audience, the larger the better, so there is a positive

---

[1] For instance, credit cards charge a fee per transaction to sellers but an annual fee to buyers (along with rebating bonus points), implying that buyers care about overall seller adoption (see Bedre-Defolie and Calvano, 2013).

[2] Exceptions include Nocke et al. (2007) and Belleflamme and Toulemonde (2009).

network effect of consumer-side size on advertiser benefits. The relation in the other direction can be positive or negative (or indeed can vary across consumers). Typically, one thinks of television and radio advertising as a net nuisance to consumers insofar as any consumer surplus enabled from the advertising (in terms of information about better purchase options, or enhanced product satisfaction) is outweighed by intrusive interruption of the program content. Specialty magazines may involve positive net benefits,[3] especially insofar as ads in magazines (and newspapers too) are more easily skipped over, and readers may want to find out more about products related to a hobby (sailing or golf mags) or purchase opportunities (classified ads in newspapers).

To be sure, some media are not financed by advertising at all. Such cases (HBO, Sirius radio, and Consumer Reports—which has a mandate not to carry ads) are easily treated as standard one-sided markets, whereby media firms set prices and consumers choose among options in a standard manner, although such cases are rather rare. Instead, whenever consumers are paying attention (even subconsciously, as with billboards), then there is a latent demand to send them advertising messages. Witness the sponsors' emblems on soccer players' shirts and the billboards around the soccer field. Thus the common form of business model is either joint finance with both advertisers and subscribers footing the bill (magazines) or advertisers only paying ultimately for the programming ("free-to-air" or "commercial" television and radio). The business model is then as follows. The platforms want to attract consumers in order to sell their attention to advertisers. The program content is the bait, or lure, which in turn is either denigrated by the ads piggy-backed upon it (when ads are a nuisance) or indeed part of the attraction (when ads have a positive value). The program is thus a conduit for the ads to reach prospective customers, who are in turn not attracted primarily by the ads (infomercials aside!) but by the entertainment content. In this context, the platforms' problem is to balance between extracting revenue from advertisers, while delivering consumers who might be put off by the ads, and switch over, or switch off.[4] Viewed in this light, one might anticipate a marginal condition for the equilibrium at which the elasticity of revenue per viewer is equal consumer participation elasticity, and that is exactly what we deliver formally below.

We next give some notation, and discuss more the three legs of the market, continuing to mix our metaphors somewhat between the various media applications.

2.2.1 Consumers

The media consumers are the readers, viewers, listeners, or (web-)surfers. They choose whether or not to subscribe to a particular channel (if there is a subscription fee) or buy a magazine, and how much time and attention to pay to it (depending in part on the quality

---

[3] See Chapter 9 (this volume) for more details on the empirical evidence for positive benefits.
[4] This is one instance of a more general trade-off between third-party financing and consumers participation that is analyzed in depth by Hagiu and Jullien (2011).

of the publication, how it matches with the consumer's tastes, and the number and types of ads carried). They may indeed consume several channels, although with most media they can only devote attention to one at a time.[5] While engaged with a channel, a consumer may register some of the ads on it, and she might buy something she otherwise would not have.

Given the complexities of modeling the effects in the previous paragraph in terms of the mapping from subscription fees and ad levels to ultimate purchases, it is not too surprising that the literature has taken some drastic simplifications. One of the least egregious is the assumption that the ad nuisance (or desire for ad exposure) can be monetized into dollar terms. Frequently it is assumed that all consumers face the same valuation/cost per ad, and that it is moreover a linear function of ad volume on the channel. Thus, the full price from watching channel i is

$$f_i = s_i + \gamma a_i, \quad i = 1, \ldots, n,$$

where $s_i \geq 0$ is the subscription price, a_i is the ad volume carried on the channel, and γ is the (net) nuisance per ad (which may be negative if ads are enjoyable).[6]

With these prices in mind, consumer choice of what to watch is determined by utility maximization. The standard assumption has been that consumers make a discrete choice of which (single) channel to engage with, and so the apparatus of discrete-choice models (or spatial competition models) has frequently been deployed. This reflects that a consumer can typically only engage a single channel at a time, and the import of this "single-homing" assumption was only recently recognized. Indeed, the modeling of "multi-homing" consumer choice is quite elaborate, and still in its infancy (more details are given in Section 2.4), even if the practice is perhaps becoming even more prevalent with increased Internet penetration (see Chapter 10, this volume). In broad terms then, consumer choice delivers a demand system of substitute products whereby the number of consumers choosing channel i is (denoting $\mathbf{f}_{-i}$ the vector of other platforms' prices)

$$N_i(f_i; \mathbf{f}_{-i}),$$

which is decreasing in the first argument and increasing in each element of the vector of all other channels' full prices.

While many contributions rely on discrete-choice models such as the Hotelling duopoly model, the Vickrey–Salop circle model, or the logit model, an alternative interpretation of N_i is that it measures the total time or attention devoted by consumers to the media platform (see Dukes, 2006; Gal-Or and Dukes, 2003). Some contributions use a representative consumer model (e.g., Kind et al., 2007, 2009). These are discussed in

---

[5] Multi-tasking across media is becoming more common with the advent of the Internet, although even with traditional media it is sometimes possible (reading the newspaper while listening to the radio).

[6] Thus the nuisance might allow for netting off expected consumer surplus from buying advertised products.

detail below, as are extensions of the Hotelling-type models, to allow for individual consumer demand for multiple platforms (multi-homing).

Consumer surplus (from the channel decisions) is then measured in standard fashion given the consumer's optimization problem and the full prices faced.

2.2.2 Advertisers

Advertisers are assumed to derive some benefit from reaching consumers. This should realistically depend on the number and types of other advertisers reaching them, and also the types and numbers of consumers reached. Both of these heterogeneities are typically set aside. That is, first, the value to a particular advertiser from reaching a consumer is usually assumed independent of the specific platform via which she is reached (thus ignoring the matching problem that readers of a motorcycling magazine are more likely to be interested in chain-lube than those of a sailing magazine).[7] Second, the value per consumer is independent of the number of consumers reached,[8] so there are constant returns to advertising (this would not be the case if there were non-constant marginal production costs for advertisers' goods, for example).[9]

Third, competition in the product market is suppressed (so GM's returns from advertising are independent of whether Ford also advertises). This assumption is most tenable when ads are from different sectors and there are negligible income effects (so that the chance the consumer buys the steak-knife is independent of whether she accepts the mortgage refinance). Dukes and Gal-Or (2003), Gal-Or and Dukes (2003, 2006), and Dukes (2004, 2006) analyze media with advertising for competing products.

Except where explicitly noted to the contrary, we assume away limited attention and congestion (Anderson and de Palma, 2009; Van Zandt, 2004) so that the return from an ad does not depend on how many other advertisers reach the same individual.

Under these assumptions, we can rank the advertiser willingness-to-pay per consumer in standard fashion, from high to low, to generate the advertiser demand curve for impressions on a per-consumer basis. Moreover, when each consumer can be reached through one platform (single-homing), the decision to buy advertising space on any platform is independent of the decision for other platforms. Hence the single-homing assumption for consumers implies that advertisers put ads on multiple platforms (they multi-home).

Let then $v(a)$ denote the willingness-to-pay per consumer for the ath highest advertiser. If a platform gets the top a advertisers, its price per ad per consumer is $v(a)$ and its revenue per ad per consumer is

---

[7] For exceptions, see the literature on targeting, such as Athey et al. (2014), discussed in the last section.

[8] In models where demand is measured by the time spent on the platform, the unit of demand is consumer time and the assumption is that the value per unit of time is constant.

[9] As Rysman (2004, p. 491) puts it, advertiser profit per look is constant. An exception is Crampes et al. (2009).

$$R(a) = av(a).$$

Assume that the corresponding marginal revenue $R'(a)$ slopes down in standard fashion.

2.2.3 Media Platforms

Media platforms are assumed to maximize their profits. Abstracting for the moment from costs (and therefore quality) of providing programming, then under pure advertising finance (so $s_i = 0$ for all i), profit is $\pi_i = P_i a_i$ with P_i the price of an ad on platform i. With mixed finance, profit is $\pi_i = P_i a_i + s_i N_i$. We unpack these profit functions and draw out tractable ways to deal with them in oligopolistic platform competition in the next section.

2.2.4 Other Players

To be sure, there are many other agents interacting in the production of the final product (such as ad agencies, content producers like journalists and program producers, cable providers and distributors, and the ilk—see especially Chapter 7 (this volume)). These are often set aside in the analyses in order to concentrate on the major market interaction we focus upon here, namely, the two-sided market interaction between advertisers and consumers as arbitrated by the platforms.

2.3. EQUILIBRIUM ANALYSIS OF SINGLE-HOMING VIEWERS/READERS/ LISTENERS/SURFERS

We start out with the analysis of pure advertising finance. For technological reasons in the difficulty of excluding and pricing access to a pure public good (the TV or radio signal, say), the early days of broadcasting involved such a business model. Only fairly recently, with the advent of signal scramblers and descramblers, did it become economically viable to have viewers pay for platform access. The case of pure ad finance is also one type of equilibrium regime in the panoply of broader tariff choices, as seen below.

The key step in finding an equilibrium is to use the structure imposed above in order to regroup and rewrite the platform's profit:

$$\begin{aligned} \pi_i &= P_i a_i \\ &= v(a_i) N_i(\gamma a_i; \gamma \mathbf{a}_{-i}) a_i \\ &= R(a_i) N_i(\gamma a_i; \gamma \mathbf{a}_{-i}). \end{aligned}$$

That is, the profit which is the product of the price per ad times the volume of ads aired can be split up and repacked as profit per ad per viewer times ad volume, and then reconstituted as the ad revenue per viewer times the number of viewers. We can thus find an equilibrium to the game between platforms by treating the a values as strategic variables. Notice that this means that the platforms can be viewed as choosing the amount of air time (or newsprint pages) to devote to ads, and then selling the ad time (or space) at the price the market will bear. Equivalently, because $v(a)$ is monotonically decreasing, we can treat *prices per ad per viewer* as the "strategic" variable. Alternatives, such as choosing ad prices *per se*, are discussed below.

The first-order condition for the ad-finance game is then readily expressed (by maximizing ln π_i) as the equality between two elasticities (Anderson and Gabszewicz, 2006), those of revenue per viewer and viewer demand. Equivalently, letting a prime denote a derivative with respect to own advertising,

$$\frac{R'}{R} = -\gamma \frac{N_i'}{N_i}, \tag{2.1}$$

where $N_i' < 0$ denotes the derivative of the demand function with respect to its first argument (i.e., the full price). This equation underscores a crucial distinction between cases when ads are a nuisance and when they are desirable to viewers. To see it, assume first that viewers are ad-neutral, so they are indifferent between having an extra ad or not. Then platforms set ad levels such that marginal revenue per viewer (R') is zero. When ad levels do not affect viewer levels, platforms simply extract maximal revenue from their viewer bases. Otherwise, there is a two-sided market effect, and platforms internalize the ad effect on viewer participation. For $\gamma > 0$ (ad nuisance), they restrain ad levels below the level at which marginal revenue is zero. This entails ad prices above the "monopoly" level even when there is competition among platforms. Conversely, for $\gamma < 0$, they sacrifice some revenue per viewer by expanding ad levels in order to entice viewers and so deliver more of them and consequently charge advertisers less per ad. That is, the ads themselves are used as part of the attraction to the platform, though the platform does not expand ad levels indefinitely because then the revenue per viewer would fall too much as more marginal willingness-to-pay advertisers would have to be attracted.

The RHS of (2.1) can readily be evaluated for standard symmetric oligopoly models with n platforms, to deliver some characteristic properties of the solution. For the Vickrey (1964)[10] and Salop (1979) circle model, it is $\gamma(n/t)$ (Anderson and Gabszewicz, 2006; Choi, 2006), where t is the "transport cost" to viewers. For the logit model (Anderson et al., 1992), it is $\gamma((n-1)/\mu n)$, where μ is the degree of product heterogeneity.[11] In both cases (as long as $R'(a)/R(a)$ is decreasing, as implied by the marginal ad revenue decreasing), a higher ad nuisance causes lower ad levels per platform. More preference heterogeneity (t or μ respectively) raises ad levels as platforms have more market power over their viewers. Increasing the number of platforms, n, decreases the ad level. The analogy is that advertising is a "price" to viewers, so naturally such prices go down with more competition. Because the advertising demand curve slopes down, this means that the ad price per viewer exacted on the advertiser side actually *rises with competition*

---

[10] The relevant analysis is republished in Vickrey et al. (1999).

[11] Similar properties hold for other discrete-choice models with i.i.d. log-concave match densities in that the corresponding expression is increasing in n: see Anderson et al. (1995).

(though the ad price itself may not because viewer bases per platform contract). This result may reverse when viewers multi-home, as discussed in Section 2.4 on multi-homing and competition for advertisers.

The oligopoly analysis can also be readily extended to allow for asymmetric platforms, with asymmetries in viewer demand functions allowing for "quality" differences such that higher qualities are associated with higher numbers of viewers for any given vector of ad levels. Anderson and Peitz (2014) engage the structure of aggregative games (which encompasses logit, among other demand structures) to deliver a number of characterization results for market equilibrium. For example, higher quality channels carry more ads, but nonetheless serve more viewers.[12]

The profit function formulation above readily extends to when subscription fees are charged to, e.g., magazine readers. Then there are two sources of revenue from each reader, the direct fee and the ad revenue. The profit expression becomes

$$\pi_i = (s_i + R(a_i))N_i(f_i; \mathbf{f}_{-i}).$$

The solution (assuming that the s and a values are determined in a simultaneous move Nash equilibrium between platforms with consumers observing subscription prices and ad levels[13]) can be determined recursively by first showing the optimal split between s_i and a_i while keeping readership constant. This device will allow us to tie down equilibrium ad levels and then determine subscription prices. That is, fix $f_i = \bar{f}_i$, and so maximize total revenue per reader, $s_i + R(a_i)$, under the constraint that $\bar{f}_i = s_i + \gamma a_i$, so $a_i^s = \text{argmax} \bar{f}_i - \gamma a_i + R(a_i)$. Then $a_i^s \geq 0$ solves $R'(a^s) = \gamma$ (Anderson and Coate, 2005).[14] This means that marginal ad revenue should equal the reader nuisance cost: if it were lower, then total revenue could be increased by decreasing ads and monetizing the subsequent nuisance reduction into the subscription price, and conversely. This relation embodies the two-sided market phenomenon mentioned by Rysman (2009), that a stronger advertising side (a rise in the revenue per visitor) implies less is earned on the other side because then there is more incentive to attract viewers.

One immediate conclusion is that pure subscription pricing prevails if $R'(0) \leq \gamma$, which occurs if the ad demand is weak, and/or if ad annoyance costs are strong. In this case, subscription prices are given by the standard Lerner/inverse elasticity conditions for oligopoly prices—the standard "one-sided market" analysis applies.

---

[12] This analysis is discussed at more length below (Section 2.3.4) when we discuss see-saw effects in media markets.

[13] For magazines, for example, subscription prices are likely determined in advance of advertising rates: it might be worthwhile to develop the analysis for the corresponding two-stage game. Another theme to develop is price discrimination between newsstand and yearly subscription prices.

[14] The result is generalized in Crampes et al. (2009) to a circle market structure and a general advertising annoyance function. Anderson and Gans (2011) extend the result to a distribution of γ in the viewer population: then the average γ determines a^s.

Note that if ads are desirable to readers ($\gamma < 0$) then ad levels are above the "monopoly" level (defined as $a^m = R'^{-1}(0)$).

The constraint that s_i be non-negative is imposed because, if not, readers would be paid for getting magazines, and would then get lots of them and throw excess copies away to collect the subsidies, which would be untenable. Assuming for the moment that $s_i > 0$, and that $R'(0) > \gamma$ so that there is at least some ad financing, the profit function is given as

$$\pi_i = (s_i + R(a^s))N_i(f_i; \mathbf{f}_{-i}), \tag{2.2}$$

where a^s solves $R'(a^s) = \gamma$ for all i and $f_i = s_i + \gamma a^s$. As pointed out by Armstrong (2006), the problem then has a familiar structure, though with an interesting twist. The profit function above, and therefore the game and its solution, is just like a standard oligopoly problem with $R(a^s)$ entering as if it were a negative marginal cost![15] The idea is that each reader carries with her an associated revenue. Hence solutions can be found from solutions to standard oligopoly models with differentiated products, modulo the caveat that subscription prices be non-negative. Indeed, while standard oligopoly models return prices above marginal cost, here an (unconstrained) solution would only return prices above $-R(a^s)$, which might well entail negative solutions for subscription prices. Therefore the subscription price non-negativity constraint might well be binding. If so, the solution is pure ad finance. This happens when a^s is above the level of advertising that would be chosen for a free service,[16] and the outcome is described already above as the elasticity equality between ad revenue per reader and reader demand.

The logic above can also explain the coexistence of pay and free services in the same market as a function of platform content. Loosely, media platforms with the highest elasticity of subscription demand would be free while others would have pay-walls. It follows also that those services charging subscription prices would have a lower advertising level (i.e., a^s) than the free services.[17] Using a model of vertical product differentiation, Gabszewicz et al. (2012) show that a free-to-air low-quality media platform may coexist with a subscription priced high-quality media platform. Anderson and Peitz (2014) use an aggregative game formulation to determine when and which platforms use pay, free, or mixed finance, based on program "quality" (by which we mean a favorable demand-shifter). Low-quality platforms are more likely to be ad-financed, and high-quality ones to use subscription pricing.

---

[15] And modulo the inclusion of γa^s in the full prices in demands, which is like a quality decrement to all platforms.

[16] Assuming quasi-concavity, the service is free if the slope $RN_i' + N_i$ is negative at a^s, which can be written as
$$\frac{R'(a^s)}{R(a^s)} < -\gamma \frac{N_i'(a^s; f_{-i})}{N_i(a^s; f_{-i})}.$$

[17] Recall that all media audiences are here assumed equivalent for advertisers. The conclusion would be modified if the consumers of the paid media were more attractive for advertisers.

We have treated so far the marginal cost to reaching consumers as zero. While this fits radio, TV, and the Internet, for magazines and newspapers there are newsprint costs. The analysis so far is readily adapted to these cases. Indeed, it suffices to include a cost c_i per reader for the basic entertainment pages, and a further cost per reader per page c_a for the ad pages, and so the profit function becomes

$$\pi_i = (s_i - c_i + R(a_i) - c_a a_i)N_i(f_i; \mathbf{f}_{-i}).$$

Thus the analysis above goes through replacing $R(a_i)$ by $\widetilde{R}(a_i) = -c_i + R(a_i) - c_a a_i$.[18] In particular, the ad level is now determined by $\widetilde{R}'(a^s) = \gamma$. When $\gamma < 0$, this may mean pricing below cost, as developed in the next section.

2.3.1 The Ad Revenue/Subscription Revenue Balance

This section both delivers a description of equilibrium finance model for a calibrated example for monopoly and illustrates some key features of pricing in two-sided markets. It also delivers results about how the market business model responds to changes in the demand strengths on the two sides of the market.[19]

Suppose that ad market demand is linear, so $v(a) = 1 - a$ and hence $R'(a) = 1 - 2a$. In any equilibrium involving ads and subscriptions, then $a^s = (1 - \gamma)/2$, so that $R(a^s) = (1 - \gamma^2)/4$, and the subscription price solves $1 + (R(a^s) + s)(N'(f)/N(f)) = 0$.

Now specify too a linear consumer demand function for the medium, $N(f) = 1 - f$, with $f = s + \gamma a$. Then $s > 0$ solves $1 - s - \gamma a^s - (R(a^s) + s) = 0$, or

$$s = \frac{1}{8}\left(3 - 2\gamma + 3\gamma^2\right).$$

When $s = 0$ we have the pure ad-finance regime which solves $R'/R = -\gamma(N_i'/N_i)$ (see 2.1), so

$$\frac{1 - 2a}{a(1 - a)} = \frac{\gamma}{1 - \gamma a}.$$

Whenever $\gamma \geq 1$, the equilibrium is in subscriptions only. Then, given the linear demand, $s = f = 1/2$. The solutions for the equilibrium values as a function of γ are given in Figures 2.1 and 2.2. Figure 2.1 shows equilibrium participation on the two sides of the market, namely, advertiser and consumer levels. Both of these are decreasing in γ up to $\gamma = 1$, whereafter there are no advertisers and subscriber numbers are constant in the subscription-only regime. Put the other way, the more consumers like ads—negative γ is ad loving, so that then the market interaction involves bilateral

---

[18] One might also include some fixed cost as an increasing function of the number of advertisers (sales force effort finding advertisers, etc.), which might be important empirically.

[19] This material is based on Anderson and Shi (2015).

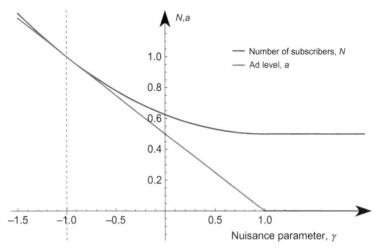

Figure 2.1 Participation on the two sides of the market.

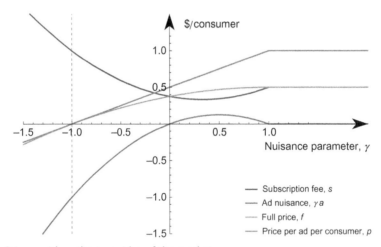

Figure 2.2 Prices paid on the two sides of the market.

positive externalities—then the more participation there is from both sides. Notice that for $\gamma < -1$ the yen for ads is so strong that the number of advertisers goes beyond 1, which can be construed as pricing ads below the marginal cost of delivering them (say, the cost of printing the pages in a magazine). This can make sense in a two-sided world because when ads are attractive it is possible to charge readers much more for the media product. For example, some newspapers carry some ads for free (such as the Hook's classified ads in Charlottesville), and some vintage car magazines carry free ads with the consumer footing all platform revenues.

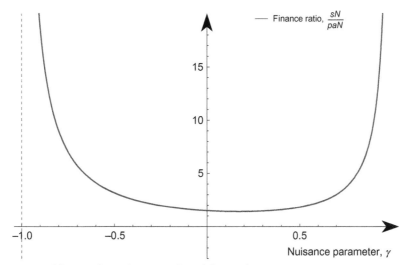

Figure 2.3 Ratio of finance from the two sides of the market.

Figure 2.2 shows the prices faced on both sides of the market (p and s) and furthermore breaks down the full price paid by the consumers into the subscription fee and the ad nuisance (or benefit, when this is negative). Notice the negative ad price (noted above) for $\gamma < -1$. For $\gamma < 0$, the more consumers like ads then the more ads they are delivered, even to the point of pricing them below marginal cost. This is the idea from two-sided market analysis of subsidizing one side of the market to extract more from the other side: consumers are charged increasingly higher subscription prices as they like ads more.

As γ rises, the price per ad per consumer, p, and the consumer full price, f, rise too (consistently with the falling participation).[20] Here the breakdown of f is interesting: because the total ad nuisance rises for $\gamma > 0$ then falls as ads disappear, the subscription fee falls and then rises in order to have the full price rise. We will see more starkly in the next example the U-shape of s, showing that a particular subscription price can be consistent with one level of ad loving, and one level of ad annoyance. When ad nuisance is large, consumers are charged quite a high price to avoid the ads, but when consumers like ads, they are charged a high price to enjoy a lot of them.

One striking recent development in magazines is the drop in subscription prices and tilt toward ad finance in the business model. Figure 2.3 plots the ratio of subscription revenue to advertising revenue as a function of γ. Above the upper bound $\gamma = 1$ there is no ad revenue, while below $\gamma = -1$ net ad revenue is negative. The fraction of ad revenue is highest in the middle region around $\gamma = 0$ where ad revenue per consumer is greatest. For higher levels of ad nuisance there are fewer ads and more is taken from

---

[20] Despite rising prices on both sides of the market, platform profits fall consistently with γ—as is clear more generally from applying the envelope theorem.

subscription prices, while for ad loving there are so many ads that little can be charged per ad to attract so many ads and consequently charge consumers a lot for the benefit from them.

For the parameters of these first three figures, the subscription price is always positive. This will not be the case for sufficiently strong ad demand. Figures 2.4 and 2.5 describe the equilibrium participation and prices respectively for the stronger ad demand $v(a) = 3 - a$ (and with the same consumer demand as before, $N = 1 - f$). These parameters lead to all three regimes being deployed as the equilibrium business model, depending on γ. The new regime—pure ad finance—arises in the middle, when subscription prices are zero. Consistent with the previous description, equilibrium participation in

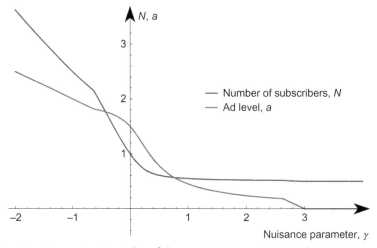

Figure 2.4 Participation on the two sides of the market with expanded ad market.

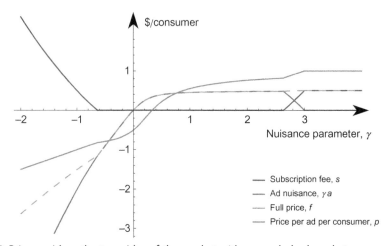

Figure 2.5 Prices paid on the two sides of the market with expanded ad market.

the market for both sides falls with γ and is reflected in rising ad price per consumer and rising consumer full price. The kinks in the participation rates occur when s hits zero and the regime shifts to ad-only finance. Once again, in order to get the consumer full price rising, the subscription price is U-shaped.

2.3.2 Representative Consumer Models

Several authors use a representative consumer approach to modeling the consumer side in media economics.[21] There are pros and cons to proceeding thus. First, it is not always clear what is obscured by aggregating explicitly heterogeneous individuals and their choices. This issue is particularly germane given we have drawn strong differences in outcomes when some consumers multi-home from the case where all single-home. The representative consumer consumes some of all platforms' offerings, and on the advertiser's side it is assumed that ads are valued on each platform the same way regardless of whether the ad(s) are seen on other platforms. The latter is consistent with the single-homing disaggregated approach. Thus, one way to interpret the representative consumer is not as "representative" in the traditional sense of aggregating disaggregate behavior, but instead more as a "typical" consumer who watches multiple channels. This brings up a benefit of the approach, which is that it can deliver a multi-homing model for the consumer side, and allow for allocation of time/attention across platforms. However, it must also be assumed that any multi-homing advertiser (MHA) puts ads on all channels at the same time so that the problem of what happens when a consumer sees more than one ad from the same advertiser does not arise. (Note that these issues are common to the advertising congestion approach deployed by Anderson and Peitz (2014), and described further below.) The model therefore may fit TV (where one can only reasonably watch at most one channel at any given time) rather than magazines, where ads are not ephemeral. Alternatively, one might indeed assume that the consumer's response to any ad is independent of how many times she sees it. Another point on the plus side is that it is important to explore alternative settings, and to check for robustness of findings.

There are two further issues. First, it is typically assumed that consumption of a medium entails a constant money price per unit of time. However, most TV channel subscriptions are "all-you-can-watch" after paying a term subscription. A second issue concerns the utility/demand functions frequently used, which are based on the Shubik and Levitan (1980) linear demand system. This particular demand system has been criticized for some perverse comparative static results in the way it deals with entry of new products: the point becomes apparent in the implicit representative consumer approach that generates it, having extra interaction effects through the number of products *per se*.[22]

---

[21] See, for example, Dewenter et al. (2011), Cunningham and Alexander (2004), and Godes et al. (2009), in addition to the other papers cited below.

[22] Nonetheless, Kind et al. (2009, footnote 9) note that their results are robust to the exact specification of consumer preferences.

Kind et al. (2007) consider a quadratic representative consumer utility function à la Shubik and Levitan (1980). They assume a three-stage game structure whereby platforms first set advertising space[23]; then advertisers choose how many ads to place on each platform; then the consumer makes her viewing choices. Advertisers are potentially heterogeneous, but each advertiser has a constant return per ad aired per viewer hour on a channel (regardless of how many ads are seen and whether or not they are on other channels). Advertisers are finite in number so, because they act before consumers observe their choices, each internalizes the negative effect of its ad levels on viewers' consumption levels. One result from the analysis is that advertisers make less profit the more platforms there are. This result broadly concurs with the analysis of the disaggregated models: platforms raise prices per viewer to reduce ad nuisance, which is how they compete for viewers. This effect reduces advertiser surplus per viewer (although the effect may be offset if the market is not covered because more viewers can be reached, and depending on the ad demand function form). Although the mechanism is a little different in the representative consumer context with the (partial) internalization of own ad nuisance, the effect is still there that set lower ad levels when there are more platforms.

Kind et al. (2009) extend the model to consider mixed finance. One other difference from Kind et al. (2007) is that platforms set (linear) ad prices (per ad) in the first stage, along with prices to the consumer per hour of watching. Because of their game timing (whereby advertisers internalize the effect of their ads on the viewer's choice), they break the $R'(a) = \gamma$ relation that comes from the usual disaggregated model. This changes some characterization results. For example, the volume of advertising is larger the less differentiated are the platforms (with the standard model, ad levels would be unaffected per platform, although indeed with partially covered markets the total level of consumer-ad-minutes would typically rise as more of the market gets covered). Kind et al. (2009) also address how the number of competitors affects the equilibrium financing balance. While more competition decreases revenues from both sources (consumers and advertisers), the share underwritten by consumers rises with the number of platforms.

2.3.3 Competitive Bottlenecks

The single-homing assumption used so far implies that each platform has a monopoly position over delivering its exclusive viewers to advertisers. While there is competition for viewers through ad nuisance, there is no direct competition for advertisers. This assumption gives rise to so-called competitive bottlenecks in the market (Armstrong, 2002, 2006, Armstrong and Wright, 2007), as evinced by the price per ad per viewer exceeding the "monopoly" rate against the advertiser demand curve (i.e., $v(a^m)$ where a^m solves $R'(a^m) = 0$). This in turn generates several strong predictions that may not hold

---

[23] They note their main results still hold if instead ad prices were chosen here.

in all contexts, and leads the discussion into the equilibrium effects of viewer multi-homing, which is continued in the next section. These anomalies were first pointed out by Ambrus and Reisinger (2006) and these "puzzles" are further discussed in Anderson et al. (2012b).

The first puzzle is that if a public broadcaster is allowed to carry ads then the private broadcasters will be *better* off because the private broadcasters pick up some of the consumers diverted by the ad nuisance on the public channel. With SHCs, there is no direct competition for advertisers, who multi-home. Anderson et al. (2015b) give some anecdotal evidence that instead private broadcasters do not relish there being ads on the public channel.[24]

Second, entry of an additional commercial broadcaster *raises* the equilibrium ad price per consumer, although we would usually expect more competition to reduce prices. This effect, already discussed above, stems from competition for consumers being in ad levels, which are the effective prices paid by consumers. These "prices" do indeed go down (just like prices go down with more competition in standard one-sided markets), but when they do so we move up the advertiser demand curve. The opposite direction of the change in prices is an example of a "see-saw effect" in two-sided media markets, as we discuss further below (Section 2.3.4).

Third, and related to the previous one, a merger *reduces* ad prices per consumer because the merged entity raises the ad level (analogous to raising the price paid by consumers in standard markets). Moreover, when the merged entity then gets a smaller market base, its price falls *a fortiori*. Evidence on this effect is mixed (see Chapters 8 and 9, this volume). Mergers in media markets are discussed further in Chapter 6 (this volume). One theme that comes up in thinking about these puzzles in the single-homing case is the realization that two-sided markets are quite different from one-sided markets. Even though the equilibrium reaction to a change (such as a merger) has the "expected" change on one side of the market (the consumer side in the above examples), it may have the opposite effect on the other side. Anderson and Peitz (2014) christen this the "see-saw effect" (see Section 2.3.4) and illustrate several instances when it occurs when consumers single-home.

A final puzzle noted by Ambrus and Reisinger (2006) is the "ITV premium" that programs with more viewers have ad prices that are more than proportionately higher. The idea is that such programs are likely delivering viewers who are hard to pick up on other programs, so this (as with the other puzzles) can be explained by the existence of MHCs, to which we turn in Section 2.4.

---

[24] Chapter 7 (this volume) gives a spirited discussion of public broadcasting in television markets. We do not enter here into the complex objective function of a public broadcaster and how to model its behavior: for the point of the current comparison, we simply assume that it moves from carrying no ads to carrying some ads.

2.3.4 See-Saw Effects in Media Markets

A "see-saw effect" (following Anderson and Peitz, 2014) arises when a change in market fundamentals causes one group of agents served by platforms to be better off while the other group is worse off. In the media context, advertisers can be better off and consumers worse off, so giving a conflicted interest to changes or legislation concerning platforms.

In standard markets, there is typically a conflict that a change (say, firm exit) can make firms better off and consumers worse off. In two-sided markets, there are three groups of agents who interact. Surprisingly, perhaps, what is good for platforms may also be good for one group (typically the advertisers, which are therefore counted on the side of platforms). The consequences for merger analysis are treated in Chapter 6 (this volume).

Anderson and Peitz (2014) apply an aggregative game framework to a two-sided media market context with competitive bottlenecks to address who are the winners and losers from changes in market circumstances (such as mergers, etc.).[25] The motivating research question was to uncover when there can be "see-saw" effects that (say) advertisers are better off while consumers are worse off from some change. This speaks to the heart of two-sided interactions.

The fundamental trade-off is seen in an elementary fashion in the advertiser demand curve for reaching consumers. The price per advertiser per viewer is on the vertical axis, while the number of advertisers is on the horizontal one. But the number of ads also represents the "price" in terms of ad nuisance that is paid by consumers in free-to-air broadcasting. So any move down the ad demand curve tends to make advertisers better off and consumers worse off.

Consider first a merger between platforms. As long as ad levels (the strategic variables) are strategic complements, such a merger makes all platforms better off, including the merged entity (so there is no "merger paradox"—this is true by analogy to models of Bertrand competition with substitute products in standard one-sided markets). What happens to advertisers depends on whether ads are a nuisance to consumers or they are desired. In both cases, ad levels move closer to the "monopoly" levels, meaning that they rise for $\gamma > 0$ and fall for $\gamma < 0$. Consumers are worse off in both cases. For $\gamma > 0$, advertisers are better off (and so there is a see-saw effect in evidence) from the fact that prices per ad per viewer fall. But this effect is mitigated by the lower audiences for the ads. As Anderson and Peitz (2014) show, advertiser surplus rises on the platforms that are not party to the merger, but the effect on the advertiser surplus that accrues on the merged platforms is more delicate. Nonetheless, there are central cases in which it rises, so then

---

[25] An aggregative game, following Selten (1970), has the simplifying structure that platforms' payoffs can be written as functions simply of own actions and an aggregate which is the sum of all platforms' actions. Judicious choice of an aggregator can render a large class of games as aggregative ones. One benefit of the approach is to deal cleanly with heterogeneity across platforms, for example in intrinsic program quality, and thus be able to give a clean cross-sectional characterization of equilibrium. See Acemoglu and Jensen (2013) and Anderson et al. (2013a) for more details on aggregative games.

the total effect is unambiguous and there is a see-saw effect in operation. For $\gamma < 0$, the effects go in the opposite directions, and so merger is bad for all the participants on both sides of the platform. These results serve to highlight the idea that the traditional conflict between firms and those they serve are much more intricate in two-sided markets: the see-saw effect draws this out.

Entry also involves see-saw effects for $\gamma > 0$. Consumers are better off (with more variety and more competition) but advertisers can be worse off if the entrant platform is a small player and the market is close enough to being fully covered. However, for $\gamma < 0$ (ad appreciation), the interests of consumers and advertisers are aligned in relishing entry.

Restricting the ad level of a platform (for example, a public broadcaster) has an unambiguous see-saw effect for $\gamma > 0$. Consumers are happier with diminished ads across the board (as the private companies respond with lower ad nuisance in the face of tougher competition for viewers). Advertisers though are worse off for the twin reasons of demand diversion to the public channel where they are denied communication with viewers, and the higher ad prices elsewhere, coupled to lower audiences.

For a mixed-finance market, Anderson and Peitz (2014) consider asymmetries between platforms to show that platforms with higher equilibrium consumer numbers have higher subscription prices because they correspond to higher "qualities" to consumers.[26] All platforms with positive subscription prices set the same advertising level, as per our earlier results to this end. Platforms with too low qualities set zero subscription prices (it is assumed negative prices are infeasible, for reasons previously discussed), and the lower the quality, the lower the ad level that is supported.

Suppose now that platforms are financed by a mix of subscription prices and ads, and consider a merger. Then, as we had for pure ad finance, ad levels on all platforms rise for $\gamma > 0$ and fall for $\gamma < 0$. Consumers in both cases are worse off, while all platforms are better off. The consequences for advertisers are also as before: there is a see-saw effect (advertisers are better off) for $\gamma > 0$ if all platforms have the same quality, for example.

See-saw effects are also apparent in other approaches. For example, Kind et al. (2007) (who consider $\gamma > 0$) find that entry raises consumer surplus but decreases advertiser surplus.[27]

There is not much work on see-saw effects with consumer multi-homing. However, one example gives the opposite effect from the single-homing case. Anderson and Peitz (2015) in their model with advertising congestion (described below) find that advertisers lose from merger while consumers gain. This is because the merged entity internalizes ad congestion to a greater degree and so places fewer ads.

---

[26] Anderson and de Palma (2001) derive analogous results for differentiated product oligopoly.
[27] Kind et al. (2009) do not consider a welfare analysis, being a Marketing Science paper, although one would expect similar see-saw effects to arise in that context. (Recall it differs from Kind et al. (2007) because it considers a mixed-finance regime.)

2.3.5 Heterogeneous Ad-Nuisance Costs, Price Discrimination, and TiVo

Ad nuisance varies across consumers. This raises two issues: platforms might offer different combinations of subscription price and ad nuisance, and consumers might be able to access technology to strip out the ad nuisance. In both cases, in equilibrium it will be those consumers most annoyed by ads who consume fewer of them.

The first of these issues is a second-degree discrimination problem. Platforms can offer different "contracts" and invite consumers to choose between them. Tag (2009) analyzes a monopoly allowing two choices, which he restricts to being an ad-only program and an ad-free pure subscription option. As he shows, allowing for the subscription option induces a higher level of advertising for those remaining on the ad-only option, in a classic illustration of the idea (going back to Dupuit, 1849) of "frightening" those with high ad nuisance to self-select into the lucrative subscription segment. While aggregate consumer surplus falls in his parameterized example, advertiser surplus rises through lower ad prices per consumer, despite a lower consumer base.

Anderson and Gans (2011) allow instead for consumers to choose a costly ad-stripping technology (such as TiVo). They find an analogous result to Tag (2009). Selection into TiVo by ad-averse consumers leads a non discriminating platform to set higher ad levels on those (less ad-averse) consumers remaining because of their lower sensitivity to ad nuisance. Ad stripping ("siphoning" off content without paying the "price" of consuming the advertising) may reduce welfare and program quality.[28] The theme of ad avoidance is further developed in Stühmeier and Wenzel (2011).

Various authors also consider mixed markets where different platforms concentrate on serving different consumers as a function of their ad sensitivity. Anderson (2003) and Lin (2011) look at a mixed duopoly with a free-to-air broadcaster and one using subscription prices only. Weeds (2013) extends the analysis to look at quality competition in a mixed duopoly with competition between a free-to-air broadcaster and one using mixed finance.

2.3.6 Market Failures in Advertising Finance

Market failures from market power are well established for oligopoly in one-sided markets. Thus, the subscription-only regime suffers from prices that are too high and the markets served are too small. Now consider the mixed-finance regime. Again, oligopoly pricing leads to insufficient site visitors. The level of ads provided under a mixed-finance system solves $R'(a^s) = \gamma$. However, the social benefit of an extra ad is the demand price, $v(a) (> R'(a))$, plus the extra advertiser surplus due to the effect of the extra ad reducing the market price of ads. This inclusive social benefit should be equal, at the optimum, to the nuisance cost, γ. This implies that the market provision of ads is below optimal

---

[28] See also Shah (2011) for more on ad avoidance as well as time-shifting of consumption.

because the social benefit exceeds the private benefit. Again, overpricing, this time in the ad market, is the usual concern with market power.

Lastly, consider pure ad financing where the upshot—too many or too few ads?—is ambiguous. To see this, first suppose that $\gamma = 0$, so readers are ad-neutral. Then, the optimum allows all ads with a positive benefit to advertisers, so $v(a) = 0$. The market solution instead delivers a lower ad level, where $R'(a) = 0$. At the other extreme, if $\gamma > v(0)$, the optimum has no ads at all by dint of the nuisance exceeding the maximal ad demand price. However, under pure ad finance, the market will always deliver some ads because they are the only source of profit. Between these extremes, there will be too little advertising for low values of γ, and too much for high enough levels of γ (Anderson and Coate, 2005).

2.3.7 Alternative Equilibrium Concepts: Price Versus Quantity

The model presented so far follows the convention adopted by most articles that the media platforms choose the amount of advertising (time length for TV, pages for newspapers, etc.) and that this choice is observed by consumers. As already pointed out, this assumption implies that we may view the choice of a as similar to choosing a vertical quality dimension. While the assumption that the media directly choose a might make sense for traditional media, it may be questionable for modern media. For instance, the amount of display on a web page may vary with the short-term fluctuations of demand for advertising slots. Auctions for ad slots often impose a reservation price so that some slots remain unfilled. Armstrong (2006) and Crampes et al. (2009) consider an alternative scenario where the platform fixes the price P_i for ads and lets the quantity a_i adjust to clear the advertising market.

If platforms choose their P_i values, the situation becomes more similar to a standard two-sided market, where the demand on one side depends on the demand on the other side. While platform i's profit is still $\pi_i = P_i a_i$, determining the quantity a_i requires solving a complex fixed-point problem to obtain the advertising levels as a function of prices. For instance, in our base model this requires inverting the system of equations:

$$P_i = v(a_i) N_i(\gamma a_i; \boldsymbol{\gamma} \mathbf{a}_{-i}); \quad i = 1, \dots, n,$$

to obtain ads quantities as function of prices $a_i = A_i(P_i; \mathbf{P}_{-i})$. Whether price-setting for ads results in lower or higher levels of advertising than quantity-setting depends on the sign of the nuisance term γ. To see this, consider the impact on demand of a marginal increase in the amount of advertising. In the quantity-setting game, the impact on subscription is just $\gamma N_i'(\gamma a_i; \boldsymbol{\gamma} \mathbf{a}_{-i})$, where N_i' denotes the derivative with respect to the first argument. In the price-setting game however, there is a transfer of demand across other platforms. When the nuisance cost (γ) is positive, this transfer of demand attracts more advertisers to competing platforms. This effect attenuates the negative impact of platform i's advertising on its subscriptions. Thus when consumers dislike advertising, the subscription demand becomes less sensitive to advertising and as a result, the equilibrium level of advertising will be higher with price-setting than with quantity-setting. The reverse holds if consumers like advertising. Hence when $\gamma > 0$, price competition for advertisers leads to a more competitive outcome for advertisers.

A similar intuition applies for the effect of the subscription price on demand. When platforms fix the *price* of advertising and advertising is a nuisance, the subscription demand is less price elastic than when platforms fix the amount of advertising. In this case, Armstrong (2006) and Crampes et al. (2009) conclude that equilibrium subscription prices will be higher. Hence when $\gamma > 0$, price competition for advertisers leads to a less competitive outcome for consumers. In both models, the equilibrium level of advertising with mixed financing is not affected by the nature of competition (price or quantity) for advertisers.[29]

2.3.8 Consumer Information

The other assumption that has been questioned and analyzed is that of the observability of advertising levels by consumers before they patronize a media platform. Non-observability may apply better in some contexts than others. Gabszewicz and Wauthy (2004, 2014) consider equilibria where each side[30] does not observe the other side's price and activity levels, and holds fixed beliefs about the other side's behavior (whose beliefs are, however, consistent in equilibrium). These are referred to as passive beliefs.[31] To see how this works, suppose that in our base model, consumers do not observe the amount of advertising a_i before they decide whether and which platform to consume. Then they expect some level a_i^e that would not vary if the platform actually decided to choose some different a_i. In this case of passive beliefs, the subscription demand is not responsive to the actual choice of advertising and the profit is

$$R(a_i)N_i\left(\gamma a_i^e; \gamma \mathbf{a}_{-i}^e\right).$$

As demand is fixed from the platform's perspective, the equilibrium level of advertising maximizes the revenue per consumer, $R(a)$, and so is set at the monopoly level a^m satisfying $R'(a^m) = 0$. Thus, under passive beliefs we obtain larger levels of advertising than

---

[29] The reason is that for any given residual demand, it is optimal to set the advertising price so that the quantity maximizes the joint surplus with the consumers $R'(a) = \gamma$ that is independent of the consumer market share, under the assumption that advertisers' value is linear in audience.

[30] The sides are advertisers and consumers in the media context: Gabszewicz and Wauthy consider bilateral positive externalities in the context of buyers and merchants holding and accepting credit cards. Their later paper assumes single-homing while the earlier one considers multi-homing. See also Section 2.4.3.

[31] See also Ferrando et al. (2008) and Gabszewicz et al. (2012). The concept was introduced by Katz and Shapiro (1985). Hagiu and Halaburda (2014) provide a general treatment in a two-sided market allowing a mix between the two types of consumers' expectations. Hurkens and Lopez (2014) look at belief formation in two-sided market in the context of telephony.

when ad levels are observed. As emphasized by Anderson et al. (2013b, 2015b), this leads to a hold-up problem. Once the consumer is committed to a platform, the platform sets the monopoly advertising level.

Consumers rationally anticipate this high level of advertising and adjust demand to $N_i(\gamma a^m, \gamma a^m)$. In particular, the aggregate participation of consumers will be lower under passive beliefs, while there will be more advertisers.

2.3.9 Nonlinear Tariffs and Insulated Equilibrium

In most industries involving some form of network externalities, firms develop business strategies aiming at facilitating consumers coordination, raising the benefit of positive network externalities or reducing the cost of negative externalities. The ability of firms to cope with externalities and to capture the value created depends in particular on the pricing instruments (see the discussion by White and Weyl (2015)).

With two-sided externalities, it is common that platforms offer complex tariffs, including tariffs that are (at least implicitly) contingent on the level of participation on the other side of the market. Examples include click-through rates which condition the total price paid by an advertiser on consumer participation, or credit card fees which condition the merchant payment to the value of transactions. As pointed out by Armstrong (2006), allowing for pricing contingent on the other side's actions results in the existence of multiple equilibria of the pricing game.

For example, suppose that in the advertising-financed regime, platforms offer two-part tariffs to advertisers so that an advertiser pays $P_i = f_i + p_i N_i$. Then for given tariffs, the advertising levels solve the system of equations

$$f_i + p_i N_i(\gamma a_i; \boldsymbol{\gamma}\mathbf{a}_{-i}) = v(a_i) N_i(\gamma a_i; \boldsymbol{\gamma}\mathbf{a}_{-i}); \quad i = 1, 2, \dots. \tag{2.3}$$

Let us fix all tariffs except for platform i, which has profit $R(a_i) N_i(\gamma a_i; \boldsymbol{\gamma}\mathbf{a}_{-i})$ with the constraints

$$v(a_j) = \frac{f_j}{N_j(\gamma a_j; \boldsymbol{\gamma}\mathbf{a}_{-j})} + p_j, \quad j \neq i. \tag{2.4}$$

Notice that only a_i enters into the profit and the constraints. In particular, any combination of fixed fee f_i and p_i that satisfies condition (2.3) is a potential best-response of platform i to the tariffs of competing platforms. With this degree of liberty, we can find multiple equilibria.

To see this, suppose that all other platforms except i choose a zero fixed fee. Then for any platform $j \neq i$, $a_j = v^{-1}(p_j)$ is independent of platform i's strategy. The problem of platform i is to maximize $v(a_i) N_i(\gamma a_i; \boldsymbol{\gamma}\mathbf{a}_{-i})$ under constraint (2.3). Any combination of f_i and p_i that yields the desired level of advertising is privately optimal. Therefore platform i may choose $f_i = 0$. Thus there is an equilibrium where all platforms set zero fixed fees. Because in this case choosing p_i is equivalent to choosing a_i, this equilibrium coincides with the equilibrium of the quantity-setting game discussed above.

Suppose instead that all platforms $j \neq i$ choose fixed fees with $p_j = 0$. The problem of platform i is to maximize $v(a_i)N_i(\gamma a_i; \boldsymbol{\gamma}\mathbf{a}_{-i})$ under constraints (2.3) and (2.4). Again, any combination of f_i and p_i that yields the desired level of advertising a_i is optimal (and gives the same values for a_{-i}). Thus platform i may choose $p_i = 0$. When all platforms choose $p_i = 0$, the situation corresponds to the price-setting game discussed above.

As shown by Armstrong (2006) for the case of pay media, there is a continuum of equilibria that can be indexed by the slopes of the per-consumer tariff p_i of each platform.[32] This raises two issues for applications. In some contexts, the choice of tariff is naturally guided by observation of business practices, as for credit cards or click-through rates. In this case, one would like to understand the reasons that motivated platforms for their choice of tariff, whether they are issues of implementation or more strategic considerations. In other contexts, there is little guidance and we need some theory to proceed.

To address this problem, Weyl (2010) and White and Weyl (2015) propose the concept of insulated equilibria. In their approach, a motivation for the choice of tariff is to improve coordination between sides by offering tariffs that offset the effect of other side's participation on the decisions of agents. They refer to this concept as insulation.

To see the implications, consider the case of a monopoly platform. The participation of consumers depends on their expectation of the advertising level. We saw above that the outcome depends on whether consumers observe or not the advertising levels. The monopoly would then want to achieve a given level of participation in a manner that is robust to the nature of the coordination process. In the above model, this is simple to achieve: the platform just has to offer to consumers a tariff contingent on the ad level, taking the form $f_i - \gamma a_i$. In this case, the full price of watching the channel is f_i independent of the level of advertising so that the platform can anticipate demand $N_i(f_i)$ irrespective of what happens on the advertising side. The advertisers' participation can also be "insulated" by setting a price p_i per consumer (see below). Weyl (2010) refers to such a tariff as an insulating tariff and shows that, for a monopoly, the choice of insulating tariffs is equivalent to the choice of quantities on each side of the market.

White and Weyl (2015) extend the concept to oligopoly. Here platforms try to secure their demand by "insulating" the demand on each side from the other side, which intuitively means that demand remains constant when demand on the other side changes (see below for a precise statement). The difficulty faced by a platform is twofold. First, the platform must account for the tariffs offered by competitors so that insulation can only be for given competitors' tariffs on the same side of the market (consumers here). Thus

---

[32] Reisinger (2014) proposes a solution based on the heterogeneity of agents with respect to their trading volumes.

the platform can only insulate consumer demand against changes in tariffs to advertisers. Second, the value of outside options for a consumer depends on the level of advertising on all the channels. This means that the platform may need to make prices contingent on all advertising levels, although we will see that this is not always the case. Formally, they suppose that each platform can offer advertisers a tariff $P_i(N_i, \mathbf{N}_{-i})$ contingent on the consumer allocation. On the other side, each platform can offer consumers a tariff $S_i(a_i, \mathbf{a}_{-i})$ contingent on the vector of advertising levels on all channels.[33] They say that platform i's tariffs are insulating for given competitors' tariffs if the following two conditions hold:

(i)   the tariff $P_i(N_i, \mathbf{N}_{-i})$ is such that the advertising demand a_i is independent of $\mathbf{N}$ given the other advertising tariffs $\mathbf{P}_{-i}$ and

(ii)   the tariff $S_i(a_i, \mathbf{a}_{-i})$ is such that the consumer demand N_i is independent of $\mathbf{a}$ given the other consumer tariffs $\mathbf{S}_{-i}$.

They show that an insulating best-reply exists for any tariffs of competitors and then define an insulated equilibrium as an equilibrium of the competition game in tariffs such that all platforms offer insulating tariffs.

Insulating tariffs have the property that the equilibrium is robust to assumptions about the coordination of the two sides and formation of expectations. They can thus be viewed as an appropriate tool for situations where platforms have enough instruments at their disposal to overcome any coordination problem and implement any desirable allocation on their residual demand curve.

To illustrate the concept, let us consider the mixed-finance regime above. Consider first the advertisers. As the benefits of the marginal advertisers for a mass a_i is $v(a_i)N_i$, it is immediately apparent that an insulating tariff takes the form $P_i(N_i, \mathbf{N}_{-i}) = p_i N_i$. Thus the media can set a price per user p_i (per reader/per viewer/per click). The amount of advertising is then $a_i = v^{-1}(p_i)$, and it is independent of consumer demand. As advertisers have a constant value per consumer, choosing the price per user or choosing the quantity a_i are equivalent.[34]

Consider now the consumer side. The demand faced by platform i is then

$$N_i\big(S_i(a_i, \mathbf{a}_{-i}) + \gamma a_i; \mathbf{S}_{-i} + \gamma \mathbf{a}_{-i}\big).$$

Intuitively if all competitors propose a tariff $S_j = f_j - \gamma a_j$, the insulating tariff for platform i is also of the form $S_i = f_i - \gamma a_i$ because then the demand is $N_i(f_i; \mathbf{f}_{-i})$ independent of advertising levels. It follows that the equilibrium that we derived before with platforms

---

[33] Whether such contingencies are feasible may be debatable, but they argue that it can be seen as a reduced form of a dynamic adjustment process.

[34] This is valid only if the value of users of one platform is independent of other platforms, and thus if consumers single-home.

choosing advertising levels and a subscription price (as in Anderson and Coate, 2005) is an insulated equilibrium. Under some generic conditions, it can be shown to be the unique insulated equilibrium.[35]

This shows that insulated equilibria may have a simple and attractive structure in some cases. In particular when consumers single-home, it provides some support to the quantity-setting model as the price-setting game would not yield an insulating equilibrium.

2.4. MULTI-HOMING VIEWERS/READERS

The models described in the previous section suppose that each media consumer chooses only one platform. However, advertisers choose to place their ads on multiple channels. The behavior of the consumers is known as single-homing while that of the advertisers is called multi-homing. This (unfortunate) nomenclature comes from common usage in the context of Internet Service Providers. The assumption that consumers single-home gives rise to the competitive bottleneck property of the equilibrium (as discussed in Section 2.3.3), which has several strong implications that may not hold in practice.

The competitive bottleneck and the ensuing predictions can change quite radically if viewers watch several channels over the course of the relative product choice span. Or, indeed, if readers subscribe to several magazines, or web-surfers go to several sites. Put simply, if ad prices are high on one platform, advertisers can avoid it by reaching viewers elsewhere, which just is not possible under single-homing. The competitive bottleneck is defanged by competition for advertisers. Several different variants on this theme are described below.

The presence of multi-homing viewers would not alter the analysis if the return to an ad on one platform were independent of whatever ads are on the other platform. However, there are several reasons why a multi-homing viewer differs from a single-homing viewer for advertisers.

First, when a consumer watches several channels or reads several newspapers, the level of attention devoted to each platform may be lower, which may reduce the efficacy of advertising. Following this logic, Ambrus and Reisinger (2006) allow for the possibility that an ad seen on a platform has diminished value if the consumer seeing it is multi-homing. They assume that the value to an advertiser of such a consumer is lower than for a consumer who single-homes.[36] Athey et al. (2014) point out that when multi-homing viewers switch between channels, a single ad may reach a multi-homing viewer

---

[35] A caveat is that if aggregate demand is fixed, $\sum_i N_i = 1$, as in the Hotelling or Salop model, there is a continuum of insulated equilibria. Thus the conclusion requires some aggregate demand elasticity.

[36] They assume that the valuations are independent of how many ads are seen overall, so there is no "information congestion" *per se*. A broader treatment might determine endogenously the value of an impression on a multi-homer through a more explicit model of information congestion.

with a smaller probability than a single-homing viewer who consumes all her content on the same platform.

Second, the return on an ad placed on one platform may depend on whether the advertiser is already reaching the consumer through another platform. While for single-homers an ad placed on two platforms is guaranteed only unique impressions, this is not so for multi-homing viewers. A second impression might have a lower value for the advertiser than the first impression. This implies that the additional value for placing an ad on a second platform will be lower if there are overlapping viewers.

We investigate below the consequences of consumer multi-homing when the value of a second impression is less than the value of the first one. A first consequence is that the price of advertising is depressed as advertisers worry that the ads they put on some platform generate second impressions rather than exclusive ones (the latter is the case with only SHCs). Building on Anderson et al. (2015b), we start with a simple presentation of the incremental pricing principle that underlies the analysis of MHCs by Ambrus and Reisinger (2006) and subsequent work. We then discuss how this affects equilibrium advertising levels depending on the context.

When demand is affected by advertising, we have the additional effect that if ad levels are low enough, multi-homing is attractive to consumers. However, low ad levels also entail high ad prices, and herein lies the confound. In particular, with high ad prices, advertisers are less likely to want to pay for ads on several channels because adding a second channel delivers some viewers they already reach on the first one. This effect fosters competition in the advertising market.

The viewer side in the duopoly analysis of Anderson–Coate was drawn from the classic Hotelling (1929) single-homing setup, whereby viewers watch the "closer" channel, corrected by ad-nuisance costs (which play the role of prices to viewers). Ambrus and Reisinger (2006) and other contributors assume that viewers who get a positive net utility from both channels (the consumers "in the middle" of the Hotelling line) multi-home and are exposed to ads from both. Thus the marginal consumer is indifferent between one of the channels alone and multi-homing.[37] For simplicity, most authors have assumed model setups such that the marginal consumer is indifferent between multi-homing and single-homing, and we follow this approach because it appears to give the strongest difference from the case of pure single-homing described in the previous section.[38]

---

[37] One might think of preference configurations in which the marginal consumer is indifferent between single-homing on two options, in which case the analysis would essentially be that of the SHC model modulated by the competition for advertisers described in the next section, or indeed there might be marginal consumers on all markets.

[38] Doganoglu and Wright (2006) consider various permutations of marginal (and infra-marginal) consumers in a two-sided platform context with bilateral positive externalities.

2.4.1 MHCs and Incremental Pricing of Ads

To see most starkly the importance of MHCs on competition in the advertising market, we start by assuming that the allocation of consumers to platforms is fixed. This would hold true when consumers are indifferent to the presence of ads. We then indicate how the results can be extended to include consumer preferences about ad content.

The role of multi-homing is brought out quite immediately in this context, and shows quite transparently how it alters market equilibrium characteristics as regards the impact of public platforms, entry, merger, etc. The analysis, which follows Anderson et al. (2015b), highlights the incremental pricing principle at work in the Ambrus and Reisinger (2006) analysis and subsequent papers.

There are n media platforms accessible for free (i.e., without a subscription price) to a population of consumers (readers/viewers/listeners/surfers). Each platform is financed by advertising. The key modification is to allow for consumers to watch more than one channel/buy more than one magazine.[39] There is some heterogeneity in the population so that some individuals may choose to consume from only one platform (single-homing) while others choose to consume from both platforms. Let N_i^E denote the number of exclusive consumers that platform i has and let N_i^S be the number of consumers i *shares* with *one* other platform. Notice that we do not specify with which other platform they are shared: we shall see that this does not matter (modulo the exception for a public broadcaster not carrying ads) given the rest of the model setup. The *total* number of consumers on platform i is $N_i \geq N_i^E + N_i^S$.[40]

The advertiser side is like Ambrus–Reisinger, extending to more than two platforms. As is assumed in all the papers discussed below, advertiser valuations are independent of how many ads are seen overall, so there is no "information congestion" *per se*. Suppose that there is a mass of A advertisers, all with the same valuation for reaching consumers, so each of the A advertisers is willing to pay v to contact a consumer. Furthermore, a consumer reached more than once on a different platform is worth $v + \beta v$ so βv is the incremental value of a second impression. Impressions beyond two have no further incremental value.[41] An ad seen on one platform is worth vN_i because it is viewed exclusively by all the viewers of the platform on which it is aired. An ad that is seen on all platforms is worth $v + \beta v N^S$, which is the full value of everyone reached once plus the incremental value of those reached twice (recalling that the mass of consumers is normalized to unity, and where $N^S = (1/2)\sum_i N_i^S$ is the fraction of viewers in the population shared one time). If an ad is placed on all platforms except platform i, the ad on platform i generates two benefits. It brings a unique impression to the exclusive consumers of platform i, and a second impression on consumers that

---

[39] See also Kim and Serfes (2006) for a multi-homing demand model.

[40] The difference between the LHS and the RHS corresponds to consumers shared with more than one platform.

[41] Anderson et al. (2015b) allow for further impressions to have value, but this is suppressed here.

platform i shares with only one other platform. The incremental value of an ad on platform i is the sum of these two benefits, $\nu N_i^E + \beta \nu N_i^S$, which we shall shortly see in the equilibrium ad price.

Assume that platforms first simultaneously set prices per ad, P_i, $i = 1, \ldots, n$. Advertisers then observe these ad prices, and then choose where to buy ads. Note first that it is an equilibrium for all platforms to price at incremental value, and for advertisers to then place ads on each platform. If all other platforms set their prices at their incremental values, then any platform would increase profit by raising its price up to its own incremental value, but would get nothing by pricing above its incremental value. Furthermore, this is the unique equilibrium: First note that all advertisers are on all platforms in equilibrium, for if a platform had no adherent advertisers it would get no profit and could certainly get something by pricing at the value of its exclusive viewers. But then, if all advertisers are to be on all platforms, prices must be at the incremental values that each platform delivers. Therefore, at the unique equilibrium, each platform sets a price per ad $P_i = \nu N_i^E + \beta \nu N_i^S$, $i = 1, \ldots, n$, so each advertiser places an ad on each platform. This is the *principle of incremental pricing*, whereby each platform prices at the value of its exclusive consumers plus the incremental value of those shared with just one other platform. Note that any consumer shared with more than one other platform has no value because they are already delivered to the advertisers at least twice elsewhere.

As pointed out by Athey et al. (2014), the principle of incremental pricing may explain why larger platforms charge higher prices per consumer, $P_i/N_i = \nu N_i^E/N_i + \beta \nu N_i^S/N_i$. Indeed, this is the case if larger platforms share a smaller percentage of their demand with other platforms so that the ratio N_i^E/N_i is higher.

Consider now (in this framework) the presence of a public broadcaster newly allowed to air ads. Then consumers shared between the public broadcaster and one private one are effectively converted from being exclusively deliverable to advertisers by the private broadcaster, so devaluing them in the ad price and hence private profit. Similarly, those shared three ways in a combination including the private broadcaster are reduced to zero value. These effects are nuanced, as described below at the end of this section, when consumer demand is ad-sensitive.

The effects of entry in this model depend on where the entrant picks up its consumer base. If all its consumers are new consumers, entry does not affect existing platforms' profits. If (as might be expected) a platform's exclusive and shared viewers both fall with entry because the market is more crowded, then ad prices fall with entry.[42] The effect on ad prices per consumer is more subtle because it depends on changes in the composition of consumers. This price goes down if there are proportionally more shared-once consumers, or if it does not fall as much as the number of exclusives (which might be the expected impact).

---

[42] That is, if $N_i^E(\mathbf{A})$ and $N_i^E(\mathbf{A}) + N_i^S(\mathbf{A})$ both decrease with entry.

Merger in this framework is quite easy to deal with. The idea is that a merged entity can still put A ads on each platform so that the situation facing other platforms is unchanged. However, the merged platform can now charge advertisers for access to consumers that are now exclusive to the merged pair but were shared-once between them before, so it can now charge $v + \beta v$ for these, up from βv each before. It can also now charge βv for any consumers attending the two merged platforms plus one other, for these were worth nothing before.

2.4.1.1 Endogenous Viewer Choices

The results above readily extend to when consumers care about the advertising levels, but do not observe them before choosing which platforms to attend. Recall that we argued in Section 2.3.8 that, in this case, consumer demand depends only on expected quantities and not realized quantities, so that with only single-homers, the platforms would choose the monopoly quantity, here $a_i = A$ (with monopoly price $P_i = vN$).

In the presence of multi-homing demand, platforms will still choose the maximal level of advertising $a_i = A$, so each advertiser places an ad on each platform.[43] Rational consumers then expect this maximal level of advertising on each platform and choose platforms accordingly. At the (unique) equilibrium, each platform sets a price per ad $P_i = vN_i^E + \beta vN_i^S$, $i = 1, \ldots, n$, where N_i^E and N_i^S correspond to demands at the expected level of advertising A per platform. Thus the principle of incremental pricing still applies, and each platform prices at the value of its exclusive consumers plus the incremental value of those shared with just one other platform.[44]

Notice that the price per ad per consumer, $p_i = P_i/N_i$, may increase or decrease with the strength of advertiser demand, A, depending on the effect of ad nuisance on the share of single-homers. Along similar lines, the price per ad per consumer decreases if the number of shared consumers goes up with entry, or if it falls less in percentage terms than the number of exclusive consumers (Anderson et al., 2015b).

The model with endogenous consumer choices also ties together the single-homing and multi-homing cases. For example, if ads are a nuisance to consumers, allowing a public platform to air ads has two contradicting forces. First, if ads are a nuisance, the public broadcaster will tend to lose consumers, and some will be picked up by the private platforms. If there is little multi-homing going on, this effect helps the private ones by expanding the base of consumers they can deliver to advertisers. Conversely though, before allowing ads, any private broadcaster sharing consumers

---

[43] For any consumer expectations of $\mathbf{a}$, platforms will price at incremental values and so all advertisers will advertise on all platforms. Thus the rational expectation is $\mathbf{a} = \mathbf{A}$.

[44] The result readily extends along the same lines when impressions beyond the second have value.

just with the public one could count these as effectively exclusives, and even those shared with the public and one another broadcaster could be charged for at βv. After allowing ads, advertisers can reach such consumers through the public broadcaster and this demotes their market value. If the value of βv is low, or there are a lot of shared links that are thus devalued, the tougher competition in the ad market will more than offset any demand diversion effect.

2.4.2 MHC Demand with Observed Ad Levels

We now extend the model to consider the effect of advertising on demand when consumers observe ad levels before choosing a platform (or can change after observation). Assume that there is some heterogeneity in the population so that some individuals may choose to consume from only one platform (single-homing) while others choose to consume from both platforms. Some contributions assume more than two platforms, but the main intuitions can be explained with $n = 2$, which we assume here.

For a given vector of advertising levels $\mathbf{a} = (a_0, a_1)$ on platforms 0 and 1, we denote by $N_i^E(\mathbf{a})$ the mass of exclusive customers and by $N_i^S(\mathbf{a})$ the mass of consumers who multi-home and thus are shared by the platforms. The total demand addressed to a platform is thus $N_i(\mathbf{a}) = N_i^E(\mathbf{a}) + N_i^S(\mathbf{a})$.

Consumer multi-homing results from the possibility of consuming contents from both platforms, when joining one platform does not exhaust all consumption possibilities. Ambrus and Reisinger (2006) assume that the two platforms are not rivals in the market for consumers so that their demands are independent. Specifically, they consider a Hotelling model with each platform at one extreme of a line and they assume that consumers located on the line consume from each platform for which their utility is positive. From the consumer side alone (i.e., in the absence of the advertising side), this would be uninteresting because the platforms would just face monopoly problems: it is the inclusion of advertisers that renders interaction. The demand structure implies that the MHCs will be "in the middle" of the interval. If the platform at 0 sets ad level a_0, its demand is the set of consumers with positive surplus, thus all consumer locations x such that $V - tx - \gamma a_0 > 0$, where V is base consumption utility and t is the consumer "transport" cost, here the disutility from distance in the program characteristics of the platform at 0. Normalizing the consumer density to one, this yields a demand

$$N_0(a_0) = \frac{V - \gamma a_0}{t} \tag{2.5}$$

(when this is below 1), and likewise for the platform at 1. Consumers overlap (in the middle) if $N_0 + N_1 > 1$, and the number of such overlappers (on both platforms) is

$$N^S(\mathbf{a}) = \max\{N_0(a_0) + N_1(a_1) - 1, 0\}.$$

Consequently, the number of exclusive viewers on platform i is

$$N_i^E(\mathbf{a}) = N_i(a_i) - N^S(\mathbf{a}), \quad i,j = 0,1, \quad i \neq j, \tag{2.6}$$

which is simply the number not served by the rival.

Note that this demand implies that when the market is covered, platform i does not control its mass of exclusive customers, which depends solely on the level of advertising of the other platform. One could easily extend the model to obtained more complex patterns (e.g., as in Gentzkow, 2007). As Ambrus et al. (2014) emphasize, (2.6) applies more generally when the valuations for the two platforms are correlated (but remain not rivals: a consumer listens/reads/views platform i if his utility is positive irrespective of the utility at the other platform, but correlation between values for the two platforms implies correlation between individuals' demands for the two platforms). The multi-homing demand then depends on the correlation between individual demands for the two platforms. In particular the share of multi-homers increases with the correlation between the utilities.

With the forces discussed above in mind, we can now think about unilateral changes that would support a particular equilibrium with advertisers multi-homing $(a_0 + a_1 > A)$.[45] An ad on both platforms is still worth $v + \beta v N^S(\mathbf{a})$, but an ad on platform j alone is just worth $v N_j(a_j)$. Differencing yields the market-clearing total ad price for platform i, in terms of N values, as

$$P_i = v N_i^E(\mathbf{a}) + \beta v N^S(\mathbf{a}),$$

and duopoly platform i's profit is

$$\pi_i = v N_i(a_i) a_i - (1 - \beta) v N^S(\mathbf{a}) a_i. \tag{2.7}$$

The first part, $v N_i(a_i) a_i$, is the profit of a (non discriminating) monopoly platform. The presence of competitors induces a reduction in profits as multi-homing reduces the attractiveness of the platform. In particular, a media platform sharing demand with others would choose a lower level a_i of advertising than a monopoly if the demand from multi-homers is more elastic with respect to advertising than the demand from single-homers, i.e., if

$$-\frac{N_i'(a_i) a_i}{N_i(a_i)} < -\frac{\partial N^S(\mathbf{a})}{\partial a_i} \frac{a_i}{N^S(\mathbf{a})}.$$

For a given total demand of a platform, the media platform would benefit from reducing the share of multi-homers among its customers so as to raise its incremental value per consumer. This means that at the margin of the monopoly level of advertising (at equal

---

[45] If $a_0 + a_1 < A$, then each advertiser patronizes one platform or none and the prices are $P_i = v N_i(a_i)$. In this case, each platform acts as a monopoly on both sides.

demand for its product), a platform serving some MHCs would raise the advertising level if this reduces the share of multi-homers. Thus entry may raise or reduce the level of advertising per platform.

One implication of incremental pricing is that when the equilibrium involves MHAs, platforms will need to leave some surplus even to homogeneous advertisers. By contrast, a discriminating monopolist owning the two platforms could price-discriminate by charging different prices for ads depending on the whether the advertiser puts an ad on one or both platforms. In doing so, the monopoly would extract the full advertiser surplus. Denoting by $A^S = a_0 + a_1 - A$ the mass of shared advertisers, the total monopolist's profit is

$$\Pi = \sum_i \nu N_i(a_i)a_i - \nu(1 - \beta)N^S(\mathbf{a})A^S.$$

It follows that the marginal profit for a monopoly is

$$\frac{\partial \Pi}{\partial a_i} = \frac{\partial \pi_i}{\partial a_i} + \nu(1 - \beta)\frac{\partial N^S(\mathbf{a})}{\partial a_i}(A - a_{-i}),$$

where π_i is the duopoly profit defined in (2.7) and $A - a_{-i}$ is the mass of advertisers exclusively on platform i. Thus, in the Ambrus and Reisinger setup, a monopoly would engineer a lower number of multi-homers, N^S, than under duopoly. In particular, this implies that a merger reduces advertising if the consumer multi-homing demand decreases with advertising.

Total welfare under discriminating monopoly is the sum of total vertical surplus Π and consumer surplus. Clearly, such a monopoly would set an excessive level of advertising as it would not internalize the negative effect of advertising on consumer surplus. The same occurs for a duopoly if N^S decreases with advertising. These conclusions, however, hold only for homogeneous advertisers (where a monopoly achieves perfect discrimination), as we have seen that with heterogeneous advertisers a monopoly would reduce the supply of advertising and advertiser surplus.

Ambrus et al. (2014) propose an alternative approach by allowing homogeneous advertisers to buy multiple ads on each platform. An advertiser which airs m_i ads on platform i gets a return of $\phi(m_i)$ for each consumer who is not exposed to the advertiser's ads on the other platform. The return on a consumer who is exposed to m_j of the advertiser's ads on the other platform is $\phi_2(m_0, m_1)$. With a unit mass of advertisers, all advertisers will advertise on both platforms and $m_i = a_i$. For given intensities of advertising a_0 and a_1, the lump-sum price charged to an advertiser for placing a_i ads on platform i is $P_i = \phi(a_i)N_i^E(\mathbf{a}) + (\phi_2(\mathbf{a}) - \phi(a_{-i}))N^S(\mathbf{a})$, which is also the profit of platform i.

In the same context of non-rival content as Ambrus and Reisinger, they confirm the result that a media platform facing competition will air more ads than a monopoly if the demand from multi-homers is sufficiently more elastic to advertising than the demand from single-homers.[46] They also show that, for a bivariate normal distribution of utility, this condition holds when the two platforms deliver negatively correlated utilities.

2.4.3 MHCs and Heterogeneous Advertisers

One drawback of the two previous models is the simplifying assumption that advertisers are homogeneous. The Anderson and Coate (2005) framework, and subsequent models in that vein, allowed for heterogeneity in the willingness-to-pay by advertisers. In the presence of MHCs, different advertisers may choose different portfolios of platform presence, and do so even if there is no correlation between advertiser demand and program choice (which remains a major outstanding research problem).

As pointed out by Doganoglu and Wright (2006), when customers of two-sided platforms are heterogeneous in their valuation of externalities, they will differ in their consumption patterns. In the context of media and advertising, this means that some advertisers will patronize only one platform while others will patronize two platforms.

Indeed, a natural framework for extending the advertiser demand is to deploy models of vertical differentiation, which describe competition between firms selling different quality products to consumers who have heterogeneous values over quality. These consumers translate naturally in the media context to advertisers which have different values for making an impression, and the "qualities" have a natural analog in the *numbers* of consumers attending each platform. Notice that the standard models of vertical differentiation (Gabszewicz and Thisse, 1979; Mussa and Rosen, 1978; Shaked and Sutton, 1983 for duopoly) have consumers making a single choice of option. In the oligopoly equilibrium, a firm with a higher quality sells at a higher price to those consumers with high valuations. The standard analysis was extended by Gabszewicz and Wauthy (2004) to allow for consumer multi-purchase. The consumers who most value quality are those who will multi-purchase in equilibrium. Their model can then be directly transposed into the advertiser demand side in a fuller-fledged two-sided market platform context with "qualities" endogenously determined via the viewer demand side. In the spirit of the multi-homing models above, overlapping consumers denigrate the "quality" of buying the bundle of both platforms (an ad on each platform), so it is not worth the sum of its parts. That is, advertisers who multi-home have to "pay twice" for overlapped viewers, so only those advertisers with high willingness-to-pay will multi-home if there are many MHCs (and second impressions are not worth much).

To see how this works, consider the duopoly model with fixed consumer demands N_i and $N^S = N_1 + N_2 - 1$. Suppose that ν is heterogeneous. Faced with ads priced at P_1 and

---

[46] Their condition compares the ratio of ads–elasticities of the two demands with the ratio of elasticities of advertising returns per consumer for multi-homers (ϕ_2) and single-homers (ϕ). For instance, if $\phi_2 = \phi(m_0) + \phi(m_1) - \phi(m_0)\phi(m_1)$, the condition of Ambrus and Reisinger is sufficient for entry to raise ad levels.

P_2, an advertiser will multi-home if the incremental value of each platform exceeds the price, thus if:

$$\nu > \nu^m = \max_i \frac{P_i}{N_i - (1-\beta)N^S}.$$

Advertisers with a lower ν will choose to single-home or stay out of the market. This means that while the incremental value is the relevant one for high-value advertisers, competition with single-homing prevails for low-value advertisers. In this setup, an advertiser which single-homes opts for platform i if $\nu N_i - P_i$ is larger than 0 and $\nu N_j - P_j$. If the return to ads is a linear function of the consumers reached, then a price competition game for advertisers may fail to have a pure strategy equilibrium.[47]

Anderson et al. (2013b) engage such a (vertically differentiated) advertiser demand side with a specific consumer demand side that allows for consumer multi-homing. They use the non-existence of a price equilibrium that we just noted for some consumer allocations to rule out some types of configurations in advertiser and consumer homing.

Their consumer model is a horizontal differentiation model quite similar to the one used by Ambrus and Reisinger (2006) that was described above.[48] The equilibrium concept is the same as that at the end of Section 2.4.1: consumers do not observe ad levels but rationally anticipate them. *A priori*, four regime combinations can arise: each side can fully single-home or have some multi-homers.

Consider first any regime with SHCs. This is the "competitive bottleneck" case so that all platforms set the monopoly ad level a^m (and are expected to do so). It is an equilibrium as long as no consumer wants to multi-home given the monopoly ad levels on all platforms. Note that all active advertisers multi-home. Hence single-homing on both sides cannot happen.[49] Another combination that cannot happen for a wide range of parameter specifications (including a uniform distribution of advertiser valuations) is partial MHC with SHAs.[50] Taken together, these results then mean that the relevant market

---

[47] For example, suppose that $N_i = N_j$. Then an outlet serves all the multi-homers if it sets the higher price but it serves all multi-homers and all single-homers if it sets the lower price. The advertising demand discontinuity implies that the price game has only mixed strategy equilibria.

[48] These models are described in more detail in Chapter 10 (this volume). The Anderson–Foros–Kind model (see Anderson et al., 2013b) has MHCs who value quality increments of their second-choice (further) product differently from their first choice. However, for the current purpose, with symmetric media product "qualities," the model is the same as that of Ambrus–Reisinger.

[49] The SHC–single-homing advertiser (SHA) combination can arise in the Ambrus–Reisinger model when the length of advertisers is large enough that the sum of each platform's advertiser level is below the total mass A.

[50] This is ruled out by the first-order conditions on the advertiser side. However, SHAs can arise with full MHC. If all consumers are multi-homing, then platforms become perfect substitutes. Equilibrium ad prices are zero, and advertisers are indifferent as to which platform to place an ad upon.

structures are restricted to MHAs together with either SHC or MHC. The former we have already described, and it involves rational anticipation of monopoly ad levels.

The MHA–MHC equilibrium is the most intricate. One result (as follows from Footnote 45 above) is that there can be no symmetric equilibria even though the model is symmetric. Asymmetries are somewhat to be expected given that the vertical differentiation model gives rise to asymmetric quality choices in its standard incarnation (e.g., Shaked and Sutton, 1983). These results above are analogous to those for the case of the model of Gabszewicz and Wauthy (2004) for bilateral positive participation externalities.

The insight that the interaction between multi-homing and vertical differentiation may be a source of asymmetry is nicely illustrated by Calvano and Polo (2014). In their duopoly model, as in Ambrus et al. (2014), homogeneous advertisers choose advertising intensity with decreasing returns to impressions, parameterized by the effectiveness of each single impression. Consumers devote more or less time to each platform, with large consumers multi-homing. They show that when each impression is very effective, and thus multiple impressions not valuable, one platform chooses to be purely ad-financed (and thus free to consumers) while the other charges consumers for a service without advertising. The reason for this asymmetry is that once one platform proposes advertising, the risk of multiple impressions and low incremental ad price deters the other from doing so. According to the same logic as Gabszewicz et al. (2012), the ad-financed platform is a low-quality/negative-cost platform that sets a zero subscription price. The duopoly then generates the same pattern of services as would a monopoly screening ad-averse consumers from others with a free-of-ads service (Tag, 2009).

Athey et al. (2014) point out that in practice platforms have limited ad capacity. Their model differs from above as they focus on the issue of tracking (the ability to follow a consumer's behavior on the platform) and account for the fact that attention of viewers is a scarce resource. In their model, MHCs spread their attention over the two platforms (they switch), so that they are less likely to be reached than single-homers, and they combine this effect with advertiser value from multiple impressions. Limited attention implies that the media platforms are constrained in their supply of advertising slots (or impressions) per consumer. With fixed SHC and MHC demands, they examine the game where each platform chooses first advertising intensity and then prices adjust. Their asymmetric equilibrium exhibits the same MHA–MHC pattern as described above, with low valuation advertisers single-homing and high valuation advertisers multi-homing. In their analysis, as more consumers switch between platforms, advertising capacity expands and the platforms' revenue decreases.

2.4.4 Information Congestion and MHCs

Information congestion in ads constitutes another channel through which multi-homing can impact market performance. The congestion idea is that a consumer is less likely to remember a particular ad when she is exposed to a higher volume of ads. The simplest way to formalize this (e.g., Anderson and de Palma, 2009) is to assume that the consumer will pay attention to at most ϕ ads.

Notice first that if consumers single-home, then platforms will just internalize ad congestion by eliminating it and ensuring higher ad prices for those advertisers with higher willingness-to-pay. Thus all that happens in a single-homing context from allowing for congestion is analogous to an ad cap of ϕ: high-quality platforms are effectively constrained while low-quality ones now compete directly against a lower number of effective competitors. Thus, when the cap that affects the high-quality platforms is tighter, ad levels tend to rise for the weaker platforms.

So suppose now that consumers multi-home. Anderson and Peitz (2015) model this situation by assuming consumers choose how much time to devote to each platform. Their time-use model is described in detail in Chapter 10 (this volume). As indicated there, higher quality programs air more ads in equilibrium but nonetheless enjoy larger consumer numbers. We here draw out the implications for the various "puzzles" of the standard single-homing model.

The economics at work are those of a common-property resource (consumer attention), modulated by platform heterogeneity (in quality). More acutely, a larger platform—one with larger quality—internalizes more the effects of an increase in its ad level because it has more at stake in the total ad level.

Then the effects of entry of a new platform are to reduce the stakes of incumbents, and so incumbents internalize to a lesser degree. This effect renders their ad levels higher, contrasting with the single-homing impact. In an analogous (but opposite) vein, a merged entity has a larger stake in total congestion. It therefore is more mindful of its ad level on total congestion, and the upshot is to set lower ad levels. Allowing a public broadcaster to carry ads has two conflicting effects on other platforms. It increases their demand through its ad nuisance, but it also increases the congestion and competition for advertisers.

2.4.5 Take-Aways and Ways Forward

Introducing actively MHCs makes a big difference to both the positive and normative analysis of media markets by inducing effective competition in the advertising market and breaking the competitive bottleneck that comes with consumer single-homing.

Analyzing a model of search diversion,[51] where platforms compete in reach and price for advertisers, Hagiu and Jullien (2014) point to a complex effect of multi-homing that may raise or reduce reach, depending on the intensity of competition on each side of the market.

---

[51] Search diversion relates to interference by the platform in the consumer search process, which includes intrusive advertising.

More work is needed on formulating tractable models of multi-homing demand, and integrating them with endogenous multi-homing by advertisers. Various models of multi-homing demand *per se* have indeed been formulated, such as Kim and Serfes (2006), and Anderson et al. (2015 forthcoming), based on the Hotelling (1929) spatial model. Anderson and Neven (1989) use a Hotelling-based model to describe consumers mixing between products (called "roll-your-own" preferences by Richardson, 2006).[52] There is also the random utility discrete-choice model of Gentzkow (2007).

While the work by Anderson et al. (2013b) described above does integrate partial multi-homing on both sides of the market, the model is not very tractable, and does not readily extend (for example, to more platforms). That model can also usefully be analyzed with the alternative equilibrium concept of observable ad levels (in that vein, repeated interaction and long-term reputation effects could be usefully addressed, and the details ought to be fleshed out).

There is therefore still a need for tractable and workable approaches to break out the two-sided interaction when both sides are partially multi-homing.[53] Indeed, one path is to develop the time-use model in Anderson and Peitz (2015): the model of ad congestion they engage is one way to deliver such interaction.

Other questions, in addition to the anti-trust treatment for such markets (see Chapter 6, this volume), include the effects of multi-homing on the other dimensions of competition, such as content provision. As discussed in the next section, content provision is impacted by multi-homing because of the desirability of attracting exclusive (i.e., single-homing) consumers so that platforms strive to provide content valued by single-homers to the exclusion of multi-homers.

2.5. EQUILIBRIUM GENRE CHOICES

In the broader perspective, program quality, type, and variety of offerings are paramount to evaluating consumer satisfaction with media. The analysis so far has concentrated on performance with respect to advertising choices while taking as given the program offerings by platforms. Yet the types and numbers of choices provided in the market are arguably at least as important to performance. We now explore these extra dimensions to performance.

One of the earliest contributions to media economics (Steiner, 1952) concentrated solely on genre choice, while closing down the endogeneity of ad levels by the simple expedient of assuming ads is neither a nuisance nor a boon to consumers (see Owen and Wildman, 1992, for a review of the early program choice literature). We start at this

---

[52] Variants of this have indeed been already deployed in the context of media economics—see, e.g., Gal-Or and Dukes (2003), Gabszewicz et al. (2004), Richardson (2006), and Hoernig and Valletti (2007).

[53] A theoretical analysis of this issue in the canonical two-sided market is Jeitschko and Tremblay (2015).

point, and are able to draw on an extant literature on product differentiation with fixed prices. We then expand the scope to consider the role of endogenous ad choices in a full two-sided market context.

Steiner (1952) enunciated the duplication principle whereby media offerings tend to concentrate (and double up) in genres with large consumer interest. Put succinctly by example, if 70% of media consumers will only listen to country music, and 30% will only listen to rock, and if there is only room for two radio stations (due to spectrum constraints), then the market equilibrium will have two country stations. A two-channel monopolist will provide one channel catering to each type and so cover the full diversity of tastes.

Beebe (1977) amended the setup to allow consumers to have second preferences, and christened the Lowest Common Denominator outcome whereby a monopolist could provide a low-tier program type that many types would listen to, while competition could provide more specialist higher-tier programming. These themes are developed more in Chapter 1 (this volume) and implications for merger analysis are developed in Chapter 6 (this volume). Of particular note is the implication that programming choices are driven by advertisers' desire to impress consumers of genres more likely to buy the advertised products. Even if many consumers are interested in Nature programs, their preferences are not given much weight in a market system with ad finance if they are unlikely to respond to ads: sitcoms with ad-responsive viewers can instead attract multiple (duplicative) offerings. The upshot is a first-degree market failure when preferences cannot be expressed through the market by viewer willingness-to-pay. Of course, such problems are likely to be largely mitigated in the modern context where product offerings are many, and consumers who are unattractive to advertisers can find their market voice through paying directly for content.

Steiner's duplication principle finds its natural parallel in Hotelling's (1929) principle of minimum differentiation. However, while Steiner envisaged fixed "buckets" of viewers, Hotelling's model allowed for a continuum of types. The "fixed-price" version of Hotelling's model was extended to multiple outlets by Eaton and Lipsey (1975), and many subsequent authors elaborated upon the theme. One feature of such spatial models of localized competition[54] is that there are multiple equilibria (for six or more outlets in the linear market case) when a fixed number of outlets choose locations simultaneously, and that different positions can earn different profits, so some locations are more profitable than others in equilibrium. This raises the question of how outlets might compete, in a broader setting, to get the better locations, and also the question of equilibrium numbers of firms under free entry. One way to tackle the problem is to consider sequential entry of foresighted outlets that accounts for both the locations of subsequent entrants and the

---

[54] The term localized competition refers to the idea that outlets compete directly only with neighboring outlets in the underlying space of program characteristics.

possibility of deterring their entry. The problem is quite complex because an outlet must consider the locations of future entrants, and how to use future entrants' incentives to their own advantage (see, for example, Prescott and Visscher, 1977). Due to the fact that entrants must fit between existing outlets (in their programming formats), the upshot can be that outlets in the market can earn substantial pure profits in equilibrium (see, e.g., Archibald et al., 1986, for a forceful argument). The market may therefore involve a far sparser coverage of product variety than would be suggested by models where outlets are spaced so that all earn zero profit.

We now introduce ad nuisance into the spatial duopoly framework. We first treat SHCs, and then allow for multi-homing.[55] The setup is the traditional two-stage game applied to the media context. That is, we seek equilibria at which platforms first choose locations while rationally anticipating the subsequent (second-stage) equilibrium in ad levels (and subscription prices, when pertinent). The overarching principles governing equilibrium locations balance two effects in the first-order conditions for best responses. First is the "direct" effect of moving toward the rival. This is positive, and picks up the idea that with full prices constant, consumer bases increase when moving inward. Notice that this is the only effect in models with fixed prices, and is the driving force behind the Principle of Minimum Differentiation noted above. The second effect is the "strategic effect" that moving in tends to intensify competition by harshening the rival's full price (in the pricing sub-game induced by locations) and so hurts profit. This effect induces the desire to move away to relax competition. A balance between the two effects characterizes an interior solution.

With these effects in mind, several results can be drawn off the shelf from existing equilibrium models of spatial competition. First of all, there is a direct mathematical equivalence between standard models of price competition and models of ad finance when advertisers all have the same willingness-to-pay, v. To see this, notice that then i's profit is given by $\pi_i = va_i N_i(\gamma a_i; \gamma a_j)$: writing $p_i = \gamma a_i$, we have $\pi_i = (v/\gamma)p_i N_i(p_i; p_j)$, so that the profit is proportional to that in an equivalent pricing game. The solutions are then those of the pricing game corresponding to the demand system induced by the spatial structure that generates the demand $N_i(p_i; p_j)$. To take a central example, suppose that consumers are located on the unit interval and consumer disutility (transport) costs are quadratic functions of distance, as per the modification of Hotelling's (1929) linear-cost model propounded by D'Aspremont et al. (1979). Then the location outcome (at least when locations are restricted to the unit interval) are the extremes, giving rise to a "maximum differentiation" result. This is because the strategic effect of relaxing competition dominates the direct effect for all interior locations for this disutility specification.

---

[55] Gabszewicz et al. (2004) analyze the free-to-air TV model allowing consumers to mix between the programs of the two channels (as in Anderson and Neven, 1989). Gabszewicz et al. (2004) assume that ad nuisance is a time-weighted sum of ad nuisances to a power $\mu > 0$ (i.e., the sum of d_0^μ and d_1^μ). When $\mu < \sqrt{2}$, they find that platforms are at the extremes (the "normal" case would indeed fall in this range because $\mu = 1$). It is only for higher μ that platforms move in.

Taken literally, then, the prediction for genre choice is maximal variety difference between competing platforms, opposite the minimum differentiation (or duplication à la Steiner) predicted when there are no ad-nuisance costs. The inclusion of the nuisance cost leads platforms to separate to avoid ruinous competition in the ad "price" paid by consumers, and so to endogenously induce mutually compatible high levels of ads. Note that the social optimum in this model is to locate at the quartiles, so the equilibrium is too extreme.

When the advertiser demand is not perfectly elastic, Peitz and Valletti (2008) show that (with a concave revenue per viewer, $R(a)$) maximal differentiation still prevails for high enough disutility (transport) rates. For lower rates, platforms move closer in equilibrium as the direct effect kicks in. Likewise, lower ad-nuisance costs, γ, decrease differentiation, although duplication (minimum differentiation) never arises for $\gamma > 0$, for then ads and profits would be zero, which platforms avoid by differentiating.

We can also use the spatial analysis of Section 2.2 to determine the equilibrium outcome for a mixed-finance system (ads and subscription prices to consumers). Recall then from (2.2) that i's profit is given by $\pi_i = (s_i + R(a^s))N_i(f_i; f_j)$, where a^s solves $R'(a^s) = \gamma$ and with $f_i = s_i + \gamma a^s$. This is therefore equivalent to a situation in the standard pricing model where platforms have negative production costs, as we previously established. Hence (modulo the caveat discussed next on non-negative subscription prices), the location outcome is maximal differentiation with platforms setting ad levels to equate marginal ad revenue per viewer to nuisance cost (Peitz and Valletti, 2008).

Gabszewicz et al. (2001) engage the model above with a surprising twist by assuming that platforms cannot feasibly set subscription prices below zero—if people were paid to take newspapers, clearly they would walk off with stacks of them. This floor can change the outcome quite dramatically. In their model, they assume no ad nuisance ($\gamma = 0$) so that the condition $R'(a^s) = \gamma$ for the ad level implies that ads are set at the per-consumer monopoly level, a^m. However, the tenor of their results applies more generally.[56] They show that if ad revenue is weak enough, then maximal differentiation attains; while if it is high enough, the outcome is minimum differentiation with free-to-air media (and both constellations are equilibria for some intermediate values).[57]

---

[56] They assume ad demand is linear. They also consider a three-stage game with locations, then subscription prices, then ad levels. However, as they show, in the last stage the ad level is set at the monopoly level, a^m, so that the upshot is the same.

[57] Bourreau (2003) analyzes a similar model appending quality investment, where quality raises consumer valuations vertically across the board. He contrasts advertising-financed and pay TV outcomes. In both cases, he finds equilibria that are symmetric in qualities (mimicking). Pay TV gives extremal horizontal location outcomes, as per D'Aspremont et al.'s (1979) classic extension to quadratic transport costs of Hotelling's (1929) model. For advertising finance, he considers a two-stage location then quality game with advertising revenues fixed per viewer. The direct location incentive is toward minimal differentiation (counter-programming); this is offset by a strategic effect of more intense quality competition. The latter effect is weaker the lower are ad revenues, and he finds that minimal differentiation is reached as ad revenues go to zero.

The reasons can be ascribed to the interplay of strategic and direct effects. For weak ad demand, subscription prices are paramount, and platforms ensure these are high by differentiating maximally, which is just an extension of the standard pricing result. However, for strong ad demand the direct effect takes over because picking up consumers to deliver to advertisers becomes predominant. When platforms are close enough together, subscription prices are floored at zero. This takes away completely the strategic effect and we are back to the model with fixed prices and hence minimum differentiation.

Gabszewicz et al. (2001) relate their finding to the idea of the "Pensee Unique," which is a social context in which discrepancies among citizens' political opinions are almost wiped out (p. 642) (see Part III of this volume, and in particular the discussion in Chapter 14).

Gabszewicz et al. (2004) relate the degree of differentiation of free broadcasters to the elasticity of the nuisance term, higher elasticity leading to less differentiation. Location choice induces a strategic effect that works through increased levels of advertising when differentiation increases, which explains why free-media platforms may choose maximal differentiation. This effect is reduced if consumer demand is very elastic to advertising, as advertising will vary little with location, and in this case differentiation will be smaller.

Many models compare free-to-air versus pay and thus take the payment technology as given (an early example is Hansen and Kyhl (2001), whose thought experiment is to consider a ban on using pay-walls for important sporting events and so put the programming into the free public domain of commercial broadcasting). For instance, Peitz and Valletti (2008) show that pay-platforms deliver more advertising and higher total welfare than free platforms when the nuisance from advertising is small. The reason is that large revenues from advertising are passed through to consumers (a see-saw effect). In the context of the Vickrey (1964)–Salop (1979) model with free entry (discussed further below), Choi (2006) shows that, contrasting with excessive entry in pay media, free media may induce insufficient or excessive product diversity. A difficulty with these comparisons is that, as pointed out by Gabszewicz et al. (2001), whether media platforms are paid or free depends on the nuisance and constraints on payments. It is when ad nuisance is small and therefore advertising revenue large, that platforms will prefer to be free rather than charging a positive subscription price.

Several papers discuss endogenous content quality in media markets. Armstrong and Weeds (2007) analyze program quality in a symmetric Hotelling duopoly under pay TV and pure advertising–funding, respectively.[58] They find that quality is lower in ad-financed duopoly than in a duopoly where both platforms use mixed financing. This is because of the higher marginal profitability when two revenue extraction instruments are available. Armstrong and Weeds (2007) get several other interesting results. Under

---

[58] The analysis is extended by Weeds (2013) to a mixed duopoly comprising a free-to-air broadcaster and another one that uses mixed finance. See also Weeds (2012).

mixed financing, equilibrium profits are a hump-shaped function of the strength of advertising demand. A weak advertising demand is bad news for platforms, but so too is a strong one because then profits are dissipated through high investments in quality to try and attract consumers. Another intriguing result (reminiscent of Grossman and Shapiro, 1984) is that platform profits are increasing in the marginal cost of quality investment. This comes from the strategic effect of softening competition.

Anderson (2005) looks at an asymmetric model of quality investment in which one platform has a central role (like a "hub" or a Lowest Common Denominator) and competes in local markets with local platforms. The central platform (think Clear Channel radio, or Hollywood movies) competes in all local markets but a local platform (Welsh language radio, or Bollywood) is also present in each local market. The structure in each local market is like the Armstrong and Weeds (2007) setup, i.e., "Hotelling" segments with ad levels being set in local markets by both the local and the global competitor, but all such local segments are effectively connected through the hub. The global producer here has an economy of scale in quality provision because its quality is "one-size-fits-all" and applies to all the local markets in which it competes. However, the local market decisions (advertising levels) are tailored to each market. Through the quality choice of the global platform, there are externalities between local producers even though they do not interact directly. In equilibrium, the large platform chooses higher quality than the local ones because it can spread its costs of providing quality over all the local markets. Each local producer's quality and audience share is larger in larger local markets, and so the disparity is largest in the smallest markets.

Kerkhof and Munster (2015) analyze a different "quality" margin. They assume that advertisers' willingness-to-pay to contact consumers is decreasing in a quality variable that consumers find desirable. For example, consumers may appreciate a serious documentary, but the framing effect of embedding ads may make them less willing to buy frivolous products. The platforms then face a classic sort of two-sided market trade-off that what is good for extracting revenue from advertisers (here "low" quality) is bad for delivering the viewers' eyeballs. Kerkhof and Munster (2015) argue that a cap on advertising in this context can be welfare improving. Their mechanism is thus different from the standard arguments about ad caps (e.g., Anderson, 2007).[59]

The models so far discussed assume single-homing by media consumers. As we argued in the previous section, MHCs can be worth substantially less (in a platform's consumer portfolio) than SHCs. This effect can lead to bias in platform positions to favor catering to SHCs and against catering to MHCs. Since the single-homers are worth more, platforms will strive to deliver such exclusive viewers while avoiding overlapped consumers. The theme is developed in Anderson et al. (2015b) in a spatial duopoly model. As noted

---

[59] The latter paper also analyzes the effects of ad caps on platform quality choice.

earlier, in the context of the Hotelling model, the MHCs will be those in the middle of the market. The less valuable these are (e.g., the lower the value of a second ad impression), the further apart will platforms locate in equilibrium, and the worse off are the multi-homers. Athey et al. (2014) discuss the supply of multiple content in a model of decreasing return per impression and imperfect tracking of viewer behavior. They show that a reduction of supply by one platform may lead the other platform to expand its supply. This points to a potential free-rider issue insofar as investment by one platform to reduce the multi-homing demand benefits all platforms.

2.5.1 Free-Entry Analysis

Classic analysis of long-run equilibrium with oligopoly or monopolistic competition closes the model with a free-entry condition, which is often taken as a zero-profit condition for symmetric firms. Equilibrium product variety is then described by the number of products in the market. This can be compared to optimal product variety to discern market failures in the overall range of diversity provided by markets. Following Spence (1976), the market delivers excessive product variety when the negative externality on other firms of entry (the "business-stealing" effect) dominates the positive externality on consumers from having better-matched products and lower prices.

The canonical models that are usually analyzed are the CES representative consumer model, the Vickrey (1964)–Salop (1979) circle model, and "random utility" discrete-choice models such as the logit. We concentrate on the latter two because they derive from explicit micro-underpinnings for individual consumers.

Consider first the mixed-finance context, whereby both subscription prices and advertising are used. Then, the characterization of the start of Section 2.3 applies so that platforms' ad choices satisfy $R'(a) = \gamma$. As we noted earlier, the implication for subscription pricing is analogous to there being a negative marginal cost. Therefore, for the class of models that assume fully covered markets and symmetric firms, because cost levels do not affect equilibrium profits, the market equilibrium is fully independent of the advertising demand. The implication is that equilibrium product variety is not impacted by the advertiser demand strength. This strong decoupling result implies that the standard Vickrey–Salop analysis goes through: there is excessive variety in equilibrium (see Choi, 2006, for the statement in the media context). The same remark applies to other covered market models (e.g., discrete-choice random utility models with covered markets). This decoupling is somewhat disconcerting for both the positive and the normative analysis, but the problem is really the assumption that the market is fully covered. While the circle model cannot be easily relaxed (apart from the trivial expedient of introducing low consumer reservation prices and hence local monopolies), the discrete-choice model can allow for uncovered markets through "outside" options, and this reconnects equilibrium variety to advertising demand strength.

The canonical model also assumes that the revenue per consumer $R(a)$ is independent of the audience, which is questionable. For instance, access to a large customer base helps Internet platforms improve the efficiency of their advertising services. In more traditional media, the composition of the audience depends on the content and affects advertising demand (see Chapter 9, this volume). A large audience with very heterogeneous consumers may not be attractive for specialized advertising. Crampes et al. (2009) point out that allowing R to depend on the consumer base is tantamount to considering variable returns to scale in the audience, with less (more) entry when the revenue R increases (decreases) with N_i.[60]

Now consider a regime of pure advertising finance. Here the advertising side is reconnected to equilibrium diversity. Under the fully covered market specification (e.g., circle and logit), equilibrium ad levels and profits are decreasing in the number of platforms (as long as $R(\cdot)$ is log-concave: see the analysis in Anderson and Gabszewicz, 2006). The important point is that a weak advertising demand delivers low equilibrium diversity because the economic impetus for entry is absent through low profitability from advertising. This indicates that market failures through underprovision of variety can be especially severe in such circumstances, for example in less-developed nations. With strong advertising demand, the classic over-entry result still attains: Choi (2006) notes the strong disconnect between optimal variety and advertising levels in this case, albeit for the first-best optimum.[61] Indeed, the disconnect holds whenever markets are fully covered: the first-best optimal ad level of ads satisfies $v(a^0) = \gamma$ regardless of the number of platforms.

Accounting for the endogeneity of the business model (free vs. pay) leads to slightly different conclusions as the free-media business model emerges only if the advertising demand is strong enough. As shown by Crampes et al. (2009), imposing a non-negativity constraint on consumer prices raises equilibrium prices (to zero) when they would be negative. This relaxes competition for consumers, raises profits, and reduces advertising and consumer surplus. As a result, there is more entry and total welfare is lower when platforms are free than if they could subsidize consumers' participation. Moreover, platforms rely more extensively on quality improvement as an indirect form of subsidy, as well as tying (Amelio and Jullien, 2012).[62]

---

[60] They also show that price competition on the advertising side delivers more entry in the media market than quantity competition.

[61] Considering a constrained optima, such as with a zero-profit constraint or the constraint that platforms choose ad levels non-cooperatively, would alleviate this separability result.

[62] Dukes (2004) analyzes free entry with advertising for competing products. Lowering product differentiation reduces entry by media, thereby intensifying their use of advertising. High media diversity (due to easy differentiation) results in excessive advertising.

2.6. FURTHER DIRECTIONS

This chapter has emphasized the theoretical insights from the recently developed literature on two-sided markets applied to the context of media markets. Big differences in predictions arise in situations where consumers single-home (and the competitive bottleneck of Section 2.3.3 applies) from when consumers multi-home (as per Section 2.4). More work would be welcome here: some preliminary thoughts in this regard are given in Section 2.4.5.

For empirical studies in the various types of media market, the reader is referred to the various Chapters 3 and 7–9 (this volume). Clearly, more work that integrates the theory and the empirics is strongly desirable.

While it is outside the scope of this chapter, we should mention the burgeoning literature on targeting. This literature is mostly motivated by the development of Internet technologies and the increased ability to tailor advertising to individual preferences revealed by consumers' behavioral history. This literature develops explicit micro-models for advertising and sales suited for discussing the effect of targeting on advertising levels and prices.[63]

Athey and Gans (2010) point out that expanding advertising messages may substitute for targeting, and they thereby relate the effect of targeting on a platform's revenue and consumers to capacity constraints in the advertising markets or limited attention. Bergemann and Bonatti (2011) develop a model of competitive advertising markets with targeting and congestion. The accuracy of targeting has an inverse-U-shaped effect on the price of advertising, which results from combining improved match values with increased product concentration on each ad market. Athey et al. (2014), discussed in Section 2.4.1, explore further implications of tracking and targeting by competing platforms for advertising contracts and platform's technological choices. Johnson (2013) examines the effect of targeting when consumers have access to a costly advertising-avoiding technology. Starting from no targeting, consumers dislike increasing accuracy of targeting due to a volume effect while they like it at high level of accuracy due to improved matches with advertisers. While this literature is at its infant stage, it is a promising development for the future.

Although the recent literature has started to investigate advertising technologies in depth, there is surprisingly little theoretical research on the tailoring of the content itself to the needs of particular advertisers. Indeed, while the literature surveyed in Section 2.1 relates the choice of content to ad revenue, it never relates consumers' taste to the particular types of advertising shown on the platforms.[64] Recent exceptions are Athey and

---

[63] For contributions analyzing the consequences of targeting on the advertised products' market, see Esteban et al. (2001), Gal-Or and Gal-Or (2005), Iyer et al. (2005), Galeotti and Moraga-Gonzalez (2008), De Cornière (2010), Taylor (2013), De Cornière and de Nijs (2013), and Anderson et al. (2015a).

[64] See Chandra (2009), Chandra and Kaiser (2014), and Goettler (1999) for empirical evidence on the advertising value of audiences, and further discussion and references in Chapter 5 (this volume).

Gans (2010), who relate local advertising to local newspapers; Athey et al. (2014), who discuss the choice between focused content and high reach content; and Crampes et al. (2009), who relate the value of an impression to the size of the audience.

ACKNOWLEDGMENTS

We thank Matthew Shi, Ben Leyden, Bill Johnson, Oystein Foros, Hans Jarle Kind, Martin Peitz, and Markus Reisinger for their comments, along with our various coauthors for their help formulating our ideas. The first author thanks the NSF for support.

REFERENCES

Acemoglu, D., Jensen, M.K., 2013. Aggregate comparative statics. Games Econ. Behav. 81, 27–49.

Ambrus, A., Reisinger, M., 2006. Exclusive Versus Overlapping Viewers in Media Markets. Working Paper.

Ambrus, A., Calvano, E., Reisinger, M., 2014. Either-or-Both Competition: A Two-Sided Theory of Advertising with Overlapping Viewerships. Working Paper.

Amelio, A., Jullien, B., 2012. Tying and freebies in two-sided markets. Int. J. Ind. Organ. 30 (5), 436–446.

Anderson, S.P., 2003. Broadcast Competition: Commercial and Pay TV. Mimeo.

Anderson, S.P., 2005. Localism and Welfare. FCC Discussion Paper.

Anderson, S.P., 2007. Regulation of television advertising. In: Seabright, P., von Hagen, J. (Eds.), The Economic Regulation of Broadcasting Markets. Cambridge University Press, Cambridge.

Anderson, S.P., Coate, S., 2005. Market provision of broadcasting: a welfare analysis. Rev. Econ. Stud. 72 (4), 947–972.

Anderson, S.P., de Palma, A., 2001. Product diversity in asymmetric oligopoly: is the quality of consumer goods too low? J. Ind. Econ. 49 (2), 113–135.

Anderson, S.P., de Palma, A., 2009. Information congestion. RAND J. Econ. 40 (4), 688–709.

Anderson, S.P., Gabszewicz, J.J., 2006. The media and advertising: a tale of two-sided markets. In: Ginsburgh, V., Throsby, D. (Eds.), Handbook of the Economics of Art and Culture. North Holland, Amsterdam.

Anderson, S.P., Gans, J., 2011. Platform siphoning: ad-avoidance and media content. Am. Econ. J. Microecon. 3 (4), 1–34.

Anderson, S.P., Neven, D., 1989. Market efficiency with combinable products. Econ. Rev. 33 (4), 707–719.

Anderson, S.P., Peitz, M., 2014. Advertising Congestion in Media Markets. Working Paper.

Anderson, S.P., Peitz, M., 2015. Media Seesaws: Winners and Losers in Platform Markets. Working Paper.

Anderson, S.P., Shi, M., 2015. Pricing in the US Magazine Industry: A Two-Sided Market Perspective. Working Paper.

Anderson, S.P., de Palma, A., Thisse, J.F., 1992. Discrete Choice Theory of Product Differentiation. MIT Press, Cambridge, MA.

Anderson, S.P., de Palma, A., Nesterov, Y., 1995. Oligopolistic competition and the optimal provision of products. Econometrica 63 (6), 1281–1301.

Anderson, S.P., Foros, Ø., Kind, H.J., 2015 forthcoming. Product Quality, Competition, and Multi-Purchasing. CEPR Discussion Paper 8923.

Anderson, S.P., Foros, Ø., Kind, H.J., Peitz, M., 2012b. Media market concentration, advertising levels, and ad prices. Int. J. Ind. Organ. 30 (3), 321–325.

Anderson, S.P., Erkal, N., Piccinin, D., 2013a. Aggregative Games with Free Entry. CEPR Discussion Paper 8923.

Anderson, S.P., Foros, Ø., Kind, H.J., 2013b. Two-Sided Multi-Homing in Media Markets: Heterogenous Advertisers and Overlapping Viewers. NHH, Bergen.

Anderson, S.P., Baik, A., Larson, N., 2015a. Personalized Pricing and Advertising: An Asymmetric Equilibrium Analysis. Working Paper.

Anderson, S.P., Foros, Ø., Kind, H.J., 2015b. Competition for Advertisers and for Viewers in Media Markets. CEPR Discussion Paper 10608.

Archibald, G.C., Eaton, B.C., Lipsey, R.G., 1986. Address models of value. In: Stiglitz, J.E., Mathewson, F.G. (Eds.), New Developments in the Analysis of Market Structure. MIT Press, Cambridge, MA.

Armstrong, M., 2002. Competition in Two-Sided Markets. MPRA Paper 24863.

Armstrong, M., 2006. Competition in two-sided-markets. RAND J. Econ. 37 (3), 668–691.

Armstrong, M., Weeds, H., 2007. Public service broadcasting in the digital world. In: Seabright, P., von Hagen, J. (Eds.), The Economic Regulation of Broadcasting Markets. Cambridge University Press, Cambridge.

Armstrong, M., Wright, J., 2007. Two-sided markets, competitive bottlenecks and exclusive contracts. Econ. Theory 32 (2), 353–380.

Athey, S., Gans, J., 2010. The impact of targeting technology on advertising markets and media competition. Am. Econ. Rev. Pap. Proc. 100 (2), 608–613.

Athey, S., Calvano, E., Gans, J., 2014. The Impact of the Internet on Advertising Markets for News Media. Working Paper.

Bedre-Defolie, O., Calvano, E., 2013. Pricing payment cards. Am. Econ. J. Microecon. 5 (3), 206–231.

Beebe, J.H., 1977. Institutional structure and program choices in television markets. Q. J. Econ. 91 (1), 15–37.

Belleflamme, P., Toulemonde, E., 2009. Negative intra-group externalities in two-sided markets. Int. Econ. Rev. 50 (1), 245–272.

Bergemann, D., Bonatti, A., 2011. Targeting in advertising markets: implications for offline versus online media. RAND J. Econ. 42 (3), 417–443.

Bourreau, M., 2003. Mimicking vs. counter-programming strategies for television programs. Inf. Econ. Policy 15 (1), 35–54.

Caillaud, B., Jullien, B., 2001. Competing cybermediaries. Eur. Econ. Rev. Paper Proc. 45 (4–6), 797–808.

Caillaud, B., Jullien, B., 2003. Chicken & egg: competition among intermediation service providers. RAND J. Econ. 34 (2), 309–328.

Calvano, E., Polo, M., 2014. Strategic Differentiation by Business Models: Free-to-Air and Pay-TV's. Working Paper.

Chandra, A., 2009. Targeted advertising: the role of subscriber characteristics in media markets. J. Ind. Econ. 57 (1), 58–84.

Chandra, A., Kaiser, U., 2014. Targeted advertising in magazine markets and the advent of the internet. Manag. Sci. 60 (7), 1829–1843.

Choi, J.P., 2006. Broadcast competition and advertising with free entry: subscription vs. free-to-air. Inf. Econ. Policy 18 (2), 181–196.

Crampes, C., Haritchabalet, C., Jullien, B., 2009. Advertising, competition and entry in media industries. J. Ind. Econ. 57 (1), 7–31.

Cunningham, B., Alexander, P., 2004. A theory of broadcast media concentration and commercial advertising. J. Public Econ. Theory 6 (4), 557–575.

D'Aspremont, C., Gabszewicz, J.J., Thisse, J.F., 1979. On Hotelling's 'stability in competition'. Econometrica 47 (5), 1145–1150.

De Cornière, A., 2010. Search Advertising. Working Paper.

De Cornière, A., de Nijs, R., 2013. Online advertising and privacy, Discussion Paper, University of Oxford.

Dewenter, R., Haucap, J., Wenzel, T., 2011. Semi-collusion in media markets. Int. Rev. Law Econ. 3 (2), 92–98.

Doganoglu, T., Wright, J., 2006. Multihoming and compatibility. Int. J. Ind. Organ. 24 (1), 45–67.

Dukes, A., 2004. The advertising market in a product oligopoly. J. Ind. Econ. 52 (3), 327–348.

Dukes, A., 2006. Media concentration and consumer product prices. Econ. Inq. 44 (1), 128–141.

Dukes, A., Gal-Or, E., 2003. Negotiations and exclusivity contracts for advertising. Mark. Sci. 22 (2), 222–245.

Dupuit, J., 1849. De l'influence des péages sur l'utilité des voies de communication. Ann. Ponts Chaussées 17 (mémoires et documents), 207.

Eaton, B.C., Lipsey, R.G., 1975. The principle of minimum differentiation reconsidered: some new developments in the theory of spatial competition. Rev. Econ. Stud. 42 (1), 27–49.

Esteban, L., Gil, A., Hernandez, J., 2001. Informative advertising and optimal targeting in a monopoly. J. Ind. Econ. 49 (2), 161–180.

Ferrando, J., Gabszewicz, J.J., Laussel, D., Sonnac, N., 2008. Intermarket network externalities and competition: an application to the media industry. Int. J. Econ. Theory 4 (3), 357–379.

Gabszewicz, J.J., Thisse, J.F., 1979. Price competition, quality and income disparities. J. Econ. Theory 20 (3), 340–359.

Gabszewicz, J.J., Wauthy, X.Y., 2004. Two-Sided Markets and Price Competition with Multi-Homing. Working Paper.

Gabszewicz, J.J., Wauthy, X.Y., 2014. Vertical product differentiation and two-sided markets. Econ. Lett. 123 (1), 58–61.

Gabszewicz, J.J., Laussel, D., Sonnac, N., 2001. Press advertising and the ascent of the 'Pensee Unique'. Eur. Econ. Rev. 45 (4–6), 641–651.

Gabszewicz, J.J., Laussel, D., Sonnac, N., 2004. Programming and advertising competition in the broadcasting industry. J. Econ. Manag. Strategy 13 (4), 657–669.

Gabszewicz, J.J., Laussel, D., Sonnac, N., 2012. Advertising and the rise of free daily newspapers. Economica 79 (313), 137–151.

Galeotti, A., Moraga-Gonzalez, J.L., 2008. Segmentation, advertising, and prices. Int. J. Ind. Organ. 26 (5), 1106–1119.

Gal-Or, E., Dukes, A., 2003. Minimum differentiation in commercial media markets. J. Econ. Manag. Strategy 12 (3), 291–325.

Gal-Or, E., Dukes, A., 2006. On the profitability of media mergers. J. Bus. 79 (2), 489–525.

Gal-Or, E., Gal-Or, M., 2005. Customized advertising via a common media distributor. Mark. Sci. 24 (2), 241–253.

Gentzkow, M.A., 2007. Valuing new goods in a model with complementarity: online newspapers. Am. Econ. Rev. 97 (3), 713–744.

Godes, D., Ofek, E., Sarvary, M., 2009. Content vs. advertising: the impact of competition on media firm strategy. Mark. Sci. 28 (1), 20–35.

Goettler, R., 1999. Advertising Rates, Audience Composition, and Competition in the Network Television Industry. Working Paper.

Grossman, G., Shapiro, C., 1984. Informative advertising with differentiated products. Rev. Econ. Stud. 51 (1), 63–81.

Hagiu, A., Halaburda, H., 2014. Information and two-sided platform profits. Int. J. Ind. Organ. 34, 25–35.

Hagiu, A., Jullien, B., 2011. Why do intermediaries divert search? RAND J. Econ. 42 (2), 337–362.

Hagiu, A., Jullien, B., 2014. Search diversion and platform competition. Int. J. Ind. Organ. 33, 48–60.

Hansen, C.T., Kyhl, S., 2001. Pay-per-view broadcasting of outstanding events: consequences of a ban. Int. J. Ind. Organ. 19, 589–609.

Hoernig, S., Valletti, T., 2007. Mixing goods with two-part tariffs. Eur. Econ. Rev. 51, 1733–1750.

Hotelling, H., 1929. Stability in competition. Econ. J. 39, 41–57.

Hurkens, S., Lopez, A.L., 2014. Who should pay for two-way interconnection? Working Papers 774, Barcelona Graduate School of Economics.

Iyer, G., Soberman, D., Villas-Boas, J.M., 2005. The targeting of advertising. Mark. Sci. 24 (3), 461–476.

Jeitschko, T., Tremblay, M., 2015. Platform Competition with Endogenous Homing. Working Paper.

Johnson, J.P., 2013. Targeted advertising and advertising avoidance. RAND J. Econ. 44 (1), 128–144.

Katz, M.L., Shapiro, C., 1985. Network externalities, competition, and compatibility. Am. Econ. Rev. 75 (3), 424–440.

Kerkhof, A., Munster, J., 2015. Quantity Restrictions on Advertising, Commercial Media Bias, and Welfare. Working Paper.

Kim, H., Serfes, K., 2006. A location model with preference for variety. J. Ind. Econ. 54 (4), 569–595.

Kind, H.J., Nilssen, T., Sörgard, L., 2007. Competition for viewers and advertisers in a TV oligopoly. J. Med. Econ. 20 (3), 211–233.

Kind, H.J., Nilssen, T., Sörgard, L., 2009. Business models for media firms: does competition matter for how they raise revenue? Mark. Sci. 28 (6), 1112–1128.

Lin, P., 2011. Market provision of program quality in the television broadcasting industry. BE J. Econ. Anal. Policy 11 (1), 1–22.

Mussa, M., Rosen, S., 1978. Monopoly and product quality. J. Econ. Theory 18 (2), 301–317.

Nocke, V., Peitz, M., Stahl, K., 2007. Platform ownership. J. Eur. Econ. Assoc. 5 (6), 1130–1160.

Owen, B., Wildman, S., 1992. Video Economics. Harvard University Press, Cambridge, MA.

Peitz, M., Valletti, T.M., 2008. Content and advertising in the media: pay-TV versus free-to-air. Int. J. Ind. Organ. 26 (4), 949–965.

Prescott, E., Visscher, M., 1977. Sequential location among firms with foresight. Bell J. Econ. 8 (2), 378–393.

Reisinger, M., 2014. Two-Part Tariff Competition Between Two-Sided Platforms. Working Paper.

Richardson, M., 2006. Commercial broadcasting and local content: cultural quotas, advertising, and public stations. Econ. J. 116, 605–625.

Rochet, J., Tirole, J., 2003. Platform competition in two-sided markets. J. Eur. Econ. Assoc. 1, 990–1029.

Rochet, J., Tirole, J., 2006. Two-sided markets: a progress report. RAND J. Econ. 37 (3), 645–667.

Rysman, M., 2004. Competition between networks: a study of the market for yellow pages. Rev. Econ. Stud. 71 (2), 483–512.

Rysman, M., 2009. The economics of two-sided markets. J. Econ. Perspect. 23 (3), 125–143.

Salop, S.C., 1979. Monopolistic competition with outside goods. Bell J. Econ. 10 (1), 141–156.

Selten, R., 1970. Preispolitik der Mehrproduktenunternehmung in der Statischen Theorie. Springer Verlag, Berlin.

Shah, S., 2011. The Effect of the DVR on Network and Consumer Behavior. Ph.D. thesis, University of Virginia.

Shaked, A., Sutton, J., 1983. Natural oligopolies. Econometrica 51 (5), 1469–1483.

Shubik, M., Levitan, R., 1980. Market Structure and Behavior. Harvard University Press, Cambridge, MA.

Spence, M., 1976. Product selection, fixed costs, and monopolistic competition. Rev. Econ. Stud. 43 (2), 217–235.

Steiner, P.O., 1952. Program patterns and the workability of competition in radio broadcasting. Q. J. Econ. 66 (2), 194–223.

Stühmeier, T., Wenzel, T., 2011. Getting beer during commercials: adverse effects of ad-avoidance. Information Economics and Policy 23 (1), 98–106.

Tag, J., 2009. Paying to remove advertisements. Inf. Econ. Policy 21 (4), 245–252.

Taylor, G., 2013. Attention Retention: Targeted Advertising and the Ex Post Role of Media Content. Working Paper.

Van Zandt, T., 2004. Information overload in a network of targeted communication. RAND J. Econ. 35, 542–560.

Vickrey, W., 1964. Microstatics. Harcourt, Brace, New York.

Vickrey, W.S., Anderson, S.P., Braid, R.M., 1999. Spatial competition, monopolistic competition, and optimum product diversity. Int. J. Ind. Organ. 17 (7), 953–963.

Weeds, H., 2012. Superstars and the long tail: the impact of technology on market structure in media industries. Inf. Econ. Policy 24 (1), 60–68.

Weeds, H., 2013. Programme Quality in Subscription and Advertising-Funded Television. Working Paper.

Weyl, E., 2010. A price theory of multi-sided platforms. Am. Econ. Rev. 100 (4), 1642–1672.

White, A., Weyl, E., 2015. Insulated Platform Competition. NET Institute Working Paper No. 10.

CHAPTER 3

Empirical Modeling for Economics of the Media: Consumer and Advertiser Demand, Firm Supply and Firm Entry Models for Media Markets

Steven T. Berry*, Joel Waldfogel[†]
*David Swensen Professor of Economics, Yale University, New Haven, CT, USA
[†]Frederick R. Kappel Chair in Applied Economics, Carlson School of Management, University of Minnesota, Minneapolis, MN, USA

Contents

Abstract

We present empirical techniques that are both familiar to students of industrial organization and useful for modeling of media markets. We first focus on demand estimation with discussion of various discrete choice models. We then turn to estimation of the demand for advertising. We next turn to the supply side of the market. We discuss the estimation of models using continuous variables that firms choose (such as prices or ad level), followed by a discussion of entry models with both homogeneous and differentiated products. We conclude with a brief discussion of future challenges.

Keywords

Demand estimation, Discrete choice, Entry modeling

JEL Codes

C01, L82

Handbook of Media Economics, Volume 1A
ISSN 2213-6630, http://dx.doi.org/10.1016/B978-0-444-62721-6.00003-2

3.1. INTRODUCTION

The goal of this chapter is to present empirical techniques useful for the empirical study of media markets. These approaches will be familiar to students of contemporary empirical industrial organization, but we will emphasize aspects and approaches most relevant to the media markets.

Our task is to describe techniques that do two things: (i) are both suitable for dealing with the fundamental economic conditions and data available of media markets; and (ii) are consistent with theory and models in ways that allow both simulation of alternative policies and the calculation of objects of theoretical interest (e.g., welfare or consumer surplus) as functions of the products entering the market. Hence we focus on "structural" approaches at the exclusion of others, even though descriptive approaches geared to causal inference are quite useful for analyses of media industries as well.

A few fundamental features of media markets (as emphasized elsewhere in this volume, see Chapter 1) include high—and almost exclusively—fixed costs, preference heterogeneity, and a mix of user and advertiser finance. These features give rise to market outcomes that can deviate in interesting ways from efficient arrangements, creating a need for empirical modeling approaches usable for counterfactual simulation of alternative arrangements, such as impacts of mergers or planners' optimal arrangements.

Media products are also special in that their consumption—for example of news products—is often a means toward the end of becoming informed. Public policy has an interest in media products in as much as the structure of the media market may have an effect on civic engagement and, in particular, voting (see Chapters 13–19). This further substantiates the need for methods for analyzing impacts of policies or regulations on product positioning and media consumption.

An additional feature that is important for facilitating empirical analysis is that many media markets have traditionally been local, with the consequence that one can observe outcomes, including entry, product positioning, and consumption, that arise in geographic areas that differ in their demographic and economic size, as well as composition. New technologies are eroding the distinctness of local markets, creating challenges that we discuss at the conclusion.

Some inherent features of media markets give rise to data availability or its lack. The ad-supported nature of media creates a need for audience measurement, which in turn tends to create good data on the number of consumers using each product. Moreover, it is possible in many contexts to observe consumption tendencies separately by demographic and geographic groups. Prices, on the other hand, are often challenging to obtain. Some products, such as terrestrial radio broadcasts and over-the-air television, have zero prices to consumers. Other products, such as daily newspapers (along with movies and music), often have uniform prices with so little variation that the identification of demand relationships can be challenging. While measures of ad prices, such as market-level ad revenue or posted spot prices of advertising, are sometimes observable, much of the relevant ad price information is not publicly available. The needs of advertisers give rise to available data on product characteristics and the number of available products. In media such as radio broadcasting and newspapers, there are directories listing the available outlets along with information on their product targeting (broadcast formats for radio, etc.).[1] Finally, changing technologies—such as Internet radio, television time-shifting devices, and streaming delivery of various kinds of media products—strain the ability of existing data infrastructure to describe the performance of media products.

This chapter proceeds in the following sections. Section 3.2 discusses relevant models of audience and advertising demand. Section 3.3 presents a brief discussion of advertiser demand for media consumers. Section 3.4 turns to models of entry and equilibrium. Along the way we make reference to examples in the media and, where appropriate, more general industrial economics literatures. Section 3.5 discusses the use of structural models for policy analysis of media industries. Section 3.6 concludes and contains a discussion of future challenges.

3.2. AUDIENCE DEMAND

3.2.1 Introduction

Audience demand is obviously key to the analysis of media markets. For some media (e.g., newspapers), direct consumers of media are at least one primary source of revenue, whereas in other markets (traditional radio) audiences are effectively part of the production process. In advertising-supported media, audience attention is "sold" to advertisers and so we can think of audiences as being "produced" for sale to the paying "consumers," who are advertisers.

Below we review a set of demand models that are now standard in empirical industrial organization, but with an emphasis on the features of media markets and on the relevant policy questions. These models are typically discrete-choice models, although at an aggregated market level they can also be given an interpretation as involving consumers with a taste for variety (see Anderson et al., 1992).

We think of potential audience members who face a set of media choices, described by various characteristics. Some of these characteristics are observed to the researcher, and some not. These consumers differ in tastes according to demographic attributes that we, as researchers, observe and they also vary with unobserved consumer attributes and tastes. In some cases consumers pay a price for consuming the good, in others not.

These models are broadly consistent with some basic stylized facts about media markets. Two such interesting stylized facts are that (i) audience size increases in the number of choices and (ii) different demographics make starkly different choices within the same

---

[1] See Chapters 7–9 of this volume.

market. Both of these are consistent with heterogeneous preferences, and the first would also be consistent with a taste for variety.

As an example of the first stylized fact, Figure 3.1 shows how the number of varieties and products available varies with the size of the market across US local radio markets. Larger markets have more radio stations as well as more varieties. As an example of the second stylized fact, Figure 3.2 shows how radio choices vary by demographic. A small number of station formats that are targeted at blacks attract almost two-thirds of black listening, while these formats attract only a small share (under 3%) of white listening. A similar pattern holds for Hispanic versus non-Hispanic listening.

Classic discrete-choice models, following on from McFadden (1974, 1981), allow for preferences that vary with observed and unobserved demographics, easily accommodating the pattern seen in Figure 3.2. In addition, they include an idiosyncratic "match" component for between each consumer and products. As the number of products increases, consumers are more likely to find a desirable match with some product and total audience size increases. In the context of some markets, this is seen as an undesirable feature of models with idiosyncratic match components. However, Figure 3.1 suggests that this is a desirable feature for media markets. Clearly, we would like the data to

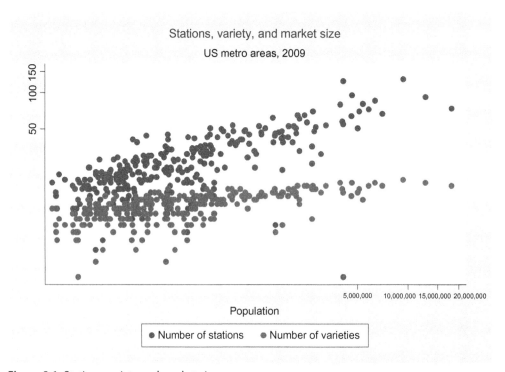

Figure 3.1 Stations variety and market size.

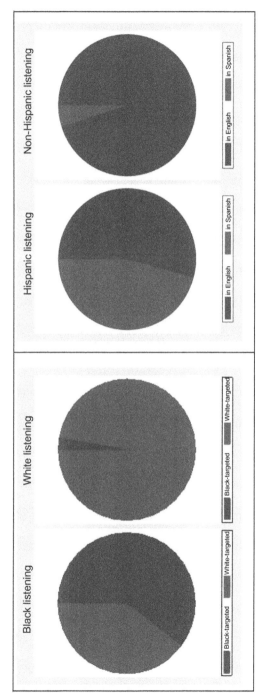

Figure 3.2 Radio listening and demographics.

somehow determine the relative importance of idiosyncratic match values and more systematic taste differences depending on observed and unobserved demographics and taste.

3.2.2 Classic Discrete Choice with Observed and Unobserved Product Characteristics

We think of a set of potential consumers (audience members) in a cross-section of markets. In each market, consumers make a discrete choice to consume one of the "within-market" products or else to choose the "outside good." For example, in Fan (2013), in each county consumers can choose to purchase one of a list of available newspapers, or can purchase no newspaper at all.

Following McFadden (1981), consider a utility function for potential consumer i for product j in market t of

$$u_{ijt} = \delta_{jt} + \mu_{ijt}, \tag{3.1}$$

where δ_{jt} is the "mean utility" of product j in market t and μ_{ijt} captures the distribution of tastes about that mean. For each consumer, the tastes μ_{ijt} can be correlated across products in ways that depend on the attributes of the consumer and the characteristics of the product.

Following Berry (1994), we model the mean utility as depending on a set of observed characteristics, x_{jt}, as well as an unobserved (to the researcher) characteristic ξ_{jt}. The unobserved characteristic captures elements of quality that are not measured in our data and its presence also helps to fix ideas about the econometric endogeneity of demand. The vector x_{jt} includes observed data on product quality, but also measures of horizontal differentiation such as type of product—for example, a dummy variable for whether a paper is an urban daily or whether a radio station plays country music. Depending on the media market, the vector x_{jt} sometimes includes price and sometimes does not. For convenience, we assume that

$$\delta_{jt} = x_{jt}\overline{\beta} + \xi_{jt}. \tag{3.2}$$

A classic random coefficients (e.g., Hausman and Wise, 1978) formulation for the distribution of consumer tastes would be

$$\mu_{ijt} = \sum_{k} x_{kjt}\beta_{ikt} + \varepsilon_{ijt}. \tag{3.3}$$

The term ε_{ijt} is consumer i's match value for product j, usually assumed to be i.i.d. across products. Most commonly ε_{ijt} is assumed to be distributed i.i.d. standard normal or else to be distributed according to the "double exponential" extreme value distribution that generates the familiar logit model of choice probabilities. The scale of utility is often normalized by holding the scale of ε_{ijt} fixed as other parameters change, although other normalizations are possible.

The summation term then introduces cross-product correlation in tastes. The term β_{ikt} is consumer i's marginal utility for characteristic k, often modeled as a function of the observed demographics and unobserved "tastes" of the consumer:

$$\beta_{ikt} = \sum_k x_{kjt}[\upsilon_{ik}\sigma_k + \gamma_k z_i]. \tag{3.4}$$

The observed demographics are the vector z_i, and the utility interaction between product characteristic k and the consumer demographics is parameterized by $\gamma_k z_i$. In empirical practice, the number of such interactions generally has to be limited. Unobserved tastes for characteristic k are captured by the scalar υ_{ik}, often assumed to be normally distributed. The variance of unobserved tastes for characteristic k is increasing in the parameter σ_k. The combination of unobserved product characteristics (as in 3.2) with a normally distributed random coefficients logit (as in 3.4) is introduced in Berry et al. (1995), referred to as "BLP."

The distribution of marginal tastes for characteristics, β_{ikt}, drives the cross-product substitution patterns implied by the model. A higher variance of marginal tastes for product characteristic k implies, *ceteris paribus*, that consumers will more closely substitute between products with similar values of x_{kjt}. For example, in radio markets a larger σ_k on the unobserved taste for country music will imply that consumers will be more "loyal" to the country music format as market conditions change. The simple reason is that when σ_k is large, those consuming country music are disproportionately those with a systematic taste for country music, whereas when σ_k is small many consumers listening to a given country music station are doing so simply because of a large idiosyncratic match value ε_{ijt}.

The idiosyncratic match value is almost always present in a classic discrete-choice demand model, in part because it "smooths out" market shares and avoids kinks in the demand function (Berry and Pakes, 2007). However, the economics of the idiosyncratic match value is sometimes questioned, as it implies that each new product is "born" with some fresh component that brings value to some subset of consumers. This assumption seems more reasonable in media markets than in some other markets. Further, the i.i.d. match value implies that the share of media consumers increases in the number of product choices, an assumption that matches our stylized fact. The degree to which the market expands is governed by the relative importance of the systematic β_{ikt} as opposed to the idiosyncratic ε_{ijt} and this relative importance is determined by the parameters σ_k and γ_k.

There are several variations and classic special cases. The nested logit (Cardell, 1991; McFadden, 1978) assumes that the only random coefficients are those on a set of "nested" product group dummies. With one level of product nests, the unobserved random taste component of utility for a product in nest k is given by[2]

---

[2] Arbitrarily rich observed interactions with consumer demographics are easily added to the nested logit model; they are omitted here only for exposition.

$$\mu_{ijt} = \nu_{ikt}(\sigma_k) + (1 - \sigma_k)\varepsilon_{ijt}, \tag{3.5}$$

with $\sigma_k \in (0, 1)$, a parameter that as σ_k moves from zero to one places less weight on the "logit" idiosyncratic taste component ε_{ijt} and more weight on the systematic "taste for nest k." The distribution of the nest-taste term ν_{ikt} changes with σ_k. At $\sigma_k = 0$, $\nu_{ikt} = 0$ and the model reduces to the pure logit. At $\sigma_k = 1$, the model places no weight on the product level ε_{ijt} and the model predicts that within each nest only the good with the highest mean utility will be purchased. An issue with the model is that the model is not well defined outside when σ_k falls outside of the range (0,1).

3.2.3 Identification of Demand Parameters

It is useful to start with an intuitive discussion of what kind of data variation will allow us to learn about demand parameters. For a more formal treatment, see Berry and Haile (2010, 2014). Mean utility levels are fairly easy: if two products have the same characteristics, higher market shares translate into higher mean utility levels. Indeed, it is in general possible to show in the discrete-choice context that given other demand parameters there is a one-to-one map between the vector of market shares and the mean utility levels, δ (see Berry et al., 2013). For example, in the case of the pure logit with no random coefficients model, the mean utility levels are just given by the classic log-odds ratio, $\ln(s_j/s_0)$, where s_j is the share of product j and s_0 is the share of the outside good. In the pure logit, then, we can estimate the parameters of Equation (3.2) via the linear relationship

$$\ln(s_j) - \ln(s_0) = x_j\beta + \xi_j. \tag{3.6}$$

If the observed and unobserved characteristics are uncorrelated, then this equation can just be estimated via OLS. However, in many of the empirical examples below it is most plausible to assume that some characteristics (such as price or observed quality) are correlated with ξ_j. This suggests the use of instrumental variables methods. In the case of price, natural instruments are exogenous cost shifters and, in the context of imperfect competition, exogenous variables that shift markups. As we see in the examples below, in media markets there is sometimes no price paid by the audience and the interesting endogeneity issues involve other product characteristics, such as the nature of the media content (radio format or newspaper political slant).

Moving to the random coefficients model of Equations (3.3) and (3.4), identification becomes more subtle. As noted, the random coefficients drive substitution patterns. Intuitively, we would learn about substitution patterns by exogenously changing the product space—the number and characteristics of products offered to consumers—and then observing the resulting change in demand. However, the model also contains product-level unobservables. If we allowed these unobservables to change freely with changes in the product space, we could always attribute all of the change in demand patterns to the unobservables and none to fundamental substitution patterns. Thus, identifying substitution patterns requires some restriction on the way the unobservables move as we make changes in the product space.

The necessary requirement is that the variables that change the product space are exogenous in the sense that they are uncorrelated with the demand unobservables. This is a familiar requirement for an instrument. Here, however, these instruments do not "instrument for" a particular variable, but rather allow us to identify the parameters that control substitution patterns. Intuitively, they have to change the product space in a manner that reveals the relevant substitution patterns. The nature of these patterns varies with the specification, which in turn is often driven by the data and questions at hand.

In the examples below, we illustrate the use of various types of instruments that are useful both for handling endogeneity problems in mean utility and for identifying substitution patterns in a random coefficients style model. We discuss several broad candidates for instruments briefly here and then elaborate and illustrate with various media examples.

A first set of instruments involves cost shifters of own and rival firms. Own-cost shifters are a natural instrument for own-price (and perhaps for other endogenous characteristics) while rivals' costs shift rivals' prices and therefore help to trace out substitution patterns in response to price. "Hausman instruments" are the prices of goods in other markets, intended as proxies for common cost shocks (see Hausman, 1996; Nevo, 2001). If the prices are responding to common demand shocks as well, then the instruments may not be valid.

A second set of instruments are direct measures of rival product characteristics, and the number of different types of products. These instruments, sometimes called "BLP" instruments following their treatment in Nevo (2001), directly change the product space and help to reveal substitution patterns. If the product characteristics are not exogenous, but are (for example) chosen in response to demand shocks, then they will not be valid instruments.

A third set of instruments are helpful when there is variation in the level of market demographics and these demographics drive product choices. It is important that these market demographic levels vary conditionally on whatever observed demographics, z_i, are in the utility specification (3.4). This is especially useful when we can model the decisions of individual consumers in markets whose overall demographic levels vary. It is also useful in a "representative consumer" model where market shares are driven by the shares of demographic groups but the product space is generated by the total population of demographic groups. In the context of newspapers, Gentzkow and Shapiro (2010) attribute this idea to George and Waldfogel (2003). Berry and Haile (2010) cite Waldfogel (2003) and refer to these instruments in general as "Waldfogel" instruments.

In addition to these three classes of instruments, identification can be aided by various panel data/timing assumptions on the unobservable demand shocks. For example, we might be willing to assume that demand follows an AR(1) process and that rival characteristics are uncorrelated with the current-period innovation in the demand shock. This amounts to a timing assumption that characteristics are chosen before the demand innovation is observed.

3.2.4 Example of a Single-Parameter Nested Logit

To illustrate, it is useful to start with a very simple model using market-level data. Consider the symmetric model of radio listening in Berry and Waldfogel (1999). In their simplest model, the only random coefficient is on a dummy variable equal to one for each inside good (and zero for the outside good of no radio listening). Although the model is too simple to capture many interesting features of radio listening, the nested logit functional form nicely parameterizes the "taste for variety" in the aggregate data. In each quarter-hour period, each listener in the metropolitan area has utility for radio station j, given by the nested logit functional form

$$u_{ijt} = \delta_t + v_{it}(\sigma) + (1-\sigma)\varepsilon_{ijt},$$

which is a simple version of Equation (3.5). In particular, Berry (1994) shows that this model can be estimated via the equation

$$\ln(s_j) - \ln(s_0) = x_j\beta + \sigma \ln\left(\frac{s_j}{1-s_0}\right) + \xi_j. \tag{3.7}$$

Note that in this model the "within-group substitution parameter" σ is the coefficient on the log of the "inside share" $\ln(s_j/(1-s_0))$. In the case in which stations are assumed symmetric, the within-group share reduces to $(1/N)$, where N is the number of stations in the market. If $\sigma = 1$, then the log-odds ratio of shares is just proportional to $1/N$ as there is no substitution from the outside good as N increases. In this case, the effect of increasing N is pure "business stealing," there is no growth in aggregate radio listening as the number of choices grows. When σ is low, however, the aggregate audience grows relatively rapidly as the number of choices increases.

If N were exogenous, we could estimate the substitution parameter via an OLS regression. However, a moment's reflection reveals that the number of stations in the market is potentially related to unobserved determinants of the tendency to listen. For example, in markets where consumers like radio, entry conditions for stations will be favorable, giving rise to a relationship between entry and listening where the causality runs from listening to entry, rather than the other way around. Hence, N is not an appropriate exogenous "instrument" to identify the substitution parameter.

The solution to this problem is a source of variation in the number of available stations that does not enter the utility function of listeners. Again, instruments should (i) be excluded from the individual-level utility function and yet (ii) shift the choice set. Plausible characterization of the entry process provides guidance on instruments. As Waldfogel has argued, media products make supply—entry and positioning—decisions based on characteristics of the entire market. Hence for local media products, variables such as local population and aggregate local income are appealing instruments for the number of local products. This approach assumes that even though individual-level demographics may affect the consumption of media products, aggregate variables based on these demographics have no direct effect on individuals' consumption. This assumes away various possible spillover and regional sorting (migration) effects.

In the case of radio, Berry and Waldfogel (1999) estimate σ at the market level by placing demographic shares in the utility function and then instrumenting $(1/N)$ with total market population. The estimates of σ are quite precise and indicate a moderately high level of "business stealing."

3.2.5 Further Examples of Audience Demand

Gentzkow and Shapiro (2010) consider demand for monopoly newspapers. The relevant substitution here is all to the outside good of not subscribing to the newspaper. Gentzkow and Shapiro focus on the question of "media slant," that is, whether the language of the news articles slants toward the political left or right. The paper develops very clever language-based measures of slant for newspapers. The measure of reader slant is based on political contributions at the level of the zip code, c, within metro newspaper markets.

In Gentzkow and Shapiro, a newspaper's measured slant in market t is denoted y_t. In zip code c, $\hat{r}_{ct}$ is an observed measure of readers' political preference based on campaign contributions. "True" reader slant is then modeled as $r_{ct} = \alpha + \beta \hat{r}_{ct}$, where the parameters α and β translate the observed measure into the same location and scale as the measure of newspaper slant. In the spirit of an "ideal point" Hotelling-style model, readers pay a utility cost based on the distance between their preferred political location and the newspaper's slant. As a function of true political preferences, utility is

$$u_{ict} = x_{ct}\beta + \gamma(r_{ct} - y_t)^2 + \xi_{ct} + \varepsilon_{ijt},$$

where ε_{ijt} is the usual logit error, x_{ct} is a vector of zip-code demographics (including a market-specific dummy to control for overall newspaper quality), and ξ_{ct} is the unobserved zip-code level taste for the newspaper in market t. Expanding the square in the ideal point model gives linear terms in $y_t r_{ct}$, r_{ct}^2, and y_t^2 so that we can write the model as

$$u_{ict} = \delta_{ct} + \varepsilon_{ijt},$$

where (after expanding the square and substituting in the observed preferences $\hat{r}_{ct}$) we have the "mean utility" term

$$\delta_{ct} = \bar{\delta}_t + x_{ct}\beta + \lambda_0 y_t \hat{r}_{ct} + \lambda_1 \hat{r}_{ct} + \lambda_2 \hat{r}_{ct}^2 + \xi_{ct}, \tag{3.8}$$

where the λ parameters are functions of the "Hotelling distance" parameter γ, and the parameters α and β relate the observed consumer slant measure to the true slant.

As in (3.6), Gentzkow and Shapiro can then invert the market logit share functions to recover δ_{ct}, which gives a linear estimating equation in the terms on the right-hand side of Equation (3.8). Gentzkow and Shapiro note that their measure of newspaper slant, despite its advantages, likely contains some measure error. This suggests the use of an instrumental variable to correct for measurement error. Such an instrumental variable would also deal with the classic endogeneity concern that the unobservables can be correlated with the right-hand side product characteristics.

Gentzkow and Shapiro suggest a "Waldfogel" instrumental variable based on the demographics of the overall market t; in particular they use the market share of Republican voters. The idea is that this variable shifts the newspaper's choice of slant. The implicit exclusion restriction is that, conditional on a given zip code's preferences, the overall market's Republican share does not directly affect newspaper demand within the zip code. This, for example, rules out spillovers across zip codes within markets.

The IV estimates in Gentzkow and Shapiro then reveal the "structural" effect of a change in newspaper slant on zip-code-level readership, which in turn generates newspaper profits. They then use a supply-side model to show that newspapers are roughly choosing slant to maximize profits, as opposed to pursuing some other personal or political agenda. We return to supply-side issues below.

Fan (2013) studies competition and mergers in the newspaper industry. As opposed to the monopoly metro markets of Gentzkow and Shapiro, she considers overlapping county-level markets for newspapers. She also emphasizes the endogeneity of both price and (non-political) newspaper characteristics, which were implicitly included in the market-newspaper term $\bar{\delta}_t$ in Gentzkow and Shapiro. Depending on the county, c, readers face different choice sets that include various suburban papers within larger metropolitan regions. The utility function of reader i in county c for newspaper j is

$$u_{ijc} = x_j \beta + y_{jc} \psi + z_c \phi - \alpha p_j + \xi_{jc} + \epsilon_{ijc}, \tag{3.9}$$

where p_j is the price of the newspaper and x_j is a vector of endogenous characteristics (news quality, local news ratio, and news content variety). The vector y_{jc} contains within-county newspaper characteristics assumed to be exogenous (e.g., whether the headquarters city is in the county) and z_c is a vector of county demographics. The term ξ_{jc} again captures unobserved tastes for the newspaper in a given county.

Once again, the vector of county-level market shares can be inverted to obtain the mean utility terms

$$\delta_{jc} = x_j \beta + y_{jc} \psi + z_c \phi - \alpha p_j + \xi_{jc}.$$

There are now four endogenous variables, price, and the vector of endogenous characteristics. It is likely that these are correlated with the unobserved taste ξ_{jc}. For example, the price is likely to be higher when the newspaper is unobservably more popular. This makes the IV problem more difficult. Broadly speaking, Fan also makes use of modified

Walfogel-style instruments, interacted with exogenous rival characteristics (BLP instruments). In her case, she uses consumer demographics in the other counties served by a rival newspaper. For example, if a paper sold in a sparsely populated suburban county is headquartered in a populous central metropolitan county, it is likely to have high levels of quality and variety. The headquarters county is taken as exogenous so that the demographic levels in that county are available as instruments that shift the choice set in the suburban county. More specifically, the population demographics of "other counties" where the newspaper is sold are excluded from the mean utility of the paper in a given county. Therefore, "other county demographics" are available as instruments for endogenous characteristics and prices in the "own county" mean utility equation. In Fan (2013), the Waldfogel-style instruments include other counties' education level, median income, median age, and urbanization.

Fan (2013) considers extending the model of (3.9) to include random coefficients on some of the characteristics. As noted, random coefficients allow for richer substitution patterns than simple logit models. For example, if some consumers have a larger than average taste for local news, they will likely substitute from one locally focused paper to another one, whereas the pure logit generates substitution patterns that vary only with demographic-specific market shares. It is not clear whether Fan has adequate instruments for this purpose, and so she models only one random coefficient (on local news). Once again, we consider Fan's supply side below.

Continuing with a discussion of random coefficients, Sweeting (2013) and Jeziorski (2014) consider listener demand models for radio that include random coefficients. In addition to demographically varying tastes for formats, both Sweeting and Jeziorski have normally distributed random coefficients on format, which in practice is very similar to the nested logit model. Though the model with normal coefficients lacks a closed form solution, it also lacks any *a priori* constraints on the value of the substitution parameters (which in the nested logit must fall between zero and one). Jeziorski also adds a random coefficient on the quantity (in minutes per unit time) of advertising, which introduces a new dimension of substitution beyond the nested logit. Both of these authors consider dynamic models on the supply side, focusing either on joint ownership (Jeziorksi) or format choice (Sweeting).

Both Sweeting and Jeziorski want to model market structure endogenously, and so do not want to assume that the numbers and formats of competing products are uncorrelated with the demand unobservable ξ_{jt} and so available as potential instruments. Instead, both use a combination of panel data and IV assumptions. For example, Jeziorski uses a "quasi-difference" in the unobserved product characteristic for station j at time t:

$$\xi_{jt} = \rho\xi_{j,t-1} + \nu_{jt} \tag{3.10}$$

and then assumes that the innovation ν_{jt} is uncorrelated with past market and product characteristics. These are the BLP instruments, but with the exogeneity (uncorrelated) assumption defined relative to the innovation ν_{jt}. This has the disadvantage of relying heavily on a specific panel data "timing" assumption, but it makes up for a lack of instruments that are uncorrelated with the undifferenced ξ_{jt}.

Another source of data variation is repeated choice or (similarly) ranked choices, including second-choice data (Berry et al., 2004). If consumers give similar ranks to products that are similar in some product dimension, that is evidence of close substitution in that dimension. This greatly aids in the estimation of substitution parameters. In many (but not all) models of repeated choice, a tendency to repeatedly choose similar products is also evidence of tight substitution. Clearly, some notion of diminishing marginal utility or a taste for variety could possibly overturn that result, so a good model might allow for both persistent taste (that generates repeated similar choices) and for some taste for variety. One common model has persistent (over time) random coefficients on product characteristics, but product-specific ϵ_{ijt} that are independent over time. If consumers make similar choices (in some product dimension) over time, then the random coefficients will be found to be important and the model will imply tight substitution in that dimension. The independent ϵ_{ijt} allows for a variety of choices over time and implies substitution patterns that are not driven by product characteristics (although nothing in the model accounts for actual diversity-seeking behavior.)

Goettler and Shachar (2001) carry this idea further in the context of television viewing. They seek to uncover the structure of product characteristics from the repeated choices of television viewers. The approach is similar to the discrete-choice analysis in political science that identifies dimensions of political differences between politicians in Congress. Goettler and Shachar also allow for switching costs (the utility cost of changing the channel) as an apparently important alternative source of persistent choices. They find persistent preference for shows along four dimensions. The first two relate to complexity of plot and the "realism" of the plot (crime dramas vs. situation comedies, for example). The last two dimensions map into similarities between the viewer demographics and the demographic pitch of the show.

Continuing with studies of television viewing, Crawford and Yurukoglu (2012) use data not just on channels watched, but also data on the time spent watching each channel. This adds additional data on the intensity of preference and does allow the estimation of diminishing marginal returns to watching a given channel.[3] This is a true taste for variety. The paper applies its demand analysis to a study of cable television channel bundling. Note that many cable channels are almost always bundled together (for example, in an "expanded basic" channel tier) so without data on time spent watching each channel it would be difficult to empirically distinguish the taste for individual channels within

---

[3] The use of discrete choice plus intensity of use data goes back at least to the Dubin and McFadden (1984) study of residential electric appliance demand.

bundles. The time-watching data allows the authors to attribute greater value to those channels that are viewed more intensely.

In Crawford and Yurukoglu (2012), the utility of household i from time t_{ic} spent watching channel c in bundle j is

$$\nu_{ij} = \sum_{c \in C_j} \gamma_{ic} \log(1 + t_{ic}), \tag{3.11}$$

where C_j is the set of channels in cable bundle j.[4] The consumer allocates total hours per day across the various channels plus an outside good of not watching television. The taste parameters γ_{ic} depend on consumer demographics. Consumer utility for bundle j then depends on the optimized values of the channel utility as well as on the price of the bundle, on the observed (z_j) and unobserved (ξ_j) characteristics of the bundle, and on random "logit" error terms

$$u_{ij} = \nu_{ij}^* + z_j \psi - \alpha p_j + \xi_j + \epsilon_{ij}. \tag{3.12}$$

Estimation proceeds as in BLP. The unobserved characteristics include important features such as the quality of bundled Internet service. Therefore, as usual, price and the unobserved characteristics are likely highly correlated. The instruments for price are direct "Hausman"-style instruments. These are the prices of similar cable bundles as charged by other firms in the same DMA. These instruments are correlated with price if there are common within-DMA shocks, as seems very likely to be true. They are uncorrelated with ξ_j if unobserved product characteristics (and other firm/bundle demand "shocks") are independent within DMAs. As usual with Hausman instruments, this second requirement could be criticized. However, the variation in other-firm price is a very powerful instrument if correctly specified.

3.3. ADVERTISER DEMAND

Audience demand is an essential component of models of revenue, but the translation of audience demand into revenue requires models of advertiser demand.

The simplest approach is to assume that the medium in question is small relative to the advertising market, in which case the media firm is a price taker in the advertising market. In such a case, the price per media consumer might nevertheless vary by type of consumer, as consumers vary in their value to advertisers depending on age, gender, income,

---

[4] Crawford et al. (2015) extend this Cobb–Douglas utility function to a more flexible form that allows for different degrees of diminishing marginal utility across channel types. In particular, sports channels appear to be a very valuable part of cable bundles even though time spent watching is not extraordinarily high. One possible explanation is that the first hours spent watching sports have a very high value, but there is also a relatively steep decline in marginal utility (e.g., once the highly valued top sports events have been viewed, extra hours of watching other events give little marginal utility).

and so forth. In some cases, advertisers may care about the racial or ethnic composition of the audience, perhaps because ethnicity is correlated with preferences for different advertised goods.

It might also be true that advertiser demand is downward sloping—that is, that the marginal willingness to purchase an advertisement is declining in the size of the total audience exposed to the ad, or in the total demographics (quantity times demographic share) of the audience. More subtly, advertisers may care about the number of times a given person is exposed to an ad, with a willingness to pay that declines in the degree of repeat exposures to the same person.

Berry and Waldfogel (1999) observe the market-level price of radio advertising as revenue per radio listener. They model advertiser demand as a simple constant-elasticity function of total market listening share, as in

$$\ln(r_t) = x_t \lambda_1 - \lambda_2 \ln(S_t) + \nu_t, \tag{3.13}$$

where x_t is a vector of market characteristics and S_t is the total share listening to radio. The unobservable advertising demand shock ν_t is likely correlated with the listening share, since a high level of ad demand will encourage station entry, which in turn leads to high listening. Possible instruments for listening share include the same variables discussed above in the context of nested logit radio demand. These include population and population by demographics.

With richer data, the specification in (3.13) can be extended. Sweeting (2013) models station-level ad prices and includes controls for station format and audience demographics. Jezkiorski, among others, attempts to model prices at the level of a 60-second ad slot. This introduces the "quantity of advertising," a_t, in addition to the quantity of listeners. In radio, the intensity of advertising presumably drives down listening share so that demand for listening should depend on a possibly endogenous quantity of ads. It will also affect the supply side, discussed below.

Rysman (2004) considers advertiser demand for traditional printed "yellow pages" directories that consist of paid advertisements for various, mostly consumer-oriented, retail and service establishments. Pre-Internet, these were a primary reference for consumers seeking service providers and retail outlets. The two sides of the market are the advertisers, who generate revenue for the directory, and consumer "users" who receive the yellow pages book for free. Advertiser demand presumably increases in the amount of usage and usage presumably increases in the amount of advertising (which increases the information value of the directory). This creates a classic network effect among competing oligopoly firms. Rysman's model features consumers who "single-home" each given search in a single yellow book and features advertisers whose "profit per look" is constant (so that competing directories are neither complements nor substitutes in price). In particular, he derives a Cobb–Douglas directory-level aggregate inverse advertising demand function for directory j in market t of

$$\ln\left(r_{jt}\right) = z_{jt}\beta + \gamma \ln\left(a_{jt}\right) + \alpha \ln\left(q_{jt}\right) + \nu_{jt},$$

where r_{jt} is advertising price, a_{jt} is quantity of advertising, and ν_{jt} is an unobservable. Rysman's instrument for usage, q_{jt}, of directory j is the number of households who have recently moved to market t. The instrument for advertising quantity includes cost shifters, such as the local wage. The demographic shifters z_{jt} include population coverage of the directory. (Note that this variable is naturally excluded from Ryman's nested logit model of usage share.)

Fan (2013) follows Rysman in modeling advertiser demand (in column inches) as a function of ad rate (in dollars), r_{jt}, audience size (circulation), q_{jt}, market number of households, H_{jt}, and an unobservable ν_{jt},

$$\ln\left(a_{jt}\right) = \lambda_0 + \lambda_1 \ln\left(H_{jt}\right) + \lambda_2 \ln\left(q_{jt}\right) + \lambda_3 \ln\left(r_{jt}\right) + \nu_{jt}. \tag{3.14}$$

Again, this equation has two endogenous variables and so requires at least two instruments. The same Waldfogel-style instruments that Fan uses in the estimation of readership (circulation) can be used to estimate (3.14). One interesting question is whether those instruments are rich enough to independently shift both quantity and ad price. Supply-side restrictions, discussed in the next section, may provide further restrictions that aid in the estimation of advertising demand parameters.

In these examples, we see that the estimation of advertiser demand depends in part on the richness of the available data. More complicated models tend to introduce further endogenous variables, increasing the demand on instruments. Luckily, the same exogenous instruments that shift choice sets in demand estimation can often serve as instruments in the advertiser demand equation as well. To the degree that instruments are not rich enough to estimate components of advertiser demand, supply-side restrictions may help improve our estimates. We turn next to that supply side.

3.4. THE SUPPLY SIDE: CHOICE OF PRICES, AD QUANTITY, AND OTHER CONTINUOUS CHARACTERISTICS

Because of high fixed costs, relatively few media firms operate in an environment of perfect competition. In a traditional oligopoly framework, differentiated products firms are often modeled as choosing prices conditional on product characteristics. In two-sided media markets, firms may be setting prices to an audience and/or to advertisers. In some cases (as noted in the previous section), we may treat the size of the audience as the "quantity" being sold to advertisers, but in other cases we treat the quantity of advertising (in, say, minutes or column-inches) as a decision separate from the size of the audience. In these cases, increases in the quantity of advertising may drive down (or, possibly, up) the size of the audience, setting up a classic marginal cost—marginal benefit analysis of ad price or ad quantity. Going further, as in other industries, we often want to model endogenous choices related to non-price product quality and horizontal positioning.

In many cases, we can treat the variables (price, ad quantity, product quality) in the last paragraph as continuous choices governed by a first-order condition. As is now traditional in empirical IO (going all the way back to the two-sided newspaper study of Rosse (1970)), these first-order conditions can also be the basis of an instrumental variables or method of moments estimating equation.

As a concrete example, Rosse (1970) considers monopoly newspaper markets. In cross-sectional market t, there are two output measures, number of subscribers, q_t, and ad quantity, a_t (say measured in column-inches per issue). These have associated prices p_t (subscription price) and r_t (ad price). In Rosse, there is one endogenous quality measure, "news space," y_t. Fan (2013) adds additional possible quality measures, but for our example we will stick to one. There are cost shifters, w_t, like plant scale (which is treated as exogenous). Demand shifters are in the form of a vector of demographics, z_t, with some elements of z_t excluded from w_t and vice versa. Rosse then specifies five equations, which are the first-order conditions for the three endogenous variables, plus subscriber and advertiser demand. We have already discussed the estimation of subscriber (audience) demand and advertiser demand and this would be even easier in Rosse's one-product (monopoly) demand example. In particular, the same kind of demand-side instrumental variable arguments holds.

Rosse's innovation was to estimate the parameters of marginal cost(s) from first-order conditions for optimal subscriber and advertising quantity. These first-order conditions set marginal revenue equal to marginal cost, and so they rely on the demand side as well. Updating Rosse slightly, we can begin with a simple single-product logit demand example, as in (3.6),

$$\ln(s_t) - \ln(1 - s_t) = z_t\beta - \alpha p_t + \gamma^a a_t + \gamma^y y_t + \xi_t. \tag{3.15}$$

This is a simplified version of the Fan (2013) demand system; she adds multiple differentiated products, multiple quality levels, and possible random coefficients. As noted in the demand section, Equation (3.15) might be estimated by itself via IV methods, but available instruments might be insufficient to identify coefficients on three endogenous variables. The supply-side choices of prices and quality can aid in identification.

To fix ideas, we begin with a market that has only subscription revenue and no ad revenue; this is a classic one-sided market. Following the more recent literature (Berry, 1994), we model marginal cost as $mc(q_t, w_t, \theta) + \omega_t$, where ω_t is an unobserved cost shock and θ is a parameter to be estimated. The first-order condition for price is, as usual, marginal revenue equals marginal cost.

$$q_t + p_t\frac{\partial q_t}{\partial p_t} = mc(q_t, w_t, \theta) + \omega_t. \tag{3.16}$$

This equation can be rewritten in a traditional form as price minus a markup equals marginal cost:

$$p_t - \frac{q_t}{|\partial q_t / \partial p_t|} = mc(q_t, w_t, \theta) + \omega_t. \tag{3.17}$$

Because we assumed that marginal costs are linear in an unobservable, this equation is linear in its "error term" and therefore can be easily estimated using traditional IV techniques. Rosse (1970), and many others, assume that the marginal cost is a linear function of the endogenous variables and cost shifters. In the model without advertising, if marginal cost depends linearly on cost shifters, w_t, and on output, Equation (3.17) becomes

$$p_t - \frac{q_t}{|\partial q_t / \partial p_t|} = \theta_1^c w_t + \theta_2^c q_t + \omega_t^c, \tag{3.18}$$

where the θs are marginal cost parameters to be estimated.

Note that the markup in (3.18) depends only on data and demand parameters; this is a general feature of static monopoly and oligopoly pricing models. Rosse (1970) models linear monopoly demand, whereas in the case of logit demand (3.15) the markup term is

$$\frac{q_t}{|\partial q_t / \partial p_t|} = \frac{1}{\alpha} \frac{1}{(1 - s_t)}.$$

Price minus this markup, substituted into the left-hand side of (3.18), can then be used as the dependent variable in a linear IV regression to uncover the parameters of marginal cost. Excluded demand shifters, together with Waldfogel- and BLP-style instruments, can then identify the parameters on the endogenous variables.

Since demand parameters enter the markup term, there can be substantial efficiency gains from estimating the demand and supply equations simultaneously, particularly if there are sufficient instruments and/or exclusion restrictions so that the cost parameters are over-identified when the markup function is known. In an extreme case, we could estimate the slope of demand exclusively from the first-order condition, using the logit form of the markup, as in

$$p_t = \frac{1}{\alpha} \frac{1}{(1 - s_t)} + mc(q_t, w_t, \theta) + \omega_t. \tag{3.19}$$

This approach relies on the logit functional form and would require some instrument that causes variation in $1/(1 - s_t)$ separately from q_t.

Even when using a demand model that is richer than the logit, pricing decisions may provide as much or more information about demand substitution patterns as does direct estimation of demand. For example, a firm whose product competes with a close substitute will choose a low markup (low price relative to marginal costs) as compared to a product that does not face close substitutes.

Equation (3.18) illustrates a general principle of estimation via a first-order condition for a continuous variable. One theme in this literature is to choose a functional form that allows us to write (or rewrite) the first-order condition as an equation with a linear error. This in turn allows estimation by traditional IV or "method of moments" techniques.

In the two-sided media case, the modeling of cost shocks within the system of first-order conditions becomes considerably more complicated and raises some issues that are still at the forefront of the literature. We consider an example, inspired by both Rosse (1970) and Fan (2013), where newspaper profit is given by revenue from both subscribers and advertisers. The profit function is subscriber plus advertising revenue minus cost,

$$p_t q_t + r_t a_t - C(q_t, a_t, y_t, x_t, \omega_t), \tag{3.20}$$

where the endogenous variables shifting cost, (q_t, a_t, y_t), are output quantity, ad quantity, and newspaper quality.

We model the firm as choosing prices p_t and r_t, with subscriber and advertising demand equilibrating according to the assumed demand functions

$$q_t = D^q\left(p_t, a_t, y_t, x_t, \xi_t, \theta^d\right), \text{ and} \tag{3.21}$$

$$a_t = D^a(r_t, q_t, z_t, \nu_t, \theta^a). \tag{3.22}$$

Again, these demand functions could be estimated prior to a consideration of supply, or they could be estimated simultaneously with supply.

Note that in the two-sided market, when demand is affected by advertising and vice versa, subscriber and advertising quantities are determined simultaneously by the joint demand system (3.21 and 3.22). This raises a question of how to compute the effect of a change in ad price on ad quantity. The direct effect is obvious, but there is an indirect effect via the subscriber response to ad quantity, which in turn affects ad demand and so forth. Rysman (2004, pp. 495–496) notes this problem: "Estimating the first-order condition in the price-setting game introduces serious difficulties because usage [consumer demand] depends directly on [advertising] quantity … taking the derivative of the demand curve with respect to price (in order to compute marginal revenue) would require solving a fixed-point equation … complicating an already involved optimization routine."

In the yellow pages example, Rysman (2004) avoids this problem by estimating a quantity-setting model, where the yellow pages firms commit to a given "size" of the directory and then receive a market-clearing price. As noted, Rysman's data has a subscription price of zero and so, following on from Equation (3.22), we can simply consider the inverse advertising demand function:

$$r_t = (D^a)^{-1}(a_t, q_t, z_t, \nu_t, \theta^a). \tag{3.23}$$

The marginal revenue from a change in advertising quantity is now well defined as

$$MR_a = \frac{\partial (D^a)^{-1}}{\partial a_t} + \frac{\partial (D^a)^{-1}}{\partial q_t}\frac{\partial D^q}{\partial a_t}.$$

This nicely breaks out the direct and indirect effects of advertising quantity on revenue. Jeziorski (2014) takes a similar approach in another industry (radio) without a subscription price.[5]

In some cases, we might be happy with a quantity-setting model. Indeed, Berry and Waldfogel (1999) consider an even simpler "Cournot" model of advertising supply. In their model, listeners are "sold" directly to advertisers, so q_t and a_t are by definition equal. Better programming choices (or new entry into a discrete radio format) increase listenership and thereby cause a movement down a market-level advertising demand curve, creating a new equilibrium ad price.

In the Jeziorski model with radio-ad minutes, the Cournot ad-quantity model might capture an intuition that stations commit to a fixed number of ad minutes as part of an implicit deal with consumers that a complementary share of the hour be devoted to programming. However, in the yellow pages market, the Cournot assumption seems less intuitive. The size of the yellow pages book can vary easily with the number of ads sold and there seems very little reason to commit to a size. Rysman presents evidence, on the other hand, that prices are posted and fixed to potential advertisers before the book is printed. This is more suggestive of a price-setting model and in fact Rysman is clear that he makes the Cournot assumption for practical reasons rather than as a necessarily preferred model of the market.

As a solution to the problem of estimating the price-setting model in two-sided markets, we propose that the derivatives of subscription quantity and ad quantity with respect to prices be computed via the implicit function theorem applied to (3.21) and (3.22).[6] We refer to these as the "total" derivatives dq_t/dp_t, dq_t/dr_t, da_t/dp_t, and da_t/dr_t. For example, the term dq_t/dp_t accounts for the direct effect of the price change, $\partial D^q/\partial p_t$, as well as the implicit indirect effect of that quantity change on a_t and back to q_t. Use of the implicit function theorem is correct when the appropriate matrix of demand derivatives is invertible. It has the great advantage of not requiring us to compute a solution to a system of two-sided multi-product demand equations, thereby avoiding much of Rysman's computational objection.

Note that one can extend the implicit function technique to the oligopoly case. In an oligopoly, the quantities of all the oligopoly competitors are equilibrating as one firm changes its prices.

---

[5] Fan (2013) avoids the issue by not placing advertising directly into the subscriber demand function, although it is plausible that some consumers might value (or dislike) ads.

[6] Fan (2013) has a related, but different, use of the implicit function theorem, which we discuss below.

We turn now from marginal revenue to costs. We model costs as depending on the endogenous variables and on a vector of cost shocks, ω_t, with one shock for each decision. As an example somewhat in the spirit of Fan (2013), we could model costs as

$$C = q_t[mc(a_t, \gamma_t, \theta^q) + \omega^q] + [F^a(a_t, \theta^a) + \omega^a a_t] + [F^\gamma(\gamma_t, \theta^\gamma) + \omega^\gamma \gamma_t]. \quad (3.24)$$

The first term is quantity times marginal cost, where marginal cost varies with advertisements and quality as well as a parameter vector and a cost shock. The second term in brackets is the fixed cost of selling and producing advertisements, also depending on a parameter and a cost shock. The third term is the fixed cost of quality. Looking forward to a relatively straightforward IV or GMM estimation method, a key feature of (3.24) is that the incremental cost of each endogenous variable is linear in its associated cost unobservable. To capture this, we might assume the more general cost function:

$$C = \bar{C}(q_t, a_t, \gamma_t, x_t, \theta) + \omega^q q_t + \omega^a a_t + \omega^\gamma \gamma_t, \quad (3.25)$$

where the specification of $\bar{C}(q_t, a_t, \gamma_t, w_t, \theta)$ would depend on the details of the application and the data.

Given the profit function defined by (3.20)–(3.22) and (3.25), the three first-order conditions (for subscription price, ad price, and quality respectively) then resemble traditional "multi-product" firm pricing first-order conditions:

$$q_t + \left[p_t - \left(\frac{\partial\bar{C}}{\partial q_t} + \omega_t^q\right)\right]\frac{dq_t}{dp_t} + \left[r_t - \left(\frac{\partial\bar{C}}{\partial a_t} + \omega_t^a\right)\right]\frac{da_t}{dp_t} = 0, \quad (3.26)$$

$$a_t + \left[r_t - \left(\frac{\partial\bar{C}}{\partial a_t} + \omega_t^a\right)\right]\frac{da_t}{dr_t} + \left[p_t - \left(\frac{\partial\bar{C}}{\partial q_t} + \omega_t^q\right)\right]\frac{dq_t}{dr_t} = 0, \text{ and} \quad (3.27)$$

$$\left[p_t - \left(\frac{\partial\bar{C}}{\partial q_t} + \omega_t^q\right)\right]\frac{\partial D^q}{\partial\gamma_t} + \left[r_t - \left(\frac{\partial\bar{C}}{\partial a_t} + \omega_t^a\right)\right]\frac{\partial D^a}{\partial q_t}\frac{\partial D^q}{\partial\gamma_t} - \left(\frac{\partial\bar{C}}{\partial\gamma_t} + \omega_t^\gamma\right) = 0. \quad (3.28)$$

For example, in Equation (3.26) a one-unit increase in subscription price increases profits by (i) subscription quantity q_t plus (ii) the price-marginal cost margin on subscriptions times the total change in q_t induced by the price change plus (iii) the advertising margin times the total change in a_t induced by the change in p_t. Again, recall that the total derivatives in the first-order conditions capture both the direct and indirect effects of price changes, via a use of the implicit function theorem.

Note that in a Nash price (and quality) setting equilibrium, the oligopoly first-order conditions take the same form as (3.26)–(3.28), except that the derivatives of the demands with respect to prices and qualities depend on the derivatives of differentiated products demand, holding other firm's prices and qualities fixed. Multi-product oligopoly first-order conditions are also easy to derive.

Another possibility, following Fan (2013), would be to model quality as being chosen prior to prices. In the oligopoly case, this will lead to a different final equilibrium prediction. Note that the two pricing first-order conditions implicitly define equilibrium prices as a function of quality, γ_t. Again, following Fan, the derivative of prices with respect to quality, say $dp_t/d\gamma_t$ and $dr_t/d\gamma_t$, can be found via the implicit function theorem applied to the pricing first-order conditions (3.26 and 3.27). This in turn allows Fan to make use of first-order conditions for newspaper quality that look forward to the later equilibrium in prices, without computing the "second-stage" pricing equilibrium.

To complete an empirical specification, Rosse (1970) assumes that incremental costs $(\partial\bar{C}/\partial q_t, \partial\bar{C}/\partial a_t, \partial\bar{C}/\partial\gamma_t)$ are all linear in data and parameters. The three first-order conditions (3.26–3.28), plus linear subscriber and advertiser demand equations, then make up the five linear equations that Rosse (1970) takes to the newspaper data.[7] Identification then follows from classic linear simultaneous equations arguments. Fan (2013) uses the oligopoly versions of these same equations, modified for a first-stage quality decision together with carefully chosen functional forms and a more realistic demand side.

BLP suggest estimating the cost parameters via classic Generalized Method of Moments (GMM) techniques that are closely related to nonlinear (in the parameters) IV methods. As usual, we need excluded instruments that are assumed to have zero covariance with the unobservable ωs. The moment conditions used in estimation are then the interaction of the implied unobservable ωs with the instruments.

To implement the GMM method, given any guess for the demand and cost parameters, it must be possible to solve the first-order conditions (3.26–3.28) for the cost shocks ω. This is very close to the supply-side estimation technique in BLP, where the first-order pricing conditions for multi-product firms have multiple cost errors in each equation and one must show how to "invert" the multi-product oligopoly first-order conditions to solve for the cost shocks. Conditional on the solution for the ωs, the GMM econometric techniques of BLP carry directly over to the case of two-side markets.

Note that the first-order conditions are linear in the cost unobservables (with coefficients that are total demand derivatives). A sufficient condition to solve (3.26)–(3.28) for the costs shocks is that the first two equations can be solved for the quantity and ad demand errors, as the third equation can then be solved for the quality error. Since the equations are linear in the ωs, this solution is unique as long as the appropriate determinant condition is satisfied; here that condition is

$$\frac{\partial q_t}{\partial p_t}\frac{\partial a_t}{\partial r_t} \neq \frac{\partial q_t}{\partial r_t}\frac{\partial a_t}{\partial p_t}.$$

---

[7] Rosse (1970), in the manner of that day, simplifies the problem by simply "tacking on error terms" (disturbances) at the end of each first-order condition, but this obscures a discussion of exclusion restrictions, which ought to be based on the idea that there are various incremental costs on the right-hand side of the first-order conditions.

This condition is the same as in the two-good multi-product pricing case: the product of the "own-good" demand slopes cannot equal the product of the cross-good pricing effects (p_t on a_t and r_t on q_t). If this knife-edged condition does not hold, then the first-order conditions can be solved for the unobservables as a function of data and parameters.

These unobservables are then interacted with instruments to form moment conditions in the same manner as in the BLP supply side. If the instrument vector is I_t, then these moment conditions are

$$E(\omega(\theta)|I_t) = 0,$$

where $\omega(\theta)$ is the vector of cost errors.

3.5. THE SUPPLY SIDE: POSITIONING AND ENTRY

The prior section discussed supply-side models of continuous choice. However, many supply decisions are discrete, most importantly the decision to enter a market or market segment at all. Many media economics questions, like the degree of product variety or the degree of competition, are often best answered via models of entry into markets and sub-markets.

The previously discussed models of user (listener, viewer, reader) demand for programming, in conjunction with advertiser demand for ads, generate important ingredients that are very useful for entry modeling. Entry modeling, in turn, has two natural applications. First, data and a demand model give predictions for revenue associated with different entry configurations; from these it is possible to infer operating costs (or at least bounds on them). Second, and perhaps more important, given estimates of costs as well as an equilibrium notion, it is also possible to calculate policy counterfactuals. For example, what is the welfare consequence of a merger or the entry consequence of a tax on operating costs?

Media markets vary substantially in the size of fixed costs in relation to market size; and this relationship in turn determines what task an entry model needs to accomplish. Newspaper markets, for example, tend to have roughly one product per market, so an entry model needs to determine both whether a firm will operate and its positioning in product space. In markets such as television and radio broadcasting, markets support multiple products (Berry and Waldfogel, 1999). Entry models need therefore to determine the number of products operating and, in some applications, a more complicated equilibrium determination of the number of products of each type.

When fixed costs are low enough to allow multiple products, then the important supply-side decisions include both whether to enter and, if so, with what characteristics. It is instructive to begin with the case in which entrants are symmetric (so that the only decision is whether to enter). We then turn to the case with differentiation.

Following on from Bresnahan and Reiss (1988, 1991), much of the empirical entry literature proceeds without demand models, instead relying only on data on the number of firms/products operating in a market. Suppose that firms offering either identical or symmetrically differentiated products may enter a market. Drawing on the broadcast media context, assume that costs are purely fixed, where fixed costs in market t are denoted F_t. In the simplest models, we assume that fixed costs are the same for every firm in a given market or market segment.

The most basic idea for estimation is just revealed preference. In a complete information pure-strategy Nash equilibrium, if we see a firm operating in a given context it must be profitable given the environment and the actions of other firms. If a potential product is not offered, then we infer that adding that product to the market would not be profitable.

In particular, if we see one firm operating in a market, we can infer that the profit accruing to the single firm is non-negative but that the per-firm profits accruing to two firms would be negative. Similarly, when we see N_t firms operating, we can infer that per-firm profits for the N_t firms are positive but would not be if $N_t + 1$ firms entered.

To be more formal, following Bresnahan and Reiss, assume that there are a large number of *ex ante* identical entrants and that per-firm post-entry revenue is $r(N_t, x_t, \theta)$, with x_t a vector of revenue shifters and θ a vector of parameters to be estimated. Profits are $\pi(N_t, x_t, F_t, \theta) = r(N_t, x_t, \theta) - F_t$. The condition for N_t firms to enter into a complete information pure-strategy Nash equilibrium is then

$$r(N_t, x_t, \theta) - F_t > 0 > r(N_t + 1, x_t, \theta) - F_t \quad \text{or}$$
$$r(N_t, x_t, \theta) > F_t > r(N_t + 1, x_t, \theta). \tag{3.29}$$

If we make a parametric functional form assumption on F_t and assume it is independent of x_t, then Bresnahan and Reiss note that this takes the form of a classic "ordered probit" or, more generally, an ordered choice model. The probability of the N_t firm equilibrium is just the probability that F_t falls within the bounds $[r(N_t + 1, x_t, \theta), r(N_t, x_t, \theta)]$. This probability then forms the basis for a straightforward method of moments estimator.

Berry and Tamer (2007) note that the competitive effect of N_t on per-firm revenue (or variable profit more generally) is highly dependent on the assumed functional forms for per-firm revenue and the distribution of F_t. Sometimes the necessary functional form restrictions are credible, and sometimes not. We might obtain more credible estimates of the fixed-cost distribution if we use information on prices and quantities to estimate the per-firm revenue function. In the context of media markets, this is done in Berry and Waldfogel (1999). They estimate the parameters of $r(N_t, x_t, \theta)$ using models of listener and advertising demand, as discussed above. Their economic question is the magnitude of excessive entry, which depends on the incremental cost of an additional product, F_t. They follow Bresnahan and Reiss in estimating the parameters of this distribution via MLE.

To illustrate, given a simple logit model and a symmetry assumption the share of population consuming the "inside share" is $\left(Ne^{\delta}/1 + Ne^{\delta}\right)$. If M is market size and p is the revenue per consumer, per-firm revenue when N products operate is $r(N) = \left(e^{\delta}/1 + Ne^{\delta}\right)pM$ and per-firm revenue with one more than the observed number of firms is $r(N + 1) = \left(e^{\delta}/1 + (N + 1)e^{\delta}\right)pM$. Given the structure of the bounds in (3.29), the ability to calculate counterfactual revenue at $N+1$ firms is particularly important.

Given estimated fixed costs for each market, we can solve the model for the free entry equilibrium. By construction, this yields the observed entry pattern. What is more useful, however, is that we can also use the estimates, along with the structure of the model, to solve for meaningful counterfactuals such as the welfare maximizing equilibrium or the equilibrium outcome that would result if a profit maximizing monopolist operated all of the firms in the market.

3.5.1 Entry Models with Differentiation

We next consider a model of entry into a differentiated product space. Imagine that there is a discrete set of product-type "bins" and that firms can freely enter into any of these product bins. In radio, these product types might be observed programming formats. Differentiation complicates entry modeling because equilibrium now involves not just a scalar number of products, but a vector consisting of the number of products of each type. Now, there is not necessarily a unique Nash equilibrium to an entry game (see Mazzeo, 2002; Tamer, 2003). The straightforward Bresnahan and Reiss MLE approach relies on a unique map from the unobservable fixed costs to the observed entry outcome, but this map is not unique in the presence of multiple equilibria. We discuss here some modeling approaches for entry and equilibrium in the presence of differentiation, beginning with a model with two types of consumers and two types of products.

When entering products are differentiated into discrete types that are imperfect substitutes for one another—as in the case of radio broadcasting—then while finding an equilibrium production configuration is more complicated than in the symmetric case, inference about fixed costs is relatively straightforward. This is the case explored in Berry et al. (2015). We observe some configuration of horizontally differentiated products, which we can summarize as a vector whose elements are the number of products of each type. Again, we assume that there are a very large number of *ex ante* identical potential entrants, who consider entry into any one of the possible horizontal entry positions (formats). Fixed costs are the same for every possible entrant in a given format. The observed configuration is by assumption profitable for each operating station, while additional entry in a particular format would render operators in that format unprofitable. Hence, observed revenue per station provides an upper bound on fixed costs for stations of that type, while demand-model-derived counterfactual estimates of revenue per station (with one more entrant in the format) serve as lower bounds on format fixed costs.

For example, with two entry positions, the fixed costs in format 1 must satisfy a condition similar to (3.29),

$$r(N_{1t}, N_{2t}, x_{1t}, \theta) > F_{1t} > r(N_{1t} + 1, N_{2t}, x_{1t}, \theta), \tag{3.30}$$

where (N_{1t}, x_{1t}, F_{1t}) are respectively the number, revenue shifters, and fixed costs in format 1, and N_{2t} is the number entering in format 2.[8] Once again, it is key that the counter-factual revenue at $N_{1t} + 1$ can be estimated from the data on format listening and advertising demand. A simple insight in Berry et al. (2015) (BEW) is that these bounds can be used directly in counterfactual analysis, with no need for further estimation of the distribution of fixed costs. By using merely the necessary condition expressed by (3.30), Berry et al. (2015) avoid the entire issue of estimation under multiple equilibria. In many cases, the bounds are quite tight and allow BEW to make relatively clear statements about the degree of excess entry.

Berry et al. (2014) pursue a different approach to entry with differentiation. One prominent feature of media markets is the sharp difference in preferences in groups between, say, blacks and whites (or Hispanics and non-Hispanics). This provides some motivation for classifying products into two types, targeting one of two groups of consumers.

If one has estimated a demand model with two types of consumers—say blacks (B) and whites (W)—and two types of products, then it will give rise to two per-station revenue functions: $r_W(N_W, N_B)$ and $r_B(N_W, N_B)$. That is, per-product revenue for each product type depends on the number of own-type products and the number of other-type products. In the extreme example that members of one group do not consume the other type of product, the functions simplify to $r_i(N_i)$, $i = B, W$.

Free entry means that products enter as long as the per-product revenue (assumed symmetric within type) exceeds fixed costs. Hence

$$r_W(N_W, N_B) > F_W > r_W(N_W + 1, N_B), \text{ and}$$
$$r_B(N_W, N_B) > F_B > r_B(N_W, N_B + 1).$$

In addition, the fact that we observe (N_W, N_B) as an equilibrium implies that no firm currently in one format would prefer to switch to the other format. These conditions provide bounds on fixed costs, as in (3.30).

Berry et al. (2014) develop a model along these lines for radio, which they use to infer the welfare weight that the fictitious planner underlying free entry attaches to black and

[8] The condition is easily extended to more than two formats. Recall that in cases with variable costs, the per-firm revenue function would be replaced by a per-firm variable profit function. We might learn about variable costs from a subscriber price first-order condition, as in the prior section, or there might be additional variable cost parameters to estimate from the entry first-order conditions. This later case requires more complex econometric "bounds" techniques.

white listeners by its choice of (N_W, N_B). In their treatment, the fictitious planner is maximizing the welfare from listeners, given the cost of operating stations:

$$\mathcal{L} = W(L_W(N_W, N_B), L_B(N_W, N_B)) + \lambda[K - F_W N_W - F_B N_B].$$

The planner's welfare weights on black and white listening are $\partial W/\partial L_W$ and $\partial W/\partial L_B$, respectively. Each of the other terms in the equations may be calculated from the demand model and as outputs from the entry model. Hence the welfare weights may be calculated directly.

While this approach does not allow a direct determination of the optimal entry configuration, it does allow a different sort of assessment. If the implied welfare weights on listener types differs, then it is clear (subject to integer constrains) that a reallocation of stations from the group with the higher weight would raise welfare for an egalitarian planner. Put more simply, it would generate more listening without raising station operating cost.

Some recent research on media has fruitfully employed dynamic models. See, for example, the studies by Sweeting (2013) and Jeziorski (2014) referenced above. Formal treatment of these approaches lies outside the scope of this chapter, but we expect these approaches to see wider application.

3.6. FUTURE CHALLENGES

Events tend to dictate both what questions are of interest and what questions can be studied. The development of the Internet has linked formerly distinct local media markets. The substitutes for a local newspaper or radio station had traditionally been other local outlets. Now, however, local products face competition from products elsewhere, with the main consequence that local products are declining in most media markets. This has been seen most acutely in newspapers, but local radio stations have also seen new competition from both satellite and Internet radio. The rise of non-local products competing with local products is of interest from a variety of perspectives.

One of the traditionally convenient features of media markets has been their geographic distinctness. The consumers in a particular geographic area motivate the entry and positioning of local products. If there are 100 distinct markets, one has 100 independent observations on both the entering products and consumer choices among their local alternatives. With the growth of non-local products, entry and positioning decisions are governed less by factors that differ across place.

Television consumption used to occur simultaneous with broadcast, making its measurement and meaning relatively straightforward. The development of time-shifting technologies (Tivo and later on-demand services) made its measurement somewhat more complicated. More recently, the development of streaming television offerings (from outlets such as Netflix and Hulu) has further complicated both the meaning and measurement of television viewing.

Radio has faced similar transformations. First, consumers obtained access to satellite offerings. Then came online radio. In principle, XM, Pandora, and iHeart Radio are simply different outlets that, while not local, are simply sources of audio programming. The development of subscription-based interactive services such as Spotify's premium offering (which gives users access to an extensive music library) presents a further complication. While it is a substitute for radio programming, it is also a substitute for the purchase of recorded music. Streaming music services are a hybrid between radio services and recorded music sales. The hybrid status complicates market definition; lack of widely available data poses an important practical challenge to research.

REFERENCES

Anderson, S., dePalma, A., Thisse, J.F., 1992. Discrete Choice Theory of Product Differentiation. MIT Press, Cambridge, MA.

Berry, S.T., 1994. Estimating discrete-choice models of product differentiation. RAND J. Econ. 25, 242–262.

Berry, S.T., Haile, P., 2010. Nonparametric Identification of Multinomial Choice Demand Models with Heterogeneous Consumers. Cowles Foundation, Yale University. Discussion Paper 1718.

Berry, S.T., Haile, P., 2014. Identification in differentiated product markets using market level data. Econometrica 82, 1749–1797.

Berry, S.T., Pakes, A., 2007. The pure characteristics demand model. Int. Econ. Rev. 48, 1193–1225.

Berry, S.T., Tamer, E., 2007. Identification in models of oligopoly entry. In: Blundell, R., Newey, W.K., Persson, T. (Eds.), Advances in Economics and Econometrics: Theory and Applications, Ninth World Congress, vol. 2. Cambridge University Press, Cambridge.

Berry, S.T., Waldfogel, J., 1999. Free entry and social inefficiency in radio broadcasting. RAND J. Econ. 30, 397–420.

Berry, S.T., Levinsohn, J., Pakes, A., 1995. Automobile prices in market equilibrium. Econometrica 63, 841–890.

Berry, S.T., Gandhi, A., Haile, P., 2013. Connected substitutes and invertibility of demand. Econometrica 81, 2087–2111.

Berry, S.T., Eizenberg, A., Waldfogel, J., 2014. Fixed Costs and the Product Market Treatment of Preference Minorities. National Bureau of Economic Research, Cambridge, MA. NBER Working Papers No. 20488.

Berry, S.T., Eizenberg, A., Waldfogel, J., 2015. Optimal Product Variety in Radio Markets. (unpublished paper).

Berry, S.T., Levinsohn, J., Pakes, A., 2004. Differentiated products demand systems from a combination of micro and macro data: the new vehicle market. J. Polit. Econ. 112, 68–105.

Bresnahan, T., Reiss, P., 1988. Do entry conditions vary across markets? Brook. Pap. Econ. Act. Microecon. Annu. 1, 833–882.

Bresnahan, T., Reiss, P., 1991. Entry and competition in concentrated markets. J. Polit. Econ. 99, 977–1009.

Cardell, N.S., 1991. Variance Components Structures for the Extreme Value and Logistic Distributions. Mimeo, Washington State University.

Crawford, G.S., Yurukoglu, A., 2012. The welfare effects of bundling in multichannel television markets. Am. Econ. Rev. 102, 643–685.

Crawford, G.S., Lee, R.S., Whinston, M.D., Yurukoglu, A., 2015. The Welfare Effects of Vertical Integration in Multichannel Television Markets. (unpublished paper).

Dubin, J., McFadden, D., 1984. An econometric analysis of residential electric appliance holdings and consumption. Econometrica 52, 345–362.

Fan, Y., 2013. Ownership consolidation and product characteristics: a study of the US daily newspaper market. Am. Econ. Rev. 103, 1598–1628.

Gentzkow, M.A., Shapiro, J.M., 2010. What drives media slant? Evidence from U.S. daily newspapers. Econometrica 78, 35–71.

George, L., Waldfogel, J., 2003. Who affects whom in Daily Newspaper Markets? J. Polit. Econ. 111, 765–768.

Goettler, R.L., Ron Shachar, R., 2001. Spatial competition in the network television industry. RAND J. Econ. 32, 624–656.

Hausman, J.A., 1996. Valuation of new goods under perfect and imperfect competition. In: Bresnahan, T., Gordon, R. (Eds.), The Economics of New Goods. In: Studies of Income and Wealth, vol. 58. National Bureau of Economic Research, Chicago, IL.

Hausman, J.A., Wise, D.A., 1978. A conditional probit model for qualitative choice: discrete decisions recognizing interdependence and heterogeneous preferences. Econometrica 46, 403–426.

Jeziorski, P., 2014. Effects of mergers in two-sided markets: the US radio industry. Am. Econ. J. Microecon. 6, 35–73.

Mazzeo, J.M., 2002. Product choice and oligopoly market structure. RAND J. Econ. 33, 221–242.

McFadden, D., 1974. Conditional logit analysis of qualitative choice behavior. In: Zarembka, P. (Ed.), Frontiers in Econometrics. Academic Press, New York, NY.

McFadden, D., 1978. Modelling the choice of residential location. In: Karlqvist, A. et al., (Ed.), Spatial Interaction Theory and Planning Models. North-Holland, Amsterdam.

McFadden, D., 1981. Econometric models of probabilistic choice. In: Manski, C.F., McFadden, D. (Eds.), Structural Analysis of Discrete Data with Econometric Applications. MIT Press, Cambridge, MA.

Nevo, A., 2001. Measuring market power in the ready-to-eat cereal industry. Econometrica 69, 307–342.

Rosse, J.N., 1970. Estimating cost function parameters without using cost data: illustrated methodology. Econometrica 38, 256–275.

Rysman, M., 2004. Competition between networks: a study of the market for yellow pages. Rev. Econ. Stud. 71, 483–512.

Sweeting, A., 2013. Dynamic product positioning in differentiated product markets: the effect of fees for musical performance rights on the commercial radio industry. Econometrica 81, 1763–1803.

Tamer, E., 2003. Incomplete simultaneous discrete response model with multiple equilibria. Rev. Econ. Stud. 70, 147–167.

Waldfogel, J., 2003. Preference externalities: an empirical study of who benefits whom in differentiated-product markets. RAND J. Econ. 34, 557–568.

CHAPTER 4

Advertising in Markets

Régis Renault
PSL, Université Paris Dauphine, LEDa, Paris, France

Contents

Handbook of Media Economics, Volume 1A
ISSN 2213-6630, http://dx.doi.org/10.1016/B978-0-444-62721-6.00004-4

Abstract

This chapter proposes an analysis of the role of advertising in the transmission of information in markets. It also describes how the economic analysis of informative advertising provides a satisfactory account of advertising practices and discusses the extent to which resorting to alternative approaches to advertising might be fruitful. In doing so, it provides an overview of what has been identified in the literature as the main incentives of firms to resort to advertising as well as the main arguments pertaining to the welfare economics of advertising. The chapter provides some simplified expositions of the various theories and describes some related empirical literature. The exposition starts with a presentation of the analysis of informative advertising. It is first explained how the informative role of advertising can be understood from the theory of search with particular attention to price advertising. Advertising that contains direct product information is then considered, looking at the nature and the amount of such information provided by advertisers and including some considerations on legal restraints on misleading advertising. Finally, the argument that advertising may provide indirect information in the form of quality signaling or as a coordination device is described and discussed. The chapter then moves on to an analysis of the technology through which advertising conveys information to consumers, considering in turn advertising costs, targeting, and information congestion. The perspective is expanded in the final part of the chapter by allowing advertising to have some role other than the transmission of information. In doing so, the welfare implications of advertising are reconsidered while accounting for a potentially persuasive role of advertising or viewing advertising as a good that complements the advertised product in the consumer's preferences. The strict consumer rationality assumption is also relaxed. The exposition ends with the dynamics of advertising resulting from its role in the accumulation of goodwill for a product or a brand.

Keywords

Informative advertising, Persuasive advertising, Complementary good approach to advertising, Welfare analysis of advertising, Consumer search, Product information, Information disclosure, Signaling

JEL Codes

D42, D82, D83, L11, L15, M37, M38

4.1. INTRODUCTION

As other chapters in this volume illustrate, advertising is a key ingredient of the media business model. According to Holcomb (2014), advertising revenue represented 69% of total media revenue in the US in 2013, down from 82% in 2006. The magnitude as well as the evolution of this ad revenue share suggest that implications of the economics of advertising are very relevant to the economics of media. In particular, they provide the basis for interpreting the demand for advertising space, which in turn determines ad revenue. Advertising is also a critical (though usually adverse) determinant of the attractiveness of a media outlet to its audience or readership. The nuisance experienced by a reader, a listener, or a viewer, because of advertising, might be somewhat mitigated by the value that the individual gets out of being reached by the ad. Again, understanding what advertising does and how it affects the consumer helps analyze this mitigating effect. Finally, a proper welfare evaluation of the media market should account for the impact of advertising on the product market outcome.

In this chapter, I present an overview of the economic analysis of advertising. Although the focus is mostly theoretical, I describe some empirical work, which is directly relevant to the theoretical issues I am discussing. The presentation is organized around the idea that a major function of advertising is to facilitate the dissemination of information to buyers. My goal is to investigate how much can be understood about advertising while considering that its sole function is to transmit information. A complementary objective is to determine how much more can be learned from alternative views on advertising.

The motivation for emphasizing information transmission is twofold. First, due to the considerable development of the economics of information since the 1960s, economic theory is well suited to the analysis of information and its impact on the market outcome. It provides a well-defined role for advertising that can be understood while viewing consumers as rational decision-makers endowed with stable tastes. In particular, this allows for standard welfare evaluations, on the basis of which policy implications can be discussed. This is why a large majority of the theoretical contributions in the last 50 years concerns informative advertising. Second, even if there might be a debate about how much of advertising is informative, there is no doubt that the market outcome cannot be fully understood while abstracting from the informative role of advertising. It gets consumers information that they would otherwise access at a very high cost or not at all. If nothing else, it tells them about the availability of new products.

Although it might now seem natural that economists study informative advertising, early writers on the subject mostly insisted on some other role. Bagwell (2007) offers a very comprehensive survey of these early works. Advertising is broadly described as a wasteful activity that enhances a firm's market power. Particular emphasis is put on its role as an effective barrier to entry. One benefit of advertising that is usually acknowledged by these authors is that, by increasing sales, it generates economies of scale. Some relevant references are Braithwaite (1928), Robinson (1933), and Kaldor (1950).

As Bagwell (2007) explains, this strand of research may be gathered into what he calls the *persuasive view*. According to this line of thought, advertising is for the most part a manipulation of tastes as in Braithwaite (1928), or a manipulation of information as in

Kaldor (1950). This approach was quite prominent until the 1960s. It has in particular contributed a large body of empirical work on the measure and determinants of market power. Major contributors in this respect are Bain (1956) and Comanor and Wilson (1967, 1974). Although different authors propose different interpretations of how advertising impacts consumer behavior, they all stress that it induces major economic inefficiencies by enhancing market power and creating barriers to entry. In particular, it induces spurious product differentiation (Braithwaite, 1928; Comanor and Wilson, 1967, 1974).

Prior to the 1960s, several authors such as Marshall (1890, 1919), Chamberlin (1933), and Kaldor (1950) had recognized an informative role for advertising. Notably Chamberlin (1933) proposes an analysis of the use of informative advertising by a monopolistically competitive firm. He distinguishes advertising that informs consumers about the existence of a product that has a market expansion effect and price advertising that makes the firm's demand more elastic. Kaldor (1950) also considers that one of the roles of advertising is to provide information about the price and the product. However, he views this information as unreliable because it is provided by an interested party. In the end, he concludes that advertising is mostly persuasive. When trying to assess the informational benefit of advertising, these authors face a major difficulty: they analyze the impact of better information for consumers in a theoretical setting that assumes that consumers have perfect information about prices and products. One contribution of the informative view is to propose some new theoretical frameworks and concepts that take into account consumers' imperfect information.

What Bagwell (2007) characterizes as the *informative view* constitutes a complete flip of perspective from the persuasive view regarding the impact of advertising on economic activity. Advertising is considered in this alternative approach as enhancing competition and economic efficiency by providing consumers with better information about the competing options. Rather than being a barrier to entry, it facilitates it and rather than softening competition by introducing more product differentiation, it intensifies it by facilitating price comparisons.[1] It should be no surprise that this line of reasoning is associated with the Chicago School. The two seminal theoretical contributions to this literature are Stigler (1961) and Nelson (1974). They constitute the main inspirations for this chapter (Sections 4.2–4.4) and I return to them repeatedly.[2]

In his grandiose introductory paragraph, Stigler (1961, p. 213) makes the point that, of all people, academics should realize that "… information is valuable: knowledge is power. And yet it occupies a slum dwelling in the town of economics." In the same paragraph, he moves on to write "And one of the information producing industries, advertising, is treated with a hostility that economists normally reserve to tariffs or monopolists."

---

[1] The influential work by Telser (1964) illustrates these ideas. See Bagwell (2007) for details.
[2] See also Ozga (1960) for an early theoretical contribution on informative advertising.

The foremost contribution of Stigler's article is to offer the first analysis of consumer search for a low price in a market where prices are dispersed. This then sets the stage for thinking of advertising as facilitating the consumers' access to information. Stigler has a first crack at such a study of informative advertising by considering that it increases the number of options a consumer is aware of and hence can choose to search through.

Although Stigler (1961, p. 213) does mention "… the relationship of commodities to consumer preferences …" as a relevant dimension about which we should suspect there is imperfect information, his analysis is solely focused on prices. By contrast, Nelson's renowned 1970 article investigates how consumers have access to product information. A fundamental insight from Nelson's investigation is that, contrary to price information, product information is not entirely accessible through consumer search. Some attributes, the *experience characteristics*, such as the taste of some food product, can be learned only after the product has been purchased. He introduces the distinction between *search goods* that the consumer can essentially evaluate through search and *experience goods* for which experience constitutes the main source of information.

Nelson draws the main implications of this distinction for advertising in Nelson (1974). He argues that much of the information transmitted through advertising is indirect and that this is especially the case when advertising concerns experience goods. Nelson further explains that this should lead to large advertising expenditures for experience goods (see Section 4.4), along with ads for search goods that include a lot of direct information (see Section 4.3). He gathers some empirical evidence in support of this view. Nelson's point is primarily to argue that advertising provides indirect information, but he also makes a number of very valuable remarks and conjectures about the provision of direct information through advertising.

Although the informative view affords a powerful explanation for how advertising impacts consumer behavior and contributes to social welfare, it is quite conceivable that advertising that has no informative content is also an effective and socially useful activity. Chicago School economists have put forward standard microeconomics to argue that advertising may be viewed as yet another commodity which can be supplied efficiently by a competitive economy.

This alternative approach to advertising is described by Bagwell (2007) as the *complementary view*. The gist of the argument is that advertising may be thought of as a complementary good to the advertised products. The increase in willingness to pay induced by advertising merely reflects the benefit the consumer draws from consuming this complementary good along with the purchased product. The idea that advertising should be viewed as a commodity had already been considered in the analyses of Kaldor (1950) and Stigler (1961). But the first systematic analysis of advertising along those lines is due to Stigler and Becker (1977). Other important contributions are Nichols (1985) and Becker and Murphy (1993). As Bagwell (2007) points out, a key difference between the complementary view and the persuasive view is that, in the former, consumers are endowed with stable preferences whereas in the latter advertising may induce a change in these preferences. I discuss the implications of these various interpretations in Section 4.6.

I hope to show through this chapter that a lot can be learned about advertising while keeping a strict informative perspective. In particular, I show that the opposition between a persuasive view that stresses how advertising adversely affects economic efficiency and an informative view that emphasizes the contribution of advertising to social welfare is in part unfounded. Even if advertising is merely used to provide information, it can be to a large extent a waste of resources used in a combative manner by firms to take over each other's market share. It can also contribute to enhance market power by improving consumer awareness of differentiation among products.

Still, the informative view has its weaknesses. It involves great strategic complexity. As a result, it assumes a lot in terms of consumer sophistication and leads to some indeterminacy in the form of multiplicity of equilibria. It overemphasizes the advertising of prices, which does not seem to mesh well with much of the advertising we see. It also seems better suited to explain advertising for new products rather than advertising for established brands. This is why alternative approaches that incorporate uninformative content or allow for some consumer naivety should not be overlooked despite the many conceptual difficulties and controversies they entail.

Before outlining the remaining content of this chapter, I should mention two very recent literature reviews that cover similar material. I have already repeatedly referred to Bagwell (2007) that offers a very comprehensive overview of the economics of advertising. In particular, it provides a very detailed discussion of the empirical literature over the years. I have drawn on it substantially to write this chapter. My goal, however, has been to propose a somewhat narrower perspective that complements the work of Bagwell (2007). One important difference is that I stress the link between search and advertising (in Section 4.2). I also cover a number of recent contributions that came out after 2007, in particular some research pertaining to product information disclosure, discussed in Section 4.3.4. Another recent survey is Dukes (2006), who offers a succinct overview of the main issues, with particular attention to how advertising interacts with competition.

Each of the following sections in the chapter ends with some concluding remarks that, whenever relevant, highlight some implications for media economics. The next three sections are devoted to the analysis of informative advertising. Section 4.2 explains how the informative role of advertising can be understood from the theory of search. It also discusses the main contributions and issues concerning price advertising. Section 4.3 concerns advertising that contains direct product information. It first discusses the literature on the role of advertising in matching horizontally differentiated products to consumers and then considers the strategic disclosure of product attributes by firms. Section 4.4 presents the vast literature inspired by Nelson's argument that much of the information transmitted through advertising is indirect. It looks more specifically at the quality signaling argument and at the coordination role of advertising. Section 4.5 focuses on various characteristics of the technology through which advertising conveys information to consumers, considering in turn advertising costs, targeting, and information congestion. I take a wider perspective in Section 4.6 by allowing advertising to have some role other than the transmission of information. In doing so, I reconsider the welfare implications of advertising while incorporating elements of the persuasive and complementary views. I also relax the strict consumer rationality assumption and I consider an important function of advertising, which is to build some goodwill for a brand. I offer a few final thoughts in Section 4.7.

4.2. SEARCH AND ADVERTISING

As I have emphasized in the introduction, in order to capture the informative role of advertising, it is necessary to consider a framework where the consumer's access to information is limited if firms do not advertise. I start by summarizing the two seminal papers on consumer search by Stigler (1961) and Diamond (1971). Stigler starts by arguing that there is price dispersion in markets that leads consumers to search. Diamond, however, shows that costly consumer search should lead to a one-price equilibrium under reasonable assumptions. I will show that combining search and advertising yields price dispersion although it does not generate search in equilibrium. I end the section with an overview of the literature on price advertising, first with homogeneous products and then with differentiated products, with particular emphasis on arguments suggesting that advertising is excessive or, on the contrary, insufficient as compared to a social optimum benchmark.

4.2.1 Stigler's Question

Stigler (1961) argues that buyers cannot be aware of all prices that are charged by different sellers of a given commodity. Obtaining such information takes time and effort and is therefore costly. Stigler suggests that perfect price information for buyers might be achieved if prices remained unchanged for a very long period of time. However, he dismisses this possibility as unrealistic. As a result of the buyers' imperfect information, they cannot systematically arbitrage price differences, which may therefore persist. This, according to Stigler, explains the dispersion in prices that characterizes actual markets. These considerations lead him to investigate how price information might reach buyers, due to their own search activity and to the sellers' advertising effort.

Much of Stigler's attention is devoted to characterizing the optimal non-sequential search rule for a consumer, given he expects some price distribution and faces a search cost that is proportional to the number of searches. An additional search decreases the expected lowest price observed by the buyer and the marginal impact on the expected minimal price of an additional observation is decreasing. Hence, there is a well-defined solution to the optimal search problem. Stigler then considers how advertising provides buyers with additional search opportunities by letting them know about the existence of a seller and how to reach him. Such advertising has some value to the buyer by increasing the expected number of sellers he is aware of, and making it more likely that this number exceeds the number of searches he wishes to perform.

The insights from Stigler's contribution as to the impact of the buyers' imperfect information on the market outcome are very partial but critical. He makes the point that buyers' ignorance leads to dispersion, which in turn makes information provided by advertising valuable. This is true even if that information is the most basic possible, namely the existence of the advertising seller. In many respects, his analysis remains very preliminary and his main merit is to set out a broad research agenda that remains relevant today. For instance, he provides some brief discussions of such issues as the role of intermediaries in facilitating the transmission of information from sellers to buyers or the implications of charging media users rather than advertisers for advertising.

Before returning to the informative role of advertising, I turn to a decisive landmark in the theory of search.

4.2.2 Diamond's Question

Although the work of Diamond (1971) may be perceived as a dramatic rebuff of the analysis of search by Stigler (1961), its starting point is quite remote from Stigler's considerations.[3] Diamond positions his article as a critique of the analysis of the stability of competitive equilibria. By contrast with that literature, he intends to propose a setup with three appealing attributes. First, the adjustment should "… reflect some realistic process …". Second, "… agents in a disequilibrium process should be aware, at least in part, of the disequilibrium …". And finally, prices should be set by agents involved in the market, buyers or sellers, rather than by an auctioneer. Diamond's original construction does not involve any price dispersion. Nor does it involve any consideration of the consumers' optimal search behavior. Rather than a distribution of prices, there is a distribution of threshold prices above which buyers would not buy. The values of these thresholds evolve over time, taking into account the actual pricing behavior of firms. In particular, a buyer's threshold increases whenever she has not purchased in the previous period. Each firm prices as a monopolist on its local demand. The source of competition is the possibility that buyers postpone their purchase, but doing so involves some cost. At any date, the profit-maximizing price is always at least as high as the lowest threshold, implying that the minimum threshold should rise over time, either because the low-threshold buyers drop out or because they observe prices at which they do not purchase. The market finally reaches a steady state at which all firms charge the monopoly price.

---

[3] As a matter of fact, Stigler is mentioned nowhere in Diamond (1971).

As I now briefly explain, non-cooperative game theory affords a much simpler and theoretically consistent approach to the same problem.[4]

Consider a market for a homogeneous product with n sellers. They share the same constant marginal cost, denoted $c \geq 0$. The market demand at price $p \geq 0$ is denoted $d(p) \geq 0$, where all buyers have the same demand.[5] The function d is such that the monopoly profit $d(p)(p-c)$ is single peaked and reaches a maximum at some price $p^m > c$. Sellers choose prices simultaneously, where p_i denotes the price of seller i. Consumers may find out additional price quotes through sequential search. The cost of an additional search is $s > 0$. All sellers are initially randomly matched with an equal fraction of the total buyer population in such a way that the corresponding demand at price p is $d(p)/n$.[6] Buyers matched with a seller get to observe its price at no cost before deciding whether or not to search on through the other sellers.[7] At each round of search, if a consumer decides to search on she is matched randomly with one of those sellers she has not yet visited.[8] The cost of recalling a price quote from some previous round is zero. What has come to be known as "the Diamond paradox" states that, *in any sequential equilibrium*[9] *of this game, all firms charge the monopoly price p^m and no consumer searches beyond the first firm visited; furthermore such an equilibrium exists.*

I now sketch a proof of the paradox. Existence is fairly immediate. If consumers expect the same price from all sellers, it is optimal for them not to search. Each seller, if it charges a price below p^m, faces demand $d(p)/n$ with a corresponding profit of $1/n$ times monopoly profit. Hence profits are no larger than what the seller earns at price p^m. For larger prices, demand is clearly at least as elastic as monopoly demand (the seller now competing with the option to search on as well as the outside option) so that pricing above p^m cannot be more profitable.[10] I now turn to the uniqueness argument for pure strategies.[11]

---

[4] Although it is arguably not the same problem because the analysis below assumes an equilibrium behavior by agents, whereas Diamond was interested in the convergence of a disequilibrium process to some long-term equilibrium.

[5] The result could also be derived assuming heterogeneous buyers with unit demands.

[6] This will be approximately the case with random matching provided that the buyer population is large enough.

[7] The analysis would go through if the first price quote costs s and all buyers have a price-sensitive demand with corresponding consumer surplus at p^m of at least s.

[8] Otherwise, search would no longer be random and other equilibrium outcomes are possible (see Arbatskaya, 2007).

[9] In this game, some players, namely the consumers, make moves at some information sets at which they are not perfectly informed of the history of play. This is why the relevant equilibrium concept is the sequential equilibrium: see Kreps and Wilson (1982).

[10] It is straightforward to specify off the equilibrium path behavior for consumers to complete the description of the equilibrium.

[11] The generalization to mixed strategies, though it is not too involved, would be slightly more technical because the sellers' strategy spaces are not countable.

I first show that the lowest equilibrium price is at least p^m. Suppose instead that the lowest equilibrium price is $p < p^m$. Consider a seller i who is charging that price. First note that, because all consumers have identical demands, marginal cost is constant and $p < p^m$, the firm's profit from selling to any particular consumer, is strictly increasing at $\underline{p}$ (using the assumption that monopoly profit is single peaked). I now show that if i increases its price by some small amount, no buyer would prefer searching to buying from i. Consider a buyer whose consumer surplus at price p is denoted $v(p)$. By searching one more time, she can expect at best $v\left(\underline{p}\right) - s$. Because consumer surplus is continuous in price, the firm can increase its price slightly so that consumer surplus decreases by less than s and the consumer prefers buying at that new price to searching on. Now, seller i faces two segments of buyers. First, buyers who end up with seller i after some rounds of search must be holding at best a surplus of $v\left(\underline{p}\right) - s$ from previous rounds. Otherwise they would not have searched, expecting a price of at least $\underline{p}$. Such buyers would therefore all buy from i if its price is slightly above $\underline{p}$. Second, demand at any price p from buyers matched in the initial round with i is $d(p)/n$. It follows that i's profit on the new buyers is $(1/n)$ times monopoly profit, which is strictly increasing at $\underline{p}$ because $\underline{p} < p^m$. Seller i would therefore wish to deviate by increasing its price.

The proof that the largest price cannot exceed p^m proceeds similarly by contradiction. Let $\bar{p} > p^m$ denote that price. The basic argument is that a seller charging that price has at most demand $d(\bar{p})/n$ (which is what it would get if all other sellers are charging that price). Hence it is better off charging p^m which, from the previous argument, is less than or equal to any other price charged in equilibrium so that the corresponding profit is at least $(1/n)d(p^m)(p^m - c)$.

The paradoxical nature of the result is threefold. First, introducing even the slightest search cost wipes out all competition in the market. An extreme version of this is when the buyers must incur the search cost even for the first price quote and they all have unit demand. Then, even if they are heterogeneous in their willingness to pay, the market unravels (this was initially pointed out by Stiglitz, 1979). Second, monopoly pricing prevails no matter how large the number of firms is. Third, this is a search model with no search in equilibrium. The literature has proposed a number of alterations of the framework that solve the paradox in one or more of the above dimensions. I exclusively concentrate on the role that can be attributed to informative advertising.

To conclude the discussion of the search framework inspired by Diamond (1971), it is worth noting that the type of advertising considered in Stigler (1961) would not modify the market outcome in terms of pricing or consumer search behavior. Recall that Stigler only considered advertising that informs buyers of the existence of sellers so buyers must still engage in search to uncover price information. Then a seller's advertising activity would only affect the share of buyers that show up at that seller's shop to get a first price quote. It would still be the case that each seller could act as a monopolist with the resulting demand and that there would be no search. This is why the research that I discuss below has considered price advertising through which each seller can commit to some pricing behavior. This, however, does not disqualify Stigler's approach altogether because he was actually considering a search technology that is different from the sequential search of the Diamond environment. Burdett and Judd (1983) have shown that, if buyers use non-sequential search as in Stigler, although the monopoly price equilibrium always exists, there can be equilibria with dispersed prices so that consumers find it optimal to sample more than one seller with positive probability. In such a context, an increased advertising intensity may be valuable to consumers and social surplus by increasing the probability that a buyer is able to sample more than one seller.

I now present the main insights from the research on price advertising with homogeneous products with sequential search or no search at all.

4.2.3 Price Advertising and Price Dispersion

The idea that price advertising might constitute a sensible solution to the Diamond paradox was first explored in the seminal paper by Butters (1977). Although the article does include a version of the model with consumer search, it is usually remembered as a model where consumers may only purchase at firms that have reached them with an ad. The ad provides them with price information and the opportunity to buy. As such, it has inspired a number of variants where advertising informs consumers about both the existence of a firm and its price. Besides Butters himself, Stegeman (1986) and Robert and Stahl (1993) have studied a model of price advertising with sequential consumer search. I first present a streamlined model that I use to present the insights from both strands of the literature.

The following stylized model shares many features with the model of Robert and Stahl (1993). Consider a duopoly for a homogeneous good. Both marginal costs are zero. There is a continuum of consumers with measure 1. When the market opens, consumers do not know a firm's price unless they see it advertised. They may, however, find out prices that are not advertised through sequential search. Each search costs $s > 0$. All consumers have identical unit demands with a valuation of $v > 3/2$ for the product. I now introduce the following simplifying assumption on the advertising and pricing game: firms may either not advertise and price the product as they wish, or advertise, in which case they must charge $p = 1$ (to be thought of as a low price). If firm i, $i = 1, 2$, advertises, it selects to reach a fraction $\Phi_i \in (0, 1]$ of the consumer population which costs $1/2\Phi_i^2$. In a first stage, firms simultaneously choose whether to advertise or not: if they advertise, they select an advertising reach; and if they do not advertise, they select a price, p_i, for firm i. In a second stage, after observing advertisements that have reached them, if any, consumers choose whether or not to enter the market, and if they do whether to search and buy. If consumers enter the market without seeing an ad, they are matched with equal probability with one of the two competitors.

I look for a symmetric equilibrium where each firm advertises with probability λ and chooses intensity Φ (so firms only randomize between two advertising intensities: zero and Φ). If a firm does not advertise, it optimally selects the price that makes a consumer just indifferent between searching and not searching (provided it is less than v). Let r denote that price. Consumers who see an ad from each firm or no ad at all split equally between the two competitors. Hence a firm's profit when advertising with intensity Φ_i and expecting its competitor to play its equilibrium strategy is given by:

$$\left[\lambda\left(\frac{\Phi_i\Phi+(1-\Phi_i)(1-\Phi)}{2}+(1-\Phi)\Phi_i\right)+(1-\lambda)\left(\Phi_i+\frac{1-\Phi_i}{2}\right)\right]-\frac{1}{2}\Phi_i^2, \quad (4.1)$$

which simplifies to

$$\left[\lambda\left(\frac{-\Phi}{2}\right)+\left(\frac{1+\Phi_i}{2}\right)\right]-\frac{1}{2}\Phi_i^2. \quad (4.2)$$

This expression is maximized at $\Phi_i=1/2$ so the equilibrium value of Φ is $1/2$. I nonetheless go through the equilibrium derivation assuming Φ takes on any value in $(0,1/2]$. If a firm does not advertise, its profit is

$$\left[\lambda\left(\frac{1-\Phi}{2}\right)+(1-\lambda)\left(\frac{1}{2}\right)\right]r. \quad (4.3)$$

In a mixed strategy equilibrium, λ should equate profit expressions (4.2) and (4.3), which yields

$$\lambda=\frac{(\Phi^2-1-\Phi)+r}{\Phi(r-1)}. \quad (4.4)$$

Recall that r is determined by the indifference of a consumer between buying at price r and searching a firm from which she has received no ad. The probability that a firm is advertising (and hence charging a low price) conditional on not receiving an ad from that firm is given from Bayes law by $(1-\Phi)\lambda/(1-\Phi\lambda)$. Hence r is a solution to

$$\frac{(1-\Phi)\lambda}{1-\Phi\lambda}(r-1)=s, \quad (4.5)$$

where the left-hand side is the expected benefit from search given the advertised price is 1. A firm that does not advertise therefore prices at

$$r=1+\frac{1-\Phi\lambda}{(1-\Phi)\lambda}s. \quad (4.6)$$

It is readily verified that, for $\Phi\leq1/2$, conditions relating λ and r given by (4.4) and (4.6) may be depicted as in Figure 4.1, provided that search cost s is not too large and advertising intensity Φ is not too close to 0 (where the equation for the CI curve is derived

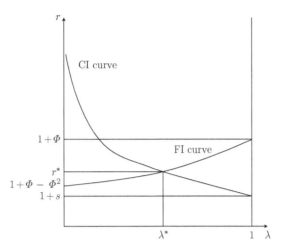

Figure 4.1 Equilibrium for some exogenous value of Φ. Along the CI curve, a consumer is indifferent between searching and not searching. Along the FI curve, a firm is indifferent between advertising and not advertising.

from (4.6) and the equation for the FI curve is derived from (4.4)). Hence, if firms are constrained to select advertising intensity Φ, the equilibrium values of λ and r are given by the coordinates of the intersection of the two curves. This is the case as long as the corresponding value of r is less than v so consumers are willing to buy at price r. This condition also ensures that consumers who do not receive any ad are willing to incur search cost s to enter the market.

This equilibrium exhibits price dispersion to the extent that a firm that does not advertise charges a higher price than a firm that does. This would still be the case if the advertised price was endogenous. There would, however, be another source of dispersion among firms that advertise. Indeed, in our simple framework, if a firm expects its competitor to advertise a price of 1, in the event that it advertises, it would be better off undercutting 1 to capture all consumers who receive an ad from both firms. A related argument rules out any mass point in the distribution of advertised prices. Robert and Stahl (1993) show that, in equilibrium, there is a continuous distribution of advertised prices. Furthermore, low prices are advertised more. Dispersion of advertised prices is also found in price advertising settings with no consumer search, such as in Butters (1977), Stegeman (1991), and Stahl (1994). However, Stahl (1994) finds that, in oligopoly, the intensity of advertising does not depend on the advertised price.

I now discuss the comparative statics with respect to search cost s, which is the only exogenous parameter that has not been set to a specific value. An increase in search costs results in a shift upward of the CI curve. Recalling that $v > 3/2 \geq 1 + \Phi$, the mixed strategy survives as long as $s < \Phi$. Then, following an increase in s, the equilibrium point moves along the FI curve so that r and λ increase. An increase in search costs therefore results in an increase in the price charged by a firm that does not advertise, as well as an increase in the probability that a firm chooses to advertise.

4.2.4 Too Much or Too Little Advertising?

A central question in the literature on price advertising has been the comparison between the equilibrium and the second-best socially optimal advertising intensity: second-best here indicates that advertising intensity is adjusted so as to maximize social surplus, assuming that firms are free to price as they wish. The original work by Butters is often remembered for establishing that the equilibrium level of advertising is socially optimal. This, however, is obtained in the model without consumer search. When he does allow for search, he finds that the equilibrium intensity is excessive. Stegeman (1991) and then Stahl (1994) have shown that the optimality result of Butters is specific to his demand specification and that, with no consumer search, advertising is typically insufficient. I first discuss the intuition behind this result and then explain, with the help of the model of the previous section, why, with consumer search, advertising can be excessive.

Consider again the model of the previous section, now assuming that consumers may purchase only if they see an ad from at least one of the firms. Advertising should then be interpreted as informing consumers about the firm's existence and location as well as its price. Still assuming that the advertised price is 1, firm i then choose the advertising intensity Φ_i that maximizes profit

$$\Phi_i\left(1 - \frac{\Phi}{2}\right) - \frac{1}{2}\Phi_i^2, \tag{4.7}$$

where Φ is the equilibrium advertising intensity chosen by the competitor. Firm i's best response is therefore $\Phi_i = 1 - \Phi/2$. The unique equilibrium is symmetric with both firms choosing advertising intensity $\Phi = 2/3$. Now for an advertising intensity Φ by each firm, the corresponding social surplus is given by

$$\left(2\Phi - \Phi^2\right)(v - s) - \Phi^2, \tag{4.8}$$

which is maximized at $\Phi^* = (v - s)/(v - s + 1)$. It follows that advertising is excessive for $v - s < 2$ and insufficient for $v - s > 2$. This ambiguous result reflects the two counter-vailing external effects associated with a firm's choice to increase its advertising intensity. On the one hand, an increase in a firm's advertising results in an increase in the proportion of consumers who buy, but for each additional sale, the firm obtains at most the corresponding social surplus (but typically less, if $v - s > 1$): this is what Tirole (1988, p. 294) calls the *non-appropriation of surplus* in the context of entry. On the other hand, the firm gets to sell to some new customers who, having received an ad from the competitor, would have bought in any case: this corresponds to what Tirole (1988, p. 294) calls *business stealing*.[12]

The ambiguous result obtained in this fixed price model does not reflect the finding in the literature. This is because the equilibria that have been obtained in the literature with endogenous prices typically involve no atom in the price distribution.[13] The welfare analysis of advertising intensity with no consumer search has been performed in monopolistic competition by Butters (1977) and Stegeman (1991), and in oligopoly by Stahl (1994). I now borrow from Stegeman (1991) the intuition for why these authors find that advertising intensity cannot be excessive and is typically insufficient. Think of ad messages that all have the same cost of being sent $b > 0$ as in Butters (1977). Consider a firm that would be charging the maximum value in the support of the price distribution. Because the price distribution is continuous, an ad by that firm steals no business from any other firm. Hence, at the optimal advertising intensity for that firm, the social surplus generated by the last ad message sent must be at least the firm's private benefit, which is no less than b from profit maximization. Now think of a firm charging a price strictly below the maximum. The social surplus generated by an ad at that price is at least as large as that generated by an ad at the maximum. It is therefore at least b. Thus, the advertising by any firm cannot be excessive. Furthermore, the social surplus from an additional ad at a price below the maximum is strictly above b if demand is elastic. This argument also explains why the advertising intensity is socially optimal in Butters (1977). Indeed, he considers homogeneous consumers with unit demands. Because the maximum price is the reservation price, the social surplus at that price coincides with the producer surplus and advertising is socially optimal at that price. Since demand is inelastic, the social surplus from an ad is the same at all prices so that the advertising level is socially optimal at all advertised prices.

In all the studies that do not involve consumer search, the social benefit of advertising stems solely from the additional sales it generates. By contrast, in the research that allows for consumer search (Butters, 1977; Robert and Stahl, 1993), the market is fully covered, independent of the advertising intensity. This is because all those who do not get any ad choose to search and buy from the first seller they encounter. From a first-best perspective (say if we constrain firms to price at marginal cost and consumers are aware of it), advertising has no social value and since it is costly, its socially optimal level is zero.

This is, however, no more the case if firms can set prices freely. Without advertising, if consumers know their valuations before searching, the market would be in a Diamond-like situation and, if consumers have unit demand, there would be no market. Hence,

---

[12] See Tirole (1988, p. 288) for how these two effects apply to entry in the model of Spence (1976).

[13] See Anderson et al. (2014) for asymmetric equilibria where some price is charged with positive probability and the equilibrium ad level is socially excessive.

firms must be allowed to engage in some advertising activity, so they have some incentive to offer low prices. Consumers who do not see any ad, expecting that such low prices might be offered, then have an incentive to participate in the market. As far as I am aware, the optimal advertising intensity that balances consumer participation with the cost of advertising has not been investigated.[14]

In the setting of Section 4.2.3, it is clear from Figure 4.1 that we may have an equilibrium with full consumer participation as long as $\Phi > s$ so the two curves cross for some $\lambda < 1$. Hence for $s < 1/2$, the advertising intensity chosen by firms $\Phi = 1/2$ is clearly excessive. An analogous result holds in the setting of Robert and Stahl (1993), where consumers are homogeneous with unit demand and identical search costs. They find that for a low enough search cost, there is full participation and the price charged by a firm that does not advertise is strictly less than the consumers' valuation. If advertising intensity was slightly decreased at all advertised prices, the strict inequality between the unadvertised price and consumer valuation would still hold and consumers would still participate. Presumably, this result may not generalize for a heterogeneous population of consumers in terms of search costs or valuations. Advertising may then have a market expansion effect as in the model with no search. This may be the case, either because it induces search by high-search-cost consumers or it makes low prices more likely, so more consumers end up buying.

Welfare results for price advertising with homogeneous products may be summarized as follows. If advertising does not induce much market expansion, consistently with a model where consumers may purchase through search, then advertising is likely to be excessive. If, on the contrary, advertising enhances market participation by consumers significantly, either because it increases consumer awareness of available sellers or because consumers are very heterogeneous in their search and purchase behavior, then we may expect the market provides too little advertising. This suggests that the diagnosis should be, to a large extent, inferred from an empirical investigation of whether advertising has a strong market expansion effect or not. Actual markets, however, are characterized by some degree of product differentiation. Advertising may then contribute to social welfare, even if it only induces a shift of demand from one product to anther. This is because consumers may be shifting to products with which they have a better match.

I now discuss the analysis of price advertising in markets for horizontally differentiated products.

---

[14] Although Butters (1977) does find excessive advertising in his model with search, he obtains this result while assuming that the market is covered independent of the advertising intensity. In his setting, advertising contributes to social welfare by saving consumer search costs because only those consumers who are not reached by any ad must incur these costs. By contrast, my discussion assumes consumers must incur search costs before buying whether or not they have received an ad.

4.2.5 Price Advertising with Product Differentiation

The existing research on this topic (Grossman and Shapiro, 1984; Christou and Vettas, 2008; Sovinsky-Goeree, 2008) has ignored the possibility of search. It therefore assumes that a consumer can buy only at firms from which she has received an ad, in which case she is perfectly informed about that firm's product and price.

Consider a simple duopoly model of price competition with differentiated products. If all consumers are perfectly informed, the demand for firm i's product is given by $\widetilde{d}_i(p_i, p_j) > 0$, for $i = 1, 2$ prices $p_i \in IR_+$, for firm i, $p_j \in IR_+$ for firm j, $i = 1, 2$, $i \neq j$. There is a measure one of consumers with unit demand and the perfect information market is assumed to be covered so that $\widetilde{d}_2(p_2, p_1) = 1 - \widetilde{d}_1(p_1, p_2)$. Firms simultaneously select an advertising intensity $\Phi_i \in [0, 1]$ and a price p_i for each firm $i = 1, 2$. Advertising intensity measures the proportion of consumers that are reached by an ad from firm i. It costs $A(\Phi_i) = (a/2)\Phi_i^2$, $a > 0$, for a firm to advertise with intensity Φ_i. The covered market assumption is extended to assume that all consumers who receive an ad only from firm i (who have measure $\phi_i(1 - \phi_j)$) buy from that firm no matter what price it charges. Furthermore, advertising is not targeted so the demand from consumers who receive an ad from both firms (who have measure $\phi_i\phi_j$) is $\hat{d}_i(p_i, p_j)$. Firm i's demand with imperfect consumer information may therefore be written as

$$d_i(p_i, p_j, \Phi_i, \Phi_j) = \Phi_i\left[(1 - \Phi_j) + \Phi_j\widetilde{d}_i(p_i, p_j)\right]. \tag{4.9}$$

Assuming firms have constant marginal production costs, $c_1 \geq 0$ and $c_2 \geq 0$, price first-order conditions are derived in a standard way as

$$p_i - c_i = -\frac{d_i(p_i, p_j, \Phi_i, \Phi_j)}{\dfrac{\partial d_i}{\partial p_i}(p_i, p_j, \Phi_i, \Phi_j)} = -\frac{1 - \Phi_j}{\Phi_j\dfrac{\partial \widetilde{d}_i}{\partial p_i}(p_i, p_j)} - \frac{\widetilde{d}_i(p_i, p_j)}{\dfrac{\partial \widetilde{d}_i}{\partial p_i}(p_i, p_j)}, \quad i = 1, 2, \ j \neq i. \tag{4.10}$$

Assuming advertising intensities are interior, $\Phi_i \in (0, 1)$, $i = 1, 2$, corresponding first-order conditions are

$$a\Phi_i = (p_i - c_i)\frac{\partial d_i(p_i, p_j, \Phi_i, \Phi_j)}{\partial \Phi_i} = -\frac{\left[1 - \Phi_j + \Phi_j\widetilde{d}_i(p_i, p_j)\right]^2}{\Phi_j\dfrac{\partial \widetilde{d}_i}{\partial p_i}(p_i, p_j)}, \quad i = 1, 2, \ j \neq i, \tag{4.11}$$

where the second equality is obtained by substituting in the price first-order condition for firm i.

Let us start by considering the first equalities in (4.10) and (4.11) and use the notation $D_i = d_i(p_i, p_j, \Phi_i, \Phi_j)$, and i's partial demand derivatives with respect to own price and advertising, D_{ip} and $D_{i\Phi}$, respectively. Further define $D_{iA} = (D_{i\Phi})/(a\Phi_i)$, which is the demand derivative with respect to advertising expenditures $A(\Phi_i)$. Then substituting

(4.10) into (4.11) and rearranging, we obtain the well-known Dorfman and Steiner (1954) relation:

$$\frac{A(\Phi_i)}{p_i D_i} = -\frac{(\Phi_i/2)D_{i\Phi}}{D_{ip}p_i} = -\frac{D_{iA}A(\Phi_i)}{D_{ip}p_i} = -\frac{\eta_A}{\eta_p}, \tag{4.12}$$

where η_A and η_p are the demand elasticities with respect to advertising expenditures and price, respectively.

This simple relation states that the share of revenue devoted to advertising should equal the ratio of the elasticity of demand with respect to advertising expenditures to the price elasticity of demand (in absolute value). A simple takeaway is that a firm facing a demand with lower price elasticity, and hence endowed with more market power, advertises more. This is the flip side of the persuasive view argument that firms use advertising to enhance their market power.[15] The present setting allows for an analysis of how advertising relates to market power and how they are jointly determined in equilibrium.

In the framework of Grossman and Shapiro (1984) and the related literature, the two sources of variation in market power are the extent of product differentiation and the number of firms. It is straightforward to discuss the impact of product differentiation in the duopoly setting above. Assume that there exists a function $\bar{d}_1$ defined on IR, such that $\hat{d}_1(p_1, p_2) = \bar{d}_1(p_1 - p_2)$, for all $(p_1, p_2) \in IR_+^2$ (a property shared by many standard discrete-choice duopoly models), and marginal costs are identical, $c_1 = c_2 = c$. The full information covered market condition then implies that $\hat{d}_2(p_2, p_1) = 1 - \bar{d}_1(p_1 - p_2)$. Further assume that there exists a symmetric equilibrium where both firms charge p^* and advertise with intensity Φ^*. Let $b = -\bar{d}_1{}'(0) = -(\partial \hat{d}_i(p^*, p^*))/\partial p_i$, $i = 1, 2$. Then, because $\hat{d}_i(p^*, p^*) = \bar{d}_1(0) = 1/2$, first-order conditions (4.10) and (4.11) may be written as

$$p^* - c = \frac{1 - \Phi^*}{\Phi^* b} + \frac{1}{2b} \tag{4.13}$$

and

$$a\Phi^* = \frac{(2 - \Phi^*)^2}{4\Phi^* b}, \tag{4.14}$$

so that equilibrium price and advertising intensity are

$$p^* = c + \sqrt{a/b}, \quad \Phi^* = \frac{2}{1 + 2\sqrt{ab}}. \tag{4.15}$$

---

[15] See Bagwell (2007) for a detailed discussion of this theme, both from a theoretical and an empirical point of view.

In commonly used models, the parameter b may be interpreted as a measure of product differentiation: it measures how many consumers a firm loses by raising its price slightly above that of its competitor and is therefore large if there is little product differentiation. For instance, in the Hotelling duopoly example of Tirole (1988, pp. 192–294), $b = 1/2t$, where t is the unit transport cost. In a random utility model with i.i.d. valuations for the two products, f, $b = \int_{-\infty}^{+\infty} f(\epsilon)^2 \mathrm{d}\epsilon$, where f is the density of the additive random utility term: it may then be interpreted as the "mass" of consumers who are just indifferent between the two products at equal prices. For the uniform distribution on $[\alpha, \beta]$ used by Christou and Vettas (2008), $b = 1/(\beta - \alpha)$. In this uniform case, a broader support means more heterogeneity in products and tastes.

From the first-order condition, (4.13) and (4.14), more differentiation, and hence a lower b, all other things being equal, moves the equilibrium price and the advertising intensity upward. Note, however, that price is decreasing in advertising intensity. This is because more advertising by the competitor means less captive consumers who only get an ad from firm i. For $\Phi^* = 1$, the pass-through rate $p^* - c$ takes its full information value $1/2b$. This opens up the possibility that more product differentiation leads to lower prices, although for the present specification with quadratic costs of advertising, this is not the case. There is, however, no ambiguity about the impact of an increase in product differentiation on advertising, which is positive.

To discuss the impact of the number of competitors on pricing and advertising, I draw on the analysis in Christou and Vettas (2008), who study a variant of the model with a random utility specification of demand. They find that more firms unambiguously lead to a decrease in the advertising activity of each firm. Although this seems coherent with the intuition from Dorfman and Steiner (1954), it does not reflect a systematic relationship between market power and advertising. Indeed, Christou and Vettas (2008) find that an increased number of competitors does not necessarily lead to lower prices. The intuition for this is simple and follows from the same strategic interplay between price and advertising that causes a potentially ambiguous impact of product differentiation on pricing. For a fixed advertising intensity by competitors, an increase in the number of firms decreases a firm's price. However, more competition leads to a lower advertising intensity, which increases market power, and hence the price. Christou and Vettas (2008) find that this price-augmenting effect may actually dominate in their setting.

The above price comparative statics results suggest that it might be extremely misleading to ignore the limited access of consumers to information when performing a structural estimation of market demand. This has been done in numerous studies in the wake of the groundbreaking work of Berry et al. (1995) on the automobile industry. Sovinsky-Goeree (2008) addresses this issue in her analysis of the US personal computer market in the late 1990s. She uses data on ad expenditures in various media (magazines, newspapers, TV, radio) as well as a survey of consumers that includes information about their exposure to the various media. This data allows her to simulate the household's exposure to advertisements, which in turn conditions the household's choice set (it can choose only among products it is aware of). This introduces some heterogeneity among buyers that affects their purchase decision independent of the product's characteristics. She jointly estimates market demand and the firms' first-order conditions for pricing and advertising.

Her focus is on the measure of market power and how it compares to what it would have been if the model had been estimated assuming that consumers had full information. She finds that market power would have been hugely underestimated (and thus demand price elasticity greatly exaggerated). She estimates a median markup for the industry of 15%, where a standard estimation using the method of Berry et al. (1995) that assumes perfect consumer information would yield an estimate of 5%. Note that from pricing first-order conditions (4.10) or (4.13), the markup with imperfect consumer information should clearly exceed what it would be with perfect consumer information. Indeed, the last term on the right-hand side in (4.13) is the full information markup and the term that precedes it is clearly positive. It is also clear that own-price elasticity is larger in absolute value for the full information setting: with imperfect information, when a firm raises its price, it only loses to the competitor consumers who were indifferent and who had received an ad from both firms. Still, there is no clear argument why estimating the full information model on data generated with imperfect information should necessarily produce higher or lower estimated markups than would be obtained by estimating the true model. In any case, the results in Sovinsky-Goeree (2008) show that the discrepancy can be very substantial.[16]

I now return to the comparison of market-provided advertising with the second-best socially optimal level. As argued by Tirole (1988), the main takeaway from the analysis of informative advertising with product differentiation is that advertising may either be insufficient or excessive. Again, as Tirole (1988, p. 294) explains, the two countervailing forces at work are *non-appropriation of social surplus*, which suggests advertising might be insufficient, and the *market stealing effect*, which induces firms to over-provide advertising. By contrast with the homogeneous product setting, the positive externality for consumers of an additional ad (associated with the non-appropriation of social surplus effect) may arise even if the ad reaches a consumer who is also getting some ad from some competing firm. This is because, due to horizontal product differentiation, the additional product that the consumer is aware of may be a better match for his tastes. Christou and Vettas (2008) find that advertising is inappropriately low with little product

---

[16] As she explains on p. 1053, if three products with identical characteristics and prices are competing, then the full information model would assume a purely random matching between products and consumers. If, however, this matching is explained to a large extent by advertisements from different firms reaching different consumers, then the corresponding demand would be much less price elastic. However, she explains in her online appendix that the inappropriate specification of the model could bias the results in the opposite direction.

differentiation and it is excessive when product differentiation is substantial.[17] This does not mean, however, that there is a systematic relationship between product differentiation and the welfare properties of market-provided advertising. Indeed, as I have explained above, it is possible to have excessive advertising with homogeneous products and no consumer search, as in the asymmetric equilibria studied by Anderson et al. (2014).

I end this discussion of advertising in differentiated product settings with some considerations on allowing for consumer search. Two preliminary remarks are in order. First, because the relevant information concerns both a price and a product, and the product information could involve multiple dimensions, if consumers are allowed to search, a firm could choose to disclose only part of the relevant information and let the consumer find out the rest on her own. I discuss this possibility in Section 4.3.3.2 in a monopoly setting. Performing such an analysis in oligopoly is non-trivial. Second, as shown by Wolinsky (1986) and Anderson and Renault (1999), costly sequential search does not yield the Diamond paradox if consumers search not only for price but also for products they like.

Consider a simple duopoly with differentiated products where consumers may search sequentially. If there is no advertising and if, in equilibrium, the two firms charge the same price, then consumers follow a simple stopping rule when deciding whether they buy from the first firm encountered or go to the next one: they stop if the utility they obtain from the first product is above some threshold value. If this is not the case then they move on to search the second firm and can then make a perfectly informed choice between the two products. Standard arguments show that this threshold value is decreasing in search costs. I further assume enough symmetry so the threshold does not depend on which firm is searched first.

Assume now that a firm may use advertising to inform the consumers about its price and product (it must reveal both) before they start searching. First notice that a consumer does not benefit from receiving an ad from only one firm (except by saving on search costs if the first search is costly). The ad merely determines which firm the consumer gets to see first. Now a consumer who receives an ad from both firms benefits differently depending on whether her utility with each product is above or below the threshold. If both her utilities are above the threshold, then she benefits from making a perfectly informed choice, which would not have been the case if she had received no ad or one ad. If both her utilities are below the threshold, then she benefits by saving on the search cost she would have had to incur to make a perfectly informed choice if she had received at most one ad. If only one of the utility levels exceeds the threshold, then the nature of the benefit depends on the order in which the consumer uncovers information.

---

[17] Hamilton (2009) obtains a similar result in the Hotelling duopoly setup.

The above argument shows that, in order for advertising to generate some social surplus, search costs must be large. Indeed, with low search costs, the threshold utility is very large and most consumers have utility levels with both products that lie below. Then the only benefit from being exposed to advertising is a cut in search costs. If search costs are low, the benefits are low as well. Now if search costs are low, firms do not benefit much from advertising. Consumers end up making a perfectly informed choice whether or not they receive ads. This suggests that with differentiated products, it is not clear that if consumers are allowed to search there will be excessive advertising as is the case for a homogeneous product.

4.2.6 Concluding Remarks

Because consumers face search costs, advertising is a socially beneficial activity. This point was first made by Stigler (1961) and is reinforced by the Diamond paradox that tells us that, with no advertising, we would get the monopoly outcome or even complete market unraveling. For homogeneous products, consumer search is motivated by the dispersion in prices and, indeed, the interaction of search and advertising yields price dispersion. Yet there is no search in equilibrium because all prices are low enough that consumers prefer not to search. However, advertising concerns for the most part markets with differentiated products. On these markets, consumers search for appropriate products as well as low prices and typically they do engage in search when they do not receive advertising from some of the sellers.

Now that a growing share of the advertising market, including advertising on online media, is on the Internet, search and advertising are much more intertwined and search costs are much smaller. Shoppers on the Internet may be exposed to ads and users of websites that provide such contents as news or entertainment may become immediate shoppers by clicking on an ad.[18] New forms of advertising have emerged, notably search advertising whereby sellers bid to obtain sponsored links that are in favorable positions on a search engine.[19] These new practices also illustrate that one important role of advertising is to direct consumer search, whereas the great majority of the analysis of consumer search assumes random search. There is a growing theoretical literature on ordered consumer search, including Arbatskaya (2007), Armstrong et al. (2009), Zhou (2011)), Haan and Moraga-González (2011), and Anderson and Renault (2015).

Advertising being socially valuable does not mean it is provided optimally by the market. It may be under-provided because of the non-appropriation of consumer surplus by advertisers or excessive because of the market-stealing externality on other advertisers. For a homogeneous product, there is an argument suggesting it is under-provided,

---

[18] See Renault (2014) for a framework that captures these features.

[19] Studies of search advertising include Varian (2007), Edelman et al. (2007), Athey and Ellison (2011), Chen and He (2011), De Cornière (2013), and Anderson and Renault (2015).

but this requires that advertising has a significant market expansion effect. If consumers can search sellers from whom they have received no ad, then advertising does not affect the market size. It is what Marshall (1890, 1919) calls "combative advertising" that merely reshuffles market shares. Then it is clearly excessive. Some empirical support for combative advertising can be found in Lambin (1976), whose results suggest that advertising does not increase demand in an industry. When allowing for product differentiation, there is no clear takeaway. Advertising may be insufficient even if it has no impact on the market size. This is because it may induce large gains in consumer surplus by improving the matching between consumers and products. I provide another perspective on the social optimality of advertising in Section 4.6 taking into account its non-informative roles.

Note finally that the above results are relevant for a proper welfare analysis of the media market. The advertisers' willingness to pay for ad space does not correctly reflect the social benefit of advertising, unless advertisers are perfectly discriminating monopolists. Conversely, because of potential inefficiencies in the market for ad space, the private advertising cost incurred by firms may differ from the social cost of advertising, making the welfare analysis presented here inappropriate. I return to this point in the concluding remarks to Section 4.5.

4.3. PRODUCT ADVERTISING

The goal of this section is to present a fairly recent body of literature that investigates the incentives of firms to provide information about their product to consumers. This research has adopted two distinct modeling strategies that are complementary. In a first set of models (Section 4.3.3), ads are viewed as informative signals about how well the product matches the consumers' taste. The firm can choose the characteristics of this signal—how informative it is or what it informs the consumer about—so as to maximize its profit. However, the firm has no private information about how good the match is. Alternatively (Section 4.3.4), other papers explicitly model how ads inform consumers about their match, by disclosing the product's attributes. In such a setting, both sides have private information about the match since the consumer knows her tastes and the firm knows the product's attributes. The disclosure game is then a signaling game. The section ends with a discussion of how we might think of misleading advertising in the context of such disclosure games.

I first introduce the general issue of the informative content of ads by briefly summarizing the seminal paper by Nelson (1974), and presenting some relevant empirical work both in economics and marketing.

4.3.1 Nelson's Question

In his famous early 1970s articles (Nelson (1970, 1974)), Philip Nelson has drawn our attention to the channels through which consumers obtain product information.

In Nelson (1974), he develops a theory of the role of advertising in this respect. To do this, he uses the distinction between search goods and experience goods that he introduced in Nelson (1970). Characteristics of search goods can be observed by a consumer before she decides whether to buy or not, whereas characteristics of experience goods are learned only once the good is consumed. His premise is that advertising may transmit information only if this information is deemed credible by potential buyers. His analysis abstracts from any government intervention in the form of laws on misleading advertising.

He argues that a claim pertaining to a product is credible only if it concerns "search attributes." Indeed, there is no point in telling major lies about such attributes because they would at best fool the consumer into incurring some visit cost but not into buying. The consumer may find out the truth before she buys. He concludes that ads for "search goods" should contain a lot of information, whereas ads for experience goods should not. And yet, in view of the anecdotal evidence provided by Nelson, ad expenditures devoted to the promotion of experience goods are much larger than what is spent on advertising search goods.

Nelson (1974) is best known for solving this puzzle. The key insight is that the information provided by experience good ads is indirect. I return to this point in the next section that discusses the role of advertising as a signal. My focus here is on Nelson's predictions on direct information in ads. His conclusions are that ads for experience goods should contain hardly any information, whereas ads for search goods should be very informative. Furthermore, the information conveyed about search goods should be credible even if there are no laws on misleading advertising. The body of research I discuss below explores these issues through models of information disclosure. I next look at some of the available evidence regarding the informative content of advertising.

4.3.2 Empirical Evidence on Advertising Content

The analysis of Nelson (1974) predicts that much of the ad money is spent on ad messages for experience goods that contain little or no direct information. He provides various indirect evidence that this is the case. Verifying it directly requires some data on the actual content of ad messages and some coding strategy that allows for measuring the amount of information it includes. Shortly after the publication of Nelson's article, though with very different motivations, some researchers in marketing have undertaken to gather such data and to construct a coding method. This line of research, called "content analysis," was initiated by Resnik and Stern (1977). They define 14 categories of "information cues" that include such items as price, quality, performance, availability, nutrition or warranties. The methodology consists of counting the number of categories present in each ad message, in order to measure its informativeness. The content of advertisements in different media has been investigated in this fashion. For instance, Abernethy and Franke

(1996) present summary statistics for a set of previous studies on US media: they find that the average number of categories per ad over four different studies of US television is 1.06, with only 27.7% of ads including at least two and 37.5% having no category whatsoever. For seven studies on US magazines, the average was 1.59, where 25.4% have three or more categories and 15.6% have no category at all. For newspapers, they find a much higher average, but still no more than 38.5% of advertisements inform about more than four categories. Newspaper ads are much more likely to include price information than magazine ads, 68% against 19%. The overall picture is that many ads include little information, if any, although a majority of ads include some information.

In recent years, there have been renewed efforts to gather and exploit data on the content of ads (e.g., Anderson et al., 2013, 2015; Bertrand et al., 2010; Liaukonyte, 2012). Anderson et al. (2013) provide a systematic analysis of the content of television ads for over-the-counter analgesics in the US. They have constructed an original dataset by coding the content of all ads over a 5-year period, recording all specific claims that are made about the medicine (such as fast or strong) as well as whether these claims were comparative or not (this particular industry being characterized by an extensive use of comparative claims in advertising). By contrast with the Resnik and Stern (1977) methodology, they do not gather information cues into general categories but rather add up the total number of information cues in a message to measure its informativeness. Over the period of investigation, 30 different attributes were mentioned, of which they keep the top 23 in terms of amount of dollars spent advertising them. They also relate these attributes to the actual characteristics of the drugs as established in medical publications. They use a simple model of a firm's choice of the informativeness of its ad messages, where the firm trades off the amount of persuasive (non-informative) content with the amount of information. The marginal benefit of an extra second of persuasion is some random variable, the realization of which varies across ads: the smaller it is, the more information cues the firm chooses to include in the ad. They find that ads for objectively higher quality products include more cues. Ads for brands with large market shares provide less information and comparative ads are more informative. Finally, ads for brands with large generic counterparts embody less information.

The results in Anderson et al. (2013) cannot be directly compared to those of marketing studies on advertising content. The focus is actually different. By using general categories that can apply to a broad range of different products, content analysis allows for comparing the informative content of ads across media, over time, across countries or across industries. The results, however, are not very conclusive. Besides, the observation that ads are not very informative because they cover only a small number of the 14 possible categories is questionable: categories are broad and only a small subset of them might be relevant for a particular advertised product. The most convincing takeaway is that the percentage of ads covering no information cue category is rather large. The approach in Anderson et al. (2013) rather focuses on the incentive of firms to provide direct information in ads. They derive predictions about which firms are more likely to include more information in their advertisements. Looking at a particular industry allows for having measures of informativeness that are more directly comparable across brands: products are sufficiently close that the relevant information is similar. It remains hard to make statements about the informativeness of ads in absolute terms because it is not clear what the most informative ad possible would look like, but comparisons among brands and products seem reasonable.

The theory of indirect information on experience goods proposed by Nelson (1974) provides one explanation of why many ads are completely uninformative. It tells us nothing, however, about the extent to which ads should include some information when that information is credible. Nor does it predict the nature of the information that a firm might choose to disclose or to keep silent. The remainder of this section presents various theoretical frameworks that help address these issues.

4.3.3 Match Advertising

Typically, we view advertising as an effort to make a firm's product more attractive to potential consumers. Intuition then suggests that a proper disclosure strategy consists of revealing favorable features while hiding unfavorable ones. This, however, implicitly assumes that all consumers agree on what is favorable and unfavorable news about a product. Yet consumer tastes are often heterogeneous and products are horizontally differentiated. As a result, information that is good news to some buyers turns away others. The social value of information is then to facilitate a good match between products and buyers. The empirical study by Anand and Shachar (2011) on ads for television shows provides an interesting illustration of this role of advertising. They find that exposure to an ad can make it less likely that a viewer watches the advertised program and that seeing one ad reduces the probability that a viewer watches the wrong program by 10%. I now discuss a seller's incentive to provide detailed product information that improves the matching.

It is useful to start with two methodological remarks. First, an obvious reason for not disclosing information is that it might be too costly. The literature has typically ignored these costs to focus on the demand-driven incentives for not disclosing information. There is actually a difficulty in specifying how disclosure costs are related to the "quantity" or the nature of the information that is being revealed (costs are introduced in Section 4.5.1). A second point is that, as I will explain in Section 4.3.4, information transmission involves some strategic complexity that often leads to multiple equilibria. Many researchers who have been concerned about the provision of march information have circumvented this problem by assuming that the firm can completely control the information that is inferred by buyers from looking at the ad, subject to some constraint that it is consistent with Bayesian updating. The advertiser can then select the inference that is most profitable. This requires in particular that the firm holds no private information about the value of the match. The analysis presented in this subsection follows this modeling strategy.

In much of the following discussion, I use a setting where a monopoly seller produces a good with constant marginal cost $c \in [0,1)$. For simplicity of exposition, there is only one buyer, who has unit demand. The buyer's willingness to pay is $r \geq 0$, which is the realization of a random variable. Initially, r is unknown to both parties but it is common knowledge that it has a uniform distribution on [0,1].

4.3.3.1 Direct Information About Experience Goods

The early contributions on the transmission of match information (Lewis and Sappington, 1994; Meurer and Stahl, 1994) assume that consumers cannot acquire pre-purchase information about products through their own endeavor. This is consistent with the classification of products as experience goods in Nelson (1970). Still, in contrast to Nelson's view, it is assumed that the disclosed product information is directly available in the ad and is credible. Following the literature, I assume that this credibility is achieved through *certification*.[20] Typically, laws on misleading advertising may achieve this as long as the claims can be verified by a court.[21]

A stripped-down version of Lewis and Sappington (1994) may be presented in the simple monopoly setting above. Before the buyer decides whether to purchase the product or not, the firm announces a price and, if it so chooses, provides some product information. If it provides such information, the buyer observes a signal $\sigma \in [0, 1]$, which is equal to her true valuation r with probability α and is uniform on [0,1] independent of r with the complementary probability $1 - \alpha$. In short, the buyer learns r perfectly with probability α and learns nothing otherwise but does not know which situation she is in. Then the larger α is, the more informative is the ad.

From the standard uniform distribution, the prior expected value of the match is $1/2$. After observing the signal σ, the buyer's expected willingness to pay is $\alpha\sigma + 1/2(1 - \alpha)$. This expected willingness to pay is increasing in α if $\sigma > 1/2$ and decreasing in α if $\sigma < 1/2$. Figure 4.2 shows the inverse demand curve given the posterior beliefs of the buyer, where price, p, is on the vertical axis and the probability that the product is purchased, q, is on the horizontal axis. As demonstrated by Johnson and Myatt (2006), the firm's problem may be analyzed graphically by letting the inverse demand curve pivot around the point A in the figure with coordinates $(1/2, 1/2)$. Indeed, if the firm sells with probability $q < 1/2$, it charges a price above $1/2$, because of the standard uniform

---

[20] As should become clear from my discussion of cheap talk in Section 4.3.5.1, in the models discussed in this subsection, information could be credible even without certification.

[21] Lewis and Sappington (1994) actually mention other possible ways of transmitting credible information like allowing consumers to test the product themselves.

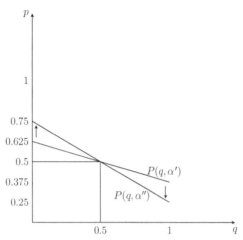

Figure 4.2 Improved match information, where $P(q, \alpha)$ denotes the inverse demand when the signal is informative with probability α.

distribution of σ: so the expected willingness to pay of the marginal consumer is increasing in α. Conversely, for a sale probability above $1/2$, the marginal consumer's expected willingness to pay is decreasing in α. Thus in the figure, $\alpha' < \alpha''$. This means that the better informed is the consumer, the steeper is the inverse demand curve. In particular, if the consumer has no information, $\alpha = 0$, then the inverse demand is flat at willingness to pay $1/2$.

If the firm can choose any $\alpha \in [0, 1]$, it chooses either $\alpha = 0$ or $\alpha = 1$. Suppose, on the contrary, that the firm chooses $\alpha \in (0, 1)$. If it sells with probability $q < 1/2$, then if it makes the demand curve steeper by providing more information, it can sell with the same probability at a higher price. Similarly, if it sells with probability $q > 1/2$, it can increase its profit by providing less information. As a result, the firm chooses between full information and no information. As Johnson and Myatt (2006) emphasize, no information means that the inverse demand is flat and the firm's strategy is to sell to the entire buyer population at an intermediate price, whereas with full information the firm chooses a steep inverse demand that allows for charging a high price to the consumers in the "niche" of the product.

Which factors determine whether the firm chooses no information or on the contrary full information? First consider changes in marginal cost. If it is zero, then by providing no information, the firm can charge a price of $1/2$ and sell with probability 1. This yields the perfect price discrimination profit $1/2$: indeed, perfect discrimination would involve charging a price of r to the consumer for all realizations, which would yield the same expected profit. Then the no-information profit clearly exceeds that under full information, which is the uniform price monopoly profit against the full information demand, $1/4$. It can be shown that the firm's profit-maximizing behavior is to hide information if marginal cost is low and reveal full information if marginal cost is large.[22] Lewis and Sappington (1994) also argue that the firm finds it profitable to fully reveal information only if match values are heterogeneous enough.[23]

The original analysis by Lewis and Sappington (1994) actually postulates a very general form for the informative signal.[24] Still, the firm cannot choose its characteristics (it only chooses the probability that a consumer receives it). As a result, they do not characterize the optimal informative signal for the firm. It turns out that this question has a very simple answer in their experience good setting. Consider a simple signal that only tells the consumer whether or not her match exceeds marginal cost c: formally $\sigma \in \{\ell, h\}$ and $\sigma = h$ with probability 1 if $r \geq c$, $\sigma = \ell$ with probability 1 if $r < c$. Now suppose the firm charges a price of $E(r|r \geq c)$. Then the consumer buys if and only if she learns that $r \geq c$. Furthermore her expected surplus from buying is zero. This implements the perfect price discrimination outcome: the firm only sells to the consumer if she is willing to pay more than marginal cost and it captures the entire social surplus. It is therefore the best the firm can achieve.[25] Hence the optimal solution involves partial information disclosure, in contrast with the finding of Lewis and Sappington (1994) and Johnson and Myatt (2006). This first-best solution should be viewed as a benchmark. There is no guarantee that the firm has access to appropriate disclosure strategies to implement it. Note however that, because the firm perfectly controls the consumer's access to product information, it can implement this solution merely by selling the access to information to the consumer at some price that extracts all *ex ante* surplus and then price at marginal cost.

Meurer and Stahl (1994) and Anderson and Renault (2009) study match information advertising in a discrete-choice, differentiated product duopoly setting. In both papers, match disclosure decisions are taken in a first stage prior to price competition and partial

---

[22] To see this, note that, using the envelop theorem on the full information profit, it is convex and decreasing in c, and it has just one crossing point with the no-information profit, which is linear and decreasing (because the no-information profit crosses from above).

[23] A simple intuition for this is that, if matches are all very close to $1/2$ and $c < 1/2$ so that the firm can sell while providing no information, then all matches are above marginal cost and no information implements the perfect discrimination profit. If, on the contrary, matches are widely spread around $1/2$, then with no information the firm sells to a significant mass of consumers whose willingness to pay is below marginal cost, so that it would be better that they are excluded from buying. If it fully reveals information, the firm can screen out those consumers and charge a price substantially above $1/2$ while still selling to the large mass of consumers with very high valuations.

[24] They merely require a first-order stochastic dominance between the consumer's posterior beliefs after observing a more or less favorable signal. The version presented here can be found in Johnson and Myatt (2006).

[25] This result was first derived by Saak (2006). It is also related to the analysis in Anderson and Renault (2006), who show, in a search good setting, that this type of threshold signal does at least as well as any other informative signal (see Section 4.3.3.2). Their argument can easily be adapted to the simpler case of experience goods.

match advertising is ruled out. In Meurer and Stahl (1994), match values for the two products are perfectly and negatively correlated so that match disclosure by either firm fully informs a consumer. By contrast, Anderson and Renault (2009) assume i.i.d. match values but they allow a firm to choose between providing no information, information on its own match only, or information on both matches thus using comparative advertising.

Anderson and Renault (2009) assume zero advertising costs. They first consider a situation with symmetric firms where, without any match information, both products would be perceived as identical by consumers. This would result in Bertrand competition with zero profits. More match information always increases both firms' profit so it is a weakly dominant strategy to reveal own-match information. As a result, full match information is disclosed, whether comparative advertising is barred or not. Meurer and Stahl (1994) also find that match information is profit enhancing. They, however, consider costly advertising reach so that there is not enough of it from the producers' point of view.[26]

Comparative advertising becomes a very relevant practice when firms are *ex ante* asymmetric enough, either in terms of production costs or because there is a systematic quality advantage $\Delta q > 0$ in favor of one of the products that consumers take into account in their purchase decision, in addition to the match difference and the price difference. Then comparative advertising is used by the "weak" firm with the small market share (high costs/low quality) so as to attract those consumers who have a very strong match preference for its product. The "strong" firm, however, prefers that limited match information be conveyed to consumers so they make their purchase decision mostly on the basis of the quality and/or price difference for which it has a large advantage. When comparative advertising is used by its competitor, it lowers its price, which benefits most consumers because they buy from the large firm. This, combined with the better match information imparted by comparative advertising, improves consumer surplus over what it would be if comparative advertising was disallowed. Total surplus, however, deteriorates because too many consumers buy the low-quality product.[27]

A few observations are noteworthy regarding the comparison between monopoly and oligopoly. First, competition may provide added incentives for the firms to disclose match information. Both in Meurer and Stahl (1994) and the symmetric version of Anderson and Renault (2009), full product information is disclosed, whereas a monopoly firm may choose to withhold such information (e.g., when its marginal cost is low

---

[26] They also find that advertising may be excessive or insufficient relative to the social optimum. See Bagwell (2007) for more details.

[27] Emons and Fluet (2012) consider a setting where consumers know horizontal match but not quality. They compare direct advertising where each firm may only advertise its own quality to comparative advertising where a firm advertises the quality difference. In the latter case, only one firm advertises in equilibrium. They analyze both the case of direct quality information and the case of quality signaling through ad expenditures.

enough).[28] The simple intuition for this is that product information relaxes price competition. This price-increasing impact of information also arises under monopoly: once information is revealed, a firm caters mostly to those consumers who have a strong preference for its product (over the competitor or the outside option). However, when firms are asymmetric, Anderson and Renault (2009) show that more match information in the form of comparative advertising may induce a drop in price for the firm with the large market share.

I now turn to the disclosure of match information for a search good so that the consumer may obtain product information before purchase even if the firm does not advertise it.

4.3.3.2 Search Goods and Advertising Content

The focus so far has been on experience goods, implying that the firm has full control over the product information that is available to consumers prior to purchase. Furthermore, the analysis in the previous subsection implicitly assumes that price information is freely available to the consumer. It is therefore not possible to discuss the availability of price information in advertisements. The framework I introduce next allows for both analyzing advertising of search goods and discussing the advertiser's choice of including price and/or product information in ads.

A search characteristics as defined by Nelson (1970) is such that the consumer may observe it prior to purchasing the product. If such information could be accessed at no cost, then there would be no role for advertising product information. The discussion of search characteristics advertising in Nelson (1974) clearly incorporates some costs for the consumer to acquire the pre-purchase information: he explicitly mentions "transportation costs of consumers" (p. 730). These costs may naturally be construed as visit costs required to get to the store (or on the seller's web page), inspect the product, and then possibly purchase it. Anderson and Renault (2006) consider a monopoly setting that captures this simple idea. It is a straightforward extension of the monopoly setting introduced above. Let us now assume that the buyer may only purchase the product after incurring a visit cost $\gamma > 0$. Once this cost is sunk, and prior to deciding whether to buy or not, she becomes perfectly informed about the product and hence knows the realization of r perfectly as well as the price charged by the firm. The firm may use advertising to inform the consumer about the product and/or the price before she decides whether to visit or not. The main objective is to determine the optimal choice of ad content for the firm. Because the consumer is initially uninformed about r, all consumer types are *ex ante* identical. I now assume that marginal cost is $c = 0$ so that, given the standard uniform distribution of the match, the unique monopoly price is 1/2.

---

[28] It is, however, not the case that competition necessarily leads to more information revelation, as I explain in Section 4.3.4.

If γ is small enough, the firm may obtain the monopoly profit without resorting to any advertising. If the consumer observes no information before deciding whether to visit, the firm cannot infer anything about the match value from observing a visit. Hence, it charges the monopoly price $1/2$. Expecting this, it is optimal for the consumer to visit as long as the visit cost is less than her expected surplus from visiting and then buying if and only if $r \geq 1/2$: this expectation is merely the standard consumer surplus, which is here $1/8$. Hence, in order for advertising to have a role, visit costs should be at least $1/8$.

I now turn to an important insight, which is a reformulation of the unraveling result of Stiglitz (1979). Suppose that the firm only advertises product information and provides full information to the consumer. The consumer, when deciding whether to visit, knows the realization of r but not the price. In equilibrium she rationally anticipates that the firm will charge some price p^*. It is then optimal to visit if and only if $r \geq p^* + \gamma$. If $p^* + \gamma < 1$ then the consumer visits whenever her match is large enough. The firm can then infer that the visiting consumer is willing to pay at least $p^* + \gamma$. But this means that it could up its price to this level and still sell to the consumer, thus making more profit than at price p^*. Hence p^* cannot be an equilibrium price. This means that, in equilibrium, the consumer must expect a price above $1 - \gamma$ so she does not visit, no matter how high her match value is. As a result the market unravels.[29] Such advertising is therefore not profitable for the firm. In short, the consumer expects to be held up.

However, a firm need not always include a price in its ad in order to circumvent the holdup problem. Suppose the firm can post an ad that merely informs the consumer whether her match is above or below the monopoly price, $1/2$. Then if the consumer learns she is willing to pay at least $1/2$, she expects her match to be uniform on $[1/2, 1]$ and choose to visit as long as γ is at most her expected surplus at price $1/2$, $\int_{1/2}^{1} (r - 1/2) 2 \mathrm{d}r = 1/4$. A consumer learning that her match is below $1/2$ will not visit. The firm anticipating that a consumer who visits is willing to pay at least $1/2$ does not choose to charge less. Charging a larger price would also yield $\hat{r}$ a lower profit because the demand elasticity at $1/2$ is -1. It is therefore credible that the firm will charge $1/2$ to a consumer who visits and we have an equilibrium. Thus, using this simple threshold disclosure strategy enables the firm to retain its monopoly profit for visit costs as high as $1/4$.

For larger visit costs, it is no longer possible for the firm to sustain monopoly profit. Nor is it possible to survive without resorting to price advertising. This is because the consumer is no longer willing to visit, expecting the monopoly price even if she is reassured that she is willing to pay that price. The firm therefore needs to further sweeten the

---

[29] This argument can readily be generalized to mixed strategies, oligopoly, and *ex ante* heterogeneous consumer types, as long as they all have a strictly positive visit cost. Such unraveling, however, would not arise if the buyer had a price-sensitive demand rather than a unit demand and the visit cost was not too large. Alternatively, if the firm sells multiple products as in Rhodes (2015), then the holdup problem is circumvented because the firm cannot infer a precise enough lower bound on a consumer's willingness to pay for each of the products.

deal by committing in its ad to price below 1/2. Indeed, Anderson and Renault (2006) establish that the firm cannot improve upon a disclosure strategy that consists of a simple binary signal that tells the consumer whether her match is above or below a threshold $\hat{r}$ with no further information. The intuition is as follows. Given the threshold match strategy, it is optimal for the firm to price so as to make the consumer just indifferent between visiting and not visiting when she learns her match exceeds the threshold. By providing more information, the firm can only improve the expected surplus of some consumer types with a match well in excess of the threshold, which does not increase sales because these types are visiting anyway and then buying with threshold information. However, because of Bayesian updating, this improved expectation for a high-match consumer necessarily implies that those consumer types who are close to the threshold learn that their match is not so good. As a result, the firm would need to lower its price to keep those consumer types onboard. By contrast with the analogous result for an experience good, this disclosure strategy does not allow the firm to achieve the full discrimination profit unless the visit cost is very large.

Anderson and Renault (2006) show that as the visit cost γ increases, the firm's advertising strategy goes from no advertising to threshold match-only advertising and then to threshold match and price advertising. In any case, a firm ideally prefers to provide only partial information to consumers. This result is to be contrasted with the prediction in Lewis and Sappington (1994) that the optimal information provision should be full if the firm wishes to inform at all. This result also does not provide much support for the prediction in Nelson (1974) that ads for search goods should contain a lot of information. Further note that price is never advertised alone. This is true, however, only if the firm can parse the information it provides sufficiently finely. If product information must be fully informative, then the firm chooses to advertise price alone for intermediate visit costs.

Thus far, I have treated γ primarily as a visit cost required to make a purchase that automatically warrants full access to product information for the consumer. If a product is elaborate enough, obtaining all relevant information may require some additional cost and the consumer might choose to purchase while uninformed so as to save on these costs. To illustrate this possibility, suppose that γ is merely a cost of acquiring full product information whereas the consumer may now purchase the product with no visit cost if she only bases her decision on advertised information. Assume γ is low and the firm's ad only informs the consumer whether she is willing to purchase the product at monopoly price 1/2 or not. If the consumer is charged 1/2, she buys without acquiring any further information. It is possible, however, for the firm to charge a price $p > 1/2$ such that the consumer learning that her match is at least 1/2 would still choose to buy without acquiring any further information: this price should satisfy $\int_{1/2}^{p} (p - r) 2 dr \leq \gamma$, where the left-hand side is what the consumer would save by not purchasing the product when her match is below p if she was perfectly informed. This allows the firm to sell the monopoly quantity at a price above monopoly price. By contrast, if it provides no information as in the Anderson and Renault (2006) setting, the consumer is informed if γ is small and the firm earns the monopoly profit. Hence, the firm chooses to provide partial product information in order to reduce the consumer's incentive to search and become perfectly informed. This possibility is explored in Wang (2014)).[30]

The analysis of disclosure used in this subsection is suitable for match information but is not well adapted for quality information. I now turn to a setting that is also relevant for the disclosure of some quality dimension.[31]

4.3.4 Advertising of Product Attributes

The literature on match revelation in Section 4.3.3 assumes a unique *ex ante* firm type. When the firm makes more or less information available to the consumer, it does not know whether it will make its product more or less attractive. The firm's incentives to reveal information do not depend on any private information it might hold and the consumer does not infer anything about such private information. Although this is a convenient way of thinking of the disclosure of match information, it does not seem appropriate for investigating the disclosure of quality information. Disclosing such information may be more or less desirable, depending on whether the firm's product quality is high or low. More generally, some horizontal match attributes may appeal more broadly to consumers than others.

In order to account for this heterogeneity of firm types, following Koessler and Renault (2012), I enrich the monopoly model of Section 4.3.3 by assuming that the willingness to pay r is now written as $r(s, t)$. The first component $s \in S$ is the firm's type summarizing the firm's private information (typically the characteristics of its product) while $t \in T$ is the consumer's type or private information (typically her tastes over product characteristics). The distribution of r is now derived from the joint distribution of (s, t). An ad for the firm now consists of revealing a subset of types in S and misleading ads are ruled out by requiring that the announced subset contains the firm's true type. Throughout I assume that the product is an experience good so the consumer may

---

[30] He actually uses the information transmission technology of Johnson and Myatt (2006) and finds that partial information ($\alpha \in (0, 1)$) is optimal when search costs are low. Bar-Isaac et al. (2010) consider the firm's choice to make information more or less costly to acquire for the consumer. They find that an intermediate search cost is a price discrimination tool, where only some consumers acquire the information (see also the recent literature on obfuscation, e.g., Ellison and Wolitzky, 2012; Wilson, 2010). Another angle considered by Mayzlin and Shin (2011) is to consider the strategic choice of which information to convey if the firm can only transmit a subset of the relevant information. They show that not revealing horizontal match information may be a way for a high-quality product to signal that it is high quality.

[31] Anderson and Renault (2013) extend Anderson and Renault (2006) by also considering the disclosure of quality attributes. They find that quality attributes are always revealed in equilibrium if the visit cost is large enough and that low-quality firms show more match and/or price information. Their analysis of quality disclosure borrows arguments from the persuasion game literature below.

not acquire any information other than that revealed by the firm. I also assume that a type s firm can always credibly reveal that its type is s. For the sake of expositional clarity, I will take three firm types $S = \{s_1, s_2, s_3\}$ and assume a marginal cost independent of the firm's type (normalized to zero unless specified otherwise).

4.3.4.1 Unraveling of Quality Information

Milgrom (1981) considered a simple example he called "the persuasion game" to analyze the disclosure of certified quality information by a monopoly firm.[32] The equilibrium analysis yields a very crisp and strong result.

In the above framework, products that only differ in quality may be introduced as follows. Assume that for all $t \in T$, $r(s_1, t) > r(s_2, t) > r(s_3, t)$. Then, all consumer types agree that s_1 is higher quality than s_2, which in turn is higher quality than s_3. Further, assume there is a finite number of consumer types. Consider a candidate equilibrium where firm type s_1 does not fully reveal that it is selling the highest quality product. Let p be the price it charges. Let t be, among consumer types who are willing to buy at that price on the basis of the information provided, a type with the lowest willingness to pay for s_1. Because the type t consumer is not sure that the quality is the highest possible, her expected willingness to pay is strictly less than $r(s_1, t)$. Then, if it reveals its type is s_1, the firm could increase its price still selling to type t. From the definition of t, it would also be selling to all other consumer types who were willing to buy at price p with imperfect information. Hence it cannot be the case that quality s_1 is not fully revealed in equilibrium. Now given that it is fully revealed, the same argument shows that type s_2 necessarily fully reveals its quality in equilibrium. This in turn implies that in equilibrium, type s_3 cannot hide it is the lowest quality.

It is rather straightforward to show, using similar arguments, that for any set of possible product qualities, quality information is fully revealed to the consumer in equilibrium. If it was not, then a higher quality firm would always find it profitable to reveal it is higher quality. It is also easy to see that such a fully revealing equilibrium can be sustained by assuming that, if a firm does not fully disclose, then the consumer believes with probability 1 that it is of the lowest quality, consistent with the information it has provided.

As I discuss in Section 4.5.1, an obvious reason why the unraveling result might not hold is that disclosure of quality information is costly. Another reason (see Shin, 1994 for the argument in a related context) is that the consumer might not know whether the seller is actually able to provide the relevant certified quality information. To illustrate, suppose all three firm types are equally likely and there is only one consumer type t with $r(s_1, t) = 5$, $r(s_2, t) = 1$, and $r(s_3, t) = 0$. Assume now that the firm is able to certify its quality only with probability $\rho \in (0, 1)$. Now consider an equilibrium where, in the event that quality can be certified, only type s_1 reveals its quality. When observing no

---

[32] Other formulations of this problem can also be found in Grossman and Hart (1980) and Grossman (1981).

information the consumer believes that, with probability ρ, the product is either s_2 or s_3 with corresponding expected match $1/2$ and with probability $1 - \rho$, the firm is merely unable to reveal so the expected match is then 2. Hence when no information is revealed the firm can charge $2 - (3/2)\rho$. For ρ small enough, this is more than 1, which is the price type s_2 could charge by proving to the consumer it is not s_3, whenever possible. This partially revealing equilibrium can therefore be sustained.

The unraveling result suggests that, as long as the firm is able to certify its quality at a low enough cost, we should expect that quality information will be widely dispersed. This, however, assumes that this is the only relevant information. I next discuss the revelation of product attributes in a broader context.

4.3.4.2 Disclosure of Horizontal Match Attributes

My discussion of horizontal match information disclosure in Section 4.3.3 suggests that a firm would like to include only a limited amount of such information in ads. This is in sharp contrast with the unraveling result for quality information. I now reconsider this question in the context of the persuasion game of this subsection. A major difference with the previous analysis is that now the consumer may make some inference about the firm's type from the content of the ad. To see how this radically changes the analysis of information disclosure, consider the following result due to Koessler and Renault (2012). They show that as long as the firm's type and the consumer's type are independently distributed, there exists an equilibrium in which product information is fully revealed to the consumer. The main argument underpinning the result can be easily understood from my three-firm-type example above. Suppose type s_1 deviates from the fully revealing equilibrium by only disclosing that its type is either s_1 or s_2 and announcing some price p. Now given the price p, it is possible to compute the demand addressed to the firm (probability of a sale) depending on whether the consumer believes its type to be s_1 or s_2. Then we may specify off the equilibrium path beliefs that put all the weight on whichever type yields the lowest sale probability and it is clear that the deviation profit of type s_1 cannot be larger than its equilibrium full information one.

This, however, is not a generalization of unraveling to a general match disclosure setting. It merely says that full revelation is an equilibrium but it does not rule out others. This can be illustrated by considering one special case of interest, investigated by Sun (2011), where the product attributes and consumer tastes are derived from the Hotelling (1929) linear city model. To illustrate, assume the set of consumer types is the unit interval $T = [0, 1]$, and $s_1 = 0$, $s_2 = 1/2$ and $s_3 = 1$. Types are independent and uniformly distributed. The match is given in a standard manner by $r(s, t) = R - |r - t|$. In this simplified setting with only three product types, product type s_2 in the middle of the segment is always revealed in equilibrium.[33] However, for R large enough, there may be an equilibrium where the two extreme products s_1 and s_3 pool by not

---

[33] When assuming that the product type is uniformly distributed over the whole interval Sun (2011) finds that for R large enough, there exists a fully pooling equilibrium where no product information is revealed.

revealing their product information. To see this note that, if this is the case, the expected match is independent of the consumer type t and given by $R - (1/2)$ (the expected transport cost does not depend on location). The profit-maximizing solution is therefore to charge $R - (1/2)$ with corresponding profit $R - (1/2)$. Now for R large, the best a firm located at the extreme can achieve if consumers know its type is to sell to all consumer types by charging $R - 1$ (so even the consumer type at the other extreme buys). Hence it is not profitable to deviate by revealing product information. However, for $R < (1/2)$ the two extreme firm types could not survive by pooling in this manner, whereas they can still survive by revealing product information and catering to their niche customers.

Sun (2011) shows that, in equilibrium with a continuum of firm types, firms selling products that are sufficiently close to the center reveal product information and that the set of such products becomes larger as R decreases. This means that, interpreting a low R as low quality, if product quality is known to consumers, low-quality products tend to provide more horizontal match information than high-quality products. However, another insight from Sun (2011) is that if quality as well as horizontal attributes are unknown to consumers, then a quality difference might not be revealed in equilibrium if it is too small. To illustrate, suppose now that a product type is characterized by a value of R in addition to a location. Locations of the three types are as before but $R = 4$ for types s_1 and s_3 and $R = 3.5$ for type s_2: matches are thus $r(s_1, t) = 4 - t$, $r(s_3, t) = 3 + t$, and $r(s_2, t) = 3.5 - |t - 1/2|$. Then there is an equilibrium where no information is revealed. It is then optimal for the firm to serve the entire market at price $10/3$. This is larger than the full information profits, 3 for all types. Hence the equilibrium can be sustained by specifying off the equilibrium beliefs that put all the weight on s_1 if $R = 4$ is revealed but the horizontal attribute is not.

The above example also illustrates a useful result due to Koessler and Renault (2012). Whenever a disclosure strategy guarantees each firm type at least as much as its full revelation profit, then there exists an equilibrium in which the firm uses this disclosure strategy. One application of this result is the case where the firm is able to implement a threshold disclosure strategy which, from the analysis in Section 4.3.3, is profit maximizing for disclosing match information for both experience and search goods. Anderson and Renault (2006) present a simple specification of firm and consumer types as well as a match function r such that threshold disclosure is feasible. Then, as discussed by Koessler and Renault (2012) for an experience good, there is an equilibrium where the firm achieves the perfect discrimination profit, which is larger than the full disclosure one.

The above discussion highlights the multiplicity of equilibria that may arise, when product information involves some horizontal attributes valued differently by different consumer types.[34] This does not mean, however, that the only case in which full disclosure is the unique equilibrium is when product information only concerns quality. First,

---

[34] Standard forward induction refinements have no bite on this multiplicity. However, Celik (2014), using the undefeated equilibrium of Mailath et al. (1993), significantly refines the set of equilibria in the Hotelling setting studied by Sun (2011).

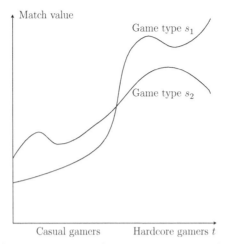

Figure 4.3 A match value for which product information is always disclosed.

in the examples above, the equilibria that do not involve full disclosure require a proper specification of the probability distribution of product types and consumer types. Second, as shown by Koessler and Renault (2012), there exists a class of match functions that are consistent with some horizontal matching, such that the unique outcome is full information disclosure independent of the probability distribution over types.

To illustrate, consider the following example adapted from Koessler and Renault (2012). A firm sells a video game whose type is either s_1 or s_2. Buyers may be ranked according to how many hardcore or casual players there are in the [0,1] interval, where a higher t means more hardcore. Matches are depicted in Figure 4.3. If the consumer is sufficiently hardcore, she is willing to pay more than a more casual gamer for both games but prefers s_1, which is more elaborate. However, the sophistication of game s_1 turns away a more casual gamer, who therefore prefers s_2. Because the match with both games is higher for a hardcore gamer, the expected match is also larger. Hence if no information is revealed, either the firm sells only to some of the hardcore gamers or it sells to all hardcore gamers and some casual ones. Then it is fairly easy to see that in the former case firm type s_1 would deviate from a pooling equilibrium and, in the latter case, firm type s_2 would deviate.[35] There must therefore be full disclosure in equilibrium.

In the above example, the match function satisfies what Koessler and Renault (2012) call pairwise monotonicity: it requires that, for any pair of product types and any pair of consumer types, either both consumer types prefer one product to the other or one consumer type has a higher match with both products than the other consumer type.

---

[35] For instance, if the firm sells to some casual gamers, then the type who has the lowest match with s_2 among those who buy is necessarily casual and therefore prefers s_2. Firm type s_2 if it outs itself can therefore increase its price without losing customers.

Pairwise monotonicity is sufficient in order for full disclosure to be the only equilibrium outcome. Furthermore, whenever it does not hold, there exists a probability distribution of firm and consumer types such that some other equilibrium can arise.

I next return to a discussion of how competition affects the disclosure incentives of advertisers.

4.3.4.3 Competition and Disclosure of Product Attributes

The work on product attribute disclosure discussed up to this point assumes a monopoly firm. One may wonder how competition might change the firm's incentives to disclose product information. In particular, is there a sense in which it induces more or less information disclosure? Note that oligopoly involves two important differences with monopoly. First, a firm may choose to reveal information pertaining not only to its own product but also to that of a competitor, as in Meurer and Stahl (1994) or Anderson and Renault (2009), discussed in Section 4.3.3. Second, the outcome may depend on whether prices are chosen simultaneously with product information disclosure or afterward.[36]

A first remark that applies quite generally is that it is straightforward to adapt the argument in Koessler and Renault (2012) for the existence of a fully revealing equilibrium to an oligopoly framework. For instance, Janssen and Teteryanikova (2014) consider a duopoly model where the firm's type and the consumer's type are represented by a location on Hotelling's linear segment. Types of the two firms and the consumer are i.i.d. and transport costs are quadratic. They show that, whether or not firms are allowed to reveal each other's location and whether product information is disclosed simultaneously with or prior to pricing decisions, there exists a fully revealing equilibrium. The general argument is that, after any deviation, it is always possible to specify worst-case consumer beliefs that put all the weight on the least profitable type consistent with the information disclosed by the firm. It is to be expected that this simple argument carries over to a fairly general class of oligopoly models.

Given the above remark, the relevant question is whether and when there exist equilibria where product information is only partially revealed or not revealed at all. For instance, Board (2009) considers a vertically differentiated duopoly with heterogeneous consumer tastes. He assumes that firms first decide whether to disclose quality and then choose prices and that a firm can only disclose its own quality. To illustrate, assume that firm 1's type/quality is 1 and firm 2's type/quality is either $\underline{s}$ or $\bar{s}$, with $0 < \underline{s} < \bar{s} < 1$. The consumer's type is $t \in [0, 1]$ and the match is $r(s, t) = st$. If the consumer holds passive beliefs at the pricing stage (meaning she bases her expectation of 2's quality on the information disclosed at the previous stage), then Board (2009) shows that firm 2's profit is concave in its expected quality and is 0 if that expected quality is either 0 or 1. Hence,

---

[36] The case where firms would commit to prices prior to disclosure seems less relevant and, to my knowledge, has not been considered.

if $\underline{s}$ is close enough to 0 while $\bar{s}$ is close enough to 1, there exists an equilibrium such that firm 2 does not reveal its quality.

The above result is in sharp contrast with the unraveling result for the persuasion game. It can be understood as follows. If firm 2's quality is too close to 0, then it cannot make much profit whereas if it is too close to 1, there is not enough product differentiation and competition is harsh so its profit is low as well. Firm 2 chooses not to disclose so its expected quality takes on some intermediate value which yields a higher profit. It chooses to hide its quality even if it is high in order to benefit from the strategic effect on firm 1's price, which is larger if firm 1 faces a competitor with low expected quality.[37] The results would be very different if firms had to commit to a price at the same time as they disclose quality information. There would then be unraveling as in the monopoly case: results in Koessler and Renault (2012) show that, because the match difference between the products of the two firms satisfies pairwise monotonicity, it is a best response for firm 2 to disclose its product information.

Consider now the following simple model of a horizontally differentiated duopoly, which is a stripped-down version of the model studied by Janssen and Teteryanikova (2014). Each firm is at either end of Hotelling's product segment with independent and equal probabilities: $s_i \in \{0, 1\}$ is firm i's type $i = 1, 2$. The consumer has type $t \in [0, 1]$ and the match is $r(s, t) = R - |s - t|$ (R is taken to be large enough that the market is covered). Firms know each other's product but the consumer does not. First consider the case where firms cannot resort to comparative advertising so they can only reveal their own type. Then it is easy to construct an equilibrium where no product information is revealed and both firms price at zero whether or not price is chosen at the disclosure stage or after product information has been disclosed. This equilibrium can be sustained by assuming that, if a firm unilaterally deviates by revealing its own product type, then the consumer believes with probability 1 that the other firm sells the same product. Since the other firm is charging zero, the deviating firm cannot earn positive profits.

The more substantial insights from the analysis in Janssen and Teteryanikova (2014) concern the case where firms can resort to comparative advertising. First consider the case where prices are chosen after firms have disclosed product information. Then it is again possible to sustain a fully pooling equilibrium, although it is very different from the one above. In this equilibrium, firms do not disclose any information in the first stage and both charge a price of 1 in the second stage. If a firm deviates to full disclosure of both product types in the first stage, then they play the full information-pricing game in the second stage (where the symmetric price is 0 if products are identical or 1 if products are different). If a firm deviates in the second stage by charging a price different from 1, then the consumer believes it is located at 0 while the other firm is located at 1.[38] Then, the

---

[37] A similar intuition underscores the analysis in the quality choice setting of Shaked and Sutton (1982).

[38] This is only a partial description of the sequential equilibrium that focuses on the most relevant deviations.

best a firm can achieve by deviating is to share the market at a price of 1, which is exactly what happens in equilibrium.

Things change drastically if pricing and disclosure decisions are simultaneous. The above equilibrium would not survive because, if both firms happen to sell the same product, each of them could profitably deviate by revealing product information and undercutting the other firm. This would yield a profit of 1 as opposed to the equilibrium profit 1/2. It can be shown that, in any equilibrium, consumers learn whether products are identical or different. In this simple example, however, this information may be conveyed through prices alone without any direct product information disclosed by firms (price is 0 if products are identical and 1 if they are different). Janssen and Teteryanikova (2014) show that, with a continuum of product types over the whole Hotelling segment, the probability that product information is not directly disclosed is zero. These results show that there is a role for comparative advertising even with *ex ante* symmetric firms, because it rules out equilibria where product information is not revealed (to be contrasted with the results in Anderson and Renault, 2009, in Section 4.3.3).

From this discussion, there are no clear theoretical grounds for arguing that competition induces more informative advertising than monopoly or the reverse. It is still the case that full revelation may emerge as an equilibrium under very general circumstances. Existing results suggest that non-disclosure of product attributes is less likely to happen when the choice of prices is concomitant to the decisions to disclose.

Up to now, I have discussed product advertising assuming that the posted information is perfectly certified, thanks to some laws against misleading advertising. Yet such laws cannot possibly apply to all relevant information because it is not always verifiable by a court. Besides, the legal implementation of such laws is likely to be imperfect.

4.3.5 Misleading Advertising

Once again, Nelson (1974) is an excellent starting point for a discussion of misleading advertising. Recall that he postulates that a firm cannot certify the advertised information. Nonetheless he argues that such information can be deemed credible by consumers. As I have already mentioned, one instance is when the information concerns search characteristics that the consumer can check on her own before purchase. But he also identifies cases where an experience characteristic may be credibly advertised. In particular, this is the case according to Nelson if "… consumers' belief in the truth of that statement does not increase the profit from initial sales …" (p. 731). I start my discussion of misleading ads by exploring to what extent these two conjectures are indeed confirmed by the recent theory on cheap-talk communication. Then I consider the implications of imperfectly implemented laws on misleading advertising and the possibility that firms indeed make false claims despite these laws.

4.3.5.1 Cheap Talk

I start by considering Nelson's claim that statements regarding search attributes are inherently more credible than those regarding experience attributes. Consider a monopoly firm selling a product for which the consumer has a price-sensitive demand $d(p, s, t) = \Theta_{s,t} - p$, where s is the product's quality, which is either high, $s = h$, or low, $s = \ell$, and t is the consumer's type, which is either high, $t = h$, or low, $t = \ell$. Further assume that $\Theta_{h,h} = 6$, $\Theta_{h,\ell} = \Theta_{\ell,h} = 2$, and $\Theta_{\ell,\ell} = 1$. All types are independent and have equal probability $1/2$. Production costs are zero. If the consumer has perfect information about quality while the firm only knows the probability distribution of t, then it is readily verified that the high-quality firm only serves the high-type consumer at a price of 3 and the low-quality firm charges a price of $3/4$ and serves both types. Corresponding profits are $9/2$ for firm type h and $9/16$ for firm type ℓ. If the product was an experience good and the consumer did not know the quality as in Section 4.3.4, the firm could convey no credible information to the consumer by advertising an unsubstantiated claim about its quality: a low-quality firm would always claim its quality is high.

Now assume that the consumer must incur a visit cost $\gamma > 0$ in order to purchase the product. If she does, she learns s as well as the price charged by the firm. Furthermore, in case of a visit, the firm incurs a processing cost $\rho > 0$, whether the product is sold or not (Nelson, 1974 mentions such processing costs as deterrents to mislead consumers for advertisers of search goods). The firm may post a cheap-talk message in an ad that the consumer can observe before she decides whether to visit or not. This cheap-talk message is a claim that s has some value $\hat{s} \in \{\ell, h\}$. Now, because the consumer observes quality before buying, a firm's profit gross of processing costs is its full information profit. Also note that no matter how small γ is, a type ℓ consumer never visits the firm if it expects it to have high quality because she then expects zero surplus. Now the high-quality firm gains nothing from inducing a visit from a type ℓ consumer but it incurs the processing cost ρ. By contrast, if ρ is not too large then a low-quality firm prefers to have both types of consumer visiting and if γ is not too large, a type ℓ consumer visits the firm if it expects it is low quality, since she expects a price of $(3/4) < 1$. Hence there is an equilibrium where the firm truthfully and credibly reveals its quality in its ad.[39]

I now turn to Nelson's insight concerning the credibility of cheap-talk messages pertaining to experience goods. He gives the example of a medicine that either cures athlete's foot or indigestion. Provided that the potential demand for the two types of medicine is similar, the firm benefits nothing from making a false claim about its product (if there are potential repeat purchases as Nelson assumes there are, then it is actually

---

[39] This simple model is adapted from that of Gardete (2013). He also finds that cheap-talk revelation of quality is possible for a search good but uses a different specification of preferences, such that it is profitable for a type ℓ firm to be matched with a type ℓ consumer and for a type h firm to be matched with a type h consumer. He has no processing costs.

strictly better off telling the truth). In terms of modeling, this can be captured by considering a product located on a circle sold to a consumer whose type is a location uniformly distributed around that circle and the match is decreasing in the distance between the locations. Then all product types have the same full information demand and the firm cannot benefit from misrepresenting its type. Chakraborty and Harbaugh (2014) use a related argument in a random utility discrete-choice model with random coefficients. In their setting, a firm may credibly claim that one of its attributes is very attractive to consumers (puffery about the best sandwich in the world) because by doing so, it induces some adverse anticipations about some other attribute (the sandwich is not very healthy).[40]

With an experience good, the firm's expected profit only depends on the buyer's beliefs about the firm's type. Hence a necessary condition for information to be credibly revealed through cheap talk is that expected profit is constant across all equilibrium beliefs of the buyer (abstracting from the potential benefits from repeat purchases that Nelson, 1974 factors in). Chakraborty and Harbaugh (2010) provide a general argument for the existence of an equilibrium where cheap talk affects the consumer's beliefs, when the relevant information is multidimensional. For instance, if the match is given by $r(t, s) = t_1 - t_2 s$, where the firm's type is $t = (t_1, t_2) \in [(1/2), 1] \times [0, 1]$ and the consumer's type is $s \in [0, 1]$, then announcing $(t_1, t_2) = (1, 0)$ yields the largest profit. Still, there is a cheap-talk equilibrium where some partial information is credibly revealed.

4.3.5.2 Imperfect Enforcement of Laws on Misleading Advertisements

In his discussion of deceptive advertising, Nelson (1974) writes: "There is another important source of misleading advertising: the law" (p. 749). This provocative statement reflects the idea that laws against misleading ads improve the consumer's confidence in the content of an ad, which in turn increases the incentives of advertisers to make false claims (provided the law is not enforced with enough vigor). If enforcement is perfect, then the analyses of Sections 4.3.3 and 4.3.4 apply. I now discuss some recent research on legal restraints on advertising that do not necessarily dissuade deception. I focus more specifically on situations where some ads involve some actual false claims and yet are partially informative, so the outcome could not be reached without advertising.[41]

---

[40] Anderson and Renault (2006) and Koessler and Renault (2012) provide other examples with a random match that allow for credible disclosure, although they abstract from credibility issues by assuming perfect certification.

[41] For instance, Barigozzi et al. (2009) consider an imperfectly enforced ban on false comparative advertising claim. However, their focus is on how such a law allows an entrant to signal it is high quality so in equilibrium there are no false claims. Similarly, Corts (2013) distinguishes laws on false claims and laws on unsubstantiated claims (that are not supported by some evidence, which is costly to generate for the firm), but also focuses on separating equilibria.

Following Rhodes and Wilson (2014), consider a monopolist selling a product whose quality is either high or low. The firm knows its quality and may claim that it is high to the consumer who is initially uninformed. Making such a claim when quality is low, however, involves some penalty. Assume the consumers demand is price sensitive so she retains some strictly positive surplus at the monopoly price. For intermediate values of the penalty, there is an equilibrium in which the low-quality firm makes a false claim with some probability strictly between 0 and 1. The consumer therefore updates her beliefs when observing a quality claim and is charged a price derived from the corresponding expected quality. However, at this price, the consumer pays too much for the good whenever the actual quality is low. Still, Rhodes and Wilson (2014) provide a range of demand and parameter conditions where the consumer may actually benefit from the existence of such false advertising and hence prefer a more lenient law enforcement. This is because in those cases, such as when the product qualities are sufficiently high, the deterioration in the expected quality associated with a high-quality claim is more than compensated by a lower price.[42]

Drugov and Martinez (2012) consider the choice of a communication strategy by a firm that is assumed to be able to manipulate the signal that the consumer receives about her match. Contrary to the match disclosure settings of Section 4.3.3, the firm may choose to bias that information to make it more favorable. However, increasing that bias makes it more likely that the firm will be prosecuted and fined. The firm also chooses the accuracy of a signal: a more vague signal makes the biased information less reliable for the buyer but decreases the probability of prosecution. It is found that in the optimal communication strategy, more bias is associated with more noise. In particular, there will be more bias and more noise if the standard of proof required to prosecute is higher.

Note that although these models explain why advertising might be misleading (in the sense that the firm uses false information in its ad), they do not involve any consumers that are systematically misled. In Rhodes and Wilson (2014), consumers understand that a high-quality claim might be sent by a low-quality firm and reduce their willingness to pay as a consequence, while in Drugov and Martinez (2012) they correctly anticipate the bias in equilibrium. Although they are sometimes induced to make choices they would not have made had they been perfectly informed, this is not any different from what happens in other models I have discussed where the equilibrium is not fully revealing. As Nelson (1974) points out, "Deception requires a misleading [...]statement, but also somebody ready to be misled by that statement" (p. 749). Assuming fully rational consumers seems to keep the second requirement out of reach. I discuss the possibility that consumers are somewhat less sophisticated in Section 4.6.2.

---

[42] Piccolo et al. (2015) find similar results in a somewhat related duopoly setting.

4.3.6 Concluding Remarks

In addition to facilitating consumer awareness of available sellers and available prices for a commodity, advertising can help consumers figure out the nature and characteristics of the various products available for sale. Although information about search goods is available prior to purchase, it comes at a cost. Advertising then can provide some information that lures consumers into incurring that cost. For experience goods, consumers cannot decipher product information before buying without the help of the seller, who may choose to use advertising to provide such help.

A common perception, supported by some evidence, is that advertisements contain little information. This, however, does not mean that advertising is not about information. Even if a firm may convey credible information at no costs to consumers, it may find it more profitable not to do so or rather to use advertising to transmit a limited amount of information. In particular, a firm whose product is *a priori* perceived as having high quality finds it profitable to keep quiet about its horizontal attributes. This is the case whether the product is a search good or an experience good. Still, there are configurations of tastes and product attributes for which a firm reveals full information. This is the case in particular when the only relevant information is quality.

More product information in advertising typically enhance the firm's market power and is associated with larger prices. Match information is used by the firm to target consumers with high valuations for its product. In a competitive setting, more horizontal match product information improves consumer awareness of product differentiation, which softens price competition. This prediction that firms use advertising to enhance their market power is consistent with the persuasive view, although here advertising is purely informative.

Although laws against misleading advertising lend credibility to the information provided, they are not applicable to all pieces of information because they might not be perfectly verifiable by a court and law enforcement might remain sufficiently lenient that false claims are not deterred. Recent work on cheap talk shows that, even if no misleading ad law is in place, advertisers can sometime convey credible direct information. As surmised by Nelson (1974), this credibility is easier to achieve for search goods. Analyzing how rigorous law enforcement should be is an important policy question that economists have only recently started to address.

I have for the most part left aside welfare considerations in my discussion of product advertising. Theoretical results are not at all conclusive as to whether firms provide too much or too little information and whether forced disclosure rules might be desirable. Still, withholding information often improves their ability to capture consumer surplus.[43] Forced disclosure laws may therefore be useful tools for consumer protection.

---

[43] This is all the more the case if, rather than a posted price, the firm uses an optimal mechanism that elicits the buyer's private information, as shown by Koessler and Skreta (2014) and Balestrieri and Izmalkov (2012).

Finally, theoretical settings involving search goods allow for analyzing the choice of disclosing price information in ads. A firm may choose to disclose only horizontal match information with no price, when it can fine-tune the amount of product information it is transmitting to the consumer. In a cheap-talk context, the provision of soft quality information may be enough to reassure the consumer that the price is not too high. Prices could also have a signaling role, along the lines of the material in the next section, and firms might choose to hide them because showing them might be an adverse signal about product information.

4.4. ADVERTISING AS A SIGNAL

From the analysis of product advertising, it appears that firms that sell high-quality products want to make this information visible to consumers to avoid the standard inefficiencies associated with adverse selection. Although they may be helped in this respect by the legal restraints on misleading advertising, it is often not feasible to make verifiable quality claims to which the law would lend the hoped-for credibility. A substantial body of economic research in the wake of Nelson (1974) has explored the indirect role that ad expenditures can play in making this information credible. I now review this literature, starting with Nelson's main arguments and moving on to the game theoretic analysis of the signaling role of advertising. I end with the related topic of advertising as a coordination device.

4.4.1 Nelson Again

As I emphasized in the previous section, Nelson (1974) argues that ads cannot provide much direct information about experience goods. His main point is that, even if ads have a very limited information content, they can still transmit information to consumers indirectly. The general argument is that consumers expect a firm that advertises more to be a "better buy" (Nelson, 1974, p. 732). He offers three arguments for why this should be the case.

The main argument is that a firm that is more efficient in "… producing the utility that consumers seek" benefits more from advertising and reaching more consumers (p. 732). What Nelson calls a greater efficiency is the ability of a firm to provide a certain level of quality at a lower cost. It is unclear how this should be formally captured. One simple way of making this formal would be to consider the difference $s - c$, where s is quality and c is marginal cost. A firm for which $s - c$ is larger earns a higher per-consumer surplus and hence has a greater incentive to advertise to get more customers. Nelson's argument also requires that a higher $s - c$ yields a higher consumer surplus. Then consumers should rationally be attracted by firms that advertise more.

Nelson provides two additional arguments to support the view that advertisements are indirectly informative. The first is that advertising might signal high-quality products because they are more likely to be purchased repeatedly. Nelson bases his reasoning on the idea that consumers tend to forget the name of the brands they have previously purchased and liked, and one role of advertising is to remind them of the brand's name. A firm that sells a bad product would not find it profitable to remind consumers of its brand name because consumers would not purchase again a product they have not enjoyed in the first place. Hence, consumers who have not tried the product yet should infer that a product that is advertised a lot has good quality. There is some form of externality exerted by informed consumers who have experienced the product's quality before on uninformed ones.[44]

The other possibility suggested by Nelson is that advertising indirectly informs consumers about how well an experience good is matched to their tastes and needs. The idea here is that a consumer expects that the products that are advertised in the media she watches, reads, or listens to are products that she is potentially interested in and will want to buy again if she tries them. This is a standard targeting argument. Yet, if a firm has the incentive to post its ad in the right media, then it should also select to make a proper cheap-talk claim in its ad about which customers should like the product. The same outcome could then be achieved with cheap talk along the lines of the analysis in Section 4.3.5.1. Indeed, as I have already pointed out, Nelson mentions that repeat purchases may constitute a basis for credible cheap talk in ads for experience goods.

Nelson's central message is that advertising may inform even if it contains no direct information. An alternative view could be that such advertising is purely persuasive or constitutes some form of complementary good as discussed in the introduction. Ackerberg (2003) uses a structural model of consumer behavior to test the two alternative views. He studies advertising for Yoplait yoghurts in the US. In his model, advertising may either affect the consumer by informing her that the product is high quality (if more ads enhance demand through this channel, it is interpreted as quality signaling). But advertising can also affect utility through a prestige effect, where more advertising means more prestige. It is possible to identify the two effects because consumers with no experience of the product are affected by both effects whereas consumers who have already consumed the product are only affected by the prestige effect. Using longitudinal user exposure data, he finds that only the information effect is significant.

Nelson stresses the self-enforcing nature of the mechanisms he describes but does not use any formal equilibrium concept. In particular, he does not explore all the strategic dimensions involved with attempts by firms to manipulate the consumers' beliefs or how these beliefs might react to unexpected changes in a firm's behavior. Although the reformulations described below are not entirely consistent with Nelson's original

---

[44] Linnemer (2002) proposes a model of advertising as a signal where some consumers are informed. See also Lauga (2012), that I discuss in Section 4.6.2, on the role of advertising as a reminder.

constructions, his work has had a considerable influence on the theoretical analysis of advertising.

4.4.2 Quality Signaling and Money Burning

I here discuss the main insights from this substantial literature, drawing on Bagwell (2007, subsections 6.1 and 6.2) and Tirole (1988, chapter 2, subsection 2.6.1.2). Typically, the frameworks used in the literature consider the signaling of quality both through advertising and price. To build intuition, and following Bagwell, I start with a static setting.

4.4.2.1 Static Quality Signaling

The following framework is inspired by Overgaard (1991). It is somewhat related to Nelson's conjecture that consumers should expect firms that are "efficient" to advertise more. A monopoly firm sells a product whose quality is either high ($s = h$) or low ($s = \ell$). After learning its exogenous quality, the firm chooses a price $p \geq 0$ and advertising expenditure $A \geq 0$. Then consumers observe (p, A) but not s and form beliefs about the probability that quality is high, $\beta = b(p, A)$. Then they purchase quantity $q = D(\beta, p, A)$, where D is differentiable on $[0, 1] \times IR_+^2$, strictly increasing in β and A, and strictly decreasing in p. Marginal production cost is constant and given by c_s for quality s. Throughout I assume that, for a given perceived quality β, a larger marginal cost implies a higher profit-maximizing price and a lower profit-maximizing level of ad expenditures. I also assume that both are increasing in β. The intuition for why a firm with a higher marginal cost might advertise less is that it finds it less profitable to expand its demand (which is also why it charges a higher price). This is what Tirole (1988) calls the Schmalensee effect after Schmalensee (1978). Finally, D is assumed to be such that the profit function $(p - c_s)D(\beta, p, A) - A$ is single peaked in p and A and reaches some strictly positive value.

Note that here advertising has a direct impact on demand, which is consistent with Nelson's argument. It could, for instance, be an increase in the number of consumers that become aware that the firm exists as in the monopoly model discussed by Bagwell (2007, p. 1752), although it is important here that all consumers who are reached by an ad can observe A perfectly (which is not the case if consumers are reached randomly by ads sent by the firm[45]). Also note that actual product quality only enters the firm's profit through its production costs. Hence, if $c_h = c_\ell$, there cannot be a separating equilibrium because whatever profit the high-quality firm can obtain by convincing consumers that it is high quality can also be achieved by the low-quality firm with the same consumer beliefs.

---

[45] There could possibly still be a signaling role for advertising, to the extent that consumers receiving multiple duplicates of the ad would infer that A is large. See Hertzendorf (1993) and Moraga-Gonzalez (2000) for settings where advertising intensity is observed with noise.

Now consider what would happen if the firm could use only one signal. First assume that it must spend some fixed amount A on advertising. Let $p_s(\beta)$ denote the profit-maximizing price for a quality s firm with consumer beliefs β. If $c_h > c_\ell$, then $p_h(\beta) > p_\ell(\beta)$ for any β. Now consider a separating equilibrium[46] where firm type s charges price p_s^*, with $p_h^* \neq p_\ell^*$. After observing p_s^*, consumers believe quality is s so $\beta = 1$ if price is p_h^* and $\beta = 0$ if price is p_ℓ^*. As is standard in the literature, I concentrate on the least cost separating equilibrium (which is selected by standard equilibrium refinements). It is the separating equilibrium at which the profit of the high-quality firm is the largest.

In a separating equilibrium, the low-quality firm charges $p_\ell(0)$ and earns its full information monopoly profit, denoted here π_ℓ.[47] If π_ℓ is strictly below the profit that a type firm earns by charging $p_h(1)$ while consumers believe it is high quality, then there is an equilibrium at which the high-quality firm earns its full information monopoly profit as well while charging $p_h^* = p_h(1)$ and this is obviously the least cost separating equilibrium. If, on the contrary, by charging $p_h(1)$ while consumers believe it is high quality, a low-quality firm can earn more than π_ℓ, then there cannot be a separating equilibrium at which firm type h charges $p_h(1)$ (the low type would then choose to mimic the high type). Because profit is single peaked in price, and $p_\ell(1) < p_h(1)$, a low-quality firm's profit is decreasing at $p_h(1)$ if consumers believe its product is high quality. Hence in order to obtain a separating equilibrium, it suffices to increase p_h^* sufficiently above $p_h(1)$ so that a type ℓ firm would earn no more than π_ℓ by deviating to p_h^* while consumers believe it is high quality.[48]

The analysis of the case $c_h < c_\ell$ is the symmetric of the analysis above. Now, $p_h(1) < p_\ell(1)$ and type ℓ's profit for $\beta = 1$ is strictly increasing at $p_h(1)$. Then, to obtain the least cost separating equilibrium, it suffices to decrease p_h^* just enough below $p_h(1)$ so that a low-quality firm earns no more than π_ℓ by deviating to p_h^* to convince consumers it is high quality.

The logic applied to price signaling can readily be adapted to the case of signaling through advertising assuming that the firm is forced to charge a price p independent of its quality. Let $A_s(\beta)$ be the profit-maximizing level of ad expenditures for firm type s if consumers hold beliefs β. Let A_s^* be the type s level of ad expenditures in the least cost separating equilibrium. Once again, the choice of the low type is not distorted from its

---

[46] I consider sequential equilibria. As in other discussions in this chapter, I do not fully describe the equilibrium: in particular I usually omit specifying beliefs off the equilibrium path that sustain the equilibrium behavior.

[47] This is because the high-quality firm has no incentive to pretend it is low quality, so an equilibrium does not require that the low-quality price be distorted.

[48] Such a price p_h^* indeed exists, thanks to the single-crossing condition that the price derivative of profit with a high marginal cost is larger than the price derivative of profit with a low marginal cost. Similar single-crossing conditions are implicitly used repeatedly in the arguments below.

full information level, $A_\ell^* = A_\ell(0)$, and I again call the corresponding profit π_ℓ. If $c_h > c_\ell$, then $A_h(1) < A_\ell(1)$ (from the Schmalensee effect) and the low type's profit if consumers believe it is high quality is strictly increasing at $A_h(1)$. Then the least cost separating equilibrium is obtained by distorting A_h^* downward from its full information profit-maximizing level $A_h(1)$ just enough that a low-quality firm could not earn more than π_ℓ by deviating to A_h^* and having consumers believe it is high quality. An analogous logic is at work when $c_h < c_\ell$ so that in the least cost separating equilibrium, ad expenditures by a high-quality firm are distorted upward from the full information profit-maximizing level.

Bagwell (2007) characterizes the least cost separating equilibrium in his setting adapted from Overgaard (1991). He shows that both signals are used jointly. If $c_h > c_\ell$, then price (respectively advertising) is distorted upward (respectively downward) from its full information profit-maximizing level. The reverse distortions arise if $c_h < c_\ell$. Only the last case is consistent with the prediction of Nelson (1974) that "good buys" advertise more. When the high quality is more costly to produce, it is unclear which product is a good buy in the sense of Nelson and his prediction holds only if the low quality is a good buy. Besides, as I already mentioned, if costs are identical for both qualities, then there is no separating equilibrium although the high-quality firm is efficient according to Nelson's interpretation.

Another important difference with Nelson is that, here, product information is transmitted through pricing as well as advertising. Recall that Nelson assumes there are no laws on misleading advertising so the price cannot be used as a joint signal with advertising (posting a price in the ad would be pure cheap talk). In Nelson's argument, consumers go to firms that advertise a lot because they expect a low price for the quality they will get. I return to this idea in Section 4.4.3.

Finally, as shown by Bagwell (2007), advertising would not be used as a signal if it was purely dissipative so that it would have no direct impact on demand. The separation of types in the equilibria described above is achieved because it is more costly for the low-quality firm than for the high-quality firm to distort its advertising level. Consider, for instance, the case where $c_h < c_\ell$. If advertising was purely dissipative, then if the high-quality firm is willing to spend an amount A on advertising so that consumers believe it is high quality, then so is the low-quality firm.[49] As I now show, things are quite different if the product can be purchased repeatedly.[50]

---

[49] In the reverse case, since both full information profit-maximizing levels are zero, it is not possible to distort them downward.

[50] Linnemer (2012) shows that dissipative advertising may be a signal of quality in a static setting where quality and cost are not perfectly correlated so private information is two-dimensional. He uses a continuum of types with full support and his results are somewhat reminiscent of Nelson's prediction that more efficient firms advertise more.

4.4.2.2 Repeat Purchase and Money Burning

Tirole (1988, p. 119) gives a simple illustration of how price or advertising can signal the quality of an experience good that is purchased repeatedly. Assume that the monopolist considered above faces one consumer with unit demand. The buyer's willingness to pay is s independent of how much is spent on advertising. If the consumer buys the product once, she may choose to purchase it again in a second period after observing s from her first period experience and observing the second period price charged by the firm. Since the consumer knows s in the second period, the best the firm can do is to charge a price of s to extract all the surplus. The firm and the consumer share the same discount factor $\delta \in (0, 1)$.

I now study the first period interaction, assuming that $s_h > c_h \geq c_\ell > s_\ell = 0$ (the important point is that $c_\ell > s_\ell$ and $s_h > c_h$, so only the high-quality product has a market under perfect consumer information). I again look for a separating equilibrium. Note that here, because only a high-quality product will be purchased again in the second period if it is purchased in the first period, the firm's quality has a direct impact on its profit even if costs are equal. If the product is purchased in the first period, the discounted second-period revenue is δs_h for a high-quality firm and 0 for a low-quality firm. In a separating equilibrium where it is identified as low quality by the consumer, the ℓ type firm makes zero profit and we can set its equilibrium price and advertising in the first period at $p_\ell^* = A_\ell^* = 0$.

I first characterize a separating equilibrium where the high-quality firm only uses advertising expenditure to signal. That is, it charges in the first period its full information price, $p_h^* = s_h$. Letting A_h^* be its equilibrium advertising expenditure, its equilibrium discounted profit is $(1 + \delta)(s_h - c_h) - A_h^*$. If the low-quality firm mimics the high-quality firm, its profit is $(s_h - c_\ell) - A_h^*$ because it is able to sell at price s_h in the first period to the consumer who believes quality is high but cannot earn any profit in the second period. In order to have an equilibrium, the high-quality firm must be at least breaking even while the low-quality firm must not find it profitable to pretend it is high quality. So we must have

$$(1 + \delta)(s_h - c_h) - A_h^* \geq 0 \geq (s_h - c_\ell) - A_h^*, \tag{4.16}$$

which requires that $\delta(s_h - c_h) > c_h - c_\ell$. The left-hand side is the discounted benefit of the seller of a high-quality product from selling again in the second period, whereas a low quality seller could not sell again (the *Nelson effect* in Tirole, 1988, p. 120). The right-hand side is the cost saving from selling a low-quality product rather than a high-quality product (the *Schmalensee effect*). As long as the former dominates the latter, there are some values of A_h^* satisfying (4.1) so that dissipative advertising can be used to signal quality. In the least cost equilibrium, the amount spent on advertising is $A_h^* = s_h - c_\ell$ (so the ℓ type is just indifferent between deviating or not).

What changes if price also signals quality? Then the h type firm picks a price $p_h^* < s_h$. This can be interpreted as an introductory offer, since the firm moves its price up to s_h in the second period. Then condition (4.16) becomes

$$\left(p_h^* - c_h\right) + \delta(s_h - c_h) - A_h^* \geq 0 \geq \left(p_h^* - c_\ell\right) - A_h^*, \qquad (4.17)$$

which still requires that $\delta(s_h - c_h) > c_h - c_\ell$. Now in the least cost separating equilibrium, the high-quality firm's price and advertising satisfy $p_h^* = A_h^* + c_\ell$. The corresponding loss in profit for the h type firm from what it would get under full information is $c_\ell - c_h$. This means that, from the point of view of the firm, price signaling and signaling through ad expenditures are perfect substitutes. In any case, the firm burns an amount of money $c_h - c_\ell$ off its full information profit to convince the consumer it has high quality. Although introductory offers and dissipative advertising are perfect substitutes for the firm, they have very different welfare implications. The former is merely a transfer from the firm to the consumer. The latter is a purely wasteful activity. Introductory offers are clearly observed in practice and hence it is unclear from this simple example why firms should resort to dissipative advertising.

The above example, however, shoots down some important dimensions of the firm's problem by assuming perfectly inelastic demand. Milgrom and Roberts (1986) analyze the same quality signaling problem while assuming consumers have a heterogeneous willingness to pay. Furthermore, in their setting, a low-quality firm may earn some profit in both periods in a separating equilibrium. Still it is assumed that more sales in the first period generate more profit in the second period for the high-quality firm even though it may have a higher marginal cost. This is due to the *Nelson effect*: the favorable first period experience increases the second period demand (there are more repeat purchasers). Bagwell (2007) offers a characterization of the least cost separating equilibrium in a reduced form version of the Milgrom and Roberts setting. I now discuss the results and provide intuition.

It is useful to recall some properties of the pure price signaling analysis in the static setting. When $c_h > c_\ell$, the high-quality firm distorts its price upward because this price increase is more harmful to the low-quality firm than to itself. For $c_h < c_\ell$, it distorts its price downward because the resulting loss in profit is less for a type h firm than for a type ℓ firm. In the two-period model, we also need to account for the impact of the first period price on the second period profit. Under the assumption that more sales in the first period increase the second period profit more for a high-quality firm, increasing the first period price is more costly for the high-quality firm. If $c_h < c_\ell$, the Nelson effect reinforces the h type's advantage over the ℓ type in reducing its price. By contrast, if $c_h > c_\ell$, the Nelson effect goes against the h type's advantage over the l type in increasing its price. Then price signaling involves an upward distortion only if $c_h - c_\ell$ is sufficiently large.

Now if the high-quality firm uses dissipative advertising alone to signal quality, in order to inflict a \$1 loss in profit to a deviating ℓ type, it must incur a \$1 loss in its own profit. If instead it uses a price distortion and $c_h < c_l$, then a drop in price that decreases the profit of the deviating ℓ type by \$1 decreases the h type's profit by a smaller amount. For this reason, dissipative advertising is never used in the least cost separating equilibrium when high quality is less costly to produce. In the reverse case, however, because of the Nelson effect it could happen that the price increase needed to decrease the deviating ℓ type profit by \$1 decreases the h type's profit by a larger amount. Milgrom and Roberts (1986) characterize situations where dissipative advertising is used in that case along with an upward price distortion.

Although this literature suggests some possible role for dissipative advertising, it does not necessarily support the view that it should be widely used, given the restriction on parameters needed for dissipative advertising to be an effective signal, when a distortion in price can also be used.[51] This suggests the theory of advertising as an indirect transmitter of information is better supported if it also has a direct demand expansion effect as in the static framework above and in accordance with the conjectures of Nelson (1974), who did not consider dissipative advertising. This is also what is suggested by the empirical study of Horstmann and MacDonald (2003) on the compact disk (CD) player market between 1983 and 1992. They find that new CD players are heavily advertised and sold at low prices, which is not consistent with the Milgrom and Roberts' (1986) results but could match the prediction of the static analysis where advertising has a direct effect.[52]

I now consider an alternative signaling role for advertising.

4.4.3 Advertising and Coordination

Another indirect role of advertising is that it may facilitate coordination. I discuss two applications.

A first application can be found in Bagwell and Ramey (1994a, b). Here I present a simple setup loosely inspired by Bagwell and Ramey (1994b).[53] A monopoly firm has three potential customers with an identical price-sensitive demand. There are increasing returns to scale in production so marginal cost is decreasing in quantity. Thus, for a well-behaved demand, monopoly price is lower if the firm can sell to more consumers. Let $p_m(n)$ be the monopoly price if the number of consumers served is $n = 1, 2, 3$. Let $S_n > 0$ be the surplus of a consumer at price $p_m(n)$ and we have $S_1 < S_2 < S_3$. The firm earns a larger monopoly profit if it sells to more customers and hence faces a higher demand at any price. Letting π_n denote monopoly profit when the number of customers is n, we have $\pi_1 < \pi_2 < \pi_3$.

---

[51] See Kihlstrom and Riordan (1984) for a purely competitive setting where prices cannot signal.

[52] Arguably, there is not much scope for a Nelson effect for CD players.

[53] The example bears several differences with Bagwell and Ramey (1994b). Their main model is a duopoly. More importantly, advertising is purely dissipative. However, in order for advertising to be used in the refined equilibria, they assume that the firm has private information about whether it is efficient or not. Bagwell and Ramey (1994a) present a monopolistic competition model of retailing. The equilibrium with advertising is in mixed strategy where firms that advertise a lot invest in large-scale operations and attract a lot of customers. See Bagwell (2007, section 5.3) for details.

Now consider the following game. Initially, only consumer 1 is aware of the firm's existence (she is the local consumer base). In a first stage, the firm decides on its capacity to serve between 1 and 3 customers while charging the corresponding monopoly price. It may also advertise its existence to consumers 2 and 3. Either it reaches them with personal flyers, in which case it costs $f > 0$ to inform each consumer, or it may post a television ad that is seen by both consumers and that costs T where $f < T < 2f$ (the increasing returns to using a TV ad are motivated by the idea that the potential population is large). Further assume that $f < \pi_2 - \pi_1, f < \pi_3 - \pi_2$, and $T - f < \pi_3 - \pi_2$, so the firm would choose television advertising if it was certain both consumers show up. In a second stage, consumer 1, and other consumers if they have been reached by an ad, decide whether or not to visit the firm and buy, where a visit costs zero for consumer 1 and γ for consumers 2 and 3. Assume $S_2 < \gamma < S_3$, so consumers 2 and 3 visit only if they expect the firm to be catering to three customers. Note that the firm cannot commit to a price in its ad, which is consistent with Nelson's assumption that there is no legal restriction on misleading ads. It is also consistent with the stylized fact that many ads contain no price.

This is a coordination game with three pure strategy equilibria that are Pareto ranked. In the Pareto-dominated equilibrium, the firm does not advertise and sells only to consumer 1 at price $p_m(1)$. It is Pareto dominated by an equilibrium where the firm sends flyers to 2 and 3 and sells to all consumers at price $p_m(3)$. This equilibrium in turn is less efficient than the equilibria where the firm posts an ad on TV and also sells to all at price $p_m(3)$. In the first equilibrium, non-local consumers, 2 and 3, rationally would not react to advertising off the equilibrium path. It is then a best response for the firm not to advertise and to serve consumer 1 alone. By contrast, in the other equilibria, the firm expects consumers to respond to the type of advertising it uses and if it uses flyers it is because non-local customers would not visit when exposed to a TV ad.

Following Bagwell and Ramey (1994b), the two least efficient equilibria can easily be refined away by using equilibrium weak dominance. If consumers see an ad on TV, they should infer that the firm is set up to sell to three customers and will charge them $p_m(3)$. Otherwise, it would not bother expending the resources. If $T > 2f$, the refinement only eliminates the no-advertising equilibrium. The equilibrium with flyers survives because it is the less costly way of reaching non-local consumers and the TV ad survives, because if the firm deviates to sending flyers, each consumer could believe that only one flyer has been sent and that the price will be $p_m(2)$. One interesting property of a TV ad is that, when one consumer gets to observe it, she may also realize that other consumers are observing it and that those other consumers themselves realize that other consumers are exposed to this same ad. In other words, as argued by Chwe (2001), advertising may be a way to achieve what game theorists call *common knowledge* of an event, where this event may merely be that a group of consumers has observed the same ad.

The second application involves a consumption externality and is inspired by Pastine and Pastine (2002) and Clark and Horstmann (2005). Two firms with zero production costs sell to a continuum of identical consumers with mass 1. The utility attached to buying the product from one firm depends on the extent of the consumption externality imparted by other consumers buying the same product. The willingness to pay for firm i's product is x_i, where x_i is the mass of consumers who buy from firm i. This externality might arise because of fashion or some network externality (among users of the same OS on a cell phone, for instance). In a first stage, a firm may decide whether or not to spend some amount $A > 0$ on dissipative advertising. In a second stage, firms compete in prices. If the outcome of the first stage is symmetric, then consumers choose the cheapest product or split equally if prices are identical. The outcome is then the standard Bertrand equilibrium with zero profit for each firm. If one and only one firm advertised in the first stage, then consumers choose that firm when indifferent in the second stage. Hence if firm a advertised, then consumers buy product b if and only if $p_b \le x_b$ and $x_b - p_b > x_a - p_a$. Then, there cannot be an equilibrium such that all consumers buy product b[54] and, if prices must be positive, the only equilibrium is such that firm a charges 1 and firm b charges 0 and all consumers buy from firm a (the situation is analogous to a Bertrand game with firms having different qualities). The first period game may then be represented by the following matrix, that shows profits of firms a and b depending on both firms' choices to advertise or not.

		Firm b	
		Yes	No
Firm a	Yes	$(-A, -A)$	$(1-A, 0)$
	No	$(0, 1-A)$	$(0, 0)$

For $0 < A < 1$, there are two pure strategy equilibria where only one firm advertises and serves the entire market in the second stage. The corresponding social surplus, $1 - A$, is entirely captured by the advertising firm. This should be compared to the social surplus of $1/2$ that accrues to consumers if neither firm advertises. By coordinating consumers on the same product, advertising raises social surplus by $1/2$. This, however, comes at a cost of A so that, for $1/2 < A < 1$, advertising is a wasteful activity.

4.4.4 Concluding Remarks

Advertising that does not contain any direct information may nonetheless inform consumers. As Nelson (1974) explains, this is the case for experience goods whose quality cannot be evaluated by consumers prior to purchase. Much theoretical effort has been devoted to understanding whether and when firms have an incentive to use advertising in this way. Nelson argues that firms should be expected to spend more on such indirectly

---

[54] Such an equilibrium could exist with a finite price grid, where firm b would charge the highest price below 1 and firm a would charge 0.

informative advertising than on directly informative advertising. This is because it is the amount spent on the former that conveys the information whereas ads that contain direct information merely need to reach consumers once. He finds some empirical support for this view by providing some empirical evidence that ad expenditures for experience goods are much larger than for search goods. The substantial theoretical investigations on this issue do not fully confirm Nelson's predictions. If prices may be used to signal a product's high quality (in particular through introductory offers), they often achieve this objective more effectively than massive advertising expenditures. If high quality is more costly to produce than low quality, it may even be the case that the seller of a high-quality product chooses to spend little on advertising to credibly signal its high quality (thus signaling that it aims at selling little at a high price).

A higher potential for repeat purchases of the product (for instance, if the product is non-durable like food items) makes massive advertising of an experience good more attractive to a high-quality seller. It is only in this case that a firm producing a high-quality item that is more costly to produce than a low-quality one sometimes chooses high ad expenditures to convince consumers its quality is high. It may then even use advertising that is purely dissipative and has no direct impact on its demand.

In practice, ads often do not include price information so that large ad expenditures can then induce consumers to incur the shopping cost that will uncover the price as in the search good settings considered in Sections 4.3.3 and 4.3.5. I am not aware of any research that investigates quality signaling in such a framework. I have illustrated however how, in this case, ad expenditures may signal a low price for a product of known quality. When there are potential increasing returns in retailing, ads may help consumers coordinate on buying from large retailers that offer low prices. This coordinating role of advertising may also arise for products characterized by consumption externalities, either because of network effects or fashion.

As a final remark, it should be stressed that in order to get definite predictions about the indirect informativeness of advertising, it is typically necessary to refine the set of equilibria. Indeed, the outcome hinges very much on how consumers interpret the firm's advertising behavior. This may even impact which media the firm chooses to use, as is the case in the simple flyers versus TV example in Section 4.4.3. This may also apply to the non-informative content of the ad. Signaling quality is not merely a matter of conveying the information that a large amount has been spent on an ad campaign. The way in which it is transmitted may matter as well. Furthermore, as I explain in the next section, it is also critical that consumers pay attention to these ads while they are exposed to an increasing quantity of information of all sorts.

4.5. ADVERTISING TECHNOLOGY

Much of the discussion up to this point ignores the specifics of how the information contained in an ad reaches consumers. I now provide an overview of some of the main insights in the literature regarding advertising technology. I start with a discussion of advertising costs. I then introduce the targeting of ads and finish with the issues raised by information congestion.

4.5.1 Advertising Costs

I first consider the cost for an advertiser to reach consumers, which I already introduced in Section 4.2, and then I discuss how the disclosure costs (that may be more than the cost of just reaching consumers) affect the firm's incentives to reveal product information.

4.5.1.1 Advertising Costs and Reach

In his groundbreaking analysis of informative advertising, Butters (1977) is very careful in specifying the technology through which advertising reaches consumers. He assumes each ad has a constant cost $b > 0$ and that it lands on one out of a population of n consumers, where each consumer is equally likely to be reached. It follows that each ad reaches each consumer with probability $1/n$ and, for n large, if a is the number of ads sent per consumer, the probability that a consumer is reached by at least one ad is approximately $\phi = 1 - e^{-a}$. This is a concave function of a, meaning that the impact of an additional ad on the reach decreases as the number of ads sent increases. This in turn begets advertising cost as a strictly convex function of reach, $A(\phi) = -bn \ln(1 - \phi)$. In other words, as noted by Stahl (1994, p. 164), although the marginal cost of sending an additional ad is constant, the marginal cost of increasing the reach is strictly increasing.

The technology used by Butters is best interpreted as advertising by means of flyers that are randomly handed out to consumers, where each flyer reaches one and exactly one consumer. Now if we think of advertising through media outlets, an ad printed or aired once reaches a potentially large population of consumers. This means that the probability that any one consumer is reached by one ad is larger than $1/n$. As discussed by Stegeman (1991, p. 216), if k/n denotes the probability that a consumer is reached by an ad, then, still taking n to be large, she is reached by at least one ad with approximate probability $\phi = 1 - e^{-ka}$ if the number of ads per consumer is a. This again is a concave function inducing a rising marginal cost of increasing the reach.

This discussion suggests that there are decreasing returns to advertising intensity, contrary to what Kaldor (1950) postulates (see Bagwell, 2007, p. 1713). Bagwell (2007, pp. 1731–1732) discusses a series of empirical works that looks at the impact of advertising on sales. The evidence from that literature is that there are diminishing returns to advertising. It is important here to make a few remarks on these empirical findings and how they relate to the theory.

First, what Kaldor had in mind was rather a persuasive form of advertising, as I discuss in the introduction. The increasing returns he envisaged had more to do with the impact of advertising on consumer tastes (or perceived tastes) than with the reach technology. Even if we focus exclusively on informative advertising, the role of advertising in the Butters environment, which is to ensure potential buyers become aware of the firm's existence, is just one possible informative role. Consider, for instance, the signaling role described by Nelson (1974). In his formal analysis, he assumes that the indirect informa-tion kicks in only if consumers are exposed to enough repetitions of the same ad and he uses this to argue that experience goods are advertised more than search goods. Then, still using the Butters technology, reach is determined by the probability that a consumer is exposed to more than $m > 1$ ads. Then it is at least theoretically possible that for a low enough ad activity, the impact of one more message on the reach probability is increasing in the total number of messages. The empirical work by Lambin (1976) does find such a threshold (see Bagwell, 2007, p. 1732).

A second point is that different media might be used by advertisers depending on how broad a reach they are trying to achieve. As I suggested in my flyers versus TV example in Section 4.4.3, using TV advertising might be less costly than flyers when trying to reach a large population. For instance, Porter (1976) finds evidence that the impact of an increase in TV advertising on industry profit is much stronger than the impact of an increase in overall advertising activity (see Bagwell, 2007, p. 1733).

Finally, an important ingredient for advertising costs is the pricing behavior of the media. The actual pricing is not publicly observed, but list prices typically incorporate some form of quantity discounts. However, an ad that is more likely to reach many con-sumers (a larger k in my analysis above), say because of a large viewership, is typically priced higher, implying a higher b.

4.5.1.2 Disclosure Costs

Now I abstract from the choice of reach by advertisers and focus on how the cost of dis-closing information affects the firm's decision. My analysis of disclosure in Section 4.3 assumes no cost and emphasizes that a firm might choose not to reveal information about its product even if such revelation involves no cost.

A first question concerns the revelation of quality information. One takeaway from Section 4.3.4 is that, if product information only concerns product quality, then it is fully revealed by the firm. It is fairly straightforward to show that if there is some fixed cost of dis-closing quality information, then producers of lower quality products keep quiet so the con-sumer only learns that quality is not so good without knowing quality precisely. One natural question is how this private choice of quality revelation compares to what would be socially optimal. Jovanovic (1982) analyzes a monopoly setting where disclosing quality is costly and finds that too much quality information is revealed as compared to the social optimum.

To understand the result, consider the following simple setting. A monopolist sells a product to a buyer with unit demand whose willingness to pay is the product's quality s that may be either s_ℓ or s_h, where $0 < s_\ell < c < s_h$ and c is the unit production cost. The firm knows s while the buyer only knows that $s = s_h$ with probability $\alpha \in (0, 1)$. Let $\bar{s}$ be the expected quality given the buyer's beliefs. As in the standard persuasion game, the firm may provide certified information about its product quality through advertising.

Now consider the incentives of a high-quality firm to reveal that $s = s_h$. By disclosing quality, it can charge the consumer s_h rather than $\bar{s}$. Hence it will do so as long as the associated cost is no more than $s_h - \bar{s} = (1-\alpha)(s_h - s_\ell)$. By contrast, the social benefit from disclosure is to avoid the product being purchased when it is low quality. The associated expected gain in social surplus is $(1-\alpha)(c - s_\ell) < (1-\alpha)(s_h - s_\ell)$. Thus, for a disclosure cost strictly between $(1-\alpha)(c - s_\ell)$ and $(1-\alpha)(s_h - s_\ell)$, the firm chooses to disclose although it is not socially desirable. An important takeaway from this analysis is that policies aimed at encouraging quality disclosure are at best wasteful (because they involve subsidies or enforcement costs[55]) and can actually be detrimental to the market outcome. Of course, with a different specification of demand, so consumer surplus is non-zero, they could be desirable for consumer protection. Furthermore, as Jovanovic (1982, p. 42) notes, if quality is endogenous, then forced disclosure may have a beneficial incentive role by increasing the firm's benefit from improving its quality.

When thinking about disclosure costs, one obvious question is how they are related to the quantity of information contained in the ad. The nature of the information provided may matter as well and it is not clear in practice that more information is necessarily associated with a larger disclosure cost. Even if it is the case, we need a measure of the quantity of information that can be applied to a general enough class of disclosure strategies. Manduchi (2013) addresses this issue in the experience good match disclosure problem discussed in Section 4.3.3.1. A monopolist sells a product to a buyer with unit demand where the match is either $r = r_h$ with probability $q \in (0, 1)$ or $r = r_\ell$. Production cost is $c > 0$ where $r_\ell < c < r_h$. The firm may devise any binary information system such that the buyer receives one of two signals $\sigma \in \{b, g\}$, where $\sigma = g$ is a good signal in the sense that it is more likely to be observed by a high-valuation buyer than by a low-valuation buyer. Absent disclosure costs, the firm would choose to have $\sigma = g$ observed with probability 1 if $r = r_h$ and with probability 0 otherwise. Manduchi uses an entropy-based measure of information called "mutual information." Using a disclosure cost that is linear in the quantity of information, he finds that the firm reveals information only if there is enough *ex ante* uncertainty about the match so that q is in some intermediate range. In that range, the information provided is mostly used to screen out a low match consumer if q is low, whereas for q large enough information is used to make sure a high match consumer buys. The probability of a sale is less (respectively larger) than q if q is small (respectively large) enough.

Next I turn to targeted advertising.

---

[55] Note, however, that the mere possibility for the firm to disclose certified information requires some enforcement of laws against misleading ads. The analysis here implicitly assumes the corresponding costs are charged to the firm. Forced disclosure laws may involve extra costs.

4.5.2 Targeted Advertising

When a firm faces a heterogeneous population of consumers, an obvious way to save on advertising costs is to target advertising, which allows for reaching primarily those consumers who have a more inelastic demand and not wasting advertisements on people who would not buy the product in any case. This can be achieved by advertising in different media that reach different consumer populations, by advertising differently to different geographic areas, by exploiting customer information or websites' tracking information (see the chapters in this volume on the economics of Internet media (Peitz and Reisinger, 2015) and user-generated content (Luca, 2015)).

On top of the obvious cost advantage of targeting, this practice allows a firm to enhance its market power by making its demand less elastic. This is the main takeaway from studies that have considered the use of targeted advertising by a monopoly firm, such as Esteban et al. (2001). Similar insights may be obtained in a competitive environment, as illustrated by the simple setting of Iyer et al. (2005). They consider a differentiated product duopoly with zero production costs. Each firm has a captive consumer base with measure $h > 0$ that is only interested in buying its product with reservation price r. There is also a measure $s = 1 - 2h > 0$ of shoppers who just buy the cheapest product available. Reaching a measure m of consumers with advertising costs Am, consumers only buy from a firm if they have received an ad from that firm.

In equilibrium, firms mix over prices. If targeted advertising is not feasible, then the firm can guarantee itself a profit of $rh - A$ by charging r and only serving its home base. It turns out this is the equilibrium profit if it is positive (that is, for $A \leq rh$). It is immediately apparent that if advertising can be targeted, a firm can improve over this by advertising only to its home base and still charging r, thus earning $h(r - A)$. This is viable for a wider range of advertising costs, $A \leq r$. In equilibrium, firms do send ads to shoppers with some probability, but prices are stochastically larger than what they would be if advertising was not targeted. Results are similar whether or not firms can price discriminate.

This reduction in a firm's demand elasticity is, however, not the only consequence of the targeting of ads. Ben Elhadj-Ben Brahim et al. (2011) study targeted advertising in the Hotelling setting with advertising reach analyzed by Tirole (1988), discussed in Section 4.2.5 of this chapter. There is one firm at each end of the Hotelling segment with identical and constant marginal costs. Each firm can select its advertising intensity for each location but must charge a uniform price. Advertising costs to achieve a reach ϕ are $A(\phi) = (1/2)a\phi^2$. Ben Elhadj-Ben Brahim et al. (2011) first show that, in equilibrium, each firm chooses two advertising intensities: a high one for locations at which, if perfectly informed, consumers would select the firm's product at the equilibrium prices, and a lower one for the remaining locations that are farther away from the firm. Note that the only benefit from advertising to the latter set of consumers comes from selling to those who do not get an ad from the competitor (which is preferred by these consumers if they are perfectly informed). It follows that, for low advertising costs (low a), because each firm advertises a lot to its local customers (it actually chooses to reach all of them), it does not advertise to the others who are certain to receive a competing ad. Prices are then larger than if targeted advertising was infeasible. In contrast, for large advertising costs, each firm advertises to both consumer segments but selects advertising intensities below 1. Prices are then lower than they would be without targeted ads.

In this setting, if a firm drops its price, the set of consumers it wishes to target with a higher advertising intensity is expanded. The jump in advertising intensity for the marginal consumers (those who would switch to the firm who has cut its price if perfectly informed) contributes to make demand more price elastic. There is no such jump if the firm advertises uniformly to all consumers.[56] The increased demand elasticity due to an increase in advertising intensity with targeted advertising is reminiscent of the analysis of Chamberlin (1933) on informative advertising that makes demand more elastic (see Bagwell, 2007, p. 1709). However, this increased advertising intensity at the margin in the case of targeting constitutes an additional marginal cost of increasing sales that pushes prices upward. As a result of the two countervailing forces, prices are higher with targeting if advertising costs are low,[57] but lower if advertising costs are high. If they are sufficiently high, then targeted advertising reduces the profitability of the market.

In the analysis above, consumers benefit from targeting directly to the extent that they are exposed to more ads pertaining to products they wish to purchase. As I just explained, the indirect impact through price may go either way. Another potential benefit that is not captured in the theoretical frameworks I have discussed so far is that consumers receive less ads that are irrelevant. Provided that there is some nuisance cost associated with being exposed to an ad, as is typically assumed in the media economics literature, such a reduction in overall ad quantity is beneficial to consumers. Johnson (2013) proposes a framework that incorporates this dimension as well as ad avoidance activity by consumers. A parameter in his model measures the precision with which a firm is able to target the consumers who are interested in its product. He finds that improved targeting has an ambiguous impact on consumer welfare. Although it improves the relevance of the ads they receive, it increases the firm's incentives to advertise to more consumers, which decreases welfare for those who get the least relevant ads.

In Johnson (2013), advertisers are subject to a negative externality imparted by consumer's ad avoidance. But in practice they also exert some negative externality on each other by sending out ads that compete for the consumer's attention. Consumers are exposed to many ads along with many other pieces of information to which they may

---

[56] From first-order condition (4.14), a firm that drops its price actually finds it optimal to drop its uniform advertising intensity.

[57] For low enough ad costs, consumers are perfectly informed with uniform advertising and there is no difference in the price elasticity of demand between the two regimes.

not pay full attention. This creates information congestion, the topic that closes this discussion of ad technology.

4.5.3 Information Congestion

Van Zandt (2004) and Anderson and De Palma (2009) propose some related models of "information overload." The general idea is that messages sent to the same recipient by different sources may crowd each other out because the recipient can or wishes to only pay limited attention to the information she receives. As a very direct illustration, Anderson and De Palma (2009, p. 688) quote a figure measuring that 46% of the bulk mail in the US remains unopened. Whether because of some exogenous inability to process a large amount of information or because processing it is too costly, consumer attention is scarce and advertisers compete for that attention.

Anderson and De Palma (2012) use an ingenious construction to analyze how this competition for attention among firms selling in different markets interacts with price competition among firms in the same market. They consider multiple markets for homogeneous products. Competition in each market is monopolistic competition, similar to Butters (1977): (i) a continuum of firms send ads with a price offer; (ii) consumers are identical with unit demand for each product and a consumer can buy from a firm only if she has received an ad from that firm; (iii) each ad must bring in zero profit because of free entry. By contrast with Butters (1977), an ad reaches all consumers but it is noticed by each consumer with some probability that is less than one so that each consumer only notices a fraction of the ads sent.[58] Furthermore, because of information congestion, the probability that a consumer notices a particular ad in one of the markets is decreasing in the total number of ads addressed to the consumer from all firms in all markets. Markets differ as to the social surplus generated by a sale. As in Butters, equilibrium in each market is characterized by a price distribution: each ad trades off a higher probability of a sale achieved by a lower price with the higher revenue per sale afforded by a higher price. Because without congestion the advertising intensity would be socially optimal as is the case in Butters (see Section 4.2.4), here advertising is excessive: each firm sending an ad does not take into account the added congestion it creates for all the other ads sent.

The model uncovers a rich pattern of externalities across sectors. If the number of active markets increases, this increases information congestion, which in turn increases prices in the pre-existing markets. The share of all those markets in total advertising goes down and the absolute advertising level decreases for the weaker markets (in terms of potential social surplus per sale). The impact of an increased consumer attention on overall advertising intensity is non-monotonic. If attention is low, few ads are sent because they are very unlikely to make a sale. If attention is very high, competition is very intense because each consumer gets to compare a lot of prices and hence advertising intensity is

---

[58] In Butters, each ad reaches only one consumer so each consumer observes only a subset of all the ads sent.

low again due to the limited profitability of a sale. It is only for intermediate levels of attention that sending an ad is very profitable so that advertising is very intense. Regarding the distribution of advertising activity across markets, it is very heterogeneous if consumer attention is low, with strong sectors advertising the most. Improved consumer attention intensifies competition in all sectors, which equalizes profit between stronger and weaker markets. This results in a more uniform advertising intensity across markets.

4.5.4 Concluding Remarks

The theoretical literature on advertising reach typically assumes decreasing returns to advertising expenditure, which ensures a well-behaved optimization problem for the firms. Butters (1977) has shown that this is consistent with an advertising technology that reaches consumers randomly. There is also some empirical support for such a specification of advertising costs. Yet there may be good reasons to think that returns to advertising expenditures can be increasing, in particular when advertising is only effective if consumers are reached by more than one ad message, or if a massive advertising reach can be achieved through such mass media as television.

A proper analysis of advertising costs actually requires taking into account how pricing decisions of media firms are determined. One important issue is whether there is some form of price discrimination involving quantity discounts. Besides, as I already alluded to in the concluding remarks of Section 4.2, the pricing of ad space has potentially major implications for the welfare analysis of advertising intensity. In other words, it is necessary to know whether the price charged for ad space is above or below its social cost. For instance, as explained by Anderson and Gabszewicz (2006, p. 294), if media platforms charge both sides (advertisers and the audience) then the price per ad unambiguously exceeds the social cost of ads, which is the nuisance cost for the platform's audience.[59] Then the social cost of advertising is actually lower than the private cost incurred by advertisers, which pulls the market outcome in the direction of an insufficient provision of ads.

But the welfare analysis of advertising must also account for the nature of the information provided by the ad. Indeed, the ad cost may depend on which information is provided. For instance, more ad space may be needed to convey the desired information either because the consumer should be exposed repeatedly (as is the case for signaling the high quality of an experience good) or because conveying a lot of information requires more space. Second, the benefit of advertising additional pieces of information (if there is any) may vary greatly depending on the nature of the information, as illustrated by the analysis in Section 4.3.

---

[59] This is assuming that the entire potential audience is served, with single homes and keeping the media content exogenous.

The analysis of targeted advertising has remained rather limited. The key role played by the media who specialize in reaching a certain type of audience is usually acknowledged, but generally abstracted from in the analysis. It is often argued that the Internet has great potential for capturing a larger share of the advertising market, not only because of the breadth of the advertising reach it offers but also because of the quality of that reach, thanks to the improved targeting facilitated by the large amount of information gathered on users. How profitable this may be depends, however, on how the profitability of product markets is affected by this improved targeting. Some additional work would be warranted that looks at this issue while taking into account the specificities of the new targeting methods available such as keywords on search engines, tracking technologies, or exploitation of user-generated contents.

Finally, information congestion has important implications for the media business model, by introducing a new externality among advertisers or among platforms (see Anderson et al. (2015) for a theoretical analysis and Choi (2014) for an empirical investigation).

4.6. ADVERTISING THAT MIGHT NOT INFORM

In all the preceding material, I keep with a strict informative interpretation of advertising. As explained in the introduction, my goal is to explore how far this approach takes us in our understanding of the role of advertising in markets. The present section extends the scope of the analysis by considering some roles for advertising that are not necessarily associated with the provision of information to consumers. As can be seen from Sections 4.3 and 4.4, information transmission provides a rich framework for interpreting advertising, even if it contains only limited information. Still, it requires that consumers are very sophisticated and also leads to a great multiplicity of equilibria. Besides, it may seem difficult to argue that massive advertising by well-established brands only has to do with informing consumers. Furthermore, if advertising is about transmitting information, it is not easy to explain why firms would not use it massively to provide price information, especially if they are facing some competition. In practice, many ads do nor include any price.[60] Here I first reconsider the welfare analysis of advertising without restricting attention to informative advertising. I then discuss two forms of consumer naivety. Finally, I consider the goodwill effect of advertising with particular attention to whether it can be interpreted as evolving consumer information.

---

[60] There are practical reasons why price information is not disclosed in ads: it may be too complex if it involves price discrimination or a national brand may not wish to commit to prices so they can be set locally and adjust to local conditions.

4.6.1 Too Much or Too Little Advertising: A Broader Perspective

I now consider a very simple problem, which I use to discuss the welfare implications of advertising. Consider a monopolist charging a uniform price that can spend money on advertising to shift its demand outward.[61] A first question concerns the contribution of advertising to social surplus. There is actually a simple unambiguous answer to this question, which is consistent with pretty much any interpretation of the impact of advertising on demand that can be found in the literature. Indeed, the monopoly quantity without advertising is typically below the socially optimal level calculated with the demand curve with zero advertising expenditure. Hence, even if advertising shifts demand while being completely irrelevant to the welfare of consumers, it may still improve social surplus if it induces an increase in the quantity that the firm chooses to produce and this increase in quantity is not too large so quantity remains below its socially optimal level. For instance, Glaeser and Ujhelyi (2010) use this argument in a context where advertising is pure misinformation that convinces consumers that the product's quality is better than it actually is (or, in the case of cigarettes, which is their main application, that the adverse effects of the product are milder than they really are).[62] As the following discussion shows, this social benefit of advertising is even larger for the alternative welfare benchmarks that have been considered in the literature.

Advertising being socially beneficial does not mean that it is provided optimally by the market. To address this issue, consider the following simple setting. A monopoly firm with constant marginal cost $c \geq 0$ sells to at most two consumers. Consumer i, $i = 1, 2$, has unit demand with reservation value $r_i(A) > c$, where A denotes advertising expenditures by the firm and r_i is strictly increasing in A. To simplify, assume the firm chooses between $A = 0$ and $A = 1$.

I now present a welfare analysis of the firm's choice to advertise that abstracts from any informative role of advertising. A first approach, and in some sense a natural starting point, is to assume that if advertising increases a consumer's willingness to pay, it increases the surplus she can obtain by consuming the product at some given price. The social benefit of advertising should then incorporate the increase in consumer valuations. It is as if advertising imparts a higher quality to the product. As noted by Becker and Murphy (1993), the welfare analysis is then similar to that of Spence (1975) regarding a firm's choice of its product's quality (see Tirole, 1988, chapter 2, subsection 2.2.1 for an analysis of the choice of quality by a monopolist). The second-best social optimum prescribes that

[61] This is what Johnson and Myatt (2006) call "hype," which has been the main focus of the literature and may be attributed to information or other forms of product promotion. They contrast it with advertising that "rotates" demand, which they call "real information" in reference to the match information disclosure discussed in Section 4.3.3.1. Match information typically turns some consumers away from the product, whereas Johnson and Myatt presume that this would not be the case for non-informative forms of advertising.

[62] They actually derive the result for a Cournot oligopoly, where the argument is the same as for monopoly.

the product's quality should maximize the social surplus generated by the sale of the monopoly quantity. This social surplus depends on the impact of quality on consumer valuations for all the units sold. By contrast, the monopolist cares about the impact of quality on its profit. This in turn depends on the impact of quality on the marginal consumer's valuation, which determines the monopoly price. Then, simple calculations show that the profit-maximizing quality is below (respectively above) the socially optimal one if the marginal impact of quality on the marginal consumer's valuation is below (respectively above) the marginal impact of quality on the average valuation taken over all units sold by the firm.

In the simple two-consumer setting above, assume that with or without advertising, the firm sells to both consumers.[63] Further assume that $r_2(A) \leq r_1(A)$, so consumer 2 is always the marginal consumer and the firm prices at $r_2(A)$, $A = 0, 1$. The firm chooses to advertise if and only if $2(r_2(1) - c) - 2(r_2(0) - c) = 2(r_2(1) - r_2(0)) \geq 1$. In contrast, advertising is socially optimal if $r_1(1) + r_2(1) - 2c - (r_1(0) + r_2(0) - 2c) = r_1(1) + r_2(1) - r_1(0) - r_2(0) \geq 1$. Hence if the average change in valuation $(r_1(2) - r_1(0) + r_2(1) - r_2(0))/2$ exceeds (respectively is below) the change in valuation for consumer 2 $r_2(1) - r_2(0)$, then the firm may under-advertise (respectively over-advertise) as compared to the social optimum.

Arguably, the above result reflects the inefficiency of imperfectly competitive markets rather than some specific property of advertising. Stigler and Becker (1977) present a model of consumer behavior on the basis of which they argue that the appropriate approach to advertising is to view increases in willingness to pay as genuine increases in consumer welfare. They develop a framework where households consume some commodities that they produce using various ingredients. Advertising is viewed as an ingredient which is used, along with the advertised product, to produce such a commodity. Advertising is therefore complementary to the advertised product. The main insight from their analysis is that advertising may then be provided by perfectly competitive firms. The idea is that there is perfect competition in the market for the commodity consumed by the household. Such a commodity could, for instance, be "prestige" and the products that might help produce it might be expensive watches or expensive shoes. The price on that market is a shadow price that reflects the marginal consumer's willingness to pay for one more unit of the commodity. Firms competing on that market may charge different prices if they provide more or less advertising, but the shadow price paid by the household is independent of which firm provides the product.

In the Stigler and Becker world, households can purchase any quantity they wish of the commodity at the equilibrium shadow price, independent of the firms' advertising decisions. This means that a firm's decision to advertise does not affect consumer surplus. Advertising may, however, enhance the firm's revenue. For instance, in the two-consumer example,

---

[63] The result can accommodate a change in the quantity sold if quantity adjusts continuously.

if consumer 2 is the marginal consumer, then the equilibrium price is $r_2(0)$. By using advertising, the firm may increase its revenue by $2(r_2(1) - r_2(0))$ and it chooses to advertise if this is larger than 1. Because this has no impact on consumer surplus or on the producer surplus of competitors, this rule is also optimal from a social surplus perspective. Nichols (1985) shows that if the commodity market is perfectly competitive, then the equilibrium advertising expenditure is socially optimal.

Although the complementary view seems like the natural approach that is consistent with the standard microeconomics of consumer behavior, many economists consider that much of advertising induces some consumer response that can only be attributed to some form of "irrationality." This is what I have described in the introduction, following Bagwell (2007), as the persuasive view. Still, there are two ways of interpreting the increase in willingness to pay that advertising triggers. A first interpretation is that it is pure manipulation that changes consumer behavior but not consumer tastes. This is, for instance, explicitly the case in Glaeser and Ujhelyi (2010), where advertising is pure misinformation. This is also coherent with the analysis of advertising by Braithwaite (1928) or Kaldor (1950). Social welfare should then be evaluated using the no-advertising valuations, $r_i(0)$, $i = 1, 2$, in my two-consumer example.

But the persuasive view has often been portrayed as considering advertising as a taste shifter (see Bagwell, 2007, p. 1720). For instance, Stigler and Becker (1977, p. 83) cite Galbraith (1958), who writes that advertising's "... central function is to create desires— to bring into being wants that previously did not exist". In a very influential and controversial article, Dixit and Norman (1978) undertake a welfare analysis of advertising that is consistent with this point of view. Because tastes change as a result of the firm's advertising, it is unclear which preferences should be taken into account to establish the welfare benchmark. Either the new preferences are treated as irrelevant to welfare and then the analysis should proceed assuming advertising only induces a change in behavior, so the original valuations should be used to compute social welfare. Or we should acknowledge that this change in tastes defines a new welfare criterion and the post-advertising valuations provide the proper welfare measure to compare the market situation with and without advertising. Dixit and Norman (1978) consider both possibilities and establish a remarkable over-provision result, which holds independent of which welfare measure is selected.

I now present the gist of Dixit and Norman's argument using the two-consumer monopoly setting. Assume that, without advertising, the firm only serves consumer 1, whereas if it advertises it serves both. This increase in quantity ensures that there is some social benefit associated with advertising. Otherwise, advertising would clearly be excessive if the firm chose to resort to it. Further assume that $r_2(1) \leq r_1(1)$ so that consumer 2 is the marginal consumer if the firm advertises. The firm's surplus is therefore $r_1(0) - c$ if it does not advertise and $2(r_2(1) - c) - 1$ if it does. Advertising thus generates the incremental producer surplus $2r_2(1) - r_1(0) - c - 1$. Using the post-advertising tastes, the incremental social welfare induced by the firm's advertising is the social surplus associated with the purchase of the product by consumer 2 minus the advertising cost $r_2(1) - c - 1$. It is readily seen that the incremental producer surplus exceeds the incremental social surplus if and only if $r_2(1) > r_1(0)$. Because the firm charges consumer 1's valuation $r_1(0)$ if it does not advertise and consumer 2's valuation $r_2(1)$ when it does advertise, this simple analysis shows that advertising is excessive if it induces a strict increase in monopoly price. Clearly, the result holds all the more if pre-advertising tastes are used instead to evaluate welfare.

The incremental analysis above underscores the analysis in Dixit and Norman (1978), which uses continuous demand curves (see Bagwell, 2007, subsection 4.2.1, for a graphical illustration of the argument). The idea is that, when it advertises and serves an additional consumer, the firm is capturing the entirety of the social surplus of the additional consumer it serves and if, in addition, it increases its price, it is also capturing additional surplus from inframarginal consumers. However, this argument is correct only as long as the additional consumer who is served is also the marginal consumer that determines the post-advertising price. This point is noted by Shapiro (1980) in a clever comment on Dixit and Norman. When using the post-advertising demand to perform their welfare analysis, they implicitly assume that the order of consumer valuations has not been modified by advertising. In the example above, assume to the contrary that $r_1(1) < r_2(1)$ so that, when it advertises, the firm charges $r_1(1)$. The social surplus generated by advertising is still $r_2(1) - c - 1$ and price is still increasing, although now from $r_1(0)$ to $r_1(1)$. However, the incremental profit is now $2r_1(1) - r_1(0) - c - 1$. If advertising only has a limited impact on consumer 1 so $r_1(1) - r_1(0)$ is small, then the firm's gain from advertising is less than the social value it generates. Advertising may therefore be undersupplied by the firm even though it induces an increase in the monopoly price. Obviously this is not the case if social surplus is measured using the advertising-free valuations $r_1(0)$ and $r_2(0)$.

From the analysis above it appears that the only case where the welfare analysis of monopoly advertising is unambiguous is when the impact of advertising on demand is considered completely irrelevant to welfare so the advertising-free valuations are used to evaluate surplus. In that case, the monopolist advertises excessively. It is not so surprising that, in the other cases, welfare results are not clear-cut, because both the persuasive approach and the complementary good approach put little structure as to the impact of advertising on inframarginal valuations as opposed to its impact on the marginal valuation. I now conclude this discussion with some remarks on how the informative view of the previous sections could be put to bear to evaluate welfare in this monopoly advertising problem.

Here I consider in turn advertising reach, discussed in detail in Section 4.2, and the advertising of product information, studied in Section 4.3. Recall that in the advertising reach analysis pioneered by Butters (1977), advertising expands a firm's demand by making more consumers aware of the firm's existence, and that awareness implies that the consumer is perfectly informed and may buy at no additional cost. As pointed out by Shapiro (1980), this can be accounted for in the demand-shifting monopoly setting by assuming that the pre-advertising valuation is zero for those consumers who are initially unaware of the firm's existence, and then using the post-advertising valuations to evaluate welfare. For instance, in the two-consumer setting, if consumer 1 is initially aware of the firm's existence and then advertising allows the firm to reach consumer 2, then we have $r_1(1) = r_1(0)$ and $r_2(1) > r_2(0) = 0$. Now also recall that in my discussion of Section 4.2.4, following Tirole (1988), I explain that it is typically ambiguous whether market-provided advertising is excessive, because of the two countervailing effects, "non-appropriation of surplus" and "market stealing." Under monopoly only the first effect remains because there are no competitors to steal the market from. This suggests that the firm does not advertise enough because it cannot fully appropriate the surplus it generates through advertising.

Returning to the application where advertising reaches consumer 2 in addition to consumer 1, either $r_2(1) \leq r_1(0)$, in which case the monopoly price would be weakly smaller with advertising, or $r_2(1) > r_1(0)$, in which case the firm charges $r_1(1) = r_1(0)$ with advertising so price is unaffected. Hence the analysis of price increasing advertising of Dixit and Norman (1978) never applies. Furthermore, it is readily seen that advertising is weakly under-provided by the firm and the only case where the firm's behavior is socially optimal is when $r_1(1) = r_2(1)$, a case where the firm can extract the entire social surplus through its monopoly price. If we allow for any form of heterogeneity in tastes, so the firm cannot fully appropriate consumer surplus, then monopoly advertising is insufficient as predicted by the discussion of Section 4.2.4.

Now consider the provision of product information. As I briefly mention in the concluding remarks to Section 4.3, there is no clear-cut general conclusion regarding the firms' incentives to provide product information as compared to what would be socially optimal. For instance, Koessler and Renault (2012, p. 645) provide an example where the firm wishes to disclose full certified information (and this is a unique equilibrium) and yet it would be preferable for social welfare that it is incapable of certifying product information (even if certification and disclosure involve no cost). And there are some obvious cases where the ability of a firm to certify and disclose product information at no cost is socially desirable. Here I just consider the canonical case of quality disclosure, as in Sections 4.3.4.1 and 4.5.1.2.

Favorable quality information should ameliorate the product's appeal to consumers and therefore shift demand outward as has been assumed above. Furthermore, post-advertising valuations are clearly the relevant measures of gross consumer surplus. Provided that price increases as a result and that the order of consumer valuations is the same whether consumers know that quality is good or not, then the analysis of Dixit and Norman (1978) shows that the monopoly firm excessively provides quality information. However, a full welfare analysis must also account for the impact of information revelation when quality turns out to be lower than expected by consumers. This is what is done in the analysis of quality disclosure in Section 4.5.1.2. I now consider a reinterpretation of the two-consumer setting above that allows for a full welfare analysis of monopoly quality disclosure.

Assume the product's quality is either high or low, where $q \in (0, 1)$ is the probability that quality is high. Then, for $i = 1, 2$, $r_i(0)$ is the valuation of consumer i if she does not know quality while $r_i(1)$ is consumer i's valuation for the high-quality product. Assume that the firm sells only to consumer 1 if consumers do not know quality, and sells to both consumers if quality is revealed and is high. Further assume that $r_2(1) \geq r_1(0)$ and that consumer 2 is the marginal consumer when quality is known to be high. Then the perfect information price of the high-quality product is at least as large as the price charged by the monopoly firm when its quality is not known. From the analysis above, the high-quality firm's incremental profit from disclosing quality is at least as large as the social surplus it generates by revealing its quality and selling to one more consumer. Let us now assume that the low-quality firm's quantity resulting from information disclosure is no larger than the quantity sold when quality information is not disclosed. Further assume that the monopolist under-provides the low-quality product even when quality is unknown so that any drop in the quantity sold as a result of quality revelation diminishes social surplus. Then quality disclosure decreases social surplus if quality is low. As a result, it is unambiguous that the high-quality firm's incentives to provide quality information are excessive as compared to what would be socially optimal.

The above result that the disclosure of quality information by the monopoly firm is excessive coincides with the result derived in Section 4.5.1.2 in my discussion of Jovanovic (1982). The underlying motive for excessive disclosure is, however, quite different. In Section 4.5.1.2, demand is inelastic and quality revelation can only contribute to social surplus by preventing the sale of some units of the low-quality product that generates a negative surplus. Here, demand is elastic and all units of the low-quality product that are sold with or without information generate some positive surplus. The point is to show that under the assumptions that induce over-provision of persuasive advertising in Dixit and Norman (1978) there is an excessive provision of quality information that is even more severe under fairly reasonable conditions (that the monopolist sells an insufficient amount of the low-quality product even if consumers do not know quality and does not sell more if quality is revealed to be low).

Returning now to persuasive advertising, the difficulty in evaluating its welfare implications is a result of the disconnection between consumer tastes and consumer behavior: there is no unambiguous manner to infer one from the other. It is also clear that in order for persuasive advertising to be possible, consumer rationality must be altered in some way. One possible route to perform a proper welfare analysis is to assume stable preferences and model the bounded rationality explicitly. I explore this direction in the next subsection by looking at some recent contributions.

4.6.2 Consumer Naivety

There is obviously a great variety of manners in which we might wish to think of consumer naivety. Here I discuss two formulations that have been proposed in some recent and influential research with some applications to advertising: consumer unawareness (or myopia) and coarse thinking.

Here again I use a simple monopoly framework to illustrate these ideas. A monopoly firm with zero costs is selling a product to a consumer with unit demand. The product is characterized by two characteristics, (x_1, x_2), where x_i, $i = 1, 2$, is either 0 or 1.

Consumer unawareness and shrouded attributes. Assume that the value to the consumer of buying the product is given by $\hat{r} = \bar{u} - \sum_{i=1,2} x_i \Delta_i$, with $\bar{u} > 0$ and where $\Delta_i > 0$ represents the loss in utility for the consumer of consuming a product with characteristic $x_i = 1$ rather than $x_i = 0$. In other words, the consumer considers each characteristic independently, in evaluating how it affects her utility. She may, however, be unaware that attribute 2 exists. This idea has been formalized in some general game theory contexts by various authors (see, for instance, Geanakoplos, 1989 or Heifetz et al., 2006) Whether she is aware or not depends on the firm's communication. The firm selling product (x_1, x_2) can send a certified message $m \in \{(x_1, \varnothing), (\varnothing, x_2), (x_1, x_2)\}$, where $\varnothing$ in the ith position indicates that the ith characteristics are not mentioned. Now assume that the consumer is aware of characteristic 1 but remains unaware of characteristic 2 unless it is mentioned by the firm. Letting A be the set of characteristics that are mentioned in message m, the consumer's willingness to pay may then be written as $r(x_1, x_2, m) = \bar{u} - \sum_{i \in \{1\} \cup A} x_i \Delta_i$.

If the consumer was, from the outset, fully aware of the existence of the two characteristics, then this would be a special case of the persuasion game of quality disclosure described in Section 4.3.4. The unique sequential equilibrium outcome would then be that the firm fully reveals (x_1, x_2) and charges the consumer her true valuation $\bar{r}$. Now assuming that there is initial consumer unawareness, consider the following candidate equilibrium. The high-quality firm type $(0,0)$ announces $m = (0, \varnothing)$ and so does firm type $(0,1)$. In both instances, the consumer is reassured that $x_1 = 0$, and since this is all she cares about, the firm can charge a price of $\bar{u}$ and she buys. The other two types announce message $m = (1, \varnothing)$ and charge $\bar{u} - \Delta_1$. Obviously, no firm type could gain by disclosing more or less information (assuming that when the firm does not disclose the first characteristics, the consumer infers that $x_1 = 1$).[64] In this equilibrium, the consumer pays her true valuation only if the product has the highest quality or if it is product $(1,0)$. If the product is either $(0,1)$ or $(1,1)$, she pays more than her valuation.

---

[64] A proper formal analysis would require writing an appropriate definition for the equilibrium concept. Heifetz et al. (2011) show more formally that unraveling may break down if there is some unawareness on the buyer's side.

This simple example illustrates that, when consumers are not fully aware of all the potential attributes, a firm may select to "shroud" some of these attributes. This is especially the case if finding out that these attributes exist can only deteriorate the consumer's expected valuation for the product, as compared to what she thought, based on the attributes she was initially aware of. This may explain why, despite the persuasion game unraveling result, some negative information might remain hidden. This idea of shrouded attributes has been applied by Gabaix and Laibson (2006) to price information. Obviously, consumers are aware that price is a relevant dimension in determining the utility associated with purchasing a product. However, relevant price information is often more complex than a single price quote. Specifically, Gabaix and Laibson consider add-ons, which are items that are complementary to the purchased product and that the consumer may end up purchasing from the same provider. They mention such examples as printer cartridges or bank account services and penalties. A rational consumer anticipates the pricing of these items if the firm does not advertise it. She also foresees that, once the base product has been bought, there will be some cost in finding out about other sources that might provide those additional items at a cheaper price. This creates a potential holdup problem similar to the one discussed in Section 4.3.3.2, which the firm might wish to fight through price advertising, especially if it faces competition.

Gabaix and Laibson, however, argue that some consumers might be "myopic" about the pricing of add-ons and this may provide a rationale for firms to keep quiet about the price of these additional complementary items. In the modeling of Gabaix and Laibson (2006), myopic consumers merely ignore the pricing of add-ons when deciding whether to buy the base product, as long as the firm makes no mention of its add-on pricing. Hence, myopic consumers may be viewed as being "unaware" of add-on prices unless one of the competitors advertises them. Gabaix and Laibson show that, even with competition, there may be an equilibrium where all firms shroud add-on prices.[65]

In sum, unawareness is an argument for why advertisers might choose to hide some relevant attributes. As such, it might provide some support for imposing some forced disclosure rules. I now present an alternative form of consumer naivety that could explain why it might be profitable for advertisers to claim some seemingly irrelevant attributes.

Coarse thinking. In the simple setup outlined at the beginning of the subsection, assume that x_2 reflects some category the product might belong to. Further assume that the consumer's true valuation is given by $\hat{r} = \bar{u} + x_1 x_2 \Delta$, where $\Delta > 0$ is the additional utility for the consumer if $x_1 = x_2 = 1$. The expression for $\bar{r}$ indicates that attribute x_1 affects the consumer's welfare only if $x_2 = 1$.

Mullainathan et al. (2008) call the consumer a "coarse thinker" when she does not know x_2. In other words, she does not know which product category she is dealing with.

---

[65] Their modeling also includes some *ex ante* investment that non-myopic consumers can undertake so as to be able to avoid the high add-on prices they anticipate from the seller of the base product.

In their application to "branding," they propose as an example that some consumers might confuse such brand labeling as "California Burgundy" for some cheap California wine with the certified labeling "Burgundy" that applies to quality wines from the French Burgundy region. In the four-product setting above, products (0,0) and (1,0) would be two cheap California wines with comparable physical characteristics but the producer might try to differentiate one of them (say (1,0)) by calling it California Burgundy. Products (0,1) and (1,1) would be two wines characterized by a quality difference so that only product (1,1) can claim a certification label such as Burgundy. Formally, assume that the producer of the generic cheap California wine, $x_2 = 0$, can choose a message $m \in \{CB, DR\}$, where CB stands for "California Burgundy" and DR stands for "Delicious Red" (following the example in Mullainathan et al., 2008). By contrast, the wine producer in the alternative category, $x_2 = 1$, chooses a message $m \in \{B, T\}$ if it is (1,1) and $m \in \{T\}$ if it is (0,1), where B stands for Burgundy and T stands for Table. The key point here is that only product (1,1) can use message B. The coarse thinker, however, not knowing x_2, confuses messages B or CB. She only realizes that $x_1 = 1$ when reading such a message but is unsure whether this certifies a high quality or not.

If the consumer is not a coarse thinker, Mullainathan et al. call her a Bayesian, in which case she knows which category of product she is dealing with, so she knows x_2. Now assume $x_2 = 0$. If a Bayesian consumer is endowed with beliefs about the product's characteristics x_1, she updates her beliefs after observing the message m, depending on the equilibrium messages she expects from products (0,0) and (0,1). Her willingness to pay, however, does not depend on these beliefs. It is $r(m) = \bar{u}$ for all $m \in \{CR, DR\}$. By contrast, a coarse thinker believes that $m = CB$ might certify quality in the event that $x_2 = 1$. Assume now, as in Mullainathan et al., that the probability assigned by a coarse thinking consumer to $x_2 = 1$ is exogenously fixed at some level strictly between zero and one.[66] A producer of cheap California wine will be able to charge a higher price to that consumer if it announces $m = CB$, rather than $m = DR$. Mullainathan et al. show that, if the consumer population comprises some Bayesians and some coarse thinkers, then it is optimal for a monopoly producer of cheap California wine to propose two brands: Delicious Red that is purchased by Bayesian consumers and California Burgundy that is purchased by coarse thinkers where the latter brand is sold at a higher price than the former.

---

[66] Mullainathan et al. (2008) also mention the possibility that coarse thinkers could be more sophisticated and update their beliefs in view of the message they receive. For instance, if they believe that product (1,1) is much more unlikely than product (0,1), then they would drastically revise the probability that $x_2 = 1$ downward after observing $m = CB$ (assuming that $m = CB$ is product (1,1)'s equilibrium strategy). Lauga (2012) explores a similar idea in a setting where consumers are confused about the past experience they have had with a product. When they remember a favorable experience, they cannot tell whether it was their actual experience or whether they have been influenced by some advertising campaign. They update their beliefs about the product quality accordingly, taking into account the firm's equilibrium advertising behavior.

Note that rather than reflecting some bounded rationality, coarse thinking is formally equivalent to restricted information regarding the state of the world. It is analogous to the situation considered by Shin (1994), where the buyer is uncertain about the ability of a producer to certify that its quality is high (see Section 4.3.4.1). This lack of information could, however, be attributed to some improper initial information processing that would explain the confusion between different messages. A more convincing story would require a full equilibrium analysis that would clarify where these different messages come from, how consumers become informed about them, and how they are used in the different categories by different agents. It would also be useful to allow for repeat purchases.

The next subsection looks at the dynamics of advertising and how much of this dynamics can be explained by the transmission of information.

4.6.3 Advertising and Goodwill

It has been recognized for a long time that advertising may have some potentially large dynamic impact. The standard argument, which is a cornerstone of the persuasive view, that advertising is a very effective barrier to entry, requires that the incumbent's advertising has some lasting impact that cannot be overcome by potential entrants. It is then natural to think of advertising as contributing to a stock of "goodwill" in favor of the advertised brand or product. A substantial strand of research that traces back to Nerlove and Arrow (1962) has investigated the dynamics of firm advertising, both theoretically and empirically.[67] This goodwill dynamics may also explain why well-established brands or products may remain heavily advertised.

A key question here, which is at the heart of this chapter's inquiry, is whether goodwill can be construed as resulting from informational dynamics, or whether it reflects some non-informative impact of advertising on consumer behavior, along the persuasive view or the complementary good interpretations. The following discussion is organized around two potential sources of information dynamics: the matching of consumers to products and the evolution of consumer awareness of a brand or product.

As suggested by Tirole (1988, subsection 2.6.1.1), goodwill may reflect consumer learning about how well the product matches tastes. In Tirole's two-period example, a monopoly firm can get more consumers to learn in a first period whether they like the product or not, by lowering its price. This in turn increases the pool of consumers who have a high willingness to pay in the second period. Hence, a low price in the first

---

[67] For instance, Roberts and Samuelson (1988) estimate a structural model of non-price rivalry in the US cigarette industry. They estimate advertising first-order conditions allowing for goodwill accumulation allowing each firm to react to its rival's advertising in the previous period (see Bagwell, 2007, for more details). Dubé et al. (2005) propose a model of goodwill accumulation where advertising only contributes to goodwill if its intensity is sufficiently high at a given time. They then use the model to explain the "pulsing" nature of firms' advertising behavior.

period is an investment that generates a more profitable market in the second period. Bergemann and Vlimki (2006) take this principle to a dynamic infinite horizon monopoly setting where the firm and consumers are forward looking and consumers may buy the product repeatedly. Consumers learn about their match through consumption of the product, in which case they randomly receive a perfectly informative signal at some exogenous rate. It is therefore an experience good model. The dynamics of pricing and consumer learning can be decomposed into two phases: an early phase and a mature phase. In the early phase, the marginal consumer is uninformed, whereas in the mature phase the marginal consumer is informed. The nature of the mature phase critically depends on two parameters: the monopoly price against a demand from a population of consumers who know their match perfectly, denoted $\hat{p}$, and the willingness to pay of an uninformed consumer who expects that the price will be $\hat{p}$ forever after time t (time is treated as continuous), which is denoted $\hat{w}$. Bergemann and Vlimki characterize the situation as a mass market if $\hat{w} > \hat{p}$. The firm then sells to both informed and uninformed consumers in the mature phase and its price decreases as more consumers become informed. In the reverse situation, labeled niche market, the firm only sells to informed consumers in the mature phase and its price is kept constant at $\hat{p}$.

Saak (2012) studies how the firm could use informative advertising in this setting. He considers two possible roles for advertising. A first role is to increase the rate at which consumers who are consuming the product learn about their match. A second role is to provide direct information to consumers about their match with the product, even if they do not purchase it. Saak varies the extent to which advertising is effective in this latter respect from no impact to a full impact, meaning that advertising is as informative for non-purchasing consumers as it is for purchasing consumers. He finds that advertising intensity typically peaks during the early stage. In a mass market, advertising stops before the end of the early stage. In that case, the firm balances a short-run benefit with a long-run loss from advertising. More advertising means that there will be more informed consumers in the mature phase, which in turn implies lower price. Indeed, informed consumers are the source of demand elasticity. The short-run benefit is then to increase the willingness to pay of uninformed consumers at time t because they expect that, if they end up liking the product, they will benefit from lower prices in the future. Because the marginal consumer is uninformed in the early stage, this enables the firm to charge a higher price. However, lower future prices mean lower future profits so that the long-term impact of advertising is detrimental. Getting closer to the end of the early phase, this negative effect dominates and the firm stops advertising. By contrast, in a niche market, in the mature phase the firm sells to informed consumers alone and price is $\hat{p}$. There is therefore a long-run benefit from advertising which is the standard expended demand effect. Then the firm keeps on advertising all the way through the mature phase. This is the case as long as the advertised information reaches some consumers who are not purchasing the product (who are the uninformed in the mature phase of a niche market).

The analysis in Saak (2012) shows that a firm may keep on advertising a product indefinitely to accumulate some goodwill that results from better consumer information. One possible testable prediction would be that this is more likely to be the case for niche markets than for mass markets. Still it would be necessary to identify to what extent this persistent advertising activity may be attributed to information rather than some alternative non-informative sources of goodwill.

As discussed by Bagwell (2007, subsection 8.1), there is a substantial empirical literature that suggests that advertising does not impact household behavior much, if the household has some previous experience with the product (e.g., Deighton et al., 1994; Erdem and Keane, 1996; Ackerberg, 2001). In his reduced-form analysis of household purchases of Yoplait yoghurts, Ackerberg (2001) makes the identifying assumption that, if advertising had a persuasive impact or was a complementary good, then it should affect the household's choice whether or not it has had some previous experience with the product or the brand. He finds that advertising only has a significant impact on purchase decisions of new customers of Yoplait yoghurts. This supports the view that the main role of advertising is to provide these consumers with information that induces then to purchase the product. Although this is broadly consistent with the theoretical setting in Saak (2012) (in particular with his assumption that yields persistent advertising in a niche market), the exact nature of that information remains to be characterized. As discussed in Section 4.4.1, Ackerberg (2003), in his structural model, proposes to interpret this new information as quality signaling. Some information about the content of the ad messages would be needed in order to know whether they might contain direct information. Ippolito and Mathios (1990) use a natural experiment to indirectly control for ad content. They study the impact of the 1985 termination of the ban on health claim advertising by cereal producers in the US on cereal brand consumption. They find that the end of the ban led to a significant increase in the consumption of fiber cereals.

Short of having detailed content information or some appropriate natural experiment as in Ippolito and Mathios (1990), it is not clear whether an improved perceived quality should be interpreted as information or as resulting from some persuasion or complementary good effect of advertising (see the discussion in Section 4.6.1 above). A recent marketing literature explores whether goodwill can be attributed to an improved perceived quality or, rather, to an improved product awareness, which is unambiguously better information. Clark et al. (2009) use a consumer survey dataset over the period 2000−2005. It provides on a yearly basis a brand awareness score and a perceived quality score for top brands (in terms of sales) in 25 broad product categories. They estimate a two-equation recursive model of perceived quality and brand awareness inspired by Nerlove and Arrow (1962). Advertising expenditure contributes to the evolution of both perceived quality and brand awareness. They use the panel structure of their data to solve for endogeneity and account for unobserved heterogeneity across brands. They find that advertising effects brand awareness positively and significantly, whereas its impact on perceived quality is insignificant. Barroso and Llobet (2012) address a related question using a structural empirical model. In their model, advertising has both an immediate impact and a dynamic impact on awareness. It also has a direct impact on consumer utility, though it is modeled as purely static. They consider the automobile market in Spain in the 1990s. Similarly to Sovinsky-Goeree (2008), they simulate consumer choice sets (see Section 4.2.5). Their main finding is that advertising has a strong role in speeding up product awareness and this is best accounted for by using a specification where advertising has a lasting impact on awareness. They also find that advertising has a significant direct impact on consumer utility that can be interpreted as perceived quality.

In summary, these various empirical studies provide some empirical support for an informative role of advertising in its contribution to a product's goodwill, either by providing product information or by contributing to product awareness.

4.6.4 Concluding Remarks

Viewing advertising, whether informative or not, as a commodity just like any other seems tempting and quite natural for economists. It then suffices to characterize the supply-side and demand-side conditions for this commodity, and to apply standard economic arguments on competition (perfect or not), technology or externalities. Surprisingly, it was only less than 40 years ago that Stigler and Becker (1977) set out to put together such a theory of advertising (along with other social phenomena). Their main objective was to show that advertising could be supplied by a competitive market. It is then possible to develop a first fundamental theorem of welfare economics argument to show that it is optimally supplied. Once we move away from the ideal world of perfect competition however, things become rapidly more complicated. For instance, market power does not necessarily induce under-provision of advertising. This is because advertising is complementary to and jointly provided with the advertised product, which is typically not sold on a competitive market. Besides, different forms of advertising may affect consumer welfare in different manners. Becker and Murphy (1993) provide a stimulating discussion of the welfare economics of advertising, depending on its impact on consumer utility and on the competitive environment. In particular, they consider the possibility of charging consumers for advertising as well as the possibility that advertising may end up being a bad because it interferes with the consumer's access to news or entertainment. These two themes are obviously very relevant for the overall inquiry of this handbook.

The complementary good approach is often presented by its proponents in stark opposition to the more traditional persuasive view, which assumes that advertising is a taste shifter. For instance, Becker and Murphy (1993, p. 956) point out the difficulties involved in performing the welfare economics of taste shifting. Yet, as explained in Section 4.6.1, the persuasive view may be characterized in a simpler way by having advertising change consumer behavior without changing tastes. Then, although advertising may have some social value in an imperfectly competitive market, by raising output it is clearly over-provided in equilibrium.[68] That persuasive advertising by a monopolist is excessive remains valid under fairly general conditions, even if welfare is measured using the post-advertising tastes. However, similar conditions also imply that the provision of quality information through informative advertising is excessive. By contrast, informative advertising by a monopolist that makes consumers aware of the product's existence and attributes is clearly insufficient.[69]

Allowing for consumer naivety is a natural way of explaining why ads do not inform consumers or contain irrelevant items that might nonetheless influence the consumer's purchase decision. For instance, consumer unawareness explains why consumers may end up paying more than their true willingness to pay, although this happens because of a lack of advertising (because some unfavorable attributes remain hidden rather than because advertising is used to manipulate as presumed by the persuasive view). Coarse thinking, on the other hand, provides an alternative explanation where it is the content of the ad that persuades consumers, although this could be attributed to a lack of information on the part of the consumer as to the credibility of the language used rather than to some bounded rationality.

The dynamic impact of advertising reflected in the accumulation of goodwill has spurred a substantial amount of theoretical and empirical work. Much of the existing evidence suggests a strong informative impact, in particular through an increase in consumer awareness of the advertised product or brand. Theory also suggests that a product's advertising activity could be sustained merely because of consumers' ongoing learning about their match or the product's quality. This ongoing learning could be all the more pervasive that consumers might not fully recall their previous experience with the product or which product they previously consumed and liked, as suggested by Nelson (1974) (see Section 4.4.1). For instance, Deighton et al. (1994) find that advertising can have some impact on consumers with some previous experience with the product, as long as that experience is not too recent.

4.7. CLOSING COMMENTS

The profitability of advertising for firms is reflected in the amount that they are willing to spend on it. Identifying the source of this profitability is a more intricate endeavor to

---

[68] Dubois et al. (2014) study the impact of banning advertising on crisps in the UK on consumer welfare. They find that the ban is detrimental to consumers under the complementary good approach, despite the fall in prices, whereas consumers benefit from the ban when the post-ban tastes are assumed to be the true tastes.

[69] The result, however, may not hold for a multi-product monopolist for the same reason why a multi-product firm may provide too many varieties (see Tirole, 1988, chapter 2, subsection 2.2.2.2).

which this chapter attempts to contribute. I have tried to argue that much of the answer has to do with the firm's efforts to communicate information to consumers. Such information may concern the product's availability, its characteristics, or pricing. This is the case even if ads are often perceived as containing very limited information, either because the firm strategically selects to provide limited information or because the information is indirect. This informative view is also consistent with the observation that much of the content of advertising is completely uninformative. Indeed, any attempt at transmitting information requires some communication strategy to catch the attention of the consumer. Advertisers must compete for the consumers' attention as emphasized by the theories of information overload. Besides, even if consumers anticipate some benefits from paying attention to advertisements, the benefits from processing the information in any one ad may be small and advertisers must strive to make the cost of doing so even smaller.

Arguably, the non-informative content of ad messages may have a role of its own in enhancing the attractiveness of the product, which may be interpreted as persuasive or as a complementary good in the consumers' preferences. Yet it does not seem necessary to appeal to this non-informative dimension to account for much of what we witness as advertising practices. Besides, there is much empirical evidence suggesting that the informative role of ads is quite significant, whereas the evidence in favor of some consumer utility-related impact of advertising is not so compelling.[70] Still, we may remain skeptical about the extreme consumer sophistication that is typically assumed in the information provision approach. Allowing for less sophistication opens up the possibility of some manipulation, which is somewhat consistent with the traditional persuasive advertising viewpoint. A close look at the content of ads may also show that some of the claims or the lack of some relevant information may only be understood as resulting from some form of manipulation. Finally, it may be fruitful to have a broader interpretation of what the relevant product information may be. For instance, in my discussion of coordination in Section 4.4.3 in this chapter I mention, for instance, fashion as a possible source of consumption externality.

It is also quite clear that, besides being profitable, advertising contributes to social welfare in markets with imperfect competition or imperfect consumer information. The difficult question there is to evaluate whether market-provided advertising is insufficient or excessive. This chapter describes a wide range of arguments pertaining to the determinants of ad expenditures as well as the determinants of the informative content of advertisements, suggesting that there is no definite answer. Even if we only focus on consumer welfare, the diagnosis remains ambiguous: although consumers benefit from being better informed by making better choices, they may be penalized by higher prices induced by more advertising (in particular when advertising provides product

---

[70] Arguably, economists are somewhat biased in favor of the informative approach for which economic theory is better suited to provide an interpretation.

information). Results on product information disclosure suggest, however, that when firms choose to provide limited information it is because it enhances their ability to capture consumer surplus, and hence forced disclosure rules are desirable for consumer protection.

ACKNOWLEDGMENTS

I wish to thank Simon Anderson, Levent Celik, David Ettinger, Justin Johnson, Frédéric Koessler, Marion Oury, Andrew Rhodes, and Chris Wilson for helpful discussions and comments.

REFERENCES

Abernethy, A.M., Franke, G.R., 1996. The information content of advertising: a meta-analysis. J. Advert. 25, 117.
Ackerberg, D.A., 2001. Empirically distinguishing informative and prestige effects of advertising. RAND J. Econ. 32, 316333.
Ackerberg, D.A., 2003. Advertising, learning, and consumer choice in experience good markets: a structural empirical examination. Int. Econ. Rev. 44, 1007–1040.
Anand, B.N., Shachar, R., 2011. Advertising, the matchmaker. RAND J. Econ. 42 (2), 205–245.
Anderson, S.P., De Palma, A., 2009. Information congestion. RAND J. Econ. 40 (4), 688–709.
Anderson, S.P., De Palma, A., 2012. Competition for attention in the information (overload) age. RAND J. Econ. 43 (1), 1–25.
Anderson, S.P., Gabszewicz, J.J., 2006. The media and advertising: a tale of two-sided markets. In: Ginsburgh, V., Throsby, D. (Eds.), Handbook of the Economics of Art and Culture. Elsevier, Amsterdam.
Anderson, S.P., Renault, R., 1999. Pricing, product diversity, and search costs: a Bertrand-Chamberlin-Diamond model. RAND J. Econ. 30, 719–735.
Anderson, S.P., Renault, R., 2006. Advertising content. Am. Econ. Rev. 96, 93–113.
Anderson, S.P., Renault, R., 2009. Comparative advertising: disclosing horizontal match information. RAND J. Econ. 40 (3), 558–581.
Anderson, S.P., Renault, R., 2013. The advertising mix for a search good. Manag. Sci. 59 (1), 69–83.
Anderson, S.P., Renault, R., 2015. Search Direction. Mimeo, Université de Cergy-Pontoise.
Anderson, S.P., Ciliberto, F., Liaukonyte, J., Renault, R., 2015. Push-Me Pull-You: Comparative Advertising in the OTC Analgesics Industry. Mimeo. Available at CESifo Working Paper No. 5418, Jun 2015.
Anderson, S.P., Ciliberto, F., Liaukonyte, J., 2013. Information content of advertising: empirical evidence from the OTC analgesic industry. Int. J. Ind. Organ. 31 (5), 355–367.
Anderson, S.P., Baik, A., Larson, N., 2014. Personalized Pricing and Advertising: An Asymmetric Equilibrium Analysis. CEPR Discussion Papers 10464.
Arbatskaya, M., 2007. Ordered search. RAND J. Econ. 38 (1), 119–126.
Armstrong, M., Vickers, J., Zhou, J., 2009. Prominence and consumer search. RAND J. Econ. 40 (2), 209–233.
Athey, S., Ellison, G., 2011. Position auctions with consumer search. Q. J. Econ. 126 (3), 1213–1270.
Bagwell, K., 2007. The economic analysis of advertising. In: Armstrong, M., Porter, R. (Eds.), Handbook of Industrial Organization, vol. 3, Elsevier, pp. 1701–1844.
Bagwell, K., Ramey, G., 1994a. Coordination economies, advertising, and search behavior in retail markets. Am. Econ. Rev. 84, 498–517.
Bagwell, K., Ramey, G., 1994b. Advertising and coordination. Rev. Econ. Stud. 61, 153–172.
Bain, J.S., 1956. Barriers to New Competition: Their Character and Consequences in Manufacturing Industries. Harvard University Press, Cambridge, MA.

Balestrieri, F., Izmalkov, S., 2012. Informed Seller in a Hotelling Market. Mimeo, New Economic School.

Barigozzi, F., Garella, P.G., Peitz, M., 2009. With a little help from my enemy: comparative advertising as a signal of quality. J. Econ. Manag. Strateg. 18 (4), 1071–1094.

Bar-Isaac, H., Caruana, G., Cuñat, V., 2010. Information gathering and marketing. J. Econ. Manag. Strateg. 19 (2), 375–401.

Barroso, A., Llobet, G., 2012. Advertising and consumer awareness of new, differentiated products. J. Market. Res. 49 (6), 773–792.

Becker, G.S., Murphy, K.M., 1993. A simple theory of advertising as a good or bad. Q. J. Econ. 108, 942–964.

Ben Elhadj-Ben Brahim, N., Lahmandi-Ayed, R., Laussel, D., 2011. Is targeted advertising always beneficial? Int. J. Ind. Organ. 29 (6), 678–689.

Bergemann, D., Vlimki, J., 2006. Dynamic pricing of new experience goods. J. Polit. Econ. 114 (4), 713–743.

Berry, S., Levinsohn, J., Pakes, A., 1995. Automobile prices in market equilibrium. Econometrica 63, 841–890.

Bertrand, M., Karlan, D., Mullainathan, S., Shafir, E., Zinman, J., 2010. What's advertising content worth? Evidence from a consumer credit marketing field experiment. Q. J. Econ. 125 (1), 263–306.

Board, O., 2009. Competition and disclosure. J. Ind. Econ. 57 (1), 197–213.

Braithwaite, D., 1928. The economic effects of advertisement. Econ. J. 38, 1637.

Burdett, K., Judd, K.L., 1983. Equilibrium price dispersion. Econometrica 51, 955–969.

Butters, G., 1977. Equilibrium distributions of sales and advertising prices. Rev. Econ. Stud. 44, 465–491.

Celik, L., 2014. Information unraveling revisited: disclosure of horizontal attributes. J. Ind. Econ. 62 (1), 113–136.

Chakraborty, A., Harbaugh, R., 2010. Persuasion by cheap talk. Am. Econ. Rev. 100, 2361–2382.

Chakraborty, A., Harbaugh, R., 2014. Persuasive puffery. Market. Sci. 33 (3), 382–400.

Chamberlin, E., 1933. The Theory of Monopolistic Competition. Harvard University Press, Cambridge, MA.

Chen, Y., He, C., 2011. Paid placement: advertising and search on the internet. Econ. J. 121, F309–F328.

Choi, D.O., 2014. Internet Advertising with Information Congestion: An Empirical Investigation. Mimeo, Université de Cergy-Pontoise.

Christou, C., Vettas, N., 2008. On informative advertising and product differentiation. Int. J. Ind. Organ. 26 (1), 92–112.

Chwe, M., 2001. Rational Ritual: Culture, Coordination, and Common Knowledge. Princeton University Press, Princeton, NJ.

Clark, C., Horstmann, I., 2005. Advertising and coordination in markets with consumption scale effects. J. Econ. Manag. Strateg. 14, 377–401.

Clark, C.R., Doraszelski, U., Draganska, M., 2009. The effect of advertising on brand awareness and perceived quality: an empirical investigation using panel data. QME 7 (2), 207–236.

Comanor, W.S., Wilson, T.A., 1967. Advertising, market structure and performance. Rev. Econ. Stat. 49, 423–440.

Comanor, W.S., Wilson, T.A., 1974. Advertising and Market Power. Harvard University Press, Cambridge, MA.

Corts, K., 2013. Prohibitions on false and unsubstantiated claims: inducing the acquisition and revelation of information through competition policy. J. Law Econ. 56, 453–486.

De Cornière, A., 2013. Search Advertising. Mimeo, Oxford University.

Deighton, J., Henderson, C.M., Neslin, S.A., 1994. The effects of advertising on brand switching and repeat purchasing. J. Market. Res. 31, 28–43.

Diamond, P.A., 1971. A model of price adjustment. J. Econ. Theory 3 (2), 156–168.

Dixit, A., Norman, V., 1978. Advertising and welfare. Bell J. Econ. 9, 1–17.

Dorfman, R., Steiner, P.O., 1954. Optimal advertising and optimal quality. Am. Econ. Rev. 44, 826–836.

Drugov, M., Martinez, M.T., 2012. Vague Lies: How to Advise Consumers When They Complain. Mimeo. CEPR DP 9201.

Dubé, J.P., Hitsch, G.J., Manchanda, P., 2005. An empirical model of advertising dynamics. Quant. Market. Econ. 3 (2), 107–144.

Dubois, P., Grifith, R., OConnell, M., 2014. The Effects of Banning Advertising on Demand, Supply and Welfare: Structural Estimation on a Junk Food Market. Mimeo, Toulouse School of Economics.

Dukes, A.J., 2006. Advertising and competition. In: Collins, W.D., Angland, J. (Eds.), Issues in Competition Law and Policy 515. ABA Section of Antitrust Law, Chicago, pp. 515–537.

Edelman, B., Ostrovsky, M., Schwarz, M., 2007. Internet Advertising and the generalized second price auction: selling billions of dollars worth of keywords. Am. Econ. Rev. 97 (1), 242–259.

Ellison, G., Wolitzky, A., 2012. A search cost model of obfuscation. RAND J. Econ. 43 (3), 417–441.

Emons, W., Fluet, C., 2012. Non-comparative versus comparative advertising of quality. Int. J. Ind. Organ. 30 (4), 352–360.

Erdem, T., Keane, M., 1996. Decision-making under uncertainty: capturing dynamic brand choice processes in turbulent consumer goods markets. Market. Sci. 15, 1–20.

Esteban, L., Gil, A., Hernandez, J.M., 2001. Informative advertising and optimal targeting in a monopoly. J. Ind. Econ. 49, 161–180.

Gabaix, X., Laibson, D., 2006. Shrouded attributes, consumer myopia, and information suppression in competitive markets. Q. J. Econ. 121, 505–540.

Galbraith, J.K., 1958. The Affluent Society. Houghton-Mifflin, Co., Boston, MA.

Gardete, P.M., 2013. Cheap-talk advertising and misrepresentation in vertically differentiated markets. Mark. Sci. 32 (4), 609–621.

Geanakoplos, J., 1989. Game theory without partitions, and applications to speculation and consensus. J. Econ. Theory.

Glaeser, E.L., Ujhelyi, G., 2010. Regulating misinformation. J. Public Econ. 94 (3), 247–257.

Grossman, S.J., 1981. The informational role of warranties and private disclosure about product quality. J. Law Econ. 24, 461–483.

Grossman, S.J., Hart, O.D., 1980. Disclosure laws and takeover bids. J. Finance 35 (2), 323–334.

Grossman, G.M., Shapiro, C., 1984. Informative advertising with differentiated products. Rev. Econ. Stud. 51, 63–81.

Haan, M.A., Moraga-González, J.L., 2011. Advertising for attention in a consumer search model. Econ. J. 121 (552), 552–579.

Hamilton, S.F., 2009. Informative advertising in differentiated oligopoly markets. Int. J. Ind. Organ. 27 (1), 60–69.

Heifetz, A., Meier, M., Schipper, B.C., 2006. Interactive unawareness. J. Econ. Theory 130 (1), 78–94.

Heifetz, A., Meier, M., Schipper, B., 2011. Prudent Rationalizability in Generalized Extensive-Form Games. Working Papers, No. 11, 4. University of California, Department of Economics.

Hertzendorf, M., 1993. I am not a high-quality firm But I play one on TV. RAND J. Econ. 24, 236–247.

Holcomb, J., 2014. News Revenue Declines Despite Growth from New Sources. Pew Research Center, Washington DC. http://www.pewresearch.org/fact-tank/2014/04/03/news-revenue-declines-despite-growth-from-new-sources/.

Horstmann, I.J., MacDonald, G.M., 2003. Is advertising a signal of product quality? Evidence from the compact disc player market, 198392. Int. J. Ind. Organ. 21, 317–345.

Hotelling, H., 1929. Stability in competition. Econ. J. 39, 41–57.

Ippolito, P.M., Mathios, A.D., 1990. Information, advertising and health choices: a study of the cereal market. RAND J. Econ. 21, 459–480.

Iyer, G., Soberman, D., Villas-Boas, J.M., 2005. The targeting of advertising. Market. Sci. 24 (3), 461–476.

Janssen, M.C.W., Teteryanikova, M., 2014. Competition and disclosure of comparative or non-comparative horizontal product information. J. Ind. Econ. (forthcoming).

Johnson, J.P., 2013. Targeted advertising and advertising avoidance. RAND J. Econ. 44 (1), 128–144.

Johnson, J.P., Myatt, D.P., 2006. On the simple economics of advertising, marketing, and product design. Am. Econ. Rev. 96, 756–784.

Jovanovic, B., 1982. Truthful disclosure of information. Bell J. Econ. 13, 36–44.

Kaldor, N.V., 1950. The economic aspects of advertising. Rev. Econ. Stud. 18, 127.

Kihlstrom, R.E., Riordan, M.H., 1984. Advertising as a signal. J. Polit. Econ. 92, 427–450.

Koessler, F., Renault, R., 2012. When does a firm disclose product information? RAND J. Econ. 43 (4), 630–649.

Koessler, F., Skreta, V., 2014. Sales Talk. Mimeo, Paris School of Economics. Available at SSRN 2465174.

Kreps, D.M., Wilson, R., 1982. Sequential equilibria. Econometrica 50, 863–894.

Lambin, J.J., 1976. Advertising, Competition and Market Conduct in Oligopoly Over Time. North-Holland, Amsterdam.

Lauga, D., 2012. Advertising with Impressionable but Sophisticated Consumer. Mimeo, Cambridge Judge Business School.

Lewis, T.R., Sappington, D.E.M., 1994. Supplying information to facilitate price discrimination. Int. Econ. Rev. 35, 309–327.

Liaukonyte, J., 2012. Is Comparative Advertising an Active Ingredient in the Market for Pain Relief? Mimeo, Cornell University.

Linnemer, L., 2002. Price and advertising as signals of quality when some consumers are informed. Int. J. Ind. Organ. 20 (7), 931–947.

Linnemer, L., 2012. Dissipative advertising signals quality: static model with a continuum of types. Econ. Lett. 114 (2), 150–153.

Luca, M., 2015. User generated content and social media. In: Anderson, S.P., Strömberg, D., Waldfogel, J. (Eds.), Handbook of Media Economics, vol. 1B. Elsevier, Amsterdam.

Mailath, G.J., Okuno-Fujiwara, M., Postlewaite, A., 1993. Belief-based refinements in signalling games. J. Econ. Theory 60 (2), 241–276.

Manduchi, A., 2013. Non-neutral information costs with match-value uncertainty. J. Econ. 109 (1), 1–25.

Marshall, A., 1890. Principles of Economics. MacMillan and Co., London.

Marshall, A., 1919. Industry and Trade: A Study of Industrial Technique and Business Organization; and of Their Influences on the Conditions of Various Classes and Nations. MacMillan and Co., London.

Mayzlin, D., Shin, J., 2011. Uninformative advertising as an invitation to search. Market. Sci. 30 (4), 666–685.

Meurer, M., Stahl II, D.O., 1994. Informative advertising and product match. Int. J. Ind. Organ. 12, 119.

Milgrom, P.R., 1981. Good news and bad news: representation theorems and applications. Bell J. Econ. 12, 380–391.

Milgrom, P., Roberts, J., 1986. Price and advertising signals of product quality. J. Polit. Econ. 94, 796–821.

Moraga-Gonzalez, J.L., 2000. Quality uncertainty and informative advertising. Int. J. Ind. Organ. 18, 615–640.

Mullainathan, S., Schwartzstein, J., Shleifer, A., 2008. Coarse thinking and persuasion*. Q. J. Econ. 123 (2), 577–619.

Nelson, P., 1970. Information and consumer behavior. J. Polit. Econ. 78, 311–329.

Nelson, P., 1974. Advertising as information. J. Polit. Econ. 82, 729–754.

Nerlove, M., Arrow, K.J., 1962. Optimal advertising policy under dynamic conditions. Economica 29, 129–142.

Nichols, L.M., 1985. Advertising and economic welfare. Am. Econ. Rev. 75, 213–218.

Overgaard, P.B., 1991. Product Quality Uncertainty. CORE, Universite Catholique de Louvain Unpublished Ph.D. Thesis.

Ozga, S.A., 1960. Imperfect markets through lack of knowledge. Q. J. Econ. 74, 29–52.

Pastine, I., Pastine, T., 2002. Consumption externalities, coordination and advertising. Int. Econ. Rev. 43, 919–943.

Peitz, M., Reisinger, M., 2015. The economics of internet media. In: Anderson, S., Strömberg, D., Waldfogel, J. (Eds.), Handbook of Media Economics, vol. 1A. Elsevier, Amsterdam.

Piccolo, S., Tedeschi, P., Ursino, G., 2015. How limiting deceptive practices harms consumers. Rand J. Econ. 46, 611–624.

Porter, M.E., 1976. Interbrand choice, media mix and market performance. Am. Econ. Rev. 66, 398–406.

Renault, R., 2014. Platform Contents. Mimeo, Université Paris-Dauphine.

Resnik, A., Stern, B., 1977. An analysis of the information content in television advertising. J. Mark. 41, 50–53.

Rhodes, A., 2015. Multiproduct retailing. Rev. Econ. Stud. 82, 360–390.

Rhodes, A., Wilson, C., 2014. False Advertising and Consumer Protection Policy. Mimeo, Loughborough University.

Robert, J., Stahl II, D.O., 1993. Informative price advertising in a sequential search model. Econometrica 61, 657–686.

Roberts, M.J., Samuelson, L., 1988. An empirical analysis of dynamic, nonprice competition in an oligopolistic industry. RAND J. Econ. 19, 200–220.

Robinson, J., 1933. Economics of Imperfect Competition. MacMillan and Co., London.

Saak, A.E., 2006. The optimal private information in single unit monopoly. Econ. Lett. 91 (2), 267–272.

Saak, A.E., 2012. Dynamic informative advertising of new experience goods. J. Ind. Econ. 60 (1), 104–135.

Schmalensee, R., 1978. A model of advertising and product quality. J. Polit. Econ. 86, 485–503.

Shaked, A., Sutton, J., 1982. Relaxing price competition through product differentiation. Rev. Econ. Stud. 49, 3–13.

Shapiro, C., 1980. Advertising and welfare: comment. Bell J. Econ. 11, 749–752.

Shin, H.S., 1994. The burden of proof in a game of persuasion. J. Econ. Theory 64 (1), 253–264.

Sovinsky-Goeree, M., 2008. Limited information and advertising in the US personal computer industry. Econometrica 76 (5), 1017–1074.

Spence, M., 1975. Monopoly, quality and regulation. Bell J. Econ. 6, 417–429.

Spence, M., 1976. Product selection, fixed costs, and monopolistic competition. Rev. Econ. Stud. 43, 217–235.

Stahl II, D.O., 1994. Oligopolistic pricing and advertising. J. Econ. Theory 64, 162–177.

Stegeman, M., 1986. Essays in Search and Speculation. Ph.D. Dissertation. Massachusetts Institute of Technology, Cambridge, MA.

Stegeman, M., 1991. Advertising in competitive markets. Am. Econ. Rev. 81, 210–223.

Stigler, G.J., 1961. The economics of information. J. Polit. Econ. 69, 213–225.

Stigler, G.J., Becker, G.S., 1977. De gustibus non est disputandum. Am. Econ. Rev. 67 (76), 90.

Stiglitz, J.E., 1979. Equilibrium in product markets with imperfect information. Am. Econ. Rev. 69, 339–345.

Sun, M., 2011. Disclosing multiple product attributes. J. Econ. Manag. Strateg. 20 (1), 195–224.

Telser, L.G., 1964. Advertising and competition. J. Polit. Econ. 72, 537–562.

Tirole, J., 1988. The Theory of Industrial Organization. MIT Press, Cambridge, MA.

Van Zandt, T., 2004. Information overload in a network of targeted communication. RAND J. Econ. 35, 542–560.

Varian, H.R., 2007. Position auctions. Int. J. Ind. Organ. 25 (6), 1163–1178.

Wang, C., 2014. Advertising as a Search Deterrent. Mimeo, University of Mannheim.

Wilson, C., 2010. Ordered search and equilibrium obfuscation. Int. J. Indust. Org. 28, 496–506.

Wolinsky, A., 1986. True monopolistic competition as a result of imperfect information. Q. J. Econ. 101, 493–511.

Zhou, J., 2011. Ordered search in differentiated markets. Int. J. Ind. Organ. 29 (2), 253–262.

CHAPTER 5

Recent Developments in Mass Media: Digitization and Multitasking

Kenneth C. Wilbur
Rady School of Management, University of California, San Diego, CA, USA

Contents

Abstract

Technology and consumer behavior are changing supply and demand for mass media. Digitization has increased consumer control over media content and advertising, with implications for advertising avoidance, advertising targeting and personalization, competition among media platforms, and media market outcomes. In addition, consumers increasingly use a "second screen" to multitask during media programs, enabling immediate online response to program and advertising content, but also offering new opportunities to divert attention. This chapter presents recent data showing that video has remained the dominant mass medium and establishing the prevalence of digitization and multitasking behavior. It then selectively reviews academic research on the antecedents and consequences of the changing picture of mass media consumption, with a particular focus on the past 5–10 years.

Keywords

Advertising, Internet, Marketing, Mass media, Media economics, Television

JEL Codes

J22, L82, L96, M30, M37

Handbook of Media Economics, Volume 1A
ISSN 2213-6630, http://dx.doi.org/10.1016/B978-0-444-62721-6.00005-6

Consumers devote more than half of all available leisure time to mass media. The purpose of this chapter is to survey recent changes in mass media consumption and research, with a particular focus on the past 5–10 years. I begin with recent data on time and advertising revenue allocations across mass media. I then selectively review academic research on how two important trends—digitization and consumer multitasking—are changing mass media industries.

To set boundaries on this review, this chapter considers mass media to be one-to-many means of communication that convey information and entertainment of primarily ephemeral value. I say "primarily ephemeral" in anticipation that, although there will be a few enduring hits, the large majority of mass media content will be consumed immediately upon, or shortly after, its distribution. For example, while some television series are archived by services like Amazon, Hulu, and Netflix, these series constitute a small fraction of the tens of thousands of hours of new television content created and distributed each year.

This definition of mass media includes television, radio, newspapers, magazines, and many other forms of digital audio, text, and video communications. However, "one-to-many" excludes personal communications services like telephony, email, search engines, and (arguably) social networks and most other forms of user-generated content. Entertainment and information content distinguish mass media from those that focus on purely commercial communications such as yellow pages or product review sites. Ephemerality excludes most books, movies, and video games, as the consumption value of these media seems to diminish more slowly with time (despite a few prominent exceptions).

Mass media industries share a particular set of economic characteristics which often distinguishes their analysis from more conventional economic settings:

- Mass media products are experience goods that are non-rival in consumption and differ in both quality and match value (i.e., horizontally and vertically differentiated product characteristics). Mass media tend to be "hits" industries in which small oligopolies of multiproduct firms compete for consumer attention.

- Many mass media recently shifted from analog to digital distribution, replacing the traditional one-way flow of information with a two-way exchange between providers and consumers. Digitization changes the information that media platforms can learn about how their consumers consume and respond to content and advertising.

- Mass media are operated as platform businesses that enable interactions between consumers and advertisers. Advertisers are charged piece rates for audiences or bundles or audiences. Consumers are normally charged a mixture of subscription fees and attention devoted to advertising interruptions. Multitasking threatens the availability of attention for advertisements, and digitization has increased control over consumer exposure to advertising.

The next section uses recent market data to establish a few facts about mass media consumption and the importance of digitization and consumer multitasking with media. Section 5.2

reviews some recent academic literature about the implications of digitization for consumer control over advertising exposure, advertising targeting, innovations in traditional media business models, and media market outcomes. Section 5.3 presents research about how multitasking—sometimes called "second screening"—is altering advertising consumption, media complementarities, and competition among media for consumer attention. The final section concludes with some directions for future research.

5.1. RECENT TRENDS IN MASS MEDIA CONSUMPTION

Before looking at media consumption data, one must first evaluate the potential sources of information. Broadly speaking, there are three types of media consumption data: measurements based on self-reports, measurements provided by media outlets, and measurements provided by third parties that are financed by media outlets.

Self-reports are known to be imperfect. Respondents may have imperfect knowledge of their own media consumption or may be unwilling to divulge it accurately. A story is often told within business schools about South American countries' switch from Nielsen diaries (self-reports) to PeopleMeters (a passive tracking device that measures television usage). After Nielsen adopted PeopleMeters, audience ratings of lowbrow comedy programs rose substantially and news programs' audience estimates fell. It seems unlikely that the change in measurement technology actually corresponded to a change in viewing habits.

In contrast to self-reports, some media companies measure and report their own audience. However, these measurements are imperfect and may be biased. For example, a magazine may know precisely how many issues it sells at retail and mails to subscribers each month. However, it does not know how many of those magazines go unread or how many are circulated to additional people after purchase. More importantly, the magazine's advertising price is likely to vary with audience size. Therefore, the magazine may want to inflate its audience report and to suppress information that might harm advertising sales.

Recognizing this incentive problem, traditional mass media industries use third-party arbiters to measure audience sizes. These organizations maintain representative samples and try to measure media usage passively. In television, Nielsen Media Research has been the de facto ratings monopoly for decades. Arbitron serves a similar function in radio. Print media report audience numbers through the Audit Bureau of Circulations. However, these third-party institutions rely primarily on the media industries for their operating budgets and rarely report information contrary to their media clients' interests. No similar set of authoritative third parties has emerged to validate audience sizes in online mass media industries.[1]

---

[1] See Wilbur and Zhu (2009) for further discussion in the context of click fraud and the search engine industry.

With these caveats in mind, I begin by looking at self-reports. The Bureau of Labor Statistics' American Time Use Survey (ATUS) surveys a stratified subsample of 7000 members of the Current Population Survey about how they spend their time. Typically 53–58% of those surveyed respond. Figure 5.1 summarizes the major categories of leisure activity in the survey.

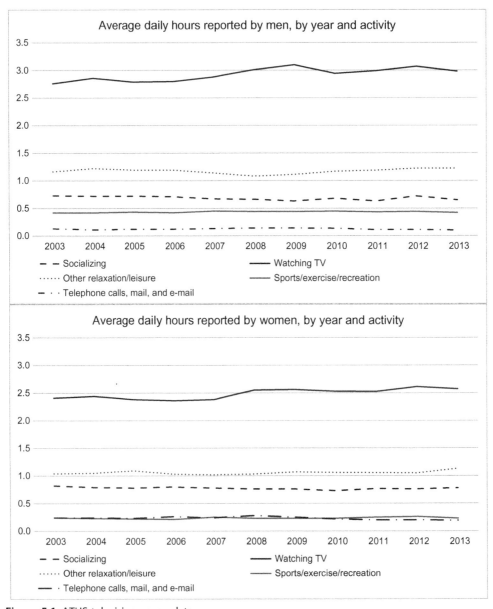

Figure 5.1 ATUS television usage data.

Two conclusions emerge. First, American consumers say they spend more than 10% of all available time, and more than 50% of their relaxation/leisure time, watching TV. (The "watching TV" category does not distinguish video consumption by source, such as traditional TV, Video on Demand, or Internet Video.) Second, viewers' reported daily video consumption time did not diminish between 2003 and 2013. If anything, video consumption rose slightly between 2003 and 2009, continuing a 50-year trend documented by Robinson and Martin (2009).

In contrast to the ATUS telephone survey, Nielsen measures television usage continuously within a stratified sample of about 37,000 households. It uses PeopleMeters to record television usage; these devices connect to the television in order to passively measure usage and tuning. The PeopleMeter augments the device-level usage information by requiring viewers to "log in" via remote control when prompted (every 20–40 min on average).

TVB (2014) and Nielsen (2014a) report figures that are interesting to compare to the ATUS data. Nielsen reports nearly twice as much television usage time as ATUS: 4.9 h per day in 2009 for American adult men, and 5.52 h per day for American adult females. The Nielsen figures corroborate the gradual rise in average daily television usage through the 2003–2009 period.

I see four possible explanations for the near-100% difference in the self-reported data and the PeopleMeter data. First, perhaps viewers do not know their actual television usage. Second, perhaps they know it, but prefer to report less than the true figure. Third, there may be multiple ways to "watch television"—e.g., as a focal activity or a peripheral activity. Perhaps viewers count focal usage time but Nielsen counts both focal and peripheral usage time. Fourth, sample selection may skew either estimate. For example, some experts believe that frequent television viewers are more likely to enroll and remain in the Nielsen sample.

I have conducted independent investigations of television usage data collected passively via digital Set-Top Boxes (STBs) by four independent companies. In order to measure daily television usage from STB records, the analyst must define a "bounce"—some time threshold at which an inactive session is assumed to terminate (a similar issue applies to measuring consumer time spent on Internet webpages). For example, if an STB is tuned to ESPN for 24 h, it is unlikely to indicate 24 h of continuous television usage. A more likely explanation is that the consumer turned off the television at some point after tuning to ESPN, but never turned off the STB. I have found that defining a bounce as about 35–45 min produced daily usage estimates comparable to Nielsen figures. Interestingly, Google (2012) claims that the average television tuning event lasts 43 min. In my view, this lends some support to the Nielsen viewing statistics.

A second measure of mass media importance is advertising revenue. Here too, television appears to be the most important mass medium. TVB (2014) reports a cross-media comparison of Kantar Media advertising data. The TVB analysis shows that television attracted about 54.4% of mass media advertising dollars, followed by newspapers

(11.7%) and Internet display (9.8%). BI (2013) summarized advertising sales revenues reported by 20 large corporations, reporting that, since 2009 at least, the large increase in online advertising revenues (including 43% from search advertising) is coming from (i) new advertising expenditures and (ii) at the expense of newspapers. It appears that aggregate television and radio advertising revenues changed little between 2009 and 2012.

A third gauge of media importance is subscription revenues. In summary, about 97% of all US households contain televisions and 87% of American households subscribe to some multichannel video service (cable, satellite, or telco), generating $95.36 billion in subscription revenues (Digital TV Research, 2014). This figure far exceeds the subscription revenue earned by any competing mass medium. However, there are some forecasts that new subscription growth will fall below the rate of new household formation, and that revenues will fall in future years as telcos such as Verizon and AT&T intensify price competition with incumbent cable and satellite companies.

A fourth way to consider the importance of various mass media is to ask consumers about their perceptions. eMarketer (2012) surveyed consumers and found that 45.2% said they trust television most as a source of news and information, followed by newspapers (20.4%), radio (17.7%), Internet-only news sources (12.5%), and social media updates (4.1%). However, when asked which sources most influence brand purchase decisions, Internet research is named most frequently (61.1%), followed by TV ads (28.3%) and radio ads (20.9%).

The sum of the data indicates that television is the most important mass medium, at least in terms of consumer attention and expenditure, with limited indications of any imminent change in position. However, two trends are changing video mass media in fundamental ways. On the supply side, *digitization* is changing the way television signals are distributed and increasing consumers' programming options. On the demand side, *screen proliferation* is changing the way television signals are consumed, making attention ever scarcer.

5.1.1 Digitization

The shift from analog to digital distribution of television signals is still fairly recent. In 2004, only 40% of US households received TV signals over digital networks; by 2011, that figure had risen above 83% (TVB, 2014).

A similar shift toward digitization has occurred in other mass media. Newspapers and magazine articles are distributed online through websites and applications on mobile devices. Terrestrial radio stations are broadcast simultaneously online and through mobile applications like "iHeartRadio." This shift has three major consequences: audience fragmentation, personalization, and increased usage information.

Digital signals require less bandwidth to convey than analog signals, so the immediate effect of digitization has been to dramatically increase the amount of mass media content available to consumers. This increase in choice has fragmented the audience. This effect is easiest to observe in television, as national broadcast networks' share of total viewing fell from 41% in 2003 to 25% in 2013 (CAB, 2014).[2] However, because total video consumption has not fallen, this loss of attention at the head of the distribution has been reallocated to more niche-oriented competitors, i.e., national cable networks.

The second consequence of digitization has been to increase consumer control over media content. An early example was the digital video recorder, which can now be found in about 47% of American households (up from 3% in 2004; LRG, 2013). The primary effect of DVR ownership is to increase the consumer's control over media, enabling such activities as time-shifting and fast-forwarding past advertisements (Wilbur, 2008).

The other way personalization impacts television consumption is by enabling video streaming services. Such "Over-The-Top" (OTT) video services have become prevalent. Nielsen (2013) estimates that 38% of US households have used Netflix, 18% have used Hulu, and 13% have used Amazon Prime Instant Video. Leichtman Research Group (2014) surveyed consumers about three personalization technologies—digital video recorders, video on demand, and Netflix—finding that 70% of American homes used at least one of those three services regularly and another one-third of households used two or more.

Perhaps the most interesting study of OTT services was reported by TiVo (2013). TiVo surveyed 9956 of its customers about their Netflix and Amazon Prime subscriptions and then analyzed those households' (passively measured) usage of the TiVo STB. Fifty-seven percent of TiVo subscribers reported patronizing Netflix, and 50% reported subscribing to Amazon Prime Video. However, there was no statistically significant difference in television usage time between self-reported Netflix subscribers and non-subscribers. These non-differences led TiVo to conclude that "Netflix does not appear to cannibalize traditional TV."

The final implication of signal digitization is that it changes wired distribution network from one-way to two-way, enabling the signal distributor to observe how consumers interact with media. For example, newspaper publishers are able to easily measure viewer attention to stories published online but not in printed newspapers. A similar shift in audience information is also occurring within the television industry. Digital signal distributors are able to retrieve complete usage information from viewers' STBs. Even television manufacturers are selling appliances that upload return usage information to their manufacturers. Return-path data have had limited impact on the television industry to date, but several analyses reviewed below suggest that they may have important consequences in the future.

---

[2] Such figures are sometimes misinterpreted as evidence of weakness in demand for television, but such reports gloss over the fact that broadcast networks' losses are mostly recaptured by cable television networks.

5.1.2 Screen Proliferation

Along with digitization, the second fundamental shift in media consumption is *screen pro-liferation*. As computers have become smaller and more convenient, sales of new form factors have risen rapidly. In the US, smartphone penetration reached 74% in 2013 and tablet ownership rose to 52% (Sahagian, 2013). In the UK, smartphone and tablet penetration rose to 51% and 24%, respectively in 2013 (Ofcom, 2013).

Smartphones and tablets are capable of receiving mass media, but this does not seem to be their primary use. Fetto (2013) reports that the typical smartphone owner in America spends about an hour per day using the device. Seventy-one percent of usage time is spent on talk, text, e-mail, and social networking. Only about 14% of usage is spent visiting websites, suggesting that mass media consumption via smartphone is less than 10 min per day.

Although smartphones and tablets are not a major vehicle for mass media consumption in the US, they nonetheless are affecting mass media consumption in fundamental ways. According to numerous recent surveys, consumers increasingly use these devices to multitask while viewing television. For example, Nielsen (2010) claimed that 34% of all Internet usage time occurred simultaneously with television consumption. Ofcom (2013) found that 81% of all tablet owners, and 53% of UK adults overall, say that they multitask by using mobile devices during television programs on a weekly basis. The most frequent self-reported media multitaskers are young, female, and high income.

The "second screen" (a tablet, smartphone, laptop, or even a desktop) may serve as either a complement or a substitute to traditional television. According to Google (2012), there are two modes consumers use while multitasking with television: simultaneous usage and sequential usage. In simultaneous usage, the viewer divides attention between unrelated activities on the two devices, for example, playing a video game during a commercial break or checking email while the television plays in the background. Consumers report that 78% of media multitasking time is spent on simultaneous usage.

The remaining 22% of media multitasking is sequential usage. This behavior can be related to either television programs or advertisements. For example, the phenomenon of posting messages about programs on social networks (e.g., Facebook or Twitter) has become sufficiently common that some practitioners now refer to it as "social television." According to Nielsen (2014b), 36% of Australian adults reported interacting with fellow viewers on social networks during or shortly after television programs they watched, up from 31% the previous year.

Sequential usage can also be driven by television advertising. Google (2012) found that 17% of multitasking search occasions were prompted by a television commercial. Television viewers can also respond to advertisements by visiting a retailer to gather product information or make an impulse purchase.

In summary, digitization and media multitasking appear to be fairly prevalent and increasingly important. The next two sections summarize recent academic research on how these two trends are changing mass media markets.

5.2. EFFECTS OF DIGITIZATION

Scholars have studied how the shift from analog to digital distribution of mass media is affecting consumers, advertisers, and media platforms. For consumers, the most studied phenomena are the increased control digitization offers by, for example, allowing consumers to selectively avoid advertisements. For advertisers, the two-way nature of digital media networks enhances their ability to target their messages to consumers. For media content platforms, digital signal delivery offers new business models. Taken as a whole, these effects change the nature of competition in mass media markets and the range of products provided.

5.2.1 Consumer Control over Advertising Exposure

A burgeoning empirical literature documents how increased viewer control has affected viewers' exposure to advertising.[3] Esteves-Sorenson and Perretti (2012) found that television remains largely a passive activity, with strong state persistence despite the small cost of switching channels. However, viewers do switch when they are annoyed by commercials. Interian et al. (2009) analyzed a large dataset of tuneaway behavior during commercials, showing that the typical advertisement loses 1–3% of the audience at the beginning of the ad slot. Schweidel and Kent (2010) presented moment-by-moment viewing data culled from digital STBs showing that program ratings fall by an average of 10% during ad breaks and that program genre can reliably predict audience retention during commercial breaks. Wilbur (2015) investigated household-level zapping behavior and found that advertising content characteristics reliably predict commercial avoidance, after controlling for program content, audience composition, and audience heterogeneity. Movie ads were zapped less often than average while auto insurance and website commercials were avoided more frequently. Tuchman et al. (2015) report that the median household in their data skips about 10% of the ads that it is exposed to.

Have elevated levels of advertising avoidance diminished the profitability of advertising? The limited evidence available suggests that the answer may be no. Zufryden et al. (1993) surprisingly found that ad exposures interrupted by zapping were more strongly associated with sales than uninterrupted exposures; they hypothesized that this difference was due to viewers' heightened attention while changing channels. More recently, Bronnenberg et al. (2010) examined data produced by a field study in which digital video recorders were given to households in a scanner panel data sample. Households' advertising exposures and brand purchases in the following year were compared to baseline

---

[3] It is important to remember that advertising avoidance is as old as advertising; Wilbur (2008) reviewed the literature on traditional modes of avoiding ads, which included leaving the room, muting the television, changing channels, or diverting attention to other activities, or engaging in conversation.

brand purchases in the previous year. The confidence interval for the effect of DVR acquisition on advertising effectiveness was tightly centered around zero, suggesting no diminution in advertising effectiveness, a result they attributed to fairly low rates of advertising avoidance among panelists.

Is this a puzzle? As advertising avoidance has gotten easier, commercial avoidance seems to become more frequent. Yet there is no evidence of diminished advertising effectiveness, and television advertising revenues have not fallen. There are three possible explanations. One is that advertisements may be designed to retain their effectiveness, even when played at high speed. For example, prominent displays of the brand logo reduce advertising avoidance (Teixeira et al., 2010), and can increase brand attitude, intention to purchase, and choice behavior (Brasel and Gips, 2008). A second possibility, which to the best of my knowledge remains unexplored, is that perhaps households do not avoid ads when they are in the market for the advertised product. In other words, an advertisement exposure that a consumer actively chooses to avoid might have offered little value to the advertiser in the event of an exposure. Further, many commercials are repeated with such frequency that even frequent ad-avoiders may receive some minimum number of exposures to the most common commercials. The third possibility is that (at least some) ads may be complements to product consumption, as originally proposed by Becker and Murphy (1993). Tuchman et al. (2015) investigated this possibility using a single-source panel database of purchases and advertising exposures. They found that greater recent brand consumption led to a lower probability of zapping the brand's television advertisement in the future.

A number of theoretical analyses have produced competing predictions about how increased levels of advertising avoidance will affect media markets. Anderson and Gans (2011) modeled a monopoly platform and examined how consumer adoption of advertising avoidance technology would alter its strategy. In equilibrium, consumers who value programming the most adopt advertising avoidance technology first, leading to rising advertising time, falling welfare and content quality, and more mass-market content. Athey et al. (2013) extended this framework to allow for competing outlets, imperfect measurement of advertising exposure, and endogenous multihoming by advertisers. As consumer switching increases, advertising levels rise and the premium paid for large audience increases, but total advertising expenditure falls.[4] In contrast, Ghosh and Stock (2010) did not model media platforms but they did consider the effect of informative advertisements on price competition in the product market. In their model, advertising avoidance leads to some consumer ignorance, which can sometimes increase advertisers' product prices and profits in equilibrium, raising the demand for advertising.

---

[4] See also Chapter 10.

5.2.2 Increased Targeting of Advertising

Digital distribution networks enable media platforms to identify individual recipients of programs and to choose the level of targeting offered to advertisers. Media vary in the targeting capabilities they offer. For example, television signal distributors could theoretically sell commercial breaks personalized to individual households, but they have so far only engaged in limited tests of more-aggregated targeting based on geodemographic segments (Deng, 2015). Most mass media platforms online allow varying degrees of audience targeting.

Bergemann and Bonatti (2011, 2014), Dukes and Gal-Or (2003), and Ghosh et al. (2013) highlight the essential trade-offs in platforms' choice of ad targeting capabilities.[5] Untargeted advertising produces many low-value, wasted exposures because most consumers are uninterested in most products. Highly targeted advertising eliminates wasted exposures, but it increases advertiser competition in the product market, driving down rents and willingness to pay for advertising. Therefore, the media platform will optimally choose between offering some intermediate degree of ad targeting, or combining ad targeting with exclusive advertising rights.

Empirical evidence on the increased targeting of advertising is more scarce. Perhaps the best known papers are Goldfarb and Tucker (2011a,b). They first investigated several thousand randomized advertising experiments, showing that matching advertising content to site content or making advertisements more obtrusive each increases advertising effectiveness individually, but doing both in conjunction backfires. This effect is likely because consumers realize they are being targeted and react negatively, as the negative interaction was largest in sensitive product categories such as health and financial services. Second, they applied a difference-in-differences framework to estimate the effect of a European restriction in advertising targeting on advertising effectiveness. They compared post-policy European advertising response to pre-policy European advertising response, as well as to US advertising response in both periods. The results indicated that display advertising became far less effective, especially so on niche-oriented websites, for smaller advertisements, and for advertisements without obtrusive (e.g., interactive, video, audio) features.

5.2.3 New Media Business Models

Although it has long been known that advertising causes audience loss, television networks have never charged per unit of audience delivered. Nielsen audience estimates are too noisy to precisely estimate audience sizes by commercial. Instead, television networks have always charged per unit of time (i.e., per 30-s spot). Advertising sales

---

[5] See also Chapter 10.

contracts do include minimum audience thresholds, but these thresholds are often set approximately two standard deviations below the expected audience size. When Nielsen's point estimate of the audience size falls short of the promised level, then the network provides "make-goods"—free advertising inventory to compensate the advertiser for the difference between the minimum guaranteed audience size and the point estimate of the audience size.

The possibility of substantial inefficiencies in advertising sales arises because of a divergence in television advertisers and networks' interests. Advertisers seek to "break through the clutter" by getting their advertisements noticed, and therefore include obtrusive stimuli which help to gain attention and reinforce their selling message. These stimuli may be aversive to some viewers who are not in the market for the advertised good, leading them to change the channel or start fast-forwarding. Often, these viewers will miss the rest of the commercial break and possibly subsequent breaks as well. Therefore, the most effective ads (i.e., those that sell very effectively) may actually reduce the network's stock of viewer attention available for sale to other advertisers. This problem is exacerbated by television networks' traditional practice of ordering advertisements within the break on a quasi-random basis.

Goldstein et al. (2013) devised an ingenious test of this hypothesis. They first hired workers online to complete a standard email categorization task while simultaneously being exposed to banner advertisements. The workers were randomly assigned to one of three pay rates and one of three advertising conditions: no ads, annoying ads, or innocuous ads. The researchers then observed each worker's output, allowing them to estimate the compensating variation of the various types of advertising content. They found that innocuous ads and no ads led to approximately equal levels of worker output, but annoying ads led to faster task abandonment. To achieve the same rate of task abandonment as caused by annoying ads, the researchers would have had to reduce the workers' pay rate by approximately $1 per 1000 impressions. This effect exceeds the market price that many websites charge for display advertising. One might speculate the effect is even larger in the context of television, as video advertisements are substantially more obtrusive than banner advertisements.

Wilbur et al. (2013) note that the rapid proliferation of digital television signal delivery networks allows the possibility of redesigning television networks' business models to better align networks' and advertisers' interests. They designed an algorithm to select, order, and price advertisements in a commercial break of endogenous length. The main idea of the algorithm is to first find the selection and ordering of advertisements that maximizes total welfare of all advertisers in the commercial break. Doing so requires the use of dynamic programming to optimize the networks' opposing goals of retaining audience and allocating each slot in the break to the advertiser with the highest willingness to pay. Payments are assigned using a second-price auction to incentivize truthful bidding and to reward advertisers with low zapping rates.

The authors estimated the primitives of their model using market data and used a series of simulations to show that it consistently finds the globally optimal solution, increases advertiser welfare and network revenues, and runs fast enough to implement at scale.

5.2.4 Media Market Outcomes

Digitization of media distribution networks is changing media markets by lowering distribution and entry costs, by altering consumer discovery of new and niche products, and by changing the resulting range of product quality offered.

Digitization has brought dramatic change in print newspaper markets. George and Waldfogel (2006) studied the effects of entry and expansion by a high-quality national newspaper (the *New York Times*) into local newspaper markets in the United States. They found that readers targeted by the national newspaper tended to adopt it in place of local newspapers, and that local papers responded by increasing content appealing to the national newspaper's non-targeted segments.

The effects of digital distribution have been studied extensively in the context of consumer products. Brynjolfsson et al. (2011) found that online distribution produces a longer tail of product sales than physical distribution even holding the selection of available products constant. They attributed the increase in the size of the tail to the improved consumer search and recommendation engines enabled by digital delivery. On the other hand, Ellison and Wolitsky (2012) investigated how firms might respond to increased competition online by raising consumers' search costs. They showed that firms have incentives to obfuscate (e.g., complicate consumer evaluation of available options) when consumer search costs are convex in effort or when consumers have imperfect information about the exogenous components of search costs.

Waldfogel (2013) examined the joint impact of digitization on sales, production, and distribution costs, and product quality in the recorded music industry. Digitization triggered three substantial changes: music piracy increased, barriers to entry fell, and new modes of music discovery (e.g., Internet radio) were invented. The result was a sharp decrease in album production by traditional music labels, a huge influx of new producers, and a steadily increasing share of commercially successful albums coming from independent producers.

Anecdotally, the print newspaper industry has experienced some changes similar to those documented by Waldfogel (2013). A common question is whether similar changes will eventually occur in the television/video industry? In the author's view, one possible differentiator is that in online video, current bandwidth constraints bind tightly. Video consumption is too high, video program files are too large, and today's cable and telco networks are too slow for all consumers to simultaneously switch from consuming broadcast video to consuming individual video streams over home Internet connections without major delays and buffering.[6] However, if Internet connection speeds rise significantly (as seems bound to happen eventually, if not yet imminently), then I expect similar changes might occur in the television industry. However, in the presence of binding video distribution constraints, it seems possible that online video will continue to exist as a supplement to traditional television consumption, a channel for niche program demand, user-generated content, delayed releases of major networks' content, and a means for incumbent programmers to identify high-value production inputs.

5.3. EFFECTS OF MEDIA MULTITASKING

A consumer who is watching television has two primary motivations to multitask: (i) information search which has been prompted by something on the television screen or (ii) seeking refuge from aversive television content (such as advertising or boring parts of a program). I will refer to these as media complementarities and competition for attention, respectively.

Multitasking behavior has been studied in laboratory experiments and in-home observational studies. For example, Pearson and Barwise (2007) analyzed videotapes recorded within 22 households. They found that viewers paid attention to 79% of commercials presented during live programming, defined as "participants looking directly at and listening to the TV while doing nothing else which required conscious attention." They also reported that usage of the digital video recorder is nearly always secondary to live viewing, even among young viewers. Jayasinghe and Ritson (2013) studied videotapes and interviews from eight Australian households, showing a variety of means by which family members engaged with or ignored advertisements. Brasel and Gips (2011) videotaped 42 college students and staff while they used television and Internet simultaneously in a lab. Subjects switched their attention between television and Internet four times per minute on average, and subsequently underestimated their own switching behavior by a factor of 8. Although findings from such small samples might not represent the broader population, they provide vivid depictions of viewer behavior in natural settings.

5.3.1 Media Complementarities

Do firms achieve economies of scope by simultaneously advertising in multiple media? These might be achieved by spreading the media budget across multiple media to reinforce

---

[6] Waldfogel (2009) surveyed college students to understand how usage of Internet video affected their television consumption. He found that the availability of unlicensed television content on youtube.com led to slightly lower network television viewing but an offsetting increase in consumption on television networks' websites.

the message with multitasking consumers in a way that single-medium advertising is unable to do. Also, advertising in more media may reach single-tasking consumers who might otherwise remain uncontacted. Numerous recent studies have found evidence of synergistic effects between television advertising and Internet advertising on offline sales (Kolsarici and Vakratsas, 2011; Naik and Peters, 2009; Naik and Raman, 2003; Naik et al., 2005; Ohnishi and Manchanda, 2012; Stephen and Galak, 2012). However, these studies mostly used aggregate data, which may have trouble disentangling multimedia synergies from other unobserved variables that may correlate with both advertising expenditures and sales. Further corroborating evidence has been found in investigations of individual-level data by Bollinger et al. (2013) and Zantedeschi et al. (2014).

There now exists substantial evidence that television advertisements can prompt consumer search. Zigmond and Stipp (2010, 2011) offered several case studies showing that search queries entered at google.com responded immediately to television advertisements broadcast during the Winter Olympics. Lewis and Reiley (2013) showed that search queries at yahoo.com for particular brands spiked instantly during Super Bowl commercial breaks when those brands advertised (and did not spike during commercial breaks when the brands did not advertise). Joo et al. (2014, 2015) investigated hourly advertising and Google search data for a mature category (financial services) over a 3-month period, showing that TV advertising generated new searches in the product category and also increased the share of searches that included branded keywords.

There is also a substantial body of evidence that Internet behavior prompted by advertising leads to online sales. Wu et al. (2005) offered the first such evidence. They showed that online-only firms' use of magazine advertising can lead shoppers to a website, and that subsequent conversion rates depend on website characteristics. They also found that joint modeling of user acquisition and conversion was required for correct inference, as unobserved characteristics in visit generation and sales leads may be correlated. More recently, Kim and Hanssens (2014) examined data on advertising, blog mentions, online search, and revenue for motion pictures. They found that pre-launch advertising generated both search and blogging, and blogging generated further search. Hu et al. (2014) brought search data collected from Google Insights for Search into a sales/advertising response model. Using aggregate data, they found that automotive advertising is associated with a positive search lift for automotive brands, as well as a heightened conversion probability among interested consumers. Liaukonyte et al. (2015) estimated how measures of online shopping behavior (traffic and sales) at 20 brand websites changed in narrow windows of time around the airing of television advertisements, and how those effects depended on ad content. They found that direct response tactics increase both visit probability and purchase probability. In contrast, informative or emotional branding tactics reduce traffic while simultaneously increasing sales among those who do visit, consistent with improving the efficiency of consumer search, as predicted by Anderson and Renault (2006).

Finally, there is substantial evidence supporting the converse effect: Internet content can influence television viewing. Early work in this area focused on the effects of online "buzz" on television viewing and book sales (Chevalier and Mayzlin, 2006; Godes and Mayzlin, 2004). More recently, Gong et al. (2015) ran field experiments in China, showing that television program ratings respond to promoted posts and content posted on a microblogging service. Hill and Benton (2012) developed a method by which consumers' Twitter accounts can be mined to generate television program recommendations. In summary, there is ample evidence that television content and advertising can drive online behavior, and that online information can influence television viewing choices.

5.3.2 Competition for Attention

Anderson and de Palma (2012) modeled how consumer attention constraints affect product market competition and advertising. They predicted that the entry of additional classes of new products would raise advertising prices and clutter, but only up to a point. At some point, so many ads are sent that product market competition intensifies and advertising profitability falls.[7]

Wallsten (2014) investigated ATUS data to determine how increasing attention paid to one medium (Internet) affects the attention paid to other activities, such as watching TV. He found that each additional minute of Internet usage is associated with 0.13 fewer minutes watching television. Woo et al. (2014) investigated similar survey data from South Korea, replicating the negative correlation between television and Internet use, but finding a much smaller negative correlation between television and Internet use on a mobile device than between television and Internet use on a desktop computer. Zentner (2012) quantified how Internet adoption changed advertising revenue in a panel dataset of 80 countries. He found negative correlations between Internet penetration and television and print advertising revenues, but no correlation with radio advertising revenues.

Perhaps the best evidence comes from Reis (2015). Reis analyzed data from a "triple-play" television/phone/Internet provider and showed, using both an instrumental variables approach and a field experiment, that increased television consumption is associated with smaller Internet download traffic. However, even this does not speak to how multitasking is influenced by television consumption, as an increase in multitasking time may be reflected as a decrease in download traffic. No study has yet presented solid evidence on simultaneous usage of both television and Internet in a large-scale sample, perhaps due to the difficulties inherent in acquiring passive measurements of individuals' simultaneous media behavior from multiple competing platforms.

---

[7] See also Chapter 10.

Finally, a small experimental literature indicates how media characteristics influence marketing effectiveness. Magee (2013) reported the results of a field experiment in which subscribers of a promotional magazine received either a print or a digital version of the magazine. Although most readers expressed a preference for the digital version, those who received the print version were more likely to open it, spend more time browsing it, and retain more information. Brasel and Gips (2013) manipulated the physical interface experimental subjects used to access the Internet. They found that touch-based interfaces, such as those found in smartphones and tablets, increase perceived psychological ownership and the endowment effect. The implications for online commerce may be substantial, as the authors conclude that "touch-based devices like tablets can lead to higher product valuations when compared to traditional computers."

5.4. DISCUSSION

Market data show very clearly that video consumption has yet to fall, despite competition from new media and the prevalence of mobile devices, though the forms in which people consume video are evolving. Digitization has increased consumer control over media by offering services such as OTT video and digital video recorders. Screen proliferation has led to an enhanced tendency to multitask using "second screen," both enabling immediate consumer response to advertisements and increasing the already-intense competition for scarce consumer attention.

Important gaps in our understanding remain. Some research opportunities are implied directly by the preceding discussion. Of first-order importance: How do media multitasking and advertising avoidance alter advertising effectiveness? How does multitasking affect consumer habit formation and the tendency to become a regular viewer of a program? How do program and advertising content affect the impulse to start, stop, or continue diverting attention to a second screen? For example, how do multitasking tendencies vary with the viewer's past experience with the program? How and why does viewer-generated content online influence, enhance, or detract from the experience of consuming a live program? How can television networks and advertisers use online channels to try to influence consumer attention during live programs?

A second important area of inquiry is the degree to which incumbent media platforms are able to generate, sample, and adopt new strategies and business models. Traditional newspapers have appeared surprisingly risk-averse as advertising budgets have moved online and newspaper revenues have fallen. Will the incumbent television networks and conglomerates take advantage of the opportunities that digitization affords, or will those opportunities be realized more effectively by a new generation of media platforms? To what extent will individual program creators start offering their content directly to consumers via OTT services or direct download, as is occurring in the recorded (audio) music and comedy markets?

Finally, and most fundamentally, it will be difficult to predict the effects of techno-logical changes on mass media industries without a more basic understanding of the needs that media industries fulfill for consumers. Most media economics research focuses on interactions between platforms or interactions between types of agents (e.g., advertisers and viewers). Yet we still do not have a great understanding of *why* the typical viewer is watching 3–5 h of video per day, why video media appear to be so prevalent and habit-forming, or what is the range of different needs (education, entertainment, information, status, social connection, etc.) that are addressed through video consumption. A basic taxonomy of viewer needs and behaviors would be very helpful in predicting the specific aspects of the current mass media industries that will evolve in response to future tech-nological changes.

ACKNOWLEDGMENTS

I thank Simon Anderson, Peter Danaher, Ron Goettler, Catherine Tucker, and Joel Waldfogel for helpful comments and discussions, with particular gratitude to Anderson and Waldfogel for inviting the chapter.

REFERENCES

Anderson, S.P., de Palma, A., 2012. Competition for attention in the information (overload) age. RAND J. Econ. 43 (1), 1–25.
Anderson, S.P., Gans, J.S., 2011. Platform siphoning ad-avoidance and media content. Am. Econ. J. Micro-econ. 3 (4), 1–34.
Anderson, S.P., Renault, R., 2006. Advertising content. Am. Econ. Rev. 39 (1), 305–326.
Athey, S., Calvano, E., Gans, J.S., 2013. The Impact of the Internet on Advertising Markets for News Media. Mimeo, University of Toronto.
Becker, G., Murphy, K., 1993. A simple theory of advertising as a good or a bad. Q. J. Econ. 108 (4), 941–964.
Bergemann, D., Bonatti, A., 2011. Targeting in advertising markets implications for offline vs. online media. RAND J. Econ. 42, 417–443.
Bergemann, D., Bonatti, A., 2014. Selling cookies. Am. Econ. J. Microecon. 7 (3), 259–294.
Bollinger, B.K., Cohen, M.A., Lai, J., 2013. Measuring Asymmetric Persistence and Interaction Effects of Media Exposures Across Platforms. Mimeo, New York University.
Brasel, S.A., Gips, J., 2008. Breaking through fast-forwarding brand information and visual attention. J. Mark. 72, 31–48.
Brasel, S.A., Gips, J., 2011. Media multitasking behavior concurrent television and computer usage. Cyberp-sychol. Behav. Soc. Netw. 14 (9), 527–534.
Brasel, S.A., Gips, J., 2013. Tablets, touchscreens and touchpads how varying touch interfaces trigger psychological ownership and endowment. J. Consum. Res. 24, 226–233.
Bronnenberg, B.J., Dube, J.-P., Mela, C.F., 2010. Do digital video recorders influence sales? J. Mark. Res. 30 (3), 447–468.
Brynjolfsson, E., Hu, J., Simester, D., 2011. Goodbye Pareto principle, hello long tail: the effect of internet commerce on the concentration of product sales. Manag. Sci. 57 (8), 1373–1387.
Business Insider (BI), 2013. The Future of Digital 2013. Slide deck.
Cable Advertising Bureau (CAB), 2014. Why Ad-Supported Cable? White Paper.
Chevalier, J., Mayzlin, D., 2006. The effect of word of mouth on sales online book reviews. J. Mark. Res. 43 (3), 345–354.
Deng, Y., 2015. DVR Advertising Targeting. Mimeo, Duke University.
Digital TV Research, 2014. North America to Add 5 Million Pay TV Subscribers. Press release.
Dukes, A., Gal-Or, E., 2003. Negotiations and exclusivity contracts for advertising. Mark. Sci. 22 (2), 222–245.

Ellison, G., Wolitsky, A.G., 2012. A search cost model of obfuscation. RAND J. Econ. 43, 417–441.

eMarketer, 2012. Traditional Media Still Most Trusted Sources of Info. Press release.

Esteves-Sorenson, C., Perretti, F., 2012. Micro-costs inertia in television viewing. Econ. J. 122 (563), 867–902.

Fetto, J., 2013. Americans Spend 58 Minutes a Day on Their Smartphones. Accessed March 2014. http://www.experian.com/blogs/marketing-forward/2013/05/28/americans-spend-58-minutes-a-day-on-their-smartphones/.

George, L.M., Waldfogel, J., 2006. The New York Times and the market for newspapers. Am. Econ. Rev. 96 (1), 435–447.

Ghosh, B., Stock, A., 2010. Advertising effectiveness, digital video recorders, and product market competition. Mark. Sci. 29 (4), 639–649.

Ghosh, B.P., Galbreth, M.R., Shang, G., 2013. The competitive impact of targeted television advertisements using DVR technology. Decis. Sci. 44 (5), 951–971.

Godes, D., Mayzlin, D., 2004. Using online conversations to study word-of-mouth communication. Mark. Sci. 23 (4), 545–560.

Goldfarb, A., Tucker, C., 2011a. Online display advertising targeting and obtrusiveness. Mark. Sci. 30 (3), 389–494.

Goldfarb, A., Tucker, C., 2011b. Privacy regulation and online advertising. Manag. Sci. 57 (1), 57–71.

Goldstein, D.G., McAfee, R.P., Suri, S., 2013. The cost of annoying ads. In: Proceedings of the 23rd International World Wide Conference.

Gong, S., Zhang, J., Zhao, P., Jiang, X., 2015. Tweeting Increases Product Demand. Working paper. Massachusetts Institute of Technology.

Google, 2012. The New Multi-Screen World Understanding Cross-Platform Consumer Behavior. White Paper.

Hill, S., Benton, A., 2012. Talkographics Using What Viewers Say Online to Calculate Audience Affinity Networks for Social TV-Based Recommendations. Mimeo, University of Pennsylvania.

Hu, Y., Du, R., Damangir, S., 2014. Decomposing the impact of advertising: augmenting sales with online search data. J. Mark. Res. 51 (3), 300–310.

Interian, Y., Dorai-Raj, S., Naverniouk, I., Opalinski, P.J., Kaustuv, Zigmond, D., 2009. Ad quality on TV: predicting television audience retention. In: Proceedings of the Third International Workshop on Data Mining and Audience Intelligence for Advertising, Paris, France, pp. 85–91. http://www.australianscience.com.au/research/google/35368.pdf.

Jayasinghe, L., Ritson, M., 2013. Everyday advertising context: an ethnography of advertising response in the living room. J. Consum. Res. 40 (1), 104–121.

Joo, M., Wilbur, K.C., Cowgill, B., Zhu, Y., 2014. Television advertising and online search. Manag. Sci. 60 (1), 56–73.

Joo, J., Wilbur, K.C., Zhu, Y., 2015. Effects of TV advertising on keyword search. Int. J. Res. Mark. forthcoming.

Kim, H., Hanssens, D.M., 2014. Paid and Earned Media, Consumer Interest and Motion Picture Revenue. Mimeo, University of California, Los Angeles.

Kolsarici, C., Vakratsas, D., 2011. The Complexity of Multi-Media Effects: Marketing Science Institute Working Paper Series 2011 Report No. 11–100. Marketing Science Institute. http://www.mcgill.ca/files/_nea/211583_MSIWP.pdf.

Leichtman Research Group (LRG), 2013. The Rise and Plateau of DVRs. White Paper.

Lewis, R.A., Reiley, D.H., 2013. Down-to-the-minute effects of super bowl advertising on online search behavior. In: 14th ACM Conference on Electronic Commerce, 9. p. 4, Article 61.

Liaukonyte, J., Teixeira, T., Wilbur, K.C., 2015. How TV ads influence online search. Mark. Sci. 34 (3), 311–330.

Magee, R.G., 2013. Can a print publication be equally effective online? Testing the effect of medium type on marketing communications. Mark. Lett. 24, 85–95.

Naik, P.A., Peters, K., 2009. A hierarchical marketing communications model of online and offline media synergies. J. Interact. Mark. 23, 288–299.

Naik, P.A., Raman, K., 2003. Understanding the impact of synergy in multimedia communications. J. Mark. Res. 13 (4), 25–34.

Naik, P.A., Raman, K., Winter, R.S., 2005. Planning marketing-mix strategies in the presence of interaction effects. Mark. Sci. 24 (1), 25–34.

Nielsen, 2010. Three Screen Report, 1st Quarter 2010. White Paper.

Nielsen, 2013. 'Binging' Is the New Viewing for Over-the-Top Streamers. Accessed March 2014. http://www.nielsen.com/us/en/insights/news/2013/binging-is-the-new-viewing-for-over-the-top-streamers.html.

Nielsen, 2014a. The Cross-Platform Report. Accessed March 2014. http://www.nielsen.com/us/en/insights/reports/2014/shifts-in-viewing-the-cross-platform-report-q2-2014.html.

Nielsen, 2014b. Social TV on the Rise: Almost One in Two Online Australians Engaging in Digital Conversation. Accessed March 2014. http://www.nielsen.com/au/en/insights/news/2014/social-tv-on-the-rise.html.

Ofcom, 2013. Communications Market Report 2013. White Paper.

Ohnishi, H., Manchanda, P., 2012. Marketing activity, blogging and sales. Int. J. Res. Mark. 29 (2012), 221–234.

Pearson, S., Barwise, P., 2007. PVRs and advertising exposure: a video ethnographic study. Qual. Mark. Res. Int. J. 11 (4), 386–399.

Reis, F., 2015. Patterns of Substitution between Internet and Television in the Era of Media Streaming - Evidence from a Randomized Experiment. Working paper. Carnegie Mellon University.

Robinson, J.P., Martin, S., 2009. Of time and television. Ann. Am. Acad. Pol. Soc. Sci. 625, 74–86.

Sahagian, J., 2013. Study U.S. Smartphone Penetration Is at 74 Percent. Accessed March 2014. http://www.emarketer.com/Article/Smartphone-Tablet-Uptake-Still-Climbing-US/1010297.

Schweidel, D.A., Kent, R.J., 2010. Predictors of the gap between program and commercial audiences: an investigation using live tuning data. J. Mark. 74 (3), 18–33.

Stephen, A.T., Galak, J., 2012. The effects of traditional and social earned media on sales: a study of a micro-lending marketplace. J. Mark. Res. 44 (Oct.), 624–639.

Teixeira, T., Wedel, M., Pieters, R., 2010. Moment-to-moment optimal branding in TV commercials preventing avoidance by pulsing. Mark. Sci. 29 (5), 783–804.

Television Bureau of Advertising (TVB), 2014. TV Basics. Accessed March 2014. http://www.tvb.org/research/95487.

TiVo, 2013. TiVo Research and Analytics Netflix Not Cannibalizing Traditional TV Viewing. http//www.marketwired.com/press-release/TiVo-Research-and-Analytics-Netflix-Not-Cannibalizing-Traditional-TV-Viewing-1815308.htm. Accessed April 2014.

Tuchman, A., Nair, H.S., Gardete, P., 2015. Complementarities in Consumption and the Consumer Demand for Advertising. Mimeo, Stanford GSB.

Waldfogel, J., 2013. Digitization and the Quality of New Media Products: The Case of Music. Working paper. University of Minnesota.

Wallsten, S., 2014. What Are We Not Doing When We're Online? Mimeo, NBER.

Wilbur, K.C., 2008. How the digital video recorder changes traditional television advertising. J. Advert. 37 (1), 143–149.

Wilbur, K.C., 2015. Television Advertising Avoidance. Mimeo, University of California, San Diego.

Wilbur, K.C., Zhu, Y., 2009. Click fraud. Mark. Sci. 28 (2), 293–308.

Wilbur, K.C., Xu, L., Kempe, D., 2013. Correcting audience externalities in television advertising. Mark. Sci. 32 (6), 892–912.

Woo, J., Choi, J.Y., Shin, J., Lee, J., 2014. The effect of new media on consumer media usage: an empirical study in South Korea. Technol. Forecast. Soc. Change 89 (Nov.), 3–11.

Wu, J., Cook Jr., V.J., Strong, E.C., 2005. A two-stage model of the promotional performance of pure online firms. Inf. Syst. Res. 16 (4), 334–351.

Zantedeschi, D., Feit, E.M., Bradlow, E.T., 2014. Measuring Multi-Channel Advertising Effectiveness Using Consumer-Level Advertising Response Data. Mimeo, University of Pennsylvania.

Zentner, A., 2012. Internet adoption and advertising expenditures on traditional media: an empirical analysis using a panel of countries. J. Econ. Manage. Strat. 21 (4), 913–926.

Zigmond, D., Stipp, H., 2010. Assessing a new advertising effect measurement of impact of television commercials on internet search queries. J. Advert. Res. 50 (2), 162–168.

Zigmond, D., Stipp, H., 2011. Multitaskers may be advertisers' best audience. Harv. Bus. Rev. 12 (1/2), 32–33.

Zufryden, F.S., Pedrick, J.H., Sankaralingam, A., 1993. Zapping and its impact on brand purchase behavior. J. Advert. Res. 33, 58–66.

CHAPTER 6

Merger Policy and Regulation in Media Industries

Øystein Foros, Hans Jarle Kind, Lars Sørgard
NHH Norwegian School of Economics, Bergen, Norway

Contents

Abstract

The aim of this chapter is to survey the media economics literature on mergers. In particular, we try to accentuate where the effects of mergers differ between conventional one-sided markets and two-sided media markets (though not all media mergers are within two-sided markets). We focus on price effects in the first part of the chapter, and in the second part we discuss how mergers affect competing media

Handbook of Media Economics, Volume 1A
ISSN 2213-6630, http://dx.doi.org/10.1016/B978-0-444-62721-6.00006-8

platforms' choice of genre. In the third part, we discuss how to take on merger control in two-sided media markets. Motivated by some actual merger cases, we also discuss how antitrust authorities might err if they use the conventional one-sided approach to evaluate mergers within media markets (even if a case-by-case assessment is undertaken).

Keywords

Two-sided markets, Mergers, Advertising, Multi-homing, Antitrust policy

JEL Codes

L11, L13, L41, L82

6.1. INTRODUCTION

Because it is media, media mergers get huge media attention. In the first dot-com era, there was a wave of entertainment and media mergers, led by the 2001 American Online (AOL)–Time Warner merger, in which AOL acquired the more traditional media company Time Warner for $165 billion.[1] Within the radio market, consolidation took place in the US market after the Telecommunication Act of 1996 (see Sweeting, 2015, this volume). Between 1996 and 2006, the US radio market experienced a merger wave, and empirical work shows that the particularities of two-sided markets have important implications for the effects of mergers on both product variety and advertising volume (Jeziorski, 2014).

The aim of this chapter is to survey the literature on the consequences of media mergers, and to summarize how the outcomes of mergers might differ between two-sided and conventional one-sided markets. In the first part, we focus on price effects, while in the second part we discuss how mergers affect competing media platforms' choice of genre. In Section 6.3, we discuss how antitrust policy takes on merger control in two-sided media markets.

The literature on two-sided markets has shown that the effects of mergers of ad-financed platforms differ from what one might expect from the conventional literature on one-sided markets. Assuming away efficiency gains, a merger that increases market power in a one-sided market leads to higher consumer prices. In a two-sided market, on the other hand, a merger that increases market power on one side of the market tends to reduce prices on the other side (see, e.g., Rochet and Tirole, 2006; Weyl, 2010). The seminal papers on two-sided media markets (Anderson and Coate, 2005) predict that a merger leads the platforms to charge *lower* ad prices if consumers dislike ads. It turns out that this puzzling result is due to the assumption that consumers visit only one media platform (e.g., watch only one TV channel or read only one newspaper), so-called

---

[1] The merger between Warner and Time took place in 1990.

single-homing. Competition for advertisers is then closed down, since the platforms have a monopoly position in delivering their exclusive eyeballs to advertisers (the competitive bottleneck problem identified by Armstrong, 2002, 2006). More recent contributions open up for competition for advertisers by allowing consumers to multi-home (Ambrus et al., 2015; Anderson and Peitz, 2014a,b; Anderson et al., 2015a,b; Athey et al., 2013). Then the puzzling prediction from the single-homing model may vanish, and ad prices may increase when ad-financed platforms are merged.

Analysis of how mergers affect diversity and differentiation incentives is considered to be an important issue in media markets, with Steiner (1952) and Beebe (1977) as the classical theoretical contributions. Steiner (1952) shows that mergers may reduce duplication of genres among ad-financed channels, and thus increase diversity. This prediction has found some empirical support within the markets for radio (see Sweeting, 2015, this volume), newspapers (see Chandra and Kaiser, 2015, this volume), and television (see Crawford, 2015, this volume). An important assumption in Steiner is that if people cannot watch their most preferred TV program, then they do not watch TV at all. Beebe (1977) relaxes this assumption, and allows consumers to have second preferences; i.e., if their favorite genre is not available, they might be willing to watch some other genre instead. Through this modification, Beebe casts doubt on Steiner's prediction that mergers tend to increase diversity. On the contrary, the opposite could be true: a merger to monopoly might reduce the number of genres broadcasted. Worse still, it could prevent consumers from being able to watch their first preferences.

More recently, Anderson et al. (2015b) formulate a Hotelling model where (some) consumers multi-home and two media platforms endogenously choose locations. They arrive at the striking result that a merger of the two platforms might have no effect on the choice of genres (location on the Hotelling line), and thus no effect on diversity.

Common for all the articles cited above is the prediction that the consequences of mergers in one-sided and two-sided markets might be very different. An important issue is how this is taken into account by the antitrust authorities in their assessment of media mergers. There are numerous examples of antitrust authorities that have applied the traditional one-sided market logic to media markets, and thereby ended up focusing on only one side of a two-sided market. Unfortunately, such a procedure might be flawed. For one thing, it fails to take into account the fact that a price increase on one side of the market can lead to a price reduction on the other side. Over the last few years, the methodology used by antitrust authorities for analyzing the price effect of mergers has improved and has been extended to a two-sided market framework. However, less progress has been made in the antitrust authorities' analysis of non-price effects of mergers, such as how mergers affect media diversity.

Not least due to the growth of the Internet, we have witnessed significant changes in market structure and technology in the media market. These changes affect both the incentives to merge and the effects thereof. Due to the transformation to online platforms, consumers have become more prone to multi-home. For ad-financed online newspapers, readers may easily browse news from multiple sources, whereas traditionally they just read one newspaper. In addition to traditional media houses going online, we have new ad-financed players, ranging from giants such as Google, Facebook, and You-Tube to smaller bloggers, which increase competition for advertisers. Furthermore, the noteworthy increase in new ways to access content, in particular by smartphones, implies that consumers simultaneously access several platforms. Ofcom (2014, p. 5) states that: "*UK adults squeeze over 11 hours' worth of communications and media activity into less than nine hours. The total volume of media and communications activities undertaken by an individual each day equate to 11 hours 7 minutes. But as some media activities are conducted simultaneously, this is squeezed into 8 hours 41 minutes per day*." As multi-homing becomes more widespread (see Peitz and Reisinger, 2015, this volume), it becomes more important to understand how competition for advertisers works, also when evaluating mergers.

Even if consumers have increased their consumption as the availability of multiple platforms has increased, there is also a limit to attention. This may give ad-financed platforms incentives to merge. As emphasized by Joshua Gans (Washington Post, September 17, 2013): "*Space on the internet is infinite, but consumer attention is scarce, and now divided between many outlets. So companies that want to reach consumers run the risk of hitting the same person more than once if they advertise with multiple publications, or only hitting a slice of them if they advertise on just one. That allows publications with a wider reach to command higher prices for their ads, since they can reach more people with a lower risk of duplication*." (Formally shown in Athey et al., 2013.)

The effects of mergers are also paid attention to in other chapters. Sweeting (2015) provides a discussion of the effects of merger in radio markets. Chandra and Kaiser (2015, this volume) discuss mergers among printed media platforms (newspapers and magazines), whereas Armstrong and Crawford (2015, this volume) discuss mergers within television.

6.2. PRICE AND QUANTITY EFFECTS OF MERGERS IN TWO-SIDED MARKETS

In two-sided markets two groups of users are mediated by a platform. At least one of the groups imposes a positive network externality on the other group (see Anderson and Jullien, 2015, this volume, for the definition of a two-sided market). In media markets, the two groups are typically advertisers and consumers (viewers/readers/listeners), and the platform is a media firm which delivers content to consumers. Ad-financed media platforms then offer eyeballs (consumers) to the advertisers. There is a positive network effect from the consumer side to the advertisers, since advertisers prefer to reach as many consumers as possible. Advertisers' impact on consumers depends on consumers' attitude to ads. If consumers dislike ads, as they typically do for television and radio (see Sweeting,

2015, this volume, on radio and Armstrong and Crawford, 2015, this volume, on television), there is a negative externality from advertisers to consumers. In contrast, for magazines, readers may like ads (see Chandra and Kaiser, 2015, this volume), in which case there is also a positive externality from advertisers to consumers. Anderson and Jullien (2015, this volume) provide a complete treatment of the economics of two-sided markets. We restrict our attention to the effects of mergers. In Section 6.3, we analyze how a merger affects media platforms' choice of genre. First, in this section, we hold product characteristics and the number of goods fixed. We do this in order to focus on pure price (and quantity) effects. General insight tells us that increased market power on one side of the market tends to reduce prices on the other side (see, e.g., Rochet and Tirole, 2006; Weyl, 2010).[2]

6.2.1 Backdrop: Price and Quantity Effects of Mergers in One-Sided Markets

Holding factors like product characteristics, costs, and the number of goods fixed, the pure price effects of mergers in one-sided markets are typically straightforward. To set the scene, consider two newspapers that are financed by subscription fees alone (no ads). Standard economic theory predicts that the closer substitutes the newspapers are in the eyes of the consumers, the less profit they will make if they compete, other things being equal. Each of the newspapers has incentives to set a low subscription price in order to steal business from the rival, and more so the more prone the consumers are to shift from one newspaper to the other. If the newspapers merge (or set prices cooperatively), the owners will internalize these business-stealing effects. Prices will thus unambiguously increase.

Farrell and Shapiro (1990) analyze possible welfare effects of mergers in a one-sided market.[3] First, they consider a potential price increase subsequent to a merger. If there are no changes in costs, they show that a merger between firms that produce substitutes will always lead to higher prices. While a reduction in fixed costs will not change this, a reduction in marginal costs will matter. In a market with Cournot competition, Farrell and Shapiro derive the criteria for how large the reduction in marginal costs must be to prevent upward price pressure after the merger. Works that are more recent have extended their analyses to other market structures, and in particular to Bertrand competition with differentiated products.[4] This approach has become quite important in antitrust authorities' analysis of mergers (see Section 6.4 for more details). One reason is that antitrust

---

[2] Weyl (2010) also provides an informal discussion of the effects of mergers in media markets.

[3] Their model builds on the more informal model in Williamson (1968), where he shows the tradeoff in welfare between reduction in competition and cost savings.

[4] See Werden (1996) for an extension to Bertrand competition and differentiated products, which was further developed in Farrell and Shapiro (2010).

authorities apply a consumer welfare standard and the price effect on final consumers then becomes very important.

The second issue Farrell and Shapiro (1990) analyze is how a merger could lead to a reallocation of production between firms. If a reallocation takes place, it might change the cost level in the industry. To see this, consider a merger between two firms that have high market shares due to low marginal costs. After the merger, they increase prices and cut down on production, while the non-merging firms produce more. This is a reallocation of production from firms with low costs to firms with high costs in production. This explains why mergers between large firms can reduce total welfare, while mergers between small firms can increase total welfare even if they lead to higher prices.

6.2.2 Two-Sided Markets and Single-Homing Consumers

In the seminal paper on two-sided media markets (Anderson and Coate, 2005), consumers are restricted to attend a single ad-financed platform. This is termed single-homing in the literature although advertisers multi-home and place ads on all platforms. The assumption of single-homing closes down price competition for advertisers; each platform has monopoly power in delivering its consumers to advertisers. This gives rise to the "competitive bottleneck" problem identified by Armstrong (2002, 2006). When considering the effects of mergers among platforms, the single-homing assumption gives rise to a puzzle when consumers dislike ads. As mentioned above, TV viewers typically dislike advertising.

Anderson and Coate (2005) consider competition between two advertising-financed TV channels, assuming that advertising is a nuisance to viewers. In their model, the TV channels compete by having few ads, thereby attracting viewers. They find that a shift to monopoly—a merger between two TV channels—leads to more advertising and lower advertising prices per viewer.[5] As in corresponding one-sided markets, competition between the merging firms is eliminated. In contrast to traditional markets, elimination of competition leads to lower advertising prices and correspondingly higher advertising volumes. The consumers on the other side of the market—the viewers—will be worse off, since they dislike advertising and their only "payment" is to incur the nuisance cost of watching ads. The total welfare effect of the merger will depend on whether there was under- or overprovision of advertising and programming (number of programs) before the merger took place.[6]

---

[5] See Anderson and Coate (2005, Proposition 5), where they consider the regime where the programming (number of programs being offered in the market) is not affected by such a merger. The counterintuitive effect of tougher competition—lower prices in the advertising market—is also shown in Barros et al. (2004).

[6] See Anderson and Coate (2005, Proposition 6). Kind et al. (2007) also discuss under- or overprovision of advertising. They compare competition with collusion, where the latter can be interpreted as monopoly. Ambrus et al. (2015) show that multi-homing will make it less likely that there is underprovision of ads in the competitive equilibrium (see Footnote 3).

Consumers' attitude toward ads—whether they like or dislike advertising—can be of importance for the effects of a merger in a two-sided market. In particular, with ad lovers, the advertising market is expected to behave in the "normal" way, i.e., higher advertising prices after a merger. Unfortunately, from the existing literature we cannot draw any clear and robust conclusions on how consumers' attitude toward advertising affects welfare consequences of a merger in a two-sided market.

6.2.3 Two-Sided Markets and Multi-Homing Consumers

Several recent papers show that introducing competition for advertisers may resolve the puzzling prediction that mergers might reduce advertising prices (Ambrus et al., 2015; Anderson and Peitz, 2014a,b; Anderson et al., 2015a; Athey et al., 2015).

Ambrus et al. (2015) supersede Ambrus and Reisinger (2006). They consider a general consumer demand function and allow (a share of) the consumers to multi-home. They also relax the standard assumption that all media consumers necessarily notice all ads to which they are exposed. More reasonably, they assume that any given consumer becomes aware of an ad only with a certain probability. This has the important implication that it might be optimal to expose a consumer to the same ad several times. In contrast to Anderson et al. (2015a), which will be discussed later in this chapter, a profit-maximizing advertiser may thus choose to advertise on several platforms even in the extreme case where all consumers multi-home.

In their baseline, Ambrus et al. (2015) consider a context with two advertising-financed TV channels ($i = 1$, 2), and initially make the non-critical assumption that the advertisers are homogeneous. The consumers differ in their preferences for the two channels, which are described by their types $q := (q_1, q_2)$. Ambrus et al. analyze a two-stage game where at stage one the platforms first non-cooperatively offer contracts to the advertisers, before the advertisers and consumers at stage two decide whether to join the platform(s).[7]

Starting with the last stage, a consumer watches channel i if and only if $q_i - \gamma n_i > 0$, where $\gamma > 0$ is the disutility of ads and $n_i > 0$ is the advertising intensity on the platform. This implies that a consumer will single-home on channel 1, say, if $q_1 - \gamma n_1 > 0$ and $q_2 - \gamma n_2 < 0$, while he will multi-home if $q_i - \gamma n_i > 0$ for $i = 1$, 2. If $q_i - \gamma n_i < 0$ for $i = 1$, 2, then the consumer will not watch either of the channels (zero-homing). Note that this formulation implies that the decision of whether to watch channel i is independent of the advertising volume on channel j. This reflects the fact that the *incremental*

---

[7] The results we focus on below hold in a setting where media firms raise revenue only through the ad market, as well as in one where they also raise revenue through subscription fees. We will only discuss the version with pure ad financing.

utility of watching a given channel is independent of the utility of watching another channel. Contrary to single-homing frameworks (like Anderson and Coate, 2005), the size of a channel's audience i is thus not increasing in the rival's advertising volume.

The value for a producer of informing a consumer of a product equals ω. The probability that a consumer who single-homes on platform i becomes aware of a given ad is $\phi_i(n_i)$, while the analog probability for a multi-homing consumer equals $\phi_{12}(n_1, n_2)$. The probability functions are increasing and concave in their arguments.

The expected gross payoff for a firm which advertises on both platforms is equal to

$$u(n_1, n_2) = \omega \left[\sum_{i=1}^{2} D_i(n_1, n_2) \phi_i(n_i) + D_{12}(n_1, n_2) \phi_{12}(n_1, n_2) \right],$$

where D_i is the number of single-homing consumers on platform i and D_{12} is the number of multi-homing consumers. With a fixed cost of advertising equal to t_i, net payoff for the advertiser equals $u(n_1, n_2) - t_1 - t_2$. In equilibrium, each platform can extract the incremental value it brings over its rival's offer, which means that

$$t_1^d = u\left(n_1^d, n_2^d\right) - u\left(0, n_2^d\right) \text{ and } t_2^d = u\left(n_1^d, n_2^d\right) - u\left(n_1^d, 0\right).$$

By advertising at both channels, the probability of reaching a multi-homer increases by $\left(\phi_{12} - \phi_j\right)$ units. Platform i can therefore charge $\omega D_{12}\left(\phi_{12} - \phi_j\right)$ for the multi-homers and $\omega D_i \phi_i$ for its exclusive viewers. The mass of advertisers is set to 1, which will also be the number of advertisers in equilibrium (since they are assumed to be homogeneous). Profits for channel i are thus equal to

$$\Pi_i^d = t_i^d = \omega \left[D_i \phi_i + D_{12}\left(\phi_{12} - \phi_j\right) \right].$$

If channel i increases the advertising intensity by one unit, the probability that an exclusive or a multi-homing consumer becomes aware of an ad increases by $\partial \phi_i / \partial n_i$ and $\partial \phi_{12} / \partial n_i$ units, respectively. The marginal value of this for the channel is $\omega[D_i(\partial \phi_i / \partial n_i) + D_{12}(\partial \phi_{12} / \partial n_i)]$. However, since the consumers dislike ads, the channel will also lose some viewers ($\partial D_i / \partial n_i$ exclusive and $\partial D_{12} / \partial n_i$ multi-homers). The marginal costs of increasing the advertising intensity thus equal $MC_i^d = \omega[\phi_i(\partial D_i / \partial n_i) + \left(\phi_{12} - \phi_j\right)(\partial \phi_{12} / \partial n_i)]$. The equilibrium advertising intensity is consequently characterized by

$$D_i \frac{\partial \phi_i}{\partial n_i} + D_{12} \frac{\partial \phi_{12}}{\partial n_i} = -\left[\phi_i \frac{\partial D_i}{\partial n_i} + \left(\phi_{12} - \phi_j\right) \frac{\partial \phi_{12}}{\partial n_i} \right].$$

Now suppose that the two channels merge, forming a *two-channel monopoly*. Since the advertisers are homogeneous, the platforms will set the fixed advertising rates such that they extract all surplus. Profits for the merged company are consequently equal to

$$\Pi^m = \omega\left[\sum_{i=1}^{2} D_i\phi_i + D_{12}\phi_{12}\right].$$

The marginal value for channel i of increasing the advertising intensity is independent of whether it has merged with channel j; the gain from increasing the advertising intensity by one unit is still equal to $\omega[D_i(\partial\phi_i/\partial n_i) + D_{12}(\partial\phi_{12}/\partial n_i)]$. However, the merged company will take into account the fact that the larger the advertising intensity of channel i, the greater is the number of exclusive viewers at channel j, $\partial D_j/\partial n_i > 0$. The marginal costs of increasing the advertising intensity are consequently equal to $\mathrm{MC}_i^m = \omega\left[\phi_i(\partial D_i/\partial n_i) + \phi_{12}(\partial D_{12}/\partial n_i) - \phi_j(\partial D_j/\partial n_i)\right]$. Recall, though, that the total size of the audience on either channel is independent of the advertising level on the other channel. This means that $\partial D_j/\partial n_i = -\partial D_{12}/\partial n_i$, which in turn implies that the marginal costs of increasing the advertising intensity are the same for a two-channel monopoly and a duopolist, $\mathrm{MC}_i^m = \omega\left[\phi_i(\partial D_i/\partial n_i) + \left(\phi_{12} - \phi_j\right)(\partial D_{12}/\partial n_i)\right] = \mathrm{MC}_i^d$. The equilibrium advertising intensity is consequently the same with a merged company as with a duopoly. Ambrus et al. thus reach the striking result that the equilibrium advertising level does not depend on the ownership structure (i.e., whether we have monopoly or duopoly). This they label the neutrality property. Ambrus et al. prove that the result survives also with heterogeneous advertisers as long as some viewers multi-home, and further that it survives if the platforms are financed both through viewer charges and through advertising.[8]

Ambrus et al. (2015) also analyze the effects of entry, and show that a previous one-channel monopoly might actually increase its advertising level if there is a change in market structure from monopoly to duopoly. This is in sharp contrast to earlier studies, which show that since viewers dislike ads, the advertising level at a platform will unambiguously fall if it faces competition. The logic behind Ambrus et al.'s result is that some viewers become less valuable once a new channel appears; this is true for those viewers who have now become multi-homers. Since the cost of losing these viewers is relatively small, it might thus be optimal to increase the advertising intensity and accept a greater reduction in the size of the audience than would otherwise be the case. Indeed, if the value of a multi-homer approaches zero, there is approximately no cost in losing him.

---

[8] From Anderson and Coate (2005), it is well known that competition between media firms might lead to underprovision of ads. Ambrus et al. (2015) demonstrate that this need not be the case with multi-homing consumers. This is seen clearly if we first consider a monopoly and homogeneous advertisers; in this case the monopoly will, as argued above, extract the whole surplus from the advertising side of the market. However, it will not internalize the viewers' disutility of ads (but will of course take into account how viewer participation varies with ad levels). In other words, the monopoly internalizes all benefits from advertising, but not all (consumer) costs. Obviously, this leads to overprovision of ads from a social point of view, and the neutrality property implies that this does not change with competition. It should be noted, though, that the overprovision result might break down with heterogeneous advertisers.

Even though they use a different equilibrium concept (passive beliefs as in Katz and Shapiro, 1985), Anderson et al. (2015a) find similar incremental pricing results as Ambrus, Calvano, and Reisinger.[9] In particular, they show that both the price per ad and the price per ad per viewer may increase when merging platforms have some multi-homing consumers. The model of Anderson et al. (2015a) is presented in more detail in Peitz and Reisinger (2015).

Both Anderson et al. (2015a) and Ambrus et al. (2015) assume that availability of more content will increase total consumption. In contrast, Athey et al. (2013) keep total media consumption per capita fixed in order to isolate the effects of the observation that consumers spend less time on traditional media and more time on online media. Importantly, their model is able to explain the collapse of advertising revenue for printed newspapers. The fraction of multi-homing consumers has increased with online platforms according to Athey et al., and when consumer attention is scarce, consumers divide their fixed consumption between more outlets. The advertisers may then reach the same person more times than necessary if they place ads on multiple platforms. On the contrary, if they place ads on just a few of the platforms, advertisers would not reach all consumers. Consequently, bigger is better: A platform with a larger audience may increase its ad prices since it reaches more consumers with a lower risk of duplication (i.e., reaching the same consumer more than once). This may obviously induce mergers among ad-financed platforms. Despite differences in assumptions, the incremental pricing mechanisms in Athey et al. are similar to those in Anderson et al. (2015a,b) and Ambrus et al. (2015).

Also two recent papers by Anderson and Peitz (2014a, b) analyze competition for advertisers. Anderson and Peitz (2014a) introduce aggregative games into media economics, i.e., games where each firm i's payoff depends on its own actions (ψ_i) and the aggregate of all n players' actions $\left(\Psi = \sum_{j=1}^{n} \psi_j \right)$.[10] Denoting profits for firm i as $\Pi^i(\psi_i, \Psi)$, its first-order condition reads

$$\Pi_1^i(\psi_i, \Psi) + \Pi_2^i(\psi_i, \Psi) = 0.$$

Under certain assumptions the best reply function of firm i, r_i, is a function of all firms' actions, $r_i = r_i(\Psi)$, with r_i being upward-sloping if actions are strategic complements. Anderson and Peitz model the advertiser side of the market in a fairly standard way, but the consumer side has several interesting features. Specifically, they use a representative consumer model, normalize the aggregate time that consumers spend on media consumption to 1, and label the fraction of the time spent on platform i as λ_i, with

[9] See Anderson and Jullien (2015, this volume) and Peitz and Reisinger (2015, this volume) for further discussions of equilibrium concepts.
[10] See Selton (1970).

$\sum_{i=1}^{n} \lambda_i = 1.$[11] Denoting the content quality and advertising level on platform i by s_i and a_i respectively, they write consumer utility as

$$U = \max_{\lambda_1, \ldots, \lambda_n} \sum_{i=1}^{n} [s_i(1-a_i)\lambda_i]^{\alpha},$$

where α is an exogenous parameter. The negative sign of a_i reflects the assumption that consumers are ad-averse and, most notably, Anderson and Peitz assume that $\alpha \in (0,1)$. This implies that each consumer will spend some time on each platform. By assumption, the consumers are thus multi-homers. Within this framework, they show that mergers among ad-financed platforms reduce consumer surplus.

Anderson and Peitz (2014b) introduce competition for advertisers by allowing for limited consumer attention. When consumers move between platforms (multi-homing), they find that a merger between ad-financed platforms reduces ad levels and increases ad prices. The result is thus similar to that of Ambrus et al. (2015) and Anderson et al. (2015a). The driving force in Anderson and Peitz (2014b) is that a merged platform internalizes the congestion problem. See Anderson and Jullien (2015, this volume) for more details on Anderson and Peitz (2014a,b).

6.2.4 Effects of Semi-Collusion Through Joint Operating Agreements

In the United States, Joint Operating Agreements have been an important feature where competing newspapers cooperate on advertising and circulation functions (see, e.g., Romeo and Dick, 2005). Policymakers have accepted these arrangements as a means to ensure ideological diversity (Gentzkow et al., 2014). See also Gentzkow et al. (2015) and Chandra and Kaiser (2015).

Dewenter et al. (2011) show that even if we abstract from diversity issues and efficiency gains:

- semi-collusion, where platforms choose ad levels cooperatively but compete in the reader market, may benefit all players (consumers, advertisers, and media platforms);
- a merger may reduce prices within a two-sided market.

Dewenter et al. (2011) consider a representative consumer framework with a continuum of advertisers and two newspapers. They assume that consumers are ad lovers such that competing newspapers seek to attract consumers from the rival by having a larger advertising volume than what would otherwise maximize profits.[12] This negatively affects the profits they earn from the advertising side of the market. Dewenter et al. consequently find that the ad volume will fall and the ad price increase if the newspapers choose ad levels collusively, compared to the outcome when they compete on both sides of

---

[11] Like Athey et al. (2013), they thus assume that consumers have a fixed amount of time to allocate among platforms.

[12] Dewenter et al. (2011) find that their main results, which we describe below, hold also with ad-averse consumers.

the market. Other things being equal, this will harm both consumers and advertisers. However, since the advertising market has now become more lucrative for the newspapers, they will have greater incentives to attract readers and sell the eyeballs to advertisers. The newspapers will therefore reduce the subscription prices so much that the size of the readership increases even though the advertising volume has fallen. The consumers thus gain from the newspapers' collaboration on the advertising market. This reflects the general insight that increased market power on one side of the market tends to reduce prices on the other side of the market (see, e.g., Rochet and Tirole, 2006; Weyl, 2010).[13]

Interestingly, and in sharp contrast to what one might expect from the logic in one-sided markets, also the advertisers might gain. This is so because even though advertising prices increase, advertisers will now reach a larger number of readers. If the latter effect dominates, which Dewenter et al. (2011) show might be the case, all agents benefit. The fact that many countries allow newspapers to collude on the advertising market might thus be fully rational even from a total welfare point of view.

Under a merger—the newspapers cooperate on both sides of the market—ad levels and subscription prices will be chosen so that overall profits for the newspapers are maximized. With no other choice variables, the outcome will then be the same as under a full merger. Whether a merger is welfare improving depends on the benchmarks. Compared with collusion in the advertising market, a merger will clearly be negative from a social point of view. The reason is that the subscription prices increase when the newspapers no longer compete in the reader market. However, if the welfare gains from the collusion in the advertising market are sufficiently strong, it could nonetheless be the case that merger is better than unrestricted competition. The likelihood for this to be true is increasing in the size of the advertising market and decreasing in the newspaper substitutability in the reader market. The intuition is that a larger advertising market tends to make it more profitable to reduce subscription prices in order to attract readers, while a high substitutability might mean that the pre-merger subscription prices were so low that it is nonetheless optimal to increase them if the newspapers are no longer competing. This shows that the possibility that a merger between two media firms might benefit both the audience and the advertisers cannot be rejected.

6.3. MERGERS AND PLATFORMS' CHOICE OF GENRES

> *I bought a bourgeois house in the Hollywood hills*
> *With a truckload of hundred thousand dollar bills*
> *Man came by to hook up my cable TV*
> *We settled in for the night my baby and me*
> *We switched 'round and 'round 'til half-past dawn*
> *There was fifty-seven channels and nothin' on*
> *"57 Channels (And Nothin' On)"*
>
> *—Bruce Springsteen (1992).*

[13] Weyl (2010) also provides an informal discussion of the effects of mergers in media markets.

6.3.1 Maximum Versus Minimum Differentiation

An idiosyncrasy of many media markets is that the firms are partially or completely ad-financed. This might affect their differentiation incentives. The economic literature on the interplay between the degree of competition and product variety goes back to Hotelling (1929)—the workhorse for the majority of recent contributions in media economics (the seminal paper by Anderson and Coate, 2005, among others). A general insight from the Hotelling model is that with the conventional assumptions of quadratic transportation costs and single-homing consumers, firms will have incentives to differentiate their products in order to soften price competition if they seek revenues from consumers directly. As shown by d'Aspremont et al. (1979), this might lead to an outcome with maximum differentiation. If, in contrast, the media platforms are purely ad-financed, and the audience is indifferent to the ad level, the platforms will want to maximize the number of viewers/readers/listeners (i.e., consumers). This might lead to co-location in the center of the market, i.e., no differentiation.

The classical contribution that analyzes differentiation incentives for advertising-financed media firms is Steiner (1952). Within a stylized simplified framework, he shows how competing platforms aim for the mass market in order to raise advertising revenue, and how this gives rise to the principle of genre duplication. In contrast to competing firms, a monopoly operating two channels would not cannibalize its own audience by duplication of genre. If the market would otherwise be uncovered, it would therefore offer diversity of genres in order to increase the total number of consumers. A multi-channel monopoly platform has no incentives to offer several identical channels. In contrast, a single-channel platform may duplicate rivals' genre if it captures more eyeballs that way than by providing a different genre than the rivals. A merger where we go from single-channel duopoly to multi-channel monopoly may thus increase diversity of genres.

Interestingly, Steiner (1952) does not build on or cite Hotelling (1929). However, it is straightforward to transfer Steiner's model into a Hotelling framework (see discussion by Anderson and Gabszewicz, 2006).

In the next section, we present Steiner (1952)'s classical duplication result. We then proceed by altering the explicit and implicit simplifying assumptions in Steiner (1952), and in particular introduce the lessons from more recent contributions on two-sided media markets.

6.3.2 Steiner (1952): Mergers May Reduce Duplication of Genres

In order to analyze how mergers affect media firms' choice of genre we first go back to the classical contribution of Steiner (1952), who developed a framework to investigate what the consequences would be of exposing the BBC to competition from a new radio station in the 1950s.

Let us translate Steiner's illustrative example into ad-financed TV channels and assume that each channel chooses between two types of genres to broadcast: football (segment F) and ballet (segment B). A critical assumption, which will be relaxed in Section 6.3.4, is that viewers are single-homing. Now, suppose that 90% of viewers want to watch football programs and 10% want to watch ballet. If their favorite genre is not aired, then they do not watch any TV at all. It is then clear that with only two channels, both will offer segment F (football) and get 45% of the viewers each (assuming equal split between identical channels). The ballet lovers will be left unserved. If the number of channels increases from two to three, we still have duplication of genres. All deliver football, now to 30% of the viewers each. If we continue this line of reasoning, we find that we need nine independent single-channel platforms before one of them will deliver ballet. Then, they will be indifferent between football and ballet since both choices provide them with 10% of the viewers.

Steiner argues that a change from two competing single-channel providers to one multiple-channel provider increases product variety. The story is simply that a multi-channel platform is concerned about the total number of viewers, and so has no incentives to air two identical channels.[14] Accordingly, when considering consequences of mergers (or entries), we need to make a distinction between the number of channels and the number of competing firms.

If we return to the case with two single-channel platforms, the lesson from Steiner (1952) is that duplication prevails as long as

$$\frac{v_A}{2} > v_B,$$

where v_i, $i = A, B$, is the fraction of consumers in segment i. Waldfogel (2009) terms this concept "preferences externalities" which refer to the fact that the majority overrides the minority when there are few alternatives (see Anderson and Waldfogel, 2015, this volume).

To compare with more recent contributions, it is straightforward to reformulate Steiner's model into a standard Hotelling framework with uniform consumer distribution. If consumers single-home, two ad-financed rivals will locate in the middle of the line (genre duplication) when consumers are ad-neutral. This was labeled the principle of minimum differentiation by Boulding (1955).

In an extension to more than two firms, Eaton and Lipsey (1975) find that the results of Boulding (1955), and other extensions of Hotelling (1929), might be sensitive to the number of firms, distribution of consumers, and changes in conjectural variations. Eaton and Lipsey show that in a one-dimensional model, the principle of minimum differentiation does not survive if we have more than two firms. However, when they extend their model to a two-dimensional space they arrive at the principle of local clustering; an entrant locates as close as possible to another firm. Thus, the principle of minimum differentiation in the two-firm case is considered by Eaton and Lipsey as a special case of the principle of clustering (or principle of pairs as they also label it).[15]

---

[14] Other early contributions that indicate such a duplication result are Rothenberg (1962) and Wiles (1963).
[15] See Hannesson (1982) for a critical assessment of the assumption made in Eaton and Lipsey (1975) on conjectural variations.

We now discuss how altering some of the (simplifying) assumptions in Steiner (1952) may alter the duplication result. For more on Steiner, see Anderson and Waldfogel (2015, this volume).

6.3.3 Consumers Have Second Preferences

In an extension of Steiner's model, Beebe (1977) allows consumers to have second preferences; i.e., if their favorite genre is not available, they still attend and watch some other genre. The message from Beebe's seminal paper is that a monopoly channel might provide content that may not be anyone's favorite, but that will be watched if nothing else is available. This is referred to as Lowest Common Denominator (LCD) programming. Take the example from above and now assume that 90% of viewers have football (F) as their *first choice*, while 10% have ballet (B) as their first choice. A third genre, reality (R), is now an option for the channels. No one has R as their favorite, but the football lovers prefer reality (R) to ballet (B) if football (F) is not available. Similarly, ballet lovers prefer reality (R) to football (F) if ballet is not available. In this setting, a monopoly provider chooses reality (LCD programming), and will run only one channel. In this sense, Beebe's extension may be considered as a caveat to Steiner's prediction that mergers reduce duplication. However, media diversity will be weakly lower. For more details on Beebe (1977) and LCD programming, see Anderson and Waldfogel (2015, this volume).

6.3.4 Advertising Effect Differs Between Genres

Empirical analyses of the television market in the United States show that advertisers' favorite genres are reality and comedy, since their experience suggests that the advertising effect is greatest when such programs are aired (Wilbur, 2008). Viewers, however, prefer action and news. Wilbur finds that the types of programs viewers would primarily watch account for only 16% of the transmission surface, while the advertisers' favorites—reality and comedy—account for 47%. This illustrates that in a two-sided market consumers are offered genres that to a greater or lesser degree are twisted in the direction of advertisers' preferences. Foros et al. (2012) show that less competition between different media—for example, through a merger—will increase this problem.

6.3.5 Dual Source of Financing: Charging Both Users and Advertisers

For media products that are financed by a combination of user payments and advertising revenue a tradeoff with respect to location incentives arises. On the one hand, in order to maximize the revenue from advertising, the platform wants to deliver a large number of eyeballs to advertisers. Under the assumption of single-homing consumers, this drives platforms to move closer to the middle of the Hotelling line. The second source of financing, payment from users, drives platforms in the opposite direction; moving apart from the rival softens price competition.

Anderson and Gabszewicz (2006) present a simple model to illustrate how introducing revenue from ads as a second source of revenue would alter the maximum differentiation principle from d'Aspremont et al. (1979). In the standard model (pure user-financed), firms' profits are given by:

$$\pi_i = (p_i - c)x_i, \text{ where } i = 1, 2,$$

where p_i is the user price, c is the marginal cost of serving one user, and x_i is the demand. If revenue from ads is introduced in addition, and the price per advertiser per viewer is *given* by β, the firms' profits equal:

$$\pi_i = (p_i - c + \beta)x_i, \text{ where } i = 1, 2.$$

The revenue from ads then acts as a unit subsidy, and Anderson and Gabszewicz (2006) show that the outcome depends on β and the transportation costs (t). If t is low and β is high, the outcome resembles Steiner's duplication result (a crucial assumption is that the user prices have to be non-negative).

Gabszewicz et al. (2001) analyze this tradeoff by modifying the game used by d'Aspremont et al. (1979). In the latter, firms choose location at stage one and user prices at stage two. Gabszewicz et al. (2001) add a third stage where firms choose advertising charges (see also Gabszewicz et al., 2002). This could change the outcome of the first stage (where firms choose location/genre) such that firms may want to locate in the middle of the Hotelling line if transportation costs (political preferences in their framework) are low or unit advertising revenues are high.

The opposing location incentives under user payments and ad financing have impact on the effects of a merger. Since purely ad-financed platforms tend to differentiate too little, while platforms with payments only from users differentiate too much, the total effects are ambiguous both under competition and under a merged multi-channel monopolist.

6.3.6 Imperfect Competition in the Product Market

The conventional way to break Steiner's duplication result is to introduce disutility of ads. If consumers dislike ads, they face an indirect price of watching TV, which is increasing in the ad volume. Under certain assumptions, this brings us back to the principle of maximum differentiation from d'Aspremont et al. (1979). However, Gal-Or and Dukes (2003) show that this may change if strategic interaction with the product market is taken into account.

Gal-Or and Dukes incorporate imperfect competition in the product market and find that the interplay between this competition and the competition between ad-financed media provides an additional explanation of the duplication of genre outcome. Both the media market and the product market are considered as spatially differentiated markets. By duplication of content, media platforms raise competition for viewers/readers/listeners. The firms in the product market then advertise less and, in turn, less product information is available for consumers in the product market. The platforms are then in a position to negotiate higher charges for ads. A crucial assumption behind this result is that consumers have disutility of ads.

6.3.7 Multi-Homing Consumers: Competition for Advertisers

A crucial assumption in the genre models discussed above is that media consumers single-home while advertisers multi-home. As noted in Section 6.2.2, this implies that each platform has monopoly power in delivering its own viewers/readers/listeners to advertisers.

If we introduce competition for advertisers by allowing consumers to multi-home, the results in the classical contributions of Steiner (1952) and Beebe (1977) may break down. Behind this there is a simple story; according to the principle of incremental pricing, multi-homing consumers are less valuable to platforms than single-homing consumers.[16] Platforms may then want to bias content against multi-homing consumers and, in contrast to Steiner's prediction, ad-financed media platforms compete by delivering media genre diversity. To see this, assume that a fraction s of the consumers is multi-homing. If the value of a second impression is zero, duplication is only profitable if

$$\frac{v_A(1-s)}{2} > v_B.$$

Thus, multi-homing consumers reduce the likelihood of duplication (we are back to Steiner if $s=0$). The presence of multi-homing among consumers may then improve resource allocation, but the benefit is reduced when second impressions of ads are valuable.

Allowing for multi-homing consumers may also alter Beebe (1977). Media platforms place more weight on the preferences of single-homing rather than multi-homing consumers. Let us consider three different consumer groups, A, B, and C, of approximately equal numbers. The three groups have as first preference content types A, B, and C, respectively. A fourth genre, D, is the second preference for all three groups. A monopolist need only provide type D (LCD programming) to have all groups on board. Similarly, when all consumers are single-homing in a duopoly, both platforms will deliver the LCD programming (type D). Assume now that group B multi-homes while A and C do not. Under the assumption of zero value of second impressions, the multi-homers (group B) are worth nothing to the two platforms. The two platforms will then

---

[16] Both Ambrus et al. (2015) and Anderson et al. (2015a) develop the incremental pricing principle, but Ambrus et al. do not consider choice of genre.

choose the genres A and B, respectively. LCD programming does not arise with duopoly, but is still the outcome under monopoly. Allowing a merger may thus reduce media diversity.

Anderson et al. (2015b) provide a formal spatial model a la Hotelling (1929), where they show that a two-platform monopoly and competition give the same choice of genres. When second impressions have no value, the social optimum is inside these locations. Hence, the market outcome gives more differentiation than the social optimum under both monopoly and competition. Consequently, a merger will not have any effect on genre diversity. Note that Anderson, Foros, and Kind assume that there is no disutility of ads; as accentuated below, introducing disutility of ads is the conventional way of breaking Steiner's duplication result under the assumption of single-homing consumers. A more formal presentation of Anderson, Foros, and Kind is given in Peitz and Reisinger (2015, this volume).

6.3.8 Limits on Ownership Concentration and Media Bias

The regulations that enforce limits on ownership concentration focus on diversity of viewpoints, and we should accentuate the difference between diversity of viewpoints and diversity of genres. The most important economic rationale that may provide support for restriction on ownership in media is supply-side media bias (see, e.g., Besley and Prat, 2006; Gentzkow and Shapiro, 2008). On the other hand, under demand-side media bias, more competition leads to more media bias (Mullainathan and Shleifer, 2005). In a recent empirical paper on ideological diversity in the US newspaper market, Gentzkow et al. (2014) analyze the impact of multi-homing consumers. The theoretical foundations of their empirical analysis are based on the models of multi-homing consumers mentioned above, but they do not specifically analyze choice of genre or mergers. However, they find that competition depends crucially on the extent of multi-homing consumers, and they find that joint ownership reduces entry. Furthermore, by fixing the number of firms, they do not find any clear relationship between ownership structure and differentiation similar to the theoretical predictions from Anderson et al. (2015a,b).

In a recent paper, Anderson and McLaren (2012) analyze how media bias may affect media mergers. In a context where media owners have political motives, they may influence opinion by withholding information. The abilities to do so are reduced by competition. Consequently, a media merger that reduces competition may then increase such media bias. Preventing mergers may then increase welfare, all other things being equal. For more on media bias, see Gentzkow et al. (2015, this volume).

6.3.9 Empirical Evidence

The theories above reveal that there are opposing effects when it comes to whether a merger will increase or decrease firms' differentiation incentives. The empirical evidence on how mergers affect diversity is also mixed. See Sweeting (2015, this volume) on the radio market and Chandra and Kaiser (2015, this volume) on the newspaper market.

In the market for ad-financed radio, the 1996 Telecommunications Act removed some merger restrictions, and Berry and Waldfogel (2001) and Sweeting (2010) find that mergers made possible by this policy change increased variety. Similarly, in the newspaper market, George (2007) finds that increased concentration may reduce duplication of genres (increase the total number of topics). In television, Baker and George (2010) and George and Oberholzer-Gee (2011) find support for business stealing and ownership effects being important. George and Oberholzer-Gee (2011) accentuate that regulations that restrict ownership concentration might reduce diversity.[17]

An important question is whether a merger causes the number of media channels to be reduced. Apparently, diversity will be reduced if the acquired company closes down. However, empirical studies indicate that this might not be true. As shown by, e.g., George (2007), the diversity within the remaining TV channels or newspapers may increase. Put differently, mergers lead to less external diversity (fewer newspapers or TV channels), but more internal diversity. This might be a beneficial change if consumers single-home.

Jeziorski (2014) estimates a structural model to find the effects from mergers in the US radio market (data from 1996 to 2006; a period with a large number of mergers in the US due to the Telecommunication Act of 1996). He takes into account the two-sidedness of the market (listeners and advertisers). Since radio is free-to-air, the main effects of mergers come through repositioning and changes in advertising prices and quantities. With respect to product variety, Jeziorsky finds that mergers lead to more product variety to the benefit of consumers (building on the results from Berry and Waldfogel, 2001; Sweeting, 2010). The increase in product variety counterweights potential negative welfare effects from mergers (advertisers are worse off by a merger).

In a recent paper, Fan (2013) estimates a structural model for the US newspaper market and allows for multi-homing consumers when she analyzes a proposed merger between two newspapers in the Minneapolis market (the US Department of Justice eventually blocked the merger). In contrast to Affeldt et al. (2013) and Filistrucchi et al. (2012), see discussion in Section 6.4. Fan takes into account how product characteristics (quality) change after the merger. Fan shows that the merged firm would reduce quality (but quality may increase among some of the rivals) compared to the outcome without a merger. Consequently, ignoring the quality change could substantially underestimate the welfare effects of such a merger. Fan also allows for multi-homing consumers (consumers read two newspapers). See Sweeting (2015, this volume) for more details on mergers in the radio market and Chandra and Kaiser (2015, this volume) for details on the newspaper market.

---

[17] See also Romeo and Dick (2005) on the radio market and Spitzer (2010) on the television market.

6.4. MERGER CONTROL IN MEDIA MARKETS

There are numerous examples of intervention by antitrust authorities toward mergers in media markets. It turns out, though, that in many cases the chosen approach differs substantially from what we would recommend based on the perspectives presented earlier in this chapter. To see this, we will first explain the method used in merger control by antitrust authorities and then discuss some cases and empirical studies of mergers. When discussing cases and empirical studies, we distinguish between price effects and non-price effects of media mergers.

6.4.1 The Method Used by Antitrust Authorities

In a majority of cases, antitrust authorities have applied what we call a traditional approach. This approach does not take into account the possible two-sidedness of media markets. To see the consequences of this, we first explain the traditional approach in detail, and show how this fails to consider the special features of two-sided media markets. We then explain an approach where the two-sidedness is taken into account, in line with the approach discussed in the previous sections of this chapter.

Note that the method, even the one extended to take the two-sidedness into account, typically starts by considering possible price effects of a merger. Then, at a later stage, other probable effects are considered, such as responses from rival firms, repositioning of the merging firms' products, and potential for entry.[18] We follow this approach by first focusing on possible unilateral price effects of the merging parties and then go on to consider other potential effects, in particular repositioning. Repositioning is commonly considered as perhaps the most important issue in media markets, so it is worth noticing at the outset that the procedure used by antitrust authorities does not necessarily focus directly on repositioning of products. In this respect, the approach that is used might be biased.

6.4.1.1 The Traditional Approach

Market definition is crucial to the decision that is made in most merger cases.[19] It is plausible that this is the case also for the sub-group of media mergers. The main idea in the antitrust authorities' approach is that if the products of two merging firms are close substitutes, then a merger might lead to higher prices. The 1982 US merger guidelines introduce the SSNIP approach—Small but Significant Non-transitory Increase in Prices. The approach starts out with a candidate market, and asks whether a hypothetical monopoly firm would find it profitable to raise prices by 5–10%. If the answer is yes, it indicates that

---

[18]   For a description of the competition authorities' procedure in merger control cases, see DG Comp (2011) concerning the EU and DOJ/FTC (2010, Sections 6.1 and 9) concerning the US.

[19]   See, for example, Baker (2007), who claims that market definition has been more decisive in competition cases in the US than any other issue.

this product does not have many very close substitutes and the relevant market is defined. If the answer is no, a new product is included and the SSNIP test is performed for the candidate market consisting of these two products. This procedure continues until the relevant market is defined, and it is then possible to calculate the merging firms' market shares. It turns out that in many merger cases antitrust authorities use market share as an important input for estimating the possible anticompetitive effect of the potential merger in question.

The SSNIP test can easily be formulated formally, which was first done in Harris and Simons (1989). Let us consider one particular product which is produced by more than one firm. The question is whether a hypothetical monopoly firm would find it profitable to increase the price of this product. Let α denote the relative price increase, and β the relative reduction in sales that leads to zero change in profit following the price increase. Furthermore, $\bar{q}$ denotes sales before the price increase and c denotes the marginal cost (assumed to be constant). If the following condition holds, then profit is identical or higher after the price increase:

$$[(1+\alpha)\bar{p}-c](1-\beta)\bar{q} \geq (\bar{p}-c)\bar{q}. \tag{6.1}$$

To simplify, let L denote the relative price-cost margin prior to the price increase; $L=(\bar{p}-c)/\bar{p}$. If we solve (6.1) with respect to β, we have the so-called critical loss $\beta=\alpha/(\alpha+L)$. This tells us the quantity of sales that the hypothetical monopoly firm can afford to lose without facing lower profits after the price increase. The critical loss must be compared to the actual loss. This can be defined as $\alpha_{\hookrightarrow}\varepsilon_{ii}$, the (negative of the) own-price elasticity of demand for this product (ε_i) multiplied by the price increase. This product is then defined as a separate market if:

$$\alpha \cdot \varepsilon_{ii} \leq \frac{\alpha}{\alpha+L}. \tag{6.2}$$

To capture the idea that the merging parties do produce differentiated goods, let us consider whether two products—each firm producing one of the two products—are belonging to the same market. We define ε_{ij} as the cross price elasticity of demand between the two products. Assuming symmetry, the condition for these two products belonging to the same relevant market is the following:

$$\underbrace{\alpha \cdot \left(\varepsilon_{ii}-\varepsilon_{ij}\right)}_{\text{Actual loss}} < \underbrace{\frac{\alpha}{\alpha+L}}_{\text{Critical loss}}. \tag{6.3}$$

The right-hand side is the critical loss we derived above. On the left-hand side, we take into account the fact that a price increase on one of the products will lead to a reduction in sales of this product that will partly be recaptured by increased sales of the other product. This explains why the price increase is multiplied by the own-price elasticity minus the cross price elasticity. Let us define the diversion ratio from product i to product j as $D_{ij} = -(\partial q_j/\partial p_i)/(\partial q_i/\partial p_i)$. It is the fraction of the reduction in sales of product i that is diverted to product j following a price increase on product i. O'Brien and Wickelgren (2003) consider the symmetric case where $D_{ij} = D_{ji} = D$ and $L_i = L_j = L$. They impose structure on the model by assuming that firms behave rationally in their (non-cooperative) pre-merger price setting. It is rational for a firm to set the price-cost margin equal to the inverse own-price elasticity of demand:

$$\frac{p-c}{p} = \frac{1}{\varepsilon_i}. \tag{6.4}$$

This is the Lerner index for one product (product i). Given such a revealed preference and symmetry, they show that products i and j belong to the same market if:

$$D \geq \frac{\alpha}{\alpha + L}. \tag{6.5}$$

These two products constitute a relevant market if the actual diversion ratio is higher than the critical loss derived above. This approach can easily be extended to a situation with asymmetries, for example one small and one large product.[20] However, the main point is still that market definition requires information about diversion ratios (or price elasticities) and margins (as well as the imposed price increase α).

Such an SSNIP approach has been criticized by economists. One criticism is that market definition is rather binary—either inside or outside the relevant market—and one should instead focus directly on the potential anticompetitive effect. Farrell and Shapiro (2010) have suggested that one should focus on the possible Upward Pricing Pressure (UPP) following a merger. They consider a merger between two firms. To check whether a merger leads to an upward pricing pressure, they combine the first-order conditions before and after the merger.

To illustrate their approach, let us consider the incentive to increase the price on one of the two products (assuming that each firm produces one product each before the merger), called product 1. We allow only for potential reductions in marginal costs of product 1. Let superscript AM denote after the merger and superscript A before the merger (where A stands for market A consisting of products 1 and 2). If we insert the first-order condition for product 1 before the merger into the first-order condition after the merger, we have the following condition for an upward pricing pressure on product 1 alone:

$$\mathrm{UPP}_1 = \left(p_2^A - c_2^A\right)D_{12}^A - \left(c_1^A - c_1^{AM}\right). \tag{6.6}$$

---

[20] See Katz and Shapiro (2003), which is further developed in Daljord et al. (2008).

The first term on the right-hand side is the value of recaptured sales: the sales that are recaptured by product 2 (the diversion ratio from product 1 to product 2) multiplied by the price-cost margin on product 2. Obviously, this gives an incentive for the merged firm to raise the price of product 1. The second term on the right-hand side is the reduction in marginal costs, which obviously leads to a downward pressure on the price of product 1. If we rearrange (6.6), and let E_1 denote the relative reduction in marginal costs on product 1, there is an upward pressure on product 1 if:

$$D_{12} > E_1 \cdot \frac{(1 - L_2)}{L_2}. \tag{6.7}$$

We see that diversion ratios and margins are important inputs to both the method for market definition and to the latter expression showing the possible upward pricing pressure. It can easily be shown that this is true even if we allow for an endogenous change in both firms' prices and for asymmetries between products.[21]

The approach we have shown here has been applied in merger control cases in the media sector. We will explain in more detail below, but for now we note that there are at least two potential errors. First, the approach does not take into account the two-sidedness which exists in many media markets. Second, it does not consider any product differentiation. For example, repositioning of products after a merger is not at all captured by such an approach. As we will show, the method has been further developed to take into account the first criticism, but not the second one.

6.4.1.2 An Extension to a Two-Sided Market

Previously, in this chapter, we have explained why the two-sidedness is of importance for the price setting on both sides of the market. The more general problem of applying one-market logic to antitrust policy in two-sided markets is discussed in, among others, Evans (2003) and Wright (2004). More specifically, methods for delineating the relevant market in two-sided markets are discussed in Evans and Noel (2005, 2008) and Filistrucchi et al. (2014). As noted above, the method for market definition points at margins and diversion ratios (or price elasticities) as crucial inputs. Let us consider a two-sided market consisting of two distinct groups of consumers, called consumer groups A and B, respectively. In the two-sided market model derived by Rochet and Tirole (2003), the Lerner index equals (assuming that c denotes the sum of the marginal costs on both sides of the market):

---

[21] As shown in Farrell and Shapiro (2010), although diversion ratios and margins are still the crucial pieces of information, the formula will differ from the one in Equation (6.7). Alternatively, absent any cost efficiencies one can estimate GUPPI (Gross Upward Pricing Pressure Index). For a discussion, see Moresi (2010) and Farrell and Shapiro (2010).

$$\frac{p^A + p^B - c}{p^A + p^B} = \frac{1}{\varepsilon_{ii}^A + \varepsilon_{ii}^B}.\tag{6.8}$$

This shows that the sum of the margins on the two sides of the market should be set equal to the inverse of the sum of the own-price elasticities. From this, it is already obvious that the traditional test for market definition, where the inputs consist of the margin and price elasticity on just one side of the market (see Equation 6.3), will fail to capture the two-sidedness. It is well known—as explained in the previous section—that margins can differ substantially between the two sides. In fact, it can be profitable to have a negative margin on one side in order to bring on board consumers from whom the other side can benefit. It is then obvious that applying data from just one side of the market to conduct a critical loss analysis can lead to major mistakes.[22] This is discussed in detail in Evans and Noel (2008), who also extend the critical loss analysis to a two-sided market.[23]

Unfortunately, it is difficult to detect the estimation bias if a one-sided market approach is applied in a two-sided market. To see this, think about a newspaper market with readers and advertisers.[24] A "naïve" approach could be that we consider a price increase for a hypothetical monopolist in the advertising market with a corresponding drop in the volume of ads, ignoring the reader side. We would then ignore the readers' response to a lower number of ads. If they are ad lovers, then a lower volume of ads would lead to a lower circulation. If so, the naïve approach would lead to a systematic under-estimation of market size since it failed to take into account the reduction in revenues on the reader side. On the other hand, the naïve approach would overestimate the market size of readers who dislike advertising.

Alternatively, we could use a more "sophisticated" version of the test where we consider the overall change in revenue resulting from a specific price increase on the advertising market only. Then we account for the change in revenues for readers. However, a change in advertising prices would make it optimal to change the reader prices as well. Since two instruments are better than one, it is obvious that allowing for changes in reader prices would make the price increase on advertising more profitable. A critical loss analysis with a change in advertising prices only would then underestimate the overall effect on profits, and therefore imply that the estimated market size would be systematically larger than the market size obtained by considering the full pricing possibilities.

---

[22] See also Evans (2003) and Oldale and Wang (2004), who both point out that there is not necessarily a relationship between market power (or no market power) and the price-cost margin on one side of the market.

[23] Hesse (2007) also warns against a one-sided market definition in a two-sided market. On the other hand, Ordover (2007) is not convinced that there is a need for new tools and new methods for antitrust policy toward two-sided markets.

[24] This distinction between a "naïve" and a "sophisticated" approach follows from Calvano and Jullien (2012).

An alternative to the critical loss analysis is to derive the upward pricing pressure. Let us extend the UPP approach to a two-sided market, consisting of market A and market R, where firms 1 and 2 are operative. Following Affeldt et al. (2013), we can derive the upward pricing pressure after a merger between the two firms. To fix ideas, think about a newspaper where A is the market for advertisers and R is the market for readers. We consider how a merger would affect the prices of firm 1. We then have the following UPP formulas for price for firm 1's product in markets A and R, respectively:

$$\text{UPP}_1^A = \left(p_2^A - c_2^A\right)D_{12}^{AA} - \left(c_1^A - c_1^{AM}\right) + \left(p_2^R - c_2^R\right)D_{12}^{AR} + \left(c_1^R - c_1^{RM}\right)D_{11}^{AR} \qquad (6.9)$$

$$\text{UPP}_1^R = \left(p_2^R - c_2^R\right)D_{12}^{RR} - \left(c_1^R - c_1^{RM}\right) + \left(p_2^A - c_2^A\right)D_{12}^{RA} + \left(c_1^A - c_1^{AM}\right)D_{11}^{RA}. \qquad (6.10)$$

The first two terms are analogous to the ones in the one-sided market: the upward pricing pressure from recapturing sales by the other firm on the same side of the market, and the downward pricing pressure from the marginal cost reduction for firm 1 on that side of the market.

The last two terms capture the cross-side effects. An increase (or decrease) in the number of units sold on one side of the market will affect the number of units that will be demanded on the other side of the market. For example, in the newspaper market, it is expected that more readers will attract more advertisers. A change in the price on one side of the market will then translate into not only changes in the number of units sold in that market, but also into the number of units sold in the other market.

The third term captures the cross-side effect from a change in the price of this firm's product in this side of the market on the other firm's revenues on the other side of the market. The change in revenue is the diversion ratio—the size of the change in the other firm's sale on the other side as a result of the change in this firm's sale on this side of the market—multiplied by the margin on the other side for the other firm. After the merger, the merged firm will take this increase in revenues on the other side of the market into account when considering a price change.

The fourth term captures the cost savings following the merger. It is the cost saving on the other side of the market for this firm.

To illustrate the effect, consider a merger between newspapers 1 and 2 with no cost reductions. After the merger, newspaper 1 sets a higher price to the readers. This leads to a diversion of some readers to newspaper 2, and this loss of readers is therefore recaptured after the merger. This is the traditional one-sided effect captured through the first term in Equation (6.10). In addition, a higher reader price leads to fewer readers for newspaper 1 and it becomes less attractive for the advertisers. This leads to a diversion of advertisers to newspaper 2, who after the merger are no longer advertisers that are lost for the firm. Such an indirect effect on the advertiser market from the reader market is captured through the third term in Equation (6.10). Interestingly, after the merger, newspaper 2 recaptures both readers and advertisers that had left newspaper 1. In contrast, in one-sided markets with only a reader side, it is only readers that are recaptured since there are no advertisers.

Note that the formulas given in Equations (6.9) and (6.10) do not include feedbacks. We have only considered in isolation each of the two prices set by firm 1. However, since there are four prices to be set, a change in one of the other three prices will feed back into the optimal choice for the price in question. As shown in Farrell and Shapiro (2010), in a one-sided market this will not change the results qualitatively. For example, a higher price on firm 2's product will make a price increase on firm 1's product even more profitable. But in a two-sided market, feedback effects can reverse the price effects. For example, consider a case where platforms 1 and 2 only overlap on side A of the market, and the demand on side A is increasing in the number of units sold on side R. The platforms could be newspapers, where the demand for advertising in each newspaper is increasing in its circulation. A merger might then lead to an upward pricing pressure on side A of the market, since this is where the firms overlapped, and the merger prevents them from competing on that side. Since each reader is then more valuable in the advertiser market, the optimal response would be to lower the price on the reader side of the market and thereby increase circulation. Ignoring the possible feedback can in such a case imply that the possible price reduction on the product on the other side of the market is not fully taken into account, and in that respect one might wrongly conclude that end consumers are worse off.

Finally, note that it is non-trivial to anticipate how consumers' attitude toward advertising might play a role. Dampening of competition on the advertising side might lead to higher advertising prices simply because the traditional business-stealing effect is dampened; the firms no longer reduce ad prices to attract advertisers. This might be true even if consumers are neither ad lovers nor ad-averse. If consumers are ad lovers, a merger would lead to an even larger upward pressure on advertising prices. As explained in Section 6.2.1, this is because ad lovers on the reader side of the market will lead to tough competition before the merger on having many ads and thereby low prices to advertisers. On the other hand, ad-averse consumers would dampen the incentive to have many ads in a competitive equilibrium. This is an argument for more ads after a merger and lower ad prices. The latter implies that the idea of testing for a price increase following a merger might be flawed; market power might lead to lower advertising prices and more advertising. Therefore, from theory we cannot conclude that the consumers' attitude toward advertising is crucial for the effect on the advertising volume of a merger.

6.4.2 The Possible Price Effect of Media Mergers

We have presented the methods used in merger control by antitrust authorities. In this section, we give some examples of how antitrust authorities have analyzed media mergers. We then contrast this approach with how media mergers have been analyzed by researchers in some recent empirical studies.

6.4.2.1 Merger Control: Some Examples

In the previous section, we distinguished between the method used for one-sided markets and the method used for two-sided markets. It turns out that competition authorities have used both methods in media mergers, and in some cases they have therefore failed to take into account the two-sidedness of the market. In what follows, we will give some examples of a one-sided approach, and then explain some examples of how the two-sided approach has been applied in some more recent media mergers.[25]

6.4.2.1.1 A One-Sided Market Approach

In merger control cases in media markets, the competition authorities have traditionally used a one-sided market approach. One example is the UK competition authorities. Both Durand (2008) and Wotton (2007) discuss several merger cases in the UK. Although they disagree on to what extent two-sidedness is taken into account, they both point at cases where the analysis has failed by only considering one side of the market, and then typically considering only the advertising market.

To illustrate this, let us consider the *Archant/Independent News and Media* merger case from 2004. This is a merger between local newspapers. When the UK Competition Commission, the phase II case handler in the UK, investigated the case, they focused exclusively on the advertising side. An important issue was the market definition. One piece of evidence was the results from a survey among advertisers. They were asked how large the price increase would have to be before they would decide to divert to advertising outside the local newspaper market. It was found that 23% of the advertising outlay would be diverted to other advertising channels than local newspapers if advertising prices increased by 5%. See Figure 6.1 for an illustration of the results from the survey.

This can be directly related to our formula for market definition (see Equation 6.3). Twenty-three percent is an estimate of the actual loss from a 5% price increase, and it can easily be seen that the local newspapers would be a relevant market if the price-cost margin is less than 17%. If so, the relevant market is rather narrow and the merger might lead to an anticompetitive effect in the advertising market for local newspapers. The Competition Commission (2007) discussed this in detail and decided that there was insufficient evidence to conclude that the merger would substantially lessen competition. As pointed out in Durand (2008) and Wotton (2007), the problem was that they considered only one side of this apparently two-sided market.

Let us assume that the competition authority had found an anticompetitive effect on the advertising side. This would most likely have led to an increase in the advertising

---

[25] We draw heavily on the surveys in Filistrucchi et al. (2010, 2014), where they provide numerous examples of how antitrust authorities have defined the relevant market. Since we focus on media mergers, we only consider what they have defined as nontransactional two-sided markets.

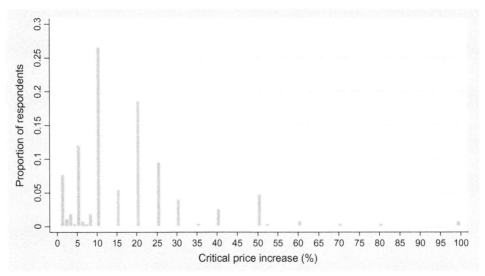

Figure 6.1 Critical price increase for advertisers considering switching to other than local newspapers.

prices, especially if the readers were ad lovers. Such a price increase would lead to a downward pressure on prices in the reader market. The reason is that higher prices in the advertising market would make each reader more valuable for the newspaper, and the optimal response would be to lower reader prices to attract more readers. The Competition Commission (2007) failed to take into account any effect on the reader side of the market. As explained in the previous section, given that readers are ad lovers, the Commission's approach would tend to underestimate the market size.

According to Durand (2008), a similar approach was used by the UK Competition Commission in the *Carlton Communications/Granada* merger in 2002. There was no overlap on the viewer side and the Commission therefore focused on the potential anticompetitive effect in the advertising market. They then failed to take into account the possible two-sidedness of the market. However, they did find that viewers might benefit from fewer ads on TV (given that ads are a nuisance), since higher ad prices could lead to less advertising. In this respect, the two-sidedness was considered to some degree. In line with this, Wotton (2007) claimed that the two-sidedness was an issue in this particular merger case.[26] The problem is, though, that in such a market it is an even more fundamental problem than in the newspaper market described above when the two-sidedness is not taken into consideration. Since the Commission argued that viewers dislike advertising, lower prices on advertising and thereby more ads after the merger

---

[26] He also noted, however, that in another merger in the radio market in the same year, *Capital Radio/GWR Group*, the Office of Fair Trading (OFT) focused exclusively on the advertising market and ignored the audience market.

(see Section 6.2.1) cannot be ruled out. The theory of harm—namely that the merger leads to higher advertising prices—is then problematic. In fact, the theory of harm could be reversed. The merger may lead to lower ad prices and more ads to the detriment of the consumers that consider ads as a nuisance.

Three other examples from television are the takeover of ProSieben/Sat1 by Axel Springer, BSkyB's acquisition of 24% of KirchPayTV, and News Corporation's acquisition of 25% of Premiere.[27] All these three cases have in common that they are mergers between one firm that is mainly financed by subscription and one that is mainly financed by advertising. It was argued that with free-to-air television there is no need to define a viewer market, since the TV channels have no direct revenue from viewers. It was also argued that pay TV has no or very limited advertising revenues, and therefore its behavior is not relevant for the advertiser market. However, as we know from the theory part, this way of reasoning is flawed. For example, one would then fail to recognize that after a merger the merged firm might have incentives to increase the advertising volume in the channel that before the merger was mainly financed by subscription revenues. This could be the case because the viewers regarded free-to-air and pay TV as fairly close substitutes, and this imposed a competitive constraint on the amount of profitable advertising. It is therefore misguided to consider the current financing structure, and from this observation conclude that one side of the market can be neglected.

6.4.2.1.2 A Two-Sided Market Approach

Already in 1995, before the theory of two-sided markets was defined, the US Supreme Court recognized the two-sidedness in the newspaper market[28]:

> *"Every newspaper is a dual trader in separate though independent markets; it sells the paper's news and advertising content to its readers."*

In recent years, we have seen several merger control cases where the two-sidedness has been discussed by parties and/or taken into account by competition authorities. Evans and Noel (2008) extended the method for market definition to a two-sided market, and they applied their method to Google's acquisition of DoubleClick, two firms active in the online advertising sector. Google operates an Internet search engine that offers search capabilities for end-users free of charge and provides online advertising space on its own websites. It also provides intermediation services to publishers and advertisers for the sale of online advertising space on partner websites through its network "AdSense." DoubleClick mainly sells ad serving, management and reporting technology worldwide to website publishers, advertisers, and agencies. Evans and Noel (2008) argue

---

[27] The first case was investigated by Bundeskartellamt in Germany, while the two other cases were investigated by the European Commission. For details concerning the cases, see Filistrucchi et al. (2014).

[28] See NAT's acquisition of the local daily newspaper Northwest Arkansas Times in Times-Picayune Publishing Co. v. United States, see 892 F. Supp. 1146 (W.D. Ark. 1995).

that these two firms operate in a two-sided market, with publishers and advertisers as two distinctly different groups of consumers. They apply a calibration technique to reveal critical and actual loss, and therefore do not have any information about demand. In line with what we explained when comparing Equations (6.8) and (6.4), they find that applying a Lerner index from one side of the market could be quite misleading. They claim that in this particular case it would lead to a too narrow market definition to only consider one of the sides of the two-sided market. Given the competition authorities' focus on market definition and market shares, this might lead to type I errors (banning welfare-enhancing mergers).

Google's acquisition of DoubleClick was investigated in detail by both the European Commission and the US Federal Trade Commission. Eventually both cleared the acquisition, and both accepted that ad networks constitute two-sided platforms serving both publishers and advertisers. For example, the European Commission stated the following:

> "Ad networks generate revenues (paid by advertisers for access to publishers' ad space inventory) that are shared between the network manager (as intermediation fee) and publishers."

In 2008, the Dutch Competition Authority (NMa) investigated an acquisition in the Dutch yellow pages market. The two companies, Truvo Netherlands and European Directories, published the only two nationwide print directories in the Netherlands. The parties argued that this was a two-sided market, where the firms provide "usage" to advertisers (look-ups or eyeballs) and provide users with information about businesses. The evidence consisted of an econometric study inspired by Rysman (2004) to detect cross price effects and two-sidedness, and two surveys among users and advertisers to detect substitution, i.e., diversion ratios among merging parties' products. According to Camesasca et al. (2009), this is one of the first merger cases where the competition authorities explicitly acknowledged the role of two-sidedness. The NMa wrote in their decision:

> "The supply of directories is thus marked by two-sidedness. It is accepted that this two-sidedness can have a certain effect. Although a limited fall in the number of users will not lead to a comparable drop in the price of advertisements, the [NMa] Board does accept that (certainly in time) a strong increase or decrease in usage will lead to a reaction from advertisers." (para 108)

The effects of the two-sidedness were decisive for NMa's decision to clear this merger.

At the same time, the European Commission investigated the US firm *Travelport*'s acquisition of *Worldspan Technologies* (another US firm). This transaction was cleared by the Commission in August 2007.[29] Both merging parties provide travel distribution services, in particular through their respective "global distribution systems" (GDS) Worldspan and Galileo (Travelport's brand). These technical platforms match travel

---

[29] The merger is discussed in Vannini (2008) and Rosati (2008), and briefly described in Filistrucchi et al. (2010).

content provided by airlines, hotel chains, car rental services, etc. on the one side, and the demand for such content as conveyed by travel agents on the other side. The Commission acknowledged that GDS was a two-sided market, and wrote:

"… [t]he existence of the GDS platform is justified by the added value it creates. A GDS coordinates the demand of [travel agents], thereby generating a positive network externality which is internalised by the [travel service providers]."

Another example is A-pressen's acquisition of Edda Media, two media firms in Norway which each owned several newspapers. The Norwegian Competition Authority did take into account the two-sidedness by investigating both the advertising and the reader market. They focused on two local areas with respect to a potential anticompetitive effect of the acquisition, and made a survey among both advertisers and readers in both areas to detect the diversion ratios. In one of the areas, they concluded from the surveys that the two newspapers were close substitutes for both readers and advertisers, and they imposed a remedy (to sell out one of the parties' newspapers). In the other area, they found that the two newspapers were close substitutes only on the advertising side, but also here they imposed a remedy (to sell out one of the parties' newspapers). In this case, they failed to take into account the fact that increased market power on the advertising side could lead to lower prices or higher quality on the reader side (see Kind and Sørgard, 2013).

Filistrucchi et al. (2014) refer to several fairly recent merger cases in the TV industry. They argue that competition authorities often fail to recognize that TV channels can be differentiated not only on content as such but also on the amount of advertising they air. One example is BSkyB's acquisition of shares in ITV.[30] The UK Competition Commission did define the two sides of the market, and discussed whether viewers would regard content of those two firms as close substitutes. But they failed to recognize that the firms could be differentiated also on the amount of advertising. As a consequence, they did not take into account any changes in the behavior in the advertiser market following the acquisition. According to Filistrucchi et al. (2014), they should have discussed whether viewers dislike advertising on TV or not. If they dislike advertising, then some theory models would predict that the merger would lead to more advertising. This could be harmful for the viewers. However, as explained in the theory part, it is not at all trivial to conclude on the welfare effect in such cases.

6.4.2.2 Empirical Studies

Let us contrast the approach we have seen in merger control with the approach used by researchers who have analyzed the effect of media mergers. One first observation is that surveys among consumers (example: readers and advertisers) are often used to analyze

---

[30] BSkyB acquired in 2007 17.9% of the shares in ITV. For details, see Filistrucchi et al. (2014).

substitution between merging firms' products, while this is seldom the case in empirical studies carried out by researchers. In contrast, researchers often estimate demand from observed quantities and prices on both sides of the market. One obvious reason for this distinction is the time constraint in merger control. Antitrust authorities will be facing a time constraint, and it may then be more feasible to conduct a survey among the consumers than to undertake a full-fledged estimation of a demand system.

Rysman (2004) is one of the first empirical studies that analyze a two-sided market (yellow pages).[31] Although this is not a study of a particular merger, he used the estimated demand system to compare monopoly and oligopoly. He found that a more competitive market is preferable. This study was the starting point for an econometric study that was applied in an acquisition in the Dutch yellow pages market (see above). There are other studies, though, that focus directly on mergers.

Chandra and Collard-Wexler (2009) study the effect of numerous mergers in the newspaper market in Canada in the late 1990s. They apply a difference-in-difference approach by comparing merging newspapers with non-merging newspapers. They find that those newspapers that were involved in mergers did not have any different price changes on either advertising prices or reader prices than the newspapers in the control groups. However, they are careful in their interpretation of their results. It is possible that the lack of price effect could be due to cost reductions following the mergers. It could also be the result of a self-selection bias, where the newspapers that merged had great market power and would have experienced even lower prices without a merger. Finally, they claim that there is some evidence of mergers having more to do with political motives and empire building than with profits.

Alternatively, one could estimate a structural model of a two-sided market in order to investigate the interplay between the two sides of the market. Examples of some early empirical studies along these lines are Rysman (2004), Kaiser and Wright (2006), and Argentesi and Fillistruchi (2007). However, there are only a few empirical studies that estimate a structural model in order to investigate the possible price effects of a merger in a two-sided market.

Both Affeldt et al. (2013) and Filistrucchi et al. (2012) estimate a structural model for the newspaper market in the Netherlands, and derive possible demand interdependencies between the advertiser and the reader side in addition to the traditional one-sided demand effects. They apply the estimated demand system to simulate possible price effects of various mergers between newspapers, and compare the results with and without incorporating the two-sidedness. They find in both studies that a one-sided approach

---

[31] See also Kaiser and Wright (2006), who test empirically the price-cost margin in the magazine market on the advertising and the reader side, respectively. They find that in this market the readers are subsidized and the magazines make most of their profits from the advertising side. Argentesi and Fillistruchi (2007) follow a similar approach by estimating a structural model for the Italian newspaper market.

might underestimate the price increase on advertising. The intuition is that the one-sided approach does not take into account the diversion on the reader side among the merging parties following a change in the prices of advertising. If readers like advertising, they will divert from the newspaper that raises advertising prices and thereby reduces the volume of advertising, and some of them will be recaptured by the other merging newspaper. After the merger, this indirect network effect is taken into account by the merging firm, leading to a stronger incentive to raise the advertising prices.

Fan (2013) also estimates a structural model for the newspaper market. She uses the model to simulate the effects of a merger between two newspapers in the Minneapolis area in the US that was blocked by the US Department of Justice. Contrary to Affeldt et al. (2013) and Filistrucchi et al. (2012), she takes into account product characteristics and the potential for a change in these following the merger. It is found that the merger would have led to a reduced quality of content, higher prices to readers, and lower circulation. She finds that ignoring the quality change could substantially underestimate the welfare effect of such a merger.

Song (2013) estimates a structural model to investigate the price effects of a merger in the market for TV magazines in Germany. It is a market with payment on both sides, advertisers and readers, and, in line with Kaiser and Wright (2006), he finds that the firms set prices below marginal costs on the reader side of the market and earn profits on the advertising side. He simulates the price effect of a merger to monopoly, and finds that advertising prices would generally increase, while the reader prices in some cases would drop after the merger.

Finally, Jeziorski (2011) investigates the effect of the merger wave in the US radio market that occurred between 1996 and 2006. He estimates a structural model and takes into account the two-sidedness of this market (listeners and advertisers). Radio is free-to-air, so the main effects of the mergers come through repositioning and changes in advertising prices and quantities. It is found that the mergers led to more product variety for the benefit of listeners, and less advertising both in small markets (with more market power) and in large markets. On average, it is found that listeners benefit from the merger wave while advertisers are worse off.

6.4.3 The Possible Non-Price Effect of Media Mergers

Although some of the empirical studies we have referred to also discuss some non-price effects, such as product quality, most of the discussion so far has focused on the possible price effect.

As explained earlier in this chapter, a merger might lead to more diversity. If media firms have been competing fiercely on location/differentiation, they will in some instances offer rather similar products and, in the extreme case, identical products. If two firms then merge, they might have incentives to reposition their products and thereby increase the differentiation. The theoretical argument is presented in Section 6.3, where we also present a brief overview of empirical findings.[32]

Repositioning has been an issue in some media mergers. One example is *GCap Media's* acquisition of *Global Radio UK* in 2008. The OFT in the UK cleared the acquisition, given that the parties accepted certain remedies. Interestingly, repositioning was explicitly considered by the OFT. They referred to the theoretical study by Gandhi et al. (2008), in which it is shown that merging parties might have an incentive to reposition their products after a merger and offer more differentiated products. In this particular case, the parties claimed that after the acquisition the radio stations would be more differentiated in terms of demographic space, and the OFT wrote the following:

> "[I]t is only upon the bringing of the different stations under common ownership that it would be rational for the owner of those stations commercially to take the decision to differentiate the stations further in terms of demographic space. This claim gains weight, because it is consistent with the U.S. evidence on product repositioning of radio stations format that occurred after a wave of mergers following U.S. deregulation of ownership restrictions, but not before it."

The OFT also referred to Berry and Waldfogel (2001) and Romeo and Dick (2005), both empirical studies of the radio market in the US (see the discussion earlier in this chapter) that found that mergers led to more product differentiation.

There are several examples from the US where the competition authorities in their merger review have taken into account the potential effects of product repositioning. Examples of merger cases are the merger between Whole Foods Market and Wild Oats Market in the retail market for organic foods, and the merger between Oracle and PeopleSoft.[33] Repositioning is mentioned in the US Horizontal Merger Guidelines, although very briefly.[34] However, as far as we know, there are no examples of merger reviews by the competition authorities in the US in media markets where repositioning has been an important issue.

6.5. CONCLUDING REMARKS

In this chapter, we present a survey of the media economics literature on mergers. We put emphasis on where the effects of mergers differ between conventional one-sided markets and two-sided media markets.

---

[32] In particular, see Berry and Waldfogel (2001), Sweeting (2010), and Romeo and Dick (2005) concerning the radio market, Spitzer (2010) concerning the television market, and George (2007) concerning the newspaper market.

[33] For a description of these and other merger cases, see Mazzeo et al. (2013).

[34] See DOJ/FTC (2010). Note that repositioning is considered as a possible constraint on the merging firms' incentives to raise prices. For example, they mention that the non-merging firms might reposition their product close to the merging firms' products (see p. 21).

In the first part of the chapter, we discuss the price effects of mergers. The two-sided markets literature has shown that the price effects of mergers of ad-financed platforms differ from predictions in the conventional one-sided merger literature. A merger that increases market power on one side of the market tends to reduce prices on the other side (see, e.g., Rochet and Tirole, 2006; Weyl, 2010). In their seminal paper on two-sided media markets, Anderson and Coate (2005) predict that a merger leads the platforms to charge *lower* ad prices if consumers dislike ads. A crucial force leading to this puzzling result is the assumption of single-homing consumers; competition for advertisers is then closed down. When allowing for competition for advertisers by allowing for multi-homing consumers, recent contributions show that ad prices may increase when ad-financed platforms are merged (Ambrus et al., 2015; Anderson and Peitz, 2014a,b; Anderson et al., 2015a; Athey et al., 2013).

In the second part of the chapter, we discuss how mergers affect competing media platforms' choice of genre. In his seminal paper, Steiner (1952) shows that mergers may reduce duplication of genres and increase diversity. The prediction is given empirical support in recent empirical papers (Baker and George, 2010; Berry and Waldfogel, 2001; George 2007; George and Oberholzer-Gee, 2011; Jeziorski, 2014; Sweeting, 2010). However, Beebe (1977) casts doubt on Steiner's prediction that mergers tend to increase diversity. If a given consumer's favorite genre is not available, he might be willing to watch some other genre instead. If so, Beebe shows that a merger to monopoly might reduce the number of genres broadcasted. In a recent two-sided Hotelling framework, Anderson et al. (2015b) allow for multi-homing consumers. They show that a merger of two platforms might have no effect on the choice of genres (location on the Hotelling line), and thus no effect on diversity.

In the third part of the chapter, we discuss how antitrust policy takes on merger control in two-sided media markets. A common message from the recent two-sided markets literature is that the consequences of mergers in one-sided and two-sided markets might be very different both with respect to effects on prices and diversity. Consequently, an important issue is how antitrust authorities take on mergers with a two-sided market nature. In numerous cases, antitrust authorities have applied the traditional one-sided market logic to media markets. Such a procedure might be flawed. With respect to the price effects, the methodology used by antitrust authorities for analyzing two-sided mergers has improved in recent years. Less progress has been made in the antitrust authorities' analysis of non-price effects of mergers (e.g., how mergers affect media diversity).

Antitrust authorities are typically concerned about horizontal mergers, and this has been the focus of this chapter. In media markets, however, antitrust authorities have also paid a lot of attention to vertical mergers (integration) and mergers between players operating in adjacent markets. We started out in the Introduction by mentioning the AOL–Time Warner merger from 2001, perhaps the most prominent merger from the dot-com era. Prior to the merger, these companies were considered to be operating in adjacent or vertically integrated markets. An issue to which we have not given attention in this chapter is the concern that such mergers might generate abilities and incentives to fore-close competing non-integrated firms that need to buy some kind of access from the ver-tically integrated firm (Rubinfeld and Singer, 2001, discuss foreclosure incentives in the AOL–Time Warner case). Much attention was also given by competition authorities to BSkyB's attempt to acquire Manchester United. Antitrust authorities were concerned about input foreclosure. The comprehensive literature on access and foreclosure is typ-ically restricted to one-sided frameworks although a few recent papers analyze the vertical relationship within two-sided markets (e.g., D'Annunzio, 2014; Stennek, 2014; Weeds, 2015).[35] Among market players, the interplay between vertical layers has gained attention as a trigger behind mergers: "*Comcast's agreement to buy Time Warner Cable was followed by AT&T's agreement to buy DirecTV for $48.5 billion. Even media giants like 21st Century Fox, run by Rupert Murdoch, looked to deal making, in part to give them more clout to use against distributors.*" (New York Times, November 17, 2014).

While complete mergers, i.e., mergers which transfer corporate control, have been the main concern among antitrust authorities, partial ownership has been a hot topic within media markets. The largest UK pay-TV provider, BSkyB, announced in 2006 that it had acquired 17.9% of the shares in ITV. The UK Competition Commission (2007) were concerned that the transaction would give BSkyB a significant degree of corporate control in ITV. If so, BSkyB would have incentives and the ability to weaken the competitive constraint of ITV on BSkyB. The Commission required that BSkyB's shareholding in ITV should be reduced to below 7.5% in order to prevent BSkyB from taking corporate control in ITV. Media and entertainment markets are also the illustrative examples used by O'Brien and Salop (2000) in their seminal paper on anticompetitive effects of partial ownership.

Merger control is in most cases restricted to structural remedies that modify the allo-cation of property rights. In addition to competition regulation, several media markets are restricted by sector-specific regulations that impose both structural and behavioral remedies. In the US market for newspapers, three remedies have been used in order to ensure ideological diversity: joint operating agreements (JOAs), restrictions on joint ownership, and provision of subsidies (Gentzkow et al., 2014, 2015).[36] Restrictions on joint ownership have also been used in radio and television markets both in the US and in Europe.

Finally, a regulatory issue in two-sided markets which has been high on the agenda in recent years is net neutrality. Weyl (2010) accentuates: "*[T]he novel element in two-sided markets is that regulators should focus most on reducing price opposite a side with a large Spence distortion. Thus regulators of ISPs should focus on limiting prices to Web sites (net neutrality) if*

[35] Armstrong (1999) considers the pure pay-TV platforms (no ads).
[36] See Chandra and Kaiser (2015, this volume) on JOAs in the newspaper market.

there is more (interaction) surplus among loyal users than among highly profitable Web sites. But if the situation is reversed, forcing ISPs to reduce prices and build more line to consumer homes may be a higher priority." The issue of net neutrality may obviously affect both vertical and horizontal merger incentives. It is, however, beyond the scope of this chapter to go into vertical mergers and sector-specific regulations.

ACKNOWLEDGMENTS

We thank Simon P. Anderson and Anna D'Annunzio for helpful discussions and comments.

REFERENCES

Affeldt, P., Filistrucchi, L., Klein, T.H., 2013. Upward pricing pressure in a two-sided market. Econ. J. 123, F505–F523.

Ambrus, A., Reisinger, M., 2006. Exclusive vs. Overlapping Viewers in Media Markets. Working Paper.

Ambrus, A., Calvano, E., Reisinger, M., 2015. Either or Both Competition: A "Two-Sided" Theory of Advertising with Overlapping Viewerships. Working Paper.

Anderson, S.P., Coate, S., 2005. Market provision of broadcasting: a welfare analysis. Rev. Econ. Stud. 72, 947–972.

Anderson, S.P., Gabszewicz, J.J., 2006. The advertising-financed business model in two-sided media markets. In: Throsby, D., Ginsburgh, V. (Eds.), Handbook of the Economics of Art and Culture. Elsevier Science.

Anderson, S.P., Jullien, B., 2015. The advertising-financed business model in two-sided media markets. In: Anderson, S.P., Strömberg, D., Waldfogel, J. (Eds.), Handbook of Media Economics, vol. 1A. Elsevier, Amsterdam.

Anderson, S.P., McLaren, J., 2012. Media mergers and media bias with rational consumers. J. Eur. Econ. Assoc. 10 (4), 831–859.

Anderson, S.P., Peitz, M., 2014a. Media See-Saws: Winners and Losers on Ad-Financed Media Platforms. Unpublished manuscript.

Anderson, S.P., Peitz, M., 2014b. Advertising Congestion in Media Markets. Unpublished manuscript.

Anderson, S.P., Waldfogel, J., 2015. Preference externalities in media markets. In: Anderson, S.P., Strömberg, D., Waldfogel, J. (Eds.), Handbook of Media Economics, vol. 1A. Elsevier, Amsterdam.

Anderson, S.P., Foros, Ø., Kind, H.J., 2015a. Competition for Advertisers and for Viewers in Media Markets. Working Paper.

Anderson, S.P., Foros, Ø., Kind, H.J., 2015b. Product Quality, Competition, and Multi-purchasing. International Economic Review, forthcoming.

Argentesi, E., Fillistruchi, L., 2007. Estimating market power in a two-sided market: the case of newspapers. J. Appl. Econ. 22, 1247–1266.

Armstrong, M., 1999. Competition in the pay-TV market. J. Jpn. Int. Econ. 13, 257–280.

Armstrong, M., 2002. Competition in Two-Sided Markets. Working Paper.

Armstrong, M., 2006. Competition in two-sided markets. RAND J. Econ. 37 (3), 668–691.

Athey, S., Calvano, E., Gans, J., 2013. The Impact of the Internet on Advertising Markets for News Media. NBER Working Paper 19419.

Baker, J., 2007. Market definition: an analytical overview. Antitrust Law J. 74, 129.

Baker, M.J., George, L.M., 2010. The role of television in household debt: evidence from the 1950's. B. E. J. Econ. Anal. Policy 10 (1), 1–36. (Advances), Article 41.

Barros, P.P., Kind, H.J., Nilssen, T., Sørgard, L., 2004. Media competition on the internet. Top. Econ. Anal. Policy. 4. Article 32.

Beebe, J.H., 1977. Institutional structure and program choices in television markets. Q. J. Econ. 91 (1), 15–37.

Berry, S., Waldfogel, J., 2001. Do mergers increase product variety? Evidence from radio broadcasting. Q. J. Econ. 116 (3), 1009–1025.

Besley, P., Prat, A., 2006. Handcups for the grabbing hand? Media capture and government accountability. Am. Econ. Rev. 96 (3), 720–736.

Boulding, K.E., 1955. Economic analysis. third ed. Harper & Bros., New York

Calvano, E., Jullien, B., 2012. Issues in on-line advertising and competition policy: a two-sided market perspective. In: Harrington, J.E., Katsoulacos, Y. (Eds.), Recent Advances in the Analysis of Competition Policy and Regulation. Edwar Elgar, Cheltenham, pp. 179–196.

Camesasca, P.D., Meulenbelt, M., Chellingsworth, T., Daems, I., Vandenbussche, J., 2009. The Dutch yellow pages merger case -2-1 will go!. Eur. Compet. Law Rev. 30 (4).

Chandra, A., Collard-Wexler, A., 2009. Mergers in two-sided markets: an application to the Canadian newspaper industry. J. Econ. Manag. Strateg. 18 (4), 1045–1070.

Chandra, A., Kaiser, U., 2015. Newspapers and magazines. In: Anderson, S.P., Strömberg, D., Waldfogel, J. (Eds.), Handbook of Media Economics, vol. 1A. Elsevier, Amsterdam.

Crawford, G., 2015. The economics of television and online video markets. In: Anderson, S.P., Strömberg, D., Waldfogel, J. (Eds.), Handbook of Media Economics, vol. 1A. Elsevier, Amsterdam.

Daljord, Ø., Sørgard, L., Thomassen, Ø., 2008. The SSNIP test and market definition with the aggregate diversion ratio: a reply to Katz and Shapiro. J. Compet. Law Econ. 4 (2), 263–270.

D'Annunzio, A., 2014. Vertical Integration in Two-Sided Markets: Exclusive Provision and Program Quality. Available at SSRN:http://ssrn.com/abstract=2359615.

d'Aspremont, C., Gabszewicz, J.J., Thisse, J.F., 1979. On Hotelling's stability in competition. Econometrica 17, 1145–1151.

Dewenter, R., Haucap, J., Wenzel, T., 2011. Semi-collusion in media markets. Int. Rev. Law Econ. 31, 92–98.

Directorate-General for Competition, 2011. Economic Evidence in Merger Analysis. Technical Report, Directory General for Competition.

DOJ/FTC, 2010. Horizontal Merger Guidelines. Jointly authored by U.S. Department of Justice and Federal Trade Commission, United States.

Durand, B., 2008. Two-sided markets: Yin and Yang—a review of recent UK mergers. Concurrences 2.

Eaton, B.C., Lipsey, R.G., 1975. The principle of minimum differentiation reconsidered: some new developments in the theory of spatial competition. Rev. Econ. Stud. 42 (1), 27–49.

Evans, D.S., 2003. The antitrust economics of multi-sided platform markets. Yale J. Regul. 20 (2), 325–381.

Evans, D.S., Noel, M.D., 2005. Defining antitrust markets when firms operate two-sided platforms. Columbia Bus. Law Rev. 2005, 667–702.

Evans, D.S., Noel, M.D., 2008. The analysis of mergers that involve multisided platform businesses. J. Compet. Law Econ. 4 (3), 663–695.

Fan, Y., 2013. Ownership consolidation and product characteristics: a study of the US daily newspaper market. Am. Econ. Rev. 103 (5), 1598–1628.

Farrell, J., Shapiro, C., 1990. Horizontal mergers: an equilibrium analysis. Am. Econ. Rev. 80 (1), 107–126.

Farrell, J., Shapiro, C., 2010. Antitrust evaluation of horizontal mergers: an economic alternative to market definition. B.E. J. Theor. Econ. 10 (1). Article 9.

Filistrucchi, L., et al., 2010. Mergers in Two-Sided Markets—A Report to the NMa. A report submitted to the Dutch Competition Authorities (NMa), June 25, 2010.

Filistrucchi, L., Klein, T.J., Michielsen, T.O., 2012. Assessing unilateral merger effects in a two-sided market: an application to the Dutch daily newspaper market. J. Compet. Law Econ. 8 (2), 297–329.

Filistrucchi, L., Geradin, D., van Damme, E., Affeld, P., 2014. Market definition in two-sided markets, theory and practice. J. Compet. Law Econ. 10 (2), 293–339.

Foros, Ø., Kind, H.J., Schjelderup, G., 2012. Ad pricing by multi-channel platforms: how to make viewers and advertisers prefer the same channel. J. Med. Econ. 25, 133–146.

Gabszewicz, J.J., Laussel, D., Sonnac, N., 2001. Press advertising and the ascent of the 'Pensée unique'. Eur. Econ. Rev. 45, 645–651.

Gabszewicz, J.J., Laussel, D., Sonnac, N., 2002. Press advertising and the political differentiation of newspapers. J. Public Econ. Theory 4, 317–334.

Gal-Or, E., Dukes, A., 2003. Minimum differentiation in commercial media markets. J. Econ. Manag. Strateg. 12, 291–325.

Gandhi, A., Froeb, L., Tschantz, S., Werden, G., 2008. Post-merger product repositioning. J. Ind. Econ. 56 (1), 49–67.

Gentzkow, M., Shapiro, J.M., 2008. Competition and truth in the market for news. J. Econ. Perspect. 22 (2), 133–154.

Gentzkow, M., Shapiro, J.M., Sinkinson, M., 2014. Competition and ideological diversity: historical evidence from US newspapers. Am. Econ. Rev. 104 (10), 3073–3114.

Gentzkow, M., Shapiro, J.M., Stone, D.F., 2015. Media bias in the marketplace: theory. In: Anderson, S.P., Strömberg, D., Waldfogel, J. (Eds.), Handbook of Media Economics, vol. 1B. Elsevier, Amsterdam.

George, L.M., 2007. What's fit to print: the effect of ownership concentration on product variety in daily newspaper markets. Inf. Econ. Policy 19 (3–4), 285–303.

George, L.M., Oberholzer-Gee, F., 2011. Diversity in Local Television News. FTC.

Hannesson, R., 1982. Defensive foresight rather than minimax: a comment on Eaton and Lipsey's model of spatial competition. Rev. Econ. Stud. 49 (4), 653–657.

Harris, B.C., Simons, J.J., 1989. Focusing market definition: how much substitution is enough? Res. Law Econ. 12, 207–226.

Hesse, R.B., 2007. Two-sided platform markets and the application of the traditional antitrust analytical framework. Compet. Policy Int. 3 (1), 191.

Hotelling, H., 1929. Stability in competition. Econ. J. 39, 41–57.

Jeziorski, P., 2011. Merger Enforcement in Two-Sided Markets. Working Paper.

Jeziorski, P., 2014. Effects of mergers in two-sided markets: the U.S. radio industry. Am. Econ. J. Microecon. 6 (4), 35–73.

Kaiser, U., Wright, J., 2006. Price structure in two-sided markets: evidence from the magazine industry. Int. J. Ind. Organ. 24, 1–28.

Katz, M.L., Shapiro, C., 1985. Network externalities, competition, and compatibility. Am. Econ. Rev. 75, 424–440.

Katz, M.L., Shapiro, C., 2003. Critical loss: let's tell the whole story. Antitrust Mag 26, 49–56.

Kind, H.J., Sørgard, L., 2013. Fusjoner i tosidige markeder. Merger in two-sided markets, MAGMA 13 (8), 51–62.

Kind, H.J., Nilssen, T., Sørgard, L., 2007. Competition for viewers and advertisers in a TV oligopoly. J. Med. Econ. 20 (3), 211–233.

Mazzeo, M., Seim, K., Varela, M., 2013. The Welfare Consequences of Mergers with Product Repositioning. Working Paper.

Moresi, S., 2010. The Use of Upward Pricing Pressures Indices in Merger Analysis. Antitrust Source.

Mullainathan, S., Shleifer, A., 2005. The market for news. Am. Econ. Rev. 95 (4), 1031–1053.

O'Brien, D.P., Salop, S., 2000. Competitive effects of partial ownership: financial interest and corporate control. Antitrust Law J. 67, 559–614.

O'Brien, D., Wickelgren, A., 2003. A critical analysis of critical loss analysis. Antitrust Law J. 71 (1), 161–184.

Ofcom, 2014. The Communications Market Report. Published 7th August 2014.

Oldale, A., Wang, E., 2004. A little knowledge can be a dangerous thing: price controls in the yellow pages industry. Eur. Common Law Rev. 25 (10), 607.

Ordover, J.A., 2007. Comments on Evans and Schmalensee's "the industrial organization of markets with Two-sided platforms" Compet. Policy Int. 3 (1), 181.

Peitz, M., Reisinger, M., 2015. The economics of internet media. In: Anderson, S.P., Strömberg, D., Waldfogel, J. (Eds.), Handbook of Media Economics, vol. 1A. Elsevier, Amsterdam.

Rochet, J.-C., Tirole, J., 2003. Platform competition in two-sided markets. J. Eur. Econ. Assoc. 1 (4), 990–1029.

Rochet, J.-C., Tirole, J., 2006. Two-sided markets: a progress report. RAND J. Econ. 37 (3), 645–667.

Romeo, C., Dick, A., 2005. The effect of format changes and ownership consolidation on radio station outcomes. Rev. Ind. Organ. 27, 351–386.

Rosati, F., 2008. Is merger assessment different in two-sided markets? Lessons from Travelport/Worldspan. Concurrences 2.

Rothenberg, J., 1962. Consumer sovereignty and the economics of television programming. Stud. Public Commun. 4, 45–54.

Rubinfeld, D.L., Singer, H.J., 2001. Vertical foreclosure in broadband access? J. Ind. Econ. 49 (3), 299–318.

Rysman, M., 2004. Competition between networks: a study of the market for yellow pages. Rev. Econ. Stud. 71 (2), 483–512.

Selten, R., 1970. Preispolitik der Mehrproduktenunternehmung in der Statischen Theorie. Springer Verlag, Berlin.

Song, M., 2013. Estimating Platform Market Power in Two-Sided Markets with an Application to Magazine Advertising. Working Paper.

Spitzer, M.L., 2010. Television mergers and diversity in small markets. J. Compet. Law Econ. 6 (3), 705–770.

Steiner, P.O., 1952. Program patterns and the workability of competition in radio broadcasting. Q. J. Econ. 66 (2), 194–223.

Stennek, J., 2014. Exclusive quality—why exclusive distribution may benefit the TV viewers. Inf. Econ. Policy 26, 42–57.

Sweeting, A., 2010. The effects of mergers on product positioning: evidence from the music radio industry. RAND J. Econ. 41 (2), 372–397.

Sweeting, A., 2015. Radio. In: Anderson, S.P., Strömberg, D., Waldfogel, J. (Eds.), Handbook of Media Economics, vol. 1A. Elsevier, Amsterdam.

The Competition Commission, 2007. Acquisition by British Sky Broadcasting Group Plc OF. Report sent to Secretary of State (BERR).

The UK Competition Commission, 2007. Acquisition by British Sky Broadcasting Group Plc OF. Report sent to Secretary of State (BERR), 14 December 2007.

Vannini, S., 2008. Bargaining and Two-Sided Markets: The Case of Global Distribution Systems (GDS) in Travelport's Acquisition of Worldspan. Competition Policy Newsletter, no. 2/2008, 43–50.

Waldfogel, J., 2009. The Tyranny of the Market: Why You Can't Always Get What You Want. Harvard University Press.

Weeds, H., 2015. TV wars: exclusive content and platform competition in pay TV. Econ. J. http://dx.doi.org/10.1111/ecoj.12195. forthcoming.

Werden, G.J., 1996. A robust test for consumer welfare enhancing mergers among sellers of differentiated products. J. Ind. Econ. 44 (4), 409–413.

Weyl, G., 2010. A price theory of multi-sided platforms. Am. Econ. Rev. 100 (4), 1642–1672.

Wilbur, K., 2008. A two-sided, empirical model of television advertising and viewer markets. Market. Sci. 27, 356–378.

Wiles, P., 1963. Pilkington and the theory of value. Econ. J. 73, 183–200.

Williamson, O.E., 1968. Economies as an antitrust defense: the welfare tradeoffs. Am. Econ. Rev. 58 (1), 18–36.

Wotton, J., 2007. Are media markets analyzed as two-sided markets. Compet. Policy Int. 3 (1), 237.

Wright, J., 2004. One-sided logic in two-sided markets. Rev. Netw. Econ. 1 (3), 42–63.

PART II

Sectors

CHAPTER 7

The Economics of Television and Online Video Markets

Gregory S. Crawford
Department of Economics, University of Zürich, and CEPR, Zurich, Switzerland

Contents

Handbook of Media Economics, Volume 1A
ISSN 2213-6630, http://dx.doi.org/10.1016/B978-0-444-62721-6.00007-X

Abstract

Television is the dominant entertainment medium for hundreds of millions. This chapter surveys the economic forces that determine the production and consumption of this content. It presents recent trends in television and online video markets, both in the US and internationally, and describes the state of theoretical and empirical research on these industries. A number of distinct themes emerge, including the growing importance of the pay-television sector, the role played by content providers (channels), distributors, and negotiations between them in determining market outcomes, and concerns about the effects of market power throughout this vertical structure. It also covers important but unsettled topics including the purpose for and effects of both the old (Public Service Broadcasters) and the new (online video markets). Open theoretical and empirical research questions are highlighted throughout.

Keywords

Economics, Television, Online video, Public service broadcasting, Advertising, Pay television, Bundling, Bargaining, Market power, Net neutrality, Foreclosure, Policy

JEL Codes

L82, L86, L32, M37, C72, D40, L40, L50

> *The need for images is universal.*
>
> **Ernst Gombrich (1990), reviewing David Freedberg (1990), The Power of Images**

> *Television: A medium—so called because it is neither rare nor well done.*
>
> **Ernie Kovacs (1950s), comedian**

7.1. INTRODUCTION

Television is special. It is special in its dominance of our leisure time.[1] It is special in its impact on political participation, political debate, and political power.[2] It is special in its

---

[1] Chapter 5 (this volume).

[2] E.g., Gentzkow (2006) and Prat and Strömberg (2011).

impact on preferences, beliefs, and culture.[3] Television influences many aspects of life in ways other products, even other media products, do not.

The goal of this chapter is to survey the economics of television and online video markets. Of course, this focus on economics means I will cover only one narrow part of the impact television has on individuals, firms, governments, and society. Entire books have been written in fields as diverse as economics, marketing, and public policy; political science; media and communications studies; and art and art history analyzing the impact television has on contemporary life. The purpose here is to explain the mechanisms generating the programming and advertising which are the primary outputs of television markets, mechanisms that I believe are essential for understanding television's potential impact in these other domains.

I therefore survey the demand and supply of television and online video markets. My scope is both theoretical and empirical, with an eye on those economic issues that have attracted the most attention of academics, regulators, and policymakers. In Section 7.2, I introduce the two main types of television commonly available to households (free and pay), describe the vertical supply structure that delivers television programming (content providers/channels and distributors/systems), and present those facts that best help understand the current functioning of the industry.[4] In Section 7.3, I introduce a simple model of two-sided television markets and assess the implications of this theory. In Section 7.4, I describe the extensions to this simple model academics and policymakers have used to understand specific features of television markets. I call these extensions "The Four Bs": (Public Service) Broadcasters, Barriers to Entry, Bargaining, and Bundling. In Section 7.5, I survey the highest profile current open policy issues in television markets. In Section 7.6, I present patterns of online video use and discuss related policy issues at the intersection of television and online video markets. Section 7.7 concludes and provides directions for future research.

While the economics of television markets are largely common across countries, the quality of data available to study the US market has made academic research more common there. This survey reflects this constraint, with the exception of my discussion of Public Service Broadcasters (PSBs) (an issue more relevant outside than inside the US) and mergers (where both US and European varieties have been important). Other chapters in this volume also cover more thoroughly topics that could sensibly have been included in my mandate. Chapter 1 of this volume introduces the economic characteristics common to all media products—high fixed costs, heterogeneous preferences, and

---

[3] E.g., Gentzkow and Shapiro (2008) and Jensen and Oster (2009).

[4] For most of the television industry's history, the typical distinction drawn in both the institutional and academic literatures has been between broadcast and pay television. The simultaneous development and diffusion of encryption technologies and multichannel (pay) digital broadcast distribution of television has weakened this distinction. I therefore choose to organize the chapter around the distinction between free and pay television, with the imperfect but still useful link between free television and broadcast television implicitly understood.

advertiser support—and these characteristics also influence outcomes in television markets. Chapter 2 of this volume covers the theory of two-sided markets in more detail. The implications of net neutrality for the delivery of online video are also covered in Chapter 10 of this volume. I discuss the economic issues at the heart of recent (mostly American) media mergers, complementing Foros, Kind, and Sorgard's largely European focus (Chapter 6, this volume). Wilbur discusses recent developments in mass media, including digitization and screen proliferation, two topics that are directly impacting television markets (Chapter 5, this volume). Chapters 14 and 15 summarize the theory and measurement of media bias. Early empirical applications were in newspaper markets, but the concerns apply equally well to television.[5] Finally, a burgeoning literature in political science and economics is analyzing both the effects of governments on television and the effects of television on economic and social outcomes, including the election and activities of governments. Chapters 16 and 17 of this volume survey these topics in depth.

7.2. THE TELEVISION INDUSTRY

7.2.1 The Types of Television

7.2.1.1 Broadcast (Free) Television

"Broadcasting" conventionally covers the distribution of both radio and television signals via electromagnetic waves, but my focus is on the television portion of this description.[6] Broadcast television in the US began in the 1930s, but gained widespread popularity and household penetration in the 1950s.[7] While the specifics vary across countries, diffusion in Western Europe followed a similar pattern, with Africa and parts of Asia starting roughly 10 years later. Television stations are generally licensed by a national regulatory authority because the electromagnetic spectrum used by broadcasters is a national resource and licensing is required to prevent interference among broadcasters. In the US, broadcast stations are licensed by the Federal Communications Commission (FCC).

There are a wide variety of station types in the US (with similar patterns internationally), but the most important distinctions are between commercial and non-commercial stations, full- and low-power stations, and analog and digital stations. The vast majority of commercial stations support themselves through the sale of advertising, while non-commercial stations rely on donations from viewers or similar sources of funding other than advertising (FCC, 2008).[8] The number of broadcast TV stations in the US has been

---

[5] See, e.g., Martin and Yurukoglu (2014).

[6] See Chapter 8 in this volume for a discussion of the broadcast radio industry.

[7] Gentzkow (2006) provides a concise survey of the early evolution of the US broadcast television industry.

[8] The US is an important exception. In the last 10 years in the US, broadcasters have successfully begun negotiating payments from pay-television distributors under a regulatory rule called Retransmission Consent. Even so, commercial broadcasters in the US still earn the majority of their revenue from sales of advertising.

stable over time at roughly 1400 full-power stations, 28 per state, and just under 7 per TV market (FCC, 2013a).

Low-power stations are smaller, local, and are often community-oriented. They are considered a secondary service and are not permitted to interfere with full-power broadcasters and are at risk of interference from them. Analog stations transmit programming using the continuous modulation of an uninterrupted sound wave, with different channels allocated to different portions of the electromagnetic spectrum, while digital signals digitally process and multiplex programming. Digital broadcasting is more efficient in its use of spectrum, freeing up spectrum previously used for analog broadcasting for other, higher-value uses.

In the US, there is often a separation of ownership between content providers (broadcast networks) and distributors (broadcast stations). Since the early days of the industry, the production of commercial broadcast programming has been organized and managed by "television networks," of which the largest are ABC, NBC, CBS, and Fox.[9] The left side of the left panel of Figure 7.1 shows the vertical structure associated with the broadcast television industry.

Table 7.1 reports aggregate statistics for US broadcast networks in 2012. Reported are measures of network costs (programming expenditure), quantity (viewership), price (advertising cost per thousand viewers, or CPM), and advertising revenue. I divide US broadcast networks into two groups: the so-called "Big Four" broadcast networks mentioned above and "minor" broadcast networks. Broadcast networks only earn advertising revenue, with the Big Four receiving between 83% and 89% of the total broadcast viewing (ratings) and revenue.

In the US, FCC regulations limit the number of stations television networks can own; the remaining stations are owned by independent firms (that typically own many stations) that negotiate with television networks to be the exclusive provider of that network's programming in a TV market. TV markets are based on geography: The Nielsen Company has divided the US into 210 mutually exclusive and exhaustive markets called Designated Market Areas that are widely used in the sale of advertising. Most network programming is shown during "prime time" (7:00 p.m. to 11:00 p.m.). News local to the station's principal community is produced by individual stations and programming in other parts of the day is either provided by the network or programmed independently with syndicators or independent program producers.

7.2.1.1.1 Public Service Broadcasters

In many countries, some portion of broadcast television service is provided by "Public Service Broadcasters" (PSBs). PSBs compete with commercial broadcasters in providing

---

[9] See Owen and Wildman (1992, Chapter 5) for a valuable discussion of the economics of television networks.

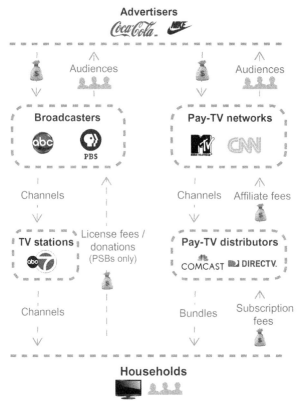

Figure 7.1 The two-sided TV market. *Notes*: Depicted is the two-sided nature of TV markets. In the left panel is the free-to-air broadcasting market and in the right panel the pay-television market. In both markets, there is a wholesale market for programming, in which content providers (broadcaster networks, pay-TV networks) negotiate with distributors (broadcast stations, pay-TV distributors) for the right to carry their content, and a retail market for distribution, in which distributors either broadcast or set prices for access to that content to households. The majority of commercial broadcasters only earn money through the sale of audiences to advertisers. Funding for Public Service Broadcasters (PSBs) comes from mandatory household license fees, sales of advertising, and/or donations from viewers. Funding for pay-television channels and distributors comes from a mix of advertising sales and subscriber payments (see Tables 7.1–7.3).

content free over the air. In the US, "the mission of public broadcasting is to advance a well-educated, well-informed society capable of self-governing the world's greatest democracy" (CPB, 2012). In the UK, the mission of the British Broadcasting Corporation (BBC) is famously to "inform, educate and entertain." In the broadest terms this captures the role of public service broadcasting in many countries; it is hard to come up with a more precise definition.[10] In practice, common aims of PSB policy are to ensure that diverse

---

[10] The UK's Peacock Committee, discussed in Section 7.4.1, noted it had experienced difficulty obtaining a definition even from the broadcasters themselves.

Table 7.1 US broadcast television networks, 2012

	Program expenditure ($ million)	Average prime time rating	Average 24-h rating	Cost per thousand (CPM) ($)	Net advertising revenue ($ million)
Big-4 B/C networks					
ABC	2763	3.9	2.4	17.6	3177
CBS	3303	5.2	2.8	16.2	4124
NBC	4041	4.7	2.6	18.5	3955
Fox	2120	3.5	3.8	33.8	2634
Total Big-4	12,226	17.4	11.6	21.5	13,891
Minor B/C networks					
The CW	439	0.7	0.6	44.1	418
Univision	234	1.7	0.7	–	641
Telemundo	204	0.6	0.3	–	374
UniMás	83	0.3	0.2	–	160
Total minor	1129	3.6	2.0	–	1752
Total B/C networks	13,355	21.0	13.6	–	15,642
Weighted average B/C networks	–	–	–	21.6	–
Big-4 share	91.5%	83.0%	85.5%	–	88.8%

Notes: Reported are aggregate statistics for US broadcast networks in 2012 (SNL Kagan, 2014a). Measures of network costs (programming expenditure), quantity (viewership), price (advertising cost per thousand, or CPM), and net advertising revenue are given. "Rating" is the average percentage of US households watching that channel across a set time interval. US broadcast networks are divided into two groups: the "Big-Four" broadcast networks (ABC, NBC, CBS, and Fox) and "minor" broadcast networks. Weighted average broadcast networks are weighted by the average 24-h rating. Big-4 share is the share of the column spent/watched/earned by the Big-4 broadcast networks.

and high-quality programming is supplied which caters to all interests and communities. In addition, programs that yield educational and other social benefits are to be encouraged, including programs that might make the population more tolerant, and also more aware of their regional and national identity. And in a related vein, there is often intervention to ensure that sufficient locally produced content is available, and that the domestic "ecology" of program production is protected.[11] These values and examples of the types and providers of programming that support these values in the UK are shown in Figure 7.2.[12]

---

[11] The UK's 2003 Communications Act defined four basic objectives for PSBs: to promote *social values*, to offer *high-quality* programming, to provide *range and balance* in its programming, and to provide *diversity* of programming. Section 7.4.1 discusses the rationale for and effects of PSBs in more detail.

[12] This figure is taken from Ofcom (2004). Similar social purposes are found in PSB systems of other countries. The PSB Charter for Ireland's Radio Telifís Éireann (RTÉ) includes among its guiding principles "the democratic, social and cultural values of Irish society." NZ On Air, the funding body for PSBs in New Zealand, states as its mission, "to reflect and foster the development of New Zealand culture and identity through broadcasting."

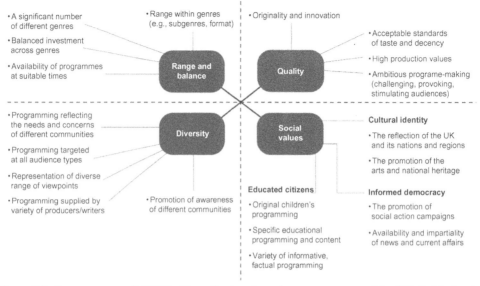

Figure 7.2 Core purposes of UK PSBs. *Notes*: Depicted are the core purposes of the UK's Public Service Broadcasters, including the BBC, and examples of the types of programming that support these purposes, as indicated by the UK media regulator, Ofcom (2004, p. 26).

Funding for PSBs comes from a variety of sources that differ across countries and across PSBs within countries, including mandatory household license fees, sales of advertising, and/or donations from viewers. The right side of the left panel of Figure 7.1 shows the vertical structure and payment flows associated with PSBs. In the UK, the oldest and largest PSB, the BBC, is the beneficiary of an annual license fee of £145.50 (approx. $20/month) and sells no advertising, while the other commercial PSBs in the market—ITV, Channel 4, and Channel 5—receive no license fee and only sell advertising. In the US, public service broadcasting is provided by public (non-commercial) television stations that provide a mix of locally and nationally produced programming. The majority of the national programming is provided by the Public Broadcasting Service, a non-profit public broadcaster jointly owned by over 350 member television stations. Funding for public broadcasting comes from a mix of sources, with contributions from individuals most important (22% on average across public television stations), followed by federal government support (18%), state and local government support (17%), university and foundation support (15%), and underwriting by businesses (13%) (CPB, 2012).

Figure 7.3 reports the aggregate amount of public (government) funding for television along with the per-household-per-month TV license paid for a selection of major world economies.[13] It shows that most developed country governments provide between

---

[13] See also Table 7.4.

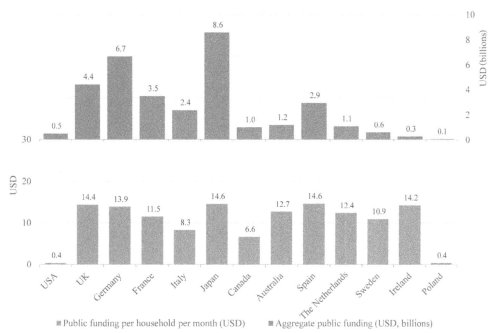

Figure 7.3 Public funding for television, 2011. *Notes*: Reported is the amount of public (government) funding for television in a range of countries in the year 2011. The top panel reports aggregate funding (in $ billion) and per-household funding (in $ per household per month). Amounts have been converted to USD using World Bank average 2011 exchange rates. Ofcom (2012), figure 3.1, author calculations.

$6 and $15 per household per month in public support for television. The US, despite being the largest television market in the world, provides only $0.40 per household per month in government support for PSBs.

7.2.1.2 Pay Television

Pay television is just that: television supported at least in part by payments from sub-scribers (households). The production of pay-television programming occurs as part of a vertical supply chain. Television channels contract with (often small) program pro-ducers for individual programs and form (often 24-h) television schedules. They then license the right to perform these programs with cable, satellite, and telecommunications companies in what is called the programming market. In turn, these distributors aggregate channels into bundles and sell access to these bundles to households in what is called the distribution market. The right panel of Figure 7.1 shows the vertical structure and pay-ment flows associated with pay-television providers. Revenues in the pay-television industry arise from a mix of subscriber and advertiser payments. Content providers (non-broadcast television channels) differ considerably in their revenue mix, but roughly

50% of upstream industry revenue comes from each source (SNL Kagan, 2014a). Distributors (cable, satellite, and Internet Protocol television (IPTV) providers) rely predominantly (90+%) on payments from subscribers.

7.2.1.2.1 Pay TV Distribution

In the US, pay television arose in the form of "cable television."[14] Cable TV began in the 1950s to transmit broadcast signals to areas that could not receive them due to interference from natural features of the local terrain (e.g., mountains). Cable systems needed access to public infrastructure and so typically reached exclusive franchise agreements with local governments granting this access in return for price, quality, and/or service guarantees. FCC regulations initially limited the provision of additional, non-broadcast, programming, but these were relaxed in the late 1970s and, with the simultaneous development and regulatory liberalization of satellite technologies, numerous programming networks were launched, including some of the most recognizable TV brands in the world (e.g., CNN and ESPN). Between 1980 and 2000, the pay (cable) TV industry experienced phases of price regulation and deregulation, and grew considerably.[15]

Entry into the pay-television distribution market is a risky and expensive undertaking. Many thought cable distribution was a natural monopoly in the early years of the industry and cable operators consequently negotiated exclusive arrangements with franchise authorities.[16] The 1992 Cable Act reversed this policy, outlawing exclusive franchises, but there was limited entry concentrated in big cities from so-called cable overbuilders.

The year 2000 was a watershed in the development of the US pay-television industry. Previous to that year, satellite companies were not permitted to distribute local broadcast signals by satellite, putting them at a competitive disadvantage relative to cable operators. The 1999 Satellite Home Viewer Improvement Act relaxed this restriction, permitting the so-called local into local carriage of local broadcast signals into local television markets. Cable subscribers peaked in 2000, despite continued annual industry subscriber growth, and are now 10% below that peak. Subscriptions to the two major national satellite providers have absorbed the majority of industry growth since that date.

The gradual convergence of television and communications (i.e., telephone) technologies in the last 20 years has given rise to entry by former telephone companies (telcos) into video markets. Most such entrants provide service using Internet Protocol (IP) technologies rather than conventional dedicated coaxial cable or satellite broadcast technologies, and are therefore called IPTV providers. In the US, telco entry was permitted by

---

[14] The material discussed in this subsection is discussed in more detail in Crawford (2013).

[15] See Hazlett and Spitzer (1997) and Crawford (2013) for discussions of this period in the industry's regulatory history.

[16] The auctioning of cable franchises was thought to be one way of controlling cable system market power and was first suggested by Williamson (1976). Zupan (1989a,b) evaluates the success of this strategy for initial franchise awards (renewals).

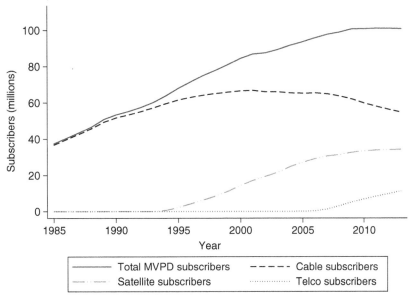

Figure 7.4 US pay-television distributor subscribers, 1985–2013. *Notes*: Depicted is the number of US pay-television subscribers (in millions) by distribution platform between 1985 and 2013 (SNL Kagan, 2014a). MVPD stands for Multi-Program Video Distributor, the FCC definition of a pay-television distributor.

the 1996 Telecommunications Act, but did not happen on a large scale until the mid-2000s with major infrastructure investments by two of the three major telcos. Since then, these two operators have grown to serve 10% of the national market despite being available to less than two-thirds of US households. Figure 7.4 shows the pattern of subscribers to US pay-television platforms from 1985 to 2013.

Using data from FCC (2012a), Figure 7.5 reports an estimate of the distribution of US cable television prices across markets in 2011, measured as the average expenditure on Basic, Expanded Basic, and Digital Basic cable services.[17] There is significant heterogeneity across cable systems in the price of Basic Services, with an average of $67.64.[18]

---

[17] These data were obtained from the FCC using a Freedom of Information request. They included information about the price for Basic, Expanded Basic, and the most popular Digital Basic service for a stratified random sample of cable systems in the US. See FCC (2012a, para. 8) for details of the sampling plan. The sample averages in the Price Survey are weighted by subscriber. Because the data provided were stripped of system and geographic identifying information, I could not weight by subscribers. Following FCC (2012a), I calculate average expenditure as the price of the Expanded Basic service plus a weighted average of the price of the Digital Basic service, with the weight given by the share of Expanded Basic subscribers that took Digital Basic in 2011. From SNL Kagan (2014a), this figure was 79.4%.

[18] See also Table 7.4.

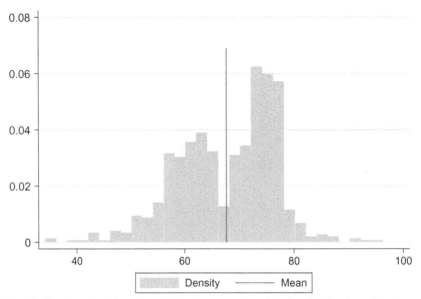

Figure 7.5 Distribution of cable prices, 2011. *Notes*: Depicted is the distribution of cable television prices as measured by average household expenditure on Basic, Expanded Basic, and Digital Basic cable services. The mean of $67.64 is indicated by the vertical line in the figure. Source: *Author calculations from FCC (2012a).*

Much of the heterogeneity in prices is likely driven by heterogeneity in the number of channels available to subscribers depicted in Figure 7.7.

A recurring concern in US pay-television markets is the persistent increase in pay-television prices over time. Figure 7.6 reports price indices from the Consumer Price Index (CPI) from December 1983 until December 2013. Reported are series for Multi-Program Video Distributor (MVPD) (i.e., cable + satellite) services and consumer non-durables. Pay-television prices have grown by 5.1% annually, almost 2% per year faster than non-durable prices.[19] This price growth has prompted recurring concerns about market power in the industry, a topic I revisit in Section 7.4.3.

7.2.1.2.2 Pay TV Program Production (Channels, Networks)

There are broadly three types of pay-television channels. *Cable programming networks* are fee- and advertising-supported general and special-interest networks distributed

---

[19] A significant challenge when interpreting pay-television price changes is accounting for differences in the quality of cable service. Crawford et al. (2008) describe how the FCC, in FCC (2009), proposed using price-per-viewer-hour as a measure of quality-adjusted cable prices. They show that between July 1997 and January 2008, price-per-viewing-hour of cable services increased by a CAGR of 5.8%, 2.8% more than the 3.1% CAGR in the non-durable CPI over the same period. Thus, cable prices have also been rising on a quality-adjusted basis.

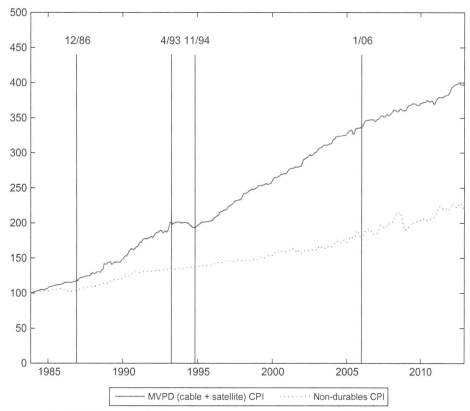

Figure 7.6 MVPD (cable + satellite) prices, 1983–2012. *Notes*: Reported are price indices from the Consumer Price Index (CPI) from December 1983 to December 2013 for MVPD (Multi-Program Video Distributor, i.e., cable + satellite) services as well as consumer non-durables. *Source: Bureau of Labor Statistics.*

nationally to distributors via satellite. Examples from the US include some of the most recognizable networks associated with pay television, including MTV, CNN, and ESPN.[20] An important subset of cable networks from a policy perspective are *Regional Sports Networks* (RSNs). As per their definition, these are regional networks that carry live broadcasts of performances of sports teams that play in and belong to the areas served by the networks. Examples include Yankees Entertainment and Sports Network (YES), Comcast SportsNet Chicago, and the Big Ten Network. While the sports carried vary somewhat across networks, a typical RSN will show those games that are not being carried on a national network from the US professional basketball (NBA), baseball (MLB),

[20] So-called cable networks earned their name by having originally been available only on cable.

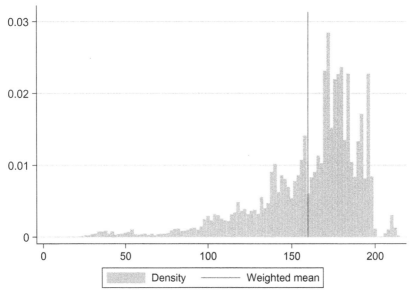

Figure 7.7 Distribution of cable channels, 2011. *Notes*: Depicted is the distribution of pay-television channels offered on Basic, Expanded Basic, and Digital Basic cable services across the 6000 systems offering service in 2011 from the Nielsen FOCUS Database. The mean, weighted by the number of subscribers served by each system, of 159.9 is depicted by the vertical line in the figure.

and hockey (NHL) leagues for the one or two franchises per sport in their service area.[21] *Premium programming networks* are advertising-free entertainment networks, typically offering full-length feature films. Examples include equally familiar networks like HBO and Showtime.

As of the 2010s, US households have access to many pay-television channels. 2011 data from Nielsen's FOCUS database on the population of US cable television lineups indicates that there are 282 television networks available to at least 1% of US households. Figure 7.7 reports the distribution of channels offered on Basic, Expanded Basic, and Digital Basic cable services across the 6000 systems offering service in 2011.[22] The distribution is very left-skewed, with a (weighted) mean of just under 160 channels. Satellite and telco systems also offer hundreds of pay-television channels.

Tables 7.2 and 7.3 report aggregate statistics for the largest US pay-television networks for which data are available. Reported in each table are measures of network costs

---

[21] The revenue these networks provide to individual sports teams are an increasingly important part of teams' businesses and an important driver of outcomes in sports markets. For example, TWC SportsNet Los Angeles recently agreed to pay the US Baseball team the Los Angeles Dodgers $8.35 *billion* to carry the team over a 25-year period.

[22] To approximate the number of channels available to a household selected at random in the US, the data are weighted by the households served by each cable system.

Table 7.2 Top-25 cable television networks, 2012

Cable networks	Prog. expenditure ($ million)	Avg. prime time rating	Avg. 24-h rating	CPM ($)	Net advert. rev.	Subs.	Avg. affil. fee	Affiliate rev. ($ million)	Total rev. ($ million)	Fee rev. share
ESPN	5333	—	0.78	19.3	1770	98.5	5.04	5973	7742	0.77
TNT	1160	—	0.83	8.8	968	99.7	1.20	1443	2411	0.60
Nickelodeon/ Nick At Nite	429	—	1.13	6.6	931	99.2	0.55	657	1589	0.41
USA	759	—	1.02	6.9	1043	99.0	0.68	815	1858	0.44
Fox News	607	—	0.92	5.0	742	97.8	0.89	1040	1782	0.58
TBS	607	—	0.64	10.4	895	99.7	0.56	673	1568	0.43
Disney Channel	306	—	1.28	—	—	—	1.09	—	—	—
MTV	579	—	0.39	13.1	817	98.1	0.40	476	1294	0.37
CNN	311	—	0.32	6.2	328	98.9	0.58	686	1014	0.68
FX Network	460	—	0.55	8.9	509	97.9	0.48	566	1075	0.53
ESPN2	496	—	0.22	10.4	270	98.5	0.67	792	1062	0.75
Discovery Channel	171	—	0.43	10.9	526	99.1	0.35	420	946	0.44
Lifetime Television	418	—	0.43	8.0	505	99.5	0.31	366	872	0.42
Food Network	278	—	0.48	9.8	609	99.4	0.18	218	826	0.26
A&E	397	—	0.60	5.3	469	98.7	0.28	334	804	0.42
History	302	—	0.72	4.7	497	98.6	0.25	291	788	0.37
HGTV	257	—	0.56	7.2	589	98.7	0.16	184	773	0.24
NFL Network	1078	—	0.19	9.0	129	68.8	0.85	645	774	0.83
Cartoon Network	250	—	0.87	4.5	462	98.9	0.20	237	699	0.34
ABC Family Channel	280	—	0.48	8.4	445	97.0	0.26	298	743	0.40
Syfy	284	—	0.42	7.8	426	98.0	0.27	312	739	0.42
Comedy Central	290	—	0.38	9.3	457	98.3	0.17	201	657	0.31
AMC	214	—	0.46	7.0	362	98.9	0.29	324	686	0.47

Continued

Table 7.2 Top-25 cable television networks, 2012—cont'd

	Prog. expenditure ($ million)	Avg. prime time rating	Avg. 24-h rating	CPM ($)	Net advert. rev.	Subs.	Avg. affil. fee	Affiliate rev. ($ million)	Total rev. ($ million)	Fee rev. share
CNBC	209	—	0.15	9.5	223	96.8	0.30	356	579	0.62
Bravo	268	—	0.31	11.8	342	94.8	0.23	262	604	0.43
Total top-25	15,746	—	14.56	7.6	14,314	97.2	16.23	18,864	33,178	0.57
Average top-25										
Total cable (198 networks)	24,066	—	30.10		21,623		41.85	28,361	49,984	0.57
Average cable		—		6.3		46.2				
Top-25 share	65.4%	—	48.4%		66.2%		38.8%	66.5%	66.4%	

Reported are aggregate statistics for the largest US pay-television networks in 2012 for which data are available from SNL Kagan (2014a). Measures of network costs (programming expenditure), quantity (viewership and subscribers), price (advertising cost per thousand, or CPM, and affiliate fees, if any), and revenue, as well as the relative importance of advertising versus fee revenue in each channel's total, are given. Affiliate fees are $ per household per month. Reported here is information for the top-25 most widely available cable networks, as well as totals for all 198 cable networks for which information is available from SNL Kagan. Top-25 share is the share of the column spent/watched/earned by the top-25 listed broadcast networks. See also Table 7.3 for information about Regional Sports and Premium Networks.

Table 7.3 Regional Sports Networks and Premium Networks, 2012

	Program expenditure	Net advert revenue	Subs.	Average affiliate fee	Affiliate fee revenue	Total revenue	Affiliate revenue share
Regional Sports Networks (RSNs)							
Fox Sports RSNs	1483	237	18.8	2.66	1782	2049	0.87
Comcast SportsNet RSNs	758	140	10.5	2.79	833	986	0.84
Yankees Entertainment (YES)	252	67	6.0	2.99	433	510	0.85
Root Sports RSNs	243	58	3.6	2.81	284	346	0.82
Madison Square Garden Network	103	61	4.3	2.71	263	336	0.78
SportsNet New York	214	38	3.8	2.55	219	258	0.85
MSG Plus	90	24	4.3	2.38	224	252	0.89
Sun Sports	168	21	3.7	2.69	207	230	0.90
New England Sports Network	151	31	2.1	3.62	178	213	0.83
Prime Ticket	144	24	3.1	2.36	169	198	0.85
Mid-Atlantic Sports Network	138	27	1.9	2.14	138	168	0.82
SportSouth	55	19	1.3	0.62	65	86	0.76
SportsTime Ohio	60	13	1.2	1.85	65	80	0.81
Altitude Sports & Entertainment	52	15	0.7	1.57	56	73	0.77
Time Warner Cable SportsNet/ Deportes	40	6	3.0	2.98	42	49	0.86
Comcast/Charter Sports Southeast	28	3	0.0	0.57	38	42	0.91
Cox Sports Television	18	8	0.6	0.74	16	24	0.66
Channel 4 San Diego	5	1	0.8	0.80	8	9	0.87
Longhorn Network	23	1	2.7	0.27	6	8	0.83
Total RSNs	4025	793	72.3		5026	5916	
Average RSNs			1.8	2.41			0.85
Premium Networks							
HBO/Cinemax	1632	0	41.5	7.68	3732	4415	1.00
Showtime/TMC/Flix	595	0	76.1	1.64	1473	1564	1.00
Starz/Encore	661	0	56.1	1.93	1259	1310	1.00
EPIX/EPIX Drive-In	217	0	9.9	1.77	206	341	1.00
Total Premium	3105	0		13.01	6670	7630	
Average Premium			45.9	3.10			1.00

Reported are aggregate statistics for the largest US pay-television networks in 2012 for which data are available from SNL Kagan (2014a). Measures of network costs (programming expenditure), quantity (subscribers), price (affiliate fees), and revenue, as well as the relative importance of advertising versus fee revenue in each channel's total, are given. Reported here is information on 40 Regional Sports Networks (RSNs), with the 13 Fox Sports, 8 Comcast SportsNet, and 3 Root Sports channels reported as single groups, and Premium Networks. See also Table 7.2 for information about the largest "cable television networks."

(programming expenditure), quantity (viewership and subscribers), price (advertising cost per thousand, or CPM, and affiliate fees, if any), and revenue, as well as the relative importance of advertising versus fee revenue in each channel's total. In Table 7.2, I report information for the top-25 most widely available cable networks, as well as totals for all 198 cable networks for which information is available from SNL Kagan.[23] In Table 7.3, I report information for all 40 RSNs and all 8 premium networks.[24]

There is considerable heterogeneity across networks both within and across types. As suggested above, premium networks only earn affiliate fee revenue, and the remaining networks earn a mix of both, with the relative importance of each differing by channel. Overall, cable networks earn the majority of advertising, affiliate fee, and total revenue. The top-25 cable networks by revenue receive approximately two-thirds of cable network advertising and affiliate fee revenue, despite accounting for less than half of cable network viewership and only 13% (25 of 198) of the networks for which such data are available. RSNs, while only relevant in those regions where they carry local sports content, are nonetheless very important in the industry, with total revenue rivaling national premium networks.

7.2.1.3 Broadcast (Pay) Television: DTT

In the mid-2000s, television regulators around the world began requiring broadcast stations to use digital instead of analog technologies.[25] Such broadcasting is often called Digital Terrestrial Television (DTT).

The Netherlands was the first country to switch, in 2006, and has since been followed by many more (ITU, 2012).[26] While economically unimportant in the US, this transition led in many countries to the growth of *multichannel* digital broadcast offerings that are a credible substitute to pay-television bundles offered via other technologies. In some countries, notably the UK with Freeview, until recently this offering relied solely on advertising revenues and was thus free to households, while in others, notably France with Télévision Numérique Terrestre, it was a mix of free and pay channels.

The relative importance of cable, satellite, and telcos (IPTV) as distributors of video programming varies considerably across the world due to the vagaries of the evolution of

---

[23] SNL Kagan, an industry resource, collects information on 198 cable networks, 40 RSNs, and 8 premium networks (in 4 corporate families). All of the summary statistics reported here rely on this subset of cable, RSN, and premium channels.

[24] For the former I group together the 13 Fox Sports, 8 Comcast SportsNet, and 3 Root Sports RSNs and report summary statistics for each of these families of RSNs.

[25] Transitioning between analog and digital broadcasting must happen simultaneously within broadcasters' transmission areas to avoid issues of interference, though it can be done either regionally (as in the UK) or nationally (as in most countries).

[26] The US made the switch by 2009, and the UK by 2012.

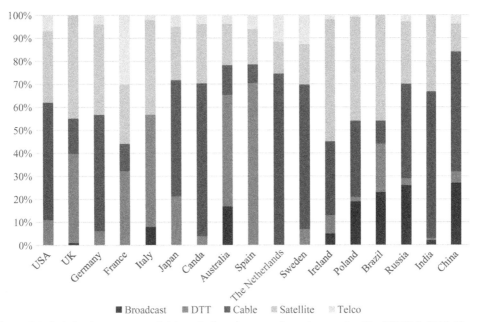

Figure 7.8 Relative importance of video platform across selected countries (% of TV HH), 2011. *Notes*: Depicted is the share of TV households across a range of countries in 2011 that obtain video service by each of five platforms: (analog) broadcast, digital broadcast (DTT), cable, satellite, and telco (IPTV). Source: *Ofcom (2012, figure 3.28).*

video markets across countries. Figure 7.8 reports the share of households that obtain video service by type of platform: (analog) broadcast, digital broadcast (DTT), cable, satellite, and telco (IPTV). The relative importance of each of the platforms shows significant heterogeneity. For example, less than 15% of households are served by cable in the UK and Brazil (and not at all in Italy), whereas almost 70% are served by cable in the Netherlands and Canada. In almost all countries, analog broadcast is free and cable, satellite, and telco provision is paid. DTT is sometimes free and sometimes paid (even within country); Figure 7.9 reports for the same countries the share of TV households served by free versus pay platforms. This varies widely, between 70% and 80% in Spain and Brazil to less than 15% in the Netherlands, the USA, and India.

7.2.2 Cross-Platform Television Statistics

Table 7.4 reports aggregate statistics about the television industry for a selection of countries in 2011. Reported is information about availability, access, use, and revenue by funding source. Information about subscribers by platform was already shown in Figure 7.8. Average individual television viewing varies substantially across the listed

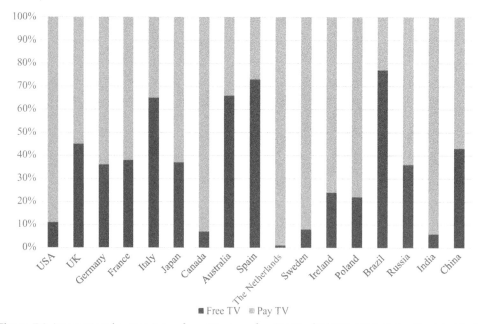

Figure 7.9 International comparison of pay TV versus free TV (% of TV HH), 2011. *Notes*: Depicted is the share of TV households served by free versus pay platforms across a range of countries in 2011. Source: *Ofcom (2012, figure 3.34).*

countries, from a low of 2.0 hours for India to a high of 4.9 hours for the US.[27] Average price data is not readily available, but a close relation, "average revenue per unit," measures the average expenditure on pay television by purchasing households. These were converted to US dollars using 2011 IMF exchange rates (Ofcom, 2012). These also vary widely, from a low of $3–4 in India and Russia to a high of over $83 in the US.[28] The US is also not surprisingly the world's largest television market, with annual aggregate revenue of $160.4 billion or $112.73 per household per month. Of this, almost two-thirds come from subscriptions and one-third from advertising, with a negligible share coming from public funding. The difference in per-household television industry revenues and the relative importance of alternative sources of funding also vary widely across countries. The reasons for this variation have to my knowledge not previously been analyzed in the academic literature.

Figure 7.10 shows total TV revenue across time by groups of countries. The US accounts for over 40% of the estimated world television revenues of $400.5 billion.

---

[27] Chapter 5 (figure 5.2, this volume) shows that, in the US, watching TV takes up almost half of the time people spend using mass media, almost double the next closest medium (listening to AM/FM radio).

[28] This likely differs from the $67.64 reported in Figure 7.5 as it includes expenditure on premium networks and ancillary fees.

Table 7.4 TV industry statistics across selected countries, 2011

	North America	Western Europe						Asia			Latin America
	USA	UK	Germany	France	Italy	Sweden	Poland	Japan	Russia	India	Brazil
Households (HHs)											
Total HHs	118.6	26.4	40.4	27.6	24.4	4.5	14.3	49.3	52.7	229.3	62.5
Television HHs	117.4	25.7	38.3	27.0	24.2	4.4	12.9	49.2	50.4	140.2	61.3
Subscribers											
Free-to-air "subs"	18.4	19.8	15.8	15.0	19.1	1.0	1.5	43.5	26.1	12.5	45.3
Pay subs	100.4	14.3	22.6	19.9	5.1	3.4	11.8	14.1	24.3	129.7	16.0
Viewing											
Hours per day	4.9	4.0	3.8	3.8	4.2	2.7	4.0	–	3.7	2.0	2.7
Subscription cost											
Monthly ARPU	$83.01	$48.39	$20.99	$39.97	$37.96	$27.13	$18.71	$47.59	$3.34	$3.74	$53.60
TV industry revenue											
Aggregate TV rev.	160.4	18.1	18.6	16.4	12.5	2.9	3.8	49.9	5.8	8.8	19.9
Subscription	102.2	8.1	6.3	8.1	3.9	1.4	2.5	18.5	1.3	6.1	8.0
Advertising	57.8	5.7	5.7	4.9	6.2	0.9	1.3	22.7	4.5	2.4	11.5
Public funding	0.5	4.3	6.6	3.5	2.3	0.6	0.1	8.7	0.0	0.3	0.4
Monthly per-HH rev.	$112.73	$57.31	$38.36	$49.44	$42.75	$53.02	$22.44	$84.35	$9.13	$3.21	$26.51
Subscription	$71.80	$25.66	$13.00	$24.33	$13.37	$25.62	$14.58	$31.33	$2.13	$2.23	$10.71
Advertising	$40.59	$18.00	$11.67	$14.69	$21.26	$16.20	$7.39	$38.41	$7.05	$0.86	$15.28
Public funding	$0.34	$13.74	$13.69	$10.47	$8.00	$11.19	$0.37	$14.67	$0.03	$0.12	$0.58
% from each source											
Subscription	63.7	44.8	33.9	49.2	31.3	48.3	65.0	37.1	23.3	69.6	40.4
Advertising	36.0	31.4	30.4	29.7	49.7	30.6	32.9	45.5	77.2	26.7	57.7
Public funding	0.3	24.0	35.7	21.2	18.7	21.1	1.7	17.4	0.3	3.8	2.2

Reported are aggregate statistics about the television industry for a selection of countries in 2011. Households and subscribers are measured in millions. Total free-to-air and pay subscribers can exceed TV households due to multiple subscriptions per household. ARPU≡ "Average Revenue per Unit," measured in US dollars per subscribing household per month, is a common industry metric measuring the average household expenditure on pay-television services. Aggregate TV industry revenue is measured in $ billions. Monthly per-household revenue is measured in US dollars per household per month.

Sources: SNL Kagan (2014a) and Ofcom (2012).

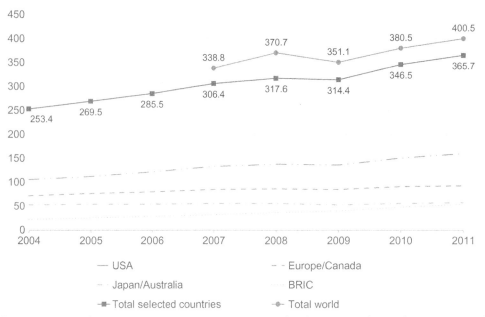

Figure 7.10 TV industry revenue over time. *Notes*: Depicted is the estimated TV industry revenue of different regions of the world, the total of these regions, and the world total between 2014 and 2011. Sources: *Ofcom (2012, figure 3.15) and PriceWaterhouseCoopers (2012, p. 57).*

Global television industry revenue has exhibited steady year-on-year increases, with significant growth coming from developing countries like the BRICs.[29] Figure 7.11 shows that in the US, as in many world markets, television advertising has not suffered from the recent growth in Internet use and advertising. As emphasized in Chapter 5 of this volume, whether measured by time spent watching, subscription revenue, or advertising revenue, "television appears to be the most important mass medium" (Chapter 5, this volume, p. 209).

Other patterns are evident from a closer look at US data. Figures 7.12 and 7.13 break out US programming market revenue by program type and revenue source across time. While broadcast network revenue has remained roughly constant across time, cable, RSN, and premium network revenue have all grown substantially. Advertising revenue has been the historical driver of programming market revenue, but was surpassed by affiliate fee revenue in 2010.

What is driving this revenue growth and what are the consequences for the distribution market? Figure 7.14 shows that patterns of programming expenditure by channels match that of revenue growth, while Figure 7.15 shows that this higher expenditure has

---

[29] BRIC = Brazil, India, and China.

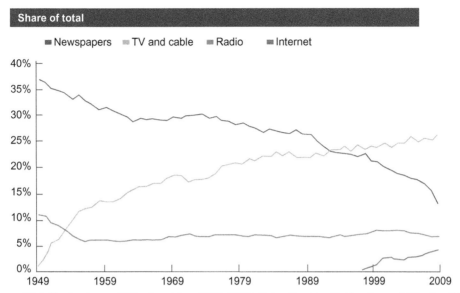

Figure 7.11 Media share of US advertising, 1949–2009. *Notes*: Depicted is the share of US advertising revenue by media type between 1949 and 2009. Sources: *FCC (2011a). Martin Langeveld at Nieman Journalism Lab; data from NAA, TVB, IAB, McCannShare.*

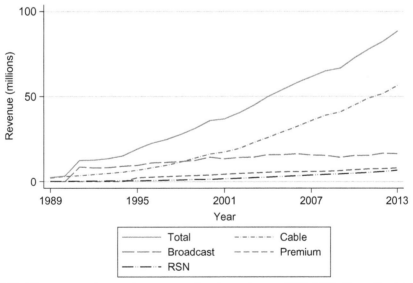

Figure 7.12 US programming market revenue by channel type, 1989–2013. *Notes*: Depicted is the revenue accruing to four different types of programming networks (channels) in the television programming market between 1989 and 2013: Broadcast, Cable, Regional Sports Network, and Premium Networks. See also Tables 7.1–7.3 for further details about revenue for these networks in 2012. Source: *SNL Kagan (2014a).*

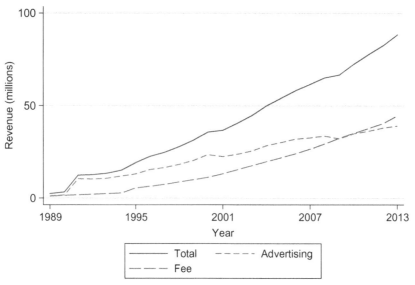

Figure 7.13 US programming market revenue by source, 1989–2013. *Notes*: Depicted is the revenue of programming networks (channels) arising from advertising versus affiliate fees in the television programming market between 1989 and 2013. See also Tables 7.1–7.3 for a breakdown by channel and channel type of revenue sources in 2012. Source: *SNL Kagan (2014a)*.

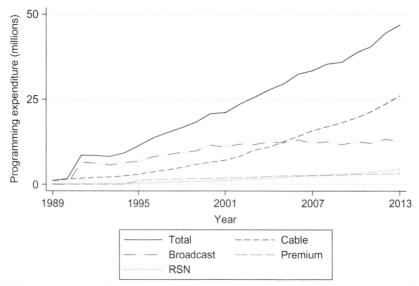

Figure 7.14 Total programming expenditure by program type, 1989–2013. *Notes*: Depicted are the expenditures on programming paid by four different types of programming networks (channels) in the television programming market between 1989 and 2013: Broadcast, Cable, Regional Sports Network, and Premium Networks. See also Tables 7.1–7.3 for further details about expenditures by these networks in 2012. Source: *SNL Kagan (2014a)*.

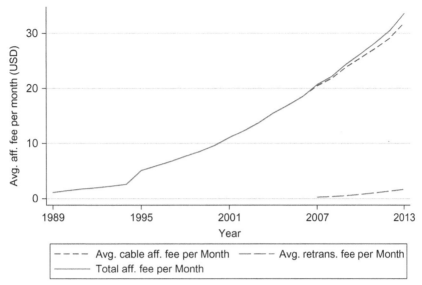

Figure 7.15 Total average affiliate fees per month, 1989–2013. *Notes*: Depicted are the total affiliate fees paid by pay-television distributors between 1989 and 2013. See also Tables 7.1–7.3 for further details about average affiliate fees by channel type and channel in 2012. Source*: SNL Kagan (2014a). Pew State of the Media, 2013.*

enabled channels to negotiate ever-increasing affiliate fees from downstream distributors. Of particular note in Figure 7.15 is the recent growth in "Retransmission Consent" fees negotiated by broadcast networks from distributors for the right to distribute broadcast signals that are otherwise available free over the air.[30] The contribution of retransmission consent fees has merely increased the already considerable growth in affiliate fees for cable networks. These, in turn, are important factors in the pattern of ever-increasing prices to households for pay-television service presented in Figure 7.6.

The overall growth in channel advertising revenue shown in Figure 7.13 hides an important compositional effect. While relative ratings for broadcast networks remain strong (e.g., compare Tables 7.1 and 7.2), Figure 7.16 shows that *total* household viewing on cable networks exceeded that on broadcast networks in the mid-2000s and has continued to grow, as of 2012 comprising 74.4% of household 24-h viewing. All these patterns point to a large and growing importance of pay television in the functioning of US television markets.

---

[30] This effect is not shown in Table 7.1 as these fees largely accrue to television stations and not to the television networks providing the majority of the programming on those stations. This is a source of dispute between broadcast networks and stations, however, as networks seek to share in these revenue streams.

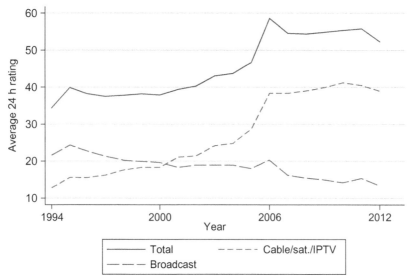

Figure 7.16 Total ratings by platform type, 1994–2012. *Notes*: Depicted is the total average 24-h rating of broadcast and pay-television networks 1994 and 2012. See also Tables 7.1 and 7.2 for further information about average 24-h ratings by channel type and channel for broadcast and pay-television networks in 2012. Source: *SNL Kagan (2014a)*.

7.3. A SIMPLE MODEL OF THE TELEVISION MARKET

As discussed in greater detail in Chapter 2 of this volume, media markets are two-sided, providing both content to households in return for subscription fees and audiences to advertisers in return for advertising payments. This two-sided structure and the relative importance of these two funding sources have important implications for prices, ad levels, programming choices, quality, and welfare.

In this section, I present a stylized model of television program production and distribution (broadcasting), which borrows elements from Armstrong and Vickers (2001), Anderson and Coate (2005), Armstrong (2005, 2006), and Peitz and Valletti (2008). I use this model to derive testable implications about outcomes in television markets which are discussed later in the section. In the next section, I highlight the specific institutional features of television markets that have required extending this stylized model in four important directions (the Four Bs).

7.3.1 The Baseline Model
7.3.1.1 Baseline Results
A broadcaster potentially makes decisions along a number of basic dimensions, including:
- the price (or more generally the tariff structure) for viewing its programs;
- the advertising intensity within its programs;

- the quality of its programs; and
- the genre of its programs.

Regulation, competitive conditions, and/or technological constraints may affect these decisions. For instance, traditional over-the-air broadcast technology does not allow viewers to be excluded from the signal, and so direct pricing of content may not be feasible. Regulations might constrain advertising intensity, or technology might allow viewers to skip advertisements. PSBs might face constraints on quality, genre, or the neutrality of news programs. We address some of these factors in the presentation to come.

We assume that a monopoly broadcaster has a unit of content (e.g., a single channel, or a single program) to supply to viewers. A viewer's gross value for this content is denoted v, and v is distributed in the population of potential viewers in some manner. All viewers are homogeneous in terms of their attitude to advertising intensity, and if they pay p for the content which has advertising intensity a, their "total price" is

$$P = \delta a + p.$$

Viewers in most cases dislike intrusive advertising, and so we assume that $\delta \geq 0$. A viewer with valuation v will then decide to watch this content when $v \geq P$, and we denote the number of viewers with $v \geq P$ by $x(P)$, the demand function for viewing.

Suppose that if the broadcaster shows a ads it obtains revenue $r(a)$ per viewer from advertisers, which we suppose is a concave function. Total revenue per viewer is therefore

$$R = p + r(a).$$

The relationship between total revenue R and total price P will depend on whether a subscription charge p can be used. If it can be used, then for any total price P, we have $P = \delta a + p$ and $R = p + R(a)$ so that $R = P + r(a) - \delta a$. The broadcaster will clearly choose advertising intensity a^* to maximize revenue for any given total price P so that

$$a^* \text{ maximizes } r(a) - \delta a.$$

Note that a^* is the advertising intensity which maximizes the joint surplus of the broadcaster and the viewer, and it ignores the surplus of advertisers themselves. We often expect advertiser surplus to increase with a, and in such cases the broadcaster chooses an inefficiently *low* level of advertising.[31] In some cases (when $r'(0) \leq \delta$) the equilibrium level of advertising is zero so that a viewer's disutility from adverting is greater even than

---

[31] Suppose, as assumed by Anderson and Coate (2005) and Peitz and Valletti (2008), that each advertiser is a separate monopolist, and can extract all consumer surplus when it sells its product. In this case, aggregate advertiser surplus is captured by the area under their demand curve. This implies that the level of advertising which maximizes total welfare is such that the advertising price, $r(a)/a$, is equal to the disutility δ. It follows that advertising is socially excessive (insufficient) if $r(a) - \delta a$ is negative (positive).

the value to the most valuable advertiser.[32] Otherwise, though, viewers are prepared to tolerate some advertising in compensation for a lower direct charge, the relationship between total revenue and total price in the pay-TV regime is

$$R_{\mathrm{pay}}(P) = P + r(a^*) - \delta a^*, \tag{7.1}$$

and an extra dollar extracted from a viewer translates into exactly one extra dollar for the broadcaster.

By contrast, in the free-to-air world with no direct viewing charge ($p \equiv 0$), there is a concave relationship between total revenue and total price, given by

$$R_{\mathrm{free}}(P) = r\left(\frac{P}{\delta}\right). \tag{7.2}$$

If regulation places a ceiling on advertising intensity, this corresponds to a cap on the total price P. The function R_{free} equals R_{pay} at one point (when $P = \delta a^*$, which implies that $p = 0$ in the pay regime), but otherwise lies below R_{pay}.[33] The intuition for this is clear: in the pay-TV regime the broadcaster has two instruments to extract revenue from the viewer, while in the free-to-air regime it has only one, and so it can more efficiently extract revenue in the pay-TV regime.

If, as is highly plausible, charging a *negative* price to viewers (i.e., $p < 0$) is not feasible, the analysis of the pay-TV regime sometimes needs modifying. When the chosen total price P is below δa^*, the corresponding direct price p is negative. Thus, when negative prices are not feasible, the revenue function continues to be given by (7.1) when $P \geq \delta a^*$, while for smaller P the pay-TV regime involves a zero price, and the revenue function coincides with R_{free} in (7.2). When $P \geq \delta a^*$, the concavity of $r(\cdot)$ can be shown to imply that $R_{\mathrm{pay}}(P)/R_{\mathrm{free}}(P)$ increases with P, so that the pay-TV regime delivers proportionally higher revenue than the free-to-air regime, not just in absolute terms.

For simplicity, suppose that the broadcaster already possesses his content, and incurs no additional costs for distributing this content to viewers. It follows that the broadcaster's total profit is

$$x(P)R(P), \tag{7.3}$$

where R is given by R_{pay} or R_{free} according to whether direct charging of viewers is feasible. Even when charging viewers is feasible, the broadcaster may choose to obtain its revenue solely from advertisers. (This is the case when the advertising intensity a which maximizes profits in the free-to-air regime, $x(\delta a)r(a)$, is below a^*, the advertising level when the firm can charge a positive viewer price.) One can show the total price P is weakly higher in the pay-TV regime than in the free-to-air regime so that viewers

---

[32] This is presumably the reason why novels and live opera typically contain no ads.

[33] This is because $R_{\mathrm{pay}}(P) = P + r(a^*) - \delta a^* \geq P + r(P/\delta) - \delta(P/\delta) = R_{\mathrm{free}}(P)$.

are worse off in the pay-TV regime.[34] Likewise, there is weakly less advertising in the pay-TV regime than in the free-to-air regime so that advertisers typically prefer the free-to-air regime.[35] While there is too little advertising in the pay-TV regime, in the free-to-air regime whether equilibrium advertising is excessive or insufficient is ambiguous. Indeed, total welfare might be higher or lower in the pay-TV regime relative to the free-to-air regime.[36]

Since the broadcaster obtains greater profit when it can charge viewers, it may be that some content can be profitably supplied *only* if viewers can be charged. As a result, even if the use of viewer charges reduces consumer surplus for a given range of content, the fact that more content might be offered in a pay-TV regime could lead to consumer gains from the practice.

In a discussion of recent developments in mass media, Chapter 5 of this volume discusses the effects of ad-avoidance technology. We also analyze that issue here. In the pay-TV regime, the widespread introduction of ad-avoidance technology will usually harm consumers once the broadcaster's response is considered. Without the ad-avoidance technology, the broadcaster chooses total price to maximize $x(P)(P+r(a^*)-\delta a^*)$, while with the technology it is in effect forced to set $a=0$ and it maximizes $x(P)P$, which induces a higher total price whenever $a^*>0$. Since a viewer dislikes advertising, it is a dominant strategy for her to avoid it when technology is available to permit this. But this behavior involves a negative spillover onto other viewers, since the broadcaster can then obtain less revenue from advertisers, and this induces it to raise its direct price. Thus, in this simple framework, a prisoner's dilemma occurs with ad avoidance, and all viewers would be better off if ad avoidance were not feasible. Of course, in a purely advertising-funded regime, the adoption of ad-avoidance technology would be catastrophic for the market.

We next consider a number of natural extensions to this basic model.

7.3.1.2 Oligopoly

The basic model above considered a single broadcaster in isolation, taking rival offerings as exogenous. Additional issues arise when the impact of one broadcaster's choices on a rival is considered. To illustrate, suppose there are just two broadcasters, *A* and *B*, and for the relevant time-slot suppose a viewer must watch the content of one or the other

---

[34] Recall that if a negative price is not feasible, that $R_{free}=R_{pay}$ for all $P\leq\delta a^*$. If the best price in the free-to-air regime satisfies $P\leq\delta a^*$, it is clear that the best price in the pay-TV regime could not be lower than this. If the best price in the free-to-air regime is greater than δa^*, the fact that R_{pay}/R_{free} increases with P for $P\geq\delta a^*$ implies that the broadcaster is better off choosing a higher total price in the pay-TV regime.

[35] Either the total price is below δa^* in both regimes or the total price above δa^* in both regimes. In the former case, advertising levels are the same. In the latter case, advertising intensity is a^* in the pay-TV regime and strictly higher in the free-to-air regime.

[36] See Anderson and Coate (2005) for further details.

(or neither). If P_A and P_B are the total prices chosen by the respective broadcasters, suppose that A gains $X_A(P_A,P_B)$ viewers, while B attracts $x_B(P_B,P_A)$. Then, as in (7.3), given the rival total price P_j, broadcaster $i=A$, B chooses its total price to maximize

$$x_i(P_i, P_j)R(P_i),$$

where R is given by R_{pay} or R_{free} according to whether direct charging of viewers is feasible.[37] In theoretical models of broadcasting, a popular specification for x_i is the symmetric Hotelling demand system, with

$$x_i(P_i, P_j) = \frac{1}{2} - \frac{P_i - P_j}{2t},$$

where t is the "transport cost" parameter, which reflects how substitutable are the two firms' offerings. In this framework, note that total prices are strategic complements, and a broadcaster's best response to its rival's total price is an increasing function of that price. In particular, if there is asymmetric regulation applied to just one broadcaster in the form of a price cap (in the pay-TV regime) or a ceiling on advertising (in the free-to-air regime), this will cause a corresponding reduction in the unregulated rival's choice of price or advertising.

In this particular case, the symmetric equilibrium choice of price P satisfies

$$\frac{R'(P)}{R(P)} = \frac{1}{t}. \tag{7.4}$$

In the pay-TV regime where R is given by (7.1), it follows that the equilibrium charge to viewers is

$$p = t - r(a^*) \tag{7.5}$$

and this charge is positive provided that $t > r(a^*)$. In the free-to-air regime the equilibrium advertising intensity satisfies

$$\frac{r'(a)}{r(a)} = \frac{\delta}{t}. \tag{7.6}$$

Since we know that $R_{\text{pay}}/R_{\text{free}}$ increases with P, it follows that $R'_{\text{pay}}/R_{\text{pay}} \geq R'_{\text{free}}/R_{\text{free}}$, and so (7.4) implies that the total price paid by viewers is higher in the pay-TV regime than in the free-to-air regime so that viewers in this model are better off in the ad-funded regime.[38] In addition, the concavity of $r(\cdot)$ implies that equilibrium advertising intensity is greater in the free-to-air regime than in the pay-TV regime.

---

[37] This presentation assumes that the competitive interaction is such that each broadcaster commits to provide a given quantity of advertising. If instead the competition is in terms of prices on the advertising side, a complicated feedback can occur in the market, as discussed in Armstrong (2006).

[38] From (7.5), if $r(a^*) \geq t$ then firms in equilibrium do not charge viewers directly, and the outcome is the same as in the free-to-air regime.

7.3.1.3 Content Choice

The main cause of market failure in the analog era was due to advertising being the sole commercial source of funds. The basic problem with advertising-funded television is that whether or not a program is profitable need not depend closely upon how *strongly* viewers like the program. If a cheap quiz show would draw the same audience as an expensive drama, then there would be no point in an advertising-funded broadcaster spending extra resources on the latter. Similarly, programs that appeal strongly to a relatively narrow audience would not be produced, even though they might generate substantial social surplus.

Moving to a subscription television system, however, greatly mitigates this problem. Since the broadcaster can extract viewers' surplus directly, we expect that it will have an incentive to show a diverse selection of programs of quality appropriate to viewers' willingness-to-pay (WTP). For instance, drama series might be unprofitable for an advertising-funded broadcaster, but not for a subscription broadcaster which can extract viewers' higher WTP for this genre compared to soaps, say.

To illustrate this, suppose for simplicity that viewers suffer no disutility from advertising (so $\delta = 0$) and the broadcaster can obtain maximum revenue r per viewer from advertisers.[39] There are a number of program options available, labeled i, which vary in audience size n and the WTP v of that audience. (Thus, each option has rectangular demand, with inelastic demand n so long as price is below v.) Program option i has audience n_i, reservation price v_i, and fixed cost F_i. If the broadcaster must choose just one of these options, then without the ability to charge for content, the broadcaster will choose the content with the highest value of

$$n_i r - F_i.$$

However, if it can charge for viewing, it will charge viewers their reservation price and so choose the content which maximizes

$$n_i(r + v_i) - F_i.$$

Since the latter choice takes into account viewer surplus, it is likely to be better aligned with total welfare (although viewers are left with no surplus). If there is a program type ("lowest common denominator" content) which is just better than nothing for most people and which costs little to produce (i.e., n_i is large, while v_i and F_i are small), this will be offered by the broadcaster in the free-to-air regime, but some other content would likely be offered in the pay-TV regime.

This discussion can be applied to the particular case of program quality.[40] Suppose that the broadcaster can choose quality, and making (or otherwise sourcing) programs with

---

[39] See also Chapters 1 and 6 of this volume for further discussion of the theoretical literature on content choice in media markets. See also Liu et al. (2004) and Godes et al. (2009) for applications to television markets.

[40] This discussion is adapted from the model presented in Armstrong (2005).

quality q requires a fixed cost $C(q)$. Suppose that viewers demand content with quality q and total viewing price P is $x(P|q)$, where x increases with q. Adapting expression (7.3) implies that the broadcaster's total profit is

$$x(P|q)R(P) - C(q), \tag{7.7}$$

where R is R_{pay} or R_{free} according to the regime.

If the broadcaster is unregulated, it chooses (P, q) to maximize this expression. The broadcaster may be regulated in one dimension and be free to choose the other. The relevant comparative statics—for example, how quality is affected by a constraint on price—depends on the precise way in which quality and price interact in the demand function. A simple case to illustrate the possibilities has quality expand the market proportionately, so that $x(P|q) = qX(P)$. In this case, (7.7) implies that the choice of P does not depend on chosen quality. This implies that a regulation which forces the broadcaster to raise its program quality, if feasible and if it does not cause it to go bankrupt, will benefit viewers.

If $X(P)R(P)$ is single-peaked in P and total price is below the maximizing price, then the broadcaster's choice of quality is an increasing function of P. Thus, as is intuitive, when it is permitted to charge viewers a higher price, the broadcaster responds by raising its quality. For example, consider a regulatory policy which puts a ceiling on advertising intensity in the free-to-air regime. For fixed quality, this policy surely benefits viewers, as it lowers the effective price they pay. But the policy reduces the revenue per viewer the broadcaster can extract from advertisers, and this may reduce its incentive to invest in quality and the combined impact on viewers could be negative. Likewise, in the pay-TV regime, a regulatory ceiling on the direct charge the broadcaster can levy on viewers might be counter-productive once the firm's quality response to the lower price is taken into account. Finally, a regime shift from free-to-air to pay TV, which we know will harm viewers with quality held constant, may benefit viewers once the firm's likely boost to its quality is factored in.

Another concern was the danger that competing broadcasters would duplicate programming, while a monopoly broadcaster could have greater incentive to provide diverse output. This is a genuine danger in a free-to-air market with limited channels, but less so with pay TV. For instance, Steiner (1952) analyzes a rather extreme model where each viewer only considers watching a single type of content, and prefers to switch off rather than watch anything else. To illustrate, suppose there are just two types of channels, A and B, with respective audiences n_A and n_B and per-viewer surpluses v_A and v_B. For simplicity, suppose that program costs are zero and there is no viewer disutility from advertising. Then a monopoly broadcaster with two channels will choose to offer both types of channels in order to maximize its total audience. (This is true in both the free-to-air and the pay-TV regime.) In the ad-funded world where each of two channels is provided by a separate broadcaster, it may be that both choose to offer the same program type.[41]

The general principle is that when broadcasters charge viewers directly for content, they have an incentive to differentiate their content in order to relax price competition. More modern treatments of this issue have tended to use a Hotelling model as a way to capture the choice of genre (or other aspects of content such as political stance). In such models, it is well known that when rivals cannot compete with price, there is a tendency to converge to the middle of the Hotelling line in a bid to maximize market share. This is a reasonable reflection of a free-to-air broadcasting market where broadcasters cannot affect advertising intensity (or viewers do not care about advertising intensity). As such, this model bears out the intuition that ad-funded broadcasters often offer the same fare. However, in a pay-TV regime where broadcasters can charge viewers directly, there is a tendency to choose locations which are far apart so as to relax price competition.[42]

Gabszewicz et al. (2001) study a Hotelling model when media duopolists first choose location and then compete for consumers. Consumers are assumed not to care about advertising intensity (i.e., $\delta = 0$ in the above notation), and so a media outlet chooses its level of advertising purely to maximize advertising revenue. If this revenue is so great that outlets offer content for free to consumers, they find that the outlets duplicate their content, while if positive prices are offered in equilibrium the outlets differentiate their offerings. This analysis was extended by Peitz and Valletti (2008) to allow for advertising disutility (which is more relevant in television markets than in the newspaper context considered by Gabszewicz et al., 2001). They find that with pay TV, broadcasters differentiate their content to the maximum extent, as in Gabszewicz et al. (2001), while in the free-to-air regime broadcasters do differentiate their content to some extent, for otherwise competition for viewers who dislike ads would force their advertising levels to zero.

7.3.2 Evaluating the Simple Model

7.3.2.1 Testable Implications

Under its maintained assumptions, the preceding model produces a number of testable implications about differences in outcomes in ad-supported and pay (ad plus subscriber-supported) television markets that I summarize here.

---

[41] This is the case when audiences are significantly skewed, in the sense that $n_A > 2n_B$, when a broadcaster prefers to get half the mass market rather than all of the niche market. However, if broadcasters can charge viewers, they are more likely to choose distinct program types in equilibrium. If they choose the same content A, say, competition drives the viewer price to zero, and they each obtain profit $(1/2)n_A r$, while if they choose distinct program types they can extract viewer surplus, and so one firm obtains $n_A(r + v_A)$ and the other obtains $n_B(r + v_B)$. It is an equilibrium to choose distinct program types when $(1/2)n_A r < n_B(r + v_B)$, which is a weaker condition than in the ad-funded regime.

[42] See d'Aspremont et al. (1979) for this analysis.

- *Prices and Welfare*: The total price to viewers (i.e., the subscription price plus the disutility from advertising) is higher in pay TV than ad TV under both monopoly and oligopoly, and so, conditional on the content being offered, viewers and advertisers are worse off in pay TV, with broadcasters better off.
- *Content Choice*: Because of this increased profitability, broadcasters will offer more content in a pay-TV environment. Furthermore, where both free and paid content are available, lowest-common-denominator programming will be offered on free channels and niche programming will be offered on pay. Finally, we should see maximal content differentiation in a pay-TV oligopoly.
- *Quality and Regulation*: Optimal quality increases with total price (and thus should be higher in pay markets). Regulations that cap prices or advertising levels will lower quality and viewer surplus.

Unfortunately, one cannot take these predictions directly to the data, as there is a sizeable gap between the simple model's maintained assumptions and the institutional characteristics of TV markets, including multi-homing consumers, multi-dimensional preferences, multichannel firms, competition within and between commercial broadcasters, public service broadcasters, and pay-television providers, and unmodeled heterogeneity in utility of content, disutility of ads, costs of program production and quality choice, and regulatory constraints across countries. As an example, a model allowing heterogeneous disutility of ads and competition between a single broadcast and pay provider offering identical content but with a different mix of advertising versus subscriber payments would likely yield, in contrast to the first prediction above, (relatively) ad-loving consumers facing a lower total price from the broadcaster, ad-hating consumers facing a lower total price from the pay operator, and the consequent self-selection of consumers into the environment that suited them best.[43]

7.3.2.2 What Can We Learn?

The theory instead has been useful in at least two distinct ways: identifying both the variables of economic interest and the mechanisms by which different economic environments (e.g., broadcast vs. pay support, monopoly vs. oligopoly) determine welfare outcomes in television markets, mechanisms that are likely to continue to operate in richer theoretical environments, and identifying relevant model primitives on which to focus empirical research. As examples of the first type, I highlight several data patterns from Section 7.2.

---

[43] My thanks to Simon Anderson for this example. As a historical note, the television theory literature's focus on the tradeoffs between broadcast and pay-television regimes going back to Steiner (1952) and Beebe (1977) reflects the combination of capacity and regulatory constraints that limited the development of the pay-television sector. Pay television's large and growing dominance of television markets evident in Figures 7.9, 7.12, 7.13, 7.14, and 7.16 has, however, largely mooted this as a policy question. We all want our MTV.

On the topic of content choice, the handful of networks in the US broadcasting sector described in Table 7.1 versus the hundreds of pay-television networks summarized in Tables 7.2 and 7.3 suggests the ability of pay-television networks to better extract viewer surplus indeed likely enables them to offer more content than can ad-supported networks, particularly in a multichannel world that limits the ability to build the kinds of large audiences of greatest value to advertisers.[44] Similarly, the immense variety of available pay-television channels in these same tables suggests significant (if not maximal) content differentiation is occurring in pay-television markets. Whether the mechanism driving this differentiation is the desire of programmers to enhance market power over their audiences with advertisers (the motivation of the effect originally developed in Peitz and Valletti (2008) using a similarly stylized modeling environment) or to enhance market power over their subscribers in negotiations with distributors (an unmodeled effect) is an interesting open research question. Regarding quality choice, Figures 7.6 and 7.14 indicating the simultaneous growth in pay-television price and quality (as measured by programming expenditure) and constancy in broadcast television quality suggests the complementarity of quality and price identified in the simple model may be a robust theoretical prediction.[45] Further theoretical work on all these questions would be welcome.

As for empirical work identifying model primitives, Wilbur (2008) and Analysys Mason and BrandScience (2010) both estimate consumer sensitivity to advertising (δ), but obtain very different results: the former, using aggregate ratings data, estimates an elasticity of approximately -2.5, while the latter, using household viewing data, estimates an elasticity indistinguishable from zero. As it is an important input into the welfare effects of advertising (and thus advertising support), further estimates of this key parameter would be useful. Furthermore, several papers have estimated preferences for programming (v), research on which I summarize in more detail in Section 7.4.4.

While welcome, there remain important features present even in the simple model that *have not* received much, if any, attention in empirical work. Examples include accounting better for the simultaneous influence of both subscriber and advertiser

---

[44] Similarly perhaps for program choice within networks of different types: Crawford (2007) found that there are important differences between the programming provided on broadcast versus cable networks, with "niche" or special-interest programming less widely available on broadcast channels than is general-interest programming (and vice versa on pay).

[45] A final example is the possible concordance between the predictions of the simple model about subscriber price caps. That such caps would reduce quality has found support in the literature evaluating such regulations imposed by the 1992 Cable Act (Besanko et al., 1987, 1988; Crawford, 2000, 2013; Crawford and Shum, 2007). Assessing the quality effects of caps on advertising minutes remains an open question; see Analysys Mason and BrandScience (2010, Annex E), Crawford et al. (2012a), and Filistrucchi et al. (2010) for related research.

payments in influencing market outcomes,[46] and analyzing content choice in television markets.[47] Other unanswered questions include how consumers trade off price versus quality, what factors influence firms' (possibly dynamic) quality choices, and determining what is the connection between competition and quality. These are all first-order inputs into television market welfare that require substantially more empirical research. The next section summarizes those extensions to the simple theory model that have been made and the empirical research that relies on them.

7.4. EXTENSIONS TO THE SIMPLE MODEL: "THE FOUR BS"

While the simple model above gives important testable predictions about outcomes in television markets, there are aspects of the industry that are not included in the model that are important to understand its functioning, as well as how television markets differ from other media markets. I call these extensions the "Four Bs": Public Service **Broadcasters**, **Bargaining**, **Barriers to Entry**, and **Bundling**. I introduce each, discuss their theoretical consequences for the functioning of television markets, and provide evidence of their effects.

7.4.1 Public Service Broadcasters
7.4.1.1 The Economic Rationale for PSBs
7.4.1.1.1 A History of PSBs
Especially in the era before pay TV, there was a clear danger of market failure in the provision of television. Advertising intensity could have been excessive, the cost of high-quality programming might not have been able to be recouped with advertising revenue alone, limited spectrum meant there could be only few rivals, and those rivals might anyway have offered duplicative content. One natural response to these problems was to promote "public service broadcasting" (PSB), either with a single designated PSB broadcaster or by imposing requirements on a number of commercial broadcasters.

---

[46] Wilbur (2008) stands out as one of the few academic papers to incorporate both viewer and advertiser demand into a model of television markets, but he does so only for the broadcast sector. By contrast, Crawford et al. (2012a) estimate a model of advertiser (inverse) demand, but do not analyze viewer demand. Similarly, recent papers in the pay-TV sector, like Crawford and Yurukoglu (2012), incorporate the advertising sector, but in a reduced-form way that prevents evaluation of advertiser welfare. This surely reflects both the modeling challenges needed to account for the pay-television supply chain and the difficulty obtaining the data necessary to analyze both the broadcast and pay-television branches and the subscriber and ad-supported sides of the market, but these barriers are being progressively lowered with time.

[47] Again Wilbur (2008) stands out, finding the programs offered on broadcast television align more closely with advertiser than viewer preferences. By contrast, research on program choice is common in radio markets; see Chapters 1 and 8 (this volume) for analyses of the impact of market size and market concentration on product selection and program variety in radio.

For example, many viewers might be made better off if advertising on television was banned or reduced for some broadcasters, and the broadcaster's funding shortfall met from other sources. Viewers might benefit if expensive dramas or documentaries were produced, which would not be offered in a laissez-faire broadcasting market.

Historically, the UK has had the best-known system of public service regulation in the world. A useful way to discuss the rationale and experience of PSBs is briefly to trace its early history in the UK, which is well documented through a number of committee reports commissioned by the UK government over the years.[48] The first such report, the 1923 Sykes Report, accompanied the formation of the BBC (initially the British Broadcasting Company, and then, from 1927, the British Broadcasting Corporation). The Sykes Report suggested that "the control of such a potential power [as radio held] over public opinion and the life of the nation ought to remain with the state," and it should not become an unregulated commercial monopoly. The report recommended that the BBC be funded using a license fee levied on owners of radio sets, and that the BBC should not broadcast advertisements.

The Sykes Report only investigated the short-run issues associated with the formation of the broadcasting service, and in 1925 the Crawford Committee was directed to formulate guidelines for the longer-term operation of the BBC. This committee invited John Reith, the first director of the BBC during the period 1923 until 1938, to present a statement of his views of broadcasting. Reith, the son of a Scottish Presbyterian minister and holding strong religious beliefs himself, presented firm opinions on the proper purposes of broadcasting: "the preservation of a high moral tone is obviously of paramount importance"; "He who prides himself on giving what he thinks the public wants is often creating a fictitious demand for lower standards which he himself will then satisfy"; and so on.[49] Reith also felt that radio had a social and political function, and could be a powerful means to national unity. He cited a broadcast speech in 1924 by King George V, the first time the monarch had been heard on radio, as having the effect of "making the nation as one man." Broadcasting could also provide the facts surrounding an issue of the day, as well as the arguments on either side, and people could make up their own minds instead of accepting "the dictated and partial versions of others." Finally, Reith argued for "unity of control"—i.e., the maintenance of the BBC's broadcasting monopoly—so that "one general policy may be maintained throughout the country and definite standards promulgated." The BBC was to keep this monopoly for the next 30 years.

---

[48] This account is mostly taken from the excellent account by Scannell (1990). Parts are also taken from Armstrong (2005) and Armstrong and Weeds (2007).

[49] In private he was more trenchant. As reported on the BBC's webpage devoted to Reith, he wrote in his diary of his admiration for Nazi-era German broadcasting: "Germany has banned hot jazz and I'm sorry that we should be behind in dealing with this filthy product of modernity." After the war he was disgusted at a broadcast of greyhound racing, "the most significant manifestation of public depravity that I have seen."

The first committee in the television era, the 1950s Beveridge Committee, had this monopoly as its focus. In its submission to the committee, the BBC argued strongly against ending its monopoly, since Gresham's Law would operate "as remorselessly in broadcasting as ever it did in currency. The good, in the long run, will inevitably be driven out by the bad. [...] And because competition in broadcasting must in the long run descend to a fight for the greatest number of listeners, it would be the lower forms of mass appetite which would more and more be catered for in programmes."

The Beveridge Committee recommended that the BBC monopoly be continued, but 2 years later, a newly elected government rejected this, and in 1955 it established commercial television in the UK, funded by advertising. This Independent Television (ITV) had strict PSB obligations, and the new second television channel was not an alternative to public service broadcasting. An advertising-funded commercial broadcaster could be induced to supply specified kinds of programming in return for its license to operate. Having one of just two television channels meant that ITV would enjoy significant scarcity rents. (The phrase "a license to print money" was coined when the first ITV licences were first awarded.) These rents could be used to fund programming that the regulatory authority wished to see provided, but which would not be supplied voluntarily by commercial broadcasters.

The next committee, the 1960s Pilkington Committee, was charged with how to allocate a new, third television channel. Sir Harry Pilkington was very much a Reithian in outlook and concerned with pervasive "triviality." The committee found a lack of variety and originality and unwillingness to try challenging subject matter, and identified commercial television as the main culprit, which was unable to "understand the nature of quality or of triviality, nor the need to maintain one and counter the other." The committee awarded the third channel to the BBC.

Finally, we fast-forward to 1986, the heyday of Margaret Thatcher's government, and to the Peacock Committee, which was set up to investigate alternatives to the BBC's license fee. This committee radically shifted the tone of the discussion in the UK, and treated broadcasting more like any other product. It wanted a broadcasting system to offer "full freedom of entry for programme makers, a transmissions system capable of carrying an indefinitely large number of programmes, [and] facilities for pay-per-programme or pay-per-channel." The committee recommended that in the medium term (the 1990s) the BBC should be funded by subscription, and that residual PSB requirements be financed from a fund open to all broadcasters.

7.4.1.1.2 PSBs as a Response to Market Failure

Armstrong and Weeds (2007) analyze in depth the extent to which PSBs can be rationalized as a response to market failure. Quoting Gavyn Davies, they give credence to the view that the mission of a PSB should not simply be to "inform, educate, and entertain," but to "inform, educate, and entertain in a way which commercial broadcasters, left unregulated, would not do." They identify two possible market failures that PSBs might solve: (1) satisfying viewer preferences that might otherwise not be served and (2) accounting for externalities associated with various types of programming.

On the first point, they argue that while such concerns may have been reasonable in a low-capacity world of the type present in the early days of the industry, they are much harder to defend now given the growth in content across countries in pay-television offerings. The second point, however, remains valid. While causality about the effects of television viewing is very hard to establish, a growing body of research argues that watching certain types of content negatively influences behavior.[50] Whether this has increased or decreased with the widespread availability of multichannel television is an open question. One thing is sure, however, while "in the early days of monopoly, the BBC could effectively force people to consume an austere diet of organ recitals, public announcements, and so on," this is less true in today's world, where audiences are becoming ever more fragmented. This suggests that even if there remains a rationale for PSBs, there is a reduced ability to implement those goals, making this a challenging issue for both policymakers and the PSBs themselves.

Finally, granting the possibility of a market failure that a PSB could address, there is a question of implementation. Armstrong and Weeds (2007) argue that singling out funding for a single entity is potentially distortionary. While proponents have argued that such a policy could force competitors to "raise their game," there is no empirical evidence in support of this view and there is the reasonable possibility that such a policy could decrease rivals' incentives to invest in programming, at minimum in the PSB's programming areas.

7.4.1.2 Effects of PSBs

Despite its significant role in the functioning of most media markets and a consensus among academics, regulators, and the public at large about the importance of PSBs for the functioning of a representative democracy, there is surprisingly little economic research supporting these beliefs.[51] Following the widespread entry of commercial broadcasters in media markets worldwide, Prat and Strömberg (2006) build a model of a monopoly provider of broadcast television facing competitive entry and analyze the impact that entry has on programming choices, channel selection, and individuals' knowledge. They then test the implications of the model using Swedish survey data taken before and after the entry of a commercial television station, finding those that start

---

[50] See, e.g., Hamilton (2000) regarding the connection between television and violence.

[51] Publicly supported broadcasters also arise in radio markets, where they are an important (sometimes leading) provider of news and information. See Chapter 8 (Section 8.4.8, this volume) for an analysis of the extent to which non-commercial content "crowds out" commercial content.

watching the commercial station increase both their level of political knowledge and their political participation.

While thought provoking, I share the views of Prat and Strömberg (2011) calling for significantly more research on the impact of PSBs, and not just on political outcomes. They argue that political information is a public good and that voters who spend resources obtaining information to keep their political leaders accountable produce a positive externality, providing one rationale for public funding of PSBs. But how big is this externality? Does a PSB provide a more valuable (e.g., less biased?) form of information compared to commercial producers? Are there other positive externalities of PSBs beyond disciplining politicians, for example on education or culture? What evidence is there for this? I share their call for greater data collection and dissemination by public broadcasters and greater emphasis on these questions by researchers.

7.4.2 Bargaining

One important feature of television markets that is frequently assumed away in theoretical models is the impact of the supply chain on market outcomes. Pay-television channel conglomerates like Disney or Viacom negotiate with pay-television distributors like Comcast or DirecTV over the price the latter will pay to the former for the right to offer the former's television channels on the latter's pay-TV bundles. Similarly, broadcast networks like ABC negotiate with stations (or station groups) over compensation for broadcast programming. This subsection describes the consequences such negotiations have on outcomes in television markets.

7.4.2.1 Bargaining Theory

In television markets, it is reasonable to think that both content providers (channels) and distributors have market power. In such cases, it's unreasonable to think that either "sets a price"; rather they bargain to determine a mutually agreeable price. In such settings, non-cooperative bargaining theory has proven to be a useful tool to help understand market outcomes.

The insights of bargaining theory can be most easily understood in the context of bilateral monopolists, A and B, bargaining over a pie of size π.[52] The set of possible agreements is given by

$$X = \{(x_A, x_B) : 0 \leq x_A \leq \pi \text{ and } x_B = \pi - x_A\}.$$

Utility to player i from an agreement is $u_i = U_i(x_i)$. If the players fail to reach an agreement, each gets a "disagreement utility" or "threat point," $d_i \geq U_i(0)$, with $d = (d_A, d_B)$. Let Ω be the set of utilities achievable through agreement, i.e.,

---

[52] The exposition here broadly follows Muthoo (1999, Chapter 2).

$$\Omega = \{(u_A, u_B) : \exists x \in X \ \text{ s.t. } U_A(x_A) = u_A \text{ and } U_B(x_B) = u_B\}.$$

Then a "bargaining problem" is given by the pair (Ω, d).

Nash (1950) established there is a unique solution to this bargaining problem that satisfies certain axioms of rational behavior.[53] This was later generalized to account for asymmetries between the two players, yielding a solution called the Asymmetric Nash Bargaining Solution (ANBS).

Let $\tau \in (0, 1)$ be the "bargaining power" for Player A (with $1 - \tau$ being Player B's bargaining power) representing the strength of each player in negotiations. The ANBS of the bargaining game (Ω, d) is the unique pair of utilities that solves

$$\max_{u_A, u_B \in \Theta} (u_A - d_A)^\tau (u_B - d_B)^{1-\tau}.$$

The solution to this problem is called the "split-the-difference rule." It says that the ANBS, (u_A^N, u_B^N), is given by

$$u_A^N = d_A + \tau(s - d_A - d_B)$$
$$u_B^N = d_B + (1 - \tau)(s - d_A - d_B),$$

where s is the "combined agreement surplus," the (utility) size of the pie to be split.

The solution indicates that each party's utility from the bargain depends on three factors: (1) their threat point, d_i; (2) the "incremental surplus," $s - d_A - d_B$, i.e., the surplus the parties could earn from an agreement above and beyond what they could earn in the absence of the agreement (i.e., the "size of the pie" to be split); and (3) their bargaining power, τ.

In addition to satisfying reasonable axioms about agent's behavior, Rubinstein (1982) later established that this ANBS solution was also the unique solution to a model of "alternating offers" that closely resembles how bargaining happens in practice. In this case, each party's bargaining power (τ or $1 - \tau$) could be related to how patient each was in negotiations.[54]

Horn and Wolinsky (1988) extended the bilateral monopoly bargaining solution to that of bilateral oligopoly. This is important in television markets because the outcomes of bargains are interdependent: negotiations yielding a low affiliate fee paid by one distributor to one channel impact the profits made by other distributors (and channels).

The equilibrium concept they introduced was a "Nash Equilibrium in Nash Bargains," or "Nash-in-Nash." Each negotiating pair reaches an agreement conditional on all other agreements (i.e., pair-wise Nash Bargaining) and, in equilibrium, no pair

---

[53] These are (1) Invariance to Equivalent Utility Representation, (2) Pareto Efficiency, (3) Symmetry, and (4) Independence of Irrelevant Alternatives (IIA).

[54] Where patience was measured by the rate at which each party discounted future profits, with lower discount rates corresponding to higher bargaining power.

wants to change their agreement given all other pairs' agreements (i.e., each pair-wise agreement is part of a Nash Equilibrium).[55] The structure of the solution for each bargaining pair nonetheless follows that for bilateral monopolists described above.

7.4.2.2 Bargaining Empirics

Crawford and Yurukoglu (2012) (hereafter CY), building on this theoretical literature and the empirical work of Ho (2009), construct an empirical model of demand, pricing, bundle choice, and bargaining to estimate bargaining parameters between channel conglomerates and large pay-television distributors in the US pay-television industry.

CY assume that the input costs (affiliate fees) paid by distributors to channels are the outcome of bilateral negotiations between upstream channels, or channel conglomerates, and downstream distributors that meet and negotiate bilaterally in a separate and simultaneous manner. Following industry practice, they assume distributors (Multiple System Operators or MSOs) negotiate on behalf of all their component systems and channel conglomerates bargain on behalf of their component channels. They bargain à la Nash to determine whether to form an agreement, and if so, at what input cost. The ultimate payoffs are determined by downstream competition at the agreed-upon input costs. Following industry practice, CY assume that the agreements between conglomerates and distributors are simple linear fees of the form $X per subscriber per month.

CY estimate that most bargaining parameters are between 0.25 and 0.75, discouraging models that assume take-it-or-leave-it offers on the part of either channels or distributors. They further estimate that distributors generally have higher bargaining parameters than channel conglomerates for small channel conglomerates (e.g., Rainbow Media or the content division of Comcast), but that the situation is reversed for large channel conglomerates (e.g., ABC Disney and Time Warner).[56] Among distributors, small cable operators and satellite providers have slightly less estimated bargaining power than large cable operators. They also find that bargaining is an important factor in determining what outcomes would be in a world where distributors were forced to offer channels à la carte, a topic I discuss further at the end of this section.

7.4.3 Barriers to Entry

As noted in Chapter 1 of this volume, media markets are generally characterized by high fixed costs, preference heterogeneity, and advertiser support. One feature that

---

[55] Like Rubinstein (1982), Collard-Wexler et al. (2012) similarly specify an alternating-offers representation of the interdependent bargains inherent in bilateral oligopoly bargaining.

[56] In the period CY study and for the 50 or so largest cable channels in their analysis, Rainbow Media owned AMC and WE: Women's Entertainment, Comcast owned E! Entertainment Television, the Golf Channel, and Versus, ABC Disney owned ABC Family Channel, Disney Channel, ESPN, ESPN2, Soap Net, and Toon Disney, and Time Warner owned the Cartoon Network, CNN, Court TV, TBS Superstation, and TNT.

distinguishes television from other media markets are the magnitudes of the fixed costs and that they are often sunk. This introduces important barriers to entry in both the upstream (channel) market as well as the downstream (distribution) market.

7.4.3.1 Market Power in Wholesale (Programming) Markets

As evidence of these fixed costs, consider again Tables 7.1 and 7.2 that report the programming expenditure for leading broadcast and cable television channels. The average annual programming expenditure for even a minor broadcast network is upward of $100 million, with $200 million required for a low-end top-25 cable network. Launching a channel requires a multi-year programming commitment, as well as administrative, technical, and marketing infrastructures that can easily push the fixed costs over $1 billion. Furthermore, most of these costs are sunk: programming investments that prove unpopular cannot be recovered, as cannot many administrative and marketing costs. Furthermore, arranging carriage agreements with leading distributors, a necessary condition for the success of a television channel, are also expensive and uncertain. All these factors lead to significant entry barriers and encourage a concentrated upstream market structure.

Table 7.5 presents the ownership pattern of leading broadcast and cable programming networks in 2013, while Figure 7.17 displays the share of this upstream industry revenue that accrues to "Big Media," "Vertically Integrated Multiple System Operators (MSOs)," and "Other" owners. The table and figure show that seven firms dominate the production of video programming in the US.[57]

There are both pro- and anti-competitive effects that could arise from this increased concentration. Increased firm size may yield economies of scale, greater facility developing and launching new program networks, and lower costs for investing in and deploying new programming and services. It may also, however, increase market power in the programming market, disadvantaging smaller channels and/or distributors. This has been a frequent issue discussed in the context of large media mergers like that between Comcast and AT&T, which created the largest downstream distributor serving nearly 25% of the US market (FCC, 2002). Some industry participants argue strongly that increasing consolidation is putting smaller distributors at a cost disadvantage in negotiations with channel conglomerates (FCC, 2013b).[58]

The conventional wisdom is that increased concentration in the distribution market improves the bargaining outcomes of those distributors, reducing affiliate fees to television channels in the programming market. The theoretical mechanisms, however, are

---

[57] Similar patterns of concentration have existed since at least 1998 (SNL Kagan, 2014a).

[58] Cox, the fifth largest distributor in the US, argues that the top four distributors exceed all others in terms of their bargaining power with programmers and this represents one of the most significant competitive threats that they face. The American Cable Association, an industry association representing small cable operators, also emphasizes the importance of scale by calling attention to the higher prices paid for video programming by small cable operators that lack scale economies.

Table 7.5 Concentration in the upstream (channel) market, 2013

Big media companies	Total revenue ($ million)	Ownership share
The Walt Disney Co.		
ABC	3161	100%
ESPN	8343	80%
Disney Channel	1459	100%
ESPN2	1098	80%
ABC Family Channel	761	100%
History	890	50%
Lifetime Television	884	50%
A&E	879	50%
Total Top Disney	17,476	14,261
Total All Disney	19,339	15,697
21st Century Fox		
Fox	2660	100%
Fox News	1917	100%
FX Network	1137	100%
Fox Sports RSNs	3616	(a)
Total Top Fox	9331	8877
Total All Fox	11,758	10,801
Viacom Inc./CBS		
CBS	4241	100%
The CW	429	50%
Nickelodeon	2117	100%
MTV	1366	100%
Comedy Central	780	100%
Spike TV	651	100%
BET	580	100%
VH1	569	100%

Vertically integrated MSOs	Total revenue ($ million)	Ownership share
Comcast Corporation		
NBC	3095	100%
Telemundo	396	100%
USA	2066	100%
Syfy	788	100%
CNBC	656	100%
Bravo	650	100%
E!	531	100%
Comcast RSNs	1427	(c)
Total Top Comcast	9609	9024
Total All Comcast	12,498	11,255
Time Warner Inc.		
The CW	429	50%
TNT	2784	100%
TBS	1817	100%
CNN	1094	100%
Cartoon Network	832	100%
Time Warner RSNs	545	(d)
HBO/Cinemax	4603	100%
Total Top Time Warner	12,103	11,903
Total All Time Warner	13,496	12,787
Cablevision		
AMC	877	100%
Cablevision RSNs	634	100%
Total Top Cablevision	1511	1511
Total All Cablevision	2193	2193
Total vertically integrated	28,187	26,236

	Revenue	Ownership Share
Showtime/TMC/Flix	1621	100%
EPIX/EPIX Drive-In	454	33%
Total Top Viacom/CBS	12,809	12,290
Total All Viacom/CBS	14,949	14,370
Liberty Global Inc.		
Starz/Encore	1385	100%
Discovery Channel	1070	100%
TLC	593	66%
Liberty RSNs	376	(b)
Total Top Liberty	3423	2762
Total All Liberty	4872	4116
Total big media	**50,918**	**44,983**

Other/Independent Companies	Revenue	Ownership Share
Univision		
Univision	692	100%
UniMás	175	95%
Scripps		
HGTV	876	100%
Food Network	867	69%
National Football League		
NFL Network	1165	100%
Total All Other/Inds	**7654**	
Total revenue all channels	**86,760**	

Notes: Reported are the revenue and share owned of the largest US broadcast, cable, Regional Sports, and premium programming networks among major multichannel owners of such networks in 2013. The left panel of the table reports this information for what are often called "big media" companies: Disney, Fox, Viacom/CBS, and Liberty. The top half of the right panel reports this information for content affiliated with large cable operators: Comcast, Time Warner, and Cablevision. The bottom half of the panel reports it for all other (i.e., "independent") owners. Revenue data is from SNL Kagan (2014a). Ownership data was collected by hand from company stock filings and industry sources for the research conducted in Crawford et al. (2015). Within each company, the highest-revenue networks are reported, as well as totals for these networks and for all their networks. Totals in the Ownership Share column are the same revenue totals weighted by ownership share. Individual RSNs are not reported; see Crawford et al. (2015) for the RSN owned by each listed company and their ownership share. Figure 7.17 displays graphically the revenue share of each company among the total revenue earned by such networks.

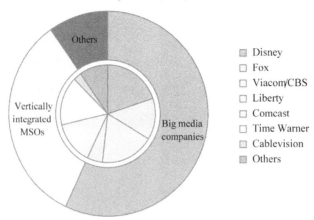

Revenue US TV channels by Owner (2013)

Figure 7.17 Concentration in the upstream market, 2013. *Notes*: Depicted is the revenue share of eight groups of owners of broadcast and pay-television programming networks in 2013: "Big Media" companies, Disney, Fox, Viacom/CBS, and Liberty, vertically integrated (cable) Multiple System Operators (MSOs), Comcast, Time Warner, and Cablevision, and Others. Revenue data is from SNL Kagan (2014a); see Table 7.5 and the notes there for further details.

not clear. In the bargaining approach summarized in the last subsection, increased size for an individual cable system reduces the viability of a program network if an agreement is not reached between the two parties. This necessarily lowers the network's "threat point." It also, however, lowers the threat point of the now-larger cable system, with the net effect unclear. Chipty and Snyder (1999) conclude that increased size downstream can actually reduce a cable system's bargaining power.[59] Similarly, Raskovich (2003) builds a bargaining model with a pivotal buyer, one with whom an agreement is necessary for a seller's viability, and finds that being pivotal is *disadvantageous* as if an agreement is not reached the seller will not trade and it is only the pivotal buyer who can guarantee this outcome. This can reduce the incentives to merge if merging would make a buyer pivotal. Inderst and Montez (2015) formalize the tradeoff articulated above and obtain sharper results. They show that when buyer bargaining power is low, as CY found for cable systems negotiating with large channel conglomerates, increases in size are *disadvantageous*, but when buyer bargaining power is high, as CY found for cable systems

---

[59] In their analysis, the size of the surplus to be split between a cable system and a programming network depends on the shape of the network's gross surplus function. They estimate this on 136 data points in the 1980s and early 1990s and find it is convex, implying it is better to act as two small operators than one big one. This convexity seems at odds both with the institutional relationship between network size and advertising revenue (which limits the ability of networks to obtain advertising revenue at low subscriber levels) as well as claims made by industry participants and observers of the benefits of increased size.

negotiating with small channel conglomerates, increases in size do indeed lower input prices. This implication remains to be tested.

Assessing the consequences of increased market power in programming markets is conceptually simple, but a lack of data on transaction prices (affiliate fees) has prevented much empirical work. Ford and Jackson (1997) exploit rarely available programming cost data reported as part of the 1992 Cable Act regulations to assess (in part) the impact of buyer size and vertical integration on programming costs. Using data from a cross-section of 283 cable systems in 1993, they find important effects of MSO size and vertical affiliation on costs: the average/smallest MSO is estimated to pay 11%/52% more than the largest MSO and vertically affiliated systems are estimated to pay 12–13% less per subscriber per month. Chipty (1995) takes a different strategy: she infers the impact of system size on bargaining power from its influence on retail prices. She also finds support for the conventional wisdom that increased buyer size reduces systems' programming costs. Finally, as discussed above, Crawford and Yurukoglu (2012) find that distributors generally have higher bargaining power than channels for small channel conglomerates, but that the situation is reversed for large channel conglomerates. The results of Inderst and Montez (2015) suggest the effects of merger depend critically on these bargaining power estimates. Further empirical research would be welcome.

7.4.3.2 Market Power in Retail (Distribution) Markets

Similar concerns about market power arise in the downstream (distribution) market.[60] The average US pay-television market is served by a single incumbent cable television system, two satellite distributors, and (in some markets) the former incumbent telephone operator. When Verizon entered the video business, they were required to invest *tens of billions* of dollars upgrading their physical infrastructure for the delivery of video programming. This despite the fact that they, like AT&T, had an advantage compared to other potential entrants in already serving the local market with telephone and Internet access services.[61] Similarly, so-called overbuilders, independent entrants in the television business, have struggled to gain more than a minuscule portion of the television market.

Figure 7.6 demonstrated that prices have consistently risen faster than the rate of inflation in the US pay-television market. Table 7.6, drawn from FCC reports on the status of competition in the programming market, reports concentration measures for the industry for several of the past 20 years. The sum of the market shares for the top 4, top 8, and top 25 MVPD providers have all increased over time, with the top 4 MVPDs serving 68% of the market and the top 8 serving 84% in 2010. The correlation between high and rising prices and increased concentration have driven concerns about high and rising market

---

[60] This subsection draws on material from Crawford (2013).

[61] The investment required is sufficiently expensive and uncertain that the third leading US telco, Century-Link, has not chosen to provide a television service except in select major urban markets.

Table 7.6 Concentration in the downstream (distribution) market, 1992–2010

Rank	Company	Market share	Company	Market share	Company	Market share
	1992		**1997**		**2000**	
1	TCI	27.3	TCI	25.5	AT&T	19.1
2	TimeWarner	15.3	TimeWarner	16.0	TimeWarner	14.9
3	Continental	7.5	MediaOne	7.0	DirecTV	10.3
4	Comcast	7.1	Comcast	5.8	Comcast	8.4
5	Cox	4.7	Cox	4.4	Charter	7.4
6	Cablevision	3.5	Cablevision	3.9	Cox	7.3
7	TimesMirror	3.3	DirecTV	3.6	Adelphia	5.9
8	Viacom	3.1	Primestar	2.4	EchoStar (Dish)	5.1
9	Century	2.5	Jones	2.0	Cablevision	4.3
10	Cablevision	2.5	Century	1.6	Insight	1.2
	Top 4	57.2	Top 4	54.3	Top 4	52.7
	Top 8	71.8	Top 8	68.6	Top 8	78.4
	Top 25	–	Top 25	84.9	Top 25	89.8
	2004		**2007**		**2010**	
1	Comcast	23.4	Comcast	24.7	Comcast	22.6
2	DirecTV	12.1	DirecTV	17.2	DirecTV	19.0
3	TimeWarner	11.9	EchoStar (Dish)	14.1	EchoStar (Dish)	14.0
4	EchoStar (Dish)	10.6	TimeWarner	13.6	TimeWarner	12.3
5	Cox	6.9	Cox	5.5	Cox	4.9
6	Charter	6.7	Charter	5.3	Charter	4.5
7	Adelphia	5.9	Cablevision	3.2	Verizon FiOS	3.5
8	Cablevision	3.2	Bright	2.4	Cablevision	3.3
9	Bright	2.4	Suddenlink	1.3	AT&T Uverse	3.0
10	Mediacom	1.7	Mediacom	1.3	Bright	2.2
	Top 4	58.0	Top4	69.6	Top4	68.0
	Top 8	80.7	Top8	86.0	Top8	84.0
	Top 25	90.4	Top 25	–	Top 25	–

Reported are the market shares of the largest distributors of pay-television services across a selection of years between 1992 and 2010 taken from annual FCC reports on the status of competition in the pay-television market. Also reported is the sum of the market shares for the largest 4, 8, and 25 such distributors.
Source: FCC (1997, 1998, 2001, 2005a,c).

power in distribution. Of course, Figure 7.14 also shows that cable television channels have been spending more on programming, raising costs to downstream operators and challenging the ability to separate out price increases due to cost increases from those to due to market power. Furthermore, the entrance of satellite providers in the late 1990s and telco providers in the late 2000s (evident in Figure 7.4) have prompted policymakers to wonder if this is "enough" competition and/or whether instead price regulations might make consumers better off.

Turning first to regulatory effects, Mayo and Otsuka (1991) examined pre-deregulation cable prices in 1982 and found regulation significantly constrained their level. Rubinovitz (1993) examines the change in prices between 1984 (when they were still regulated) and 1990 (when they were not), finding the increased exercise of market power was responsible for 43% of the price increase in the period. Crawford and Shum (2007) find that regulation is associated with higher offered qualities, despite (slightly) higher prices.

As for satellite competition, Goolsbee and Petrin (2004) estimate a flexible probit model of cable and satellite bundle demand, infer (otherwise unobservable) bundle quality from these estimates, and relate cable prices to satellite penetration controlling for quality. They find reducing satellite penetration to the minimum observed in their data would be associated with a 15% increase in cable prices. Chu (2010) extends this by analyzing system quality responses and finds that, while there is widespread variation across systems in their strategic response, on average cable prices are slightly lower, but cable quality is significantly higher.

The period since 2006 has witnessed a third wave of cable entry, that from telco operators. Industry accounts associated their entry with significant price competition, but only for the first several years after entry. Once they established a moderate presence, the conventional wisdom is that both significantly increased prices. More research on both the short- and long-run effects of telco entry is needed.

7.4.3.3 Horizontal Merger Review

Concerns about market power both upstream and down arise most frequently in the context of horizontal merger review in television markets.[62] Because most cable systems have non-overlapping service areas, mergers between cable operators often do not reduce competition in local pay-television markets. As such, most recent proposals have been approved, both in the US and Europe.[63]

---

[62] I discuss vertical merger review in Section 7.5.2. See also Chapter 6 of this volume for general issues with mergers in media markets.

[63] The Comcast—Time Warner Cable merger announced in February 2014 was withdrawn after news broke in April 2015 that the US Department of Justice (DOJ) intended to challenge the merger. The concerns raised by the merger were largely not horizontal issues in the pay-television market, but horizontal issues in the broadband Internet access market and vertical issues arising from Comcast's ownership of significant programming assets. Charter Communications has since announced their intention to purchase Time Warner Cable. Previous to this, the last big US challenge to a horizontal pay-television merger was the Echostar—DirecTV deal in 2001, which would have combined the two national US satellite operators. By contrast, Europe has seen a horizontal merger wave in recent years (Willems, 2014). Recent deals in the distribution market include Canal Plus—Movistar TV in Spain, Kabel—UnityMedia (Liberty Media) in Germany, Ziggo—UPC Netherlands (Liberty Media) in the Netherlands, and Vodafone—ONO in Spain. Much of this activity is transnational and may be driven by the anticipation of a single European digital market, with Liberty Global and Vodafone leading players in collecting (and perhaps ultimately connecting) pay-television systems across Europe.

Conducting horizontal merger reviews would benefit from answers to several questions about television markets that the academic literature has not yet provided. Should programming markets be defined broadly or narrowly?[64] What is the impact of increased size on bargaining power in programming markets? Are merger-related efficiencies likely? What of tacit collusion, upstream and/or down? Much more work is needed to address the basic questions regularly facing regulators and competition policymakers.

7.4.4 Preference Heterogeneity and Bundling

One common feature of preferences in media markets is their heterogeneity. Some people like to read the *New York Times*, while others prefer *USA Today*. Some like Miley Cyrus while others prefer J.S. Bach. And some like Fox News while others like MSNBC. Anderson and Waldfogel discuss the implications of preference heterogeneity and preference externalities in media markets, finding important connections between the size of media markets and outcomes like the number, variety, and quality of media products (Chapter 1, this volume).

Television markets are both similar and different. They are similar in that consumers of television, as in other media markets, have significant heterogeneity in their preferences. They differ, however, in that the television channels bought by consumers are *bundled* together and sold as a package.[65] In this subsection, I discuss the implications of this bundling for outcomes in television markets.

7.4.4.1 Bundling Theory

In practice, many broadcasters supply a range of content to viewers, and heterogeneous viewers may prefer some kinds of content to other kinds. A particularly simple case is when a viewer values each piece of content additively so that her WTP for content i is not affected by whether she also has access to content j. In this additive case, when the broadcaster retails its content independently, so that the price of a piece of content is independent of her consumption of other content, then the previous analysis applies without change. Both values and prices are additive, and there is no interaction between different content.

---

[64] In the BSkyB–Ofcom PayTV inquiry, separate programming markets were defined (narrowly) for premium movies and premium sports. In the Comcast–NBCU merger, the FCC implicitly defined news and business news markets narrowly when imposing a "neighborhooding" condition in its approval of the proposed merger. Determining this question requires an understanding of substitutability of programs and program networks from the perspective of viewers and, ultimately, pay-television distributors. Data exists in principle to evaluate the former (though indeed while substitutes at any point in time, channels may instead be complements in access decisions), while the latter depends on accurately modeling bargaining outcomes, particularly households' willingness to switch providers in the absence of content they value.

[65] Newspapers may also be considered bundles of heterogeneous content. Some of the effects discussed here may also apply in this setting.

However, in the pay-TV regime the broadcaster in most cases can do better than this by bundling its content together as a package.[66] (Clearly, in the free-to-air context, channel bundling has no role to play. For simplicity, suppose in the following discussion that the broadcaster does not use advertising at all.) To illustrate most transparently, suppose instead of retailing its various content separately that the broadcaster sells its full range of content as a single bundle in return for a single price.[67]

The key point is that a viewer's valuation for the whole bundle is often more predictable (i.e., less idiosyncratic) than her values for individual pieces of content (Bakos and Brynjolfsson, 1999; Crawford, 2008). This might be because of negative correlation in values for different types of content, so that those viewers who particularly like content i place less value on content j, and vice versa.[68] A deeper reason is that, even without negative correlation, idiosyncrasies in valuations tend to get "averaged out" when bundling is used. (The phenomenon is similar to the insight that a diversified portfolio is less risky for an investor than holding a single asset.) If a viewer's valuation of one kind of content is independently distributed from her tastes for other kinds of content, and if there are many pieces of content on offer, then the law of large numbers implies that her value for the bundle is highly predictable. The result may be that the broadcaster can extract a large fraction of viewer surplus with bundling, and relative to non-bundled pricing viewers may be harmed and total welfare may rise.[69]

As with the comparison between advertising-funded and pay-TV regimes, the fact that a broadcaster typically makes more profit when bundling is used implies that some content can be profitably supplied *only* if bundling is used. As a result, even if bundling often reduces consumer surplus for a given range of content, the fact that more content might be offered with bundling could lead to consumer gains from the practice.[70] For

---

[66] The pioneering articles on bundling are Stigler (1968) and Adams and Yellen (1976). The many-product discussion which follows is taken from Armstrong (1999b) and Bakos and Brynjolfsson (1999).

[67] More ornate schemes would allow viewers to pick and choose between different content, but the basic insight is seen most clearly with this "pure bundling" format.

[68] For example, suppose half the population value a sports channel at $10 and a news channel at $2, and remaining viewers have the reverse preferences. If the broadcaster had to set a separate price for each channel, it would charge $10 for either channel and viewers would see only their preferred channel. However, if it set a price of $12 for the bundle of both channels, all viewers would just be willing to pay this, and profit and welfare both rise.

[69] Continuing with the example in the previous footnote, suppose for any given piece of content half the viewers have value $10 and the rest have value $2, and valuations are independently distributed across products. As before, with per-channel pricing, the broadcaster would set the price at $10 per channel, viewers would see only the content they value highly and average revenue per subscriber per channel is $5. However, if there are many channels, most viewers place a high value on around 50% of these channels, and so most people are willing to pay around $6 per channel for the bundle. The result is that the broadcaster can extract most of the surplus from most of the viewers by giving them the whole bundle, and welfare increases since most people see all available content.

[70] See Crawford and Cullen (2007) for an investigation of this tradeoff.

similar reasons, an incumbent broadcaster with an existing portfolio of content may be willing to pay more for new content than a new entrant, since the latter is less able to achieve extra revenue obtained with bundling.[71] The result may support a tendency toward concentration in the market for content discussed in the previous subsection, due here to demand-side economies of scope rather than any supply-side economies of scope.

7.4.4.2 Bundling Empirics

A sizeable empirical literature has analyzed consumer demand for bundles of television channels. Mayo and Otsuka (1991) and Rubinovitz (1993) estimate demand for cable bundles and attempt to measure the impact of regulation on cable prices. Crandall and Furchtgott-Roth (1996, Chapter 3) and Crawford (2000) also estimate bundle demand and calculate the welfare effects of changes in prices and product offerings.

Goolsbee and Petrin (2004), Chu (2010), and Crawford and Yurukoglu (2012) are the most recent and comprehensive empirical papers analyzing demand for pay-television bundles.[72] I summarize here CY, as it builds demand for bundles from heterogeneous preferences for individual channels.

A challenge when estimating demand for bundles is to determine the relative importance of each channel in the purchase of the bundle when the bundle contains as many channels (50+) as is common in the pay-television industry. Variation in the contents of bundles across cable markets, or across bundles of different size within cable markets, helps to trace out the demand for each component channel, but generally is not rich enough to recover the full *distribution* of preferences for individual channels. Furthermore, these distributions are critical to understanding the core issues of pricing, content choice, and welfare both in existing television markets and how they may differ in different economic environments.

CY resolve this issue by pairing data on bundle composition and price with complementary data on individuals' viewing habits. The latter, both in the form of average ratings for channels across markets as well as individual households' viewing behavior, provide rich information at the level of individual channels, but do not have price information. It is only the combination of viewing data that allows estimation of the relative utility of alternative channels, and bundle purchase data that allows the translation of channel utility into bundle WTP, that allow them to recover demand curves for individual channels.

---

[71] In the running example, an incumbent broadcaster which already possesses many pieces of content would be willing to pay up to $6 per subscriber for an extra channel, while a stand-alone entrant could pay only $5.

[72] Other recent work includes Rennhoff and Serfes (2008), Byzalov (2010), and Crawford et al. (2012b).

Supported by evidence from viewing patterns in their data, CY also accommodate the "long-tail" feature of preferences for media products.[73] They do so by assuming that with some probability depending on demographics, households have a zero preference for cable channels. If positive, they further assume that the marginal distribution of preferences across households is distributed as an exponential. They then estimate the zero-taste probabilities and exponential parameters for each channel. They also estimate distributions for preferences allowing for positive or negative correlations in tastes for pairs of channels, an important consideration in the bundling literature.[74]

Figure 7.18 reports both the share of positive WTP and, among those that are positive, the estimated WTP for each of nine popular cable channels arising from their analysis. Preference heterogeneity is evident: some people (32%) do not value the cable news channel CNN at all, while others value it at more than $20/month.[75] Furthermore, preferences for each channel are estimated to have a long tail, with many valuing channels at or around $2/month and only few at values at or above $10/month.

7.4.4.3 Welfare Effects of à la Carte

Crawford and Yurukoglu (2012) use the results of their analysis to evaluate the implications of the bundling theory summarized earlier as well as the policy of forcing cable channels to be offered on an à la carte basis, a policy sometimes proposed by policymakers in the pay-television industry.[76] The results both confirm the bundling theory summarized above and refute its application to the specific case of television channels due to bargaining between channels and distributors.

---

[73] See Anderson (2006) for a general exposition of this issue and Shiller and Waldfogel (2011) for evidence of long-tail preferences for music.

[74] In subsequent research analyzing demand for both national cable television channels and Regional Sports Networks, Crawford et al. (2015) extend this demand model to allow for heterogeneous value of time between sports and non-sports channels, finding this to be an important extension which is necessary to explain the relatively large affiliate fees sports networks are able to obtain in negotiations with distributors.

[75] Furthermore, table 4 in Crawford and Yurukoglu (2012) lists, for each of the 50 cable channels in their analysis, the second channel for which households had most positively correlated preferences. For the nine channels listed in Figure 7.18, these were TV Land (ABC Family), MTV2 (BET), Fox News (CNN), MTV (Comedy Central), Nickelodeon (Disney Channel), ESPN2 (ESPN), VH1 (MTV), USA (TNT), and TNT (USA).

[76] They also analyze the impact of channels being offered as a part of Theme Tiers as well as the Bundle-Sized Pricing strategy proposed in Chu et al. (2011).

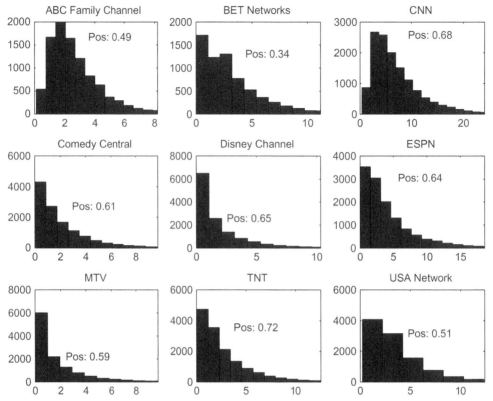

Figure 7.18 Estimated WTP for a subset of television channels. *Notes*: Reported from Crawford and Yurukoglu (2012), the estimated share of 20,000 simulated households that value each of nine large pay-television networks positively (Pos) and the estimated distribution of their willingness-to-pay (WTP) for each network are shown. In each figure, the *y*-axis reports households and the *x*-axis reports WTP in 2000 dollars.

In their counterfactual analysis, CY simulate market outcomes in one large and one small cable market, both competing with a "national" satellite provider. Outcomes are compared for two scenarios. In the first, baseline, scenario, distributors are assumed to set a fixed (bundle) fee for the 49 cable channels included in their analysis. In the second, "full à la carte" scenario, distributors are assumed to set a fixed fee for access to any channels and then individual channel prices for each of these 49 channels. Competition is between the single cable operator serving each market and the national satellite operator setting a common price in both markets.

Their baseline results confirm the predictions of the discriminatory theory of bundling summarized above: in an à la carte world, households would choose only 22 of 49 channels, expenditure on cable would fall by an estimated 23.8%, and consumer surplus would rise by 19.2%. Total industry profits would fall by 12.7%, but the gains to consumers would outweigh the losses to firms and total surplus would increase.[77]

There is an important weakness in these baseline results shared by previous papers looking at this topic: they treat the affiliate fees paid by cable systems to programmers as given. While consistent with most of the theory literature,[78] this is contrary to both the nature of programming contracts in the pay-television industry (which typically require systems to pay sometimes much higher fees if channels are offered à la carte) as well as bargaining incentives in an à la carte world. Crawford and Yurukoglu (2012) use their industry model of pay-television markets to evaluate the welfare effects of à la carte *allowing for renegotiation* between programmers and distributors in an à la carte environment, and find this has an important impact on the merits of such a policy. They estimate that renegotiation in an à la carte world would cause affiliate fees to rise by more than 100% on average, raising à la carte prices to households and lowering both consumer surplus and firm profits. On average, they find consumers would be no better off under à la carte and that any implementation or marketing costs would likely make them worse off. This should give pause to policymakers eyeing à la carte as a policy tool to increase consumer welfare in pay-television markets.

7.5. OPEN POLICY ISSUES IN TELEVISION MARKETS

A number of open theoretical and empirical policy issues currently demand the attention of regulators and policymakers around the world, drawing also the attention of academic research.[79] This section briefly summarizes these topics.

---

[77] Previous research yielded qualitatively similar conclusions for consumer and firm surplus (though not for total surplus). Crawford (2008) tested the implications of the discriminatory theory and found qualified support for it, finding that bundling an average top-15 *special-interest* cable networks was estimated to increase profits and reduce consumer welfare, with an average effect of 4.7% (4.0%). In a simulation study, Crawford and Cullen (2007) confirmed these effects and also found that bundling enhances industry incentives to provide networks more than would à la carte sales, but may do so at significant cost to consumers. Work by Rennhoff and Serfes (2008), under somewhat restrictive assumptions, reaches similar conclusions about welfare effects of à la carte, while Byzalov (2010) finds the opposite result. CY's total surplus results are contrary to those predicted by theory, but can be rationalized as, in their counterfactual, consumers pay fixed fees in order to access channels on an à la carte basis. This fixed fee itself acts similarly to a bundle as consumers only pay it if the surplus given by the sum across channels of their WTP for each channel less its price exceeds the fixed fee. Many do so, purchasing a small number of channels, and this additional sales channel not present in the standard theory increases consumer and firm surplus sufficiently to make the total surplus effect positive.

[78] For an important exception, see Rennhoff and Serfes (2009).

[79] For a view contrary to the belief that more television is always to the good, see the interesting discussion citing sociological research in Armstrong (2005, IV.3).

7.5.1 Wholesale Bundling and Competition in Programming Markets

Bundling may not only be used to price discriminate.[80] Another recent literature analyzes how bundling can also be used to extend market power or deter entry (e.g., Hurkens et al., 2013; Nalebuff, 2004; Peitz, 2008; Whinston, 1990). Both Whinston (1990) and Nalebuff (2004) demonstrate settings in which a monopolist in one product bundles a potentially or partially competitive second product with his monopoly product and either prevents entry or reduces the profitability of a potential entrant in the second product. As highlighted by Peitz (2008), Whinston (1990) requires commitment on the part of the monopolist (in the case entry was not foreclosed, she would prefer not to bundle) and Nalebuff (2004) requires sequentiality (if both choose prices simultaneously rather than having the monopolist go first, then independent pricing rather than bundling is more effective at preventing entry).

Hurkens et al. (2013), building on this literature (and especially Peitz, 2008), demonstrate that a dominant firm can, in some cases, credibly build an entry barrier by bundling. The intuition stems from the two effects bundling has on consumer demand: it increases it (what the authors call the *demand size effect*) and it makes it more elastic (the *demand elasticity effect*).[81] A key parameter in their model is α, measuring the extent to which the goods offered by a dominant firm are preferred to those offered by its rival. For intermediate values of dominance, they find that bundling can favor a dominant incumbent and disadvantage a rival. Allowing for entry costs, bundling can therefore foreclose competitive entry, with uncertain welfare effects.

The potential for bundling to impact competition between channels in television markets has long been a concern of industry participants and policymakers in the US. In this context, bundling refers to the requirement that distributors negotiating with channel conglomerates that own both more and less valuable channels distribute the less valuable channels they do not necessarily like or want in order to distribute the valuable channels they feel are essential.[82] This may impact the ability of independent channels to enter and compete in the programming market.

Distributors have complained about the bundling of affiliated program networks, both when negotiating rights to broadcast networks under retransmission consent as well as critical non-broadcast networks (FCC, 2005a, paragraphs 162; 2005b, footnote 232). One small cable operator called such tying, along with restrictions on tiering, "[one of the] two biggest issues that small and rural [cable] operators face today"

---

[80] See Section 7.4.4.

[81] See also Crawford (2008) for an exposition of these two effects in an empirical application to the cable industry.

[82] Since it is typically only one or a small number of channels that are driving this behavior by channel conglomerates, this issue has also been called "tying" in the trade press. A bundle is no more than a two-sided tie; the economic incentives are similar.

(Communications Daily, 2011). In early 2013, Cablevision, a major US cable operator, sued Viacom, a major content provider, over the practice, claiming "Viacom's abuse of its market power over access to commercially critical networks ... force Cablevision to license and distribute ... some dozen other Viacom networks ... that many Cablevision subscribers do not watch and for which Cablevision would prefer to substitute competing networks" (Cablevision Systems Corp, 2013).

Policy responses to this issue are ongoing. The FCC announced a new proceeding to investigate the issue in late 2007, but no formal rulemaking appears to have come from it (Cauley, 2007). In May 2013, Senator John McCain introduced a bill promoting à la carte at both wholesale and retail levels, but this too has stalled. Despite both strong theoretical grounds for its possibility and industry and policymaker interest in the issue, I know of no empirical evidence of either entry deterrence or competitive effects of bundling or tying by channel conglomerates in the television programming market, so empirical studies of this topic would be welcome.

7.5.2 Vertical Integration and Foreclosure

Access to essential (must-have) content has become an increasingly important issue in pay-television markets. Exactly which channels qualify for this designation is not clear, with distributors in US pay-television markets emphasizing sports and broadcast channels (FCC, 2011b) and regulators in the UK market emphasizing sports and film (movie) content (Ofcom, 2009a). The analysis of the competitive and welfare effects of exclusive access to valuable content by distributors integrated with the relevant content providers is therefore an active topic of economic research.[83]

7.5.2.1 Vertical Integration

Anti-competitive concerns are germane when a single firm owns both essential content and a distribution platform. When an integrated operator owns access to essential content, it may not allow at all the distribution of that content to rival distributors (so-called "refusal to deal") and/or it may negotiate prices that raise rival distributors' costs. Rey and Tirole (2007) call these "complete" and "partial foreclosure." Riordan (2008) summarizes the theoretical justification for concerns about vertical integration in general. Most relevant to video markets are theories relating to complete foreclosure, or refusal to deal, raising (downstream) rivals' costs, and reducing (upstream) rivals' revenues.

Even if they agree to license such content to rivals, an integrated programmer–distributor could raise the costs they pay relative to those of its integrated downstream division or reduce the revenue they receive relative to its integrated upstream division

---

[83] There is also a literature analyzing the competitive effects of exclusive dealing between unintegrated channels and distributors, particularly of premium movie and sports content. See Armstrong (1999a), Harbord and Ottaviani (2001), Stennek (2014), Madden and Pezzino (2013), and Weeds (2015).

(Ordover et al., 1990; Riordan, 1984; Salop and Scheffman, 1983). Downstream foreclosure was the primary motivator underlying the exclusivity prohibition for affiliated content in the US program access rules (discussed below) as well as the reason for several merger conditions required by the FCC in its approval of the 2011 Comcast–NBC/Universal merger (FCC, 2011b). Similarly, concerns about upstream foreclosure drove the news neighborhooding condition in that merger due to concerns about the incipient integration of MSNBC, the dominant network for business news, with Comcast, the largest MVPD and one with important footprints in several very large markets for business news. The latter case is instructive, as the concern addressed by the merger condition was not (necessarily) one of complete foreclosure, i.e., that Comcast would no longer carry rival business news networks, but that it would disadvantage them in terms of channel placement, reducing viewership and thus rivals' advertising revenue. This highlights the subtle ways in which an integrated firm with market power in one market can disadvantage rivals in vertically related markets.

Of course, there are also efficiency reasons programmers and distributors may want to integrate. Bresnahan and Levin (2012) summarize the efficiency motivations for merger in general; several of these are salient for television markets. For example, vertical integration could eliminate double marginalization, as discussed above a potentially serious issue due to the widespread use of linear fees for content.[84] Similarly, it could minimize transactions costs and reduce the risk of new program development, or better coordinate investments in complementary technologies, a particularly important issue given the challenging licensing issues posed by the advent of online video. It could also internalize important externalities between programmers and distributors in the areas of product choice, service quality, and brand development. Or it could eliminate inefficiencies in the bargaining process, a potentially important issue given the increasing frequency of disruptions in this process.

Determining whether vertical integration is motivated by strategic or efficiency considerations is a challenging undertaking. Existing empirical research has universally found that vertically integrated MVPDs are more likely to carry their affiliated program networks, but whether this is pro- or anti-competitive remains an open issue. Waterman and Weiss (1996) examine the impact of vertical relationships between pay networks and cable operators in 1989. They find that affiliated MSOs are more likely to carry their own and less likely to carry rival networks. Subscribership follows the same pattern,

---

[84] Bonanno and Vickers (1988) demonstrate that when two manufacturers (channels) compete, selling through an independent retailer using a two-part tariff with positive markup helps soften competition between them. In their setting, each channel extracts all the surplus from the retailer with the fixed (franchise) fee. In a related paper, Gal-Or (1991) shows that the same effects arise with simple linear fees: upstream manufacturers (channels) raise (upstream) markups above zero, trading off profit losses from double marginalization against profit gains from softer competition downstream.

though they find no estimated effect on prices.[85] Chipty (2001) addresses similar questions, including whether integration influences MVPD carriage of basic cable networks. Using 1991 data, she finds integration with premium networks is associated with fewer premium nets, fewer basic movie networks (AMC), *higher* premium prices, and higher premium subscriptions. On balance she finds households in integrated markets have higher welfare than those in unintegrated markets, although the effects are not statistically significant. As in the studies analyzing the impact of regulation, however, it is difficult to assess if differences across cable systems in product offerings and prices are driven exclusively by integration or by other features of integrated systems (e.g., size, marketing, etc.).

Crawford et al. (2015) measure the efficiency and foreclosure incentives in the carriage and pricing of US RSNs as well as the welfare effects of vertical integration in the presence of regulatory controls. They parameterize and estimate the incentives of upstream RSNs and their integrated downstream distributors to internalize both (1) the costs of double marginalization and (2) the benefits to the integrated downstream distributor of foreclosing his rivals' access to the RSN. They find large but not complete internalization of both efficiency and foreclosure incentives. They further find that vertical integration in the presence of (perfect) regulation requiring non-discriminatory access to integrated content (like the Program Access rules discussed below) leads to significant gains in both consumer and total surplus, but that in the absence of such regulations, integrated RSNs either completely foreclose or raise costs to rivals by 30%, lowering consumer surplus.

7.5.2.2 Policy Responses

There have been a number of policy responses to concerns about vertical integration and foreclosure in television markets.[86] In the US, the 1992 Cable Act included regulations designed to promote non-discrimination in whole television markets. These are called the "Program Access" and "Program Carriage" rules. These forbid affiliated MVPDs and networks from discriminating against unaffiliated rivals in either the programming (Program Carriage) or distribution (Program Access) markets (FCC, 2013b). They also ruled out exclusive agreements between cable operators and their affiliated networks for rolling 5-year periods.[87] This prohibition was allowed to lapse in 2012 and was replaced by rules giving the Commission the right to review any programming agreement for anti-competitive effects on a case-by-case basis under the 2010 "unfair acts" rules

---

[85] See also Waterman and Weiss (1997) for the impact of integration on carriage of basic cable networks.

[86] In this subsection, I focus on policy responses in television markets. In the next section, I revisit this issue for online video markets.

[87] But for programming that was delivered by terrestrial technologies (i.e., microwave not satellite). This so-called "terrestrial loophole" was used by distributors in a handful of geographic television markets to exclusively offer highly valued Regional Sports Networks (RSNs). This loophole was closed in 2010 as part of a new set of rules prohibiting "unfair acts" (FCC, 2012b).

(FCC, 2012d). The new case-by-case rules include a (rebuttable) presumption that exclusive deals with RSNs are unfair.

As discussed in many of the FCC documents cited above, the Program Access rules are perceived to have been a very successful policy to promote competition in the distribution market. Fostering this success has been the historical development of the cable industry. Because there are many cable operators licensing the same content across the US, including multiple operators of similar (large) size, there are useful comparators when evaluating whether an agreement reached between a content provider and an unaffiliated distributor is discriminatory. This is more challenging, however, for Program Carriage complaints. When a channel argues that it's being discriminated against, the best comparator would be contracts between the distributor in question and a "comparable" channel. Because the programming on each channel is different, however, finding a good comparison can be challenging.

Internationally, pay-television distribution tends to be dominated within a given country by a small of distributors, limiting the feasibility of regulations modeled on the US Program Access rules. Instead, many media and communications regulators have chosen more direct interventions in the market. In the UK, Ofcom in 2010 implemented a wholesale must-offer regime for the distribution of sports channels Sky Sports 1 and 2, with prices set by the regulator (Ofcom, 2010a). They later the same year referred the licensing of pay (movie) television packages to the UK Competition Commission (UKCC) for a market investigation (Ofcom, 2010b), but the UKCC found in 2012 that Sky's market position in relation to the acquisition and distribution of movies in the first pay window does not adversely affect competition in the pay-TV retail (distribution) market (UK Competition Commission, 2012). On the continent, the EC and national competition regulators have imposed various types of wholesale must-offer regulations as conditions of approval of mergers between major pay-television distributors in Italy, France, and Spain (Ofcom, 2009b). These have been largely perceived to be unsuccessful as they did not cover the content identified by rival distributors as essential to offering a competitive pay-TV package. Furthermore, it is not clear if and how sector regulators can address these deficiencies. Further research on the functioning of content licensing across pay-television markets would be useful to establish best practices to enhance the functioning of these markets.

7.5.2.3 Vertical Merger Review

Policymakers' primary inflection point in addressing concerns about vertical foreclosure in television markets is in the context of reviews of vertical mergers.[88] Almost all of the highest profile competition reviews in television markets have focused on vertical issues;

---

[88] I discuss horizontal merger review in Section 7.4.3. See also Chapter 6 of this volume for general issues with mergers in media markets.

Figure 7.19 shows the vertical links between major content conglomerates and pay-television distributors in 2012. In the US, this includes mergers like Comcast/TimeWarner—Adelphia (2005, approved with conditions), Comcast—NBC/Universal (2011, approved with conditions), and Comcast—TimeWarner (2014—15, challenged and withdrawn).[89] Similarly in Europe, with major cases including the CanalSat—TPS merger (France, 2006, approved with conditions) and the BSkyB—Ofcom pay-television investigation (UK, 2012, wholesale must-offer regime imposed).

Conducting vertical merger reviews would also benefit from answers to several questions about television markets that the academic literature has not yet provided. Articulating the incentives facing integrated operators to raise rivals' costs, reduce rivals' revenues, and/or foreclose is straightforward, but *measuring* the key factors can be difficult. For example, what is the cross-elasticity of demand between downstream rivals *in the absence of critical integrated content?*[90] Furthermore, what are integrated firms' *dynamic* incentives to foreclosure (e.g., via changes in quality investment upstream, in infrastructure investment downstream)? How well do merger conditions and/or sector regulations mitigate harm? And how can one measure vertical efficiencies? Further work building knowledge that might serve as reference points to regulators, particularly but not exclusively in Europe, would be welcome.

7.6. ONLINE VIDEO MARKETS

Online video means watching video programming through an Internet distribution channel. In this sense, it is only differentiated from free or pay television by its distribution access technology and the specific device on which it is watched. Across the world, there are a large number of online video distributors (OVDs), distribution technologies, consumer devices, and business models. This section surveys this growing industry and discusses two policy issues that touch on its development: net neutrality and foreclosure.[91]

---

[89] The analyses in these decisions often make for good reading about the relevant issues, e.g., FCC (2011b).

[90] This is a key input when evaluating the incentives to foreclose a downstream rival by withholding critical upstream content. As it is not generally measurable using existing data (as the key content is typically everywhere available pre-merger), a structural industry model like that used by Crawford et al. (2015) can provide an estimate of just such a counterfactual elasticity, but the detailed modeling and estimation involved is likely to be infeasible in the context of a typical merger review.

[91] In this section, I will follow the strategy taken by FCC (2013b, pp. 111—157) and analyze only "entities that offer video content akin to the professional programming traditionally offered by broadcast stations, or broadcast and cable networks, and which is usually created or produced by media and entertainment companies using professional-grade equipment, talent, and production crews that hold or maintain the rights for distribution." This excludes user-generated content of the type publicly available on video-sharing sites like YouTube.

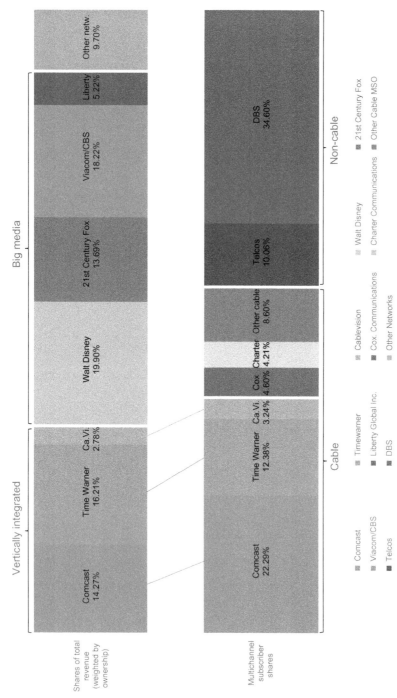

Figure 7.19 Vertical integration between channels and distributors, 2012. *Notes:* Depicted is the nature of vertical links between owners of programming networks and owners of pay-television distribution platforms. Revenue and ownership shares for the programming market are as described in the notes to Table 7.5. Shares in the distribution market are subscriber shares drawn from SNL Kagan (2014a). DBS stands for Direct Broadcast Satellite and is the sum of the subscriber shares for DirecTV and Dish Network. Ownership data was collected by hand from company stock filings and industry sources for the research conducted in Crawford et al. (2015).

7.6.1 Online Video Facts

With the rise of broadband Internet access to households and Internet-ready devices has come an increase in households' desire to watch video distributed through the Internet.[92] In the US, an estimated 85.7% of US households will purchase a high-speed data (HSD) connection in 2014, making the consumption of online video feasible for the majority of US households. Figure 7.20 shows that over-the-top Internet television (OTT) is estimated to be a significant and growing part of the television and online video industry. As discussed in Chapter 5 of this volume, by 2013 smartphone and tablet penetration in the US reached 74% and 52% respectively.[93]

While relationships governing the distribution of video content are well established in the free and pay segments of the television industry, they are still being formed in the online video segment. While owners of programming content like movie studios

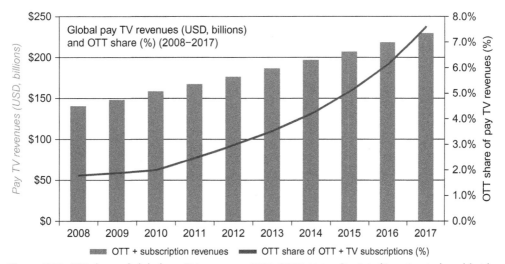

Figure 7.20 OTT share of global pay-TV revenues, 2008–2017. *Notes*: Depicted is estimated worldwide pay-television plus over-the-top Internet television (OTT) revenue and the share of this revenue accruing to OTT services. Source: *PriceWaterhouseCoopers (2013)*.

---

[92] Broadband is defined in different ways by different organizations. FCC (2013b, p. 125), citing Bernstein Research and SNL Kagan, estimates standard definition video requires an Internet connection of 2 megabits per second (Mbps) and high-definition video requires one of 4–8 Mbps. The National Broadband Plan, when discussing broadband availability in the US, reports on the availability of service by distributors providing actual download speeds of 4 Mbps (FCC (2010a, p. 20)).

[93] That being said, Wilbur notes that, despite their proliferation, most consumers are not choosing to watch online video on these devices, (presumably) preferring either a computer or an Internet-connected television.

generally license the distribution of that content through well-established distribution windows (premium channels like HBO, cable channels like A&E, broadcast channels like ABC), different owners of content have taken different strategies for making that content available online. All are sensitive about disrupting existing distribution relationships with conventional distributors, but are eager for the incremental revenue online access can provide. For example, at the time of publication, Sony Pictures Entertainment licenses many of the television programs and films in its television and movie library for distribution on conventional linear television channels as well as on an on-demand basis on the advertising-supported online video service, Crackle. Crackle is itself available online at crackle.com, as an app for smartphones and tablets for both iOS and Android operating systems, on game consoles PS3 and Xbox 360, on Sony Blu-ray players, on Roku boxes and Apple TVs, and integrated with Bravia TVs. By contrast, some of the content already licensed to the premium channel HBO may be accessed via HBO Go (formerly HBO on Broadband) from a similarly wide variety of devices and platforms.

Distributors of online video content in the US can be divided into four (not necessarily mutually exclusive) types[94]:

1. Over-the-top aggregators (**OTT aggregators**) of original and licensed content.[95]
2. Conventional pay-television distributors that provide access to live linear and on-demand content on multiple screens, typically but not exclusively within the home (e.g., **TV Everywhere**).
3. Individual **content owners**, especially sports leagues (MLB, NBA).
4. **Device manufacturers** that either license content directly or partner with providers in one of the previous three groups.[96]

A survey by SNL Kagan of online video services across 35 countries reported 710 OTT aggregators, TV everywhere providers, and device manufacturers, an average of 20.3 services per country (SNL Kagan, 2012).

At the end of 2012, North American Internet usage on fixed networks had grown by 120% (Haider, 2012). Much of this was driven by the growth in online video consumption, particularly Netflix. "Audio and video streaming account for 65% of all downstream traffic [on North America fixed networks] from 9 p.m. to 12 a.m. and half of that [33.0%]

---

[94] While they could reasonably be included, for reasons of data availability I exclude from this short survey "catch-up" TV services that allow for temporary, "sync and go," downloading of content for later (perhaps offline) viewing like Tivo in the US and the BBC iPlayer in the UK. These are usually free to households that subscribe to another type of broadcast or pay television service.

[95] Examples of providers in this group include fee- and ad-supported subscription services (Netflix, Hulu, and Amazon Prime) and rental and electronic sell-through (EST) (transactional) service providers (iTunes, Amazon Instant Video, and Vudu).

[96] Examples of providers in this group include manufacturers of stand-alone OTT devices (Roku, Apple TV), tablet and smartphone manufacturers (iPad, Kindle Fire, iPhone, and Samsung Galaxy), game console manufacturers (Sony PlayStation 3, Microsoft Xbox 360), and manufacturers of "connected TVs" (Sony, Samsung, Sharp, and Vizio).

is Netflix traffic." Amazon, Hulu, and HBO Go accounted for 1.8%, 1.4%, and 0.5% of peak traffic. Real-time entertainment, dominated by streaming audio and video, accounted for 67.4% of peak download traffic, with Netflix accounting for 46.9% of that amount. Peak traffic in Europe is less dominated by audio and video (47.4%), but this is no doubt due to lesser availability of OTT providers.[97]

OVDs differ in both their sources and amounts of revenue. According to SNL Kagan, paid subscription services (Netflix, Hulu Plus) earned $2.6 billion in revenue, or 40.0% of the online video industry's estimated total of $6.4 billion (SNL Kagan, 2014a). Video advertising, including both ad-supported subscription services (Hulu) and non-professional video (YouTube), earned an estimated $2.5 billion, or 38.7%.[98] Transactional services (EST and rentals) earned the remaining 21.3%.[99] OVDs also differ in whether or not viewers can access live linear television, from where they access it (inside/outside their home), the number of titles in their film and television libraries, whether they include advertising or not, and their price. All of these relationships are in a state of flux.

7.6.2 Net Neutrality and Foreclosure in Online Video Markets

Two policy issues have arisen with the growth of online video: net neutrality and foreclosure.[100]

7.6.2.1 Net Neutrality and Online Video

Proponents of net neutrality articulate it as a principle of openness such that all Internet traffic is treated equally by distributors. In practice, this principle has been interpreted as preventing both (1) charging content (edge) providers from accessing users (i.e., requiring "zero-pricing") and (2) price discriminating across content providers for access (Lee and Wu, 2009).

In the US, the FCC has argued that an open Internet promotes innovation, investment, competition, free expression, and other important policy goals (FCC, 2010b). In 2005, the FCC articulated a Broadband (Internet) Policy Statement articulating four principles of an open Internet and followed this in 2010 with an Open Internet Order adopting three basic rules: transparency, no blocking, and no unreasonable discrimination (FCC, 2010b). In January 2014, the US Court of Appeals for the District of

---

[97] Similarly, file sharing's share of peak download traffic on European fixed-line networks is just over double that in North America, although it has been declining over time.

[98] This is mostly due to non-professional video. Hulu's estimated 2012 revenues were $441 million, or 17.7% of this total.

[99] TV everywhere services in the US are uniformly offered as an add-on service to a conventional pay-television bundle and so earn no subscription revenue, although they do earn some advertising revenue.

[100] Some of this section draws on similar material from Crawford (2013). Chapter 10 of this volume discusses net neutrality in further detail.

Columbia Circuit vacated the anti-blocking and anti-discrimination aspects of the Open Internet Order. Netflix saw its share price drop by 5% on the morning of the news and by 13% from its pre-Christmas peak as analysts envisioned "hundreds of millions of dollars in data subsidies" (SNL Kagan, 2014b). This followed an early January announcement by AT&T allowing content providers the ability to pay for customers' data use, a clear example of behavior such regulations were trying to prevent. Zero-pricing was clearly under threat.

In March 2015, the FCC responded to the courts by setting strong rules in favor of net neutrality (FCC, 2015). These included regulating broadband Internet access providers under Title II of the Communications Act, giving them much broader regulatory powers, and explicitly prohibiting three practices that embody a non-neutral Internet: blocking, throttling, and paid prioritization. It applied the rules equally to both fixed *and* mobile Internet providers.[101] In the EU, by contrast, there are no clear pan-national rules. As part of the "Digital Agenda for Europe," the European Commission in September 2013 proposed measures that include a guarantee of net neutrality, and in April 2014, the European Parliament strengthened these proposals. The 28 member states need to next agree to the rules within the Parliament. At the time of this writing, this process is very much in doubt (Robinson, 2014).

The tradeoffs embodied in arguments over net neutrality are particularly salient for online video given its dominance of broadband traffic. Proponents of net neutrality argue it is needed to foster innovation and prevent the foreclosure of online video entrants. Opponents argue discrimination allows for more efficient network management and would enhance investments by both content providers and distributors, increasing consumer welfare. While the academic literature is replete with theoretical models incorporating such tradeoffs, empirical evidence of these effects are scarce. The only paper I know that addresses the issue with observational data is Nurski (2014), who explores the issue in using detailed UK data. She estimates demand for broadband video access and online video consumption, finding that both are sensitive to connection speeds.[102] She then simulates the effect of the entry of online video content in a world with net neutrality and another with discrimination, finding discrimination only increases entry for content providers with high fixed costs of production. Much more work is needed in this area.

7.6.2.2 Foreclosure in Online Video Markets

The non-discrimination terms vacated by the US Appeals Court also raise the possibility that issues similar to those discussed in Section 7.5.2 regarding the incentives an

---

[101] The Order did not, however, apply these rules to connections between content and broadband providers that were the focus of Netflix's agreements with Comcast and Verizon, instead choosing to review these on a case-by-case basis.

[102] Lee and Kim (2014) also look at the issue by surveying roughly 500 Internet users.

integrated pay-television provider might have to foreclose, either partially or completely, a rival upstream content provider. OVDs must necessarily rely on a high-speed broadband connection to households in order to deliver their programming, the vast majority of which are also owned by existing cable or telco MVPDs. There are therefore legitimate concerns that MVPDs will somehow manipulate their broadband networks in ways that disadvantage rival OVDs, perhaps by offering differential download speeds for rival online content, imposing data caps that lower the value of an Internet-delivered video service, or setting usage-based prices with similar effects.[103] Furthermore, it is hard to determine if such strategies are anti-competitive, as they can also help MVPDs efficiently manage their network traffic.

The market for online video distribution is in its infancy, so appropriate policies are difficult to determine on either a theoretical or empirical basis. Rubinfeld and Singer (2001) demonstrate the typical foreclosure calculus in the context of the AOL−Time Warner merger, and Farrell and Weiser (2003) analyze foreclosure incentives in the context of the FCC's Computer Inquires, the *Microsoft* case, and the then-nascent FCC Broadband proceedings.

In the Comcast/NBC−Universal merger, FCC (2011b) evaluated the potential for foreclosure online by analyzing the merged entities' historical tendency to favor integrated and discriminate against unintegrated programming in television markets. Furthermore, the potential for online foreclosure motivated many of the conditions imposed by the FCC in its ultimate approval of the merger (Baker et al., 2011; FCC, 2011b). That ruling found that, absent conditions preventing it, the merged entity would have the ability and incentive to hinder the development of competition in the online video marketplace. A key element of its merger approval was a condition requiring the merged entity to license NBC content on non-discriminatory terms to rival unintegrated OVDs in a manner similar to the Program Access rules, imposing a new baseball-style arbitration procedure to help enforce it in a timely manner.

These are all contentious policy issues that are being debated by competition and sector regulators around the world. More empirical research establishing some basic facts about the nature of traditional and online television substitutability, measuring the incentives to foreclosure, and distinguishing between efficient and foreclosing MVPD management practices would be welcome.

7.7. CONCLUSIONS

Watching television is the dominant leisure activity for hundreds of millions of individuals and, unlike many media markets, it has continued to grow despite the rising popularity of the Internet and online video. This is particularly true of pay television,

---

[103] The same issues are at play in the issue of search bias discussed in Chapter 10 of this volume.

now the dominant medium in the US in terms of both ratings and revenue, and well established abroad.

The purpose of this chapter has been to summarize the state of academic research on television and online video markets. Looking across the material surveyed here, it is somewhat difficult to connect the disparate themes. Economic research in television markets resembles an archipelago of distinct topics rather than a coherent canon. The theory literature has identified important differences in predicted ad levels, program content, prices, and welfare in simple models of ad-supported and mixed (ad- and subscriber-supported) television markets and (perhaps declining) rationales for the support of public service broadcasting. Bundling and bargaining (and their combination) have proven important (and estimable) features of television markets. Policymakers regularly turn their gaze on the industry with concerns about increasing consolidation in both the programming and distribution markets, and especially the potential for foreclosure due to vertical ownership affiliations between them. Similar concerns arise in online video markets, the development of which is (typically) outpacing research on its structure and effects.

Television is an important economic, social, political, and cultural force, and there remains much to do to improve our understanding of the economic mechanisms which govern its production. Further developing theories of television markets to reflect their multi-homing, multichannel, and multi-product nature is one, as is better connecting empirical research to both the extant theory and any such extensions. Better understanding the effects, economic and otherwise, of public service broadcasters is also essential, particularly as their advertising and license fee revenue come under increasing threat from economic and political forces. Building robust insights for practicing policymakers would be welcome, for both the television and online video markets as well as their interdependence. Finally, analyzing what drives the significant heterogeneity in the organization of television markets across countries and what are the consequences of these organizational differences for both economic and non-economic outcomes would be welcome.

ACKNOWLEDGMENTS

I would like to thank Simon Anderson, Joel Waldfogel, Ali Yurukoglu, and especially Mark Armstrong for helpful comments. The material in Sections 7.3.1, 7.4.1, and 7.4.4 was developed with the help of the latter's significant input.

REFERENCES

Adams, W.J., Yellen, J.L., 1976. Commodity bundling and the burden of monopoly. Q. J. Econ. 90 (3), 475–498.
Analysys Mason and BrandScience, An Econometric Analysis of the TV Advertising Market: Final Report. Technical Report, Office of Communications 2010. Published May 2010. Available from: http://stakeholders.ofcom.org.uk/market-data-research/other/tv-research/arr/.

Anderson, C., 2006. The Long Tail: Why the Future of Business is Selling Less of More. Hyperion, New York, NY.

Anderson, S., Coate, S., 2005. Market provision of broadcasting: a welfare analysis. Rev. Econ. Stud. 72, 947–972.

Armstrong, M., 1999a. Competition in the pay-TV market. J. Jpn. Int. Econ. 13 (4), 257–280.

Armstrong, M., 1999b. Price discrimination by a many-product firm. Rev. Econ. Stud. 66 (1), 151–168.

Armstrong, M., 2005. Public service broadcasting. Fisc. Stud. 26 (3), 281–299.

Armstrong, M., 2006. Competition in two-sided markets. Rand. J. Econ. 37 (3), 668–691.

Armstrong, M., Vickers, J., 2001. Competitive price discrimination. Rand. J. Econ. 32 (4), 579–605.

Armstrong, M., Weeds, H., 2007. Public service broadcasting in the digital world. In: The Economic Regulation of Broadcasting Markets. Cambridge University Press, Cambridge.

Baker, J.B., Bykowsky, M., DeGraba, P., LaFontaine, P., Ralph, E., Sharkey, W., 2011. The year in economics at the FCC, 2010–11: protecting competition online. Rev. Ind. Organ. 39 (4), 297–309.

Bakos, Y., Brynjolfsson, E., 1999. Bundling information goods: pricing, profits, and efficiency. Manag. Sci. 45 (2), 1613–1630.

Beebe, J., 1977. Institutional structure and program choices in television markets. Q. J. Econ. 91, 15–37.

Besanko, D., Donnenfeld, S., White, L.J., 1987. Monopoly and quality distortion: effects and remedies. Q. J. Econ. 102 (4), 743–767.

Besanko, D., Donnenfeld, S., White, L.J., 1988. The multiproduct firm, quality choice, and regulation. J. Ind. Econ. 36 (4), 411–429.

Bonanno, G., Vickers, J., 1988. Vertical separation. J. Ind. Econ. 36, 257–266.

Bresnahan, T.F., Levin, J.D., 2012. Vertical Integration and Market Structure. Working Paper, National Bureau of Economic Research.

Byzalov, D., 2010. Unbundling Cable Television: An Empirical Investigation. Working Paper, Temple University.

Cablevision Systems Corp, 2013. Cablevision Systems Corporation and CSC Holdings, LLC, Plaintiffs, Against Viacom International Inc. and Black Entertainment Television LLC, Defendants: Complaint. Technical Report, United States District Court, Southern District of New York 2013. Filed March 7, 2013.

Cauley, L., 2007. FCC Puts 'A La Carte' on the Menu. USA Today, September 11, 2007.

Chipty, T., 1995. Horizontal integration for bargaining power: evidence from the cable television industry. J. Econ. Manag. Strategy 4 (2), 375–397.

Chipty, T., 2001. Vertical integration, market foreclosure, and consumer welfare in the cable television industry. Am. Econ. Rev. 91 (3), 428–453.

Chipty, T., Snyder, C.M., 1999. The role of firm size in bilateral bargaining: a study of the cable television industry. Rev. Econ. Stat. 31 (2), 326–340.

Chu, C.S., 2010. The effects of satellite entry on cable television prices and product quality. Rand. J. Econ. 41 (4), 730–764.

Chu, C.S., Leslie, P., Sorensen, A., 2011. Bundle-size pricing as an approximation to mixed bundling. Am. Econ. Rev. 101 (1), 263–303.

Collard-Wexler, A., Gowrisankaran, G., Lee, R.S., 2012. An Alternating Offers Representation of the Nash-in-Nash Bargaining Solution. New York University, Stern School of Business, New York, NY.

Communications Daily, 2011. NARUC Panel Urges Ending Unfair Content Pricing, Tiering, Tying. Communications Daily, July 20, 2011.

CPB, 2012. Alternative Sources of Funding for Public Broadcasting Stations. Technical Report, Corporation for Public Broadcasting 2012. Available from: http://www.cpb.org/aboutcpb/Alternative_Sources_of_Funding_for_Public_Broadcasting_Stations.pdf.

Crandall, R., Furchtgott-Roth, H., 1996. Cable TV: Regulation or Competition? Brookings Institution Press, Washington, DC.

Crawford, G.S., 2000. The impact of the 1992 cable act on household demand and welfare. Rand. J. Econ. 31 (3), 422–449.

Crawford, G.S., 2007. Television Station Ownership Structure and the Quantity and Quality of Television Programming. Technical Report, Federal Communications Commission July 2007. Available from: http://www.fcc.gov/mb/mbpapers.html.

Crawford, G.S., 2008. The discriminatory incentives to bundle in the cable television industry. Quant. Mark. Econ. 6 (1), 41–78.

Crawford, G.S., 2013. Cable regulation in the internet era. In: Rose, N. (Ed.), Economic Regulation and Its Reform: What Have We Learned? University of Chicago Press, Chicago. Chapter 6. Chapters available from: http://www.nber.org/books_in_progress/econ-reg/.

Crawford, G.S., Cullen, J., 2007. Bundling, product choice, and efficiency: should cable television networks be offered à la carte? Inf. Econ. Policy 19 (3–4), 379–404.

Crawford, G.S., Shum, M., 2007. Monopoly quality degradation in the cable television industry. J. Law Econ. 50 (1), 181–219.

Crawford, G.S., Yurukoglu, A., 2012. The welfare effects of bundling in multichannel television markets. Am. Econ. Rev. 102 (2), 643–685.

Crawford, G.S., Kwerel, E., Levy, J., 2008. Economics at the federal communications commission, 2007–08. Rev. Ind. Organ. 33, 187–210.

Crawford, G.S., Smith, J., Sturgeon, P., 2012a. The (Inverse) Demand for Advertising in the UK: Should There Be More Advertising on Television? Working Paper, University of Warwick.

Crawford, G.S., Shcherbakov, O., Shum, M., 2012b. The Welfare Effects of Endogenous Quality Choice: Evidence from Cable Television Markets. Working Paper, University of Warwick.

Crawford, G.S., Lee, R., Whinston, M., Yurukoglu, A., 2015. The Welfare Effects of Vertical Integration in Multichannel Television Markets. University of Zurich.

d'Aspremont, C., Gabszewicz, J., Thisse, J.-F., 1979. On Hotelling's stability in competition. Econometrica 47, 1145–1150.

Farrell, J., Weiser, P.J., 2003. Modularity, vertical integration, and open access policies: towards a convergence of antitrust and regulation in the internet age. Harvard J. Law Technol. 17, 85.

FCC, 1997. Third Annual Report on the Status of Competition in the Market for the Delivery of Video Programming (1996 Report). Technical Report, Federal Communications Commission 1997. CS Docket No. 96–133, Released January 2, 1997.

FCC, 1998. Fourth Annual Report on the Status of Competition in the Market for the Delivery of Video Programming (1997 Report). Technical Report, Federal Communications Commission 1998. FCC 97–423, Released January 13, 1998.

FCC, 2001. Seventh Annual Report on the Status of Competition in the Market for the Delivery of Video Programming (2000 Report). Technical Report, Federal Communications Commission 2001. FCC 01–1, Released January 8, 2001.

FCC, 2002. Memorandum Opinion and Order in the Matter of Applications for Consent to the Transfer of Control of Licenses from Comcast Corporation and AT&T Corp., Transferors, to AT&T Comcast Corporation, Transferee. Technical Report, Federal Communications Commission 2002. MB Docket No. 02–70, FCC 02–310.

FCC, 2005a. Eleventh Annual Report on the Status of Competition in the Market for the Delivery of Video Programming (2004 Report). Technical Report, Federal Communications Commission 2005. FCC 05–13, Released February 4, 2005.

FCC, 2005b. Second Further Notice of Proposed Rulemaking. Technical Report, Federal Communications Commission 2005. MM Docket No. 92–264, FCC 05–96.

FCC, 2008. The Public and Broadcasting. Technical Report, Federal Communications Commission 2008, DA-08-940A2, Released July 2008. Available from: http://www.fcc.gov/guides/public-and-broadcasting-july-2008.

FCC, 2009. 2006–2008 Report on Cable Industry Prices. Technical Report, Federal Communications Commission 2009, FCC 09–53, Released January 16, 2009.

FCC, 2010a. Connecting America: The National Broadband Plan. Technical Report, Federal Communications Commission 2010, Released March 16, 2010. Available from: http://www.broadband.gov/download-plan/.

FCC, 2010b. Report and Order in the Matter of Preserving the Open Internet Broadband Industry Practices. Technical Report, Federal Communications Commission 2010, FCC 10–201.

FCC, 2011a. The Information Needs of Communities. Technical Report, Federal Communications Commission 2011. Available from: http://www.fcc.gov/info-needs-communities.

FCC, 2011b. Memorandum Opinion and Order in the Matter of Applications of Comcast Corporation, General Electric Company and NBC Universal, Inc. For Consent to Assign Licenses and Transfer Control of Licensees. Technical Report, Federal Communications Commission 2011. MB Docket No. 10–56.

FCC, 2012a. 2011 Report on Cable Industry Prices. Technical Report, Federal Communications Commission 2012, DA 12–1322, Released August 13, 2012.

FCC, 2012b. First Report and Order. Technical Report 2012, FCC 10–17, Released January 20, 2012.

FCC, 2012c. Fourteenth Annual Assessment on the Status of Competition in the Market for the Delivery of Video Programming (2007–2010 Report). Technical Report, Federal Communications Commission 2012, FCC 12–81, Released July 20, 2012.

FCC, 2012d. Report and Order in MB Docket Nos. 12–68, 07–18, 05–192. Further Notice of Proposed Rulemaking in MB Docket No. 12–68; Order on Reconsideration in MB Docket No. 07–29. Technical Report 2012, FCC 12–123, Released October 5, 2012.

FCC, 2013a. Broadcast Radio AM and FM Application Status Lists. Technical Report, Federal Communications Commission April 2013. Available from: http://www.fcc.gov/encyclopedia/broadcast-radio-am-and-fm-application-status-lists (accessed December 9, 2013).

FCC, 2013b. Fifteenth Annual Assessment on the Status of Competition in the Market for the Delivery of Video Programming (2011–2012 Report). Technical Report, Federal Communications Commission 2013, FCC 13–99, Released July 22, 2013.

FCC, 2015. Report and Order on Remand, Declaratory Ruling, and Order in the matter of Protecting and Promoting the Open Internet. Technical Report, Federal Communications Commission 2015, FCC 15–24, Released March 12, 2015.

Filistrucchi, L., Luini, L., Mangani, A., 2010. Regulating One Side of a Two-Sided Market: The French Advertising Ban On Prime-Time State Television. Working Paper, Department of Economics, CentER and TILEC, Tilburg University.

Ford, G., Jackson, J., 1997. Horizontal concentration and vertical integration in the cable television industry. Rev. Ind. Organ. 12 (4), 501–518.

Gabszewicz, J.J., Laussel, D., Sonnac, N., 2001. Press advertising and the ascent of the 'Pen-sée Unique'. Eur. Econ. Rev. 45 (4), 641–651.

Gal-Or, E., 1991. Duopolistic vertical restraints. Eur. Econ. Rev. 35, 1237–1253.

Gentzkow, M., 2006. Television and voter turnout. Q. J. Econ. 121 (3), 931–972.

Gentzkow, M., Shapiro, J., 2008. Preschool television viewing and adolescent test scores: historical evidence from the Coleman Study. Q. J. Econ. 123 (1), 279–323.

Godes, D., Ofek, E., Sarvary, M., 2009. Content vs. advertising: the impact of competition on media firm strategy. Market. Sci. 28 (1), 20–35.

Goolsbee, A., Petrin, A., 2004. Consumer gains from direct broadcast satellites and the competition with cable TV. Econometrica 72 (2), 351–381.

Haider, A., 2012. Research Roundup, M&C Edition: Internet Data Usage Climbs, Netflix Dominates North American Fixed Networks. Technical Report, SNL Financial 2012. November 11, 2012.

Hamilton, J.T., 2000. Channeling Violence: The Economic Market for Violent Television Programming. Princeton University Press, Princeton, NJ.

Harbord, D., Ottaviani, M., 2001. Contracts and Competition in the Pay TV Market. Working Paper, University College London.

Hazlett, T., Spitzer, M., 1997. Public Policy Towards Cable Television: The Economics of Rate Controls. MIT Press, Cambridge.

Ho, K., 2009. Insurer-provider networks in the medical care market. Am. Econ. Rev. 99 (1), 393–430.

Horn, H., Wolinsky, A., 1988. Bilateral monopoly and incentives for merger. Rand. J. Econ. 19, 408–419.

Hurkens, S., Jeon, D.-S., Menicucci, D., 2013. Dominance and Competitive Bundling. Working Paper, Toulouse School of Economics.

Inderst, R., Montez, J., 2015. Buyer Power and Dependency in a Model of Negotiations. Working Paper, London Business School.

ITU, 2012. Guidelines for the Transition from Analogue to Digital Broadcasting. Technical Report, International Telecommunications Union 2012. August 2012.

Jensen, R., Oster, E., 2009. The power of TV: cable television and women's status in India. Q. J. Econ. 124 (3), 1057–1094.

Lee, D., Kim, Y.-H., 2014. Empirical evidence of network neutrality: the incentives for discrimination. Inf. Econ. Policy 29, 1–9.

Lee, R.S., Wu, T., 2009. Subsidizing creativity through network design: zero-pricing and net neutrality. J. Econ. Perspect. 23 (3), 61–76.

Liu, Y., Putler, D.S., Weinberg, C.B., 2004. Is having more channels really better? A model of competition among commercial television broadcasters. Market. Sci. 23 (1), 120–133.

Madden, P., Pezzino, M., 2013. Sports League Quality, Broadcaster TV Rights Bids and Wholesale Regulation of Sports Channels. Working Paper, University of Manchester.

Martin, G.J., Yurukoglu, A., 2014. Bias in Cable News: Real Effects and Polarization. Stanford University, California.

Mayo, J., Otsuka, Y., 1991. Demand, pricing, and regulation: evidence from the cable TV industry. Rand. J. Econ. 22 (3), 396–410.

Muthoo, A., 1999. Bargaining Theory with Applications. Cambridge University Press, Cambridge.

Nalebuff, B., 2004. Bundling as an entry barrier. Q. J. Econ. 119 (1), 159–187.

Nash, J.F., 1950. The bargaining problem. Econometrica 18 (2), 155–162.

Nurski, L., 2014. Net Neutrality and Online Innovation: An Empirical Study of the UK. Working Paper, University of Leuven.

Ofcom, 2004. Ofcom Review of Public Service Broadcasting Phase 1: Is Television Special?. Technical Report, UK Office of Communications 2004. Available from: http://stakeholders.ofcom.org.uk/consultations/psb/.

Ofcom, 2009a. Pay TV Phase Three Document: Proposed Remedies. Technical Report, Office of Communications 2009. Published 26 June 2009. Available from: http://stakeholders.ofcom.org.uk/consultations/third_paytv/.

Ofcom, 2009b. Wholesale Must-Offer Remedies: International Examples. Technical Report, Office of Communications 2009. Published 26 June 2009. Available from: http://stakeholders.ofcom.org.uk/consultations/third_paytv/.

Ofcom, 2010a. Pay TV Statement. Technical Report, Office of Communications 2010. Published 31 March 2010. Available from: http://stakeholders.ofcom.org.uk/consultations/third_paytv/.

Ofcom, 2010b. Premium Pay TV Movies. Technical Report, Office of Communications 2010. Published August 4, 2010. Available from: http://stakeholders.ofcom.org.uk/consultations/movies_reference/statement/.

Ofcom, 2012. International Communications Market Report 2012. Technical Report, Office of Communications 2012. Published December 13, 2012. Available from: http://stakeholders.ofcom.org.uk/market-data-research/market-data/communications-market-reports/.

Ordover, J., Saloner, G., Salop, S., 1990. Equilibrium vertical foreclosure. Am. Econ. Rev. 80, 127–142.

Owen, B., Wildman, S., 1992. Video Economics. Harvard University Press, Cambridge, MA.

Peitz, M., 2008. Bundling may blockade entry. Int. J. Ind. Organ. 26 (1), 41–58.

Peitz, M., Valletti, T., 2008. Content and advertising in the media: pay-tv versus free-to-air. Int. J. Ind. Organ. 26 (4), 949–965.

Prat, A., Strömberg, D., 2006. Commercial Television and Voter Information. Working Paper, LSE.

Prat, A., Strömberg, D., 2011. The Political Economy of Mass Media. Working Paper, LSE.

PriceWaterhouseCoopers, 2012. Global Entertainment and Media Outlook. Technical Report, PriceWaterhouse-Coopers June 2012.

PriceWaterhouseCoopers, 2013. Global Entertainment and Media Outlook. Technical Report, PriceWaterhouseCoopers June 2013.

Raskovich, A., 2003. Pivotal buyers and bargaining position. J. Ind. Econ. 51 (4), 405–426.

Rennhoff, A.D., Serfes, K., 2008. Estimating the Effects of A La Carte Pricing: The Case of Cable Television. Drexel University, Philadelphia, PA.

Rennhoff, A.D., Serfes, K., 2009. The role of upstream-downstream competition on bundling decisions: should regulators force firms to unbundle? J. Econ. Manag. Strategy 18 (2), 547–588.

Rey, P., Tirole, J., 2007. A primer on foreclosure. In: Armstrong, M., Porter, R. (Eds.), Handbook of Industrial Organization, vol. 3. North-Holland, Amsterdam (Chapter 33).

Riordan, M., 1984. On delegating price authority to a regulated firm. Rand. J. Econ. 15 (1), 108–115.

Riordan, M., 2008. Competitive effects of vertical integration. In: Buccirossi, P. (Ed.), Handbook of Antitrust Economics. MIT Press, Cambridge, MA.

Robinson, F., 2014. Italian EU presidency puts net neutrality on hold. *Wall Street Journal*, 2014. November 25, 2014.

Rubinfeld, D.L., Singer, H.J., 2001. Vertical foreclosure in broadband access? J. Ind. Econ. 49 (3), 299–318.

Rubinovitz, R., 1993. Market power and price increases for basic cable service since deregulation. Rand. J. Econ. 24 (1), 1–18.

Rubinstein, A., 1982. Perfect equilibrium in a bargaining model. Econometrica 50 (1), 97–109.

Salop, S., Scheffman, D., 1983. Raising rivals' costs. Am. Econ. Rev. 74 (2), 267–271.

Scannell, P., 1990. Public Service Broadcasting: The History of a Concept. Routledge, London.

Shiller, B., Waldfogel, J., 2011. Music for a song: an empirical look at uniform song pricing and its alternatives. J. Ind. Econ. 59 (4), 630–660.

SNL Kagan, 2012. OTT Entities in 35 Global Markets. Technical Report, SNL Financial 2012. November 8, 2012.

SNL Kagan, 2014a. Media and Communications Database. http://www.snl.com/Sectors/Media/Default.aspx (Licensed in 2014 from Kagan World Media).

SNL Kagan, 2014b. Neflix Rocked By Net Neutrality Ruling. Technical Report, SNL Financial 2014. January 17, 2014.

Steiner, P., 1952. Program patterns and preferences and the workability of competition in radio broadcasting. Q. J. Econ. 66 (2), 194–223.

Stennek, J., 2014. Exclusive quality—why exclusive distribution may benefit the TV-viewers. Inf. Econ. Policy 26, 42–57.

Stigler, G.J., 1968. A note on block booking. In: Stigler, G. (Ed.), The Organization of Industry. Richard D. Irwin, Homewood, IL.

UK Competition Commission, 2012. Movies on Pay TV Market Investigation. Technical Report, UK Competition Commission, 2012. Published August 2, 2012. Available from: http://www.competition-commission.org.uk/our-work/directory-of-all-inquiries/movies-on-pay-tv-market-investigation.

Waterman, D.H., Weiss, A.A., 1996. The effects of vertical integration between cable television systems and pay cable networks. J. Econ. 72 (1–2), 357–395.

Waterman, D.H., Weiss, A.A., 1997. Vertical Integration in Cable Television. MIT Press and AEI Press, Cambridge, MA.

Weeds, H., 2015. TV wars: exclusive content and platform competition in pay TV. Econ. J. http://onlinelibrarywiley.com/doi/10.1111/ecoj.12195/full.

Whinston, M., 1990. Tying, foreclosure, and exclusion. Am. Econ. Rev. 80 (4), 837–859.

Wilbur, K.C., 2008. An two-sided, empirical model of television advertising and viewing markets. Market. Sci. 27 (3), 356–378.

Willems, M., 2014. Cable's Flirtations with Telcos Turn into Full-Blown Love Affair. *SNL Blogs*, March 12, 2014.

Williamson, O., 1976. Franchise bidding for natural monopolies: in general and with respect to CATV. Bell J. Econ. 7 (1), 73–104.

Zupan, M.A., 1989a. Cable franchise renewals: do incumbent firms behave opportunistically. Rand. J. Econ. 20 (4), 473–482.

Zupan, M.A., 1989b. The efficacy of franchise bidding schemes in the case of cable television: some systematic evidence. J. Law Econ. 32 (1), 401–436.

CHAPTER 8

Radio

Andrew Sweeting
Department of Economics, University of Maryland, College Park, MD, USA

Contents

Abstract

This chapter surveys the literature on the economics of radio, focusing on the broadcast industry in the United States. The first parts of the chapter provide a history of the radio industry and its regulation, and a guide to the data available for empirical research. The next part surveys the large empirical literature analyzing the effects of the wave of consolidation that took place after the Telecommunications Act of 1996, explaining which empirical results appear robust (for example, the effects of local consolidation on programming differentiation) and which remain unclear (for example, the effects of consolidation on advertising prices and quantities). The remaining parts survey the literature on whether there are too many radio stations; the strategies that stations use to boost the effectiveness of advertising; the effects of non-commercial stations on the commercial sector; and the interaction between the radio and music industries, including payola and copyright issues. The chapter emphasizes several topics that seem ripe for additional research.

Handbook of Media Economics, Volume 1A
ISSN 2213-6630, http://dx.doi.org/10.1016/B978-0-444-62721-6.00008-1

Keywords

Radio, Two-sided markets, Advertising, Mergers, Variety, Product differentiation, Synergies, Localism, Payola, Copyright

JEL Codes

L13, L41, L51, L82, M37

8.1. INTRODUCTION

Even though the inventor Thomas Edison argued in 1922 that radio was a "craze [that] will soon fade,"[1] radio has proved to be a medium of enduring popularity. In the United States, where almost everyone now has access to more modern media alternatives, 92% of the population still listens to the radio every week and the average listener tunes in for 2.5 h each day (Arbitron Company, 2013). US radio advertising revenues in 2013 were almost $15 billion, or roughly 75% of local TV advertising revenues.[2] In developing countries, broadcast radio remains the primary means of accessing news and information for millions of people because radios are cheap and require little infrastructure or literacy to operate. For example, in Kenya 87% of households own a radio, while only 47% own televisions (Bowen and Goldstein, 2010). Radio programming is also often argued to have significant effects on a country's culture: in the US, the development of personality-driven talk radio has been cited as a primary cause of political polarization (Hillard and Keith (2005), p. 80) and a perceived narrowing of playlists on music stations has often been blamed for the problems faced by the music industry (Future of Music Coalition, 2008). The importance of radio has led governments in many countries to tightly regulate or directly provide programming.

This chapter aims to introduce the reader to the economics of the radio industry and to describe empirical research that has tried both to understand these economics and to use radio as a setting to examine broader questions to do with two-sided markets, the effects of competition on product variety and deregulation. It will emphasize that our understanding is far from complete in many areas, and that recent changes to local media markets provide new questions to study and mean that answers to existing questions based on historical data may no longer be appropriate. The focus will be on the broadcast (free-to-air) radio industry in the United States in the last 25 years, but I will explain the history of the industry from its inception so that contemporary issues can be placed in their historical context. Indeed, understanding the history is necessary to understand why many

---

[1] http://rockradioscrapbook.ca/quotes (accessed February 27, 2014).

[2] http://www.biakelsey.com/Company/Press-Releases/140326-WTOP-Leads-Radio-Station-Revenues-for-Fourth-Consecutive-Year.asp and http://www.biakelsey.com/Company/Press-Releases/140424-Local-Television-Revenue-Expected-to-Reach-Over-$20-Billion-in-2014.asp (accessed February 14, 2015).

reforms that might seem natural to economists have aroused controversy. At certain points I will also mention how the radio industry in the US differs from the radio industries in other countries, for example in the role of publicly funded radio. I will also describe some of the challenges faced by the contemporary broadcast radio industry given the growing importance of satellite and online radio platforms, and non-radio digital media that have successfully captured a large share of both local and national advertising dollars.

Like broadcast television, important features of the broadcast radio industry are that (a) stations operate as two-sided platforms, attracting listeners with free programming and selling these audiences to advertisers who reach listeners with commercials or sponsored programming; (b) some types of programming—typically news and educational programming—might be considered merit or partially public goods; (c) the marginal cost of reaching additional listeners within a given coverage area is essentially zero; and (d) entry is limited by constraints on the broadcast spectrum available for radio stations to use, and stations must coordinate their frequencies and coverage areas in order for their broadcasts to be audible for listeners. This last point naturally creates a role for licensing and regulating stations. The fact that spectrum is seen as public, not private, property has also been used to argue that radio stations should operate, in the words of the 1927 Radio Act, for the "public convenience, interest or necessity," leading to a degree of content regulation that has never been applied to the US newspaper industry (at least outside of wartime). Chapter 9 in this volume discusses the newspaper industry in more detail.

While broadcast radio and television share these important economic characteristics, there are at least two significant differences between the media. First, radio is a much more portable medium with the majority of listening taking place outside of the home, a pattern that has become even more pronounced in recent years and for younger listeners.[3] The peak hours of radio listening are during the day, and especially during the morning and evening drivetime periods, whereas, since the late 1950s, television has dominated in the evening primetime period.[4] Portability also explains why most radio listening is still accounted for by traditional over-the-air broadcasts, whereas most television viewed in the US is delivered via cable or satellite even though broadcast stations remain popular. Second, the fixed costs of operating a radio station are low and the spectrum constraints are weak enough that local markets can be served by quite a large

---

[3] In Spring 2007, Arbitron identified 40% of listening as taking place at home. The remainder was split roughly equally between in car and at work (figures from Arbitron's Radio Listening Trends reports, http://wargod.arbitron.com/scripts/ndb/ndbradio2.asp, accessed February 18, 2014). By 2011, the share taking place at home had fallen to 36% (Arbitron Company, 2011), and for listeners aged 18–34 it was estimated to be 28% in 2014 (Nielsen Company, 2014).

[4] The data comes from Arbitron's Radio Listening Trends reports, http://wargod.arbitron.com/scripts/ndb/ndbradio2.asp (accessed February 18, 2014).

number of stations.[5] For example, Duncan (2002) estimated that there were 23 viable radio stations in the Washington, DC market (with another seven marginal stations), compared to 13 local television stations.[6] In Billings, Montana there were 12 viable radio stations, compared to only four TV stations, with one viable radio station for every 8736 residents aged 12 and above. In this sense, one might hope for quite competitive economic outcomes without regulation.

The costs of providing programming also differ across the media. Television production is typically expensive so that smaller stations must rely on large amounts of programming provided by the networks or syndication. In radio, producing local programming is potentially quite cheap, especially as stations are currently only charged a small proportion of their revenues for the rights to perform music (see Section 8.9.2 for a discussion of licensing arrangements). I will return to the question of whether local programming is necessarily desirable below. One consequence is that stations are able to vary their programming in response to the local competitive landscape, and in the last two decades this has resulted in the emergence of quite narrow programming formats, which may, for example, offer only a particular kind of rock music or serve listeners with a particular religious adherence. However, in spite of this cost structure and these patterns, there is an active debate about whether the types of programming that stations provide is optimal, both in the sense of whether it is of the optimal quality or whether stations offer too much of the same types of music (Future of Music Coalition, 2003).

The structure of this chapter is as follows. Section 8.2 provides a brief history of the broadcast radio industry in the US, from its inception to the present. Section 8.3 discusses the data that has been used in empirical research. Section 8.4 outlines some of the economic theory that can be used to understand the possible effects of mergers in the radio industry. Section 8.5, divided into four parts, describes empirical research examining the effects of ownership deregulation and the subsequent consolidation that took place in the 1990s and early 2000s. Section 8.6 looks at the question of whether there are too many stations in most radio markets. Sections 8.7–8.9 examine strategies that stations use to make sure listeners hear their commercials, the effects of public radio, and the effects of radio on political outcomes and its interactions with the music industry. Section 8.10 concludes.

---

[5] Many interesting questions in television arise from the vertical relationships between content providers and platform operators (such as cable companies). See Chapter 7 in this volume for an in-depth discussion. Vertical issues also exist in radio—with syndicated programming being broadcast on stations owned by many different companies, and major station owners also producing some of this programming—but it has not been the focus of attention in the economics literature.

[6] Duncan identified "viable" stations as those with signals that reached a large proportion of the market and had at least a 1% share of listening. Most markets have a number of smaller stations listed in their Arbitron market reports that can be considered marginal. Additional low-power stations would typically have too few listeners to be listed by Arbitron at all.

8.2. A BRIEF HISTORY OF THE RADIO INDUSTRY IN THE UNITED STATES

As we shall see below, some of the most interesting economic questions in the context of the contemporary radio industry concern the effects of ownership consolidation and corporate control; the response of the medium to new competitors and opportunities created by technological change; the tension that can exist between exploiting economies of scope and serving local demand; and the appropriate role for regulation in any industry that is far from being a natural monopoly but which makes use of public airwaves. Interestingly, many of these questions are recurrent themes in the history of the broadcast radio industry in the US, and this brief history is intended to help place contemporary issues in context.[7]

Radio technologies had been developed for maritime and military purposes in the years leading up to and during World War I, and, under the Radio Act of 1912, there were over 13,000 licensed amateur radio operators in the US by 1917. KDKA in Pittsburgh was the first US station to provide a regular programming schedule in November 1920. KDKA was owned by Westinghouse, which viewed the provision of programming as a natural way to drive sales of its radio receivers. Westinghouse, together with General Electric and AT&T, formed the Radio Corporation of America (RCA) in 1919. Similarly, New York station WEAF, in 1922, the first station to broadcast a commercial (for an apartment complex in Jackson Heights, with the developer paying the station $100), was owned by AT&T, which claimed a monopoly on producing transmission equipment (Hillard and Keith, 2005, p. 26). After KDKA's success there was a rapid growth of the industry, with 622 stations licensed to provide general broadcasts by the end of 1922.

Unfortunately, these stations were licensed to just two frequencies (750 and 833 kHz) so that there was considerable interference and many stations were regularly inaudible. Despite this problem, sales of radio receivers grew rapidly and Commerce Secretary Herbert Hoover organized a series of "radio conferences" in the mid-1920s in an attempt to bring some organization and coordination to the industry. Hoover's power to allocate stations to specific frequencies and time slots was successfully challenged in court. This led Congress to pass the Radio Act of 1927, which created the Federal Radio Commission (FRC), succeeded by the Federal Communications Commission (FCC) under the Communications Act of 1934, with the power to issue and deny licenses and regulate the industry with the goal of making sure that the industry operated for the "public convenience, interest or necessity."[8]

At this point, one could have imagined radio developing in at least two different ways. One way might have involved a large number of local stations operating largely

---

[7] The facts in this section can be found in Albarran and Pitts (2001) unless otherwise noted.
[8] Communications Act of 1934, ch. 652, § 303 (codified in 47 U.S.C. § 303, 1994).

or completely independently. An alternative would have been for national networks to provide common programming through a small number of powerful stations. The latter was the successful model from the late 1920s through to the 1950s. RCA launched its NBC network in 1926, with the programming being provided to local affiliates through special telephone wires provided by AT&T. RCA added a second NBC network 2 months later, with the networks being known as the Red and Blue networks. CBS entered in 1927, followed by a cooperative network, the Mutual Broadcasting System, in 1934. The FRC supported the development of national networks through its licensing policies. In particular, it licensed a relatively small number of 50,000-W "clear channel" stations. These could reach hundreds of thousands or millions of listeners, especially at night when their AM signals would travel further as they reflected off the Kennelly–Heaviside layer in the atmosphere. This was important in making big-city programming available to rural listeners, and 21 out of the 24 initial clear channel assignments went to network affiliates. Local stations were licensed but typically they were restricted to operate at much lower powers, such as 250 or 500 W, with hours of operation limited to the daytime when most family listening took place in the evening. The network structure was very successful in commercial terms and radio spread rapidly. By 1935, 60% of American households owned radios, and, because listening to the radio was free once the receiver had been purchased, the medium flourished during the Depression.

Network programming was initially oriented toward music (classical, dance, and jazz) but over time comedy shows and drama played an increasing role. The networks also carried a very large number of commercials, which was perhaps natural at a time when national and regional brands were starting to develop, radio was the only national medium and the networks formed a concentrated oligopoly where competition for listeners may have been limited. In 1932 CBS and NBC carried 12,546 commercial interruptions in 2365 h of programming, an average of 5.3 interruptions per hour. In comparison, Sweeting (2006, 2009) found that music stations in the period 1998–2001 carried between two and three commercial breaks per hour.

More surprisingly, the networks did not initially broadcast much news programming. In 1933, NBC and CBS agreed with the American News Publishers Association and the wire services, in what was known as the "Biltmore program" (after the New York hotel in which the deal was negotiated), that they would forgo developing their own news-gathering organizations and instead carry only two 5-min newscasts every day, with each news item limited to 30 words, and to not carry news that was less than 12 h old (Barnouw, 1968, p. 20)![9] For the networks, there were probably two economic

[9] While the Biltmore program may seem surprising to us, in the UK the BBC also carried a very limited amount of news and did not develop its own news department when it was first created because of pressure from newspapers. See http://en.wikipedia.org/wiki/BBC (accessed February 28, 2014).

motivations for what to us now seems a startling agreement. First, they may have wanted to avoid starting a race between themselves in programming quality that would likely increase their costs quite dramatically, especially if they tried to cover local news. Second, radio stations relied on newspapers to publish their schedules and so needed their co-operation. Indeed, when WOR in New York started running its own extended news-casts that proved to be popular with listeners, the newspaper association tried to pressure their New York members not to publish WOR's schedule. However, they refused to do so as WOR was owned by R. H. Macy's, the department store, one of the biggest news-paper advertisers in the city (Barnouw, 1968, p. 21). This example, the willingness of large companies, such as Esso, to sponsor radio news shows, and the desire of non-network stations to use news to compete for listeners undermined the Biltmore program and by the late 1930s all of the radio networks had their own news departments. However, there was also a trend toward newspapers taking over radio stations. In 1940, one-third of all radio stations were owned by newspapers, and in 100 US cities, local newspapers owned the city's only radio station.

While radio continued to grow into the 1950s, when it began to face increasing com-petition from television, which was operated by the same networks, federal regulations started to impose important limits on the networks in the 1940s. In 1941, the FCC issued its *Report on Chain Broadcasting* (the network structure was referred to as "chain broadcasting" because the links were AT&T's telephone cables). This led to new rules that made ties between stations and networks non-exclusive (allowing affiliated stations to buy programming from multiple networks), prevented the networks from demanding options on large amounts of station time (which allowed stations to develop their own programming), and shortened the length of time that a station was bound by a network contract from 5 years to 1 year (Hillard and Keith, 2005, pp. 50–52). It also prohibited licenses from being issued to stations that were affiliated with a network organization that maintained more than one network, which was true of NBC.

When the new rules were upheld by the Supreme Court in 1943, NBC divested the Blue network, which became ABC (Hillard and Keith, 2005, p. 52). The shift of regu-lation toward favoring independent broadcasters continued until the 1980s. For example, in 1975 the FCC prohibited a newspaper from owning broadcast stations (radio or TV) in the same market (Gomery, 2002), a rule that was only relaxed in 2007 when the FCC adopted an approach of considering cross-ownership on a case-by-case basis (FCC, 2010), partly because of the declining finances of the newspaper industry.

The FCC also used regulations to promote locally produced and focused program-ming. In 1946, the Main Studio Rule required stations to have their main studio in their city of license, while Program Origination rules required that at least 50% of pro-gramming was locally produced, although this was achieved initially by airing local programming outside of primetime (Hillard and Keith, 2005, p. 46; Silverman and Tobenkin, 2001). In 1950, an FCC *Report and Order* defined radio transmission as an "opportunity which provides for the development and expression of local interests, ideas, and talents for the production of programs of special interest to a particular community ... a station cannot serve as a medium for local self-expression unless it provides a reasonably accessible studio for the origination of local programs" (Hillard and Keith, 2005, p. 48).

Faced by the expansion of television, with largely national programming, in the 1950s, a focus on local service was a natural commercial response too. At the same time, the spread of portable transistor radios and the development of car radios also led radio stations to focus more on daytime programming rather than trying to compete with television during primetime. While the 1950s is often viewed as a time of decline for radio, and it certainly did lose listeners to television, the industry did not decline financially. Radio's total advertising revenues increased from $624 million to $692 million over the decade. The networks' share of those revenues did, however, fall dramatically, from 25% to only 6% during the same time period (Sterling and Kitross, 2002, p. 362).

The new focus also shifted the type of programming that stations offered toward music, first with the development of the Middle of the Road (MOR) format, offering a wide range of music with broad appeal, and then to the development of the Top 40 programming with a limited playlist of songs played frequently.[10] This way of programming, combined with the fact that radio was the primary way in which listeners could learn about new songs, meant that it was very valuable for musicians and record labels to secure places for their songs in the rotation. Therefore it is not surprising that the 1950s saw a number of so-called payola scandals where DJs were found to have accepted payments in return for playing particular songs (see Section 8.9.2 for more details).

The 1960s and 1970s also saw the steady transition of radio listeners from the AM band to the FM band, with FM first accounting for the majority of listenership in 1978. As well as the greater sound quality of FM (FM stereo broadcasts were allowed after 1961, while AM stereo was only approved in 1980), the rise of FM was also helped by a freeze on issuance of new AM licenses in the mid-1960s because of concerns about crowding and interference on the AM band.

The rise of FM was associated with two significant changes in radio programming. First, greater sound quality aided the rise of music programming, and there was a particularly rapid growth in the number of specialized music formats, many of them orientated toward rock music, which was relatively little played on the MOR and Top 40 stations on the AM band. On the AM band, stations began to specialize into News, Talk, Sports and, at least in some regions of the country, commercial Religious programming. Second, the growth of FM listenership contributed to the rise of public radio broadcasting in the US, as a portion of the FM band (88.1–91.9) had been reserved for non-commercial

---

[10] The name "Top 40" is often attributed to the fact that jukeboxes held 40 records, and it was from seeing how jukebox users chose the same songs repeatedly that radio programmers started developing the format.

broadcasters since 1945, whereas there was no similar reservation of AM spectrum.[11] The 1967 Public Broadcasting Act led to the creation of the Corporation for Public Broadcasting, with National Public Radio (NPR) being created in 1971.

In the 1970s, the FCC also enforced rules that required commercial stations to allocate 6–8% of their broadcasting time to public affairs. Since 1949, the so-called Fairness Doctrine required stations to "devote a reasonable percentage of their broadcasting time to the discussion of public issues of interest in the community served by their stations and that such programs be designed so that the public has a reasonable opportunity to hear different opposing positions on the public issues of interest and importance in the community" (Hillard and Keith, 2005, p. 60).[12]

While most academic work on the radio industry has focused on what happened following the 1996 Telecommunications Act, this Act was only one of a series of deregulatory reforms that started under the Carter Administration, and which relaxed both regulations on ownership and regulations on programming content.

In 1987, the Fairness Doctrine was removed, under pressure from broadcasters who believed that it violated their rights under the First Amendment and tended to increase production costs. The rise of political, personality-driven talk radio on AM stations, involving controversial personalities such as Rush Limbaugh, is often attributed to the demise of the Fairness Doctrine (Soley, 1999).[13] The Main Studio Rule, which was also seen as being expensive for stations to implement (Silverman and Tobenkin, 2001), was relaxed so that broadcasters were only required to have a local studio *capable* of producing programming rather than actually using it. This started a trend toward more stations being operated remotely, and this trend was strengthened as it became possible to provide programming to local stations via satellite. The FCC also abandoned rules about regulating the amount of local content.

Changes in ownership rules involved a steady progression toward more relaxed standards. Prior to 1984, a broadcaster was limited to own nationally a maximum of 7 AM stations, 7 FM stations, and 7 TV stations *nationally* (the rule of the 7s). That year the caps were raised to 12, 12, and 12, then in 1992 to 18, 18, and 12, respectively. The 1996 Act removed national ownership limits for radio stations entirely (FCC, 2010).

---

[11] The FCC first reserved spectrum for non-commercial educational radio use in 1938 (41–42 MHz band), before changing the reserved band to 88–92 MHz in 1945 (http://transition.fcc.gov/osp/inc-report/INoC-31-Nonprofit-Media.pdf, accessed February 15, 2015).

[12] Specifically in 1974 the FCC argued that previously it had not exercised its powers because broadcast stations had followed the spirit of the Fairness Doctrine voluntarily, but "would future experience indicate that [voluntary compliance] is inadequate, either in its expectations or in its results, the Commission will have the opportunity—and the responsibility—for such further reassessment and action as would be mandated" (FCC, 1974).

[13] In response to a Supreme Court ruling that the FCC was not required to enforce the Fairness Doctrine, both houses of Congress passed new legislation requiring the FCC to do so. However, President Reagan vetoed this bill.

At the local level, prior to 1992 a broadcaster was allowed to own at most one AM station and one FM station, even in the largest markets where there might be 50 or more local stations. The 1992 reform relaxed these restrictions so that three stations (with at most two on one band) could be owned in markets with less than 14 stations, and up to four stations in larger markets (as long as they had a combined audience share of less than 25%). The 1996 Act relaxed the rules so that firms could own five stations where three could be owned before, and up to eight stations in larger markets.

The 1996 Act was followed by a tidal wave of consolidation, with 4000 stations (out of 11,000) changing hands within 2 years and concentration increasing rapidly at both the local and national levels (Hillard and Keith, 2005, p. 72). For example, in the largest 10 radio markets, the average four-firm concentration ratio (based on audience shares) increased from 0.61 in March 1996 to 0.82 in March 2001, while across all markets the average ratio reached 0.93 (these and the following figures are taken from FCC, 2001). This represented a significant tightening of the oligopoly structure of local radio markets. At a national level, in March 1996, CBS Radio was the largest station owner (by revenues) with revenues of $496 million (6% of the industry total) and 39 stations, and it was focused in the largest markets. In March 2001, Clear Channel Communications had revenues of $3.4 billion (26.2%) and owned 972 stations spread across the complete range of market sizes. It would have owned even more stations except for divestitures required by the Department of Justice in analyzing mergers such as its mammoth 2000 merger with AM/FM Inc., where the firms were required to sell 99 stations in 27 markets (United States Department of Justice, 2000a). In practice, therefore, one might view the regular antitrust laws, which, when applied to radio, were focused entirely on the possibility that broadcasters might exercise market power over *advertisers*, as being as much of a barrier to concentration as FCC regulations designed to promote media plurality and to make sure that stations would serve the public interest of their *listeners* and the public more broadly. This represented a dramatic change from the situation 30 years earlier.

While many of these policy changes reflected the general move toward deregulation that affected industries from airlines to electricity, it also reflected the fact that from the early 1980s radio was facing pressure as audiences declined. Radio listening peaked in 1982, when people listened for 18.2% of the time, but they listened only 10.3% of the time in 2012.[14] On the other hand, financially the industry as a whole performed relatively well both before and immediately after deregulation. In nominal terms, industry revenues rose from $2.7 billion in 1981 (Duncan (1981), p. 70, taken from numbers reported by the FCC which were used to collect station financial information), $8.0 billion in 1991, $11.4 billion in 1996, to $17.1 billion in 2000 (numbers from Duncan (2001), p. 7).

---

[14] Statistics based on Arbitron estimates for people aged 12 and above on the hours of 6 a.m. to midnight (Radio Research Consortium, 2012).

While most academic research has ended around 2006, it is worth noting a number of recent developments, many of them associated with media convergence, that may have changed the economics of the industry.

First, the Great Recession had a large impact on advertising revenues. BIA/Kelsey estimates that industry revenues fell from $18.1 billion in 2006 to $13.3 billion in 2009, and had only recovered to $14.9 billion in 2013.[15] This decline was associated with the bankruptcy of several large radio groups, such as Citadel Broadcasting, that had bought stations at significant multiples of revenues during the boom, and major layoffs at others, including Clear Channel (renamed as iHeartMedia in 2014).[16] Partly because of financial pressures, station transactions have continued to happen at a relatively rapid rate (for example, BIA/Kelsey recorded 869 station ownership changes in 2010).[17]

Second, while stations still derive the vast majority of their revenues from broadcast advertising, online advertising (whether in the form of website banners, email advertising or audio ads placed in the online audio stream) are becoming progressively more important, and bring radio stations into much more immediate competition with other local media that also compete online. Online distribution may also weaken some of the traditional barriers dividing geographic markets. For example, BIA/Kelsey estimates that online advertising accounts for 4% of radio industry revenues in 2014, and forecasts them to grow at 10% per year over the next 4 years, compared to 2% for traditional revenues.[18]

Third, non-broadcast sources of audio programming have become more numerous. Satellite radio has increasingly penetrated, particularly into vehicles. Since 2005, satellite has offered channels providing local weather and traffic information in larger urban areas. However, satellite radio has grown much more slowly than its initial backers hoped, and in 2013 only 10% of car listeners reported that they used satellite radio all or most of the time compared with 58% for regular AM/FM radio (Edison Media Research, 2013).[19]

---

[15] http://www.biakelsey.com/Events/Webinars/Tracking-the-Broadcast-Industry-MAPro.pdf   and http://www.biakelsey.com/Company/Press-Releases/140326-WTOP-Leads-Radio-Station-Revenues-for-Fourth-Consecutive-Year.asp (accessed February 14, 2015).

[16] http://www.cbsnews.com/news/radio-giant-citadel-declares-bankruptcy/ (accessed February 15, 2015) and http://www.nytimes.com/2009/04/30/business/media/30clear.html?_r=0 (accessed February 15, 2015).

[17] http://www.biakelsey.com/Events/Webinars/Tracking-the-Broadcast-Industry-MAPro.pdf (accessed February 14, 2015).

[18] http://www.biakelsey.com/Company/Press-Releases/140326-WTOP-Leads-Radio-Station-Revenues-for-Fourth-Consecutive-Year.asp (accessed February 15, 2015).

[19] In its prospectus for an IPO in 1999, XM radio, one of the two satellite radio companies at that time, cited estimates that 43 million people would be willing to pay $200 for a satellite radio and XM's monthly subscription fee (http://www.nasdaq.com/markets/ipos/filing.ashx?filingid=1004217, accessed March 20, 2015). By 2008, XM Sirius, formed when the two companies merged, has 19 million subscribers (http://www.forbes.com/sites/greatspeculations/2013/04/12/can-sirius-xm-tune-in-big-subscriber-growth-this-year/, accessed March 20, 2015).

Internet radio services, including Pandora's music streaming service, also provide a threat, although traditional broadcasters have tried to develop online services to exploit the medium. For example, Clear Channel's platform, iHeart Radio, carries both terrestrial stations and offers services that allow users to create their own playlists that are designed to compete with Pandora. In 2013, 45% of the population reported listening to online radio in the last month, and these people listened for an average of 12 h per week. The threat that Pandora offers to traditional radio's revenues, as well as its listenership, has also increased as the platform now sells local advertising in large markets.[20] At the same time, however, broadcast stations have exploited new technology to proliferate their channels, both by offering channels in HD and using translator and booster stations to offer more programming to their broadcast stations.[21]

Finally, while syndicated political talk radio, usually of a conservative bent, was one of the big growth areas of radio programming in the 1990s and early 2000s, especially for AM stations, it may now be in retreat.[22] While personalities such as Rush Limbaugh and Sean Hannity attract widespread media attention, pressure from social media has also made some advertisers reluctant to advertise on their programs, causing a shift back to less controversial News or music programming.[23]

8.3. DATA

To study any industry in detail requires reliable data, and this is especially important when trying to study and interpret *changes over time* as much of the empirical literature on radio has tried to do. In this section, I identify some of the sources that have been used most frequently by empirical researchers, and try to indicate some of the issues that need to be considered when using them.

Unfortunately for researchers, the FCC stopped collecting information on advertising revenues and programming content in the early 1980s. In its recent work on the industry, the FCC has relied primarily on the radio version of BIA/Kelsey's *Media Access Pro*

---

[20] http://www.crainsnewyork.com/article/20140421/MEDIA_ENTERTAINMENT/304209988/pandora-unleashes-sales-force-on-local-market (accessed February 14, 2015).

[21] For example, AM stations use FM translators to put AM programming onto the FM band, while boosters are sometimes used to carry FM signals into places where FM signals cannot easily be received because of terrain. However, these services can also be used to carry programming that the station is carrying on its HD channels rather than on its primary AM or FM channel, and they are not included in the station counts used to determine whether a station satisfies ownership caps (conversation with Mark Fratrik of BIA/Kelsey, February 13, 2015).

[22] The number of stations carrying political talk radio increased from 400 in 1990 to 1400 in 2006 (http://www.stateofthemedia.org/2007/radio-intro/talk-radio/, accessed February 15, 2015).

[23] http://www.wsj.com/articles/talk-radios-advertising-problem-1423011395 (article February 6, 2015, accessed February 15, 2015).

database (BIA hereafter).[24] This data has also been used by academic researchers, including Jeziorski (2014a,b) and Sweeting (2009, 2013), who have focused on the post-1996 period. This database contains Arbitron (now Nielsen)[25] station ratings data for at least the Spring and Fall reporting periods each year, including some measures for demographic sub-groups, detailed programming format classifications, technical information (e.g., licensed transmitter power, signal coverage, including contour maps), information on station personnel, and BIA's estimates of annual station, as well as market, revenues. As one would expect, these revenue estimates are closely related to audience size, market share and format, but it is unclear whether this relationship reflects a very close relationship that exists in reality or just the relationship that BIA assumes when making its estimates. The database also contains a detailed ownership and transaction history for each station, dating back to well before 1996. For some transactions, a price is recorded, but when groups of stations, possibly from different markets, are traded, it may be very difficult to impute a price for each station. Recent additions to the BIA database include information on HD and multicast programming, and market-level estimates of online revenues.

Arbitron estimates commercial station ratings in over 270 geographic markets (the exact set of smaller markets has changed over time due to changes in market population). Arbitron markets are smaller than the designated marketing areas used to analyze local television markets, and many of them coincide almost exactly with the Metropolitan Statistical Areas used by the US Census (Arbitron Company, 2009). Listening in rural areas outside of these urban markets is unmeasured. As part of its surveys, Arbitron also collects data on non-commercial listening. Examples of this data are available through the Radio Research Consortium (http://www.rrconline.org). While simple market share data is reported on a number of radio-related websites, detailed data for listening by specific demographics, which is valuable to advertisers who want to target specific population groups, is available through BIA subscriptions and through Arbitron.

The traditional way that Arbitron has measured audiences is by recruiting a sample of the population and getting them to complete diaries that record stations that they listened to for at least 5 min during quarter-hour periods. An obvious concern is that diary data may contain systematic misreporting, especially when listeners change stations frequently and may not always be aware of exactly which station they are listening to. In response to this concern, as well as a desire to get data to advertisers and stations more quickly, Arbitron began to switch to using electronic Portable People Meters (PPMs) in larger

---

[24] http://www.biakelsey.com/Broadcast-Media/Media-Access-Pro (accessed March 1, 2015).

[25] Nielsen purchased Arbitron in 2013, rebranding Arbitron as Nielsen Audio (http://www.nielsen.com/us/en/press-room/2013/nielsen-acquires-arbitron.html, accessed February 15, 2015). As all of the work discussed in this chapter used data prior to 2013, I will refer to "Arbitron" data.

urban markets in 2010.[26] This technology is able to record the programming that the wearer is able to hear, but of course not all people actively take in the programming that they are exposed to. For example, many people may encounter radio programs when they are at a dentist's office, for example, without actively listening to it.

One result of this difference in what is being recorded is that PPMs have lead to higher estimates of station "cume" ratings (the proportion of the population who listen to a station for at least 5 min during a particular daypart), but station shares, the average proportion of the population listening to a station at any given time, remained pretty much the same as diarists actually reported the stations that they listened to a lot quite accurately. The relationship between shares and cume is potentially important because, as will be discussed below, listeners who only listen to a single station (single-homing) may be much more valuable to stations than listeners who multi-home. There has been no formal research to date into whether this change in measurement technology has led to changes in station programming, even though, as will be discussed in Section 8.5.2, its introduction was especially controversial with minority-oriented broadcasters whose estimated ratings fell. In Section 8.7, I will also cite some evidence that suggests that PPM data may, for example, change traditional perceptions about how listeners respond to commercials. PPMs may also have made it more attractive for stations to have "special programming" segments (for example, a high-profile sports event), as the more accurate PPM data allows them to make a more convincing case to advertisers that people actually listen to it.[27]

To look at quarters before 1996 researchers cannot make use of BIA, but widespread use has been made of Duncan's *American Radio* quarterly Reports and annual Market Guides. Duncan ceased publication in 2002, but most of the reports back through the 1970s are available in PDF format, together with a wealth of information from other publications, on the website http://www.americanradiohistory.com. The Duncan reports contain Arbitron ratings and estimates of station revenues (see Duncan (2002) for a discussion of the sources used for these estimates). Some of Duncan's revenue numbers actually come from stations that simply passed on the revenue numbers calculated by the auditing firms that provide revenue information to licensing organizations such as ASCAP and BMI. Duncan also contains station ownership information and information on recent station sales.

The Duncan reports also contain station format information. One thing to be aware of when using format information in Duncan (a caveat which may also be relevant for BIA) is that Duncan's format classification became finer over time. For example,

---

[26] Unless otherwise noted, this discussion is based on "Arbitron PPM President Pierre Bouvard: It's Radio's Turn to Eat at the Adult's Table", *Radio Ink*, August 1, 2009, article by Reed Bunzel. http://www.radioink.com/listingsEntry.asp?ID=370205 (accessed February 18, 2014).
[27] Conversation with Mark Fratrik of BIA/Kelsey, February 13, 2015.

Duncan's *American Radio* market report publications had 10 format categories in 1977, 12 in 1986, 21 in 1995, and 37 in 1998. In part, this is to capture changes in radio station programming, as music formats did become increasingly specialized, partly because regulatory changes meant that stations did not have to broadcast a certain amount of news programming, but it also may reflect the fact that over time it became easier for Duncan to collect and record more detailed information on what stations were doing.

While the BIA or Duncan revenue estimates are useful, they do not facilitate estimation of fundamental demand and supply relationships in advertising markets, as they do not distinguish between the prices at which advertisers purchased commercials and the quantities of advertising that are sold. A common source of price data is "SQAD" estimates of CPMs (the cost of reaching a thousand listeners) and CPPs (the cost of reaching one ratings point of listeners), which are based on actual transactions reported by media buyers.[28] This data is available at the market level, broken down by demographics and daypart. One limitation of this data is that it is not station-specific, so estimating the number of commercials by simply dividing estimated station revenues by prices (which researchers do in many contexts to estimate quantities) requires the strong assumption that different stations charge the same prices per listener. Such an assumption is likely incorrect, given an older literature noting that per-listener prices tend to increase with market share (Fisher et al., 1980) and the ability of station groups to potentially extract more surplus by bundling commercials. In addition, using average prices across stations will tend to make it harder to identify the effects of particular station mergers, especially when the number of stations is large.

Data on the quantity of commercials aired is more difficult to find, and typically relies on creating or identifying detailed airplay data. Knowing whether the quantity of commercials has increased or decreased is potentially important for understanding how consolidation has affected the welfare of advertisers. For example, Duncan (2004, p. 5) argues that most of the growth in radio industry revenues in the mid and late 1990s, when rapid consolidation happened, was "caused by expanded inventory of radio spots. The healthy economy used up the increased inventory but only at compressed prices." As part of its 2006 media ownership review, the FCC commissioned a detailed analysis of airplay data that recorded information on many different types of content, including the amount of time spent on commercials. This data on 1014 stations has been used by Chipty (2007) and Mooney (2010a). The limitations are that it contains information only on a single cross-section and that because the material was collected by a team of listeners, there is only 2 h of programming for each station. As a result there may be considerable noise in inferring the average behavior of each station even in the quarter that the cross-section was taken. Sweeting (2009, 2010) uses panel data from 1998 to 2001 that was collected by

---

[28] Details of this data is available at http://sqad.com/products/#spot-radio. SQAD data also appears in the Standard Rate and Data Service reports, http://next.srds.com/for-media/premium-data.

Mediabase, an electronic monitoring service that compiles data on the airplay of contemporary music stations. In this data, the start time of each song is recorded, together with information on whether commercials or recorded promotional material appeared between the songs. This data allows for a rich analysis of the music that is played, and provides some measure of the amount of time that individual stations spent on commercials for a large number of hours, where the length of the commercials is imputed from the time between songs.

Unfortunately, I am unaware of systematic sources of information looking at the use of syndicated programming, which plays a very important role in political and sports talk radio, but also provides significant amounts of morning drive, evening, and weekend programming on music radio stations. Potentially this type of data could be used to understand the effects of vertical integration as some of the main station owners also own producers of syndicated programming such as Premiere Radio Networks (Clear Channel). I am also unaware of any systematic data on stations that are operated remotely or use voice tracking, with the exception of one case study mentioned in Section 8.5.3. This type of data would be very important in an analysis of localism or of the effects of the changing interpretation of the main studio rule. Below I describe some work that has been undertaken on voice tracking based on case studies of individual markets.

8.4. THE EFFECTS OF INDUSTRY CONSOLIDATION ON MARKET OUTCOMES: THEORETICAL CONSIDERATIONS

Given the rapid consolidation of the radio industry following the 1996 Telecommunications Act, most empirical work on radio has focused on trying to identify how consolidation has affected market outcomes, either in the market for advertising, where the outcomes include the prices and quantities of commercials and the welfare of advertisers, or the market for listeners, where the outcomes also include the available degree of programming variety. In this section, I briefly review the theoretical literature that predicts how consolidation should affect these outcomes. Readers should consult Chapters 2 and 6 in this volume for a more detailed discussion of the theory, including for cases where listeners pay for access to programming.

At the most basic level, how consolidation should affect the quantities and prices of commercials will depend on whether merged firms have more incentives to try to exercise market power in the market for listeners, where an increase in the "price," which is the nuisance value of advertising that listeners have to listen to, will be associated with an increase in the quantity of commercials or the market for advertisers, where an increase in the price will be associated with a decrease in the quantity of commercials. The two-sided nature of the market means that one side may benefit from a merger that creates market power even in the absence of cost synergies. I now follow Anderson et al. (2012), who provide a concise description of different types of modeling assumptions under which mergers may lead to market power being exercised primarily over one side of the market.

The most well-known model in the literature is the Anderson and Coate (2005) model of competition between symmetric horizontally differentiated stations. Listeners are assumed to dislike commercials and to single-home, meaning that they listen to at most one station. Stations choose how many advertisements to carry, where the market price of a listener declines in the number of commercials, reflecting the fact that advertisers are likely to be differentiated with some advertisers valuing reaching consumers more than others. Denoting the revenue per listener on station i as $R_i(a_i)$ and the number of listeners as $N_i(a_i, a_{-i})$, then the first-order condition determining i's optimal number of ads can be expressed as

$$\frac{R_i'(a_i)}{R_i(a_i)} = -\frac{N_i'(a_i, a_{-i})}{N_i(a_i, a_{-i})},$$

which implies that the elasticity of the revenue per listener will be set equal to the elasticity of the number of listeners with respect to the number of commercials aired. Under the standard assumption that the left-hand side of this equation is decreasing in a_i, a merger between all of the stations in this model will lead to *more* commercials being aired. This happens because, in this model, each station is always a monopolist in selling its listeners to advertiser so that competition between stations is only for listeners and not for advertisers. Therefore, after a merger there is only increased market power in the listening market and the number of commercials will tend to increase.[29] Because advertising quantities are strategic complements in this model, a partial merger will also lead to an increase in the number of commercials played on all stations, and a fall in the per-listener price paid by advertisers.

While the focus of the Anderson and Coate model is on advertising quantities, one can also ask what this pricing rule implies for how much stations want to differentiate from each other. Considering the simplified example of a two-station Hotelling line model of differentiation and assuming that only listeners care about programming differentiation, that is, from an advertiser's perspective a listener to a Rock station is as valuable as a listener to a Sports station, there are two quite standard forces at work. First, there is an incentive for independent stations to gravitate toward the center of the line in order to take listeners from the other station, increasing the value of their commercials. This is consistent with the logic of Steiner's (1952) analysis, where he argued that advertiser-funded television would lead to programming that is too similar in the sense that stations would cater to the modal taste. However, a second incentive can operate in the other direction. Assuming that locations are chosen prior to the number of commercials being

---

[29] In contrast, an increase in the number of competing stations will tend to reduce how many commercials are played in equilibrium, by increasing the elasticity of listener demand for each station.

chosen, stations have an incentive to strategically differentiate so that they are less close substitutes for listeners, which reduces the elasticity of demand and allows them to play more commercials. As in standard formulations of the Hotelling line model with price competition between firms, excessive product differentiation may result, and a merger might be expected to reduce differentiation of stations' programming.

Anderson et al. (2012) emphasize that a couple of different changes to the Anderson and Coate model may cause mergers to have quite different effects on advertising prices. Particularly relevant for radio is what happens when stations set a price per commercial to advertisers but at least some listeners "multi-home," meaning that they choose to listen to more than one station. Suppose that advertisers value reaching a consumer once, but do not value reaching them additional times. A multi-homing listener can be reached through either station, which are then perfect substitutes from the perspective of advertisers who want to reach these listeners. In this case, a radio company can only extract value from advertisers for listeners who are exclusive to its stations.[30] If a merger makes more listeners exclusive to a single company, then it is natural to expect that advertising prices will increase after a merger even if the number of commercials played on each station remains unchanged. The effect on advertising quantities will depend on the specific assumptions that are made about the heterogeneity of advertiser demands, the ability of stations to discriminate between different advertisers when setting prices, and how listeners respond to advertising congestion on different stations.[31]

How does multi-homing affect incentives to strategically differentiate programming? Under the assumption that listeners will multi-home less when stations are more differentiated, Anderson et al. (2012) suggest that, if multi-homing listeners are less valuable, the incentive for competing stations to strategically differentiate will be strengthened. In this case, a merger between stations, which will reduce competition in the advertising market over multi-homing consumers, might be expected to make programming more similar.

In the context of radio it is not clear to me that the assumption that differentiation will reduce multi-homing is valid. When choosing which stations to preset on their car radios,

---

[30] This logic ignores the fact that when an advertiser runs an ad on a station it may fail to reach a specific listener if, at the time that the ad is run, that listener is not tuned in. However, even in a more general setup that accounts for this (Ambrus et al. (2013) is an example), multi-homing will tend to reduce the marginal value of running an ad on an additional station. Of course, if hearing a commercial multiple times in different contexts reinforces the message being conveyed by the advertiser then the logic would reverse and multi-homing listeners would become more valuable.

[31] Cunningham and Alexander (2004) present a model, based on a representative listener framework, which can generate a variety of effects on the quantity of commercials. Ambrus et al. (2013) develop a model of competition between media platforms where some consumers and advertisers multi-home. They show that under a variety of conditions for listeners the quantity of commercials aired is the same when platforms compete or when they are owned by the same firm, and that the quantity of commercials may rise after entry. They present some evidence for the latter effect on cable television channels.

for example, people may choose to have stations that are relatively different in order to cater to different moods at different times of the day (e.g., a favorite News station, a Sports station, a Lite Adult Contemporary station, and a Top 40 station), while tending not to pre-program multiple stations that are very similar in nature. In this case, one might expect that the desire to avoid multi-homing might lead to at least some pairs of competing stations becoming very similar. Unfortunately, this is a conjecture and very little is known about the empirical relationship between programming variety and multi-homing, even though the theory clearly indicates that it is important.[32]

On the question of whether multi-homing could lead to a common owner choosing to make its stations more similar than competing owners would, it is true that owners often choose to operate multiple local stations in similar formats. Berry and Waldfogel (2001) note this empirical pattern in the context of their examination of how consolidation affects product variety, where they find that 27% of randomly drawn pairs of local sibling (commonly owned) stations are in similar but not identical formats (e.g., Adult Contemporary and Hot Adult Contemporary), compared with 18% of randomly drawn local station pairs (ownership ignored). However, at the same time, they are less likely to operate them in exactly the same format, suggesting that a common owner's preferred strategy balances some incentive to cluster stations, which may be generated by economies of scope or a desire to deter entry into that area of the product space, and incentives to differentiate in order to avoid excessive cannibalization.[33,34]

8.5. EMPIRICAL EVIDENCE ON THE EFFECTS OF OWNERSHIP CONSOLIDATION IN RADIO

The rapid growth of empirical research in Industrial Organization in the 1990s coincided with the consolidation of the radio industry following the various rounds of ownership

---

[32] In the context of the local newspaper industry, Gentzkow et al. (2014) estimate a model of demand that allows for multi-homing and for how multi-homing across newspapers owned by different firms reduces the amount that newspapers can extract from advertisers, and how this affects incentives for product differentiation. To do so, they use data from the 1920s and information from a number of surveys of readership that measure multi-homing. Arbitron's individual market reports do contain some of this information in the form of "cume duplication" tables.

[33] Sweeting (2004) reports an Infinity Programming Director in Cleveland, quoted in Billboard on October 14, 2000, describing how "I initially made that mistake when I was programming KPNT (The Point) in St. Louis. We made sure The Point and [sister station] The River were programmed so far away from each other that you could drop something in the middle of them and that's what the competition wants you to do."

[34] Of course, if a common owner does feel threatened by the possibility that other firms will program their stations too close to one of their existing stations, then this would cast doubt on the argument that competing owners naturally want to differentiate to reduce multi-homing.

deregulation. Radio was therefore a natural place for researchers to look at when trying to understand several different effects that mergers might have. I have divided this section into four parts. Sections 8.5.1 and 8.5.2 consider the effects of consolidation in local markets on outcomes in the advertising market and programming, respectively. Sections 8.5.3 and 8.5.4 describe the more limited work that has tried to pinpoint the effects of consolidation at the national level and the size of cost efficiencies that consolidation may have realized.

8.5.1 The Effects of Local Market Consolidation on the Advertising Market

A number of papers, taking markedly different approaches, have tried to test whether increased ownership concentration in local radio markets has increased or decreased the price an advertiser must pay to reach a listener. Initially this literature was motivated by the fact that the antitrust analysis of radio mergers by the Department of Justice was focused on the welfare of advertisers, as the only customers of broadcast radio stations who actually make monetary payments (Klein, 1997). Given the recent theoretical literature, this empirical work can also be viewed as shedding light on whether models where listeners single-home, which predict that mergers will lower advertising prices, or models that assume multi-homing, which can make the opposite prediction, give a more accurate description of the industry.

Most of the literature has focused on trying to establish the *average* relationship between consolidation and prices, although the ambiguity of the theory suggests that we might well expect to see significant positive effects in some settings and significant negative effects in others. Distinguishing these cases would potentially be important given the fact that mergers are analyzed on a case-by-case basis and that the authorities are often able to negotiate carefully targeted divestitures (e.g., United States Department of Justice, 2000a), and, as we shall see, two recent structural papers find evidence of different effects.

The approach that most researchers have taken is to use a "reduced-form analysis" where advertising prices are regressed on measures of ownership concentration. Brown and Williams (2002) use a panel of data from 1996 to 2001, a period when local concentration, ownership concentration at the national level, and real radio advertising prices all increased substantially. They regress the market-level, SQAD-estimated advertising price per 1000 listeners aged 18–49 on measures of local concentration and ownership by national radio firms, market fixed effects and proxies for local advertising demand, such as market population and real income, and, to capture changes in national demand, either time effects or national GDP growth. They find that increases in local market concentration, as measured by revenue-based Herfindahl–Hirschmann indices (HHI), are positively correlated with changes in local advertising prices, but that these changes only explain around 5% of the large increase in advertising prices during the period of their data.[35] They find that greater ownership by large national radio companies is associated with lower advertising prices. However, as they note, to interpret this second correlation, it is important to recognize that SQAD-estimated prices are largely based on prices charged to regional and national advertisers who may be simultaneously buying commercials in several markets. The fact that national radio firms reduce prices to these buyers, with whom they may enjoy some economies of scale or scope by selling commercials in many markets simultaneously, does not necessarily imply that they also reduce prices to local advertisers. This matters because local advertisers account for the majority of station revenues (2006 BIA data would put the average at around 70%, and it has subsequently risen to around 75%)[36], and one might imagine that local advertisers are less able to substitute to other media than national advertisers.

Chipty (2007) also estimates reduced-form regressions to examine the relationship between concentration and advertising prices, using a cross-section of data from 2006, but also using a wider range of SQAD prices (for example, for different dayparts, and measures based on both costs per thousand listeners and costs per share point) than Brown and Williams. Chipty finds no significant relationship between local concentration and her measures of advertising prices but, like Brown and Williams, she finds a weak negative correlation between ownership by national radio firms at the local level and prices once she controls for market demographics. However, this carries the same caveat about interpretation as the Brown and Williams study, and in fact, using a sample of data on programming content, she shows that there is no significant relationship between the national ownership and the quantity of advertising on the radio, whereas a general decline in advertising prices would have led one to expect an increase in the amount of advertising. Sweeting (2008) does find a positive effect of ownership by large, national radio companies on the number of minutes of advertising using a panel of playlist data from relatively large music stations during the time period 1998–2001. The effect is of moderate size: around 0.6 more minutes of commercials per hour, or roughly 5% of the average commercial load for one of the stations in the sample.[37] Consistent with the lack of price effects of changes in local concentration in the other reduced form papers, Sweeting

---

[35] As part of its investigation into the merger between Global Radio and the Guardian Media Group's radio business, the United Kingdom Competition Commission (2013) performed a detailed price-concentration analysis, and found that "the presence of fewer good radio alternatives, and/or where the radio alternatives are not as good, is associated with higher advertising prices" (Appendix I, p. I1). Unfortunately, the magnitudes are not disclosed in the published report for confidentiality reasons.

[36] Conversation with Mark Fratrik of BIA/Kelsey, February 13, 2015.

[37] Sweeting's analysis is based on imputing the number of minutes of commercials using gaps between songs when some commercials were being played. It is therefore possible that this result instead reflects the fact that national owners tend to insert more non-commercial talk programming (e.g., promotions, sponsorship information) around commercial breaks rather than increases in the length of breaks themselves. Sweeting also looks at hours outside the morning drivetime period, which has been the focus of other studies.

finds no significant effects of changes in local concentration on how many commercials are played. Therefore, one can summarize the reduced-form literature as finding no significant effects of local consolidation, and some evidence that national consolidation raised advertising quantities and reduced prices to national advertisers.

Two recent papers, Mooney (2010b) and Jeziorski (2014a), have taken structural approaches to understanding the relationships between local concentration and market power in the advertising and listening markets. The potential advantage of structural approaches is that they may be able to disentangle complicated relationships in the limited available data by imposing the structure of an economic model and assumptions about firm behavior, and they can also allow us to translate changes in the amount or price of advertising into effects on welfare. On the other hand, the conclusions may depend on how modeling assumptions made by the researcher interpret the data. This may be particularly true in this case, as, for example, the models used both assume that listeners single-home, by estimating discrete-choice models of listener demand, rather than explicitly modeling the possibility of multi-homing. Unlike in standard Anderson and Coate-style theoretical models with single-homing listeners, however, they allow for the price of advertising on a particular station to depend on the quantities of commercials that are aired on all stations so that, potentially, a common owner might restrict the quantity of commercials to raise advertising prices. Therefore, even though listeners single-home, it is not imposed by construction that station mergers should lead to more commercials being aired.[38]

Jeziorski (2014a) estimates an equilibrium model of a two-sided market using a panel of data from 1996 to 2006. The data includes market-level SQAD advertising price estimates, Arbitron data on station audiences, and BIA data on station formats, ownership and BIA's estimates of station revenues. Jeziorski estimates that local consolidation led to quite large, 17%, reductions in the amount of advertising heard by the average listener, with a corresponding 6.5% increase in per-listener advertising prices. These changes are estimated to be largest in smaller markets, where the advertiser demand for radio advertising is estimated to be less elastic, reflecting the fact that there may be more limited alternatives to radio for advertisers in smaller cities. As I will return to Section 8.5.2, the effects on listeners can be quite complicated because of the way that a common owner may redistribute commercials across stations, and the way that changes in advertising quantities interact with changes in station formats.

Mooney (2010b) estimates a similar type of model using data from 1998 and 2003, and reaches the conclusion that, on average, the effect of increased concentration was to increase the quantity of advertising. The overall conclusion about how advertising changed is therefore the opposite of Jeziorski. The difference may be due to the fact that the

---

[38] On the other hand, a valid objection is that these models do not provide an explicit rationale for why stations would be substitutes for advertisers.

papers treat what is known about the quantity of commercials quite differently. Jeziorski assumes that the quantity of advertising on each station can be calculated using BIA's estimates of station revenues, SQAD advertising prices (per-share point), and station ratings. Mooney assumes that it is not observed. Instead, she matches a moment based on the average amount of advertising reported in Sweeting (2008). Sweeting's measure is based on a sample of successful music stations, so it may not be representative of the industry as a whole.[39] Jeziorski's approach has the potential advantage that it creates an advertising quantity variable for almost all stations (BIA does not provide revenue estimates for some smaller stations, but for this exercise this problem should not be too important) that can be used in estimation of listener and advertiser demand. In contrast, Mooney's estimates are likely to be more dependent on the assumed structure of the model to give predictions about how the quantity of commercials varies across stations and over time. However, Jeziorski's approach obviously depends on any systematic errors in the revenue estimates and SQAD prices not being correlated with changes in consolidation.[40] Future work using better data on the quantity of commercials could clearly help us to understand what the true relationships are with more confidence.

While they may disagree on the direction of the average effects, both papers emphasize that the effects of consolidation may be heterogeneous, causing significant increases in advertising prices in situations where advertisers' demand is less elastic. Mooney finds that this is likely to be the case for minority populations, which radio might be more effective at reaching than other media. In Mooney (2010a), she finds additional support for this conclusion using the advertising quantity data reported by Chipty (2007), which suggests that when a single firm owns a group of Urban stations, which appeal to black audiences, they tend to restrict how many commercials are played. Jeziorski estimates that advertiser demand is less elastic in smaller markets, where there may be fewer media alternatives. Both papers therefore make the plausible point that some mergers may be much more troubling from an antitrust perspective than others, and they give some guidance on where (smaller markets or minority-focused stations) the antitrust authorities should look for problems or require stronger evidence of efficiencies.

---

[39] Jeziorski estimates that stations played, on average, 37.5 min of commercials per day between 1996 and 2006. This estimate is much lower than estimates based on airplay data (e.g., Sweeting, 2010) or contemporaneous industry reports (Radio and Records, April 21, 2000 cited by SchardtMedia, http://schardtmedia.org/?page_id=80, accessed February 21, 2015) that indicate that stations played around 12 min of commercials per hour on average in 2000 and 2001. Of course, for the conclusions of the study, what would matter is if differences between imputed and actual quantities vary systematically with station ownership or over time.

[40] As discussed in Section 8.3, SQAD prices may be more reflective of the prices paid by national advertisers, who disproportionally advertise on stations owned by large firms, rather than those paid by local advertisers.

There have been no academic studies of what has happened to advertising prices after 2006. However, discussions with at least one industry expert indicate that the quantity of commercials aired on most stations may have fallen quite significantly to around 8 min per hour in 2015, from the 12 or more minutes per hour observed around 2000.[41] Understanding whether this change has been driven by the exercise of market power, or changes in demand, as listeners or advertisers have become more able to substitute to other media seems to present an interesting topic for future research that could also help to improve our understanding of what happened in earlier years.

8.5.2 The Effects of Local Market Consolidation on Product Differentiation and Variety

Another strand of the empirical literature has studied the relationship between local market ownership concentration and either the aggregate variety of programming that is available or measures of differentiation between different stations. These studies have been motivated by the fact that, even though antitrust analysis of radio mergers has focused on advertising price effects, changes in product variety or positioning may themselves have large effects on listener welfare as well as affecting how mergers change advertising prices.[42] In addition, changes in station programming occur quite frequently, although format changes can be costly (Jeziorski, 2014b; Sweeting, 2013 provide estimates of these costs). Another motivation comes from the perception that radio programming has become more homogeneous across the country in the last two decades, and there is interest in testing whether the popular presumption that this is due to the increasing role of media conglomerates such as Clear Channel is correct.[43]

Before discussing the empirical evidence in more detail, it is worth pointing out that one can think of measuring differentiation or variety in radio programming in a number of different ways. In a standard, two-firm Hotelling line model, it is usual to think of an increase in the degree of differentiation between the firms as synonymous with an increase in variety. But things become potentially more complicated when we enrich the model so that it can more realistically be applied to radio markets. For example, within many formats in large urban markets, there are three or more stations. How should we measure variety when some sub-groups of stations are quite similar to each other? Even more importantly, how should we account for the fact that a given station may play

---

[41] Conversation with John Lund of Lund Media Research, February 20, 2015. As will be discussed in Section 8.7, Clear Channel was one of the first firms to explicitly have a policy of reducing the number of commercials, with its "Less is More" strategy in 2004.

[42] Readers should consult section 6.4 of Chapter 6 in this volume for a discussion of the relevant theory for antitrust analysis.

[43] Future of Music Coalition (2003) provide evidence that formats have become increasingly homogeneous and link this to consolidation. Foege (2009) argues that Clear Channel, in particular, has been responsible for a decline in the variety on radio.

several different programs and, in the case of music stations, hundreds of songs in the course of a single day? For example, if two stations both use identical playlists with 500 songs, but rarely play the same songs at the same time, is there more or less variety than if the stations use two playlists that do not overlap at all but only have 50 songs each? In the empirical literature, a number of different metrics have been used, and some of the differences in the results may reflect these choices.

Berry and Waldfogel (2001) examine how ownership concentration affects aggregate variety using quasi-experimental variation created by the 1996 Telecommunications Act. While the Act raised the limit on how many stations a single firm could own in all markets, the increases were greater in larger markets, or more specifically markets with more stations. For example, in markets with more than 45 stations (true of the largest US cities such as New York and Chicago), the limit increased from four to eight stations, while in markets with 15–30 stations, the limit only increased from four to six stations.[44] Berry and Waldfogel therefore try to infer the effect of increases in common station ownership by examining how variety, measured by a count of the number of programming formats available in a market, based on format definitions in Duncan's *American Radio* publications, changed differentially across markets of different sizes between Spring 1993 and Spring 1997, around the time of the Act. This identification strategy assumes, of course, that other formatting trends affected markets of different sizes in the same way over this time period.[45] Their results are consistent with ownership concentration increasing variety, although they also show that firms owning multiple stations tend to cluster stations in similar, but not identical, formats (for example, Soft Adult Contemporary and Hot Adult Contemporary). At the same time, in their working paper (Berry and Waldfogel, 1999b), they find no effect of ownership on total listenership, using the same identification strategy.

In contrast, Sweeting (2010) uses detailed station-level playlist and station-level Arbitron audience data for a sample of contemporary music stations to examine how common ownership affects product differentiation between particular stations and station-level audiences. The focus is on stations in the same broadly defined format category (part of BIA's detailed format classification system), which collects together

---

[44] Originally, the rules were defined using so-called contour rules that examined how many stations' signal coverage areas overlapped. However, these rules were fairly opaque to apply, which created a degree of legal uncertainty for firms considering ownership transactions. In 2003, the FCC decided to use station counts based on Arbitron market definitions. See FCC Report, Order and Notice of Proposed Rule Making 03-127 (http://hraunfoss.fcc.gov/edocs_public/attachmatch/FCC-03-127A1.pdf, accessed January 2, 2014). However, this change led to some strategic manipulations of which stations were included in Arbitron local markets, so some additional rules were introduced (see discussion in http://www.commlawblog.com/tags/arbitron-market-definition/, accessed January 2, 2014).

[45] Berry and Waldfogel try to address this using earlier data and a difference-in-difference-in-difference specification. However, the possibility that there were some changes in formatting or music classification that particularly affected the largest radio markets in the mid-1990s remains a potential concern.

stations in similar formats. For example, the "Adult Contemporary" format category contains formats such as Adult Contemporary, Soft AC, Lite AC, Lite Rock, and Soft Rock. The identification strategy involves looking at how the similarity of station playlists, measured in various ways, changes when pairs, or small groups, of stations become commonly owned or cease to be commonly owned.[46] Consistent with the spirit of Berry and Waldfogel's results, in the sense that they view the driving force behind increased variety as a desire to avoid audience cannibalization, Sweeting finds that common owners tend to differentiate their stations. He also finds that the merging stations tend to significantly increase their combined audience.

However, Sweeting also shows that, at the same time, common owners make at least some of their stations more similar to stations owned by other firms, and that the listenership of these stations tends to fall, by about as much as the merging stations gain, so that when one looks at format listening as a whole, ownership consolidation is not associated with significant changes, consistent with Berry and Waldfogel's 1999b listenership result. To capture the intuition for what seems to happen, suppose that there are three independent stations, A, B, and C, arranged in a two-dimensional product space, and that initially they are arranged symmetrically (say, at the vertices of an equilateral triangle). Following a merger between the owners of stations A and B, suppose that the new common owner differentiates them by moving B further away from A. Potentially it could do so by making the station more differentiated from C as well, but the data suggests that it actually makes at least one of its stations more similar to C than it was pre-merger, to try to take listeners from C, as might happen in a spatial model where price competition is relatively limited, and, as seems plausible for radio, there is limited scope to increase total radio or format listenership by introducing completely new programming.[47]

Sweeting's results come with the caveat that there is no quasi-experimental variation in ownership at the station level. Reassuringly, however, the patterns in the data are quite similar looking at both changes in local market structure that result from very large national transactions involving many hundreds of stations in different markets and different formats, such as the 2000 AMFM–Clear Channel transaction, and local transactions involving trades of stations in an individual market. For large transactions, the claim that

---

[46] One approach defines different artists as different dimensions of the product space, and then uses a station's playlist to identify a location in this high-dimensional space. The difference between two playlists can be measured by the angle between the location vectors at the origin. Alternative approaches include simply looking at the proportion of playtime devoted to artists who are not played at all on other stations, and, for small groups of stations, the total number of different artists played. In a working paper (Sweeting, 2004), Sweeting also projected the main artists in a format category into a two-dimensional space and then placed the stations in this product space based on the artists appearing on their playlists. All of these measures produce qualitatively similar results.

[47] Studies by Borenstein (1986) and Rogers and Woodbury (1996), using data from prior to ownership deregulation, support the contention that there is significant cannibalization both within programming formats and at the aggregate level.

an omitted variable that was causing changes in differentiation to occur could also have caused the change in ownership seems particularly unlikely.

Subsequent research using station-level data on programming content has found results consistent with the claim that common owners differentiate their stations when they are in the same or similar formats. For example, Chipty (2007), using her cross-section of data collected by the FCC, finds some evidence that this is true for both music and non-music (e.g., news and sports) programming. On the other hand, recent results using stations' reported format labels, such as Waldfogel (2011a), who examines how ownership affected news programming in 2005 and 2007, have tended to find weaker relationships. As well as reflecting the fact that format names are necessarily coarse measures of content (for example, a politically right-leaning and a politically left-leaning talk station might be quite different, but both would usually be reported as being in the "Talk" format), this pattern may also reflect the fact that the type of detailed format names used in this type of study could often reflect differences in station marketing rather than real differences in content. From a research perspective, the fact that format names may be of limited use for some questions of interest is unfortunate because these labels are much more accessible to researchers than airplay data.[48]

As mentioned in the previous subsection, Jeziorski (2014a) quantifies the welfare effects of changes in consolidation between 1996 and 2006. His structural model allows him to identify effects that come through station owners being able to change their station formats. The effects, and the implications for welfare, are quite complicated because common owners are predicted to engage in some redistribution of commercials across stations (see his table 15 for a full breakdown of the results). Jeziorski estimates that, holding advertising quantities fixed, the increase in format variety between 1996 and 2006 would have raised listener welfare by 0.3%. Changes in advertising quantities—where owners of multiple stations tend to redistribute commercials toward their more popular stations—tend to slightly reduce the gain to listeners (so their welfare only goes up by 0.2%), but advertiser surplus falls substantially by 21.4% as advertising prices rise and listeners redistribute across stations to avoid commercials.[49] In contrast, advertiser welfare would only fall by 5%, and listener welfare would be essentially unchanged, if advertising quantities were allowed to change with formats held fixed. Unfortunately, because listeners do not pay a price for listening to the radio, it is not possible to compare the effects

---

[48] Of course, format labels are useful for asking questions about the provision of (say) news, classical music or Spanish-language programming where a coarse classification is sufficient. One should, however, be aware that format classifications can, in some ways, be both too coarse but also sometimes too fine. For example, Soft Rock and Soft AC stations often have almost indistinguishable playlists.

[49] One feature of Jeziorski's model that leads to this result is that common owners can increase the price of advertising by redistributing commercials from their least popular to most stations even if this increases the total number of advertising exposures. This would not be possible if the advertising price per 1000 was assumed to be declining in the number of exposures.

on listeners and advertisers in dollar terms. However, for both sides of the market, Jeziorski's results suggest that welfare effects that come through changes in product positioning are greater than the changes that come through advertising prices when programming is held fixed. This is an important conclusion, which is also consistent with the results of Fan (2013) from local newspaper markets, as most merger analyses consider only price and quantity changes, treating product varieties as given.

A separate but related strand of the literature has examined how well radio serves minority audiences, and how this may have been influenced by ownership consolidation. This is partly motivated by the concern in early theoretical work, such as Steiner (1952), that competing media outlets would provide insufficiently differentiated programming as they competed for the ears or eyes of the majority. A different concern is that large, publicly-traded corporations may be less willing or able to serve minority audiences than local broadcasters and/or businesses owned by minorities, an issue which may be compounded by the fact that minority listeners may be less valued by potential advertisers. In the 1970s, the government started the Minority Telecommunications Development Program to facilitate minority ownership of broadcast stations,[50] and as part of its 2004 decision requiring the FCC to re-examine a number of relaxations to ownership rules for radio and television stations, the Court of Appeals for the Third Circuit reaffirmed the validity of promoting minority ownership as a goal for media policy.[51]

One reason why this question is interesting is that the black and Hispanic populations tend to have different programming tastes to the rest of the population. For example, around 50% of black (Hispanic) listening is to stations in Urban (Spanish-language) formats, whereas Urban stations account for less than 5% of non-black listening and Spanish-language stations, unsurprisingly, attract almost no non-Hispanic listeners.[52] As part of his research on preference externalities (see also Chapter 1 in this volume), Waldfogel (2003) shows that increases in the number of blacks or Hispanics in a market has a large and statistically significant effect on the number of Urban or Spanish-language stations so that it is minority populations in markets where they really are minorities that are most likely to be underserved. One issue that has affected minority-oriented stations in recent years has been the introduction of Arbitron's PPM measurement technology. PPM estimates of Spanish-language and Urban station listenership were significantly lower than estimates based on more traditional diaries, and industry experts have suggested that these lower estimates, by making advertisers less willing to pay for commercial time, may have led to a significant reduction in the number of minority stations in recent years.[53]

---

[50] http://en.wikipedia.org/wiki/Minority_ownership_of_media_outlets_in_the_United_States (accessed February 25, 2014).

[51] 373F.3d 372, p. 35.

[52] Religious programming also attracts large minority audiences. See Arbitron Company (2012b,c) for details on format listenership for minority groups.

[53] Conversation with John Lund of Lund Media Research, February 20, 2015. See Napoli (2010) for an extended discussion of controversies regarding PPM.

This leaves open the question of whether station ownership affects the extent to which minorities are served, as stations owned by non-minorities might still seek to serve minority audiences. Siegelman and Waldfogel (2001), using data from the 1990s, and Waldfogel (2011b), using data from 2005 to 2009, provide some results. They show that while there may be no general relationship between ownership concentration and the provision of minority programming, when minorities actually own stations the number of stations targeted at minorities tends to increase. This, of course, suggests the need to better understand how allowing greater consolidation affects the number of stations that are minority-owned. Here, evidence presented by pressure groups, such as Free Press (2007), suggest that minority groups only control a relatively small proportion of radio stations even in markets where minorities actually constitute a large majority of the population.[54] The lack of female ownership or control is also more striking, with only 6% of stations owned by females and less than 5% of stations being owned by companies with a female CEO.[55] This is surprising in the sense that women make the vast majority of retail purchases and it is these shoppers that advertisers would really like to reach.

One consequence of pressure to expand minority ownership in the face of increasing consolidation of the radio industry has been the licensing of "Low Power FM" stations, most recently under the Local Community Radio Act of 2010.[56] These stations have limited range (typically around 5 miles), but around 759 of these stations are currently on air.[57] With the exception of Brand (2004), who describes an earlier program for licensing these stations in the early 2000s, there has been no research studying how successful these stations have been at expanding diversity of ownership or programming, and, indeed, there is almost no data available on how many listeners these stations have been able to capture.

8.5.3 The Effects of National Consolidation on Listeners and Advertisers

In line with the vast majority of the literature, so far I have concentrated on how *local* ownership consolidation affects programming content and equilibrium advertising quantities and prices. On the other hand, consolidation at the national level, by firms owning stations in many local markets, may also have important effects. Unfortunately, these

---

[54] Table 22 of Free Press (2007) indicates that only Laredo, TX, where 95% of the population is minority, has a majority of stations owned by minorities. Overall, 7.7% of full-power commercial stations are owned by minorities. Unfortunately, the FCC only started tracking racial and ethnic ownership after 1996, so it is not possible to do a comparison with the period prior to the Telecommunications Act.

[55] On the other hand, Radio One, a market leader in the Urban format, was founded by a black female who remains President of the company (http://en.wikipedia.org/wiki/Cathy_Hughes, accessed February 27, 2014).

[56] http://en.wikipedia.org/wiki/Low-power_broadcasting (accessed February 25, 2014).

[57] This number is taken from the LPFM database at http://www.angelfire.com/nj2/piratejim/lpfm.html (accessed February 25, 2014).

questions have not really been studied even though the phenomenon that chains are active in many different local markets is a common feature of retail industries, and, because of a tradition of regulating national ownership, radio appears to be a good setting for looking at the effects of chain ownership.

There are at least two ways in which national ownership might have quite positive effects on at least one side of the market. First, national owners may be able to sell advertising more efficiently to large regional or national advertisers by using national sales teams, possibly by bundling commercials across different stations.[58] This may tend to increase the equilibrium amount of advertising, as suggested by some of the evidence in Section 8.5.1, although it may squeeze the amount of time available to local advertisers. National advertisers may also benefit from firms developing a set of radio "brands" that appeal to similar listeners across the country so that ads can be tailored to match programming in a natural way.[59]

Second, national owners may be able to increase programming quality for listeners, especially if their stations are concentrated in similar formats. One way they might do this, as laid out in a model in Sweeting (2004), would be by pooling the results of their (imperfect) research into what listeners want to hear from across many different markets so that in the end they are more likely to pick better music selections.[60]

However, there are also models where this type of homogenization is much less desirable. In a model with two manufacturers and two retail outlets located in different local markets, Inderst and Shaffer (2007) show how a multimarket retailer may choose to inefficiently single-source products for markets with different tastes in order to extract more rents from manufacturers in a bargaining game. They argue that this type of single-sourcing could lead to more negative welfare consequences than within-market concentration, consistent with the evidence cited above that changes in product characteristics can have larger welfare effects than changes in pricing. This model could potentially apply to radio if we replace "retailer" with "station" and "manufacturers" with the "producers

---

[58] The United Kingdom Competition Commission's (2013) report on the merger of Global Radio and Guardian Media Group provides a discussion of how Global served large, national advertisers through a specialized sales force. It also sold advertising time to national advertisers for some small radio firms. Smaller advertisers would negotiate with stations directly.

[59] For example, in its report on the Global Radio and Guardian Media Group merger, the United Kingdom Competition Commission (2013) noted that "one agency said that Global had shown its commitment to building and investing in strong national brands that could compete against the BBC for listeners and that this had helped to make commercial radio more attractive to advertisers. Another large agency said that Global had contributed significantly to a revitalized radio industry making radio attractive to advertisers through an increase in audiences, better quality programming and easier access to larger audiences through branded networks." (p. 87).

[60] This model is consistent with the fact that the CEO of Clear Channel estimated that it spent $70 million on music research (Rolling Stone.com, August 13, 2004) and that programmers in different markets at large companies usually hold weekly conference calls to discuss what they are adding to playlists (an article in Billboard, November 16, 2000, discussed how this worked at Infinity Radio).

of syndicated programming." At least in music radio, however, one reason why this model may not work is that music has traditionally been licensed using blanket licenses issued by ASCAP, SESAC, or BMI, with terms that do not vary across companies, thereby removing the bargaining stage that drives Inderst and Shaffer's results.[61]

An alternative story would be that national owners reduce quality because, by doing so, they can reduce production costs using methods that might not be feasible for independent stations. An example here is the use of "voice tracking," where a DJ located in one city can produce pre-recorded programming to be aired in a number of other, usually smaller, cities, but which still "sounds local" in the sense that listeners are not told that the programming is pre-recorded and produced outside the market, and may contain references to local places or events.[62,63]

There are two divergent attitudes to voice tracking. The first view is that it allows high-quality talent to be used in smaller markets, where talent of this type could never be afforded if the presenter had to be physically present in the market where the broadcast was aired. The alternative view is that even if the outside presenter is skilled, some important element of quality must be lost when the presenter is not familiar with the local market or simply that many listeners would dislike the fact that the programming is produced outside the market if they were actually aware of it. While it may be hard to rationalize why consumers should dislike the fact that presenters are outside of the market *per se*, such preferences are not necessarily invalid and it provides a possible explanation for the fact that broadcasters try to disguise the fact that out-of-market presenters are being used. A practical concern is that when all programming is produced outside of the market and stations are operated remotely, they may not be able to provide vital information in the case of sudden local emergencies.[64]

[61] As will be discussed in Section 8.9.2, the use of general blanket licenses has recently begun to change as some large radio station owners, such as Clear Channel, have struck deals regarding fees for performance rights with record labels. Therefore one might believe that even if the insights of the Inderst and Shaffer model have not been relevant in the past, they may be in the future.

[62] For an example of how Clear Channel used voice tracking in the early 2000s, see "Clear Channel Uses High-Tech Gear to Perfect the Art of Sounding Local", Wall Street Journal, February 25, 2002 (http://online.wsj.com/news/articles/SB1014589283422253080, accessed January 2, 2014).

[63] The use of pre-recorded programming is not new, as stations have used pre-recorded programming since the 1970s. However, prior to 1987, the FCC required that a majority of non-network programming should be produced at a local studio (FCC Report on Broadcast Localism and Notice of Proposed Rule-Making 07–218, 2007, p. 15, http://hraunfoss.fcc.gov/edocs_public/attachmatch/FCC-07-218A1.pdf, accessed January 2, 2014). Recent technical innovations have also made it much easier to attain a local sound more efficiently using out-of-market presenters (for example, allowing a 3-h music show to be produced in less than half an hour).

[64] The example that is usually cited is a 2002 train derailment near Minot, North Dakota that led to a poisonous gas cloud spreading toward the town. All six local stations were owned by Clear Channel and operated remotely, and local emergency services were unable to get information broadcast in a timely fashion. One person died and 1000 people were injured in the disaster (Klinenberg, 2007).

The welfare issues associated with voice tracking may differ quite substantially across programming formats. In music formats, any loss of welfare will likely depend on whether the pre-recorded programming contains a selection of music that is appropriate for the market. As long as it does so, and in fact music selection can vary across markets even if the DJ's talk segments are being voice-tracked, the fact that the presenter is based elsewhere is unlikely to affect quality very much, if at all.

Empirical evidence on homogenization and the use of out-of-market programming is extremely limited. Hood (2007) provides a detailed case study of news programming over 1 week in one medium-sized market in the Western US, where the news stations primarily used newscasts produced from outside the market. Stations missed important local stories such as local flooding and a forest fire. It would obviously be interesting to assess the importance of local news coverage from a welfare perspective, but this will be difficult because the effects of local residents lacking adequate information about local issues may only show up slowly in measurable outcomes such as participation in local elections (see Section 8.9.1 for some related discussion).[65]

Sweeting (2004) provides some evidence on whether firms that own stations in the same format but different geographic markets homogenize their playlists, using his panel of airplay data over the period 1998–2001. The results indicate that common owners do tend to increase the amount of playlist overlap, but the effects are quite small in magnitude. An interesting case study involves Clear Channel's "KISS-FM" stations, in the Top 40/Contemporary Hit Radio format.[66] Clear Channel developed the KISS-FM brand and stations in multiple markets had almost identical logos and websites. However, stations' playlists displayed significant differences across stations. For example, in the first week of November 2001, KZZP-FM in Phoenix, AZ played 159 different songs (i.e., artist–song title combinations). However, only 49 of these songs were also played on the similarly branded KIIS-FM in Los Angeles, CA. At the same time, KIIS played 109 songs that were not played at all on KZZP. One can infer that these differences reflect the fact that tailoring playlists to meet local tastes or local competition remains important. Sweeting (2004) also shows that stations owned by the largest national radio companies were able to increase commercial loads without losing listeners. This suggests that changes in programming tended to increase the quality of stations for listeners, at least on average.[67]

---

[65] Schulhofer-Wohl and Garrido (2013) provide an interesting analysis of the effects of the closure of a local newspaper in Cincinnati.

[66] While KISS-FM is a Top 40/CHR brand primarily developed by Clear Channel, the station KISS-FM, based in San Antonio, TX (ironically Clear Channel's home city), is not a Clear Channel station and is in the Rock format.

[67] Of course, it is possible that national firms are more able to tailor programming to attract the average listener, whereas they may reduce quality for music lovers who desire greater variety in the music that they hear.

8.5.4 Economies of Scale and Scope

As well as understanding the effects of increased consolidation on advertisers and listeners, another strand of the literature has sought to provide estimates of the cost-side benefits to consolidation, which are relevant for welfare calculations even if consumers on neither side of the market are affected. Cost-side efficiencies potentially provide an explanation for why there was such rapid local consolidation after the 1996 Telecommunications Act, given the fact that the empirical evidence indicates that the effects on both programming and advertising markets may have been relatively small.

The legislation was also partly motivated by a desire to allow owners, especially in smaller markets, to exploit economies of scale from operating multiple stations, allowing more stations to remain open in the face of declining radio listening and the recession of the early 1990s. Sources of possible economies might include lower costs of selling radio advertising time in the form of multi-station packages, lower costs of increasing programming quality, and lower fixed costs of operating as a result of being able to share employees and managers across stations.[68]

As in the vast majority of industries, the costs of running radio stations cannot be observed directly both because accounting data is insufficiently detailed and, even when it is available, it does not classify costs in the way an economist might want to do so.[69] Therefore it is only possible to learn about efficiencies from using information on other choices (advertising loads, formatting choices, ownership transactions), a structural model, and assumptions on equilibrium behavior to infer what costs must have been to justify these choices. To date there has been no attempt to link the estimates to specific programming practices, such as voice tracking or remote operation, and doing so would be an interesting direction for future research to understand the welfare benefits, as well as costs, of these controversial innovations.

Jeziorski (2014a,b) provides recent examples of the structural approach to estimating synergies. In both cases, only synergies from local consolidation are considered. As part of his model of the advertising market, Jeziorski (2014a) allows firms that own multiple stations in the same format in the same market to have a lower marginal cost of selling advertising. He estimates that these efficiencies are significant (reducing marginal costs by 20%), an effect that is identified by the fact that commonly owned stations appear to reduce advertising quantities (recall the discussion in Sections 8.3 and 8.5.1 about how these are imputed) less than market power considerations alone would predict.

---

[68] Some direct evidence that some economies of scope result from operating multiple local stations comes from the fact that an owner often operates multiple stations from the same location. For example, the 2010 Broadcasting & Cable Yearbook (Bowker 2010) lists all four of Infinity's FM stations that were licensed to the city of Boston as having their studio at the same address. Jeziorski (2014b) provides several interesting statistics on decreases in employment in the radio industry after 1996.

[69] Audley and Boyer (2007) do provide some estimates of the different costs of running radio stations of different sizes in Canada.

Jeziorski (2014b) estimates the fixed-cost synergies associated with operating multiple stations that are either in the same market but in different formats, or in both the same market and the same format using a dynamic model of endogenous mergers and product repositioning.[70] He finds that both types of efficiency are substantial. In particular, the fixed cost of operating a second station in the same local market is estimated to be only 44% of the fixed cost of operating the first station, although the synergies become smaller when more stations are added, while operating a second station in the same format is estimated to reduce fixed costs by an additional 38%. The dollar value of these proportional efficiencies are estimated to vary greatly with market size, as per station fixed costs, for independent owners, and are estimated to be more than $10 million in the largest markets, but less than $100,000 in small markets.

Three features of the data and the model lead to the large percentage estimates of synergies. First, there was rapid consolidation in the period after 1996 and, while this pattern can partly be rationalized by market power motivations, the fixed-cost synergies provide an additional motivation, in particular for adding a second station. Second, firms were more likely to buy, and maintain, additional stations that were in the same format as their existing stations than would be justified by revenue maximization given the estimated parameters. Third, multi-station firms choose not to take stations off air even though they are cannibalizing audiences. This final source of identification is problematic, as the FCC would likely have removed the licenses of firms that kept stations off the air and reissued them to competitors. This threat would likely remove the incentive to take stations off air even without synergies.

O'Gorman and Smith (2008) estimate large efficiencies from operating multiple stations in the same local market using a static model where firms choose how many stations to operate. For example, their estimates imply that operating a second station only incurs an additional fixed cost equal to around 50% of the cost of operating one station. This estimate is therefore quite consistent with Jeziorski's, although their model is far simpler. However, this model also fails to account for the fact that if one firm does not operate a station, the FCC would likely license a competitor to do so. Based on a dynamic model estimated using only information on format-switching decisions, and not merger decisions, Sweeting (2013) also finds some evidence of efficiencies of operating multiple local stations in the same format, although they are generally not statistically significant and they are smaller than those in Jeziorski.[71]

---

[70] In Jeziorski (2014b), marginal cost efficiencies in selling advertising time are not considered, so some of these efficiencies may be attributed to fixed costs.

[71] For computational reasons, Sweeting also ignores observations where a firm moves multiple stations at the same time. However, as many of these moves involve moving stations into the same format, including these in the estimation would likely produce larger estimates of efficiencies. Therefore, Sweeting's estimates are almost certainly underestimates.

Less attention has been given to the question of whether there are substantial cost benefits to operating stations across different markets, either because they can share programming or some aspects of management (e.g., programming or news directors). These benefits would be interesting to understand given the growth of large, national radio companies described in the introduction and the emergence of firms that specialize in particular formats, such as Radio One in the Urban format or Univision Radio in Spanish-language formats.

8.6. EXCESS ENTRY

While most of the empirical literature has focused on understanding the effects of consolidation, a separate literature has asked whether, from a social welfare perspective, there are simply too many stations or too many stations of a particular type. As well as the fact that there are many stations in most radio markets, two features of the radio industry lead one to expect that "excess entry," in the sense of Mankiw and Whinston (1986), is likely: radio listenership is relatively inelastic, so new stations typically gain audience at the expense of existing ones, and many station costs are fixed, in the sense of not varying directly with the number of listeners served.

The first papers in this literature, Borenstein (1986) and Rogers and Woodbury (1996), used limited data on station listening in local radio markets to show strong evidence of business (audience) stealing in the listener market both at the aggregate level and within specific programming formats.

Berry and Waldfogel (1999a) estimated an endogenous entry model, combined with a model of post-entry competition where stations compete symmetrically for listeners and advertising prices decline in the number of listeners, using a cross-section of data from 1993. Stations are treated as being independent, which is also a reasonable simplifying assumption given that the data come from before the Telecommunications Act (although after ownership rules began to be relaxed). They ignore the value of product variety to listeners because, without prices, they cannot estimate listener welfare in dollars. Under their assumptions and ignoring integer constraints, excess entry is implied, so the interest in their results comes from the fact that they estimate that the degree of excess entry is really large. For example, they estimate that welfare would have been maximized by reducing the number of stations in the San Diego market from 31 to 9, and in Jackson, MS from 17 to 3.

Two limitations of this analysis are that it is assumed that, having entered, all stations have the same quality and are symmetrically horizontally differentiated, and that all stations pay the same fixed costs from entering. In practice, this is not an appropriate assumption because while stations may pay similar prices for licenses (of a given power and signal coverage) and transmission equipment, they may then invest very different amounts in programming quality. A better model of the industry is therefore one in which fixed costs are largely endogenous and determined in equilibrium. A recent paper by Berry et al. (2013)

addresses some of these limitations by allowing for endogenous entry, format differentiation, and endogenous quality choices in certain formats, such as News/Talk, where they allow stations to choose to be either high or low quality (to be high quality requires a higher fixed cost). Using this more general framework, they estimate that there is still substantial excess entry and also excess investment in quality. The intuition for the latter is quite similar to the logic for why there is excess entry. When total listening (or format listening) is fairly inelastic, when a station invests in higher quality it is largely going to be gaining listeners, and their associated advertising revenues, from other stations. This type of business stealing, for quality improvement rather than entry, still implies that there will be excessive investment from a social perspective. Overall they find that welfare would be increased by reducing the number of both high- and low-quality stations by around one-half in formats where there tends to be more than one station in a market.

One could imagine relaxing their remaining assumptions in several directions. For example, a more realistic model of the advertising market might allow advertisers to benefit when they can reach homogeneous audiences that can only be achieved when there are many stations offering niche programming. Alternatively, one might model investment in programming quality in a richer way to capture the fact that there is a lot of persistent heterogeneity in the audiences of stations in the same format. For example, in markets with multiple news stations in Fall 2006, the leading station has, on average, an audience that is two-and-a-half times as large as the second-ranked station, and in 82% of these markets the same station was the leader 10 years earlier (author's calculation using BIA data). Of course, a model of programming investments could also be used to extend our understanding of how consolidation has affected listeners and advertisers.[72]

Another interesting direction would be to analyze whether, even though there may be excess entry into radio markets as a whole, certain formats are underserved. Underprovision could result from listeners in these formats being less valued by advertisers; extra fixed costs that make it too costly for any firms to serve them in small markets; or some extra social value to the programming that stations and listeners may not internalize. As mentioned in Section 8.5.2, this question has arisen in relation to minorities, and I will return to it in Section 8.8 when considering the role of non-commercial broadcasters.

8.7. STRATEGIES FOR RETAINING LISTENERS

As mentioned many times already, the business model of commercial radio is to sell audiences to advertisers. A challenge for this model is that listeners typically do not want to listen to commercials, and so may seek to avoid them, potentially undermining the value of a station's advertising inventory (interested readers should read Chapter 5 in this volume). The problem is even more severe for radio stations, especially music stations, than

---

[72] For example, in the structural models of Jeziorski (2014b), Mooney (2010b), and Sweeting (2013), station quality is treated as exogenous even if it can vary over time.

for local television stations because radio listeners are usually less concerned about missing the programming immediately following the break, so they may be more willing to switch stations.[73] Indeed, when there are several stations playing similar music programming, it is quite plausible that a listener who switches to avoid an ad will never return. If multi-homing listeners are more valued than single-homing listeners, then station-switching may be even more of a commercial problem. In this section, I will review evidence on how widespread station-switching and commercial avoidance really are, before considering strategies that stations may use to limit switching.

The traditional view of people in the industry is that avoidance of commercial breaks is widespread. An Arbitron-sponsored survey by Generali et al. (2011) found that 362 advertising agency executives reported that they believe that station audiences are, on average, 32% lower during commercial breaks than in the minutes leading up to the break, while station managers believe that they are 22% lower. Empirical evidence supported this view. For example, Abernethy (1991) placed cassette recorders in the cars of a sample of listeners and found that, on average, listeners switch stations 29 times per hour, primarily in response to commercials. Dick and McDowell (2003) estimate that in-car listeners missed half of the commercials that they would hear if they did not switch stations. These statistics on in-car listeners are relevant because about 35% of listening takes place in-car,[74] with an even higher proportion during the morning and afternoon drivetime periods. In-car listeners have been estimated to be more than twice as likely to switch during commercial breaks than listeners who are at home or at work.[75]

On the other hand, Generali et al. (2011) claim that confidential PPM data shows that there is much less ad avoidance.[76] They estimate that, on average, only 7% of the audience is lost during a commercial break, and only 4% during breaks that are 3 min or shorter. However, the fall in audience is greater for listeners aged 18–34 (11%), which is one of the demographics most valued by advertisers, and for music stations (12%, vs. only 1% for "spoken word" stations).[77] Given the difference between these estimates

---

[73] Television programmers try to exploit the fact that viewers will not want to miss the conclusion of a show by scheduling more frequent breaks toward the end of a program (Epstein, 1998).

[74] This statistic is based on 2007 listening and data reported in Arbitron's Persons Using Radio report (http://wargod.arbitron.com/scripts/ndb/ndbradio2.asp, accessed January 3, 2014). The number is similar in earlier years.

[75] MacFarland (1997, p. 89) reports that, based on a 1994 survey, 70% of in-car listeners switch at least once during a commercial break compared with 41% and 29% of listeners who are at home or at work, respectively.

[76] As noted in Section 8.3, PPMs measure any contact the wearer has with commercial radio (for example, at the dentist's office), rather than active listening. The earlier cited estimates are likely to be focused on active listeners.

[77] Unfortunately the study does not break out avoidance by location, but it does find that avoidance is particularly low during the morning drivetime period. This may be explained by many music stations carrying more talk programming during the morning drive than they do at other times of the day.

and both industry perceptions and earlier results, it seems clear that more analysis of how much avoidance of commercials takes place, and who avoids them, would be valuable.

Based on the traditional perception, Brydon (1994), an advertising consultant, argues that "for advertisers, the key point is this: if, at the touch of a button, you can continue to listen to that [music] for which you tuned in, why should you listen to something which is imposing itself upon you, namely a commercial break?" He suggests that either stations should play very short breaks which would not make switching worthwhile or stations should "transmit breaks at universally agreed uniform times. Why tune to other stations if it's certain that they will be broadcasting commercials as well?" Unfortunately explicit coordination between stations is both potentially a violation of the antitrust laws, and, from a practical perspective, the fact that most stations in larger markets do not use pre-recorded programming makes it difficult to coordinate by starting and ending commercial breaks at precisely the same time. However, it is still plausible that stations might try to align their commercial breaks as much as possible even if they cannot do so either explicitly or perfectly.

In aggregate, stations do tend to play commercials at the same time. Based on Sweeting (2009), Figure 8.1 shows how many music stations played commercials each minute between 5 and 6 p.m., using data from the first week of each month in 2001. At least 15 times more stations play commercials at 5:23, 5:37, and 5:52 than play them at 5:05. An obvious question is whether this pattern arises from a desire to coordinate on

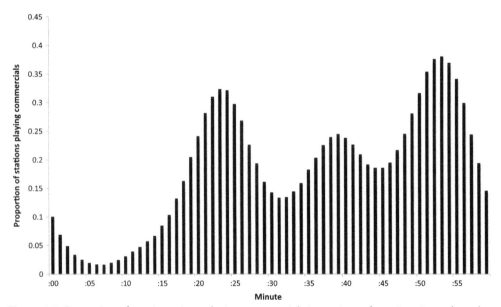

Figure 8.1 Proportion of music stations playing commercials in a minute from 5 to 6 p.m. based on data in December 2001. *Source: Sweeting (2009).*

playing commercials at the same time or some exogenous factor that makes playing commercials at these times (and at similar times in other hours) especially attractive. Two such factors can be identified from radio programming manuals and discussions with radio programmers. First, listeners tend to switch on around the start of the hour, and they tend to be particularly likely to switch stations if they hear a commercial as soon as they switch on (Keith, 1987). Therefore stations avoid playing commercials at the top of the hour. Second, the way that Arbitron has traditionally measured station ratings means that a station's ratings may be increased if it keeps listeners over the quarter-hours (Warren, 2001, pp. 23–24).[78]

Sweeting (2006, 2009) analyzes how far this pattern is driven by stations trying to coordinate stations using his sample of airplay logs from contemporary music stations. These logs identify not only the songs that are played, but also where commercial breaks or promotions are placed between songs. One can then use information on when songs started and the length of songs to estimate whether stations in a market were playing commercials at the same time.

Sweeting (2006) presents a model where stations may either want to coordinate on breaks, which follows from the logic above, or they may want to have commercials at different times. As he shows, this could happen if stations, instead of trying to maximize the audience of their commercials, try to maximize their average audience. It is not unreasonable that this could be stations' objective, as Arbitron reports measures of average audience size, not the audience of the commercials.[79] Average audience may increase if stations play commercials at different times when coordination results in some listeners switching off the radio. These models give different comparative statics for how the degree of overlap should vary with observable market characteristics, such as the number of stations, station ownership structure, and asymmetries in station listenership. In both cases, the relationships should be stronger when listeners are more inclined to switch stations when they hear commercials, as they are during the afternoon drivetime, when there are many in-car listeners and few of the music stations in Sweeting's sample have talk programming.

The empirical evidence lines up fairly consistently in favor of the version of the model where stations prefer to play commercials at the same time even when exogenous factors that make some times good for playing commercials in all markets are controlled for. This suggests both that strategic factors contribute to the degree of overlap observed in the data and, perhaps more interestingly from an economic perspective, that, despite the fact that

[78] To be precise, a station is credited with a listener for a quarter-hour if that listener listens to the station for at least 5 min during the quarter-hour. Therefore a listener who keeps listening between 5:25 and 5:35 can count as much as one who listens from 5:15 to 5:45.
[79] Arbitron continues to aggregate PPM data into average quarter-hour listening data for advertisers, even though much finer data is collected.

advertisers cannot directly observe how many people listen to their commercials, stations do appear to act to increase the audiences of the commercials, even if this might reduce their average audience. One reason for this may be that local advertisers actually have a good sense of how ads on different stations affect their sales,[80] and this effectiveness determines how willing they are to pay for future advertising time. If this is the case, stations will want to maximize how many people actually hear their commercials.

Sweeting (2009) takes the analysis further by building a semi-structural model of the commercial timing decisions, in the form of a coordination game, that allows for the performance of counterfactuals.[81] In particular, he considers what would happen if each station internalized the externality that its timing decisions imposes on other stations. For example, if station A does not play its commercials at the same time as station B, then as well as reducing the audience for its own commercials it will also reduce the audience of B's commercials. The estimates suggest that while the preference to coordinate commercials has quite limited effects on the timing of commercials in equilibrium, in the sense that non-strategic factors lead to the basic pattern shown in Figure 8.1, commercials would overlap almost perfectly if these externalities were internalized, at least during drivetime hours. This also suggests another route through which ownership consolidation—which should incentivize and facilitate more coordination—should be profitable.

Of course, there are other strategies that stations may try to use to increase the effectiveness of ads, although these have not received attention in the economics literature. An interesting issue here is that ads that are effective, in the sense that listeners can recall the product being advertised, may not be ads that listeners particularly like, creating a balancing act for stations who want to both carry effective commercials and also encourage listener loyalty. A set of studies have looked at different aspects of Clear Channel's "Less is More" strategy, which was introduced in 2004 in order to try to reduce audience perceptions of advertising clutter.[82] The strategy had three components: (i) reducing the total number of minutes of advertising; (ii) reducing the number of commercial breaks (or "pods") so that there were fewer interruptions to programming; and (iii) increasing the number of shorter commercials (e.g., 30 s) at the expense of traditional 60-s commercials.

---

[80] For example, if listeners have to make a telephone call to make a purchase, then it is quite common for an advertiser to list different numbers on different stations so that they can monitor where their adverts are most effective.

[81] A motivation of doing so is that, in common with many discrete-choice games, the game has multiple equilibria when strategic incentives are strong enough. The paper shows how the existence of multiple equilibria, here in the form of stations coordinating on playing commercials at slightly different times in different markets, helps to identify the strategic parameters.

[82] "A Radio Giant Moves to Limit Commercials", New York Times, July 19, 2004, http://www.nytimes.com/2004/07/19/business/media/19adcol.html (accessed January 3, 2014).

Together these strategies would allow Clear Channel to potentially carry as many or more advertisements using a smaller number of commercial minutes.

Allan (2005) used laboratory experiments to compare the effectiveness of 30- and 60-s commercials on listener recall of the brand being described, finding that the shorter commercials are only half as effective, even though the price of these slots was believed to be 60–70% of that for the longer commercial.[83] Potter (2009) also finds that listeners become more disengaged when there are more commercials within a pod, and that more, but shorter, ads lead to listeners overestimating the total time spent listening to commercials. Potter et al. (2008) report the results from experiments that show that distributing the same number of commercials in a greater number of advertising pods leads listeners to perceiving that there are more commercials and displaying greater irritation at them, but that it also leads to superior recall.

8.8. NON-COMMERCIAL RADIO AND THE EFFECTS OF COMPETITION BETWEEN NON-COMMERCIAL AND COMMERCIAL BROADCASTERS

In most countries, some of the oldest and still most successful radio stations are publicly owned, with prominent examples including the national and local radio channels of the British Broadcasting Corporation (BBC) and the Canadian Broadcasting Corporation (CBC).[84] While these broadcasters also carry entertainment programming that is very similar to that aired by commercial broadcasters, they also usually have objectives to provide cultural services that could be viewed as merit goods or public goods, which commercial broadcasters might be expected to underprovide. For example, Section 4 of the BBC's current charter lists the purposes of the BBC as being: "(a) sustaining citizenship and civil society; (b) promoting education and learning; (c) stimulating creativity and cultural excellence; (d) representing the UK, its nations, regions and communities; (e) bringing the UK to the world and the world to the UK; (f) in promoting its other purposes, helping to deliver to the public the benefit of emerging communications technologies and services and, in addition, taking a leading role in the switchover to digital television."[85]

Non-commercial radio in the US has had a somewhat different history, but the importance of non-commercial radio has increased quite dramatically in the last 30 years. In this section, I briefly describe the development of non-commercial radio in the US and

[83] "Clear Channel Changes Its Tune on Radio Strategy", New York Times, February 14, 2008, http://online.wsj.com/news/articles/SB120295626450067289 (accessed January 3, 2014).
[84] The BBC was, however, initially established as a private corporation created by the Post Office and a consortium of equipment manufacturers. In 1927, a Royal Charter was issued establishing the BBC as a public corporation that should act independently of the government.
[85] http://downloads.bbc.co.uk/bbctrust/assets/files/pdf/about/how_we_govern/charter.pdf (accessed February 28, 2014).

what is known about how competition with non-commercial radio may have affected the commercial sector.

While many universities were among the earliest institutions to create radio stations, in the 1920s and 1930s, most educational broadcasters were squeezed out as the networks and other commercial interests competed for AM licenses. Therefore, in 1941 the FCC reserved part of the FM spectrum (88.1–91.9) that was just starting to be used for "non-commercial educational" use. However, non-commercial radio only really became strongly established in the US following the 1967 Public Broadcasting Act, which created the Corporation for Public Broadcasting (CPB), which distributed federal funds, in the form of grants, to non-commercial stations meeting certain criteria.

Non-commercial stations can be divided into four groups (Albarran and Pitts, 2001, p. 134). The first type, which includes the largest and well-known "public" radio stations, consisting of about 560 stations in 1999, are CPB-qualified and members of NPR, which produces news programming and operates a satellite distribution network on behalf of its members. Most public radio stations are in news-related formats, and these account for the vast majority of public radio listening, but there are also significant numbers of Classical, Jazz, and Adult Album Alternative (AAA) stations.[86] As well as CPB grants, public stations are funded by listener and member donations, and donations from both non-profit and for-profit companies that can sponsor or underwrite programming. The remaining types of non-commercial stations, amounting to around 2000 stations but accounting for a much smaller share of listening, are: non-commercial religious stations, often affiliated with a network such as the Christian Broadcasting Network; student or campus stations, many of which operate on low power[87]; and community stations not affiliated with an educational establishment, many of which are run and operated by volunteers.

Since the 1980s, public radio audiences have grown significantly, even though commercial radio audiences have been falling. The Radio Research Consortium (2012) estimates that the number of people listening to public radio for at least a quarter-hour each week increased from 5.3 million in 1980 to a peak of 31.6 million in 2011. Public radio has been particularly successful in attracting older and higher-income listeners. For example, Arbitron Company (2012a) estimates that 86% of the audience of public News stations is above age 35, with 50% of listeners having annual household incomes greater than

---

[86] Arbitron Company (2012a) estimates that News, Classical, Jazz, and AAA stations accounted for 49.0%, 16.2%, 4.1%, and 6.3% of public radio listening in Fall 2011. The remainder was accounted for by stations using a mixture of programming in different formats, such as News during the day and music in the evening.

[87] Campus radio stations should be distinguished from large public radio stations that operate in association with universities such as WUNC-FM in Raleigh/Durham and WAMU-FM in Washington, DC. In the last few years, there has been a rapid growth of low-power FM stations following the Local Community Radio Act of 2010. See FCC (2012) for more details.

$75,000 and 70% of them having a college degree. In many college towns, including Madison, WI and Ann Arbor, MI, the public radio station is the largest or second-largest station in the market across all formats.[88] The ability of public radio to attract high-income audiences provides a particular challenge for commercial radio, as these listeners should be particularly valuable to advertisers.

One natural question is whether the existence of non-commercial radio stations "crowds out" commercial stations. There is excess demand for commercial licenses in larger urban markets, so the focus is, instead, on whether public stations crowd out commercial stations from particular formats.[89] Berry and Waldfogel (1999c) use a cross-section of data from 1993 to examine whether local public classical and jazz stations crowd out commercial stations in the same formats. A prerequisite for crowding out is that public and commercial stations compete for the same listeners, and they show that there is evidence that the presence of public classical or jazz stations reduces the audience size of commercial stations in these formats, and that in the classical format, the music selections of commercial and non-commercial stations are quite similar, suggesting that substitution and, therefore, crowd-out are plausible. They also find that crowd-out is likely to be concentrated in the largest radio markets because it is only in these markets where commercial jazz and (especially) classical stations are found even when public stations are absent.[90]

How important are these results? On the one hand, if the number of stations is fixed, crowd-out in a particular format implies that listeners in other formats will be benefitting from greater commercial station variety. On the other hand, these results do suggest valuable public funds are being spent providing programming that the market would likely provide anyway, and which also may be consumed disproportionately by more affluent groups in the population who do not lack for access to many kinds of media.

Waldfogel (2011b) revisits these questions using data from 2005 to 2009. The results are broadly similar, suggesting, for example, that the presence of a public classical station reduces the expected number of commercial classical stations by between 0.3 and 0.4 in large markets. However, unlike the earlier research, this paper also finds some evidence of crowding out of news stations. Given that public news stations and commercial news

[88] Author's calculations based on 2014 data available at http://www.rrconline.org/reports/pdf/Fa14%20eRanks.pdf (public stations) and http://ratings.radio-online.com/cgi-bin/rol.exe/arb581 (commercial stations) (both accessed March 18, 2015).

[89] For example, the Department of Justice has argued that spectrum constraints prevent new entry of FM stations in medium-sized markets such as Harrisburg, PA and Colorado Springs, CO (United States Department of Justice, 2000b). Of course, given excess demand for licenses, the reservation of spectrum for non-commercial stations is almost certainly crowding out commercial programming.

[90] For classical programming, they find evidence of crowd-out for markets in the two largest population quintiles in their sample. These were markets with populations above 561,000 in 1993. In 2013, the Syracuse, NY radio market had a population of 567,000 (Nielsen Fall 2013 Market Survey Schedule and Population Rankings).

stations, which often mix personality-based talk programming and quick-fire headline reporting, tend to sound quite different, this effect is more surprising. At the same time, given the different political orientation of public stations and most commercial talk radio, this result is also potentially important.

The focus of the crowding-out literature to date has been on competition for listeners. However, although they are subject to regulations on exactly what messages they can carry,[91] non-commercial stations also compete for advertising in the form of program underwriting and sponsorship. Interesting evidence on this aspect of competition between public and commercial stations may come in the future from Canada, where the Canadian Radio, Television and Telecommunications Commission (CRTC) is going to allow CBC stations to carry 4 min of commercials per hour for 3 years, at which point CBC will have to prove that this is not harming either programming quality or commercial stations.[92]

8.9. EFFECTS OF RADIO ON THE MUSIC INDUSTRY, AND CULTURAL AND POLITICAL OUTCOMES

In many countries, one of the main roles of publicly funded broadcasters is to support local culture, music, and language. For example, the CRTC requires that at least 50% of the popular music aired on CBC Radio and its French-language counterpart Radio-Canada are Canadian, based on a precise set of definitions of what constitutes Canadian music, with the aim of introducing listeners to new Canadian music and artists and supporting a vibrant Canadian music industry.[93] These mandates on the public sector are also often supported by local content regulations on commercial stations. For example, commercial stations in Canada must make sure that at least 35% of their popular music is Canadian,[94] while all Canadian stations are required to have active local studio

---

[91] http://transition.fcc.gov/osp/inc-report/INoC-31-Nonprofit-Media.pdf (accessed February 27, 2014).

[92] Decision reported in "Ads Coming to CBC Radio 2 in October," The Globe and Mail, August 19, 2013 (http://www.theglobeandmail.com/report-on-business/ads-coming-to-cbc-radio-2-in-october/article13842467/, accessed January 3, 2014).

[93] http://www.crtc.gc.ca/eng/cancon/r_cdn.htm (accessed December 30, 2013). CBC claims that at least 99% of its content is Canadian (http://www.cbc.radio-canada.ca/en/explore/who-we-are-what-we-do/), although it is not clear how it defines Canadian for the purposes of this claim. The CRTC's website explains that content regulations, which originated in the 1972 Broadcasting Act, are aimed at ensuring that the broadcasting system encourages "the development of Canadian expression by: providing a wide range of programming that reflects Canadian attitudes, opinions, ideas, values and artistic creativity; displaying Canadian talent in entertainment programming; and offering information and analysis concerning Canada and other countries from a Canadian point of view" (http://www.crtc.gc.ca/eng/cancon/mandate.htm).

[94] http://www.crtc.gc.ca/eng/cancon/r_cdn.htm (accessed December 30, 2013). A diverse set of other countries, including France, South Africa, Nigeria, and the Philippines, also have quotas for local content during at least some hours of the day (Bernier, 2012, p. 7).

facilities, which rules out the possibility of programming stations solely using voice-tracked satellite programming.

Of course, one should ask the question of how local content regulations affect welfare. Richardson (2004) argues, using a Hotelling line model, that requiring that commercial stations provide local content will tend to reduce the total amount of music variety that is available on the radio and reduce total welfare. On the other hand, it may be argued that in the long run consumers will benefit from the promotion of a vibrant local music industry, as this will increase both the variety and quality of the music that is available. Consistent with this, Ferreira and Waldfogel (2013) provide evidence that sales of local music increased after local content regulations were introduced in Canada, France, Australia, and New Zealand, although whether this is associated with increases in the total quantity and quality of local music that is produced is obviously difficult to test.

However, even absent explicit content regulation, it is interesting to understand the broader effects of radio programming. The two dimensions that have attracted most of the attention in the literature are how News and Talk programming may affect political outcomes, and how music airplay affects the demand for music in the form of CD or digital sales.

8.9.1 Politics[95]

As discussed in Prat and Strömberg (2011), there are various possible ways in which the media might affect public policy or political outcomes. For example, news coverage might affect voter turnout or affect the advantage associated with incumbency by making voters more aware of candidates and the issues involved in elections, even if it does not change the decisions actually made by policy-makers. On the other hand, the threat of criticism by local media outlets could help to reduce corruption but it could also lead to policy-makers choosing policies that favor the interests of the firms or individuals who own local media outlets.

The empirical evidence on the interactions between radio and politics or policy-making is somewhat more limited than the evidence concerning television and newspapers (e.g., Della Vigna and Kaplan, 2007; Obholzer-Gee and Waldfogel, 2009; readers should also see Chapter 14 in this volume for a related theoretical discussion for why the content of media coverage may be biased, and Chapter 15 on evidence for bias). This is especially true for recent years in the US.

Looking at the 1930s, when the coverage of radio was spreading quickly and economic policy was being revolutionized, Snyder and Strömberg (2010) provides evidence that counties where there was a greater penetration of radio were able to secure a statistically and economically significant larger share of the New Deal relief funds distributed

---

[95] Readers should also consult Chapter 13 in this volume on media coverage and its influence on government.

by state governments, with especially large effects for rural counties. At the same time, increased radio penetration also tended to increase voter turnout, which helps to explain why governors might want to favor these counties when distributing funds.[96] These relationships hold up when Strömberg instruments for the penetration of radio using exogenous factors affect the quality of reception, and the finding of local effects is especially interesting given that radio programming in the 1930s was not especially local or focused on news coverage, as discussed in Section 8.2. Ferraz and Finan (2008) provide additional evidence on how local radio can affect electoral outcomes using data from Brazilian municipalities around the 2004 election. They show that when federal government audits uncovered corruption, incumbent mayors were less likely to get re-elected, but that this effect was significantly larger when there was a local radio station to report the results. At the same time, non-corrupt incumbents were more likely to get re-elected when the municipality had a local station.

8.9.2 Contemporary Music

Radio can potentially play two quite different roles vis-à-vis sales of music. On the one hand, listening to music on the radio can be a substitute for listening to music that has been purchased,[97] but, on the other hand, being played on the radio may increase the demand for a particular piece of music either because listening to a song on the radio increases the utility of listening to it at other times or because it makes listeners aware of songs that they would not otherwise know anything about. Therefore when reading this literature, it is important to take note of whether papers are trying to measure the effect of airplay on total music purchases, where substitution is likely, or for particular songs, where one might expect to find that airplay increases sales.

Liebowitz (2004) provides empirical evidence that, when looking at sales of pre-recorded music in aggregate, radio and music sales are substitutes, although the evidence comes from the growth of radio in the US in the 1920s and 1930s and the emergence of commercial radio in the UK in the 1970s and 1980s, and so may not reflect the way that the radio and music markets interact today. Dertouzos (2008), in a study sponsored by the National Association of Broadcasters, provides evidence for the fact that airplay increases the sales of the songs that are played. Bandookwala (2010), using data for New Zealand, finds that airplay has a positive effect on the digital sales of the songs that are being played, while having no effect on aggregate digital sales.

---

[96] Gentzkow (2006) shows that the spread of television after the Second World War was associated with significant decline in turnout, suggesting that local newspapers and radio provided more informative coverage of local politics and political issues. It is, however, unclear whether local radio plays the same role today, as Snyder and Strömberg (2010) suggest that neither radio listening or TV viewing are correlated with whether US citizens know information about their congressmen.

[97] For example, someone driving to work in their car might either listen to music on the radio or on a CD.

One might also be interested in why airplay increases sales of the music that is played. Hendricks and Sorensen (2009) suggest that radio plays a key informative role in introducing consumers to new music. They show that when an artist has a successful second or third album, this increases the sales of the artist's first album, suggesting that consumers failed to buy the first album when it was released because they were not aware of it, and they attribute this ignorance to the narrow playlists of most radio stations.[98] However, one might also explain this pattern by arguing that listening to an artist on the radio and from a CD or digital recording are simply complements so that when the artist receives more airplay consumers want to buy more of their music. It is also unknown whether the success of a later album might lead a station to play more of an artist's back catalog.

The relationships between broadcast radio and the music industry are likely to be changing because of innovation both in the production and distribution of music (digitization) and the growth of Internet and satellite alternatives to broadcast radio. Waldfogel (2012) investigates these changes using an exceptionally long panel of data covering 1980–2010. He argues that prior to digitization recording, promotion and distribution were expensive and this led to a concentrated music recording industry that heavily promoted a relatively narrow range of music. In contrast, the last decade has seen an increase in the total amount of music that has been released, especially by independent (indie) labels, and some of it has been commercially successful even though it has received relatively little airplay on broadcast radio. However, these songs have sometimes been played heavily on Internet radio providers such as Pandora and last.fm.

One reason why it is interesting to identify how airplay affects sales of music is because it has implications for how one might expect money to flow between the industries. If radio airplay increases the sales, or concert demand, of the music that is played, then we would expect that performers and recording companies would be willing to pay radio stations in order to be played, in the same way that consumer package goods manufacturers may pay grocery stores slotting allowances to be prominently displayed in stores, or might pay a magazine to carry an advert or a free sample of the product. The incentives to pay for airplay are strengthened by the fact that the playlist capacity of broadcast stations is limited. The fact that some recording companies have been willing to pay has given rise to the controversial practice of "payola" within the radio industry. On the other hand, if

---

[98] While this explanation may be correct, it is worth noting that stations' playlists involve many more songs than is widely believed. Based on his playlist panel from contemporary music stations, covering 1998–2001, Sweeting (2008) reports that music stations play an average of 177 different artists (standard deviation 67) during a 5-day (Monday–Friday) week. Even in the "Contemporary Hit Radio/Top 40" format, the KISS-FM stations described in Section 8.5.3, which are representative of the format, play more than 150 different artist–song title combinations. On the other hand, the most popular artists on each station do receive a disproportionate amount of airplay: on average, the 20 most played artists in each station-week account for 47% of spins (on average, a station has 1367 spins in a 5-day week).

music plays a key role in attracting listeners and advertisers to the station, while possibly depressing music sales, then we might expect that radio stations should provide compensation to the music industry for using its creations. This issue has recently attracted significant policy attention as the music industry has pushed for broadcast stations to be made to pay for the "performance rights" to the music that they play. Performers and the recording companies own these rights, and they are distinct from the "composition rights," owned by the composers and music writers, that stations have traditionally paid for. However, even if the artists played were to receive compensation, this would not compensate the artists that are not aired, but whose sales might be reduced by airplay.

Coase (1979) provides a fascinating history of payola on radio and television, making it clear that the music industry paid performers to advertise their music long before the development of radio. The practice of payola is distinguished from other types of promotional activity by the fact that the audience is not informed of the fact that a payment has been made to secure the airplay, as they would be if songs were aired in promotional "infomercials."

From an economic perspective, there are potentially efficiency arguments for why music publishers should be able to pay for airplay. In particular, if some music publishers are particularly efficient at producing music, or have private information about the fact their songs are likely to be popular with listeners, then one might expect that some type of multi-unit auction of the radio station's airplay capacity would achieve an efficient allocation of airtime among different songs. This auction would also provide station owners with strong incentives to increase their audiences in order to increase the value of their airtime to the music industry as well as non-music advertisers.[99] However, there are several arguments that can be made for why airplay time should not be sold to music companies. First, it might increase the costs of creating and distributing new music, and could allow dominant music companies to exclude weaker rivals by locking up all of the available airtime. Second, listeners may be misled if they believe that a station is choosing music based on its objective assessment of quality rather than the price that is paid, and they might prefer a system where a station does try to provide an objective assessment.[100]

After a range of Congressional investigations into payola on both radio and television in the late 1950s, the FCC issued a new set of regulations in 1960 to regulate payola, and in particular introduced an explicit requirement that stations had to inform listeners when songs were aired of any consideration that either the station or its employees had received

---

[99] To the extent that listeners to music radio like music and dislike standard commercials, one would expect listeners would prefer an arrangement where it was recording companies that purchased advertising time on the radio.

[100] Coase (1979) describes how it was the Federal Trade Commission, rather than the FCC, that initially intervened against the practice of payola on the basis that it was a deceptive practice.

in return.[101,102] This rule is consistent with the logic of the economic argument that listeners are only really likely to be harmed when they are not made aware of the fact that the content has partly been chosen because the recording company is paying for it. Rennhoff (2010) examines how the characteristics of the weekly Billboard Hot 100 airplay charts changed around the time of these regulations, although the analysis is limited by being based on a single time-series, from January 1959 to December 1961, where it is unclear exactly how the set of available music that might have entered the charts was changing over time. He finds evidence that, after the regulations, more songs by smaller labels appeared in the top 100 and that there were more frequent changes in which song was "Number 1" in the charts. However, a measure of music variety, created based on artist characteristics, declines after the change, suggesting at least the possibility that larger labels may be less able or less willing to market more innovative music when it is harder for them to pay for airplay.

Despite the rules and the changing structure of the music industry, concerns about payola persist and some have alleged that consolidation in the radio industry has allowed payola to flourish (Future of Music Coalition, 2003). In 2005, then New York AG Elliot Spitzer investigated the behavior of several music labels, including Sony BMG, and found that they did offer stations significant financial and non-financial inducements, either directly or through so-called independent promoters, and that they also conspired with stations to offer fictitious promotions, such as a competition to receive tickets to a Celine Dion concert in Las Vegas, when in fact the award might actually be made to a station employee.[103] After this investigation, the FCC came to agreements[104] with the four large radio companies, Clear Channel, Entercom, Citadel, and CBS Radio, in which they agreed to new restrictions on their relationships with recording companies and they agreed to devote a share of their airtime to music produced by independent labels. However, Future of Music Coalition (2008, 2009) suggests that after the agreement the vast majority of songs on commercial music radio were still produced by the major recording companies, suggesting either that these relationships persist, or that financial inducements were not responsible for the pattern of programming.[105]

---

[101] Restrictions on payola apply to broadcast stations. Cable stations, such as MTV, are able to have contracts with labels which give them preferential access to the label's content.

[102] In March 2015, a group of the largest broadcasters approached the FCC to request changes in the disclosure rules for paid programming so that they would not have to announce the payments on air at the time that the programming was broadcast (see http://www.nytimes.com/2015/03/17/business/media/radio-broadcasters-seek-changes-in-disclosure-rules-for-paid-programming.html?_r=1, accessed March 19, 2015).

[103] http://www.ag.ny.gov/press-release/sony-settles-payola-investigation (accessed December 29, 2013).

[104] For example, http://transition.fcc.gov/eb/Orders/2007/FCC-07-28A1.html with Citadel Broadcasting. Future of Music Coalition (2009) discusses the airplay provisions of the agreement.

[105] Future of Music Coalition (2009) finds that independent labels secure substantially more airtime on non-commercial Rock stations. Of course, it is also plausible that non-commercial stations appeal to listeners with different music tastes to mainstream commercial radio.

The claim that broadcast radio tends to increase the sales of music has been one argument for why in the US broadcast stations have not had to pay for the performance rights to the music that they play. This position is, however, somewhat anomalous, as broadcast stations in many other countries do pay for performance rights and, since the 1994 Digital Performance Rights Act, cable, Internet and satellite radio stations in the US have been paying quite substantial fees for performance rights. In 2009, the Performance Rights Act was introduced into Congress, with some support from both parties and the Obama Administration, to make commercial broadcast music stations pay for performance rights. In line with how music stations pay for composition rights, it was envisaged that music stations would pay a proportion of their advertising revenues for so-called blanket licenses which would give them the rights to air music in any of the repertoires owned by organizations such as ASCAP, BMI, or SESAC. Non-commercial stations and stations playing only small amounts of music were to be exempted.

The effects on the radio industry of having to pay for performance rights would obviously depend on how expensive these blanket licenses would be (United States Government Accountability Office, 2010). Currently, stations pay about 1–2% of their revenues for composition rights, but the charges for performance rights might be much greater, potentially as high as 25% based on how much is paid by cable, Internet, and satellite services.[106] Audley and Boyer (2007) and Watt (2010) provide potential methodologies for assessing the value of music to radio in order to set appropriate performance rights fees.

One likely effect of introducing performance rights fees would be that some stations would switch from music to non-music formats, which could potentially affect the welfare of listeners, advertisers who want to reach the types of consumers who tend to listen to music, and the music industry itself if aggregate music airplay and the number of people listening to music radio were reduced. Sweeting (2013) uses a dynamic model of station format choice to try to predict how large this type of supply-side substitution effect would be in both the short run, for example in the 2–3 years after fees were introduced (assuming that they arrived as an unanticipated shock), and in the long run. The size and

---

[106] See, for example, http://www.broadcastlawblog.com/2010/03/articles/music-rights/copyright-royalty-board-approves-settlement-for-sound-recording-royalty-rates-for-new-subscription-services-any-hints-as-to-what-a-broadcast-performance-royalty-would-be/ (accessed December 5, 2010). XM Sirius paid 8% of its subscription revenues for performance rights in 2010–2012, even though some of its programming is not musical, and this fee included a discount recognizing that satellite radio was struggling to become established (Federal Register vol. 75, p. 5513, 2010-02-03). Companies providing audio programming on cable pay 15% of revenues (Federal Register vol. 75, p. 14075, 2010-03-24). Pandora, the leading Internet radio service, pays 25% of its revenue or one-twelfth of a cent per song, whichever is greater. However, because its revenues are low, the absolute amount of money paid by Pandora in performance rights is controversially small given the number of songs that it plays (http://www.businessweek.com/articles/2013-07-01/should-pandora-pay-less-in-music-royalties, accessed December 31, 2013).

distribution of format-switching costs play a key role in the analysis, as they might also be following mergers or other types of market shocks. Even though performance rights fees are not observed in the data, the size of switching costs are potentially identified from how many and how quickly stations switch in response to changes in the demand for different formats driven, for example, by changes in market demographics such as the growth of Hispanic populations in many cities.

Sweeting's results suggest that in the long run (e.g., after 20 years) the number of music stations would fall by around 9.5% if fees equal to 10% of music station revenues were introduced, with most of this adjustment happening within 2–3 years. One factor limiting how many stations switch to non-music formats is that the types of listeners who are most valued by advertisers (for example, whites aged 25–49) have relatively strong preferences for music programming so that when some stations switch to non-music programming the audience of the remaining music stations tends to increase, offsetting the effects of fees, although in aggregate the post-fee revenues of the industry tend to fall. The paper does not address the question of whether, in the long run, this fall in revenues would tend to reduce the quality of broadcast radio, or the total number of stations.

While the Performance Rights Act was not passed, it remains quite possible that similar legislation will be passed in the future, allowing for the predictions of the model to be tested and an investigation of whether other margins adjust as well. At the same time, a trend has begun to evolve where major radio companies, most notably Clear Channel, have started to strike private deals with both major recording labels, such as Warner Bros, and some smaller independent labels, where the radio companies do pay for performance rights on broadcast stations but also receive lower rates for performance rights for their online media services (for example, Clear Channel's iHeartRadio), which is rapidly growing.[107] While private deals potentially provide an alternative to federal legislation, they may also come to favor larger companies, who can realize economies of scale in negotiating contracts, on both sides of the market.

8.10. CONCLUSIONS

This chapter has summarized a wide range of research on the radio industry. Most of the research in the mainstream economics literature has focused on understanding the effects of the rapid consolidation in local radio markets that took place after the Telecommunications Act of 1996. The main conclusions from this literature are that owners tried to reduce the extent to which their stations cannibalize each other's audiences and that they

---

[107] http://www.nytimes.com/2013/09/13/business/media/clear-channel-warner-music-deal-rewrites-the-rules-on-royalties.html (accessed December 31, 2013) and http://www.nytimes.com/2012/06/11/business/media/radio-royalty-deal-offers-hope-for-industrywide-pact.html (accessed December 31, 2013).

benefitted from some economies of scope at the local level from being able to operate multiple stations. It is much less clear how local consolidation affected the welfare of advertisers, as it is unclear whether it has had a significant effect on the quantity of commercials that stations play or advertising prices; or of listeners, as it is unclear whether, in markets taken as a whole, the quality and overall variety of programming were affected. One might view this lack of a clear conclusion on welfare effects as disappointing given the amount of careful empirical work that has tried to look at ownership in the radio industry, but it could simply reflect the fact that there have been different effects in different parts of the industry and that, to date, researchers have not been able to fully develop empirical models, or access the appropriate data, that can account for the type of complicated multi-homing patterns, by both listeners and advertisers, that exist in radio markets.

There are many other possible topics for research that have hardly been touched on at all, and it is appropriate to list a couple of them here. First, how does radio fit into the modern media landscape? Both antitrust policy and FCC regulations place constraints on concentration in radio that may be less appropriate in an era when competition from other media for both listeners' attention and advertising dollars is becoming increasingly fierce. This increased competition might imply, for example, that common station ownership, either locally or nationally, may have quite different effects today than it had in the late 1990s. Second, what value do listeners, or society as a whole, place on local programming? Radio has moved from being dominated by national networks to being a local medium and, in the last 20 years, it has moved back toward a national model even if much of the programming can be made to "sound local" due to the clever use of voice-tracking technology. This is especially important to understand in the context of local news programming, and its possible effects on political participation and civic engagement.

ACKNOWLEDGMENTS

I thank the Editors, Mark Fratrik of BIA/Kelsey and John Lund of Lund Media Research for useful comments on earlier drafts of this chapter and for discussions about certain features of the radio industry. All errors are my own.

REFERENCES

Abernethy, A., 1991. Differences between advertising and program exposure for car radio listening. J. Advert. Res. 31, 33–42.
Albarran, A.B., Pitts, G.G., 2001. The Radio Broadcasting Industry. Pearson, Needham Heights, MA.
Allan, D., 2005. Comparative Effectiveness of 30- Versus 60-Second Radio Commercials on Memory and Money. Saint Joseph's University.
Ambrus, A., Calvano, E., Reisinger, M., 2013. Either or Both Competition: A 'Two-Sided' Theory of Advertising with Overlapping Viewerships. Duke University.
Anderson, S.P., Coate, S., 2005. Market provision of broadcasting: a welfare analysis. Rev. Econ. Stud. 72 (4), 947–972.

Anderson, S.P., Foros, Ø., Kind, H.J., Peitz, M., 2012. Media market concentration, advertising levels, and ad prices. Int. J. Ind. Organ. 30, 321–325.

Arbitron Company, 2009. Understanding and Using Radio Audience Estimates: Fall 2009 Update. http://www.arbitron.com/downloads/purple_book_2010.pdf (accessed February 18, 2014).

Arbitron Company, 2011. Radio Today 2012: How America Listens to Radio. http://www.arbitron.com/downloads/radiotoday_2012.pdf (accessed February 27, 2014).

Arbitron Company, 2012a. Public Radio Today 2012: How America Listens to Radio. http://www.arbitron.com/downloads/publicradiotoday_2012.pdf (accessed February 27, 2014).

Arbitron Company, 2012b. Black Radio Today 2012: How America Listens to Radio. http://www.arbitron.com/downloads/blackradiotoday_2012.pdf (accessed February 27, 2014).

Arbitron Company, 2012c. Hispanic Radio Today 2012: How America Listens to Radio. http://www.arbitron.com/downloads/hispanicradiotoday_2012.pdf (accessed February 27, 2014).

Arbitron Company, 2013. Radio Today by the Numbers—Fall 2013. http://www.nielsen.com/us/en/nielsen-solutions/audience-measurement/nielsen-audio/additional-resources.html (downloaded February 18, 2014).

Audley, P., Boyer, M., 2007. The 'competitive' value of music to commercial radio stations. Rev. Econ. Res. Copyright Issues 4 (2), 29–50.

Bandookwala, M., 2010. Radio airplay, digital music sales and the fallacy of composition in New Zealand. Rev. Econ. Res. Copyright Issues 7 (1), 67–81.

Barnouw, E., 1968. A History of Broadcasting in the United States: Volume 2—The Golden Web. 1933 to 1953. Oxford University Press, New York, NY.

Bernier, I., 2012. Local content requirements for film, radio and television as a means of protecting cultural diversity: theory and reality. http://www.diversite-culturelle.qc.ca/fileadmin/documents/pdf/update031112section1.pdf (accessed February 27, 2014).

Berry, S.T., Waldfogel, J., 1999a. Free entry and social inefficiency in radio broadcasting. RAND J. Econ. 30 (2), 397–420.

Berry, S.T., Waldfogel, J., 1999b. Mergers, Station Entry and Programming Variety in Radio Broadcasting. NBER Working Paper No. 7080.

Berry, S.T., Waldfogel, J., 1999c. Public radio in the United States: does in correct market failure or cannibalize commercial stations? J. Public Econ. 71 (2), 189–211.

Berry, S.T., Waldfogel, J., 2001. Do mergers increase product variety? Evidence from radio broadcasting. Q. J. Econ. 116 (3), 1009–1025.

Berry, S.T., Eizenberg, A., Waldfogel, J., 2013. Optimal Product Variety. Hebrew University.

BIA Financial Network Inc, 2006. Media Access Pro User's Manual, Version 3.0. BIA Financial Network Inc, Chantilly, VA.

Borenstein, S., 1986. Too Much Rock and Roll? Business Stealing Effects in Radio Station Format Choice. University of Michigan.

Bowen, H., Goldstein, P., 2010. AudienceScapes: Africa Development Research Brief. Intermedia. http://www.audiencescapes.org/sites/default/files/AScapes%20Briefs%20New%20Media_Final.pdf (downloaded February 18, 2014).

Bowker, R.R., 2010. Broadcasting and Cable Yearbook 2010. R.R. Bowker, New Providence, NJ.

Brand, K., 2004. The rebirth of low-power FM broadcasting in the US. J. Radio Stud. 11 (2), 153–168.

Brown, K., Williams, G., 2002. Consolidation and Advertising Prices in Local Radio Markets. Federal Communications Commission, Washington, DC.

Brydon, A., 1994. Radio must prove its merit as an advertising medium. Campaign 3, 25–26.

Chipty, T., 2007. FCC Media Ownership Study #5: station ownership and programming in radio. http://hraunfoss.fcc.gov/edocs_public/attachmatch/DA-07-3470A6.pdf (accessed February 18, 2014).

Coase, R.H., 1979. Payola in radio and television broadcasting. J. Law Econ. 22 (2), 269–328.

Cunningham, B.M., Alexander, P.J., 2004. A theory of broadcast media competition and advertising. J. Public Econ. Theory 6 (4), 537–636.

Della Vigna, S., Kaplan, E., 2007. The Fox News effect: media bias and voting. Q. J. Econ. 122 (3), 1187–1234.

Dertouzos, J.N., 2008. Radio airplay and the record industry: an economic analysis for the national association of broadcasters. https://www.nab.org/documents/resources/061008_Dertouzos_Ptax.pdf (accessed February 26, 2014).

Dick, S.J., McDowell, W., 2003. Estimating Relative Commercial Zapping Among Radio Stations Using Standard Arbitron Ratings. University of Miami at Coral Gables.

Duncan, J.H., 1981. American Radio Spring 1981. Duncan's American Radio LLC, Cincinnati, OH. (accessed February 18, 2014).

Duncan, Jr., J.H. 2001. American Radio Market Guide. Duncan's American Radio LLC, Cincinnati, OH. http://www.americanradiohistory.com/Archive-Duncan-American-Radio (accessed February 18, 2014).

Duncan, Jr., J.H. 2002. American Radio Market Guide. Duncan's American Radio LLC, Cincinnati, OH. http://www.americanradiohistory.com/Archive-Duncan-American-Radio (accessed February 18, 2014).

Duncan Jr., J.H. 2004. An American Radio Trilogy: Part I: The Markets 1975–2004. Duncan's American Radio LLC, Cincinnati, OH. http://www.americanradiohistory.com/Archive-Duncan-American-Radio (accessed February 18, 2014).

Edison Media Research, 2013. The Infinite Dial 2013. http://www.edisonresearch.com/wp-content/uploads/2013/04/Edison_Research_Arbitron_Infinite_Dial_2013.pdf (accessed February 18, 2014).

Epstein, G.S., 1998. Network competition and the timing of commercials. Manag. Sci. 44 (3), 370–387.

Fan, Y., 2013. Ownership consolidation and product characteristics: a study of the US daily newspaper market. Am. Econ. Rev. 103 (5), 1598–1628.

Federal Communications Commission (FCC), 1974. In the Matter of the Handling of Public Issues Under the Fairness Doctrine and the Public Interest Standards of the Communications Act. 48F.C.C.2d 1. Federal Communications Commission, Washington, DC.

Federal Communications Commission (FCC), 2001. Review of the Radio Industry, 2001. Mass Media Bureau, Policy and Rules Division, Washington, DC. http://transition.fcc.gov/mb/policy/docs/radio01.pdf (accessed February 27, 2014).

Federal Communications Commission (FCC), 2010. FCC Consumer Facts: FCC's Review of the Broadcast Ownership Rules. Washington, DC. http://www.fcc.gov/guides/review-broadcast-ownership-rules(accessed February 18, 2014).

Federal Communications Commission (FCC), 2012. In the Matter of the Economic Impact of Low-Power FM Stations on Commercial FM Radio: Report to Congress Pursuant to Section 8 of the Local Community Radio Act of 2010. MB Docket No. 11-83, Washington, DC. http://transition.fcc.gov/Daily_Releases/Daily_Business/2012/db0105/DA-12-2A1.pdf(accessed March 18, 2015).

Ferraz, C., Finan, F., 2008. Exposing corrupt politicians: the effects of Brazil's publicly released audits on electoral outcomes. Q. J. Econ. 123 (2), 703–745.

Ferreira, F., Waldfogel, J., 2013. Pop internationalism: has half a century of world music trade displaced local culture? Econ. J. 123 (569), 634–664.

Fisher, F.M., McGowan, J.F., Evans, D.S., 1980. The audience–revenue relationship for local television stations. Bell J. Econ. 11 (2), 694–708.

Foege, A., 2009. Right of the Dial: The Rise of Clear Channel and the Fall of Commercial Radio. Faber & Faber, New York, NY.

Free Press, 2007. Off the Dial: Female and Minority Radio Station Ownership in the United States. June 2007, http://www.freepress.net/sites/default/files/resources/off_the_dial.pdf(accessed February 27, 2014).

Future of Music Coalition, 2003. Radio deregulation: has it served citizens and musicians? In: Testimony of the Future of Music Coalition submitted to the Senate Committee on Commerce, Science and Transportation, January 30, 2003.

Future of Music Coalition, 2008. Change That Tune: How the Payola Settlements Will Affect Radio Airplay for Independent Artists. https://www.futureofmusic.org/sites/default//files/FMC.payolaeducationguide.pdf(accessed February 18, 2014).

Future of Music Coalition, 2009. Same Old Song: An Analysis of Radio Playlists in a Post-FCC Consent Decree World. https://futureofmusic.org/article/research/same-old-song(accessed February 27, 2014).

Generali, P., Kurtzman, W., Rose, W., 2011. What Happens When the Spots Come On? 2011 Edition. http://www.rab.com/public/reports/WhatHappens2011.pdf(accessed February 27, 2014).

Gentzkow, M., 2006. Television and voter turnout. Q. J. Econ. 121 (3), 931–972.

Gentzkow, M., Shapiro, J., Sinkinson, M., 2014. Competition and ideological diversity: historical evidence from US newspapers. Am. Econ. Rev. 104 (10), 3073–3114.

Gomery, D., 2002. The FCC's Newspaper–Broadcast Cross-Ownership Rule: An Analysis. Economic Policy Institute, Washington, DC. http://s2.epi.org/files/page/-/old/books/cross-ownership.pdf (accessed February 27, 2014).

Hendricks, K., Sorensen, A., 2009. Information and the skewness of music sales. J. Polit. Econ. 117 (2), 324–369.

Hillard, R.L., Keith, M.C., 2005. The Quieted Voice: The Rise and Demise of Localism in American Radio. Southern Illinois University Press, Carbondale, IL.

Hood, L., 2007. Radio reverb: the impact of 'Local' news reimported to its own community. J. Broadcast. Electron. Media 51 (1), 1–19.

Inderst, R., Shaffer, G., 2007. Retail mergers, buyer power and product variety. Econ. J. 117 (516), 45–67.

Jeziorski, P., 2014a. Effects of mergers in two-sided markets: the US radio industry. Am. Econ. J. Microecon. 6 (4), 35–73.

Jeziorski, P., 2014b. Estimation of cost efficiencies from mergers: an application to US radio. RAND J. Econ. 45 (4), 816–846.

Keith, M.C., 1987. Radio Programming. Focal Press, Boston, MA.

Klein, J.I., 1997. DOJ Analysis of Radio Mergers. Transcript of a Speech Delivered in Washington, DC, February 19, http://www.usdoj.gov/atr/public/speeches/1055.pdf(accessed February 26, 2014).

Klinenberg, E., 2007. Fighting for Air. Metropolitan Books, New York, NY.

Liebowitz, S.J., 2004. The Elusive Symbiosis: The Impact of Radio on the Record Industry. Unpublished working paper. University of Texas at Dallas.

MacFarland, D.T., 1997. Future Radio Programming Strategies, second ed. Erlbaum, Mahwah, NJ.

Mankiw, N.G., Whinston, M.D., 1986. Free entry and social inefficiency. RAND J. Econ. 17 (1), 48–58.

Mooney, C.T., 2010a. Market Power, Audience Segmentation and Radio Advertising Levels. Unpublished working paper. University of Oklahoma.

Mooney, C.T., 2010b. A Two-Sided Market Analysis of Radio Ownership Caps. Unpublished working paper. Unpublished working paper. University of Oklahoma.

Napoli, P., 2010. The Local People Meter, the Portable People Meter and the Unsettled Law and Policy of Audience Measurement in the U.S. Fordham University.

Nielsen Company, 2014. State of the Media: Audio Today 2014—How America Listens. http://www.nielsen.com/content/dam/corporate/us/en/reports-downloads/2014%20Reports/state-of-the-media-audio-today-feb-2014.pdf(accessed February 14, 2015).

Oberholzer-Gee, F., Waldfogel, J., 2009. Media markets and localism: does local news en Español boost Hispanic voter turnout? Amer. Econ. Rev. 99 (5), 2120–2128.

O'Gorman, C., Smith, H., 2008. Efficiency Gain from Ownership Deregulation: Estimates for the Radio Industry. Unpublished working paper. University of Oxford.

Potter, R.F., 2009. Double the units: how increasing the number of advertisements while keeping the overall duration of commercial breaks constant affects radio listeners. J. Broadcast. Electron. Media 53 (4), 584–598.

Potter, R.F., Callison, C., Chamber, T., Edison, A., 2008. Radio's clutter conundrum: better memory for ads, worse attitudes toward stations. Int. J. Media Manage. 10, 139–147.

Prat, A., Strömberg, D., 2011. In Advances in Economics and Econometrics: Theory and Applications, Proceedings of the Tenth World Congress of the Econometric Society. Cambridge University Press, 2013.

Radio Research Consortium, 2012. Public Radio National Trends 2012. http://www.rrconline.org/reports/reports_list.php?ID=32(accessed February 18, 2014).

Rennhoff, A.D., 2010. The consequences of 'consideration payments': lessons from radio payola. Rev. Ind. Organ. 36, 133–147.

Richardson, M., 2004. Cultural Quotas in Broadcasting I: A Model. Unpublished working paper. Australian National University.

Rogers, R.P., Woodbury, J.R., 1996. Market structure, program diversity and radio audience size. Contemp. Econ. Policy XIV (1), 81–91.

Schulhofer-Wohl, S., Garrido, M., 2013. Do newspapers matter? Short-run and long-run evidence from the closure of the Cincinnati post. J. Media Econ. 26 (2), 60–81.

Siegelman, P., Waldfogel, J., 2001. Race and radio: preference externalities, minority ownership and the provision of programming to minorities. Adv. Appl. Microecon. 10, 73–107.

Silverman, D.M., Tobenkin, D.N., 2001. The FCC's Main Studio Rule: Achieving Little for Localism at a Great Cost to Broadcasters. Fed. Commun. Law J. 53 (3), 469–508, Article 4.

Soley, L., 1999. Free Radio: Electronic Civil Disobedience. Westview Press, Boulder, CO.

Steiner, P.O., 1952. Program patterns and preferences, and the workability of competition in radio broadcasting. Q. J. Econ. 66 (2), 194–223.

Sterling, C., Kitross, J.M., 2002. Stay Tuned, third ed. Erlbaum Associates, Mahweh, NJ.

Snyder, J.M., Strömberg, D., 2010. Press coverage and political accountability. J. Politic. Econ. 118 (2), 355–408.

Sweeting, A.T., 2004. Music Variety, Station Listenership and Station Ownership in the Radio Industry. Working Paper No. 49. Northwestern University, Center for the Study of Industrial Organization.

Sweeting, A.T., 2006. Coordination, differentiation, and the timing of radio commercials. J. Econ. Manag. Strategy 15 (4), 909–942.

Sweeting, A.T., 2008. The Effects of Horizontal Mergers on Product Positioning: Evidence from the Music Radio Industry. Duke University.

Sweeting, A.T., 2009. The strategic timing incentives of commercial radio stations: an empirical analysis using multiple equilibria. RAND J. Econ. 40 (4), 710–742.

Sweeting, A.T., 2010. The effects of horizontal mergers on product positioning: evidence from the music radio industry. RAND J. Econ. 41 (2), 372–397.

Sweeting, A.T., 2013. Dynamic product positioning in differentiated product markets: the effect of fees for musical performance rights on the commercial radio industry. Econometrica 81 (5), 1763–1803.

United Kingdom Competition Commission, 2013. A Report on the Completed Acquisition of Global Radio Holdings Limited of GMG Radio Holdings Limited. http://www.competition-commission. org.uk/assets/competitioncommission/docs/2012/global-radio-gmg/130521_global_radio_gmg_ final_report.pdf(accessed February 26, 2014).

United States Department of Justice, 2000a. Justice Department Requires Clear Channel and AMFM to Divest 99 Radio Stations in 27 Markets. Press Release, July 20, 2000, Washington, DC. http:// www.justice.gov/atr/public/press_releases/2000/5183.htm(accessed February 27, 2014).

United States Department of Justice, 2000b. United States v. Clear Channel Communications Inc. and AMFM Inc.: Competitive Impact Statement. November 15, 2000, Washington, DC. http://www. justice.gov/atr/cases/f6900/6985.htm(accessed March 19, 2015).

United States Government Accountability Office, 2010. The Proposed Performance Rights Act Would Result in Additional Costs for Broadcast Radio Stations and Additional Revenue for Record Companies, Musicians, and Performers. GAO-10-826, August 2010, Washington, DC.

Waldfogel, J., 2003. Preference externalities: an empirical study of who benefits whom in differentiated product markets. RAND J. Econ. 34 (3), 557–568.

Waldfogel, J., 2011a. Station Ownership and the Provision and Consumption of Radio News. 2010 FCC Media Ownership Studies, No. 5, http://www.fcc.gov/encyclopedia/2010-media-ownership-studies(accessed February 27, 2014).

Waldfogel, J., 2011b. Radio Station Ownership Structure and the Provision of Programming to Minority Audiences: Evidence from 2005–2009. 2010 FCC Media Ownership Studies, No. 7, http://www.fcc. gov/encyclopedia/2010-media-ownership-studies(accessed February 27, 2014).

Waldfogel, J., 2012. And the Bands Played On: Digital Disintermediation and the Quality of New Recorded Music. University of Minnesota.

Warren, S., 2001. The Programming Operations Manual. Warren Consulting, San Marcos, TX.

Watt, R., 2010. Fair copyright remuneration: the case of music radio. Rev. Econ. Res. Copyright Issues 7 (2), 21–37.

CHAPTER 9

Newspapers and Magazines

Ambarish Chandra*,†, Ulrich Kaiser‡,§,¶,‖

*Department of Management, University of Toronto at Scarborough, Toronto, Ontario, Canada
†Rotman School of Management, University of Toronto, Toronto, Ontario, Canada
‡Department of Business Administration, Chair for Entrepreneurship, University of Zurich, Zurich, Switzerland
§Centre for European Economic Research, Mannheim, Germany
¶Centre for Industrial Economics at the University of Copenhagen, Copenhagen, Denmark
‖Institute for the Study of Labor, Bonn, Germany

Contents

Handbook of Media Economics, Volume 1A
ISSN 2213-6630, http://dx.doi.org/10.1016/B978-0-444-62721-6.00009-3

Abstract

We review the Economics literature on newspapers and magazines. Our emphasis is on the newspaper industry, especially in the United States, given that this has been the focus of existing research. We first discuss the structure of print media markets, describing the rise in the number of daily newspapers during the early twentieth century and then the steady decline since the 1940s. We discuss print media in the context of two-sided markets, noting that empirical papers on the newspaper industry were some of the earliest studies to use the techniques of two-sided market estimation. We then review the research on advertising in print media, particularly the question of whether readers value print advertising as a good or a bad thing. We summarize the research on antitrust-related issues in newspaper markets, including mergers, joint operating agreements, and vertical price restrictions. We then review recent research on how print media have been affected by the growth of the Internet. Finally, we offer suggestions for future research and provide thoughts on the future of this industry.

Keywords

Magazines, Newspapers, Two-sided markets, History of newspapers, Pricing behavior, Advertising, Joint operating agreements, Mergers, Vertical price restrictions, Online competition

JEL Codes

D4, D21, D22, D24, K21, L82, L86, M37

9.1. INTRODUCTION

This chapter reviews the Economics literature on newspapers and magazines, possibly the two oldest and most influential media in history. We attempt to summarize a vast literature, both theoretical and empirical, on print media. This is especially challenging since this industry has undergone enormous changes since its inception, continues to evolve at a rapid speed today, and also varies in form and structure across cities and countries. Our emphasis will be on the newspaper industry, given the preponderance of research in this area. Out of necessity, our review of empirical research will also focus mostly on the newspaper industry in the United States, again reflecting the great majority of empirical research thus far.

Print media, especially newspapers, are vital in political and economic discourse. Society tends to attach particular importance to the newspaper industry as it has traditionally been an important source of information that affects civic participation, but has also often been monopolized in small local markets.[1] This chapter will examine the economic forces surrounding these issues, as well as summarize research on the history of print media, on advertising in these media, and on the relationship between print media and the Internet.

The importance of newspapers to the democratic process, and in informing citizens, has long been recognized. In the early years of the United States, its founders viewed

---

[1] This issue is discussed further in Chapters 8, 14, 15, 16, 17, and 19.

newspapers as critical for the development of the new country. They provided the newspapers of the day with subsidized postal rates and helped create a reliable distribution network (Federal Communications Commission, 2011). Newspapers have been considered so integral to civic participation that policymakers are not content with relying on market provision of this good, and have often exempted newspapers from regulations that would normally apply in other industries. Perhaps the most famous example of this is the US Newspaper Preservation Act of 1970, which carved out an exemption for newspapers from the usual provisions of antitrust laws. Under the Act, newspapers that would normally compete in the same market were allowed to form joint operating agreements (JOAs), which allowed them to combine their business operations—in particular, the advertising side of the business—while maintaining separate news divisions. The stated goal of the legislation was to allow certain markets to support multiple newspapers, where otherwise circulation declines would have led to a monopoly.

At the same time, newspapers have usually been given free rein with regard to their content, in contrast to broadcast media such as radio. As discussed in Chapter 8, the fact that broadcast media use publicly owned spectrum has allowed a certain level of content regulation that has never been the case in the newspaper industry. Indeed, Gentzkow et al. (2006), discussed in more detail in Section 9.2, point out that in the past US newspapers never even made an attempt to claim an independent position, instead advertising their allegiance to certain political parties and publishing overtly partisan coverage of events.

Another major difference between the newspaper industry and broadcast media lies in market structure. There are often a large number of radio and television stations within a metropolitan area, and television, in particular, offers most consumers a wide range of local as well as national programming. By contrast, most newspaper consumption, in North America at least, tends to be strongly local. Moreover, the importance of economies of scale in this industry leads most cities to be local monopolies or duopolies at best, with recent years seeing a sharp decline in competition. Understanding the economic causes and consequences of local concentration is therefore extremely important.

Undoubtedly, though, the most important issue affecting the industry these days is the dramatic decline in both circulation and advertising revenues, particularly in newspapers, and the challenges posed by online media. As we will see later in this chapter, real advertising revenues in US newspapers have dropped by almost 70% since 2000, driven by a combination of declining circulation, cheaper and more effective online advertising options, and the severe effects of the 2008 financial crisis and its aftermath. Whether print newspapers will survive in their current form is an open question. Some industry observers believe that over the long term newspapers will simply change their form to purely digital versions. Even if so, it remains to be seen whether the electronic press can take the place of traditional daily newspapers with regard to providing factual, informative coverage of news events.

For magazines, the situation is not quite the same. While the two industries have much in common, the greatest difference lies in market structure. Newspapers, especially in North America, have traditionally operated in local markets, which is one reason why the Internet has disrupted this business so much, by suddenly introducing competition from around the country and the world. Magazines, by contrast, have always operated on a national scale and have therefore not been affected severely by digital media. Moreover, magazines have always needed to find ways to differentiate themselves through their choice of subject matter, in a way that newspapers have often not needed.

These differences perhaps explain the divergent fortunes of the newspaper and magazine industries in recent years. While newspapers have experienced dramatic declines, many countries have experienced a growth in the number of magazines in recent years. Data in the US suggests that magazine circulation and advertising revenues have remained relatively strong over the past two decades, as we will discuss in more detail in Section 9.2. Moreover, while a number of magazine titles have closed, there has also been entry in recent years. As with newspapers, however, the advent of the Internet may radically affect the physical form that magazines take, and it remains to be seen whether digital advertising revenues can match those of print editions.

The rest of this chapter organizes the economic literature on print media according to what we believe to be the most natural division of topics. In Section 9.2, we provide an overview of the print media industry, with an emphasis on the history of the newspaper industry, particularly that of the United States. We present some stylized facts on the industry and also discuss data sources for empirical researchers.

In Section 9.3, we discuss market structure in print media, in particular—the number of firms that the industry can support and the importance of economies of scale in this industry. We discuss in detail the structure of newspaper markets in the United States, and examine the reasons that the number of daily newspapers has fluctuated considerably over time, rising rapidly from the mid-1800s until about 1920, and then declining steadily since then.

In Section 9.4, we discuss the economics of print media, especially in the context of the recent and rapidly growing literature on two-sided markets. In fact, economists working on the print media industry were confronted with the challenges of two-sided markets—such as the estimation of multiple, interrelated demand models and cross-price elasticities—well before the development of the current literature on two-sided markets and its associated tools. We therefore first discuss an older literature on demand estimation in newspapers and magazines, before surveying the more recent research in this area.

In Section 9.5, we review the literature on advertising in newspapers and magazines. Our focus in this section is on papers that examine the intermediary role of print media in transmitting advertising messages to readers, as opposed to a more general analysis of the literature on advertising, which is enormous. In particular, we review the research on whether readers of print media value advertising positively or negatively, which has important consequences for the pricing model of newspapers and magazines. We also review research on targeted advertising in print media.

In Section 9.6, we review the literature on market power and antitrust in newspaper and magazine markets, with a particular emphasis on the literature on mergers. We also discuss joint operating agreements, vertical price restrictions, and restrictions on cross-ownership of newspapers and other media.

In Section 9.7, we turn to the effects of the Internet on traditional print media, on both the subscription and advertising sides. We review the literature on whether a publication's print and electronic editions are substitutes or complements. We then discuss the research on how online competition affects print newspapers and magazines.

Finally, in Section 9.8 we offer our concluding thoughts on the future of print media and the challenges that this industry faces.

9.2. AN OVERVIEW OF THE PRINT MEDIA INDUSTRY

In this section, we present some stylized facts on print media. We begin with a history of these media, emphasizing the newspaper industry in the United States. We then present statistics and charts that summarize the current state of these industries. We also provide references to standard data sources that researchers have relied on in the past.

9.2.1 A Short History of Newspapers

As we briefly mentioned in Section 9.1, the founders of the new United States provided considerable support for the establishment of a reliable distribution network in the early nineteenth century. At the time, both newsgathering and newspaper delivery were dependent on horses and, to a certain extent, boats. This severely affected the time it took to report on events: up to 28% of news stories were a month or more out of date (Blondheim, 1994). This situation would have also severely limited the geographic reach of newspapers, but for the fact that they were granted subsidized postal rates, which helped newspapers in the early nineteenth century to expand beyond extremely local markets. In 1794, Congress set mailing rates for newspapers and magazines at less than one-sixth of the cost of letters, and later many periodicals enjoyed free postal delivery.[2]

New technologies in the 1830s reduced the cost of both ink and paper, as well as improved the quality of printing presses (Mott, 1950). With lower costs, newspapers could afford to sharply reduce prices, which in turn led to large jumps in circulation. A higher number of readers led to interesting changes in the political stances of newspapers, as we discuss in Section 9.2.2, and was a factor in changing the focus of newspapers to cover more local news.

---

[2] https://about.usps.com/who-we-are/postal-history/periodicals-postage-history.pdf

The advent of the telegraph in the 1840s sharply reduced the time to report stories, which also made newspapers far more valuable and appealing to a broader audience. In the 1870s and beyond, advertising became more important in newspaper markets. Large national brands were emerging, led by the shrinking of distances brought about by the railroads. At the same time, printing presses were becoming far more sophisticated but also more expensive, thereby raising barriers to entry in the industry (Hamilton, 2004).

Gentzkow et al. (2006) provide an informative discussion of how technological changes in the late eighteenth and early nineteenth centuries allowed newspapers to greatly increase their scale. They document how the introduction of a new process for making paper from pulp in 1867 led to a sharp drop in the price of newsprint. This made it feasible for newspapers to invest in other production improvements such as high-speed printing technology. These investments, coupled with dramatic improvements in communication brought on by the telegraph and the transatlantic cable, allowed news-papers to substantially increase their scale of production. This also led a drop in newspaper prices and, as a result, US newspaper subscriptions increased 12-fold between 1870 and 1920. By the end of this period, the average urban adult was purchasing more than one newspaper per day and was very likely reading even more. These technological improvements also led to a large increase in the number of newspapers, particularly independent ones.

By the early twentieth century, newspapers had been growing without interruption in terms of both circulation and influence. This would start to change with the introduction of rival news media. The first challenge was posed by radio in the 1930s. Newspapers' ad revenue dropped by 28% between 1929 and 1941 (FCC, 2011). Radio stations were accused of copying newspaper stories, a charge that is being repeated with regard to the Internet today. The steady growth in newspaper circulation began to slow during this period, although it would take the introduction of another news medium for newspaper circulation to actually start to decline.

The growth of television in the 1950s and beyond marked the start of a long-term decline in newspapers in North America. Gentzkow (2006) shows that television expanded rapidly across the country: typically it took less than 5 years after the introduc-tion of television in a given market for penetration to reach 70%. Gentzkow shows that the growth of television is correlated with a decline in newspaper circulation. Moreover, these forces end up reducing voter turnout, a topic to which we return in Section 9.2.3.

Genesove (1999) discusses in detail the adoption of two new technologies in the US newspaper industry in the 1960s: photocomposition and offset printing. Together, these technologies reduced labor requirements, increased the print quality of the newspaper, and also lowered the marginal costs of production. These came at the expense of considerable one-time investment costs. Thus, adoption of the new technologies was a strategic decision that depended not just on the newspaper's own scale, but also on the existing market structure. Genesove shows that the pattern of adoption of offset printing, in particular, was partially consistent with an economic model of preemption. Among the set of monopoly newspapers, those of smaller scale were quicker to adopt the technology. However, within duopoly markets, the newspaper with the smaller market share was, on average, 4 years slower to adopt the offset press. Genesove stresses that this was a period when a number of duopoly markets saw, or expected to see, exit by one of the competitors, which complicated the adoption decision.

We postpone a detailed examination of the decline of newspapers to Section 9.3. Briefly, though, it is now clear that the deleterious effects of radio and television on newspaper circulation continued throughout the twentieth century, in conjunction with other factors. Newspapers have been steadily losing readers and revenue; when measured in real terms and on a per-capita basis, these losses have been staggering, as we discuss in detail in Section 9.2.4. The challenges posed by the Internet have been immense, but the Internet also provides a glimmer of hope for newspapers and magazines to possibly continue, and perhaps even thrive, in a new form, a topic that we return to in Sections 9.7 and 9.8.

9.2.2 Partisanship in Print Media

Television and radio news shows in contemporary America are often accused of political bias. However, such accusations are leveled far less often against print media, with the exception of influential national newspapers. This would seem strange by the standards of the nineteenth century, when most newspapers were overtly partisan, in many cases declaring explicit affiliations with one of the two major political parties. This led, in many cases, to newspapers receiving funding not only from the parties, but also from the government. Baldasty (1992) describes how printing contracts for the executive branch, and for each chamber of Congress, went to three separate Washington, DC newspapers in the 1820s, with opposing political views.

Academic research on newspapers has covered the industry as early as the nineteenth century, and the natural topic to examine from this time period was partisanship. Gentzkow et al. (2006) point out that, unlike today, there was no expectation of unbiased news coverage during most of the nineteenth century. As late as 1870, 89% of daily newspapers in urban areas were affiliated with a political party. This situation changed dramatically over the next 50 years, with a sharp rise in the proportion of newspapers that were independent, along with a focus on hard news instead of on political scandals and partisan reporting. Gentzkow et al. (2006) document the rise of the informative press by showing that the fraction of newspapers that claimed to be independent rose from 11% to 62% between 1870 and 1920. This was due both to the switching of previously partisan papers to becoming non-partisan, as well as the entry of independent papers. They use textual analysis of newspaper articles over this period to show that there was a substantial drop in partisan and biased language over this period. They also analyze newspaper coverage of two major scandals: the Credit Mobilier scandal of the 1870s and the Teapot Dome scandal of the 1920s. They show that the language used to cover these events changed significantly over this 50-year period, with even partisan newspapers reducing their use of inflammatory and accusatory language. Moreover, this period also saw the growth of independent newspapers, which covered stories that were suppressed by the partisan publications.

The reason for the growing independence of newspapers in this period was at least partly due to improvements in technology, as described in Section 9.2.1, which increased the ability of newspapers to reach a much wider audience than before. Appealing to larger audiences required newspapers to take less partisan positions. Newspapers therefore focused more on hard news, often local in scope, instead of reporting on Washington scandals and partisan positions (see Hamilton, 2004; Starr, 2004).

Gentzkow et al. (2006) also show that the increase in the size of the newspaper market between 1870 and 1920 was accompanied by an increase in the number of newspapers. This increase in competition led newspapers to provide more information relative to spin. Moreover, newspapers with higher circulation were more likely to be informative, and to provide factual, important stories in a timely manner.

On the same topic, Petrova (2011) uses data on American newspapers from 1880 to 1885 to show that the growth of an advertising market promotes media independence from political influence groups. Specifically, she shows that in areas with faster-growing advertising markets, newspapers were more likely to be independent. As was the case in Gentzkow et al. (2006), Petrova shows that this was due both to existing partisan newspapers becoming independent, and the entry of new, independent papers.

9.2.3 Newspapers and the Electoral Process

Perhaps the most important effect of newspapers on society is their influence over the electoral process. Recent empirical research has studied the relationship between newspapers and the electoral process, and we attempt to summarize some of this research here. Note that this chapter will not deal specifically with issues concerning media bias. We refer readers to Chapters 14 and 15 for detailed discussions of these issues.

Gentzkow et al. (2011) examine how the entry and exit of newspapers affects electoral politics. They show that the presence of an additional newspaper increases voter turnout in both presidential and congressional elections by about 0.3 percentage points. This effect is mostly driven by the entry of the first newspaper in a market, which increases turnout by 1 percentage point; subsequent increases in competition have a much smaller effect on political participation. This implies that, for the average adult, reading at least one paper increases the probability of voting by 4 percentage points.

Chiang and Knight (2011) estimate the extent to which newspaper endorsements affect voting intentions in the US using survey data at the time of the 2000 and 2004 elections. They point out that many voters view the media as biased, and therefore it is not clear that endorsements should sway voters' minds, either because voters choose to subscribe to newspapers which endorse their own political opinions, or because they discount media opinions that are at odds with their own. Therefore, in their model, Chiang and Knight allow readers to account for the credibility of endorsements. Nevertheless, they find that newspaper endorsements do increase the likelihood of voting for the endorsed candidate, but that this effect depends on the credibility of the endorsement. Thus, an endorsement of a Democratic candidate from a left-leaning newspaper carries less influence than one by a centrist of a right-leaning newspaper.

George and Waldfogel (2006) provide evidence that the national expansion of the *New York Times* between 1996 and 2000 had a significant effect on local newspapers. In particular, markets where the *Times* expanded its home delivery service saw circulation declines in local newspapers among the type of readers targeted by the *Times*, which the authors proxy by the share of the population that is college educated. As a result, there is some evidence that local newspapers then repositioned their products, by providing more local and less national coverage. This in turn may have led consumers of the type not targeted by the *Times* to increase their consumption of the local paper. Concretely, the results indicate that in areas with the highest penetration of the *Times*, local newspaper circulation was 16% lower among highly educated readers and 7% higher among less educated readers than in markets with the lowest penetration of the *Times*. They also speculate on the possible effects on readers who do switch to consuming the *Times*. Presumably these readers are now exposed to less local news, which may reduce their engagement with local affairs, including local political participation.

The importance of the newspaper industry that these studies have highlighted perhaps gives us some cause for concern. Newspapers have been instrumental in stimulating political discourse, and Gentzkow et al. (2006) show that an increase in the number and circulation of newspapers in the early twentieth century was accompanied by an increase in their informative content. But newspapers in their traditional form have been declining at a rapid rate in a number of countries in recent decades. It is by no means clear that electronic media are ready to take the place of the world's oldest and most powerful medium of disseminating information.

9.2.4 Stylized Facts on Newspapers and Magazines

Table 9.1 plots the number of daily newspapers in the United States since 1940, using data from the Newspaper Association of America. Two trends are apparent: first, that evening newspapers, which used to be ubiquitous in mid-sized American cities, have rapidly declined since the 1980s. Some of these evening papers converted to morning editions,

Table 9.1 Number of newspapers and aggregate circulation, by country

	Daily newspapers (paid)		Daily circulation (paid)	
	Total	Per million residents	Total (1000s)	Per thousand residents
Britain	94	1.48	10,737	169.4
Canada	95	2.75	4210	121.7
Germany	350	4.32	18,021	222.2
Japan	105	0.82	47,777	375.3
USA	1427	4.51	43,433	137.1

Note that Japan's circulation of "set papers" (morning plus evening editions) is counted only once per day.
Source: World Press Trends. Population figures for per-capita calculations were obtained from the CIA's World Factbook (2013).

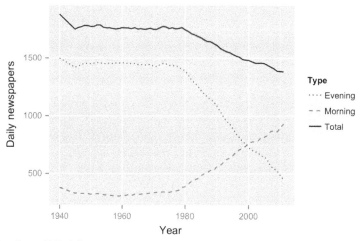

Figure 9.1 Number of US daily newspapers.

while others have simply shut down. Second, the number of morning papers has risen, but not enough to compensate for the decline of evening papers. As a result, the total number of US daily newspapers has declined from around 1750 in 1980 to about 1350 today.

The trends in Figure 9.1, however, understate the difficulties faced by the newspaper industry because they do not account for the rapid increase in America's population. On a per-capita basis, newspapers have faced sharper declines in the past few decades, and this has accelerated in recent years. Figure 9.2 presents the number of newspapers, as well as average national newspaper circulation, normalized by population. By both measures, newspapers have been declining steadily since the 1940s.

In Figure 9.3, we present data on newspaper revenues, expressed in constant 2012 dollars. Circulation revenues have been mostly stable over the past few decades, although

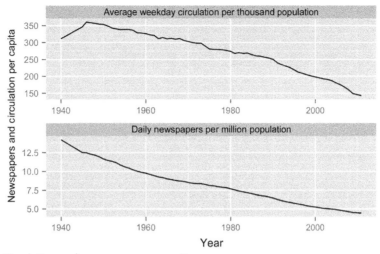

Figure 9.2 Circulation and newspapers per capita.

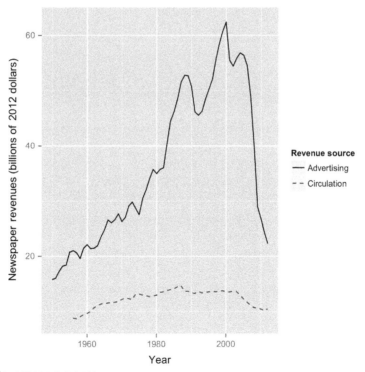

Figure 9.3 Newspaper revenues.

the decline since 2004 is striking. However, this decline is dwarfed by the enormous loss of advertising revenues, which fell by about 50% in real terms between 2004 and 2012.

9.2.5 Data Sources

From the point of view of empirical researchers, a major advantage of studying print media is that sales data are generally available on both sides of the market, i.e., with regard to both subscribers and advertisers. This is in contrast to broadcast media, where the free availability of media content often makes it difficult to acquire reliable estimates of audience sizes and characteristics; see Chapter 8 for a discussion.

Circulation data are, in fact, carefully followed figures, since they are both the main drivers of advertisers' willingness-to-pay, and barometers of the health of the industry. As a result, a number of organizations audit print media sales, and often provide detailed demographic and geographic micro-data as well.

The Audit Bureau of Circulations (ABC) is probably the best-known source of circulation data for newspapers and magazines. ABC—known as the Alliance for Audited Media in North America—is a federation of member organizations in a number of countries, each of which audits the circulation data of print media in that country. In recent years, many of these member organizations have also taken on the task of verifying the electronic reach of media.

Newspaper data in the United States are also available, at various levels of disaggregation, from the Newspaper Association of America, and Editor & Publisher Magazine. The latter used to publish an annual "International Yearbook" with detailed information on all newspapers in the United States. In recent years, this database has moved online and is available by subscription.

Magazine data in the United States are available from a number of sources: The Association of Magazine Media; Standard Rate and Data Service; and the Publishers Information Bureau. Empirical researchers will note that a number of articles on the magazine industry study the German market; this is probably due to excellent data on magazines available in Germany. Sources include IVW, which is the German equivalent to the ABC, and an organization called AG.MA, which provides truly remarkable publication-level data on the demographic characteristics of readers.

Kantar Media is an important source of data on advertising expenditures. Their AdSpender database provides monthly advertising spending, disaggregated by the type of media, at the brand level for most US metropolitan areas. It is therefore possible to track how various industries allocate their advertising budgets across media, which provides an insight into how effective firms perceive different kinds of advertising to be.

The advent of the Internet is making data more widely available, a trend that economists in all fields are exploiting. With regard to media, the consumption of newspaper and magazine websites can be easily tracked, which generates reliable audience figures as well as, in some cases, detailed data on the characteristics of each user. Well-known organizations such as comScore and Nielsen provide accurate audience figures. Media companies that have instituted paywalls often generate databases of the characteristics and the reading habits of their online audience.

9.3. MARKET STRUCTURE IN NEWSPAPERS AND MAGAZINES

We now discuss market structure in print media markets. The majority of this section is devoted to an examination of newspaper markets, due to the interesting economic issues that arise in this industry and the wealth of research in this area. As discussed in Section 9.1, empirical research on the newspaper industry has focused on the United States, and therefore our emphasis in this section will also be on market structure in the US newspaper industry, although we will point out important differences between US newspapers and those in other countries.[3] We direct readers to Chapter 1 for a more theoretical treatment of issues related to the number of firms that markets can support.

We first briefly discuss magazine markets, since the magazine industry appears so different from newspapers in terms of market structure. This is perhaps surprising given that, in many regards, the two industries are similar. Both the newspaper and magazine industries have subscription prices that are subsidized, or at least supported, by advertising revenues. Moreover, both industries are characterized by high fixed costs and low marginal costs, which are usually favorable conditions for high concentration. But measures of concentration depend, of course, on the definition of the relevant market, an often-fraught issue in the Industrial Organization literature.

Unlike with newspapers, magazines tend not to have local markets defined by cities or metro areas. This is probably a consequence of the fact that magazines' subject matter rarely deals with specific geographic areas, but is more often a general subject, such as news, sports, health, fashion, etc. Consequently, advertisers in magazines tend to target readers' demographic characteristics, rather than their geographic location. Therefore, it appears intuitive to define the relevant market for magazines at the national level. This choice is reflected in empirical research in the magazine industry: see, for example, Depken and Wilson (2004) and Oster and Scott Morton (2005) for the US, Kaiser and Wright (2006) for Germany, and Ferrari and Verboven (2012) for Belgium.

Newspapers, by contrast, vary considerably in their news coverage, their geographic appeal, and their target audience. In North America, newspapers have historically been local in nature, confining their coverage to events in the surrounding city or metropolitan

---

[3] Research specific to other countries will be reviewed in this chapter as appropriate. Examples of research on newspaper markets in other countries include the following examples: Australia (Merrilees, 1983), Belgium (van Cayseele and Vanormelingen, 2009), Canada (Chandra and Collard-Wexler, 2009), Italy (Argentesi and Filistrucchi, 2007), Japan (Flath, 2012), the Netherlands (Filistrucchi et al, 2012), Sweden (Asplund et al., 2005, 2008), and the UK (Thompson, 1989).

area. In these cases, the natural definition of a newspaper market is at the local level as well. In other countries, though, newspapers are often better characterized as competing at the national level. For example, Thompson (1989) estimates a model of circulation and advertising prices using a sample of 34 paid Sunday and morning papers in Britain and Ireland. Noam (2009) points out that countries such as the UK and Japan essentially have national, rather than local, newspaper markets.

9.3.1 The Number of Newspapers in a Market

We first pose the question: How many newspapers can a market support? Defining the market as a city or metropolitan area, which is generally appropriate in the case of the US, the answer is usually no more than one. The number of cities in the United States that can support multiple daily newspapers is fast declining, and has done so for years, as we discussed in Section 9.2. In fact, the decline in the number of multi-newspaper cities was most pronounced during the mid-twentieth century. Rosse (1967) states "In 1923 and 1963, respectively, 38.7% and 3.4% of US cities with daily newspapers contained more than one. If multiple firms could exist in 1923, why not today?"[4] On the same topic, Rosse (1980a) states: "[T]here was only one chance in nine that a paper in 1923 did not have face-to-face competition, while the odds were more than two out of three in 1978." Dertouzos and Trautman (1990) wrote that, at the time, less than 1% of US newspapers faced competition from a newspaper published in the same city.

In fact, numerous authors in the literature have pointed to decreasing competition in newspaper markets, at various points of time and in different settings. As long as 50 years ago, Reddaway (1963), writing about UK newspapers, pointed to "… the historic process whereby the number of towns with more than one evening paper has steadily dwindled – and the number with more than one independent evening newspaper has dwindled even farther." We will return, in Section 9.3.2, to the specific question of how large cities must be to sustain multiple newspapers.

We attempted to analyze data on the number of newspaper firms nationally, as well as aggregate readership, across a sample of countries. Although there is excellent data on newspapers in North America, from the Newspaper Associations of the US and Canada, recent and reliable data for other countries is harder to acquire, and the year of the most recent data varies. Moreover, since auditing standards are not necessarily the same across countries, a cross-country comparison should be interpreted with caution. With these caveats in mind, Table 9.1 presents data for five countries on the number of newspapers and total circulation, both in levels and adjusted for population.

---

[4] Using more recent data from Editor & Publisher (2012), we estimate that only about 2.5% of US cities with daily newspapers in 2012 had more than one, and this number drops further if we do not consider jointly owned newspapers or those operating under joint operating agreements.

The table shows that Japan is the clear leader in terms of total readership per capita. Japan is, in fact, a curious outlier in the newspaper industry. It has the fewest newspapers, adjusted for population, of any developed country. However, at the same time, it has the highest readership per capita. This is explained by the extraordinary readership concentration in Japanese newspapers; the two most popular newspapers in Japan—*Yomiuri Shinbun* and *Asahi Shinbun*—are also the top two newspapers worldwide and each command an audience of over 8 million readers daily.

In terms of the *number* of newspapers, the United States is the leader among this group of countries, both in absolute terms and adjusted for population. This reflects the distinctively local nature of the US newspaper industry. In fact, the large number of newspapers in the United States has been the case almost since the founding of the country and was even commented upon by Alexis de Tocqueville back in 1836. In *Democracy in America*, de Tocqueville comments on the "enormous number of American newspapers." In Vol. 1, Part 2, Chapter 3 he states: "[T]he number of periodicals and occasional publications in the United States exceeds all belief" and "in the United States, scarcely a hamlet lacks its newspaper." De Tocqueville (2004, Vol. 2, Part 2, Chapter 6) provides an explanation based on the extent of decentralization of administration in the US, and the relative power of local governments, rather than a centralized government, compared to other countries. He states: "This bizarre multiplication of American newspapers has more to do with the extraordinary subdivision of administrative power than the extensive freedom of politics or the absolute independence of the press."

9.3.2 The Decline of Newspapers

The number of daily newspapers in the US has declined from 1878 in 1940 to 1382 in 2011.[5] As recently as 1980 there were 1745 daily newspapers, implying a decline of over 20% in the last three decades or so. The nature of the industry has changed in other ways too. For most of the twentieth century, the industry consisted mostly of evening newspapers. In 1980, there were four times as many newspapers published in the evening than in the morning. By the year 2000, however, roughly equal numbers of newspapers were published in the morning as in the evening, and today there are more than twice as many morning papers than evening papers. Morning papers have always had higher circulation on average, but the disparity has grown over time and today the paid daily circulation of morning papers is more than 10 times that of evening papers. Reasons may include a rise in the popularity of evening news shows on television, a decline in the number of factory jobs that let out workers in the mid-afternoon, and the migration of readers from central cities to the suburbs where home delivery is harder (FCC, 2011; Romeo et al., 2003).

In the last several years, a number of large US cities that earlier supported two daily newspapers have seen one of them shut down—either entirely, or become weekly papers

[5] Newspaper Association of America and Editor & Publisher International Yearbook.

or else solely digital editions. These cities include Tucson, Denver, Baltimore, Cincinnati, Seattle, and Albuquerque.

A number of smaller US cities that could earlier support a daily newspaper have also lost their local papers in recent years. These include the major university towns of Ann Arbor (MI) and Madison (WI), which would generally be considered to have the population and demographics to support a newspaper. Starting in April 2012, the *New Orleans Times-Picayune* did not publish a daily edition, making New Orleans the largest American city without a daily newspaper; however, the newspaper resumed a daily print edition in 2013. As of 2013, however, the major—and only—daily newspapers in Portland (OR), Cleveland (OH), and Newark (NJ) were moving toward reduced home delivery or daily editions on less than 4 days a week, and increasing emphasis on their online editions.

Noam (2009) presents data to establish the population sizes required to sustain various levels of newspaper competition. The population size required for cities to generally be assured of sustaining a daily newspaper was 100,000 in the year 2000, while this cutoff was around 50,000 in 1980. Cities of a million or more could generally sustain three newspapers in 2000, but similar-sized cities in 1980 could support more than five. These numbers bear out at the local level the same trends that we illustrated nationally in Section 9.2: the number of newspapers in America has simply not kept pace with the growth of population. As a result, most newspaper readers today must live in a very large city in order to be assured of a choice between local newspapers. Berry and Waldfogel (2010), which we discuss in more detail in the next section, also provide evidence that the number of newspapers in a market does not increase linearly with population.

Circulation declines and newspaper closings have direct effects on other metrics in the newspaper industry. As we discussed in Section 9.2, advertising revenue in this industry has plunged. While all categories of advertising have declined sharply, the biggest losses have taken place in classified advertising, an area where local newspapers used to charge monopoly rates for listings, but now face competition from cheap or free websites such as Craigslist and Monster.com. Another measure of how much newspapers have declined is in their employment: the number of full-time journalists at daily newspapers fell from 57,000 in 1989 to around 41,000 in 2010 according to the American Society for Newsroom Editors.[6]

The empirical observation that newspapers have steadily declined in their number and circulation over a period of decades has prompted research into the causes. Bucklin et al. (1989) study predation in the newspaper industry. The stated motivation for their analysis is the declining number of US cities that can support multiple newspapers, and they discuss conditions under which firms in a duopoly or triopoly may try to force rivals out of the market. They stress that the high fixed costs in the newspaper industry—first-copy

---

[6] See http://asne.org/. Similar data are provided by PEW: http://stateofthemedia.org/.

costs are between 40% and 50% of total production costs according to research cited by them—increase the payoff for predatory action by a duopolist.

Bucklin et al. also point out that the interdependence of advertising and circulation—in other words, the two-sided nature of the industry, as we would describe it today—amplifies the importance of newspaper output, since a decline in circulation hurts both sources of newspaper revenues. Importantly, this makes it easier to financially ruin a rival, since even a small decrease in a firm's output can make it impractical to stay in business. They conclude by predicting that the slide toward monopoly in US central-city newspaper markets is inevitable. Indeed, their predictions have largely been borne out in the 24-year period since their article was written.

Rosse (1980a) discusses reasons for the decline of direct newspaper competition. Among the many reasons he considers, two in particular stand out as interesting. First, the rise of television and, especially, that medium's more efficient role in the advertising market has affected newspapers, particularly those in big cities. Second, Rosse describes the effect on newspapers of the suburbanization of America in the post-war period. Rosse suggests that this was a further hit to big-city papers, since there was no longer sufficient market segmentation to support multiple newspapers in the same city. Further, suburban newspapers faced a smaller, more homogeneous audience, and thus there was little need for multiple newspapers in these areas.

The increased pace of newspaper shutdowns in recent years is no doubt due to stiff competition from online sources. This competition affects newspapers both due to a loss of readers, which then directly lowers advertising revenue, but also due to a loss of classified advertising, which is traditionally an extremely profitable revenue source for print newspapers. Kroft and Pope (2014) document that entry by the classified website Craigslist has directly reduced the amount of classified advertising in print newspapers, and Seamans and Zhu (2014) show that these effects then propagate to the other sides of the newspaper—circulation and display advertising.[7] We discuss the effects of the Internet on print media in more detail in Section 9.6.

The decline of newspapers in the US has prompted policymakers to consider changes to help the industry. The most prominent example is the Newspaper Preservation Act of 1970, which allowed the formation of JOAs. We discuss the literature on JOAs in more detail in Section 9.5.

9.3.3 Economies of Scale in Newspaper Markets

A number of studies have pointed to the importance of economies of scale in newspaper markets, and suggested that these explain the high concentration in this industry. Dertouzos and Trautman (1990) show that there are significant economies of scale in

---

[7] See Chapter 12 for a related discussion.

both circulation and newspaper content. Rosse (1967) also finds important economies of scale in both the circulation and advertising sides.

Reddaway (1963) provides evidence on the importance of fixed costs in the UK newspaper industry, using detailed information on the cost structure of various papers, including the differences between local and national papers, as well as between quality and popular papers. Reddaway asks how it can be that the "quality" national papers in Britain could compete with the "popular" papers, when the former had a tenth of the circulation of the latter, as well as higher per-copy costs stemming from their larger physical size. The answer, of course, lies in the greater ability of quality papers to charge advertisers for delivering the most desirable audiences to them.

Berry and Waldfogel (2010) examine how market size affects the quality and variety of products. They focus on two markets that are often defined at the level of a city or metropolitan area: restaurants and newspapers. They show that while the range of qualities in the restaurant industry increases linearly with market size, the same is not true of newspapers. Although the *average* quality of newspapers is higher in bigger markets, these markets do not offer much additional variety. Berry and Waldfogel suggest that fixed costs are the explanation. In particular, they argue that quality improvements in newspaper markets depend on investments in fixed costs, such as more or better reporters and editors, rather than on marginal costs, such as paper, printing, and distribution. They note that, while some economies of scale in newspaper production seem clear, it is not the case that newspapers in even very small markets charge much higher prices, suggesting some upper bound on how important economies of scale are. Of course, this argument de-emphasizes the importance of the advertising side of the industry, and in fact Berry and Waldfogel focus entirely on the circulation side of the market, treating advertising revenue as a per-reader subsidy.

Berry and Waldfogel show that, even in very large markets, the market size of the largest newspaper remains at least 20%, and usually considerably more, in sharp contrast to the restaurant industry. The results appear to support the idea that, as market size increases, at least one newspaper has the incentive to invest considerably in quality in order to retain readers. Newspapers in larger markets tend to have a bigger staff of journalists, be physically bigger in terms of page size, and have a higher quality of reporting, as measured by the number of Pulitzer Prizes won per staff member.

George and Waldfogel (2003) examine the relationship between consumer preferences and the number of daily newspapers that a market can support. They use zip-code level newspaper circulation data in the US to show that race has an important relationship with the number of newspapers in a market. In particular, the tendency for blacks to purchase a daily paper increases with the aggregate number of blacks in the market but decreases with the number of whites. The tendency for whites to purchase a newspaper increases with the number of whites but is not affected by the number of blacks. There is a similar finding with regard to Hispanics and non-Hispanics, but other characteristics, such as age and income, do not influence newspaper sales in this manner. George and Waldfogel present evidence showing that these results are driven by product positioning; in other words, newspaper content responds to the racial makeup of readers.

What are the reasons why the newspaper industry in the United States is dominated by local monopolies? Economies of scale are, of course, an important reason, as discussed above. However, the other obvious candidate is the two-sided nature of the industry and, especially, the unique effect of advertising in the newspaper industry. Unlike in media such as television and radio, newspaper readers do not necessarily dislike advertising. It is not clear that newspaper publishers impose a tradeoff between column inches devoted to content versus advertising, unlike the obvious such tradeoff in broadcast media. Newspaper readers should find it costless to skip over advertising, and there are good reasons why certain types of advertising, such as classifieds, may be positively valued by consumers. A similar argument holds in magazine markets.

If we assume, then, that print media advertising is at least weakly positive in the consumer utility function, it implies that there are positive cross-elasticities of demand with respect to both goods provided by publishers. This can lead to a positive spiral whereby firms with greater circulation attract more advertising, which then further attracts readers and so on. In the limit, these spirals can imply a monopoly situation, abstracting away from other factors, such as consumers' taste for variety, which may support differentiated products. In fact, newspapers and magazines are not the most extreme example of such a model. Rysman (2004) shows that in the Yellow Page industry, advertisers naturally prefer directories with greater circulation, and consumers consult directories with more advertising. Kaiser and Song (2009) confirm the hypothesis that readers in print media may value advertising positively by examining German consumer magazines. See Section 9.5 for a more detailed discussion of this topic.

This argument relating to network effects can be an important complement to the scale economies hypothesis to explain newspaper concentration. Yet there remains little work showing how such positive spirals affect market structure in newspaper and magazine markets. Two examples of studies that model this phenomenon are Gabszewicz et al. (2007) as well as Häckner and Nyberg (2008). However, there is no empirical study we are aware of that investigates this matter. In fact, most structural analyses of newspaper and magazine markets model readers as being indifferent to advertising; see Fan (2013) for a recent example.

9.3.4 Newspaper Chains

An interesting development in the newspaper industry is that the number of newspapers that are part of chains has risen tremendously. Noam (2009) attributes this phenomenon to economies of scale, which, as discussed in the previous section, grew in importance with the advent of faster presses, and typesetting equipment, all of which was quite expensive. Noam emphasizes that chain ownership has steadily replaced independent, local newspapers. The fraction of daily papers owned by newspaper groups rose from 15% in 1930 to 65% in 1980. While this trend has slowed in recent years, it remains the case that 70% of newspapers today are owned by an out-of-town company.

Fu (2003) documents the increasing importance of newspaper chains in the US and points out that, by 1997, the top 20 newspaper chains owned 32% of daily news-papers, but 62% of daily circulation, showing that chain newspapers tend to be larger. Chandra and Collard-Wexler (2009) document a similar phenomenon of chain con-solidation in Canada. They describe how 75% of Canadian daily newspapers changed ownership between 1995 and 1999, primarily driven by the expansion of two nation-wide chains.

The growth of newspaper chains raises two concerns: the first is that it can reduce the variety of opinions put forward by the media. This is especially the case as chain news-papers tend to carry the same syndicated columnists in all of their papers. The second concern—potentially more important from an Industrial Organization perspective—is that the rise in chain ownership increases the possibility of multi-market contact between publishers and raises concerns about tacit collusion. Both papers mentioned above discuss these issues. Fu (2003), in particular, examines multi-market contact between newspaper chains in detail and shows that newspaper publishers who compete with each other in multiple markets tend to have higher advertising prices. Ferguson (1983) provides evi-dence that newspapers that are part of chains tend to have higher advertising rates. Dertouzos and Trautman (1990) note that the rise of newspaper chains has been subject to both Congressional hearings and investigations by the Federal Trade Commission. We discuss their paper in more detail in Section 9.4.1, but note for now that they find no evidence that chain newspapers are more efficient than independents.

9.4. NEWSPAPERS AND MAGAZINES AS TWO-SIDED MARKETS

An important feature of print media is that they cater to two different types of consumers: readers and advertisers. Advertisers value circulation so that advertising demand and mag-azine demand are related. At the same time, readers may have a (dis-)taste for advertising, leading to the two sides of the market being interrelated. These two-way network exter-nalities create a two-sided market, and print media markets are prototypical examples of it. In this section, we review papers that use the two-sided markets framework to analyze print media markets, although we note that a large number of studies on this topic existed well before the recent development of the two-sided market literature. We also review some special topics on pricing in these industries. Readers should see Chapter 2 for a more comprehensive review of the two-sided market literature. Our focus in this section is on empirical studies but we also discuss theoretical contributions where appropriate.

9.4.1 The Older Literature on Cross-Externalities in Print Media Markets

Common to the older literature on print media markets and cross-externalities is that it primarily is what we would nowadays call "structural." These papers derive (inverse) demand equations for circulation and advertising, which are subsequently estimated. These equations are linear and therefore do not allow for competition. Like recent structural studies, the early scholars use their models to conduct counterfactual analyses and to calculate own-price elasticities.

Network externalities in newspaper markets had been recognized decades ago with the diagrammatic exposition of the newspaper firm's profit maximization problem by Corden (1952–1953). In other early work, Reddaway (1963)—then President of the British Royal Commission on the Press—emphasized the role of circulation in the demand for advertising.

The first paper to actually estimate a "structural" model with interrelated demand was Rosse (1967), who studies why the newspaper industry had become more concentrated over time. One of the explanations for increased concentration is economies of scale in production, as we discussed in Section 9.3. Rosse's (1967) paper has two parts, an analysis of economies of scale in newspaper and advertisement production, and an analysis of advertising space. The first part endogenizes the number of content pages, cover prices, ad rates, circulation and advertising space, and separately estimates each (interrelated) equation. He uses the parameters of these equations to back out estimates for marginal production cost, finding evidence for returns to scale in newspaper and advertisement production. In fact, Rosse's (1967) is the first paper to estimate marginal cost based on functional form assumptions and under the absence of actual cost data.[8]

The second part of Rosse (1967) deals with the estimation of demand elasticities and serves to corroborate the earlier findings regarding economies of scale using a longer time span and a broader set of newspaper firms. The second study does in fact confirm the initial finding of returns to scale in production. It also indicates that returns to scale have remained fairly constant since 1939, which may not explain the observed increase in newspaper concentration. The second part of Rosse (1967), explained in much greater detail in Rosse (1970), constitutes the first true estimated two-sided market model as he makes advertising demand dependent on circulation, and circulation dependent on advertising.

In a paper that analyzes the importance of audience characteristics for advertising rates, Thompson (1989) deals with the tradeoff between newspaper circulation and the share of high-income newspaper readers. The paper also explicitly accounts for the two-sidedness of the newspaper market, and estimates a system of simultaneous equations for circulation, cover prices, and advertising rates.

---

[8] Rosse (1967) was also among the first to take Chamberlin's (1960) model of monopolistic competition to data.

Much of the literature that followed also concerned itself with concentration in print media markets, often motivated by the occurrence of "one-newspaper cities" in Australia (Chaudhri, 1998; Merrilees, 1983) and the US (Blair and Romano, 1993; Bucklin et al., 1989; Dertouzos and Trautman, 1990; Ferguson, 1983).

Merrilees (1983) provides a primarily descriptive event study of a price war between Sydney-based newspapers in the 1980s. His theoretical considerations include an equation for the demand for advertising that depends on circulation. He does not, however, account for reverse network effects. Bucklin et al. (1989) estimate a system of simultaneous equations where newspapers set ad rates, cover prices, and editorial quality to maximize profits. They show that feedbacks between each market side exist and argue that these feedback structures make the newspaper industry prone to what they refer to as "ruinous competition."

In their study of US newspapers, Dertouzos and Trautman (1990) also focus on the competitive situation of media firms and estimate a model that takes into account the interrelatedness between circulation and advertising. Their main findings are that there exist scale economies in newspaper production, that these are not larger for chain newspapers than for independent ones, and that newspapers in adjacent geographical areas put competitive pressure on local newspapers. They do not, however, find evidence for competitive pressure from radio broadcasting.

In an earlier study of media cross-ownership that, however, does not consider feedbacks from either market side, Ferguson (1983) examines cross-ownership of newspapers and other media; we discuss this paper in more detail in Section 9.6.

9.4.2 The Two-Sided Market Framework

The earlier papers on the newspaper market typically assumed monopoly with respect to the readership side. As a result, the literature does not consider how the structure of prices emerges from competition between two platforms that strategically set prices to each side to take into account interrelated demands. This actually constitutes a key question in print media markets and two-sided markets more generally: How does a print medium as a platform price each distinct type of user? Armstrong (2006), Gabszewicz et al. (2001), as well as Rochet and Tirole (2003) provide theoretical frameworks of two-sided markets to explain the pricing structure of these firms, and Weyl (2010) generalizes Rochet and Tirole's model.

A central finding of Armstrong (2006) is that prices on either market side are determined by the size of cross-group externalities—the network effects that run from the reader market to advertising and vice versa—the way fees are charged (lump-sum or on a transaction basis) and whether advertisers multi-home, i.e., advertise in multiple print media. Cross-group externalities make competition fiercer and reduce platform profits. He shows that there is under-advertisement compared to the social optimum since platforms operate as monopolists on the advertising market. Armstrong (2006) also coins the term "competitive bottleneck" model, where readers single-home and advertisers multi-home. He additionally considers two other types of platform competition, monopoly platforms and competing platforms.

That publishers have an incentive to cross-subsidize one side of the market by the other has been discussed in earlier theoretical work by Rochet and Tirole (2003).[9] They show that it may pay off for publishers to set copy prices even below marginal cost in order to make the print medium more attractive for advertisers. In their paper, which is primarily written with the credit-card market in mind, Rochet and Tirole (2003) distinguish for-profit and not-for-profit platforms. They compare the respective market outcomes in each case to the social optimum and recognize that prices on one market side depend on the degree of multi-homing on the respective other market side. The consequences of multi-homing for market outcomes is an issue that is the focus of a few of the subsequent papers that we shall review below.

Gabszewicz et al. (2001) also use a Hotelling setup to explain the pricing structure in newspaper markets. They consider what later was termed a competitive bottleneck model and show that advertising revenues are used to subsidize the reader market.

We now turn to recent empirical work that uses structural methods based on the two-sided markets framework. Rysman (2004) was the first to derive a structural model for a market with externalities where only advertisers are priced: Yellow Pages. He establishes that network cross-effects exist in both directions in the Yellow Pages market: advertisers value the number of readers and readers value advertising. He estimates a nested logit model for the demand for Yellow Pages and an inverse demand equation for advertising. His inverse advertising demand function assumes that readers of Yellow Pages single-home, i.e., they read at most one Yellow Page directory, an assumption that appears reasonable in this setting. His estimates suggest that an internalization of these network effects would significantly increase surplus.

Kaiser and Wright (2006) was the first paper to estimate a structural model of two-sided markets where both sides are priced. This is not the case in Rysman's Yellow Page analysis because directories are usually given free to consumers. Kaiser and Wright build on the generic two-sided market model of Armstrong (2006), discussed above, to set up an estimable structural model for German duopoly magazine markets. They derive magazine and advertising demand from a Hotelling specification where magazines compete in differentiated Bertrand fashion. The parameters of these demand equations are subsequently used to back out the subsidies publishers pay to each market side, as well as marginal cost, distribution cost, and profits. Kaiser and Wright (2006) also conduct

---

[9] Armstrong's (2006) model has a general setup quite similar to Rochet and Tirole (2003), but differs in important ways in how the benefits of joining a platform are defined, which changes the definition of profit-maximizing prices in the two papers.

comparative-static analyses whose results are consistent with the perception that prices for readers are subsidized (cover prices are around or even below marginal cost) and that magazines generate their profits from advertisements. They also find that advertisers value readers more than readers value advertisements. This implies that higher demand for copies raises ad rates and that an increased demand for advertisements decreases copy prices. They also show that their estimated production costs are similar to those reported by industry sources. Finally, they show that their results are qualitatively invariant to accounting for multi-homing on behalf of advertisers (advertisers who place their ads in multiple magazines) and readers (readers who purchase multiple magazines).

In a study of market power in the Italian national newspaper industry that also uses structural econometric modeling and that we discuss in more detail in Section 9.5, Argentesi and Filistrucchi (2007) assume away feedbacks from the advertising market to the reader market. Advertising demand and circulation are both specified as logit-type demand models. They back out markups from their estimations and compare estimated and actual markups to infer market conduct.

In a recent study of the US newspaper industry that we discuss in more detail in Section 9.5, Fan (2013) assumes that newspaper readers do not care about advertising, which implies that network externalities only flow from readers to advertisers but not vice versa. This assumption is supported by her estimation results.

Van Cayseele and Vanormelingen (2009) also provide evidence for advertising neutrality of newspaper readers. Their paper generalizes Kaiser and Wright (2006) by allowing for oligopoly (instead of duopoly) competition and multi-market contact of publishers. They derive a model of supply and demand for newspapers and advertising, using a nested logit model for circulation and a linear inverse demand function for advertising similar to that of Rysman (2004). Their data on Belgian newspapers allows them to assess newspapers' market power and market competitiveness before the background of a major market consolidation. They also evaluate an actual merger that occurred in the Belgian newspaper industry.

In an attempt to test theories derived from behavioral economics in an Industrial Organization setting, Oster and Scott Morton (2005) use US magazine data to analyze whether wedges between subscription and news-stand prices are larger for magazines that generate future benefits (like investment magazines) and that generate instantaneous benefits (like leisure magazines). They argue that this wedge should be relatively larger for investment magazines than for leisure magazines since news-stand consumers fully value the leisure good but discount future payoffs from investment magazines. In their data for 300 consumer magazines, they find evidence that such wedges do in fact exist, which implies that publishers are aware of the time-inconsistent behavior of their customers. Oster and Scott Morton (2005) also consider feedbacks from the advertising market to the reader market by including advertising rates in their equations for relative news-stand

and subscription prices, finding negative effects of ad rates on relative magazine prices. This is consistent with the view that publishers have incentives to lower reader prices to increase advertising revenues.

The interrelatedness between advertising and readership does not only have implications for pricing structures. It may also have effects on the political diversity of media. Assuming that readers dislike advertising, Gabszewicz et al. (2001) derive a three-stage game for publishers who first set their political leaning, then ad rates, and finally cover prices. They show that the feedback from readers to advertisers induces publishers to locate their political opinion in the center. The feedback from readers to advertising therefore generates a "median voter behavior" result whereas a model that excludes advertising (where only political leaning and cover prices were state variables) would generate classical Hotelling results: publishers position themselves at the two extremes of the political spectrum.

A more recent study of ideological diversity of US newspapers in 1924 that accounts for network effects from readers to advertisers (but that assumes readers are ad-neutral) is Gentzkow et al. (2012). They estimate a model of demand for newspapers, cost, entry, and revenues to show that media competition increases diversity, and that competition policy needs to take into account the print media market's two-sidedness.

9.4.3 Pricing Issues in Print Media

We now discuss a few issues related to pricing in newspapers and magazines. While the two-sided market framework suggests that advertising and circulation prices are determined jointly and therefore need to be considered at the same time, there are a few interesting pricing phenomena that need to be considered outside of this framework.

More importantly, while Media Economics usually falls squarely within the purview of Industrial Organization, some aspects of print media pricing are of interest to other economists too. Specifically, the macroeconomics literature on the frequency of price adjustment has devoted some attention to media markets. Cecchetti (1986) examines the frequency of price adjustment in US magazine markets using news-stand pricing and sales data for 38 magazines between 1953 and 1979. He shows that magazines' cover prices exhibit substantial stickiness, allowing their real value to erode by as much as a quarter before the next price adjustment. However, he also shows that prices change more frequently during periods of high inflation. Willis (2006) uses the same data to confirm some of Cecchetti's findings.

Knotek (2008) examines newspaper prices—specifically, the fact that news-stand prices are usually a multiple of a quarter. He points out that newspaper prices have typically not required pennies for more than the last 40 years. The point is that these round-number prices facilitate quick transactions and are more convenient than other prices. Knotek develops a model of how the convenience of transactions affects the choice of round-number pricing and shows that quarterly data from six large US newspapers are generally consistent with the predictions of the model.

Asplund et al. (2005) examine how likely newspapers are to vary prices on the circulation versus the advertising side in response to financial constraints. They argue that newspaper advertisers are not locked in to any given newspaper and therefore will exhibit a much more elastic demand. Readers, on the other hand, develop tastes and preferences for certain newspapers and therefore face high switching costs and are less likely to switch papers in the event of a price increase. They examine Swedish newspapers in the midst of the deep recession of 1990–1992 and show that publishers, who were faced with liquidity constraints during this period, were far more likely to raise subscription rather than advertising prices.

9.5. ADVERTISING IN NEWSPAPERS AND MAGAZINES

We devote this section to a discussion of the special role of advertising in newspapers and magazines. While the role of advertising is, of course, important in all advertising-financed media, it is particularly interesting, from a research perspective, in the case of print media. Unlike in the radio and television industries, it is not obvious that advertising imposes a cost on the circulation side. There are two reasons for this: first, print media do not necessarily involve the platform having to trade off between advertising and content; second, consumers may be able to skip advertising more easily in print media.

The question of whether consumers value advertising positively or negatively is therefore important in newspapers and magazines. We will review the theoretical literature on this question in Section 9.5.1 and the empirical literature in Section 9.5.2. We will address the related issue of multi-homing by readers in Section 9.5.3. Finally, in Section 9.5.4, we discuss how audience characteristics determine advertising rates in print media.

9.5.1 Reader Valuation of Advertising: Theory

We have laid out the effects of the interrelatedness between advertising and circulation in Section 9.4. The network effects exist no matter whether readers like or dislike advertising. While it is clear that advertisers appreciate higher circulation, at least given reader characteristics (Thompson, 1989), it is not obvious whether the same is true in reverse; i.e., whether readers like advertising in print media, or if advertising constitutes a nuisance. A positive mapping between advertising and circulation implies that publishers have incentives to subsidize circulation through advertising revenues, as in Kaiser and Wright (2006). If readers appreciate advertising, they simultaneously have incentives to subsidize advertising. The degree to which each market side subsidizes the other depends on the relative appreciation of each market side. If readers dislike advertising (but advertisers appreciate circulation), the reader side of the market will not subsidize advertising (but subsidies will still flow from advertising to circulation).

Reader preferences with respect to advertising are therefore central to the analysis of pricing structures in print media markets. Most theoretical studies of media markets—of which we shall review some below—assume that readers dislike advertising (Ambrus and Reisinger, 2005; Ambrus et al., 2012; Anderson, 2005; Anderson and Coate, 2005; Gabszewicz et al., 2001; Häckner and Nyberg, 2008; Jullien et al., 2009; Kind et al., 2003, 2007; Kohlschein, 2004; Kremhelmer and Zenger, 2004; Reisinger et al., 2009).

Reader neutrality with respect to advertising is assumed by Gabszewicz et al. (2001), a paper we briefly discussed in Section 9.4.2 and to that we shall return to below, who argue that it is simple to avoid advertisements in newspapers since it is easy to get past them. Empirical studies that assume advertising neutrality include Gentzkow et al. (2012) and Fan (2012). This shuts down the network effect from advertising to readers and collapses the two-sided market into a market with network externalities from readers to advertisers, thereby simplifying the analysis and avoiding fixed-point problems. By contrast, the models in Kaiser and Wright (2006) as well as Chandra and Collard-Wexler (2009) do not impose *a priori* restrictions on reader's attitude toward advertising.

The importance of the degree to which readers dislike advertising is highlighted by Anderson and Coate (2005), who study the under- or over-provision of ads in a two-sided TV market setting. In an extension to previous work, Anderson and Coate (2005) allow the degree to which viewers dislike advertising to vary. They assume that viewers are distributed on a Hotelling line and that platforms are located at each end of the line. Viewers are allowed to watch a single channel, while advertisers can multi-home. They show that advertising volume may be too high or too low, depending on how much viewers dislike advertising.

In an extension to Anderson and Coate (2005), who do not allow for multi-homing viewers, Gabszewicz et al. (2004) allow viewers to mix their time between channels. They set up a sequential Hotelling game where channels first choose programming and subsequently determine the ratio of ads to content. They show that when advertising is a nuisance, programs will be differentiated, which contrasts with the very early finding of Steiner (1952), who predicts duplication of content among competing channels.

That the degree of advertising nuisance is important for market outcomes is also underscored by Peitz and Valletti (2008), who analyze optimal locations of stations in terms of programming. They show that if viewers strongly dislike advertising, the ratio of advertising to content is larger in free-to-air TV, where all revenues are from advertising, than in pay TV. They predict that free-to-air TV comes with less differentiated content whereas program differentiation is maximal for pay-TV stations. The analogy to the business model of newspapers and magazines here is that free-to-air TV is comparable to free newspapers while pay TV compares to paid newspapers and magazines.

Free newspapers and their impact on market structure have, however, not been systematically studied so far.

Choi (2006) also compares free-to-air and pay TV and studies the types and extent of market failures under the two regimes under free entry. Similarly, Jullien et al. (2009) investigate the effects of free platform entry where platforms are financed both from ad revenues and subscriptions. They predict excessive entry and too-low ad levels compared to the social optimum. Both papers assume that advertising is a nuisance.

Finally, the importance of nuisance costs is highlighted by Reisinger (2012), who shows that profits may increase the more viewers dislike advertisements and that channels make revenues from advertising despite price competition for advertisers. In his model, there are single-homing advertisers and channels are differentiated from a viewer's perspective.

9.5.2 Reader Valuation of Advertising: Empirics

Our discussion of the theoretical literature has shown that reader's attitude toward advertising is important for market outcomes. We now review the empirical literature that has dealt with this topic. This literature has arrived at very mixed results. The older papers on two-sided market by Bucklin et al. (1989), Dertouzos and Trautman (1990), and Thompson (1989) for US and British newspapers respectively find that readers appreciate advertising. Sonnac (2000) conducts a cross-country descriptive analysis and finds that readers' attitudes toward advertising vary across countries.

The more recent literature tends to find positive effects of advertising pages on print media demand. Kaiser and Wright (2006) show that readers appreciate advertising for their sample of German magazines. Their data set is, however, not representative of the German magazine market since it comprises only magazine markets with duopoly competition. Filistrucchi et al. (2012) also find evidence for readers of Dutch newspapers appreciating advertising while van Cayseele and Vanormelingen (2009) show that Belgian newspaper readers are advertising-neutral.

In their analysis of the entire German magazine market, Kaiser and Song (2009) find evidence that advertising is valued positively by readers. They estimate logit demand models (with and without random effects), finding little evidence for advertising being a nuisance to readers. On the contrary, in markets where there is a close relationship between advertising and content, such as in Women's magazines, Business and politics magazines as well as car magazines, readers in fact have a clear appreciation of advertisements. To study the role of informative vs. persuasive advertising more closely, Kaiser and Song (2009) categorize each magazine in terms of advertisement informativeness. They subsequently link the degree of informativeness to reader's perception of advertising and demonstrate that there is a positive link between informative advertising and reader's appreciation of advertising.

Depken and Wilson (2004) use data on 94 US consumer magazines to study the effect of advertising on advertising rates and advertising demand. They define advertising as "unambiguously good" if advertising increases both sales and prices, and as "ambiguously good" if it decreases sales but increases ad rates (and vice versa for "bad" effects of advertising on sales and ad rates). The main finding of the paper is that advertising tends to be "unambiguously good" for 45 magazines and "ambiguously good" for 19 magazines. For 31 magazines it is an ambiguous bad.

9.5.3 Multi-Homing

A central aspect of theoretical work on two-sided markets apart from the nuisance cost to readers or viewers is multi-homing by readers and advertisers. Armstrong (2006) coins the term "competitive bottleneck" model where readers single-home and advertisers multi-home, a model that found widespread use in the theoretical literature, e.g., by Anderson and Coate (2005) that we discussed above. Apart from the results already discussed, Armstrong (2006) shows that there is under-advertisement compared to the social optimum since platforms operate as monopolists on advertising market.

The other main puzzle that the early theoretical study by Steiner (1952) generated apart from content duplication is that advertising levels unambiguously increase with competition. Ambrus and Reisinger (2005) were the first to notice that both anomalies may be reversed if the models allow for multi-homing viewers. In their follow-up paper, Ambrus et al. (2012) find that advertising levels can go up or down depending on how viewer tastes are correlated. In their setting, viewers are allowed to use multiple platforms, platforms do not steal viewers from one another but competition changes the composition and hence the value that advertisers attach to consumers—multi-homing viewers are worth less to advertisers than single-homers. Ambrus et al. (2012) coin this type of competition "either or both competition" (viewers watch either or both channels). They find that entry increases ad levels if viewer preferences are negatively correlated. The paper also comes with an empirical analysis that is based on 68 cable channels received by a viewer on a base lineup observed between 1989 and 2002 that validates theoretical implications. Ambrus et al. (2012) regress the number of supply choices on the number of channels in each market segment (news, sport, infotainment) and find large positive effects of competition on the number of avails.

In a related paper, Anderson and McLaren (2012) also demonstrate how to resolve the early Steiner (1952) puzzles by allowing for viewer multi-homing.[10] In their model, platforms become more differentiated when faced by competition in order to attract exclusive (single-homing) viewers. They show how multi-homing viewers affect platform differentiation, finding that platforms have incentives to make content unattractive to multi-homing viewers, which works against Steiner's duplication result. Anderson and

---

[10] This issue is also discussed in Chapter 6.

McLaren (2012) allow, in contrast to Ambrus et al. (2012), for both multi-homing viewers and endogenous platform quality, which is assumed to be fixed in Ambrus et al. (2012).

Multi-homing also is a major issue in Athey et al. (2011), a paper that discusses alternative viewer-tracking technologies and the implications they have for pricing and advertising demand. They consider multi-homing viewers and let advertising effectiveness differ between single- and multi-viewing viewers by allowing viewer tracking to be imperfect. They implicitly assume exogenous ad levels and allow for heterogeneous advertiser demands.

A key assumption of the theoretical literature is that multi-homing viewers have lower value for advertisers than single-homers have. This assumption is questioned by Chandra and Kaiser (2014), who show that contacting potential consumers via alternative channels may actually increase the value that multi-homing readers generate.

9.5.4 The Determinants of Advertising Rates

The determinants of advertising rates have long been studied in empirical papers, while there is no related theoretical treatment. The study by Thompson (1989), which was mentioned in Section 9.2, was among the first to recognize the importance of certain types of readers for advertisers. He finds that high-income readers are more valuable to advertisers than are low-income readers in his sample of 34 British and Irish quality and tabloid newspapers. This leads him to conclude that there exists a tradeoff between circulation and a newspaper's ability to target certain types of readers. He estimates a four-equation structural model for circulation, cover price, and two types of advertising rates. As in other earlier studies, the demand for copies and the (inverse) demand for advertising space are linear and are not dependent on prices of competing newspapers. Thompson (1989) estimates a simultaneous equation model and backs out own-price elasticities of demand.

The importance of reader characteristics has subsequently been studied by Koschat and Putsis (2000a,b) in their analysis of 101 US magazines. They essentially estimate a linear hedonic pricing equation where all variables are assumed to be exogenous. They find that young and affluent readers have a positive effect on advertising rates. In Koschat and Putsis (2000a), it is argued that advertiser's preferences for particular types of readers may induce publishers to—as they phrase it—"skew" content toward those types of readers. Koschat and Putsis (2000b) additionally conduct a counterfactual analysis where they analyze the returns to fully target (which they refer to as "unbundling") the most relevant audiences from an advertiser's perspective. They find that if publishers indeed targeted the most profitable audiences, they would be able to considerably increase profits. A critical assumption of their paper is, however, that targeting has no effects on circulation.

In another paper on the US magazine industry, Depken (2004) uses the same data as Depken and Wilson (2004) to show that both reader income and, in contrast to Koschat and Putsis (2000a,b), age have positive effects on advertising rates.

While these studies use magazine data and readership characteristics data at the magazine level, Chandra (2009) uses zip-code level on circulation and readership characteristics for US newspapers. He finds that newspapers that operate in a more competitive environment charge lower cover prices but higher ad rates compared to similar newspapers that face less competition. To explain his results, Chandra subsequently shows that newspapers in more competitive markets are better able to segment readers according to their location and demographics, thereby catering to a more homogeneous "targeted" audience that is appreciated by advertisers.

Given that magazines are highly segmented across reader characteristics (one can think of fashion magazines where it is sometimes hard to distinguish between advertisements and content), and therefore almost arbitrarily targetable, it can be argued that magazine readers may be more likely to appreciate advertisements than newspaper readers since newspapers are targeted to a lesser extent and instead cater to a geographically segmented audience. At the same time, it may be the case that advertisements are more easily skipped in newspapers, precisely because it can be difficult to distinguish ads from content in magazines. However, studies that deal systematically with such differences do not currently exist.

9.6. ANTITRUST ISSUES IN NEWSPAPERS AND MAGAZINES

Issues related to antitrust and market power in print media deserve a special discussion. As this section will show, numerous authors have noted that the antitrust economics of media, and of two-sided markets in general, have unexpected or counter-intuitive features. Evans (2002) points out that, in two-sided industries, an analysis of market definition and market power that focuses on a single side will be misleading. As Rysman (2009) notes, two-sided markets generally exhibit network effects and are therefore liable to tip toward a single dominant platform, which makes these markets of interest to competition authorities.

In addition, the common feature exhibited by media, such as newspapers, of setting price below marginal cost on one side of the market can lead to surprising policy prescriptions with regard to mergers and market concentration. As with other two-sided industries, mergers in these markets can theoretically raise prices, for both sets of consumers (Evans and Schmalensee, 2012). This section provides an overview of research concerning market power and mergers in print media. We direct the reader to X-FKS on media mergers for a more general treatment. We will also discuss two antitrust-related topics that are of special interest in the newspaper industry: joint operating agreements and vertical price restrictions.

The first issue we discuss is estimating market power in the newspaper industry. Argentesi and Filistrucchi (2007), briefly discussed in Section 9.3, estimate a structural model of newspaper demand by both sets of newspaper consumers. Their goal is to examine whether the observed pattern of prices in the Italian newspaper industry is consistent with competitive behavior rather than with coordinated behavior, and they analyze this issue separately for each side of the market while taking into account the two-sided nature of the newspaper industry. As they point out, a naïve examination of price elasticities on one side of the market does not necessarily imply anything about the degree of market power that firms enjoy. The authors specify a nested logit model of demand on the subscriber side and a simple logit model on the advertiser side, for the four main national newspapers in Italy. Two points are worth noting: first, they assume that readers are neutral toward advertising and, second, they assume single-homing on both sides of the market. While this assumption may be reasonable for readers, it is a definite simplification on the advertiser side, but is driven by data limitations. Finally, the authors specify the supply side by modeling newspaper publishers as setting both prices simultaneously.

Argentesi and Filistrucchi estimate the implied markups that publishers would set under four different scenarios, which correspond to competition or collusion on each side of the market. They then compare these implied markups with estimates of the actual markups that publishers set, based on data on newspapers' revenues and costs. They conclude that the data are most likely to be consistent with competition on the advertising side but collusion on the subscription side.

9.6.1 Mergers

Ownership consolidation and mergers are a particularly important topic in newspaper markets. As with any industry, consolidation leads to concerns about higher prices, and this is especially the case in a market such as the US newspaper industry, which already tends toward local monopolies. But the newspaper industry also raises concerns about the diversity of opinion, and as a result this matter is particularly controversial. Anderson and McLaren (2012) state: "The controversy is both political and economic: even if a media merger increases profit, it affects how well informed is the public and hence political outcomes. This means that traditional IO merger analysis is inadequate for media mergers, and until recently policy debates have been dominated by non-economists."

Nevertheless, in recent years there have been a number of studies that examine the issue of newspaper mergers, both from the traditional Industrial Organization perspective of prices, and from the issue of diversity of opinion. George (2007) studies the effect of ownership consolidation on the variety of topics covered by US daily newspapers. As multi-product firms internalize business-stealing externalities, she points out that mergers can lead owners to eliminate duplicative products and change the content of others.

She measures the variety of topics covered by newspapers using Burelle's Media Directory, which provides data on the titles of newspaper staff. She examines the period from 1993 to 2001, which saw a large number of newspaper acquisitions. Her results show that a reduction in the number of newspaper owners in a market leads to an increase in the degree of separation among the existing newspapers. Moreover, the aggregate number of topics covered per market increases with ownership consolidation. Thus, there is support for the notion that consolidation may actually benefit consumers by increasing the variety of topics covered by daily newspapers. George also finds that the increased ownership concentration did not reduce newspaper readership.

Chandra and Collard-Wexler (2009) also examine the issue of ownership consolidation in newspapers. Their study focuses on the price effects of mergers among Canadian newspapers, in contrast to the focus on content in George (2007). They first develop a Hotelling model of newspaper competition for readers and advertisers which shows that joint ownership of newspapers has no clear effect on prices for either subscribers or advertisers. A key feature of their model is that advertisers value not just the number of readers at a given newspaper, but also their characteristics. Given heterogeneity in reader characteristics, it is possible that in a duopoly equilibrium some readers provide a negative value to the newspaper publishers. These readers are the least desirable from the point of view of advertisers, yet continue to enjoy the per-reader subsidy that newspapers implicitly provide by setting price below marginal cost on the subscription side. Thus, duopoly newspaper firms may end up setting higher prices in equilibrium, in order to try to screen out these undesirable readers. However, under joint ownership of these newspapers, prices will fall because the monopolist will internalize the effect of high prices on both newspapers, in an analog of the traditional Hotelling model where joint ownership raises prices since the marginal consumer provides positive value to firms. They also show that advertising prices will move in the same direction as subscription prices, i.e., the effect on advertising prices is ambiguous as well.

Chandra and Collard-Wexler then empirically examine the price effects of ownership consolidation, relying on a series of newspaper mergers in Canada in the late 1990s, when about 75% of Canada's daily newspapers changed hands. They find that ownership consolidation had no discernible effect on either circulation or advertising prices.

Fan (2013) develops a structural model of the newspaper industry to analyze the welfare consequences of newspaper mergers. Her paper accounts not just for post-merger price changes, but also for newspapers adjusting their product characteristics. In addition, she generalizes the model of demand for newspapers by allowing households to purchase at most two daily newspapers, in contrast to most previous work, which assumed single-homing on the subscription side. She uses county-level circulation data on US newspapers between 1997 and 2005.

Fan uses the structural estimates to perform counterfactual simulations. In particular, she examines a proposed merger in the Minneapolis market that was blocked by the

Department of Justice. She shows that an analysis of reader surplus that only focuses on price effects, and ignores changes to newspaper quality, understates the loss in consumer welfare. Both newspapers will raise prices post-merger, but Fan's analysis of endogenous product characteristics shows that they will also reduce product quality, which then further reduces circulation and reader welfare. Advertiser welfare also falls by more when product characteristics are endogenized. Not surprisingly, the surplus captured by newspaper publishers is higher when they are permitted to adjust newspaper quality. In addition, Fan also simulates the effects of newspaper mergers in all US markets with two or three daily newspapers, obtaining results similar to the specific case of the Minneapolis market.

Filistrucchi et al. (2012) examine a hypothetical merger in the Dutch newspaper industry. They point out that in a number of recent newspaper mergers, competition authorities in various European jurisdictions have analyzed either a single side of the market, or each of the two sides separately, instead of incorporating the feedback between the two sides. On the subscription side, Filistrucchi et al. model consumer demand as a differentiated products discrete-choice problem. On the advertising side, similar to Rysman (2004) and other prior studies, the authors assume that the decision to advertise in any given newspaper is separable from advertising decisions at other publications. They model the quantity of advertising demanded at each newspaper as a function of the advertising price per reader, acknowledging that this variable is endogenous. As an instrument, they use the number of content pages in the newspaper, reasoning that content affects total subscriptions, and hence the advertising price per reader, but should not otherwise affect advertising demand.

They use a method laid out in a companion paper, and recover estimates of newspaper publishers' marginal costs. Somewhat surprisingly, their results suggest that newspaper publishers make positive margins on the readership side, and in fact higher margins than on the advertising side. Their results suggest that readers attach a positive value to newspaper advertising. Their main contribution comes from the analysis of a hypothetical merger in the Dutch newspaper market. Their results suggest that such a merger would not directly affect advertising prices. However, it would raise subscription prices, and the resulting loss of subscribers would reduce advertising demand and would also raise advertising prices per reader; nevertheless, the estimated effects are small.

9.6.2 Newspaper Joint Operating Agreements

A unique feature of newspaper markets in the United States is the JOA. As discussed in Section 9.1, this is a consequence of the Newspaper Preservation Act of 1970, which endeavored to preserve the diversity of newspaper voices. Romeo et al. (2003) explain the rationale behind the JOA:

"Under the protected JOA arrangement, two previously competing papers maintain separate news gathering, news reporting, and other editorial functions while combining their advertising and circulation functions: a single entity sells subscriptions to both papers and sells advertising in both papers."

Gentzkow et al. (2012) point out that newspaper JOAs are one of three instruments that policymakers have employed to increase ideological diversity, the other two being limits on joint ownership, and explicit subsidies.

Thus, JOAs are intended to permit a diversity of opinion and news in markets that would otherwise only be able to sustain a single newspaper, and publishers are given a special exemption from antitrust laws to allow them to combine their advertising and circulation operations.

What are the welfare effects of this policy? Current research on this issue is divided. Gentzkow et al. (2012) argue that allowing newspapers to form JOAs leads to a rise in both economic surplus as well as diversity. They show that allowing newspapers to collude on circulation prices alone leads to inefficient outcomes because the rise in newspaper profits does not offset the loss of surplus to consumers and advertisers, and also reduces the share of households who read diverse papers. By contrast, allowing papers to collude on advertising prices increases both economic welfare and diversity. This is because, in this situation, publishers slash circulation prices in order to increase readership and thereby profit in the advertising market in which they now have substantially greater market power. Even though publishers now have an incentive to differentiate from competitors, the effect is weak, and many more households end up reading diverse papers. In a JOA, where publishers coordinate prices on both sides of the market, the advertising effect dominates.

Antonielli and Filistrucchi (2012), by contrast, question the rationale for JOAs. Similar to Gabszewicz et al. (2001, 2002), they allow publishers to first choose their political position and then advertising and circulation prices. They analyze two forms of newspaper collusion: In the first, newspapers are allowed to jointly set prices on both sides of the market and also cooperate on their editorial lines. In the second, they can cooperate on prices but not on political position, which is exactly the situation with JOAs. The authors find that editorial lines converge much more in the latter situation, using reasoning similar to George (2007). Antonielli and Filistrucchi conclude, therefore, that the logic of JOAs is self-defeating. A possible explanation of their result is that they model newspaper readers as single-homers. By contrast, Gentzkow et al. (2012) argue that the multihoming of readers is a critical component in their finding that newspaper JOAs raise overall welfare.

Romeo et al. (2003) focus exclusively on the advertising side of the market in their examination of the economic consequences of JOAs. They point out that, since JOAs are intended to allow once competing newspapers to combine their advertising operations, the effect should normally be to raise advertising prices to monopoly levels. However, they reason that, since newspapers in the JOA still need to publish separate editions and maintain the look and feel of a newspaper in each of its editions, the actual consequence may be that the two newspapers carry more advertising than a monopolist would. Moreover, since JOAs eventually end at some point, the assets of both newspapers will eventually be available for sale. Rather than force the weaker of two newspapers in a JOA to disappear, it may be rational to have it remain a viable publication, in the hopes that a future investor will acquire it, and this also requires that this newspaper carry sufficient advertising. They estimate models of advertising rates for newspapers in 30 large cities during 1989–1999. They find evidence that JOAs act as constrained, rather than unconstrained, monopolists while setting ad rates. Thus they conclude: "The loss of economic competition inherent in the formation of a JOA may not have as serious a welfare effect as is sometimes assumed."

Bucklin et al. (1989) predict in their study of newspaper predation (discussed in Section 9.2) that the monopolies in US central-city newspaper markets are inevitable. They conclude, therefore: "little can be said against joint operating agreements that preserve an independent editorial voice even if they do not preserve competition in advertising." By contrast, Noam (2009) argues that JOAs have largely failed due to their focus on the wrong side of the market; he argues that newspapers have far greater economies of scale in newsgathering, and on the content side more generally, than on the advertising side.

9.6.3 Vertical Price Restrictions

Issues concerning resale price maintenance occur periodically in the newspaper industry. Readers with an interest in antitrust economics will recall the case of *Albrecht* vs. *The Herald Co.*, decided in 1968 by the US Supreme Court. The Herald Co. was a newspaper firm owning a number of periodicals including the *Globe Democrat*, published daily in St. Louis. The company hired carriers to deliver newspapers to subscribers, giving these carriers exclusive territories. The *Globe Democrat* printed its suggested retail price on the cover.[11]

One of the carriers hired by the *Globe* was Albrecht, which exploited its monopoly carrier status among the 1200 subscribers in its territory, to charge a higher cover price than the one suggested by the newspaper. The two firms ended up in court, and eventually the Supreme Court found in favor of Albrecht, ruling that the Herald's efforts to force a specific retail price amounted to price fixing in violation of the Sherman Act.

As economists would recognize, this situation was an excellent example of the double marginalization problem and there are strong arguments to support the Herald company's position. Indeed the Supreme Court reversed its stand on the issue in a 1997 court case.

---

[11] The material in this description is drawn from Albrecht v. The Herald Co., 390 U.S. 150 (1968), and summarized in Pepall et al. (2005).

Rosse (1980b) provides a vivid description of how restrictions against resale price maintenance are particularly harmful in the newspaper industry, showing how the usual efficiency concerns are magnified due to the advertising side of the industry being affected as well. More recently, Flath (2012) documents an interesting case of newspaper resale price maintenance in Japan. He shows that the vertical restrictions in this industry actually lead to a *floor* on prices, rather than a ceiling, and argues that this supports collusive behavior by newspapers.

9.6.4 Cross-Ownership of Newspapers and Other Media

In 1975, the FCC implemented a ban on newspapers owning either radio or television stations in the same market, with some exceptions for those media firms that already engaged in such cross-ownership. The rationale for the ban was to prevent a single media company from dominating the communication of news and information, and to ensure a diversity of opinions.

Ferguson (1983) investigated some of the consequences of this regulation. He finds that when a daily newspaper owns either a radio or television station in the same local market, it tends to increase the newspaper's circulation. In the case of a newspaper owning a television station, it also reduces advertising rates in the newspaper.

The FCC in 2007 voted to modestly relax its 1975 ban on cross-ownership, a move that was seen to be helping the ailing newspaper industry (FCC, 2010). See Chapter 8 for a discussion of how this relates to the radio industry.

9.7. PRINT MEDIA AND THE INTERNET

Publishers, and media firms more generally, have traditionally been wary of the rise of new media or new media outlets. British publishers feared that readers would substitute from buying newspapers to reading them in public libraries, radio broadcasting stations were afraid of competition from TV and, nowadays, publishers feel the threat from online media.

So far, the majority of research in this area has concerned itself with the potential for self-cannibalization, i.e., with the question of what launching a companion website does to the demand of the print version. In 2005, the *New York Times* cited an analyst at J.P. Morgan who claimed that "Newspapers are cannibalizing themselves."[12] Germany's leading news magazine, *Der Spiegel*, published a skeptical article about the future of print media, ironically on its own companion website, with the suggestive title "Too much to die, too little to survive." These fears trace back to the earlier days of the Internet. A Vice President of the media consultancy Jupiter Media Metrix is reported to have said: "Seize

---

[12] Seelye, K.Q. "Can papers end the free ride online?," The *New York Times*, March 14, 2005.

the day! Either you are going to cannibalize yourself or somebody else is going to cannibalize you" Hickey (1997, p. 38).

At least in the beginning, companion websites tended to contain "shovelware"—content that had been directly copied from the print version to the online edition. The threat of the Internet therefore appeared to be quite imminent. It had, however, also been recognized that online companions entail the possibility of providing a bundle of goods rather than a single product, the print edition and additional complementary information on the online companion. Kaiser and Kongsted (2012) describe three main ways in which the online companion may influence print demand: (i) "awareness," (ii) online subscription, and (iii) additional service. Online companions generate awareness by offering a preview of the contents of the print edition or views of current and past articles. Consumers may thus sample the print edition, thereby raising print demand, an issue that has been theoretically studied by Peitz and Waelbroeck (2004) as well as by Halbheer et al. (2014), and empirically studied by Oberholzer-Gee and Strumpf (2007) for music downloads.

Similarly, print and online audiences may differ in their audience characteristics, which implies that online companions may reach out to an audience different from that of the print version (Joukhadar, 2004; Nicholson, 2001). Online companions also offer online subscriptions, a feature that has been found to be important for the publishing industry (Barsh et al., 2001; Capell, 2004). Most importantly perhaps is that online companions allow publishers to post complementary information. Studies by Barsh et al. (1999) and Silk et al. (2001) identify the relative positioning of the online companion compared to the print version as a key determinant of self-cannibalization. This relative positioning argument has been emphasized by econometric work by Deleersnyder et al. (2002), Pauwels and Dans (2001) as well as Simon and Kadiyali (2007). If the companion websites are just shovelware, substitution is more likely. By contrast, if the companion website offers additional service, it might well complement the print edition. Complementarity may be more likely for magazines than for newspapers since a magazine's online companion allows magazines to post current news, thereby enabling magazines to overcome the disadvantage of infrequent periodicity.

To analyze whether the online companion is a substitute or complement to the print version, and since traditional models of differentiated product demand only allow products to be substitutes, Gentzkow (2007) develops a more general structural approach where products can be either complements or substitutes and derives a novel identification strategy that is based on one good being free of charge, the online companion, while the other, the print version, is not. He uses consumer survey data on two regionally competing newspapers, the *Washington Post* and the *Washington Times*, to find that online companions and print versions are substitutes and that this result is not driven by unobserved consumer heterogeneity.

Other papers that use structural demand models to gauge the effects of online companion on print version sales include Filistrucchi (2005) and Kaiser (2006). Both papers assume that the launch of a website is uncorrelated with the respective print medium's unobserved characteristics and they also both use nested logit-type demand models for circulation. Filistrucchi (2005) studies Italian national newspapers' launch of companion websites and shows that print demand statistically and economically decreases once an online outlet channel is introduced. Kaiser (2006) also estimates overall negative effects but shows that these vary substantially across different consumer age groups and across time. He claims that time may have mattered since publishers may have become better at positioning the online companion.

George (2008) also underscores the importance of readership characteristics in the relationship between the Internet and the demand for US newspapers. She estimates reduced-form equations for local Internet penetration and per-capita local newspaper circulation. Like George (2008) and Gentzkow (2007), Hong (2007) also uses consumer survey data to estimate the effect of the Internet on media demand. His dependent variable is household expenditures for different types of entertainment goods, among others newspapers and magazines. He estimates reduced-form equations and tries to identify causal effects by running difference-in-difference regressions, treating general growth in Internet penetration as exogenous.

Another strand of the literature uses time-series variation to explore the mapping between online and offline media. In earlier work, Deleersnyder et al. (2002) test for structural breaks (the introduction of the companion website) in monthly circulation time series of British and Dutch newspapers, observed between 1990 and 2001. They find that few newspapers experience a drop in circulation and advertising demand due to the existence of a companion website. The effects are, however, disperse across newspapers and economically fairly small. More recently, Kaiser and Kongsted (2012) run Granger causality tests on German magazine data. They find that online companion page visits decrease total sales. This result is driven by a decrease in kiosk sales, which is not compensated by an increase in subscriptions. Like Kaiser (2006), they show that the relationship between the online companion and the printed magazine depends on reader characteristics.

Cho et al. (2014) use a cross-country data set to study how Internet adoption affects print newspaper circulation and the survival of newspaper firms. Their data covers over 90 countries for the years 2000–2009, which encompasses the most rapid period of Internet adoption, but unfortunately ends just before the dramatic slowdown in newspaper circulation following the financial crisis. Cho et al. show that Internet adoption directly contributes to newspaper shutdowns in a number of countries, although the Internet appears to have little effect on the net circulation of those firms that survive.

While existing research has primarily concerned itself with the effect of the Internet on print demand, less is known about the reverse effect, which seems surprising given the rapid gain in the importance of online advertising. Kaiser and Kongsted (2012) do not find any evidence that print circulation affects page visits, which contrasts with an earlier study of a panel of 12 Spanish newspapers by Pauwels and Dans (2001), which finds evidence that print circulation increases website visits.

Economic research has recently started to become more interested in the effect the Internet has on advertising demand and ad rates for print media.[13] Zentner (2012) uses data on 87 countries for 11 years to document a negative relationship between Internet penetration and advertising spending in traditional media for newspapers, magazines, and TV. Chandra and Kaiser (2014) study the effect that online companions and Internet use by readers has on the value of targeted advertising for German consumer magazines. They find a complementarity between the offline and online channels: the value of targeting homogeneous consumer groups increases both with the Internet use of readers and with the existence of a companion website. They hypothesize that this result is driven by multi-homing consumers who enhance the value of targeted advertising. While they do find evidence that online channels increase the value of targeting, they also show that the overall effect of online companions and Internet use by readers on advertising rates is negative.

One fundamental problem inherent in almost all of the empirical studies of offline/online competition (or complementarity) is identification. Most studies assume the launch of a companion website to be an exogenous event (Filistrucchi, 2005; Gentzkow, 2007; George, 2008; Kaiser, 2006; Kaiser and Kongsted, 2012), which clearly is questionable. The literature has so far been lacking good natural or quasi-experiments such as the one used by Goldfarb and Tucker (2011), who use an advertising ban to tease out causal effects, or denial of service attacks as used by Goldfarb (2006), who asks whether consumers return to online channels after such an attack.

Another relevant issue from a managerial point of view is the setting up of paywalls for access to online content. US websites used to be hesitant to charge access fees in order to generate visits and thus to sell online advertising (Barsh et al., 2001; Deleersnyder et al., 2002). There has, however, been a tendency toward charging, but results had not been encouraging until recently (Hickey, 1997; Robins, 2001). In 2011, the *New York Times*, however, re-opened a paywall for its online content and several other international quality newspapers followed suit.[14] Chiou and Tucker (2013) provide descriptive evidence for the effects of paywall introduction on website visits using data from an experiment conducted by a publisher, differentiating their findings by reader demographics. Studies that also look into the effect of paywalls on offline reader demand as well as on advertising are lacking so far.

Print media markets have hitherto been considered as a prototypical two-sided market. Given the growing importance of online companions for both readers and advertisers, future research may want to concern itself with the resulting four-sided market and the implication that such an interrelationship has on pricing structures.

---

[13] Lambert and Pregibon (2008), Joo et al. (2012), and Goldfarb and Tucker (2011) study the relationship between offline and online advertising for media markets other than print.

[14] McAthy, R. "Two years in: Reflections on the New York Times Paywall," journalism.co.uk, 2013.

News aggregators that consolidate information from different websites into a single newsfeed of information have only recently become the subject of empirical research. Using a data set that tracks users' browsing behavior, Athey and Mobius (2012) show that a user's adoption of the Google News localization feature is associated with an increase in local news consumption. George and Hogendorn (2012) use very similar data to demonstrate that the adoption of geo-targeted news reduces the access cost of local news but does not seem to have economically significant effects on local publishers. In a similar context, George and Peukert (2013) use data on monthly local and non-local visits to news outlets online to demonstrate a positive mapping between group population size in local markets and the consumption of national media over the Internet. In addition, aggregated news and news collected from social media sources—so-called "robot journalism"—may substitute possibly censored or biased traditional media as in the context of the Arab Spring of 2010/2011, an issue that has not been systematically studied so far.

Finally, one may argue that the threat of online cannibalization is more imminent for newspapers than for magazines since the latter cover longer in-depth articles while the former feature current news, which can also be called up on the Internet. Indeed, studies that analyze newspapers tend to find negative effects of online companions on sales (Filistrucchi, 2005; George, 2008), while there is more heterogeneity in the results for magazines (Deleersnyder et al., 2002; Kaiser, 2006; Kaiser and Kongsted, 2012; Simon and Kadiyali, 2007). A systematic analysis of potential differences is yet to be compiled, however.

9.8. THOUGHTS FOR FUTURE RESEARCH AND CONCLUSIONS

Throughout this chapter we have highlighted areas where further research would be valuable. We now summarize some of these open research questions, and then offer our thoughts on the future of print media.

Most of the fertile research areas for economists interested in newspapers and magazines lie in how these media tackle the advent of the Internet. A basic problem in studies of the competition between online and offline channels is identification. Previous studies have generally assumed that the launch of an online edition is exogenous, which is clearly less than ideal. A useful study would carefully estimate the causal effect of a newspaper or magazine's online edition on the sales and advertising revenues of the print edition. In a similar vein, studies that examine the effect of online paywalls on offline reader demand as well as on advertising are lacking so far, as are studies of news aggregators and robot journalism.

On this note, we ask whether existing models of two-sided markets will be sufficient to analyze the media properties of the future, which are likely to have hybrid structures with significant numbers of both online and offline readers; indeed, there already exist examples such as the *New York Times*, which now enjoys significant revenues from both digital and print audiences, as well as from advertisers in both forms, but must grapple with cannibalization and optimal pricing. Empirical researchers may have to devise four-sided models of media, and also wrestle with issues of multi-homing which are often intractable.

We have discussed a large literature on whether readers of print media view advertising positively or negatively, but the empirical results are frustratingly inconclusive. It is surprising that the answer to this question is not yet known, given that economists have acknowledged the importance of feedback effects in two-sided markets; positive or negative feedback effects from advertising have radically different predictions for optimal pricing in media markets. We previously alluded to the possibility that readers may view advertisements differently in newspapers versus magazines, given that the latter targets readers by content instead of geography and is therefore perhaps more likely to have readers that derive a positive value from reading advertisements relative to them. Research in this area would be an important addition to the literature.

Industry observers have long pointed out that online advertising revenues are tiny compared with revenues in print media, even when normalized by the number of readers. This appears to be a puzzle, although some explanations have been offered. Chief among them are that online readers spend less time on a news website than they do with a printed paper, and that switching costs online are extremely low. Moreover, a large portion of the surplus in online advertising may be appropriated by firms that provide the technology to track readers across websites, or by Google, which enjoys immense market power in the online advertising market. Nevertheless, there has not yet been any systematic academic study of this issue. Research into this area will be of enormous importance, given that many newspapers are now pinning their hopes of survival on generating a large and loyal online readership, but this may be futile if advertising revenues remain low.

Research has long established that newspapers are an important driver of voter turnout and civic participation, as we discussed in Section 9.2. Moreover, Gentzkow (2006) showed that voting declined as newspapers were supplanted by television, since the latter did not have the same effect on galvanizing citizens to participate in the electoral process. An important question, therefore, is whether the same will be true with the Internet as readers consume online content. One recent paper suggesting that this may be indeed the case is Falck et al. (2014).

Within the realm of traditional print media, two questions stand out to us. First, there is little research on free print newspapers, perhaps because the lack of sales data makes credible circulation figures difficult to obtain. Nevertheless, such newspapers are extremely important in a number of large cities, particularly among users of public transportation who are excellent captive audiences for advertisers. Moreover, the economics of free print newspapers is similar to that of online media that do not impose a paywall, which applies to a large number of news sources. Understanding the impact of free newspapers on market structure, and examining whether the advertising market plays out differently in such media, is of direct economic interest and also provides a useful benchmark with which to predict the evolution of online news competition.

Throughout this chapter, we have focused on the US newspaper industry, with a few exceptions to cover print media in countries such as Canada, the UK, and Germany. As we have emphasized, this is because the existing literature is so heavily focused on the US—perhaps a common problem in Industrial Organization. Nevertheless, there is huge potential for research into the media industries in other parts of the world, particularly in developing countries where newspapers continue to thrive. Rising incomes and education levels have led to a flourishing newspaper market in countries such as India. A fruitful area of research would be a comparative analysis of print media across countries, a short example of which we provided in Table 9.1. To our knowledge, Zentner (2012) and Cho et al. (2014) are among the only studies along these lines. Such a comparative analysis is often useful for identifying interesting phenomena in certain countries, such as the remarkable circulation figures in Japan that we described in Section 9.3.1. In general, the decline of newspaper markets in North America should lead to a natural interest in how this industry operates in other countries, where similar declines are not yet apparent.

We now offer some brief concluding thoughts on this industry. Newspapers and magazines are easily the oldest of the major media that exist today. Print media have created enormous value since their inception, even as they have evolved considerably from their early days. Policymakers have long recognized that newspapers have a unique role in the civic discourse of a country, and have important consequences for informing the citizenry, encouraging electoral participation and providing a check on powerful forces in government and business.

Yet, today, print media are struggling. Newspapers, in particular, have faced devastating losses over the past two decades, even as magazines retain a stable position for now. Given long-term trends, both in the sales of print media and in the advent of digital media, it is hard to see how long printed newspapers will continue to exist, with the exception of certain well-established brands.

It is possible, though by no means assured, that newspapers and magazines will transition to digital editions, and continue operating in a new physical form for the foreseeable future. Indeed, for a number of periodicals, the online edition now provides the only positive note, being one of the few areas on which readers and revenues steadily increase. After faltering in the early years, a number of newspapers have now launched sophisticated paywalls in conjunction with well-executed digital strategies, that actually have readers willing to pay for content. And in fact, the advent of the Internet has clearly helped some newspapers—well-known media names such as the *Wall Street Journal*, the *New York Times*, and the *Daily Mail* have secured commanding positions in the flow of online news, and as voices of authority in the online mélange of blogs, news aggregators and social media.

At the same time, the simple fact is that online advertising revenues are only a fraction of what the print equivalent used to be. Even the surviving news outlets operate with ever-shrinking budgets and staffs, and occasionally have to sacrifice news bureaus in major cities, or the luxury of investigative journalism. Therefore, as we have mentioned earlier, it remains to be seen whether online newspapers can continue to command the same respect and reputation for providing balanced, reasoned, and well-researched reporting that their print counterparts once did.

ACKNOWLEDGMENTS

We thank Simon Anderson, Matthew Shi, and Joel Waldfogel for very helpful comments, Teemu Henriksson and David Flath for generously sharing data, and Christian Peukert for a thorough reading of the draft and for additional suggestions.

REFERENCES

Ambrus, A., Reisinger, M., 2005. Platform Competition and Welfare: Media Markets Reconsidered. Mimeo.
Ambrus, A., Calvano, E., Reisinger, M., 2012. Either or Both Competition: A "Two-Sided" Theory of Advertising with Overlapping Viewerships. Working Paper, University of Chicago.
Anderson, S.P., 2005. Localism and Welfare. Mimeo.
Anderson, S.P., Coate, S., 2005. Market provision of broadcasting: a welfare analysis. Rev. Econ. Stud. 72 (4), 947–972.
Anderson, S.P., McLaren, J., 2012. Media mergers and media bias with rational consumers. J. Eur. Econ. Assoc. 10 (4), 831–859.
Antonielli, M., Filistrucchi, L., 2012. Collusion and the Political Differentiation of Newspapers. TILEC Discussion Paper No. 2012-014, Tilburg University.
Argentesi, E., Filistrucchi, L., 2007. Estimating market power in a two-sided market: the case of newspapers. J. Appl. Econ. 22, 1247–1266.
Armstrong, M., 2006. Competition in two-sided markets. RAND J. Econ. 37 (3), 668–691.
Asplund, M., Eriksson, R., Strand, N., 2005. Prices, margins and liquidity constraints: Swedish newspapers, 1990–1992. Economica 72 (286), 349–359.
Asplund, M., Eriksson, R., Strand, N., 2008. Price discrimination in oligopoly: evidence from regional newspapers. J. Ind. Econ. 56 (2), 333–346.
Athey, S., Mobius, M., 2012. The Impact of News Aggregators on Internet News Consumption: The Case of Localization. Working Paper.
Athey, S., Calvano, E., Gans, J.S., 2011. The Impact of the Internet on Advertising Markets for News Media. Working Paper, Harvard University.
Baldasty, G.J., 1992. The Commercialization of News in the Nineteenth Century. University of Wisconsin Press, Madison, WI.
Barsh, J., Lee, G., Miles, A., 1999. Beyond print: a future for magazines. McKinsey Q. 3, 122–130.
Barsh, J., Kramer, E., Maue, D., Zuckerman, N., 2001. Magazines' home companion. McKinsey Q. 2, 83–91.
Berry, S., Waldfogel, J., 2010. Product quality and market size. J. Ind. Econ. 58 (1), 1–31.
Blair, R.D., Romano, R.E., 1993. Pricing decisions of the newspaper monopolist. South. Econ. J. 59 (4), 721–732.

Blondheim, M., 1994. News over the Wires: The Telegraph and the Flow of Public Information in America 1844-1897. Harvard University Press, Cambridge.

Bucklin, R.E., Caves, R.E., Lo, A.W., 1989. Games of survival in the US newspaper industry. Appl. Econ. 21 (5), 631–649.

Capell, D., 2004. Circulation at the crossroads. Circ. Manag. 19 (9), 30–34.

Cecchetti, S.G., 1986. The frequency of price adjustment: a study of the newsstand prices of magazines. J. Econ. 31 (3), 255–274.

Central Intelligence Agency, 2013. The World Factbook 2013-14. Washington, DC. https://www.cia.gov/library/publications/the-world-factbook/index.html.

Chamberlin, E.H., 1960. The Theory of Monopolistic Competition. Harvard University Press, Cambridge, MA.

Chandra, A., 2009. Targeted advertising: the role of subscriber characteristics in advertising markets. J. Ind. Econ. 57 (1), 58–84.

Chandra, A., Collard-Wexler, A., 2009. Mergers in two-sided markets: an application to the Canadian newspaper industry. J. Econ. Manag. Strateg. 18 (4), 1045–1070.

Chandra, A., Kaiser, U., 2014. Targeted advertising in magazine markets and the advent of the Internet. Manag. Sci. 60 (7), 1829–1843.

Chaudhri, V., 1998. Pricing and efficiency of a circulation industry: the case of newspapers. Inf. Econ. Policy 10 (1), 59–76.

Chiang, C.-F., Knight, B., 2011. Media bias and influence: evidence from newspaper endorsements. Rev. Econ. Stud. 78, 795–820.

Chiou, L., Tucker, C., 2013. Paywalls and the demand for news. Inf. Econ. Policy 25, 61–69.

Cho, D., Smith, M., Zentner, A., 2014. Internet Adoption and the Survival of Print Newspapers: A Country-Level Examination. Working Paper, University of Texas.

Choi, J.P., 2006. Broadcast competition and advertising with free entry: Subscription vs. free-to-air. Inf. Econ. Policy 18, 181–196.

Corden, W.M., 1952–1953. The maximisation of profit by a newspaper firm. Rev. Econ. Stud. 20 (3), 181–190.

De Tocqueville, A., 2004. Democracy in America (Vol. 147). Digireads.com.

Deleersnyder, B., Geyskens, I., Gielens, K., Dekimpe, M., 2002. How cannibalistic is the Internet channel? A study of the newspaper industry in the United Kingdom and the Netherlands. Int. J. Res. Mark. 19, 337–348.

Depken, C.A., 2004. Audience characteristics and the price of advertising in a circulation industry: evidence from US magazines. Inf. Econ. Policy 16, 179–196.

Depken, C.A., Wilson, D.P., 2004. Is advertising a good or bad? Evidence from U.S. magazine subscriptions. J. Bus. 77 (2), S61–S80.

Dertouzos, J.N., Trautman, W.B., 1990. Economic effects of media concentration: estimates from a model of the newspaper firm. J. Ind. Econ. 39 (1), 1–14.

Editor & Publisher, 2012. International Year Book. Editor & Publisher, New York, NY.

Evans, D.S., 2002. The Antitrust Economics of Two-Sided Markets. Mimeo.

Evans, D., Schmalensee, R., 2012. The antitrust analysis of multi-sided platform businesses. In: Blair, R.D., Sokol, D.D. (Eds.), In: Oxford Handbook on International Antitrust Economics, vol. 1. Oxford University Press, Oxford.

Falck, O., Heblich, S., Gold, R., 2014. E-lections: voting behavior and the Internet. Am. Econ. Rev. 104 (7), 2238–2265.

Fan, Y., 2013. Ownership consolidation and product characteristics: a study of the US daily newspaper market. Am. Econ. Rev. 103 (5), 1598–1628.

Federal Communications Commission, 2010. FCC Consumer Facts: FCC's Review of the Broadcast Ownership Rules. Federal Communications Commission, Washington, DC.

Federal Communications Commission, 2011. The Information Needs of Communities. Federal Communications Commission, Washington, DC.

Ferguson, J.M., 1983. Daily newspaper advertising rates, local media cross-ownership. J. Law Econ. 26 (3), 635–654.

Ferrari, S., Verboven, F., 2012. Vertical control of a distribution network—an empirical analysis of magazines. RAND J. Econ. 43 (1), 26–50.

Filistrucchi, L., 2005. The Impact of Internet on the Market for Daily Newspapers in Italy. EUI Working Paper 12/2005.

Filistrucchi, L., Klein, T.J., Michielsen, T., 2012. Assessing unilateral effects in a two-sided market: an application to the Dutch daily newspaper market. J. Compet. Law Econ. 8 (2), 297–329.

Flath, D., 2012. Japanese Newspapers. Working Paper, Osaka University.

Fu, W.W., 2003. Multimarket contact of US newspaper chains: circulation competition and market coordination. Inf. Econ. Policy 15 (4), 501–519.

Gabszewicz, J.J., Laussel, D., Sonnac, S., 2001. Press advertising and the ascent of the 'Pensée Unique'. Eur. Econ. Rev. 45, 641–645.

Gabszewicz, J.J., Laussel, D., Sonnac, N., 2004. Programming and advertising competition in the broadcasting industry. J. Econ. Manag. Strateg. 13 (4), 657–669.

Gabszewicz, J.J., Garella, P.G., Sonnac, N., 2007. Newspapers' market shares and the theory of the circulation spiral. Inf. Econ. Policy 19, 405–413.

Genesove, D., 1999. The Adoption of Offset Presses in the Daily Newspaper Industry in the United States. Working Paper 7076, National Bureau of Economic Research.

Gentzkow, M., 2006. Television and voter turnout. Q. J. Econ. 121 (3), 931–972.

Gentzkow, M., 2007. Valuing new goods in a model with complementarity: online newspapers. Am. Econ. Rev. 97 (3), 713–744.

Gentzkow, M., Glaeser, E.L., Goldin, C., 2006. The rise of the fourth estate: how newspapers became informative and why it mattered. In: Glaeser, E.L., Goldin, C. (Eds.), Corruption and Reform: Lessons from America's Economic History. University of Chicago Press, Chicago.

Gentzkow, M., Shapiro, J.M., Sinkinson, M., 2011. The effect of newspaper entry and exit on electoral politics. Am. Econ. Rev. 101 (7), 2980–3018.

Gentzkow, M., Shapiro, J.M., Sinkinson, M., 2012. Competition and Ideological Diversity: Historical Evidence from US Newspapers. Working Paper, University of Chicago.

George, L.M., 2007. What's fit to print: the effect of ownership concentration on product variety in daily newspaper markets. Inf. Econ. Policy 19, 285–303.

George, L.M., 2008. The Internet and the market for daily newspapers. B. E. J. Econ. Anal. Policy 8 (1), 1–33.

George, L.M., Hogendorn, C., 2012. Aggregators, search and the economics of new media institutions. Inf. Econ. Policy 24 (1), 40–51.

George, L., Peukert, C., 2013. Social Networks and the Demand for News. Hunter College Mimeo.

George, L.M., Waldfogel, J., 2003. Who affects whom in daily newspaper markets? J. Polit. Econ. 111, 765–784.

George, L.M., Waldfogel, J., 2006. The New York Times and the market for local newspapers. Am. Econ. Rev. 96 (1), 435–447.

Goldfarb, A., 2006. The medium-term effects of unavailability. Quant. Mark. Econ. 4 (2), 143–171.

Goldfarb, A., Tucker, C.E., 2011. Advertising bans and the substitutability of online and offline advertising. J. Mark. Res. 48 (2), 207–227.

Häckner, J., Nyberg, S., 2008. Advertising and media market concentration. J. Med. Econ. 21 (2), 79–96.

Halbheer, D., Stahl, F., Koenigsberg, O., Lehmann, D.R., 2014. Choosing a digital content strategy: how much should be free? Int. J. Res. Mark. 31 (2), 192–206.

Hamilton, J., 2004. All the News That's Fit to Sell: How the Market Transforms Information into News. Princeton University Press, Princeton.

Hickey, N., 1997. Will Gates Crush Newspapers? Columbia Journalism Review November/December, 28–36.

Hong, S.-H., 2007. The recent growth of the Internet and changes in household-level demand for entertainment. Inf. Econ. Policy 19, 304–318.

Joo, M., Wilbur, K.C., Zhu, Y., 2012. Television Advertising and Online Search. Working Paper, Duke University Fuqua School of Business.

Joukhadar, K., 2004. The 8 challenges of digital publishing. Circ. Manag. 19 (9), 24–29.

Jullien, B., Haritchabalet, C., Crampes, C., 2009. Advertising, competition and entry in media industries. J. Ind. Econ. 57 (1), 7–31.

Kaiser, U., 2006. Magazines and their companion websites: competing outlet channels? Rev. Mark. Sci. 4 (3) Article 3.

Kaiser, U., Kongsted, H.C., 2012. Magazine "companion websites" and the demand for newsstand sales and subscriptions. J. Med. Econ. 25 (4), 184–197.

Kaiser, U., Song, M., 2009. Do media consumers really dislike advertising? An empirical assessment of the role of advertising in print media markets. Int. J. Ind. Organ. 27 (2), 292–301.

Kaiser, U., Wright, J., 2006. Price structure in two-sided markets: evidence from the magazine industry. Int. J. Ind. Organ. 24, 1–28.

Kind, H.J., Nilssen, T., Sørgard, L., 2003. Advertising on TV: Under- or Overprovision? Mimeo.

Kind, H.J., Nilssen, T., Sørgard, L., 2007. Competition for viewers and advertisers in a TV oligopoly. J. Med. Econ. 20 (3), 211–233.

Knotek, E.S., 2008. Convenient prices, currency, and nominal rigidity: theory with evidence from newspaper prices. J. Monet. Econ. 55 (7), 1303–1316.

Kohlschein, I., 2004. Economic Distortions Caused by Public Funding of Broadcasting in Europe. Mimeo.

Koschat, M.A., Putsis, W.A., 2000a. Who wants you when you're old and poor? Exploring the economics of media pricing. J. Med. Econ. 13 (4), 215–232.

Koschat, M.A., Putsis, W.A., 2000b. Audience characteristics and bundling: a hedonic analysis of magazine advertising rates. J. Mark. Res. 39 (2), 262–273.

Kremhelmer, S., Zenger, H., 2004. Advertising and the screening role of mass media. Inf. Econ. Policy 20 (2), 107–119.

Kroft, K., Pope, D., 2014. Does online search crowd-out traditional search and improve matching efficiency? Evidence from Craigslist. J. Lab. Econ. 32 (2), 259–303.

Lambert, D., Pregibon, D., 2008. Online effects of offine ads. In: Proceedings of the Second International Workshop on Data Mining and Audience Intelligence for Advertising, Las Vegas, Nevada.

Merrilees, W.J., 1983. Anatomy of a price leadership challenge: an evaluation of pricing strategies in the Australian newspaper industry. J. Ind. Econ. 31 (3), 291–311.

Mott, F.L., 1950. American Journalism: A History of Newspapers in the United States Through 260 Years: 1690 to 1950. Macmillan, London.

Nicholson, J., 2001. Cannibals on the web? Don't you believe it!. Editor Publisher 134 (18), 1–3.

Noam, E.M., 2009. Media Ownership and Concentration in America. Oxford University Press, New York.

Oberholzer-Gee, F., Strumpf, K., 2007. The effect of file sharing on record sales: an empirical analysis. J. Polit. Econ. 115 (1), 1–42.

Oster, S., Scott Morton, F., 2005. Behavioral biases meet the market: the case of magazine subscription prices. Adv. Econ. Anal. Policy. 5 (1)Article 1.

Pauwels, K., Dans, E., 2001. Internet marketing the news: leveraging brand equity from marketplace to marketspace. Brand Manag. 8 (4), 303–314.

Peitz, M., Valetti, T., 2008. Content and advertising in the media: pay-TV versus free-to-air. Int. J. Ind. Organ. 26, 949–965.

Peitz, M., Waelbroeck, P., 2004. The Effect of Internet Piracy on CD sales: Cross-Section Evidence. CESifo Working Paper Series No. 1122.

Pepall, L., Richards, D.J., Norman, G., 2005. Industrial organization: contemporary theory and practice. Thomson/South-Western, Mason.

Petrova, M., 2011. Newspapers and parties: how advertising revenues created an independent press. Am. Polit. Sci. Rev. 105 (4), 790–808.

Reddaway, W.B., 1963. The economics of newspapers. Econ. J. 73 (290), 201–218.

Reisinger, M., 2012. Platform competition for advertisers and users in media markets. Int. J. Ind. Organ. 30 (2), 243–252.

Reisinger, M., Ressner, L., Schmidtke, R., 2009. Two-sided markets with pecuniary and participation externalities. J. Ind. Econ. 57 (1), 32–37.

Robins, W., 2001. Newspaper websites seize on a capital idea. Editor Publisher 134 (18), 3–11.

Rochet, J.-C., Tirole, J., 2003. Platform competition in two-sided markets. J. Eur. Econ. Assoc. 1 (1), 990–1029.

Romeo, C., Pittman, R., Familant, N., 2003. Do newspaper JOAs charge monopoly advertising rates? Rev. Ind. Organ. 22 (2), 121–138.

Rosse, J.N., 1967. Daily newspapers, monopolistic competition, and economies of scale. Am. Econ. Rev. 57, 522–533.

Rosse, J.N., 1970. Estimating cost function parameters without using cost data: illustrated methodology. Econometrica 38, 256–274.

Rosse, J.N., 1980a. The decline of direct newspaper competition. J. Commun. 30 (2), 65–71.

Rosse, J.N., 1980b. Vertical Price Fixing in Newspaper Distribution: A Per-Se Rule That Makes Everyone Worse Off. Unpublished manuscript, Stanford University.

Rysman, M., 2004. Competition between networks: a study of the market for yellow pages. Rev. Econ. Stud. 71 (2), 483–512.

Rysman, M., 2009. The economics of two-sided markets. J. Econ. Perspect. 23 (3), 125–143.

Seamans, R., Zhu, F., 2014. Responses to entry in multi-sided markets: the impact of Craigslist on local newspapers. Manag. Sci. 60 (2), 476–493.

Silk, A.J., Klein, L.R., Berndt, E.R., 2001. The emerging position of the Internet as an advertising medium. Netnomics 3, 129–148.

Simon, D., Kadiyali, V., 2007. The effect of a magazine's free digital content on its print circulation: cannibalization or complementarity? Inf. Econ. Policy 19, 344–361.

Sonnac, N., 2000. Readers' attitudes toward press advertising: are they ad-lovers or ad-averse? J. Med. Econ. 13 (4), 249–259.

Starr, P., 2004. The Creation of the Media: Political Origins of Modern Communications. Basic Books, New York.

Steiner, P.O., 1952. Program patterns and the workability of competition in radio broadcasting. Q. J. Econ. 66 (2), 194–223.

Thompson, R.S., 1989. Circulation versus advertiser appeal in the newspaper industry. J. Ind. Econ. 37 (3), 259–271.

Van Cayseele, P.J., Vanormelingen, S., 2009. Prices and Network Effects in Two-Sided Markets: The Belgian Newspaper Industry. Working Paper, Catholic University of Leuven.

Weyl, R.G., 2010. A price theory of multi-sided platforms. Am. Econ. Rev. 100 (4), 1642–1672.

Willis, J.L., 2006. Magazine prices revisited. J. Appl. Econ. 21 (3), 337–344.

Zentner, A., 2012. Internet adoption and advertising expenditures on traditional media: an empirical analysis using a panel of countries. J. Econ. Manag. Strateg. 21 (4), 913–926.

CHAPTER 10

The Economics of Internet Media

Martin Peitz*, Markus Reisinger[†]
*Department of Economics, University of Mannheim, Mannheim, Germany
[†]Department of Economics, Frankfurt School of Finance & Management, Frankfurt, Germany

Contents

Abstract

We survey the economics literature on media as it applies to the Internet. The Internet is an important driver behind media convergence and connects information and communication technologies. While new Internet media share some properties with traditional media, several novel features have appeared: On the content side, aggregation by third parties that have no editorial policy and user-generated content has become increasingly important. On the advertiser side, fine-tuned tailoring and targeting of ads based on individual user characteristics are common features on many Internet media and social networks. On the user side, we observe increased possibilities of time-shifting, multi-homing, and active search. These changes have gone hand-in-hand with new players entering media markets, including search engines and Internet service providers. Some of these players face novel

Handbook of Media Economics, Volume 1A
ISSN 2213-6630, http://dx.doi.org/10.1016/B978-0-444-62721-6.00010-X

strategic considerations, such as how to present search results. In response to these changes, an emerging economics literature focuses on the allocative and welfare implications of this new media landscape. This chapter is an attempt to organize these contributions and provide a selective account of novel economic mechanisms that shape market outcomes of Internet media. A large body of work has focused on the advertising part of the industry, while some studies also look at content provision and the interaction between the two.

Keywords

Internet, Media economics, Digital media, Targeting, News aggregation, Search advertising, Display advertising, Two-sided markets

JEL Codes

L82, L86, M37, L13, D21, D22

10.1. INTRODUCTION

The Internet has changed the lives of most people, in both business and leisure activities. It allows for a previously unknown immediacy of news coverage from a large number of sources. In a sense, Internet media cover unexpected events in real time over the whole world (see, e.g., Salaverría, 2005).[1] Searching on Google, social networking on Facebook, and video streaming on YouTube are ways to spread and receive such news. The providers of these services have become increasingly important, affecting media markets in general and Internet media in particular.

Due to technological progress, firms have new and unparalleled opportunities to advertise their products to Internet users, through methods such as fine-tuned targeting. Therefore, Internet companies use business models that are different from the ones used in more traditional media markets and are often purely ad-financed. This raises questions on the efficiency of media markets on the Internet and (potentially) their optimal regulation.[2]

These are two reasons why media on the Internet is an important topic for research. In addition, we observe that Internet media influence political diversity and, in contrast to traditional media, can quickly leverage the success (or failure) of civic movements to attract public support. This chapter provides a guide to the recent literature on the economics of Internet media. After reporting some facts in Section 10.2, we provide four themes along which Internet media markets can be analyzed.

---

[1] This holds as long as governments and commercial providers (Internet Service Providers, search engines) do not restrict the flow of information. In some countries, certain topics do not appear as search results when using a search engine. To allow for a wide circulation of this article, we do not give concrete examples.

[2] For a survey on antitrust issues in Internet platforms industries, see Calvano and Jullien (2012).

First, as covered in Section 10.3, Internet affects content provision of media players. We note a tendency of different media to converge. For example, a user interested in news may visit the website of a newspaper or the one of a television channel. This makes it increasingly difficult to classify a media outlet on the Internet as belonging purely to one of the traditional media formats.[3] In particular, the web presence of several newspapers and television channels offer text and video. This is more than a labeling issue to the extent that different types of media are subject to different legal rules and that different traditions for media design may become closer substitutes on the Internet since they are only one click away.

While traditional media businesses have built a presence on the Internet (e.g., BBC and CNN) and some have adjusted their business models, new actors are appearing. Big Internet players such as network operators and software platforms have become "infomediaries" by aggregating information or signing specific contracts with content providers. These aggregators do not have editorial policies but make content suggestions based on algorithms and user feedback (e.g., Google and Facebook). Neither Google nor Facebook started out as news aggregators, but they have evolved into them. For some users, Facebook has become a personalized magazine, as they read the posts on Facebook pages they have subscribed to. Given the reach of Facebook, this can have a fundamental impact on media consumption.[4] Similarly, YouTube started out providing short amateur videos, which could be considered pure entertainment and outside the media world. However, nowadays, YouTube can be seen as a source of information that functions like media. In addition to revamped old media and big Internet companies moving into media, new media models and players, such as personal blogs and threads, have appeared. These include new formats (e.g., messaging networks such as Twitter and blogs) and pure Internet formats of newspapers (e.g., *Huffington Post*).

To qualify as media in our view, a website has to update information frequently and to replace old content with new content (or to give more visibility to new than to old content).[5] This distinguishes media from, for example, an encyclopedia. Hence, we would not call Wikipedia media, at least in its current form. However, if Wikipedia adjusted to include news items or propose updated Wikipedia entries according to recent developments, Wikipedia could become Internet media.[6]

Second, as covered in Section 10.4, the Internet affects user consumption of media content. The Internet has attracted many users, and their behavior online may be different compared to behavior documented in traditional media markets. We observe that for

---

[3] Traditional media formats are newspapers, magazines, radio, and television. See Chapters 7–9 in this volume for details on these traditional media.

[4] See Section 10.2, on some facts of Internet media consumption.

[5] This is, among other things, driven by an inherent ephemerality in content value.

[6] On user-generated content, see Chapter 12.

many people in OECD countries, the Internet has become the main source of media consumption. According to GlobalWebIndex, in a large number of countries, the average user spends more time consuming media online than offline (see Section 10.2).

While it is true that paper has simply been replaced by a screen on a laptop, electronic reader or smart phone, this change in technology, though noteworthy, may not change the underlying economics of media markets. If this were the only change, the economics of Internet media would probably not deserve a full chapter. Similarly, if people watch a live sports event on their laptop via some streaming service instead of using a television screen, this also constitutes a change of device but would not be a reason by itself to reconsider television media. Finally, if somebody listens only to Internet radio instead of relying on radio frequencies, this constitutes a change in habit, but for our purposes is otherwise irrelevant.

However, users may act differently on the Internet compared to how they consume linear television programming, radio broadcasting, and newspapers. While multi-homing is also often a feature of consumer behavior for television programming, the ad-financed media on the Internet are particularly prone to encountering multi-homing users who click themselves through different websites. Thus, the impact of multi-homing on media competition is particularly relevant on the Internet.

Users search for media content primarily via search engines. Thus, the functioning of these search engines is likely to affect media consumption. In particular, an important question is whether search engines bias their results to search queries and whether this affects market outcomes.

In general, consumers play a more active part in media consumption. Media content on the Internet can be subject to reader feedback, which affects the further diffusion of content. This can take the form of comments and recommendations. These also play out on social networks, where user decisions determine the spread of content (e.g., users can share an article or video with their friends). Here, users become, in a sense, curators of the media environment. In addition, they become creators by uploading their own images or videos, which may have news content for small online communities and thus may constitute "local" news. This relates to the observation that, in general, a key characteristic of media, in contrast to communication, is that information moves in only one direction, from one sender to many receivers; and this distinction becomes less clear-cut on the Internet, as social networks have resulted in (interactive) user-generated content and limits to exposure. The former implies that some Internet media have incorporated elements of interactions. The latter implies that only a select group (e.g., the Facebook friends of a particular person or cause) obtains access to the available information.

Third, as covered in Section 10.5, media on the Internet match advertising to content. Most Internet media are primarily and exclusively financed through advertising, which can be display advertising or search advertising, among other forms. The former is similar to advertising in traditional media. However, in traditional media, content and advertising tend to be unrelated (with the caveat that some media have narrow target groups—in specialized magazines, for example—that allow for targeted advertising). On the Internet, however, it is feasible to have context-specific ads that depend on the requested content. Such tailoring of ads affects media competition. For example, targeting allows firms with a potentially small customer group to actively participate in the advertising market—a phenomenon known as the "long tail" hypothesis of Internet advertising (Anderson, 2006). This affects advertising prices and thus the advertising intensity of big companies with a broad customer base. In addition, better targeting has implications for the interaction between offline and online media.

Of particular relevance is keyword advertising, which consists of advertisements linked to a specific word or phrase. Keyword advertising increases the precision with which advertisers convey their "message" to the right audience, but the general welfare consequences of this type of advertising are not obvious. Also, the incentive of a search engine to offer the best match to consumers is not evident. The matching precision may have consequences for competition between advertisers, thereby affecting the revenue stream of the search engine. Another important question is the effectiveness of such keyword advertising, measured by conversion and click-through rates (CTRs). Again, it is not clear whether search engines are interested in displaying the results in the most efficient rank order.

We note a great reduction in classified ads in print media. In many cases, their substitutes have become disconnected from media (as in the case of Craigslist) and thus are outside the scope of this chapter.[7]

Fourth, as covered in Section 10.6, media on the Internet match users to advertising directly. With the increasing amount of data available about Internet users (including information obtained from cookies), the Internet allows for tracking and individual ad targeting, disconnecting advertising from media content. Again, this has implications for the functioning of media markets. For example, holding ad and product prices constant, better tracking should be beneficial to advertisers because their messages are wasted with a lower probability. Thus, websites should be able to reap higher advertising revenues. At the same time, better tracking may increase competition between advertisers since consumers become better informed. This tension affects the outcome in media markets and, in turn, has consequences for Internet users. An obvious one is that users are less likely to block ads if ads, *per se*, provide a better match. At the same time, there can be more subtle effects. For example, in order to reap more advertising revenues, platforms have an incentive to prevent users from switching to other platforms. A way to achieve this could be to offer higher-quality content so that, for example, a user consuming news becomes fully informed on a single website and therefore has

---

[7] Classified ads on the Internet are similar to ads in print yellow pages, but they allow for better tailoring and search.

no incentive to consult an alternative website. Hence, content is also affected by the tracking technology.

The improved tracking technology also creates an additional revenue source for websites, given that websites provide data to advertisers. Websites not only can charge users for content and producers for placing ads, but also can offer data to producers. Since this helps producers to make advertising more effective, producers are willing to pay for these data. In addition to providing a better match, better tracking has further advantages to producers. For example, it allows them to retarget users, thereby increasing users' attention span for a particular ad.

With the increasing amount of time users spend on the Internet and websites' strong reliance on ad revenues, users appear to be more likely not to recall all advertising; thus, congestion issues—already a problem in traditional media—appear to be even more relevant on the Internet since users often visit a large number of ad-financed websites.

The literature on media economics, both in general and in how it applies to the Internet, is evolving rapidly. This chapter does not aim to provide an exhaustive overview of the economics of Internet media, but presents a selection of recent works on the topics addressed above.

10.2. MEDIA AND ADVERTISING ON THE INTERNET: SOME FACTS

10.2.1 Facts About Internet Media Use

Internet media include traditional media going online (such as the *New York Times*); pure online media, which in its editorial policies resemble traditional media (such as *Huffington Post*); and pure online platforms (such as Yahoo) that may lack a clear editorial policy and, instead, rely on sources such as Reuters news. Internet media are becoming increasingly important as a source of news. The Pew Research Center runs surveys asking people whether they got news "yesterday" from a particular type of media (data are made available by Pew Research Center). While in 1991 more than two-thirds of respondents said that they got news from television (68%), in 2012 only 55% said so. A similar pattern holds for radio: in 1991 more than half of the respondents said that they got news from radio (54%), while only 29% said so in 2012. Even stronger is the change with respect to newspapers. Here, 56% of respondents said that they got news from newspapers in 1991, and only 29% said so in 2012. So-called digital news has only recently been included in the survey: in 2012, 50% of the respondents said that they got news as digital news.

To the extent that users replace a subscription to a print edition with a subscription to an electronic submission, this merely reflects a change in technology. However, the switch to digital media certainly may affect the type of news and the way that it is consumed. The move to the Internet also affects the production technology of the Internet; in particular, it is less costly to provide more frequent updates, and the variable costs are reduced, compared to print (no printing and low delivery costs).

For the economics of Internet media, it is more important that there are changes in the way that media on the Internet operate. Many newspapers have not made strong inroads into Internet distribution, and those that do must seriously alter their business model. In addition, emerging players in Internet media have attracted a lot of attention, as we document next and treat more systematically in Section 10.3.

Several online measurement firms (in particular, comScore, Nielsen, and Experian Hitwise) provide information on digital traffic. Since they compute traffic in different ways, their numbers look somewhat different. Here, we report only the numbers released by Experian Hitwise (taken from Pew Research Center, 2013a).

Table 10.1 provides information on the most frequented news websites based on hits in 2012. We find that new and traditional media are both popular. Three general observations can be made. First, the 2012 numbers suggest that different types of traditional media (newspapers such as the *New York Times* and television such as CNN) co-exist on the Internet. Second, new media players have entered—in particular, news portals

Table 10.1 Internet news sites by visits in the US in 2012

	Share (%)	Total visits
news.yahoo.com	9.96	5,061,468,962
www.huffingtonpost.com	5.45	2,772,623,500
www.weather.com	3.8	1,937,665,856
www.msnbc.msn.com	2.13	1,096,295,903
www.cnn.com	2.02	1,006,425,806
gma.yahoo.com	1.70	871,463,749
www.foxnews.com	1.70	838,014,419
news.google.com	1.38	694,071,244
usnews.msnbc.msn.com	1.21	643,412,705
weather.yahoo.com	1.06	541,483,467
cityguides.msn.com	1.05	536,032,331
www.nytimes.com	1.04	522,225,600
www.drudgereport.com	0.98	481,470,727
home.now.msn.com	0.95	497,616,015
www.usatoday.com	0.82	420,809,971
www.accuweather.com	0.82	417,186,293
www.weatherunderground.com	0.81	412,512,889
abcnews.go.com	0.80	404,226,736
usnews.nbcnews.com	0.72	356,936,414
local.yahoo.com	0.72	367,295,141
www.people.com	0.67	341,541,090
www.newser.com	0.63	318,767,914
www.washingtonpost.com	0.57	286,614,807
www.foxnews.com/us	0.57	291,019,495
www.dailyfinance.com	0.56	283,381,243

Source: Pew Research Center (2013a) using Experian Hitwise.

such as Yahoo and Microsoft's MSN. Third, Google, as a news aggregator and search engine, has entered the game. To the extent that users consider both types of media as sources of news or information, we observe that the online market of news platforms is more diverse than traditional media markets. In addition, we observe media convergence in the sense that some media that, in the offline world, belong to separate markets now arguably belong to the same market. For instance, portals of newspapers and television broadcasters offer news in text, photo, and video formats. In Table 10.1, we observe that the newspapers *New York Times* and *USA Today* have a strong online presence, as do television broadcasters CNN and Fox News.

There are multiple ways in which a user may access the media platform. An obvious, necessary condition is that the user has access to the Internet. Here, the user has a contractual relationship with an Internet Service Provider (ISP). The standard business model of the (user's) ISP is to charge the user a tariff. While not so a common feature, an ISP may also receive payments from the content/media side for delivering traffic. We address the role of ISPs in Section 10.3 in the context of the net neutrality debate.

News aggregators provide a means to find news. For example, Google News can be the first stop for a user looking for news on a particular event. While there is (currently) no financial transaction between media platform and media aggregator, this issue is looming in the public debate (see Section 10.3). Users may not turn directly to a news aggregator and may, instead, initiate their search using a general search engine. The user then finds search results by news aggregators and media platforms. Thus, the set of actors include content providers, advertisers, media platforms, news aggregators, search engines, ISPs, and users. Figure 10.1 illustrates how content and advertising can reach users. On the advertiser side, our illustration is a bit simplistic. Large media platforms do, indeed, have direct contact with advertisers. However, many websites sell ad space to advertising networks that act as intermediaries between media platforms and advertisers. Additional players, not included in our analysis, are firms offering advertising software tools; these firms offer separate tools to media platforms and advertisers.[8]

Media operate in a richer environment on the Internet than in the offline world. As in many traditional media, a media platform on the Internet typically combines content and ads. When the platform does not vertically integrate with the content provider side, it has contracts with content providers and advertisers. The most common business model, then, is to offer such bundles of content and advertising to Internet users. The Internet user derives a benefit from the content offer, while advertising may also affect her utility.

---

[8] For more details, we refer to Evans (2008). This part of the industry is also characterized by vertical integration. For instance, Google, which is also a major advertising network for display advertising, acquired DoubleClick in 2008. DoubleClick offers software that allows advertisers and media platforms to track users (with the help of cookies) and to organize advertising campaigns. DoubleClick also offers software for search advertising.

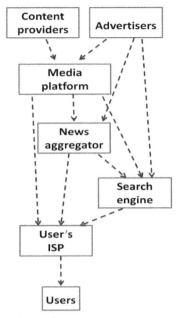

Figure 10.1 A stylized Internet media market.

Advertisers pay media platforms for placing their ads and delivering them to Internet users. Content providers receive payments from the media platform for delivering content. In purely ad-financed media, Internet users do not make monetary payments to the media platform. However, viewers of these ads are valuable, as they pay with their eyeballs, similar to free-to-air television.[9]

In the presence of multiple media platforms, the standard assumption is that users make a discrete choice among the platforms. Although this assumption appears to be appropriate in the traditional newspaper market, it is questionable how well it fits in the case of television, and even more so in the context of Internet media, where the alternative media platform is just one click away. We discuss alternative models of user behavior (in particular, multi-homing) and their implications in Section 10.4.

News consumption via social network plays an increasingly important role for a large number of users. News is defined here as "information about events and issues that involve more than just your friends or family" (see, e.g., Pew Research Center, 2013c).

---

[9] If users consider advertising to be a nuisance, a media model on the Internet can be developed along the lines of traditional media, as is formalized, for instance, in the Anderson and Coate (2005) model (for a recent, more general treatment, see Anderson and Peitz, 2014b). This model formalizes the interaction among advertisers, media platforms, and users. This media model connects to the literature on two-sided markets, with seminal contributions by Rochet and Tirole (2003) and Armstrong (2006), among others. For a textbook treatment, see Belleflamme and Peitz (2010).

To document the user base, Pew Research Center (2013b) provides survey results for the US adult population. Among adult Internet users, 71% are active on Facebook, while the corresponding numbers are 46% for those over age 65 and 90% for those aged between 18 and 29. A more recent phenomenon is social networking on mobile phones; in September 2013, 40% of all Internet users were active with social networking on mobile phones. The engagement on several social networking sites, especially on Facebook, is strong: 63% of Facebook users visit the site at least once a day, and 40% do so multiple times throughout the day.

In particular, Facebook has become an important platform for users to get news. According to Pew Research Center (2013c), with survey data from September 2013, 64% of US adults use Facebook, and 30% of US adults use Facebook to get news on the site; thus, for around half of its users, Facebook is a news site. Another popular site is YouTube. While 51% of US adults use YouTube, only 10% of US adults get news from it, which is around one in five. Only Twitter exhibits a ratio similar to that on Facebook: 16% of US adults are on Twitter, and 8% get news from it.

Social networks play a role in the creation and spread of information; we note that some users may become creators by posting their own images and videos, while others become curators by reposting and sharing existing material. Pew Research Center (2013d), based on a survey data from 2013, classified 54% of social network users as creators and 47% as curators (some users are both). According to a July–August 2012 survey, two-thirds of social network users have shown political engagement on the network—e.g., by encouraging others to vote, expressing their political opinion or sharing others' political expressions (Pew Research Center, 2013e). This shows that social networks do not only carry information relevant for a small set of people, but also contribute to the general debate on civic issues. In our survey, we address the information-spreading aspect of Internet media in Section 10.4.

10.2.2 Facts About Internet Advertising

The previous subsection provided some facts about Internet media use and the content side. Next, we present some facts on Internet advertising, which started only in 1994 with the sale of the first banner ad (see Kaye and Medoff, 2000). As pointed out in Section 10.1, the Internet has changed the landscape for advertisers. To the extent that advertisers have replaced some of their advertising on traditional media with Internet advertising, this has a direct impact on those media. A striking example has been the move of classified ads from print media to electronic platforms. While classified ads used to bring in substantial advertising revenues for newspapers (which possibly cross-subsidized other parts of the newspaper), Internet platforms have drastically cut those revenues for newspapers unless they have been able to dominate the respective market segment on the Internet. This loss in revenues on the advertising side has implications for the pricing of

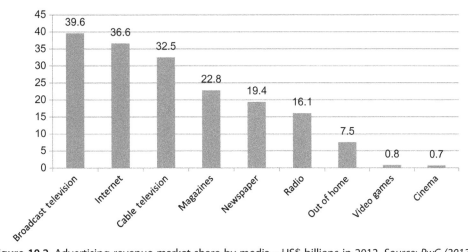

Figure 10.2 Advertising revenue market share by media—US$ billions in 2012. *Source: PwC (2013).*

newspapers. In particular, newspapers increase subscription prices, sacrifice circulation, and set lower ad prices (see Seamans and Zhu, 2014).

After television advertising, Internet advertising has become the most important medium in terms of ad revenues, at least in the US. As Figure 10.2 illustrates, in 2012 advertising revenues for Internet media were close to 37 billion US$. As in other media, advertising can play different roles for advertisers. It can inform about product availability, price, and product characteristics; it may allow consumers to draw inferences about product characteristics (advertising as a signal: Milgrom and Roberts, 1986; Nelson, 1974); it may change consumer preferences to the benefit of the advertiser and thus be persuasive; or it may serve as a complement to the product (Becker and Murphy, 1993).[10] We return to these views on advertising when discussing different Internet advertising formats.[11]

Figure 10.3, in turn, shows the rapid increase in advertising spending on Internet media, with an annual growth rate of about 20% over the last 10 years. Only at the height of the financial crisis in the US from 2008 to 2009 can one observe a small dip in ad revenues. This contrasts with the development of newspaper advertising revenues. In 2000, ad revenues stood at around 49 billion US$; in 2012, they totaled less than 20 billion US$.[12]

---

[10] Bagwell (2007) provides an excellent survey of the economics of advertising.

[11] See also Chapter 4 in this volume.

[12] There is compelling evidence that Internet advertising can be effective in stimulating purchases. This does not hold only for online purchases, but also for offline ones. For example, Lewis and Reiley (2014) find in a controlled field experiment with a large retail store that more than 90% of purchase increases occur in brick-and-mortar stores. Similarly, Johnson et al. (2014) demonstrate that repeated exposure to online ads was highly profitable for the retail store whose data were analyzed.

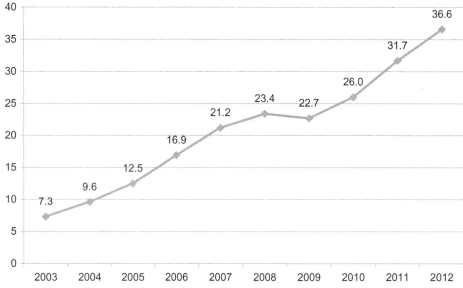

Figure 10.3 Internet ad revenues 2003–2012—US$ billions. *Source: PwC (2013).*

Internet advertising can take different forms.[13] Here, we mention the most common: *search advertising* accounts for a large fraction of total Internet ad revenues. To the extent that it makes consumers aware of certain offerings, this type of advertising can be seen as directly informative. Consumers may also consider it to be indirectly informative about the quality of a match through a signaling role of the ad—e.g., if an offering appears at the top of the page of sponsored search results.

The dominant platform for search advertising is Google; in the US it first took the top position in 2003, relegating Yahoo to second place. In 2013, around two-thirds of all search requests on general search engines were made on Google, while 18% were made on Microsoft sites (using Bing) and 11% on Yahoo (according to comScore qSearch). In Europe, Google is even more dominant, accounting for more than 90% of searches in 2013. Google is stronger yet in terms of revenues. An explanation for this finding is that the larger platform is more attractive to advertisers.

The second big category of ad revenues is *display advertising*. Display advertising can be contextual, as it can be linked to particular keywords or phrases. We can also refer to such a strategy as tailoring. In addition, display advertising on the Internet can be personalized if the advertising platform has knowledge about consumer characteristics. This then leads

---

[13] We refer to Evans (2008) for a detailed explanation of search and display advertising. See Goldfarb (2014) for a discussion of the different forms of online advertising.

to targeted advertising on the Internet,[14] which improves the match between the advertised product and the consumer. In general, such advertising can be informative, persuasive, or complementary.

The third major category of advertising revenues used to be *classified ads*; however, revenues have been decreasing over the last years in the US. In the early 2000s, classified ads moved quickly from newspapers to Internet platforms (e.g., Craiglist in the US)—one reason for the fast decline of advertising revenues at many newspapers. Classified ads on the Internet allow users to apply individual searches rather than using a predetermined classification scheme. Otherwise, the economics of classified ads did not change because of the move to the Internet. One would often consider this advertising format informative, as it makes consumers aware of an offering.

Additional formats, which are listed in Figure 10.4, include mobile advertising and digital video advertising. Mobile advertising, which saw a quick increase between 2010 and 2012, has the potential to add another tailoring dimension: the displayed ad may depend on a consumer being physically close to a particular location at which a product or service is available. Advertisers' hope is that mobile advertising is a means to generate immediate purchases. Here, advertising may play mainly an informative role, as it makes consumers aware of a product or service that they may be interested in at a particular location. Digital video advertising is akin to television advertising, with the important difference that it allows for tailoring and targeting (we note that television advertising also allows for some tailoring). This format may be more attractive for advertising that is persuasive or serves as a complement. Figure 10.4 reports advertising revenues according to the ad format for the US in 2012.

Media platforms on the Internet offer the possibility of measuring the impact of advertising—by counting the number of clicks an ad generates, for example. This has opened up the possibility of using a pricing model that is different from simply counting the number of impressions, as is done traditionally in media. The measure for the latter is cost per mille (CPM—i.e., the cost per 1000 impressions). If the ad price depends, instead, on the number of clicks (or possibly even the number of purchases), the traditional pricing model is replaced by one that is performance-based. As Figure 10.5 illustrates, performance-based ad pricing has been gaining the upper hand on the Internet, accounting for close to two-thirds of all Internet ad revenues in 2012. Ad revenues accruing to Google, through sponsored search results, make up the majority of these revenues.

Internet advertising may affect not only own-product sales. Several researchers have conducted natural experiments on Internet advertising to analyze spillovers of advertising campaign on competitors. For example, Lewis and Nguyen (2014) used display

---

[14] Athey and Gans (2010) make the distinction between tailored and targeted advertising. See Sections 10.5 and 10.6 for more details.

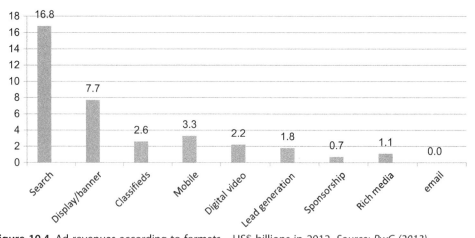

Figure 10.4 Ad revenues according to formats—US$ billions in 2012. *Source: PwC (2013).*

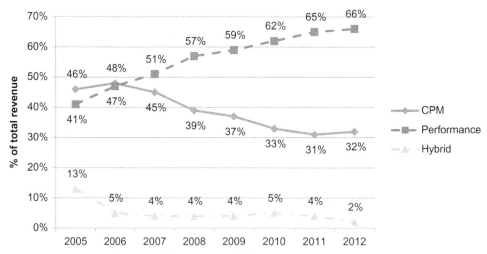

Figure 10.5 Internet ad revenues by pricing model. *Source: PwC (2013).*

advertising on Yahoo!'s front page. On some days, Yahoo! sells ads on its front page as ad-splits, which entail two display ads being alternately shown throughout the day, one every even second and the other every odd second. This allows naturally for exogenous variation because there is no systematic difference between even-second and odd-second visitors, thereby providing a test group (visitors exposed to the target ad) and a control group (visitors exposed to the other ad-split ad). Lewis and Nguyen (2014) find that display ads caused an increase in searches not only for the advertised brand (35–40%) but also for competitors' brands (1–6%). The effect on searches by brand can be up to 23% for competing brands. Sahni (2015) finds similar results using data from restaurant search websites. He also shows that the extent of the spillover depends on the advertising intensity. If the intensity is low, spillovers are particularly large, perhaps because advertising then has mainly the effect of reminding consumers about similar options. By contrast, if the intensity is high, spillovers disappear and the advertiser receives more searches.

The business model of most news websites is ad-financed. However, there are a few exceptions, primarily newspapers. For example, in the UK, almost all major newspapers require readers to subscribe to their online content. *The Times* has a paywall for all of its content. Other newspapers, such as *The New York Times* or *The Wall Street Journal*, offer limited free access with some number of free articles per month. Therefore, these newspapers have a mixed business model—that is, partly ad-financed and partly subscription-financed.

10.3. PROVIDING MEDIA CONTENT

Media content on the Internet reaches users through multiple channels. In this section, we discuss some of the issues of media content provision and how users access this content. We address the various layers of the value chain, as illustrated in Figure 10.1, with a focus on the provision of content. While a large part of this section will be informal, the section contains a formal analysis of media platforms as gatekeepers and of the role of news aggregators. We take a broad view and also shortly discuss the role of search engines (formally investigated in Section 10.4) in the context of user choice, and the role of ISPs with a guide to the net neutrality debate.

10.3.1 Internet Media Consumption and Convergence

The availability of media content on the Internet dilutes or even removes the boundaries between newspaper and television channels. For instance, in the case of news programming, a consumer can visit the website of a news channel or one of a newspaper. Each of these media typically has combined offerings of electronic articles (containing text and often photos) and videos. This describes the convergence of different media. We may view this convergence as market integration, implying that offerings that used to be independent (newspaper versus television) become substitutes. How this convergence affects market structure is an issue that deserves investigation.

One issue is the coverage of different topics. Media platforms have to choose topics that differ in their success probability, with success meaning that the topic attracts users' attention and generates a reward (e.g., through ad revenues). In such markets, the quality of the media platform and its ability to predict the success of a topic affects its choice of topic.[15]

---

[15] For a theory contribution on this point, see Katona et al. (2013).

Another issue (for empirical research) is whether the Internet alters the way news is consumed. In particular, news on the Internet facilitates the combined consumption of news and background information. For instance, a particular news item may lead a user to consult Wikipedia for additional information or background. While we typically would not classify Wikipedia as media, the overall portfolio of information on a topic consumed over the Internet may look very different from the product consumed in traditional media.

The convergence of different types of traditional media also leads to important policy questions. As newspapers and television channels on the Internet become closer substitutes, policymakers have to tackle the fact that newspapers and television channels are, in many places, subject to different regulations. Furthermore, in many countries, public service broadcasters play an important role in traditional radio and television markets. As television channels develop an Internet presence, they start to compete with newspapers on the Internet. While we do not intend to address these policy issues directly, this section helps to understand the functioning of Internet media markets and may therefore also be helpful from a policy perspective.

10.3.2 Media Platforms as Gatekeepers

The gatekeeper role of media appears to be of particular relevance on the Internet—the issue also arises in traditional media, as discussed below. Media platforms on the Internet (and traditional media) can be seen as managing the amount and type of information a user can digest. In particular, if a user has a limited attention span for news and is unable or unwilling to push herself to read more news, a media platform, by recommending a selection of news, can emphasize the most relevant news items. This is especially the case if the platform has information on the user's tastes and tailors the news selection to them, as is the case with Internet media. Since the role of Internet media platforms as gatekeepers is widely discussed, it is useful to provide a simple formal exposition, which gives some structure to think about this issue. To this end, we reinterpret the model by Anderson and de Palma (2009), in that we include individual news providers that compete for users' attention. Access to users is managed by a media platform.

Consider a media platform that selects among alternative news providers and offers a selection of news items to a user. Suppose that there are n potential news providers, each contributing up to one piece of news. A news provider of type θ obtains advertising revenue $\pi(\theta)$. Advertising revenue is increasing in the value of content θ because we assume that a news provider with more valuable content is more likely to deliver advertising to the user.

The user has an attention span φ for news items, which will be derived below; i.e., she randomly selects φ news items if she is presented with more than φ.[16] In particular, if

[16] Somewhat related, in Section 10.6 we present a setting in which users have a limited attention span for advertising.

there is no selection among news, each available news item is seen with probability min $\{\varphi/n, 1\}$. Suppose that delivering a news item costs κ. Under free entry and appropriate boundary conditions, there is a marginal type $\theta^* = n$ such that $(\pi(\theta^*)\varphi)/n = \kappa$. This determines the number of news items $n(\varphi; \kappa)$ under free entry.

The user's cost of sampling messages is denoted by $C(\varphi)$. Given the total number of news items n, each randomly sampled news item gives an expected surplus of $S^e(n) = \frac{1}{n}\int_0^n s(\theta)\mathrm{d}\theta$. The utility-maximizing attention span is arg max$_\varphi \varphi S^e(n) - C(\varphi)$. The first-order condition $S^e(n) = C'(\varphi)$ determines the chosen attention span when $\varphi \leq n$. Hence, $\varphi(n) = \min\left\{n, C'^{-1}(S^e(n))\right\}$. In equilibrium, for low values of κ, there may be information overload—i.e., $\varphi^* \leq n^*$.

The media platform can manage the amount of news being offered to users. In other words, the media platform can become a gatekeeper. Traditional media partly filled this role by selecting articles provided by news agencies and other sources. In the case of newspapers, they traditionally charge readers for the active selection of content. While they may also provide unique content, an important role of both traditional and new media is this selection role. Whether this selection is based on an editorial policy or is software-based is irrelevant in this context. Limiting the amount of content on the platform can reduce or even eliminate information overload. In particular, a monopoly gatekeeper would price out information overload. It may do so by charging news providers for access. If the provision of news is costly, payments may flow in the opposite direction. Then, the media platform pays less than what it would do in the case of an unlimited attention span. Thus, the overall message is that a limited attention span for news may give a role to a platform to limit the amount of news included on its website.

To the extent that users frequent multiple media platforms, these platforms do not fully internalize that additional content on their platform reduces the probability that content on other platforms will receive the users' attention. Hence, information overload remains an issue for competing media platforms. A characterizing feature of the Internet is that users often visit many media platforms.[17] Therefore, the Internet is particularly prone to the problem of information overload.

The media platform's role as gatekeeper is not restricted only to the amount of content, but also to content selection and quality. These two dimensions are also highly influenced by the ad-financed business model. For example, Sun and Zhu (2013) conduct a study on how the content and quality of blogs are affected by an ad-revenue-sharing program of a Chinese portal site. In particular, this portal site launched the program and invited around 3000 bloggers to participate. Bloggers who allowed the portal site to

---

[17] See Section 10.4 for a more detailed discussion of this issue in an advertising context.

run ads on their blogs received 50% of the ad revenues generated on the site. Around 1000 bloggers decided to participate.

Sun and Zhu (2013) find that the decision to participate in this program has led to a shift to more popular content by around 13%. Around 50% of this increase comes from shifts to topics from three domains: stock market blogs, salacious content, and blogs about celebrities. The blog posts of participants in these domains increased by 6.6% relative to non-participants.

In addition, participating bloggers also increased their content quality. This is measured, for example, by the number of users who bookmark a post as one of their favorites and by the average number of characters, pictures, and video clips. (For example, more characters means that the blogger invests more effort in writing and goes deeper into the focal topic, whereas more pictures often make the blog more attractive.) This suggests that bloggers exert more effort on blogging content that they are not necessarily intrinsically interested in, and that they do so to obtain higher revenues from advertising.

Sun and Zhu (2013) also show that these effects are strongest for moderately popular bloggers and, in particular, stronger than for very popular bloggers (and non-participating bloggers). A possible explanation is that very popular bloggers have always covered popular topics and/or maintained a high level of quality. Hence, there is not much space for improvement. Non-participating bloggers, by contrast, may have a large disutility from blogging about content that does not reflect their tastes, and thus they choose not to participate.

10.3.3 News Aggregators and the Selection of News

News aggregators such as Google News have added another layer in the market for Internet media. Users may use an aggregator as the main access point and select news items based on this aggregator's listings. A few academic studies have tried to shed light on the link between quality choice of media platforms and the presence of news aggregators.

Here, the role of a news aggregator such as Google News is to help users to easily find high-quality content. As Dellarocas et al. (2013) point out, absent news aggregator, users may find their way to different news because media platforms may provide links to a rival's content. They present a model in which users are interested in a particular event, and different media platforms cover this event with different quality. Users are not informed *ex ante* about the quality and therefore visit media platforms randomly. While users appreciate the provision of external links (toward higher-quality content), and this increases the overall attractiveness of a media platform, users reduce their time spent on a particular platform, which decreases ad revenues for the media platform. Despite such links, there is a role for the news aggregator, as it actively selects among content, allowing users to avoid the hassle of moving from one media platform to another that provides higher quality. The news aggregator improves the overall performance of the market, which is in the overall interest of media platforms, as this increases user participation in the market; however, the news aggregator also absorbs some of the rents generated in the market, thereby reducing what is on the table of media platforms. Dellarocas et al. (2013) show that if content providers offer links to each other's content, entry of an aggregator may lead to less competition among content providers to provide high quality. If, by contrast, content providers cannot link to rivals' content, entry of an aggregator tends to lead to more competition among content providers.

Rutt (2011) analyzes quality choice by media platforms when some users are loyal to a particular media platform, and others search for free high-quality content. Loyal users are willing to pay for content, but searchers are also valuable, as additional traffic generates advertising revenue. The presence of an aggregator is assumed to be essential for searchers to identify the quality of content. A platform may charge for content but then loses searchers. Platforms simultaneously set price on the user side and the quality of content. Under some conditions, a mixed-strategy symmetric equilibrium exists, with the feature that media platforms randomize over price and quality by choosing from a probability distribution among qualities at a price of zero or by setting a particular quality at a positive price.[18] If a platform ends up doing the latter, it serves only loyal users (and extracts all the surplus from them), while in the former equilibrium, it competes with other platforms for searchers. The main finding is that as the fraction of searchers increases, platforms with free content increase their content quality (in the sense of first-order stochastic dominance), while platforms with positive prices decrease their content quality. In addition, as the fraction of searchers increases, content is provided more often for free. Thus, existing searchers benefit from more searchers. Also, loyal searchers benefit, as it becomes more likely that they can enjoy content for free.

Jeon and Nasr (2013) study media competition, where users can access content either by going directly to a media platform or by accessing news via an aggregator, such as Google News. The presence of such a news aggregator affects competition between media platforms, especially in the long run, when they react to changes by adjusting the quality of their news items.

To analyze this issue, Jeon and Nasr (2013) propose a stylized model of competing media platforms that offer news items from a full set of news categories. Each news item is either of high or of low quality. Media platforms may operate in an environment without a news aggregator or in an environment in which the news aggregator selects high-quality news items for all news categories for which high quality is available. Low quality is selected only for those news categories for which media platforms fail to make high quality available.

---

[18] The intuition for the existence of a mixed-strategy equilibrium is similar to the one of equilibrium price dispersion in a model of sales (e.g., Varian, 1980).

It is instructive to see the formal setup how a news aggregator can deal with news from different categories. Each of two media platforms cover a continuum of categories $[0, 1]$. Each platform chooses a subset I_i of categories for which it offers high-quality news. We can then associate the quality of the media platform with the measure of high-quality news issues $q_i = \mu(I_i)$, where it is assumed that $\mu([0, 1]) = 1$.[19] Users are identical with respect to their valuation of high-quality coverage.

In addition to differences in high-quality coverage, platforms are horizontally differentiated, where differentiation may reflect different political views or different styles (such as using British or American English). This horizontal difference applies to each news category. Users are heterogeneous with respect to these horizontal platform characteristics. This is formalized following the standard Hotelling representation with platforms being located at the extreme ends of the $[0, 1]$ interval and users being uniformly distributed over this interval. A user located at x incurs a disutility of τx if she consumes all news from platform 1 and $\tau(1 - x)$ if she consumes all news from platform 2. Then, the utility of a user x choosing platform 1 is $v_1(x) = u_0 + q_1 - \tau x$, where the marginal utility from increasing high-quality coverage is normalized to 1. Correspondingly, the utility of x choosing platform 2 is $v_2(x) = u_0 + q_2 - \tau(1 - x)$. In the absence of a media aggregator, users face a discrete-choice problem between two media platforms.

Platforms obtain revenues from advertising. Jeon and Nasr (2013) assume that platform revenues are proportional to the amount of time users spend on a platform, which is implied by a constant advertising price per exposure and exposure being proportional to the amount of time spent on the platform. It is assumed that users spend a total of one unit of time on low-quality media. High-quality coverage makes them investigate a category longer, increasing the time spent on news consumption by δ per category. Hence, a user who consumes news only on platform 1 spends time $1 + \delta q_1$ on platform 1. Each unit of time spent on the platform generates ad revenues A. Denoting the number of users of platform 1 by D_1 in the absence of a news aggregator, the profit of platform 1 is

$$\pi_1(I_1) = AD_1(1 + \delta\mu(I_1)) - C(\mu(I_1)),$$

where the cost of increasing high-quality coverage is convex (in particular, $C(s) = cq^2$ for $q \leq 1/2$ and infinity for larger q). Here, the parameter c is assumed to be sufficiently large such that in all environments, platforms choose high-quality coverage with q_i strictly lower than $1/2$.

In the absence of a media aggregator, platforms simultaneously choose their high-quality coverage I_i across news categories. Then, users make a discrete choice between the two media platforms. Because users cannot combine news from different platforms, for any given q_i, each media platform i is indifferent to which particular category it offers

[19] The cost of quality provision is assumed to satisfy the condition that a media platform always chooses a policy with $\mu([0, 1]) \leq 1/2$.

high quality. Straightforward calculations show that qualities are strategic substitutes; i.e., if the competing platform increases its amount of quality coverage, the best response by the media platform is to decrease its own quality coverage. One can then show that in a symmetric equilibrium, quality coverage is decreasing in the differentiation parameter τ, while profits are increasing. In other words, if users consider platforms as weak substitutes, media platforms invest less in quality coverage. This finding is in line with the basic intuition that more differentiation makes competition less intense.

How does the presence of a news aggregator affect competition between media platforms? Its presence changes the picture considerably because the aggregator proposes a mix of news from different platforms. In this respect, users see the news aggregator as a device to multi-home—that is, it allows them to, indeed, mix across platforms.[20] In the presence of a news aggregator, media platforms are no longer indifferent about which particular category contains high-quality news, as it is relevant whether there is duplication of high-quality coverage for the different categories. In particular, if platforms fully specialize—i.e., $I_1 \cap I_2 = \varnothing$—we have that $\mu(I_1 \cap I_2) = 0$. By contrast, if platforms choose maximal overlap, we have that $\mu(I_1 \cap I_2) = \min\{\mu(I_1), \mu(I_2)\}$.

To illustrate the functioning of a news aggregator, suppose that there are six (instead of a continuum of) news categories. Furthermore, suppose that platform 1 offers the vector $(1,0,1,1,0,0)$, where 1 stands for high quality and 0 for low quality, while platform 2 offers $(0,1,0,1,1,0)$. By choosing maximal quality, the news aggregator then offers $(1,1,1,1,1,0)$, where, in the case of the same quality, we postulate that each media platform is listed with probability $1/2$. Thus, the news aggregator provides higher quality than each individual media platform. From the user's perspective, while the aggregator offers higher quality, using the aggregator comes at the cost of a worse fit for consumers (with $x \neq 1/2$).

Returning to the model with a continuum of categories, a user located at x who obtains news through the news aggregator receives utility

$$v_{12}(x) = u_0 + \mu(I_1 \cup I_2) - \eta_1 \tau x - \eta_2 \tau(1-x),$$

where η_i is the fraction of news items that are linked to media platform i. This fraction is the sum of the fraction of categories with exclusive high-quality news items on media platform i, $\mu(I_i) - \mu(I_1 \cap I_2)$; one-half of the fraction of news categories with two high-quality news items, $(1/2)\mu(I_1 \cap I_2)$; and one-half of the fraction of news categories that do not contain any high-quality news items, $(1/2)(1 - \mu(I_1 \cup I_2))$. Thus, we can write

$$v_{12}(x) = u_0 + \mu(I_1 \cup I_2) - \frac{\tau}{2} + \tau\left(x - \frac{1}{2}\right)(\mu(I_2) - \mu(I_1)).$$

[20] For an analysis of the effect of multi-homing users on advertising revenues, see Section 10.4.

A user $x < 1/2$ prefers the news aggregator to media platform 1 if $v_{12}(x) > v_1(x)$. This is equivalent to

$$\mu(I_1 \cup I_2) - \mu(I_1) > \tau\left(\frac{1}{2} - x\right)(1 + \mu(I_2) - \mu(I_1)).$$

The left-hand side contains the gain due to higher quality from the news aggregator and the right-hand side the loss due to the larger preference mismatch with respect to horizontal characteristics. Whenever there are some categories for which only platform 1 offers high quality and some others where the reverse holds, a user at $x = 1/2$ strictly prefers the mix provided by the news aggregator over the offers by the two media platforms. Hence, users fall into up to three sets: users around $1/2$ rely on the news aggregator, while users at the extreme points tend to rely on the respective media platform. By contrast, if $I_1 = I_2$, there is no room for a news aggregator.

It can be shown that media platforms either choose full specialization such that $\mu(I_1 \cap I_2) = 0$, or that they provide maximal overlap such that $\mu(I_1 \cap I_2) = \min\{\mu(I_1), \mu(I_2)\}$. In any symmetric equilibrium with $\mu(I_1) = \mu(I_2) = \mu$, media platforms choose full separation if exposure due to high-quality news is sufficiently large, $\delta\mu > 1$. It can then be shown that, for large δ, there is a unique symmetric equilibrium in which platforms choose full separation and the news aggregator is active. In this environment, qualities are strategic complements, and the market-expansion effect due to higher quality dominates the business-stealing effect. In the reverse case, the business-stealing effect dominates the market-expansion effect, and there are equilibria in which media platforms choose the same categories for high-quality news items. This suggests that the viability of the news aggregators depends on the demand expansion of high-quality news items.

When the media platforms fully separate their high-quality coverage, users benefit from the presence of the news aggregator. While the effect on media platforms' profits is ambiguous, total surplus is also higher. Thus, to the benefit of society, the presence of news aggregators can give incentives to media to specialize their high-quality coverage, which in turn leads to an overall wider high-quality coverage of news items and categories.

The overall message that emerges from the analysis of news aggregators is that they affect the media platforms' incentives to invest in the quality of content. The above-discussed works have identified situations in which the presence of news aggregators is beneficial for society; however, the opposite result may well hold true, in particular since the news aggregator is an additional player extracting—also at the margin—rents from the market.

10.3.4 Search Engines and Media Content

Search engines are an important entry point for readers. Readers may be interested in a certain topic or event and simply use Google or some other search engine (e.g., Bing,

Baidu in China, Yandex in Russia, or Naver in South Korea) to click on a particular news item. This traffic generates profits for the search engines, as it allows them to place ads together with the organic search results. As news items are linked, a click by the reader on a particular news item moves the reader to a particular news site. When searching on Google, for example, the reader receives information on the news provider (e.g., the Internet site of a newspaper or television channel) and a snippet from the news item, which provides some context in which the search item appears. The distinction between a search engine and a news aggregator is, in some cases, a bit blurred, as a reader may use Google or Google News to access news, where we would label the former a search engine and the latter a news aggregator. An issue in both cases is, first, whether search engines have the right to provide links or need an explicit agreement from the website owner to provide a link and, second, whether search engines have an obligation to treat all content in a transparent and "non-biased" way.

Concerning the former, some interested parties have asked to be compensated for the extraction of snippets. For instance, the industry association of German newspapers has asked to receive payments. We note that, before this request, Google had already offered newspapers the option to delist their content. In this case, neither snippets nor links are provided in the organic search results on Google. Newspapers see themselves as providing content to Google without receiving any monetary payment, allowing Google to make money on advertising. Google, by contrast, claims to deliver additional traffic to newspapers and does not charge directly for the service. Following this logic, newspapers can derive benefit from this traffic (e.g., via advertising, pay-per-view or offering subscriptions). Therefore, it is not clear which economic mechanism would warrant public intervention to satisfy the newspapers' demands for payments by Google. Under a new law,[21] a group of German media companies hopes to extract license fees from Google for making snippets available (it is apparently unclear what length of the snippet would justify such a license fee). Essentially, this group of media companies aims to sustain a positive price vis-à-vis Google by coordinating their actions; this would not be possible if they acted independently.

The second issue has been analyzed in the context of search neutrality. While we are not aware of academic work on the first issue, several contributions have considered search neutrality, which applies not only to searches for news items, but also to broader searches, including those for products. We discuss search neutrality in Section 10.4.2.

---

[21] This is the ancillary copyright for press publishers (Leistungsschutzrecht für Presseverleger), which came into force on August 1, 2013. In its initial draft, it was intended to introduce a fee even for short snippets, but this has been removed from the final version.

10.3.5 ISPs, Net Neutrality, and Media Content

To enjoy media content, users need an Internet connection. Thus, a user obtains her consumption utility from jointly consuming both the content and the connectivity service. If the user is not using public wi-fi, she typically will have a contract with an ISP. This ISP offers her download and upload services at a contractually agreed-upon speed.

When content travels from the content provider to the consumer, the provider accesses the Internet via its ISP. Content is then sent through the Internet to the consumer's ISP. Traditionally, the content provider makes payments to its ISP. The ISP then ensures that content is delivered to the consumer's ISP. The consumer pays her ISP for the access product. There are no payments from the content provider to the consumer's ISP. In addition, all material is treated equally according to the best-effort principle.

Due to the explosion in data volume, a new issue is congestion, which leads to delays at certain times or to the breakdown of some services. Internet media are part of the congestion issue; according to Sandvine (2014), real-time entertainment, which includes media, constitutes a large fraction of the traffic. For instance, on mobile networks in Europe, YouTube contributes 20.62% and Facebook 11.04% to downstream traffic; as reported in Section 10.2.1, a large fraction of this traffic stems from news accessed by users. The OECD predicts that video streaming and IP-based television will increase traffic volumes (OECD, 2014).

Congestion issues are particularly relevant with mobile access where capacities are lower, but may also take place on landlines (DSL, cable). Some content providers have opted for the possibility of bypassing the public Internet and the risk of delay at interconnection points by operating content-delivery networks. Also, some ISPs offer media products (e.g., TV) that are treated differently from other content. Furthermore, as part of the net neutrality debate, there is discussion about whether a consumer's ISP can also charge on the content-provider side, thus introducing two-sided pricing. In addition, ISPs may inspect the data that they are handling and decide—based on the characteristics of the data in question—which type should receive priority treatment (deep packet inspection). Furthermore, as a number of countries are currently considering, content providers might self-select into different service classes, as ISPs offer both a slow and a fast lane. Such tiering would be legal according to the European Commission's proposal. Content providers could pay for prioritized access (while the "slow" lane is typically considered to be free). It has become mostly a political question whether these more flexible approaches should be allowed.

Proponents of strict net neutrality want to rule out such approaches, forcing ISPs to obtain all their revenues on the consumer side and not allowing them to deviate from the best-effort principle, which treats all traffic symmetrically. Critics of strict net neutrality point out that a one-sided price structure in a two-sided market tends to lead to rents on one side while reducing rents on the other. In particular, ruling out payments by content providers to consumer ISPs may lead to low overall revenues for user ISPs and may reduce their incentives to invest in a more powerful access network. While the exact competitive effects of imposing net neutrality rules are complex, when investment incentives by ISPs are considered (see, e.g., Bourreau et al., 2015; Choi and Kim, 2010; Economides and Hermalin, 2012; Krämer and Wiewiorra, 2012), a general issue is that unrestricted transmission may lead to congestion problems. Here, the capacity at a particular point (e.g., a switch close to the user) constitutes a common property resource.

An important observation is that some types of traffic are time-sensitive, meaning that consumer's utility is strongly negatively affected by delay (e.g., video calls or online gaming), while other traffic is not (e.g., video-on-demand or emails). For media, live sports events tend to be time-sensitive, whereas most other types of content can be delivered with short delays without costs for consumers, provided that they have equipment at home that allows for buffering.

A first basic result can be obtained in a model with a monopoly ISP. If the ISP is not allowed to discriminate between time-sensitive and time-insensitive traffic (by treating these types of traffic differently or by charging for priority access), both types of traffic are treated in the same way based on best effort. For any given composition of time-sensitive and time-insensitive traffic, this implies that in times of congestion, the allocation could be improved if time-sensitive traffic received priority. Since suppliers of time-sensitive traffic have an incentive to deliver on time, they also have an incentive to obtain prioritized access even if it carries a positive price. Taking into account that some traffic is more time-sensitive than other traffic makes the introduction of a priority lane potentially welfare-improving. Prioritized delivery may be secured through a price charged on the priority lane. Then, the priority lane serves as a screening device, and ISPs do not need to know the type of data they are delivering. Alternatively, ISPs may inspect the data packages and decide whom to give priority. This typically requires ISPs to look into the packet, which, however, raises privacy and data protection issues.

As Choi et al. (2013) and Peitz and Schuett (2015) point out, inframarginal content providers can also adjust their traffic volume. For instance, to deal with congestion, they may invest in compression technologies to reduce the volume of traffic.[22] While deep packet inspection addresses the inefficiency caused by treating time-sensitive and time-insensitive traffic equally, it is not a useful tool to tackle the incentive issues faced by content providers (see Peitz and Schuett, 2015). This holds since deep packet inspection does not put a price on congestion, in contrast to charging a price for prioritized delivery under tiering. By putting a price on time-sensitive traffic, which might be passed on to final users, the ISP creates an incentive for content providers to avoid such

---

[22] Alternatively, this can be done by making traffic less time-sensitive, which can be achieved through buffering and thus removing the need to obtain prioritized delivery.

payments. In particular, content providers have an incentive to reduce the volume of time-sensitive traffic that they send.

Summarizing the state of the net neutrality debate is beyond the scope of this article (for a recent survey on the academic analysis of net neutrality, see Krämer et al., 2013). The important lesson emerging from the debate is that regulatory decisions affect the rent distribution between content providers and ISPs. This, in turn, may affect the strategy of media platforms. In particular, if congestion is not priced, content providers may add a lot of traffic stemming from advertising (e.g., advertising preceding videos). If congestion is priced, media platforms may obtain a larger fraction of revenues from charging consumers directly.[23]

10.4. USERS CHOOSING MEDIA CONTENT

In traditional audiovisual media, such as television, consumers usually need to choose which content to consume at any given point in time and which to dismiss. Consider a television viewer who is interested in two different movies and one sports game broadcast by different stations on the same evening. This viewer has to choose one program to watch but, by making this choice, misses the other programs. This problem of linearly progressing content of TV or radio is absent in online media offers.

Content provided by Internet platforms can be quite durable. For example, media libraries allow users to access content at any time. Thus, the Internet is a nonlinear medium in which each consumer can choose her preferred time and order of content consumption.

In this respect, Internet media offer content at the individually preferred time, in contrast to the predefined time slots of traditional audiovisual media. So it shares important features of (digital) VCRs and on-demand content with respect to time shifting, but unlike these other forms of on-demand content, the cost to obtain the same content at different points in time on the Internet is almost negligible. In fact, another website is "just one click away," and accessing it does not require costly hardware. For traditional media, time shifting requires special hardware devices such as VCR or PVR setup boxes (e.g., offered by TiVo or DirecTV). In addition, accessing multiple websites is often an almost mindless activity, while deciding which content to videotape is a more conscious decision.

Consequently, online media consumers are usually multi-homers, whereas in traditional media markets, consumers are more likely to choose one outlet and stick to it. Consider, for example, the market for newspapers: Most consumers read only one daily

---

[23] Moreover, the pricing of congestion may affect the choice of format of media content. For instance, video consumes more bandwidth than text, and with video, a higher resolution requires more transmission capacity.

newspaper (if any) due to time constraints and often stick to this choice for a long time.[24] Also, during the course of an evening, TV viewers who want to watch a movie usually choose one and single-home on the channel showing the movie. For the other side of the market, this implies that an advertiser can reach a particular consumer only by placing ads in the particular newspaper that this consumer is reading, or by placing commercials during the movie that the viewer is watching. To inform a large number of consumers, advertisers need to buy ads on multiple outlets due to consumers' single-homing behavior. This problem is captured by the seminal competitive bottleneck model of Anderson and Coate (2005) and follow-ups.

If, instead, consumers choose multiple outlets, an advertiser can reach a consumer not only on a single platform but also on multiple ones. In this respect, platforms lose their monopoly power of delivering consumers' attention to advertisers. In the competitive bottleneck model, in order to attain such a monopoly position, platforms fight for the exclusive turf of consumers, thereby capturing rents on the advertiser side but dissipating parts of these rents to consumers. In a market with multi-homing on both sides, this is no longer necessarily true. This implies that the well-known force that competition intensity is determined by the strength of business stealing on the consumer side is less relevant in online media markets. Since consumers are active on multiple platforms, new forces come into play and old ones are probably disabled. This can affect platforms' content choice.

In Section 10.4.1, we provide different formalizations of multi-homing on the consumer side. We focus particularly on implications for competition and distinguish them from models with single-homing consumers. Before doing so, we note that if advertisers could perfectly coordinate their messages, then multi-homing would be equivalent to single-homing. Consider the situation in which advertising has decreasing returns-to-scale—that is, the first impression is very valuable, but further impressions are less valuable because there is a probability that the consumer has already noticed the ad on another platform. If advertisers can perfectly coordinate their messages, they can prevent a consumer from being exposed to the ad multiple times. For example, on TV, this requires that an advertiser choose the same time slot for its ads on each station. Therefore, competition in this model is equivalent to competition in a model with single-homing consumers. Anderson and Peitz (2014a) use the formulation to study advertising congestion. We discuss this paper in more detail in Section 10.6.2.

---

[24] However, Gentzkow et al. (2014), using historical data on newspaper readership, find that even in the newspaper market, multiple readership is quantitatively important. In particular, in their data, 15% of households that read a daily newspaper read two or more newspapers.

10.4.1 Consumer Choice with Multi-Homing and Its Implications on Content

One of the first attempts to allow consumers to combine consumption of multiple products was done in the Hotelling (1929) framework in a one-sided market. Suppose that there are two platforms, 1 and 2. The content provided by each platform is interpreted as its location on the Hotelling line. Platform 1 offers content α and platform 2 offers content $1 - \beta$. Most of the literature works under the assumption that a consumer subscribes to only one platform. This implies that the disutility of a consumer located at x from not consuming the preferred content is $g(|x - \alpha|)$ or $g(|1 - \beta - x|)$, depending on which platform the consumer is active, where g is an increasing function. Anderson and Neven (1989) extend this formulation by allowing a consumer to consume any mix of the two contents of

$$\omega\alpha + (1 - \omega)(1 - \beta),$$

with $0 \leq \omega \leq 1$. The disutility incurred by a consumer at x under the assumption of quadratic disutility is $(\omega\alpha + (1 - \omega)(1 - \beta) - x)^2$. Therefore, the consumer can obtain her optimal content by combining the existing content in the right way. The Hotelling model with content mixing can be straightforwardly interpreted in the media market context. Suppose that each consumer has some amount of time that she can allocate between the two platforms. Then, the consumer spends a share $\omega(x)$ of this amount on platform 1 and $1 - \omega(x)$ on platform 2.

Suppose that consumers are uniformly distributed on the interval between 0 and 1. Although the utility formulation is very different from the standard single-homing Hotelling model, the resulting aggregate demand function is exactly the same if consumers pay for the amount of time they spend on a platform.[25] To see this, recall, first, that in a traditional Hotelling model, the aggregate demand of firm 1 is

$$D_1 = \frac{1 + \alpha - \beta}{2} + \frac{p_2 - p_1}{2(1 - \alpha - \beta)}. \tag{10.1}$$

Let us now briefly derive the aggregate demand in the mixing model. The utility function of a consumer located at x is

$$v(p_1, p_2, \alpha, \beta, x) = u_0 - (\omega\alpha + (1 - \omega)(1 - \beta) - x)^2 - \omega p_1 - (1 - \omega)p_2,$$

where u_0 is the gross utility from using the platform. Maximizing with respect to ω, we obtain

---

[25] Anderson and Neven (1989) consider such linear pricing and find that the model gives similar results as the standard Hotelling model. Hoernig and Valletti (2007) analyze two-part tariffs and find that consumers then do not necessarily choose their preferred product mix because they need to pay fixed fees to both platforms.

$$\omega(x) = \frac{2(1-\alpha-\beta)(1-\beta-x) - p_1 + p_2}{2(1-\alpha-\beta)^2}$$

for

$$\alpha + \frac{p_2 - p_1}{2(1-\alpha-\beta)} < x < 1 - \beta + \frac{p_2 - p_1}{2(1-\alpha-\beta)},$$

while $\omega = 1$ for $x \leq \alpha + (p_2 - p_1)/(2(1-\alpha-\beta))$ and $\omega = 0$ for $x \geq 1 - \beta + (p_2 - p_1)/(2(1-\alpha-\beta))$. Therefore, consumers whose preference is close to the content of one of the platforms do not mix, while those located at less extreme positions choose to mix the content. Determining the aggregate demand of firm 1, we obtain

$$D_1 = \alpha + \frac{p_2 - p_1}{2(1-\alpha-\beta)} + \int_{\alpha + \frac{p_2-p_1}{2(1-\alpha-\beta)}}^{1 - \beta + \frac{p_2-p_1}{2(1-\alpha-\beta)}} \omega(x) \mathrm{d}x = \frac{1 + \alpha - \beta}{2} + \frac{p_2 - p_1}{2(1-\alpha-\beta)},$$

which equals (10.1), implying that the two formulations are equivalent. In other words, single-homing in the Hotelling model can also be interpreted as multi-homing of consumers who mix content. As a consequence, competition plays out in exactly the same way in the two models.

Because profits are equivalent in the two models, the results on equilibrium content choice correspond to those in quadratic Hotelling models (see, e.g., d'Aspremont et al., 1979). In particular, if α and β are restricted to be positive, firms in a two-stage location-cum-price game choose maximal differentiation in equilibrium. That is, $\alpha = \beta = 0$, and firm 1 is located at 0 whereas firm 2 is located at 1.[26] If α and β can be negative, in equilibrium $\alpha = \beta = -1/4$, implying that firms choose content outside the unit interval. In media markets, this means that platforms may polarize content even if it does not match the heterogeneity of tastes.

Although the positive results of content mixing in the Hotelling model coincide with the ones of the standard analysis, the normative economics are different. For example, as shown by Anderson and Neven (1989), the socially optimal locations in the mixing model are indeed 0 and 1. Hence, if firms are bounded to choose locations within the consumer taste space, they choose the welfare-optimal ones. By contrast, in the traditional Hotelling model, welfare-optimal locations are in the interior of the taste space (at $\alpha = \beta = 1/4$), leading to excessive differentiation.

We now extend the framework of mixing content to a two-sided ad-financed media model—i.e., platforms obtain their revenues from advertisers instead of consumers. That is, prices p_1 and p_2 are equal to zero, but consumers view advertising levels a_1 and a_2 on the platforms as a nuisance. Therefore, the utility function of a consumer located at x is

---

[26] Peitz and Valletti (2008) show that this result holds true also in the context of advertising-financed media, in which platforms receive revenues from consumers and advertisers.

$$v(a_1, a_2, \alpha, \beta, x) = u_0 - (\omega\alpha + (1-\omega)(1-\beta) - x)^2 - \gamma\omega a_1 - \gamma(1-\omega)a_2,$$

where γ represents the nuisance parameter of advertising.

Gal-Or and Dukes (2003) use this framework to analyze content choice in media markets. They find that platforms choose the same location on the Hotelling line, a result in stark contrast to the one obtained in the traditional framework. In the model of Gal-Or and Dukes (2003), consumers obtain content for free but incur a disutility from advertising. Advertisers compete in the product market and inform consumers about their products via advertising. A lower advertising intensity leads to less-intense product market competition, implying that advertisers' prices and profits are higher. Each platform and advertiser negotiate about the payment made by the advertiser in return for advertising on the platform. In this negotiation, the two parties maximize their joint surplus and share it equally. By choosing minimal differentiation, platforms reduce the amount of advertising in equilibrium because advertising is a nuisance to consumers. Hence, intense competition for consumers in the media market results in low advertising levels. Via minimal differentiation platforms commit to a low advertising intensity, thereby reducing product market competition. This, in turn, allows advertisers to reap higher profits. Since platforms do not set advertising prices but negotiate with producers, minimal differentiation does not lead to zero advertising prices but increases the surplus in the negotiation.[27]

Gabszewicz et al. (2004) also consider multi-homing consumers but do not consider advertiser competition in the product market. Instead, they assume that the disutility of consumers is convex in the advertising level—that is, the disutility from advertising is a_i^θ, with $\theta \geq 1$. As they show, in equilibrium, platforms may choose a location in the interior range of the Hotelling line; that is, the content is relatively similar.[28] In fact, the equilibrium locations are closer to each other, the larger is θ. That is, the program diversity is smaller, the larger is the advertising aversion of consumers (measured by increasing marginal disutility of advertising).

These papers are based on the idea that consumers mix the time that they spend on different platforms, keeping the total amount of time fixed. However, in most markets, the availability of content increases consumption. These features have been incorporated

---

[27] Exclusive advertising contracts are a different means to mitigate competition between advertisers. These contracts are standard practice, e.g., in the US television industry. By offering single-category advertising rights, a platform guarantees not to sell another slot in the same advertising break to any close competitor. Therefore, consumers are less informed about competing products, yielding higher profits for advertising firms. For a detailed analysis, see Dukes and Gal-Or (2003).

[28] Peitz and Valletti (2008) also find that platforms do not choose "maximal" differentiation to obtain higher surplus from advertisers in case consumers obtain content for free. Their model is cast in a framework in which all consumers single-home and advertisers multi-home. However, as they note, their results carry over to a setting in which consumers mix content.

into several models; we begin with those that keep the assumption of consumers being distributed on the Hotelling line and incurring a disutility in distance.

In Ambrus and Reisinger (2006), platforms are located at the endpoints of the Hotelling line, with platform 1 located at point 0 and platform 2 located at point 1. The utility of a consumer located at x is then $u_0 - \gamma a_1 - tx$ when consuming from platform 1 and $u_0 - \gamma n_2 - t(1-x)$ when consuming from platform 2. A consumer can be active on both platforms and optimally does so if the utility she obtains on each platform is positive.

Deriving the demand functions, consumers located close to platform 1 will be exclusive consumers of platform 1, while consumers who are located close to platform 2 will be exclusive consumers of platform 2. However, consumers in the middle segment of the Hotelling line enjoy a positive utility on each platform (given that advertising levels are not too high). These consumers are therefore overlapping consumers active on both platforms. Denoting the demand of exclusive and overlapping consumers of platform $i = 1, 2$ by D_i we obtain $D_1 = (u_0 - \gamma a_1)/\tau$ and $D_2 = 1 - (u_0 - \gamma a_2)/\tau$. Overall, there are $D_{12} = [2u_0 - \gamma(a_1 + a_2)]/\tau - 1$ overlapping consumers, $D_1 - D_{12} = 1 - (u_0 - \gamma a_2)/\tau$ exclusive consumers on platform 1, and $D_2 - D_{12} = 1 - (u_0 - \gamma a_1)/\tau$ exclusive consumers on platform 2. The demand configuration is displayed in Figure 10.6.

An advertiser's profit from reaching a consumer can be different for overlapping and exclusive consumers. For example, an overlapping consumer may spend less time on a platform than a consumer who is exclusively active on a single platform. Similarly, an advertiser who buys advertising space on both platforms may receive a lower benefit from an overlapping consumer than an advertiser who displays ads on only one platform because the overlapping consumer may become aware that the advertisement is already on the other platform. This implies that an (additional) advertisement on platform i is less valuable for an advertiser who is also active on platform j than for an advertiser who is active only on platform i.

Ambrus and Reisinger (2006) characterize the equilibrium advertising levels in the cases of monopoly and duopoly. They find that multi-homing on the consumer side

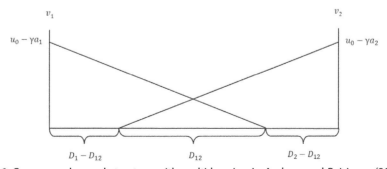

Figure 10.6 Consumer demand structure with multi-homing in Ambrus and Reisinger (2006).

reduces the competitive pressure in advertising levels. As a consequence, advertising levels are socially excessive under the assumption that advertisers are homogeneous.

Anderson et al. (2010) also analyze multi-homing consumers in the Hotelling setting. In their model, media platforms do not carry advertising but, rather, charge viewers directly and thus their model is not a two-sided market model. In their model, a consumer located at x obtains a utility of

$$v_1 = (r - \tau x)q_1 - p_1$$

when subscribing to platform 1 only. Here, q_1 represents the coverage of platform 1 and p_1 the price of platform 1. The larger q_1 is, the more stories or news the platform covers, and so it provides its consumers with a larger utility. The parameter r represents the reservation value of a consumer while τ is, as before, the transportation parameter. Therefore, a consumer benefits more from high coverage if her preferences are better aligned with the content of the platform. Correspondingly, the utility from being active on platform 2 is $v_2 = (r - \tau(1 - x))q_2 - p_2$.

When active on both platforms, the consumer obtains an additional utility. In particular, Anderson et al. (2010) distinguish between two types of multi-homing consumers by explicitly allowing multi-homing consumers to first consume the content of the platform they prefer most and then consume the content of the other platform. The additional value a consumer obtains from subscribing to the second platform depends on the extent of overlap in the content of the two platforms. This overlap is given by $q_1 q_2$, as platforms cannot coordinate their content coverage. Therefore, platform 2 covers $(1 - q_1)q_2$ stories that are not covered by platform 1. The consumer also obtains an additional value when reading the same story twice because each platform presents it in a different way. This additional value can be captured by $1 - b$, with $b \in [0, 1]$; that is, the lower b, the higher the additional value of reading the same story a second time. This implies that the additional benefit of consuming an amount q_2 of news or stories when first consuming an amount q_1 is

$$(1 - q_1)q_2 + (1 - b)q_1 q_2 = (1 - bq_1)q_2.$$

Therefore, the utility of a consumer who visits platform 1 and then platform 2 is given by

$$v_{12} = v_1 + (r - \tau(1 - x))(1 - bq_1)q_2 - p_2.$$

Similarly, the utility of a consumer who first visits platform 2 and then platform 1 is

$$v_{21} = v_2 + (r - \tau x)(1 - bq_2)q_1 - p_1.$$

The locations of consumers indifferent between different pairs of options are illustrated in Figure 10.7, in which the marginal consumers are denoted by $x_{1,12}$, $x_{12,21}$, and $x_{21,2}$.

In this framework, Anderson et al. (2010) solve for the equilibrium prices and profits. They find that profits are decreasing in the transportation cost parameter τ. In a standard

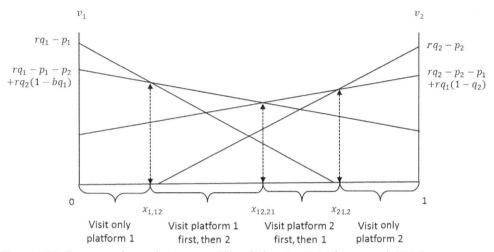

Figure 10.7 Consumer demand structure with multi-homing in Anderson et al. (2010).

Hotelling model, τ measures the degree of competition, and a higher τ implies that plat-forms are more differentiated and so profits are larger. By contrast, with multi-homing, the result is reversed because the total demand of platform 1 is independent of the price charged by platform 2. To see this, note that the total demand of platform 1 includes all consumers between 0 and $x_{21,2}$. When determining the consumer who is indifferent between, on the one hand, visiting platform 2 first and platform 1 next and, on the other hand, visiting only platform 2, we have $v_1 = v_{12}$. In this expression, the price of platform 2 is canceled out. Therefore, each platform's total demand is independent of the rival's price. A platform charges a price equal to the incremental value it brings to a consumer who is also active on the rival platform. Therefore, platforms act as monopolists in their pricing decisions. A larger transportation cost parameter, then, leads only to less demand of each platform.

While the assumption that consumers' preferences are distributed along the Hotelling line has the advantage of tractability and straightforward interpretation, it imposes a strait-jacket on preferences and thus on demand. In particular, the sum of demand of both firms is perfectly price-inelastic (up to some upper bound of prices). Therefore, a price cut leads only to business stealing but does not increase overall demand in the market. Second, the preference structure is, by definition, perfectly negatively correlated; that is, the con-sumer who has the strongest preference for the content of platform 1 has the weakest preference for the content of platform 2, and vice versa. Therefore, it is impossible to analyze effects of content or ideology correlation on competition, which is often at the heart of media markets.

Two recent papers consider different preferences and demand. Ambrus et al. (2015) propose a model in which a consumer's choice to visit one platform is independent of the choice to visit another. This implies that a consumer chooses to visit the platform if her utility is positive. Advertisers are homogeneous and can post multiple ads on a platform. The value of informing a consumer is normalized to 1. Platforms offer contracts to advertisers consisting of an advertising level m_i in exchange for a transfer payment t_i. An exclusive consumer of platform i becomes informed about an advertiser's product with probability $\phi_i(m_i)$, with ϕ_i strictly increasing and concave. This captures the idea that the consumer might be exposed to the same ad twice, implying decreasing marginal returns from advertising. Similarly, a consumer active on both platforms becomes informed with probability $\phi_{12}(m_1, m_2)$, with ϕ_{12} strictly increasing and concave in each argument and a negative cross-partial derivative.

Because advertisers are homogeneous in this framework, they all put the same advertising level on a platform. Due to the concavity of the advertising technology, a platform can make more profits by having all advertisers on board instead of just a fraction of it. Therefore, in equilibrium, all advertisers accept the contracts of both platforms. If the mass of advertisers equals 1, the aggregate advertising level equals the one of an individual advertiser. This implies $m_i = a_i$, where a_i is the aggregate advertising level on platform i. In equilibrium, a platform cannot extract the full surplus from advertisers even though advertisers are homogeneous. Instead, a platform can extract only the incremental surplus, which is the surplus that it delivers in addition to the surplus that an advertiser can obtain when rejecting the contract and being active only on the other platform. Hence, incremental pricing also emerges in this model.

More formally, denote the demand of exclusive consumers by $D_i(a_1, a_2)$, $i = 1, 2$, and the demand of multi-homing users by $D_{12}(a_1, a_2)$. An advertiser who accepts both contracts gets a benefit of

$$D_1(a_1, a_2)\phi_1(a_1) + D_2(a_1, a_2)\phi_2(a_2) + D_{12}(a_1, a_2)\phi_{12}(a_1, a_2) - t_1 - t_2.$$

Instead, when accepting the contract of platform j only, he gets

$$\left(D_j(a_1, a_2) + D_{12}(a_1, a_2)\right)\phi_j(a_j) - t_j$$

because the advertiser reaches consumers only on platform j. As a consequence, platform i can demand only

$$t_i = D_i(a_1, a_2)\phi_i(a_i) + D_{12}(a_1, a_2)\left(\phi_{12}(a_1, a_2) - \phi_j(a_j)\right).$$

This leaves a profit of $D_{12}(a_1, a_2)(\phi_1(a_1) + \phi_2(a_2) - \phi_{12}(a_1, a_2))$ to each advertiser, which is positive due to the concavity of the advertising technology.

To understand how competition works in this model, compare the market with duopolistic platforms with a monopoly market. The monopoly platform can extract the full surplus of advertisers. There are two effects from entry. First, each multi-homing consumer can now get informed about an advertiser's product on both platforms. Therefore, the single ad is worth less, a *duplication effect*. Due to this effect, the advertising intensity in duopoly falls. However, there is also a more subtle countervailing effect. For the single platform, all consumers are exclusive consumers. Relative to overlapping consumers, these consumers are more valuable, and losing them is relatively costly for the platform. This curbs its incentive to increase the advertising level. By contrast, in duopoly, some of the lost business due to increased advertising levels comes from overlapping consumers. The duopolist shares business with its rival, and losing this shared business is less detrimental than losing exclusive consumers. As a consequence, due to this *business-sharing effect*, the duopolist has a greater incentive to increase the advertising level. This shows that competition is driven by the *composition* of consumer demand and not just by the mere *size* of the demand. The paper demonstrates that if the business-sharing effect dominates the duplication effect, advertising levels in a duopoly are larger than in a monopoly, and vice versa.

It is also possible to relate the strength of the business-sharing and the duplication effects to consumers' preferences and the content provided by the platforms. Suppose, for example, that platforms' contents are relatively similar in the sense that consumers who like the content of platform 1 have a high probability of also liking the content of platform 2. In this case of a positive consumer preference correlation, platforms have many overlapping consumers. If platforms are symmetric and have a similar advertising intensity, a platform, by reducing its advertising intensity, attracts many exclusive consumers relative to its current demand composition. Therefore, the gains from reducing advertising levels are relatively high, implying that platforms with positively correlated content are likely to have lower advertising levels. By contrast, suppose that platforms are news platforms and that one caters to a more right-wing audience and the other to a more left-wing audience. Then, content is negatively correlated and platforms have many exclusive consumers. By reducing the advertising intensity, a platform attracts mainly consumers with moderate preferences, and some of them will visit both platforms. These consumers are, on average, less valuable than the existing ones, who are mainly exclusives. Therefore, each platform has only little incentive to lower the advertising intensity, which leads to a high equilibrium level of ads. Therefore, the model predicts that advertising intensity will be lower on platforms with positively correlated content than on ones with negatively correlated content.

Anderson et al. (2014) analyze a different model with multi-homing consumers. Let us again focus on the case of two platforms and suppose that $D_i(a_1, a_2)$, $i = 1, 2$, denotes the exclusive consumers of platform i, whereas $D_{12}(a_1, a_2)$ denotes the overlapping consumers. An advertiser can choose whether or not to advertise on a platform—that is, the advertising level of an individual advertiser is either 0 or 1. Suppose that the value of informing an exclusive consumer equals ϑ, while the value of informing a multi-homing consumer equals $\vartheta(1 + \lambda)$, with $\lambda \in [0, 1]$. A possible interpretation is that the probability with which a consumer becomes aware of the ad is x on each platform. An ad to the same consumer on another platform raises the chance that she becomes aware of the ad by $x(1 - x)$. Therefore, normalizing the value of informing a consumer to 1, we have that $\vartheta = x$ and $\lambda = 1 - x$.

In Anderson et al.'s (2014) model, first, consumers form an expectation about the advertising intensity on each platform. Then, platforms set a price per ad, and advertisers rationally anticipate the number of consumers and choose to buy ads. Finally, consumers decide which platform to join. Due to the game structure, consumers do not react to the actual number of ads, which simplifies the solution of the game.[29]

In equilibrium, each platform charges a price of (omitting arguments)

$$D_i \vartheta + D_{12} \vartheta \lambda,$$

and all advertisers are active on both platforms. Hence, platforms can extract the full surplus an advertiser obtains when informing an exclusive consumer, but only part of the surplus that an advertiser obtains when informing an overlapping consumer. An advertiser obtains a positive profit of $D_{12}\vartheta(1 - \lambda)$. Therefore, the principle of incremental pricing reemerges.

Anderson et al. (2014) then focus on several important aspects of media markets that are influenced by the presence of multi-homing consumers. Consider the well-known problem of content duplication and suppose that each media platform has the choice of providing content A or B. If consumers only single-home and more than two-thirds of them are interested in content A instead of content B, then both platforms will specialize in content A. This is because if half of the consumers choose platform 1 and the other half platform 2 when both have the same content, then each platform gets more than one-third of the consumers. By contrast, when choosing content B, a platform gets less than one-third of the consumers. In general, duplication of content occurs in equilibrium if and only if

$$\frac{D_A}{2} > D_B,$$

where D_j, $j = A, B$, denotes the consumership for content j.

---

[29] The game involves passive expectations as in the classic model by Katz and Shapiro (1985). This form of expectation building implies that consumers form their expectations before observing the prices set by platforms. Hagiu and Halaburda (2014) and Belleflamme and Peitz (2014) use related assumptions in two-sided market models, in which all or a fraction of the agents of one side cannot observe the prices charged on the other side. The opposite assumption involves agents forming expectations after observing all prices and is (usually) denoted responsive expectations. For a discussion of the different implications of the two assumptions on termination charges of communication networks, see Hurkens and López (2014).

Now, suppose that consumers can multi-home. If both platforms have the same content, a fraction d_{12} of consumers multi-home. If both platforms choose content A, then each of them obtains a profit of

$$\frac{D_A}{2}\vartheta((1-d_{12})+d_{12}\lambda).$$

By contrast, if one platform chooses content B, it obtains a profit of $D_B\vartheta$. Comparing the two profits shows that choosing content A is preferred if and only if

$$\frac{D_A}{2}(1-d_{12}(1-\lambda))>D_B.$$

Compared to the situation without multi-homing consumers, it is evident that content duplication occurs under a strictly smaller parameter range. Hence, if multi-homing consumers are present, the problem of content duplication is less severe.

To sum up, the work on multi-homing provides two important lessons. First, platforms set their tariffs for advertising according to incremental pricing. This is because the consumer's first impression is usually more valuable than the second, and consumers can now be reached on multiple platforms. Therefore, although consumers are no longer the bottleneck, platforms cannot extract the full surplus from advertisers. Second, platforms do not care only about the size of demand, but also about how it is composed of single- and multi-homing consumers; thus, the composition of demand affects market outcomes.

10.4.2 Search Engines and Search Bias

So far, we have simplified our presentation by assuming that users know which websites' content they are interested in and can access it directly. This implies that no intermediary is needed to help users select their preferred websites. However, the Internet offers a multitude of information, and finding the most relevant bits is often impossible without the help of a search engine. In fact, worldwide, there are billions of queries each day on different search engines. As described in Section 10.2, the most prominent one is clearly Google, with a market share of more than 90% in European countries and a global average of more than 80%. However, other search engines dominate in some countries; for example, in China, the search engine Baidu has a market share of more than 75%, whereas Google China has only slightly more than 15%.[30]

If the only role of search engines were to efficiently allocate users to their preferred websites, then search engines would not be particularly relevant to this chapter. In that limited role, the information gatekeeper directs users to the appropriate media content, and its presence has no economic implications. However, the business model of a search

---

[30] See http://www.chinainternetwatch.com/category/search-engine/ (accessed April 25, 2014).

engine, like that of most media platforms, centers around attracting users and obtaining revenues from advertisers. It is therefore not obvious that the incentives of users and search engines are perfectly aligned. In particular, search engines may bias their search results to obtain high revenues from advertisers. Suppose, for example, that a user wants to watch the video of a particular song and searches for it via Google. The video is available through multiple video portals, such as YouTube, MyVideo, or Clipfish, and Google can choose the order in which to display the search results. Since Google owns YouTube but not the other video portals, Google may have an incentive to bias its search results in favor of its own video portal and away from others.

Establishing such a search engine bias empirically is not always straightforward. Tarantino (2013) reports that, in response to a query with the keyword "finance," Google lists Google Finance first, whereas Yahoo! lists Yahoo! Finance first. This suggests that at least one of the two search engines is biased if consumers on one search engine are comparable to those on the other.

Edelman and Lai (2015) consider the following quasi-experiment: In December 2011, Google introduced a tool called Google Flight Search, which helps users to search for a flight from A to B. When Google Flight Search appeared, it always appeared in a box at the top position. However, the appearance of Google Flight Search was very unsystematic, and minor changes in the entry could lead to the appearance or disappearance of the box.[31] Edelman and Lai (2015) estimate the change in the CTR when the Google Flight Search box appeared. They find that with the box, the CTR for paid advertising increased by 65%, whereas the CTRs for non-paid search of other travel agencies decreased by 55%. Therefore, the study provides evidence that search engines are able to influence user behavior by the layout and format with which the search results are presented.

Search engines usually have two different kinds of links, organic (or non-paid-for) links and sponsored (or paid-for) links. The organic links reflect the relative importance or relevance of listings according to some algorithm. The sponsored links are paid for by advertisers. As outlined in Section 10.2, selling those advertising slots represents the largest revenue source of Internet advertising.

The major commercial search engines sell the sponsored links via second-price auctions with a reserve price for each auction. Since a search engine observes whether or not a user clicks on a sponsored link, advertisers pay per click. Thus, the price is called the per-click price (PCP). If an advertiser bids a higher PCP, this secures a rank closer to the top. However, the advertiser with the highest bid does not necessarily receive the first slot on top of page one of the search results. The search engine's goal is to maximize revenue from selling slots and therefore it also takes into account the number of times users click

---

[31] For example, the box was shown when typing in "flights to orlando," but it did not appear when searching for "flights to orlando fl."

on an ad. As a consequence, the search engine needs to estimate the CTR and may put ads with a lower PCP in a higher position if their CTR is high. Google uses a quality score that reflects the estimated CTR to determine the slots for the respective advertisers.[32] There are several studies analyzing the auction mechanism in detail, including the seminal papers by Edelman et al. (2007) and Varian (2007). More recent papers are Katona and Sarvary (2008), who analyze the interaction between sponsored and organic links, and Börgers et al. (2013), who explore the bidding behavior for sponsored links on Yahoo's search pages.

Do search engines list search results in the best interest of consumers? The economics literature has uncovered several reasons why search engines may have an incentive to bias their search results. We start with reasons that are to be considered even if a search engine is not integrated with a media platform. First, distinguishing between organic and sponsored links can provide one answer to why search engines bias their search results. As Xu et al. (2012), Taylor (2013a), and White (2013) point out, organic links give producers a free substitute to sponsored links on the search engine. Therefore, if the search engine provides high quality in its organic links, it cannibalizes its revenue from sponsored links. At the same time, providing better (i.e., more reliable) organic search results makes the search engine more attractive. If consumers have search costs, a more attractive search engine obtains a larger demand. However, if the latter effect is (partially) dominated by self-cannibalization, a search engine optimally distorts its organic search results.

Chen and He (2011) and Eliaz and Spiegler (2011) provide a further reason why search engines may bias their search results. Since the search engine obtains profits from advertisers, it is in its best interest that advertisers' valuation of sponsored links is high. This valuation increases if product market competition between advertisers is relatively mild. Therefore, the search engine may distort search results to relax product market competition between advertisers. In Chen and He (2011) and Eliaz and Spiegler (2011), the search engine has an incentive to decrease the relevance of its search results, thereby discouraging users from searching extensively. This quality degradation leads to lower competition between producers and therefore to higher prices.[33]

We now turn to the case in which the search engine is integrated with a media platform (as is the case with YouTube and Google). Does this lead to additional worries about search engine bias, or can integration possibly reduce search engine bias? In what follows, we present the models of de Cornière and Taylor (2014) and Burguet et al. (2014) to systematically analyze the costs and benefits of search engine integration.

In de Cornière and Taylor's (2014) model, there are a monopoly search engine $i = 0$ and two media platforms $i = 1, 2$. The media platforms are located at the ends of a Hotelling line, with platform 1 located at point 0 and platform 2 at point 1. Users are

---

[32] For a more detailed discussion, see Evans (2008).
[33] See Xu et al. (2010, 2011) for related models.

distributed on the unit interval, but before deciding to search, they are not aware of their location. This implies that without searching, a user cannot identify which media platform has the content she is interested in most. A user incurs search costs s when using the search engine, where s is distributed according to a cumulative distribution function denoted by F.

Both the media platforms and the search engine obtain revenues exclusively from advertising. The quantity of advertising on website i is denoted by a_i. Users dislike advertising, implying that the disutility of a user who will be directed by the search engine to website i is $\gamma_i(a_i)$, which is strictly increasing. A user's utility is also decreasing in the distance between her location and the location of website i. The utility a user receives from website i is

$$v(d, a_i) = u(d) - \gamma_i(a_i) - s,$$

where d denotes the distance between the location of website i and the location of the user and $u'(d) < 0$.

The search engine works as follows: If a user decides to use the search engine, she enters a query. The search engine then maps the user's query into a latent location on the Hotelling segment and directs the user to one of the platforms. The search engine's decision rule is a threshold rule such that all users with $x < \bar{x}$ are directed to platform 1 and those with $x \geq \bar{x}$ are directed to platform 2.

Advertising is informative, and there is a representative advertiser. The expected per-user revenue of the advertiser is

$$R(a_0, a_1, a_2, \bar{x}) = r_0(a_0) + \bar{x} r_1(a_0, a_1) + (1 - \bar{x}) r_2(a_0, a_2),$$

where $r_i, i = 0, 1, 2$ represents the revenue from contacting users on the search engines or the respective media platform. A key assumption is that ads on the search engine and on the media platforms are imperfect substitutes. That is, the marginal value of an ad on one outlet decreases as the number of advertisements on the other outlet increases. Formally,

$$\frac{\partial^2 r_i(a_0, a_i)}{\partial a_0 \partial a_i} \leq 0.$$

This implies that the advertising revenue generated by a media platform falls if a_0 rises. The advertiser pays platforms on a per-impression basis, and the respective prices are denoted by p_i. Therefore, the expected per-user profit of an advertiser is

$$\pi_a = R(a_0, a_1, a_2, \bar{x}) - a_0 p_0 - \bar{x} a_1 p_1 - (1 - \bar{x}) a_2 p_2.$$

Given that a fraction of users D use the search engine, the profit of the search engine is $\pi_0 = D a_0 p_0$, while the profits of the media platforms are $\pi_1 = \bar{x} D a_1 p_1$ and $\pi_2 = (1 - \bar{x}) D a_2 p_2$, respectively. To simplify the exposition, de Cornière and Taylor (2014) keep a_0 fixed and focus on the choice of a_1, a_2, and $\bar{x}$.

The timing of the game is as follows: First, media platforms choose their advertising levels a_1 and a_2 and the search engine chooses $\bar{x}$. In the second stage, the advertising market clears—that is, p_0, p_1, and p_2 equalize demand and supply for each outlet. In the third stage, consumers decide whether or not to use the search engine. Finally, those consumers who use the search engine type in a query and visit the media platform suggested by the search engine.

When deciding whether or not to use the search engine, a consumer knows $\bar{x}$ and has an expectation about the advertising levels on the media platforms, denoted by a_i^e. The expected utility of a consumer from using the search engine is therefore given by

$$E[v] = \int_0^{\bar{x}} u(z)\mathrm{d}z + \int_{\bar{x}}^1 u(1-z)\mathrm{d}z - \bar{x}\gamma_1\left(a_1^e\right) - (1-\bar{x})\gamma_2\left(a_2^e\right) - s.$$

Since the outside option of a consumer is normalized to 0, she will use the search engine as long as $E[v] \geq 0$, which determines the user demand D. We denote the value of $\bar{x}$ that maximizes the expected consumer utility and thus the participation rate by x^D.

A *search bias* can then be defined as follows: The search engine is biased as long as $\bar{x} \neq x^D$. In particular, the search engine is biased in favor of media outlet 1 (media outlet 2) when $\bar{x} > x^D$ ($\bar{x} < x^D$).

When deciding about its optimal cutoff value $\bar{x}$, the search engine faces the following problem. First, it wants to have high user participation. Other things being equal, a larger number of search engine users leads to higher profits because the willingness-to-pay of advertisers increases. Therefore, the search engine cares about relevance to users, but this is not the only important characteristic of concern to users. Users also dislike advertising, implying that they prefer to be directed to a site that shows a low number of ads. As a consequence, the fewer the advertisements on outlet 1 relative to outlet 2, the higher the search engine sets $\bar{x}$, and vice versa. These considerations align the incentives of the search engine with those of users. However, the search engine obtains profits from advertisers and therefore aims to maintain a high price p_0 for its own links. With that, a strategic consideration comes into play. If ads on media platform i are particularly high substitutes for ads on the search engine, the search engine prefers to bias results against this platform. This allows the search engine to keep p_0 high and to obtain higher profits. Formally, clearing of the advertising market implies that the price of ads is equal to the advertiser's marginal willingness-to-pay; that is (omitting arguments),

$$p_0 = \frac{\partial r_0}{\partial a_0} + \bar{x}\frac{\partial r_1}{\partial a_0} + (1-\bar{x})\frac{\partial r_2}{\partial a_0}.$$

Therefore, p_0 is non-increasing in a_1 and a_2. It follows that the search engine biases its results against the media outlet for which $\partial r_i/\partial a_0$ is more negative. As a consequence, too many consumers are directed to media outlet 1 if $\partial r_1/\partial a_0 > \partial r_2/\partial a_0$, and too many consumers are directed to media outlet 2 if the reverse holds true. If the two media platforms are symmetric, or if the advertising demands are independent, then no bias occurs.

De Cornière and Taylor (2014) then analyze the effects of integration of the search engine with one of the media platforms. Suppose that there is partial integration without control of ad levels. That is, media platform i shares a fraction ρ_i of its profit with the search engine but obtains full control with respect to the ad level a_i. In reality, this case is relevant for two reasons: First, Google owns subsidiaries, such as DoubleClick, which sell advertising technologies to media outlets. Therefore, the search engine already obtains some revenues from media outlets. Second, even when fully integrated, a media outlet might still be independently managed.

The profit of the media outlet is, then, $\pi_i = (1 - \rho_i)\bar{x}Da_ip_i$, which implies that the optimal advertising level is the same as in the non–integrated case since the profit function is just multiplied by a constant. The search engine's profit is now $\pi_0 = D(a_0p_0 + \rho_i\bar{x}a_ip_i)$. There are two immediate consequences: First, the search engine has an incentive to bias its result in favor of media platform i because it benefits directly from this platform's revenues. Second, it also benefits more from higher consumer participation, implying that the search engine wants to implement higher quality (i.e., less biased results).

Because of these two potentially opposing forces, partial integration can increase or decrease the level of bias. In particular, if the search engine were biased to the detriment of platform i without integration, partial integration might mitigate this bias. However, even if the search engine were biased in favor of media outlet i without integration, partial integration could lead to a reduction in the bias because the search engine would care more about quality. De Cornière and Taylor (2014) show that this occurs if the elasticity of user participation with respect to quality is large.

When considering full instead of partial integration, similar effects are at work. Here, the ad level of the integrated media platform will fall after integration due to the internalization of the price effect—i.e., advertising levels are substitutes. With respect to the bias, the search engine again has the incentive to increase consumer participation. Therefore, it may benefit from a reduction in the bias. This result is most likely if the two media platforms are very different with respect to the substitutability of their ads to the search engine's ads; in other words, one is a close substitute, while the other is a mild substitute for the search engine's ads. In general, if the media platforms are symmetric, partial or full integration always leads to an increase in bias but can still benefit consumers through lower ad levels.

Burguet et al. (2014) propose a different setup to analyze the problem of search engine bias and integration. They do not allow for ad nuisance but explicitly model consumer search for advertisers' products. In what follows, we present a simplified version of their model, which nevertheless captures the main tradeoff.

There is a mass one of users, indexed by i. Users are interested in the content of a website. There are N websites, indexed by n, and each user i has a specific content that matches her interests and generates net utility $u > 0$. This content is denoted by $n(i)$. Any other content generates a net utility of zero. Users do not know which website matches their interests. Therefore, they need the help of a search engine, denoted by 0. The search engine can perfectly identify the relevant website $n(i)$ after a user has typed in the query. Websites are symmetric in the sense that each website's content interests the same fraction of users, $1/N$. When using the search engine, a user incurs search cost s, where s is distributed according to a c.d.f. denoted by F.

The search engine displays a link to a website after a user has typed in the query. The search engine can choose the probability that the link leads to the content matching the user's interest. We denote this probability by ϕ^O. The superscript O stands for organic link, representing the fact that the links to websites are non-paid and therefore organic.

The search engine and websites obtain profits from producers who pay to advertise their products. There are J different product categories, indexed by $j \in \{1, 2, ..., J\}$. User i values only one category $j(i)$ and buys one unit. There are two producers of products $k \in [1, 2]$ in each category. Producer 1 provides the best match to a user, leading to a net utility of v_1. Producer 2 provides only the second-best match, leading to a net utility of v_2, with $0 < v_2 < v_1$. The margins earned by the producers are given by m_1 and m_2, respectively. To simplify the exposition, Burguet et al. (2014) assume that users' and producers' interests are misaligned, in the sense that for each category, $m_2 > m_1$.[34] Moreover, to simplify the welfare analysis in all categories, $m_1 + v_1 > m_2 + v_2$, implying that the social optimum involves only transactions of the best-match product. As above, categories are symmetric in the sense that each category's products interest the same fraction of users, $1/J$.

The search engine provides a single link after a user has typed in a query for product search in a particular category.[35] It also has full market power and sets a pay-per-click price. The search engine chooses to display the link of producer 1 with probability ϕ^S and the link of producer 2 with probability $1 - \phi^S$. The superscript S stands for sponsored link, representing the fact that producers pay for the links to websites.[36]

---

[34] This is an extreme assumption. However, for the main result to hold, it is sufficient that there are some categories for which this misalignment holds true.

[35] In Burguet et al. (2014) and de Cornière and Taylor (2014), users visit only a single website after typing in a query. However, users sometimes click on multiple search results (in sequential order) broadly following the respective ranking of the results. This implies that advertisers exert externalities on each other, e.g., through bidding for more prominent placement. Athey and Ellison (2011) and Kempe and Mahdian (2008) provide models that explore the effects of these externalities on the optimal selling mechanism of the search engine.

[36] The description of the game departs from the original model considered by Burguet et al. (2014). Instead of having only two producers in each category, Burguet et al. (2014) consider four, two for the best-match product and two for the second-best product. These firms are in Bertrand competition for links. The search engine runs a second-price auction with the twist that it partially discounts second-best products, to allow best-match products to win the auction. Burguet et al. (2014) show that the discount is set in such a way that all four producers choose the same bid after discounting. Then, ϕ^S represents the probability that the search engine chooses a best-match product as the winner.

Users can also buy the products on websites. In particular, each website offers a "display-ad" slot for a link to a producer. If a user i visits website $n(i)$ (i.e., the website with the content she is interested in), she notices the ad with probability α, with $0 < \alpha \le 1$. By contrast, if she is directed to a website different from the one with the content that interests her, the probability is $\alpha\beta$, with $0 < \beta < 1$. The targeting of websites is less accurate than that of the search engine. Formally, the website gets user i's product category right with only probability $\sigma < 1$. That is, the website obtains a signal of each visiting user's product category interest, and this signal equals $j(i)$ with probability σ. The websites also have full bargaining power vis-à-vis producers.

The timing of the game is as follows: In the first stage, the search engine and the website announce prices to merchants. In addition, the search engine announces its design variables ϕ^O and ϕ^S. In the second stage, users decide whether or not to use the search engine. If they participate, they first search for content and can visit the website displayed by the search engine. When consuming the content, they may click on the ad for the producer displayed by the website and may buy the producer's product. They then either leave the market or type in a product query and can visit the website of the producer displayed by the search engine and buy the product.[37] Therefore, the search order is first content and then product.

Figure 10.8 depicts all actors in the model and the interaction between users' search for content and products. The solid arrows represent products and the dashed arrow content. Downward arrows indicate links of advertisers (producers) and media platforms (websites), and upward arrows depict users visiting the respective websites.

In this model, the *search bias* is defined as follows: The search engine is biased as long as $\phi^O < 1$ and/or $\phi^S < 1$. In particular, since $u > 0$, (i.e., directing a user to her preferred content provides a higher benefit than directing the user to any other content), a social planner optimally chooses $r^O = 1$. Moreover, since $m_1 + v_1 > m_2 + v_2$, a social planner optimally chooses $r^S = 1$.

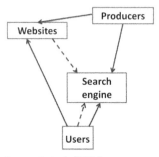

Figure 10.8 The media market in Burguet et al. (2014).

---

[37] Note that users pay the search costs only once—that is, the search participation decision is a single one.

The game can be solved by backward induction: Users' choices are immediate once stated, except for the participation decision. In particular, users click on the links provided by the search engine. In the product search stage, they buy the advertised product, whether it is the best match or the second-best, provided that it is in their preferred category. When a link to a preferred product is displayed on the website, a user buys the product only if it is the best match because she anticipates that she can buy at least the second-match product and, with probability ϕ^S, the best-match product in the next stage.

To determine the mass of participating users, we first determine the margins of the search engine and the websites. Since the search engine and the website make take-it-or-leave-it offers to producers, they will charge a price of m_1 to type 1 producers and m_2 to type 2 producers. This implies that the average margin of the search engine equals $\phi^S m_1 + (1 - \phi^S)m_2$. Turning to the website, it will display ads only for best-match products since users will never buy second-best-match products when clicking on the link from websites. Since a website offers the product category a user is interested in with probability σ, and the user becomes aware of the link with probability α (given that the user is interested in the content of the website), the expected margin of the website is $\sigma \alpha m_1$. By contrast, if the user is not interested in the content of the website, she realizes the ad only with probability $\alpha\beta < \alpha$, implying that the corresponding margin is $\sigma\alpha\beta m_1$.

The share of users who buy from organic display advertising on websites is then

$$\mu = \sigma\alpha\left(\phi^O + \left(1 - \phi^O\right)\beta\right).$$

The utility of a user from using the search engine is given by

$$\phi^O u + \left(\mu + (1 - \mu)\phi^S\right)v_1 + (1 - \mu)\left(1 - \phi^S\right)v_2 - s.$$

Let us denote the critical value of s, at which the last expression equals zero, by $\bar{s}$. The mass of participating users is then $F(\bar{s})$. This yields the profit of a search engine:

$$\pi_0 = F(\bar{s})(1 - \mu)\left(\phi^S m_1 + \left(1 - \phi^S\right)m_2\right). \tag{10.2}$$

What are the levels ϕ^O and ϕ^S that the search engine wants to set? Let us start with ϕ^O. Increasing ϕ^O raises participation because the search engine becomes more reliable on content search (the first term of (10.2), $F(\bar{s})$, increases). At the same time, increasing ϕ^O makes advertising on platforms more effective. Since the search engine and the websites compete for advertisers (producers), this reduces π_0 (the second term, $(1 - \mu)$, falls). Turning to ϕ^S, an increase in ϕ^S raises the reliability of the search engine with respect to product search and therefore increases user participation (the first term increases). However, because $m_2 > m_1$, the average margin of the search engine falls (the third term, $\left(\phi^S m_1 + \left(1 - \phi^S\right)m_2\right)$, decreases).

Burguet et al. (2014) show that the incentive of the search engine to distort content search and product search, starting from $\phi^O = \phi^S = 1$, depends on the ratio of the following terms:

$$\frac{u}{\sigma\alpha(1-\beta)m_1} \text{ versus } \frac{v_1 - v_2}{m_2 - m_1}.$$

The first expression refers to the costs and benefits of distorting content search, while the second refers to the costs and benefits of distorting product search. When distorting content search (with no distortion of product search), consumer surplus falls by a rate u, but the advertising revenues of the search engine rise at a rate $\sigma\alpha(1-\beta)m_1$.[38] Instead, distorting product search reduces consumer surplus at a rate $v_1 > v_2$ but increases the value for the search engine by $m_2 - m_1$. Burguet et al. (2014) show that, generically, the search engine will distort at most one type of search, setting the other at the optimal value. Specifically, if the expression on the left is larger than the one on the right, only product search is distorted, whereas only content search is distorted if the reverse holds true. Only if both expressions are the same might both searches be distorted.

Overall, this shows that even without integration of a website with the search engine, the search engine might have an incentive to distort search due to competition with websites for advertising. The question is, again, whether vertical integration with a website exacerbates this distortion or reduces it.

To see the incentives of the search engine under integration, suppose, first, that the search engine is integrated with all websites. Then, the profit of the search engine becomes

$$\pi_0 = F(\bar{s})\left[(1-\mu)\left(\phi^S m_1 + \left(1-\phi^S\right)m_2\right) + \mu m_1\right].$$

The search engine internalizes the externality exerted on websites by distorting ϕ^O or ϕ^S because it fully participates in the profits of the websites. This induces the search engine to improve its reliability, for both content and product search. Thus, the effect of integration is positive.

To understand the negative effects, consider the more realistic case in which the search engine is integrated with only a fraction of the websites. Then, it has an incentive to divert search from non-affiliated websites to affiliated ones. This leads to a different level of ϕ^O for affiliated websites than for non-affiliated ones. For example, if $\phi^O = \phi^S = 1$ without integration, then integration lowers consumer surplus because it may induce the search engine to reduce ϕ^O for non-affiliated websites.

To sum up, the literature on search engines shows that even without integration of a search engine with content providers, the search engine may have an incentive to bias search results. This bias occurs due to competition for advertisers between the search

---

[38] This is because a reduction of r^S reduces the probability that a user buys a product through a display link on a website from $\sigma\alpha$ to $\sigma\alpha\beta$.

engine and content providers. Integration between the search engine and a content provider affects the way that competition for advertisers plays out; integration leads to higher or lower social welfare, depending on the circumstances.

10.4.3 Information Spreading on the Internet

In the previous subsection, we restricted our attention to search engines as the only intermediaries between users and content-providing websites. However, there exist several other online channels allowing users to find out which website they are potentially interested in. In what follows, we discuss some of these channels and mechanisms, with a particular focus on their implications for the spread of information across the Internet. Specifically, we are interested in whether different users receive the same or differing information, according to the channel they use. Because few papers in the literature analyze these issues, we will confine our discussion to a description of the phenomenon and the tentative implications for competition and plurality, without presenting a rigorous analysis.

A popular way that users access content apart from using a search engine is to visit a news website and search for "most-read news" or "most-popular stories." This device is offered by most news websites, such as BBC or Bloomberg, the websites of most newspapers, and also by video-sharing websites, such as YouTube. The standard way in which websites decide to classify content as most popular or as must-read news is by counting the absolute number of clicks on this content in the past (correcting for up-to-dateness and other factors). In this respect, the popularity of stories is similar to a classic network effect; that is, the more people read a story, the more attractive it will be to others.[39] The effect of most-popular stories is that users are more likely to obtain the same information. Even if users are heterogeneous and are interested in different content *ex ante*, the pre-selected content of websites is the same, and users access only content within this pre-selected sample. Therefore, users obtain the same information, which implies that they become more homogeneous regarding their information. This exerts a negative effect on plurality.[40] This issue is not (or to a much smaller extent) present in traditional media, in which the tool of counting the number of clicks and, therefore, a direct measure of popularity is not feasible.

Additionally, most-popular stories often have a tendency to be self-reinforcing as most popular. If a story is recommended as highly popular, then more users will read it, implying that the number of clicks increases, thereby making the story even more popular. This effect is known as observational learning and is documented by, among others, Cai et al. (2009), Zhang (2010), and Chen et al. (2011). As a consequence, it is not

---

[39] See Katz and Shapiro (1985, 1994) for seminal papers on network effects.

[40] Another effect is that the selection of the content usually depends on the absolute number of clicks but not on the time users spend on the website. Therefore, it is not clear if websites accurately measure how interesting the respective content is to users.

obvious whether users read the same stories because they are actually interesting for a majority of users or if users read them merely because they are recommended.

Contrasting this hypothesis, Tucker and Zhang (2011) present a mechanism for why listing "most-read" stories can benefit stories with niche content or narrow appeal. Users usually have an *ex-ante* expectation if particular content is of broad versus narrow appeal. In this respect, a story with content that appeals to a majority of users is more likely to make it onto the most-read list. Now suppose that a story of broad-appeal content is ranked fourth on the most-read list, whereas a story of narrow-appeal content is ranked fifth. Since the broad-appeal story has a higher probability of being part of the most-read list, users will infer from this ranking that the narrow-appeal story is probably of higher quality or has particularly interesting insights. Therefore, if both stories are ranked almost equally, users will be more attracted by the story with narrow-appeal content. Tucker and Zhang (2011) test this hypothesis in a field experiment. A website that lists wedding service vendors switched from an alphabetical listing to one in which listings are ranked by the number of clicks the vendor received. They measure vendors as broad-appeal ones when located in towns with a large population and as narrow-appeal ones when located in small towns. Tucker and Zhang (2011) find strong evidence that narrow-appeal vendors, indeed, receive more clicks than broad-appeal vendors when ranked equally.

Oestreicher-Singer and Sundararajan (2012) also conduct an analysis to determine if popular or niche items benefit most from recommendations. In particular, they analyze the demand effects in recommendation networks by using data about the co-purchase network of more than 250,000 products sold on Amazon.com. They use the feature of Amazon.com to provide hyperlinks to connected products. To identify the effect that the visible presence of hyperlinks brings about, the authors control for unobserved sources of complementarity by constructing alternative sets of complementary products. For example, they construct a complementary set using data from the co-purchase network of Barnes & Noble (B&N). The B&N website provides a recommendation network similar to Amazon.com's, but the product links might be different, and those on the B&N website are invisible to Amazon.com customers. Therefore, the products linked on the former website but not on the latter provide an alternative complementary set.[41] Oestreicher-Singer and Sundararajan (2012) find that visibility of the product network has very large demand effects—i.e., the influence that complementary products can have on the demand for each other can be up to a threefold average increase. Newer and more popular products use the attention induced by their network position more efficiently.

The results of Oestreicher-Singer and Sundararajan (2012) differ from those of Tucker and Zhang (2011). In particular, the former paper finds that popular products benefit more

---

[41] Similarly, products that are linked in the future on the Amazon.com website but not today can be assumed to be complementary to the focal product today and can be used to construct an alternative complementary set.

from recommendation, while the latter find that niche products receive larger benefits. A potential explanation is that consumers may be more inclined to browse niche websites when looking for products for a special occasion (such as weddings dresses) than when looking for more standard products. The contrasting findings could also reflect different reasons underlying the demand effect—i.e., attention in Oestreicher-Singer and Sundararajan (2012) and observational learning in Tucker and Zhang (2011).

Another way for users to access content is to read what other users recommend. For example, via the "share" command on Twitter or other social media, users recommend content to their friends or followers (for some facts on users as curators, see Section 10.2.1). These friends are highly likely to read what the recommenders "like," which is not necessarily what the majority of users are interested in or what friends of other users like. Therefore, in contrast to the "most-popular" stories, sharing content leads to different users obtaining different information and therefore does not necessarily lead to a reduction in plurality. However, users may access only content of a particular type because they largely ignore or are not aware of recommendations by users who are not their friends or whom they do not follow. In this respect, sharing content can lead to narrow or exaggerated views. It is therefore prone to media bias, which is discussed extensively in Chapters 14 and 15.

It is evident that the flow and diversity of the information depends on the architecture of the (social) network. For example, the architecture of Twitter is similar to the star network, in which the user in the middle spreads information to all its followers. However, two followers may not necessarily exchange information directly with each other but only through the user they follow. By contrast, on Facebook, mostly groups of users interact, implying that there are more direct links and direct information sharing among these users.[42]

Most-read news and individual users sharing news are two extreme forms of spreading information on the Internet. Whereas the former depends only on the absolute number of clicks, the latter depends on a user's subjective evaluation.[43] In between these two forms are recommendations provided by websites. These recommendations are based partly on content (as in the case of most-popular stories) and partly on the specific user (as in the case of sharing information by users).

Regarding content, a website has many different forms of selecting recommendations to users. An extreme one is based purely on an algorithm, such as the absolute number of clicks in the past, and does not involve any editorial selection.[44] The other extreme is a

---

[42] For detailed analyses of network formation, see, e.g., Jackson and Wolinsky (1996) or Jackson (2010). Banerjee et al. (2014) provide a recent analysis of how gossip spreads within a network.

[43] Thus, to formalize the former, standard models with aggregate network effects can be used, whereas for the latter, the link structure of the social network has to be taken into account.

[44] For example, this is the case with Google News. For a more detailed discussion on news aggregators, see Section 10.3.3.

purely curated selection, based on editorial policy. While the latter is evidently more subjective, it usually involves real journalism—that is, journalists becoming well informed about particular topics. An interesting question regards the benefits of these two forms of news selection for different classes of content. In particular, it is interesting to explore whether both types can survive for a particular content category since users value differentiation and/or multi-home, or whether one type tends to become dominant. Regarding recommendations based on the specific user, a website is informed about the history of the user's browsing behavior. Therefore, it can tailor its recommendation to this behavior and recommend stories or news according to the user's past preferences. In contrast to the case when other users recommend stories or news, here a user's own past behavior determines the stories that she becomes aware of. Again, this may lead to a loss in plurality.

These devices to obtain information compete with search engines. As an example, consider Amazon versus Google. Many users searching for books now directly use Amazon's website and no longer search on Google. In the case of media, a similar pattern can be observed, with users who are looking for news bypassing the search engines and immediately visiting the website of their preferred news provider. An interesting question is how such behavior affects the bias of search engines and (potentially) of news websites.

10.5. MEDIA PLATFORMS MATCHING ADVERTISING TO CONTENT

The success of a firm's advertising campaign is driven mainly by the effectiveness of its ads. Foremost, the recipients of the ads (i.e., the potential consumers) should be primarily individuals or companies with an inherent interest in the firm's products. Otherwise, informing potential consumers about characteristics of the product is unlikely to lead to actual purchases. To increase advertising effectiveness and reduce wasted impressions, firms match their advertisements to content on media outlets in such a way that consumers who are interested in the content are also likely to be interested in the advertised product. This practice is called *content matching* or *tailoring* and can be seen as a particular instance of targeting.

Consider, for example, a local bookstore. The store has higher returns from placing ads in a local newspaper than in a global one. The local newspaper is read by a local audience, which consists of the potential consumer group for the bookstore. By contrast, a large portion of ads in the global newspaper are wasted since many readers do not live in the vicinity of the bookstore. Similar examples apply to content instead of geography. The advertisements of a cosmetics company are usually more effective in a women's magazine than in a computing magazine, and a sports apparel manufacturer's ads are likely to be more effective during televised sports than during a comedy show. However, in traditional media, the degree and effectiveness of such tailoring is limited. As argued by

Goldfarb (2014), for example, the distinguishing feature of Internet advertising is its reduction in targeting costs compared to traditional media.

On the Internet, targeting is not limited to linking advertising to specific content. Advertisements can be targeted to the intentions of the consumer (reader/viewer/listener) as inferred from past behavior or based on specific circumstances, such as the weather conditions at the consumer's location. For example, media platforms can expose different users to different advertisements, even when those users browse the same website at the same time. The particular advertisement can be conditioned on many different parameters. For instance, the website may engage in geo-targeting and display advertisements relevant to the user's geography (inferred from IP addresses). Similarly, the website may keep track of ad exposure to users, thereby reducing repetitive exposure of ads, or search engines may display ads conditional on queries conducted, a practice called keyword advertising. Clearly, both practices lower the number of wasted impressions, allowing the website or search engine to charge higher prices to advertisers, everything else given. A highly debated form of targeting is called behavioral targeting. Here, a website customizes the display advertisement to information collected in the past about a user. The website uses cookies based on pages that the user has visited and displays ads that could be of particular interest to the user;[45] cookies are small pieces of data sent from a website, which track the user's activities. These cookies give precise information about the user's past web-browsing behavior and therefore about her preferences. We analyze implications of behavioral targeting in Section 10.6.

In Section 10.5.1, we discuss different formalizations of targeting (in the wider sense), focusing on tailoring on the Internet and how it differs from general tailoring. In Section 10.5.2, we then discuss the practice of "keyword targeting" in more detail.

10.5.1 How to Formalize Targeting

In the economics literature, targeted advertising has been shown to be able to segment the market. Esteban et al. (2001) consider targeted advertising by a monopolist and show that the monopolist will target primarily consumers with high reservation values, thereby extracting a higher surplus.

Targeting also affects market outcomes under imperfect competition between advertisers. In particular, segmentation due to targeting may relax product market competition and thus allow firms to charge higher equilibrium prices. Iyer et al. (2005) consider a model with two competing firms that need to advertise to inform consumers about the existence of their products. There are three different consumer segments. Consumers belonging to the first have a high preference for the first firm in that its members consider buying only from that firm; those belonging to the second have a high preference for the second firm; and those belonging to the third are indifferent between the firms, and buy

---

[45] For an in-depth discussion and analysis of behavioral targeting, see Chen and Staellert (2014).

the lower-priced product.[46] Advertising is costly to firms. Iyer et al. (2005) show that without targeting, equilibrium profits are zero because firms spend their entire product market profit to inform consumers. By contrast, with the possibility of targeting consumers, firms advertise with a higher probability to the market segment that prefers the firm's product than to the indifferent consumers, enabling the firms to reap strictly positive profits. Roy (2000) and Galeotti and Moraga-Gonzalez (2008), analyzing different models, also show that targeting can lead to full or partial market segmentation, allowing firms to obtain positive profits.[47]

In what follows, we provide a more detailed discussion of the models by Athey and Gans (2010) and Bergemann and Bonatti (2011); both works explicitly consider targeting strategies on the Internet. The former focuses on the supply side and keeps consumer demand simple, whereas the latter explicitly models the demand side and keeps the supply side simple.[48] We then briefly discuss the model by Rutt (2012).

Athey and Gans (2010) present a model that is cast in terms of geo-targeting. However, it can be adjusted to other forms of targeting. Specifically, consider a set of localities $x \in \{1, ..., X\}$, where each locality consists of N consumers. In each locality, there is one local media outlet. There is also one general outlet denoted by g, which is active in all locations. Consumers single-home—that is, they visit only one outlet. The market shares for local and global outlets in each locality are the same and given by n_g for the global outlet and $N - n_g$ for the local outlet.

Each advertiser i is only local and therefore values only impressions to consumers in the respective locality. The value to advertiser i of informing a consumer is v_i. Outlets track advertisers, which implies that they offer each advertiser a single impression per consumer. There is a continuum of advertisers with values $v_i \in [0, 1]$ with cumulative distribution function $F(v_i)$. Each outlet chooses the number of ads, $a_j, j \in \{1, ..., X, g\}$, that can be impressed on a consumer. We denote by p_j the impression price of outlet j. Finally, the probability of informing a consumer with an impression on outlet j is given by ϕ_j. There is no nuisance of advertising.

For each local outlet l, the probability of informing a consumer equals 1. Instead, for the global outlet, this probability depends on targeting being possible or not. If targeting is

---

[46] Chen et al. (2001) consider a similar demand structure to analyze the implications of targeting. In contrast to Iyer et al. (2005), they assume that firms can charge different prices to the consumers in different segments and show that imperfect targeting softens competition.

[47] Other models of targeted advertising include van Zandt (2004), who analyzes information overload; Gal-Or and Gal-Or (2005), who analyze targeting by a common marketing agency; and Johnson (2013), who studies ad-avoidance behavior by consumers when targeting is possible. The latter will be analyzed in Section 10.6.1.

[48] For an in-depth discussion of the different parameters influencing supply and demand of Internet advertising, see Evans (2009).

not possible, this probability is $\phi_g = 1/X$ because market shares are the same in all localities. By contrast, if targeting is possible, the probability is $\phi_g = 1$.

Solving for the equilibrium number of ads when targeting is not possible, the first observation is that an advertiser will buy impressions on outlet j if $\phi_j v_i \geq p_j$. Since $\phi_l = 1$ for local outlets, the total demand for impressions to a given consumer is $1 - F(p_l)$ for a local outlet l. In equilibrium, demand equals supply, implying that $1 - F(p_l) = a_l$ or $p_l = F^{-1}(1 - a_l)$ for a local outlet in a given locality. The profit function of outlet l is therefore $a_l F^{-1}(1 - a_l)$, which is to be maximized over a_l. We now turn to the global outlet. An advertiser will buy impressions on outlet g if $v_g \geq X p_g$. Since a_g are the impressions *per consumer* and there are X localities, the overall demand is $X(1 - F(X p_g))$, leading to an equilibrium that is characterized by $X(1 - F(X p_g)) = a_g$ or $p_g = (1/X) F^{-1}(1 - (1/X) a_g)$. The profit function is $a_g (1/X) F^{-1}(1 - (1/X) a_g)$, which is to be maximized over a_g.

It is easy to see that the problem of the global outlet is the same as that of the local outlets, adjusted by a scaling factor. Hence, $a_g^* = X a_l^*$ and $p_l^* = X p_g^*$, implying that per-consumer profits are the same. If targeting is possible, the problem of the global outlet becomes exactly the same as that of the local outlet. In this case, the number of ads and the ad price are the same for both types of outlets.[49] Athey and Gans (2010) obtain that, without targeting, the global outlet expands its number of advertisements to X times what a local outlet would provide due to wasteful impressions. Therefore, the price it charges is only $1/X$ times that of a local outlet. However, per-consumer profits are not affected, and the global outlet replicates the outcome of the local outlet.

To easily grasp the tradeoff in the model of Athey and Gans (2010), it is instructive to look at the model for the case in which advertising space is fixed for the global outlet. Is the advertising price of the global outlet with targeting higher or lower than without? The obvious effect is that advertising on the global outlet is less effective since advertisements are mismatched with probability $(X - 1)/X$. By contrast, advertising on a local outlet is effective with probability 1. In addition to this *efficiency effect*, there is also a *scarcity effect*. Without targeting, an advertiser from a locality competes with advertisers from other localities for scarce advertising space. This increases the price on the global outlet. Formally, comparing the advertising price on the global outlet with and without targeting gives

$$F^{-1}(1 - a_g) > \frac{1}{X} F^{-1}\left(1 - \frac{1}{X} a_g\right).$$

The advertising price with targeting is higher than that without targeting only if the last inequality is satisfied. As shown by Athey and Gans (2010), this holds true as long as a_g is not particularly high.

---

[49] Note that the problems of local and global outlets are separated, implying that a change in the number of ads of one outlet does not affect the number of ads on the other.

Athey and Gans's (2010) model demonstrates that targeting primarily allows an outlet to reduce wasteful impressions. As long as there are no costs of these impressions, targeting does not help an outlet to achieve higher profits. However, under many circumstances, there are such costs. For example, in most of the models discussed above, consumers dislike advertising. If there are nuisance costs to advertising, consumer demand is lower, the larger the number of ads. Targeting then reduces this problem and allows the global outlet to realize higher demand. Athey and Gans (2010) provide other reasons for such costs of impressions. Suppose, for example, that there is a constraint on advertising space that prevents the global outlet from just raising its number of impressions. Targeting then makes the use of the scarce advertising space more effective and allows the global outlet to reap higher profits. (A similar reasoning holds for the case in which providing advertising space is costly.) Alternatively, in the model presented above, demand across localities was assumed to be homogeneous. However, a more realistic model would consider hetero-geneous demand so that the global outlet has higher demand in some localities than in others. This implies that advertisers in these localities have a higher willingness-to-pay for advertising space. Thus, targeting allows the global outlet to price discriminate between advertisers of different localities and obtain higher profits.

It is worth mentioning that targeting does not necessarily increase profits for the global outlet. Consider an extension of the basic model in which outlets compete for advertisers. This could be due to the fact that advertisers value, at most, one consumer impression. As Athey and Gans (2010) show, targeting can spur competition between local and global outlets because the two types of outlets are vertically differentiated with-out targeting. When implementing targeting, both outlets provide a similar service to advertisers, leading to reduced prices. As a consequence, profits may fall with targeting. Anecdotal evidence of excessively fine targeting reported by Levin and Milgrom (2010) supports the relevance of this result.

Athey and Gans's (2010) model focuses on the supply side and reveals that increasing the supply of advertising can be a substitute for targeting. Therefore, targeting is partic-ularly effective if an outlet can increase its advertising space only by incurring a cost.

Bergemann and Bonatti (2011) pursue a different route by modeling the demand side in a detailed way and keeping the supply side as simple as possible. In particular, they explicitly introduce the idea that targeting on the Internet allows for unbundling of content, thereby splitting a single advertising market into multiple ones. For example, readers of a traditional newspaper have to buy the whole newspaper to access the content they are interested in. Therefore, advertisers with niche products will probably find it too expensive to place an ad. By contrast, online consumers may access (and pay for) only selected articles. This implies that a producer of a niche product may find it profitable to pay for an ad that targets only the consumer group interested in the particular article.[50] A similar effect holds for Internet TV.

---

[50] This phenomenon has been called the "long tail of advertising"; see Anderson (2006). It also applies to keyword advertising and behavioral targeting.

Major broadcasting networks usually focus on the taste of the masses to increase their advertising revenues. For example, sports channels do not devote much air time to niche sports, such as shot put or weight lifting. However, followers of these sports can access reports online and watch them at any time. This allows small businesses whose target groups are people interested in such niche sports to access these advertising markets.

Bergemann and Bonatti (2011) examine these effects and their implications for offline versus online media. Suppose that there is a continuum of products and a continuum of advertising markets. A product is denoted by y and is produced by a single firm y with $y \in [0, \infty)$. Similarly, advertising markets are denoted by $z \in [0, \infty)$. There is a continuum of buyers with a mass of one. Each buyer has a preference for a particular product and is located in one advertising market. The joint distribution of consumers across advertising markets and product markets is $F(z, y)$ with density $f(z, y)$. The fraction of consumers interested in product y can be written as $f(y) = \int_0^\infty f(z', y) dz'$, when integrating over all advertising markets. Similarly, the size of advertising market z can be written as $(z) = \int_0^\infty f(z, y') dy'$, integrating over all products. The conditional distribution of advertising markets for a given product y is $f(z| y) = f(z, y)/f(y)$. Product differences can be expressed by differences in the size $f(y)$ to distinguish mass from niche products.

Each firm y can inform consumers about its product by sending a number of advertising messages $a_{z,y}$ in advertising market z. Each message reaches a random consumer with a uniform probability, as in the model of Butters (1977): With probability

$$\mathrm{pr}\big(a_{z,y}, f(z)\big) = 1 - \mathrm{e}^{-a_{z,y}/f(z)},$$

a given consumer in advertising market z of size $f(z)$ becomes aware of product y.

In each advertising market z, the supply of messages M_z is fixed. This supply is proportional to the size $f(z)$ of the advertising market—that is, $M_z = f(z)M$. Here, M can be interpreted as the average time a consumer spends on advertising messages. In each advertising market, there are a large number of media outlets. Outlets act as price takers, implying that a firm y can purchase messages at a price p_z in each market. The profit of firm y can then be written as[51]

$$\pi_y = \int_0^\infty \big[f(z, y)\mathrm{pr}\big(a_{z,y}, f(z)\big) - p_z a_{z,y} \big] dz.$$

To easily distinguish between mass and niche products, Bergemann and Bonatti (2011) impose that $f(y) = \alpha \mathrm{e}^{-\alpha y}$. Here, a larger parameter value α represents a more concentrated product market. With this formulation, firms can be ranked in decreasing order of market size—i.e., a firm with a higher index y is smaller in the sense that fewer consumers are interested in its product.

---

[51] The value of informing a consumer is normalized to 1.

The advertising markets are also ranked according to the mass of consumers interested in the market. Advertising market 0 is a large market in which all advertisers are interested, and advertising markets become smaller and more specialized with an increasing index. To formalize this, suppose that firm y is interested only in consumers in markets with $z \leq y$. For each firm y, the advertising market $z = y$ is the one with the highest density of consumers, conditional on market size. The conditional distribution of consumers with interest in product y over advertising markets z is given by the following truncated exponential distribution:

$$\frac{f(z, y)}{f(y)} = \begin{cases} \beta e^{-\beta(y-z)} & \text{if } 0 < z \leq y, \\ 0 & \text{if } y < z < \infty, \end{cases}$$

for all advertising markets $z > 0$. There is a mass point at $z = 0$ and the conditional distribution is $f(z, y)/f(y) = e^{-\beta y}$ if $z = 0$. The parameter β measures the concentration of consumers in advertising markets. We will explain below how the possibility of targeting consumers can be measured by β. Combining the definition of market size with the conditional distribution gives the unconditional distribution

$$f(z, y) = \begin{cases} \alpha \beta e^{-(\alpha+\beta)y} e^{\beta z} & \text{if } 0 < z \leq y, \\ 0 & \text{if } y < z < \infty, \end{cases}$$

with a mass point at $z = 0$, where the unconditional distribution is $f(z, y) = \alpha e^{-(\alpha+\beta)y}$. The market size can then be calculated by integrating over the population shares. Since consumers who are potential buyers of product y are present in all advertising markets $z \leq y$ but not in advertising markets $z > y$, we have

$$f(z > 0) = \int_z^\infty \alpha \beta e^{-(\alpha+\beta)y} e^{\beta z} \mathrm{d}y = \frac{\alpha \beta}{\alpha + \beta} e^{-\alpha z}$$

and

$$f(z = 0) \int_0^\infty \alpha e^{-(\alpha+\beta)y} \mathrm{d}y = \frac{\alpha}{\alpha + \beta}.$$

The distribution of consumers across product and advertising space has a natural interpretation in terms of specialization of preferences and audiences. First, a product with a larger index is a more specialized product in the sense that there are fewer potential buyers. Similarly, an advertising market with a higher index z is a market with a more narrow audience. Second, potential consumers of larger firms are distributed over a smaller number of advertising markets. This can be seen by the assumption above that $f(z, y)$ is positive only for $z \leq y$. For example, potential buyers of product $y = 0$ are concentrated in the advertising market $z = 0$. Interpreting advertising markets as media outlets, this implies that a consumer interested in a mass product does not visit a website with advertisements for niche products.

Third, the variable β, ranging from 0 to ∞, captures in a simple way the ability of firms to target consumers. For example, as $\beta \to 0$, all consumers are concentrated in advertising market 0, implying that there is a single advertising market. By contrast, as $\beta \to \infty$, then all potential buyers of product y are in advertising market y, and so there is perfect targeting. In general, an increase in β implies that consumers are spread over more advertising markets and can be better targeted by firms. Overall, the highest conditional density of potential consumers of firm y is in advertising market $z = y$. As β gets larger, more consumers move away from the large advertising markets (near $z = 0$) to the smaller advertising markets (near $z = y$).

To illustrate how the model works, let us look at the benchmark case in which all consumers are present in a single advertising market $z = 0$. We solve for the equilibrium amount of advertising and the equilibrium price. Since there is a single advertising market, we drop the subscript z in the notation. The profit function of firm y is then $\pi_y = f(y)\text{pr}(a_y) - p a_y$. Determining the first-order conditions and using the definition of $f(y)$ yields

$$a_y = \begin{cases} \ln(f(y)/p) & \text{if } f(y) \geq p, \\ 0 & \text{if } f(y) < p. \end{cases} \tag{10.3}$$

As is evident, firms with a larger market size optimally choose a larger amount of advertising. Therefore, in equilibrium, only firms with the largest market size find it optimal to advertise. Let M be the total number of advertising messages and denote by Y the marginal advertiser. The market-clearing condition is given by $\int_0^Y a_y dy = M$. Using demand for ads given by (10.3) and $f(y) = \alpha e^{-\alpha y}$ yields

$$\int_0^Y \left(\ln\left(\frac{\alpha}{p}\right) - \alpha y \right) dy = M.$$

Using $a_Y = 0$ together with the last equation, we can solve for the equilibrium price and the marginal advertiser. This gives $p^* = \alpha e^{-\sqrt{2\alpha M}}$ and $Y^* = \alpha \sqrt{2M/\alpha}$. Inserting back into the demand function of advertiser y yields

$$a_y^* = \begin{cases} \alpha\sqrt{2M/\alpha} - \alpha y & \text{if } y \leq Y^*, \\ 0 & \text{if } y > Y^*. \end{cases} \tag{10.4}$$

Therefore, only the largest firms advertise, and the equilibrium number of advertising messages is linearly decreasing in the rank y of the firm. As the concentration in the product market measured by α increases, fewer advertising messages are wasted, leading to an increase in social welfare. In particular, the allocation adjusts to firms with a larger market size, implying that fewer firms advertise as α increases.

To analyze the effect of targeting, Bergemann and Bonatti (2011) examine the situation with a continuum of advertising markets and a positive targeting parameter $\beta \in (0, \infty)$. The allocation of advertising messages is then given by a generalization of (10.4):

$$a^*_{z,\gamma} = \begin{cases} \alpha\beta e^{-az}\left(\sqrt{2M/(\alpha+\beta)} - (\gamma-z)\right) & \text{if } z>0, \\ \alpha\sqrt{2M/(\alpha+\beta)} - \alpha\gamma & \text{if } z=0. \end{cases}$$

Does targeting improve social welfare and do firms benefit from targeting? Bergemann and Bonatti (2011) show that the social value of advertising is increasing in the targeting ability β. The intuition is that targeting increases the value of advertising for a firm γ in its "natural" advertising markets $z \approx \gamma$. This leads to an increased volume of matches between firms and potential consumers, which improves social welfare.

However, looking at the cross-sectional implications of targeting, not all firms benefit from improved targeting. In particular, only the small firms that are not active in the mass advertising market $z=0$ and the largest firms, which are primarily active in that market, benefit. By contrast, medium-sized firms, which are active in the mass market and also in several other markets $0<z\leq\gamma$, are hurt. To grasp the intuition behind this result, observe, first, that for small firms (those not active in market $z=0$), the mass of potential buyers in their natural advertising markets $z \approx \gamma$ increases, allowing them to reach a larger fraction of consumers. A similar effect is present for large firms. Their customers are concentrated in a small number of markets, and an increase in the targeting ability increases the chances of achieving a match. By contrast, medium-sized firms are hurt by the decrease in consumers participating in market $z=0$, and this decline cannot be compensated by the rise in participation in their natural markets $z \approx \gamma$.

The model can be used to analyze the implications of targeting for "online" versus "offline" media. In the offline medium, there is only a single advertising market, whereas there is a continuum of advertising markets in the online medium. For simplicity, suppose that the online medium allows for perfect targeting of advertising messages to consumers. Consumers are dual-homing and spend a total amount of M_1 on the offline medium and M_2 on a single online market z. More specifically, $f(z)M_2$ is the supply of advertising messages in each targeted market z. So, the online medium consists of a continuum of specialized websites that display firms' advertisements. There is competition between the two media because each firm views the advertising messages sent online and offline as substitutes due to the risk of duplication. Bergemann and Bonatti (2011) show that the price for offline advertising decreases in M_2, reflecting the decreased willingness-to-pay for regular ads if a better-targeted market is present. The price for online advertising decreases in M_1 only on those websites that carry advertisements of firms that are also active offline. However, advertising markets with a high index z carry only the advertisements of niche firms, which are not affected by the allocation in the offline medium because they do not advertise there. This implies that online advertising reaches new consumer segments that are distinct from the audience reached by offline advertising.

Suppose, in addition, that each consumer is endowed with an amount of time equal to M and allocates a fraction σ of this time to the online medium. This implies that $M_1 = (1-\sigma)M$ and $M_2 = \sigma M$. It is now possible to analyze what happens when consumers spend more time online—that is, when σ increases. The effect on the offline advertising price is then non-monotonic. If σ is low (i.e., online exposure is low), the marginal willingness-to-pay for offline advertising falls because online advertising is more efficient. This induces a decrease in the offline advertising price, although the supply of offline advertising messages decreases. However, as σ increases further, the composition of firms active in offline advertising changes. In particular, only the largest firms display advertising messages offline, implying that the marginal advertiser has a high willingness-to-pay. This leads to an increase in the offline advertising price with σ. With regard to firm revenue, this implies that if consumers spend more time online, firms that are active solely in the online market unambiguously benefit. These are rather small firms. The effect on large firms is ambiguous: Since they are active on the offline medium, they may pay a larger advertising price, which reduces their profits.

In summary, Bergemann and Bonatti (2011) show that targeting on the Internet allows platforms to split up a single advertising market into multiple ones. This allows producers of niche products, who are not active in the single large advertising market, to advertise, thereby increasing advertising efficiency. Small and also large firms benefit from targeting. By contrast, medium-sized firms are worse off because attention of consumers migrates to smaller advertising markets.

Rutt (2012) proposes a different formalization of targeting. He considers a model with n platforms which are distributed equidistantly on a circle, single-homing users, and multi-homing advertisers. A user's valuation for an advertiser's product is binary, namely either of high or of low valuation (with the low valuation being set equal to 0).[52] Advertisers are uncertain about the true valuation. In particular, advertiser j does not know consumer i's valuation for her product with certainty but only has an expectation. Each advertiser receives an informative signal about a consumer's true valuation. The realization of the signal induces an advertiser to update the expectation. The targeting technology can now be modeled as a change in the informativeness of the signal.[53] In the extreme case that targeting is impossible and signals are pure noise, the updated expectation equals the prior expectation. By contrast, when the signal is perfect, the advertiser knows the consumer's valuation with certainty. As a result, an increase in the informativeness leads some advertisers to revise their beliefs upward, while others revise them downward. Advertisers receiving a positive signal become more optimistic, whereas advertisers with a negative signal become more pessimistic.[54]

---

[52] Pan and Yang (2015) consider a similar market structure with two platforms to analyze the effects of targeting; they specify user demand and thus improved targeting differently.

[53] A simple example of a signal structure which fits this description is the truth-or-noise information structure: suppose that the prior expectation about consumer i having a high valuation for the product is X, the signal is Y, and the signal reveals the true consumer valuation with probability Z. Then, the posterior expectation is $ZY + (1-Z)X$.

[54] In this respect, the information structure is similar to the demand rotation considered in Johnson and Myatt (2006).

With regard to the timing, platforms first select their advertising levels and advertisers then submit their conditional demands specifying which types of users they wish to be matched with for a given advertising price. For example, advertisers announce that they want to have ads displayed only to users who show an interest with a probability higher than some cutoff level. After users have decided which media platform to consume from, advertisers observe the signals and update their valuations. The advertising price then adjusts to clear the market. Afterward, consumers enjoy the media content, observe the advertisement, and make purchases.

In this setting, Rutt (2012) shows that targeting increases the advertising price and thereby allows platforms to receive higher profits. This effect is the stronger the more competitive is the market and the more users are averse to ads. This is because in markets satisfying these conditions, the equilibrium features only few advertisements, implying that the marginal advertiser received a particularly high signal. As a consequence, improved targeting increases this advertiser's willingness-to-pay, resulting in a strong increase in the advertising price. In the case of free entry of platforms (at some setup costs), improved targeting may exacerbate excessive entry and leads to insufficient advertising due to high prices. Overall, the model therefore predicts a heterogeneous effect of targeting in different media markets.

The models of Athey and Gans (2010) and Bergemann and Bonatti (2011) share the assumption that offline and online advertising are substitutes.[55,56] If a potential consumer can be contacted via an advertisement through one channel, a conditional contact through the other channel is worth less. Goldfarb and Tucker (2011a) provide empirical support. They use data on estimated advertising prices paid by lawyers to contact potential clients with recent personal injuries. Goldfarb and Tucker (2011a) exploit state-level variation in the ability of lawyers to solicit those customers. In particular, this "ambulance-chasing" behavior is regulated in some states by the state bar associations, which forbid written communication (including direct electronic communication via email) with potential clients for 30–45 days after the accident. Goldfarb and Tucker (2011a) use data on estimated auction prices of 139 Google search terms on personal injury in 195 regional city markets to analyze the effects of these regulations.[57] They find that, compared to the prices for personal injury keywords in non-regulated states, in states with solicitation

---

[55] Rutt (2012) considers only online platforms. When interpreting some platforms as online and others as offline media outlets in his model, online and offline advertising would be independent. This is because users only visit a single platform and so advertisers can reach each particular user exclusively via online or via offline advertising.

[56] More generally, there is a link between offline and online in the sense that advertising offline affects consumer purchase online. In particular, Liaukonyte et al. (2015) study the effect of television commercials on actual purchase behavior on the Internet. They find a positive effect, even immediately after a viewer is exposed to the commercial.

[57] Search terms on personal injury can be identified objectively because there is a precise legal definition by the bar association.

restrictions, such keyword prices are between 5% and 7% higher. Therefore, when offline marketing communication is not possible, firms appear to switch to online advertising. This suggests that there is substitution between the two forms of advertising. In addition, Goldfarb and Tucker (2011a) demonstrate that this effect is larger in locations with a small number of potential clients. One interpretation is that mass-media advertising may not be cost-effective when consumers are hard to reach. Therefore, the possibility of direct off-line advertising is particularly valuable. If this advertising channel is closed, online advertising prices rise. This implies that in markets with fewer customers, online advertising allows firms to reach the hardest-to-find customers, thereby lending support to the "long tail" hypothesis in Internet advertising (Anderson, 2006).

We also note that targeting on the Internet can take many different forms beyond geographical or contextual targeting. For example, social targeting has become increasingly popular. Socially targeted ads, when displaying the ad to a particular user, refer to another user (e.g., a friend on Facebook). More precisely, a social ad is an online ad that "incorporates user interactions that the consumer has agreed to display and be shared. The resulting ads display these interactions along with the user's persona (picture and/or name) within the ad's content" (IAB, 2009). Tucker (2012) compares the effectiveness of socially targeted ads to that of conventionally (demographically) targeted ads and non-targeted ads. She conducted a field experiment on Facebook involving a non-profit charity organization that provides educational scholarships for girls to attend high school in East Africa. The non-profit organization launched a standard advertising campaign and a social variant of it. In this social variant, the recipients of the ads were only Facebook users who are friends of existing fans of the charity. Tucker (2012) finds that these socially targeted ads were more effective than regular display advertising. This holds both for randomly selected users and users who previously expressed their interest in either charity or education. For example, the aggregate click-through-rate of the socially targeted ads was around twice as large as that of non-socially targeted ads.

10.5.2 Keyword Advertising

A very effective form of targeted advertising is keyword advertising. Keyword targeting refers to any form of advertising that is linked to specific words or phrases and is displayed when a user is looking for information. Therefore, such advertising is not necessarily a nuisance to users and is wasted with a lower probability than, say, TV advertising or banner ads, as the ad is relevant to the user's query and therefore valuable. Nowadays, almost all search engines offer keyword advertising. The most well-known form is probably Google AdWords.[58] It also engages in contextual advertising; that is, Google's system scans the text on the websites that are most relevant to the search query and displays ads based on the keywords found in the respective texts. A main question is whether this form of targeting is welfare-enhancing.

---

[58] The study by Goldfarb and Tucker (2011a) discussed above uses keyword advertising by Google.

In this subsection, we focus on keyword advertising on search engines. The question has been raised whether search engines have an incentive to present the most relevant ads according to the keyword entered by the user. To address this question, de Cornière (2013) proposes a model with a single search engine that matches potential consumers and producers. Consumers are uniformly distributed along a circle with circumference 1. Each consumer is described by a two-dimensional vector: first, by the consumer's location on the circle, which describes her favorite product denoted by $\omega \in [0; 1]$; and second, by her willingness-to-pay, denoted by $\theta \in [0, \bar{\theta}]$. In particular, in each location, there is a continuum of mass 1 of consumers whose reservation price θ is distributed with c.d.f. F. Both variables ω and θ are private information. Each consumer buys, at most, one unit and obtains a utility of

$$v(\theta, d, P) = \theta - c(d) - P,$$

where P is the price of the product and $d = d(\chi, \omega)$ measures the distance between the product's location χ and the consumer's location ω. The function $c(d)$, therefore measures the mismatch costs and is assumed to be increasing and weakly convex.

Products are continuously distributed on the circle. There is a continuum of entrants for each product. Each product can be described by a keyword, which is denoted by $\chi \in [0; 1]$; that is, the keyword is identical to the location of the product. The parameter χ is private information to the producer, implying that consumers know neither the position of a firm on the circle nor the price; hence, they need to use the search engine. When a firm wants to advertise on the search engine, it incurs a fixed cost of C to launch an advertising campaign. (This cost is not a payment to the search engine.)

The search process works as follows: Firms select a set of keywords that they want to target. The set is assumed to be symmetric around χ—that is, $\Sigma(\chi) = [\chi - D_\chi; \chi + D_\chi]$, where the meaning of D_χ becomes clear below. Consumers enter the keyword of their preferred product ω. After entry of the keyword ω, the search engine randomly selects a firm χ such that $\omega \in \Sigma(\chi)$. Once a consumer has decided to use the search engine, she incurs search costs of s and learns the price and location of the firm selected by the search engine. The firm then pays an amount p to the search engine; therefore, p represents the price-per-click. The consumer can then buy the product or not buy it and stop searching, or she can hold the offer and continue searching. That is, recall is costless. For each additional search, the consumer again incurs costs of s.

The timing of the game is as follows: In the first stage, the search engine chooses the per-click-price $p,$[59] which is public information to producers and consumers. In the

[59] For a model of click fraud, in which publishers affiliated with the search engine's advertising network or competing advertisers artificially drive up clicks (e.g., by impersonating consumers) without increasing sales, see Wilbur and Zhu (2009).

second stage, producers make their decisions. They first decide whether to be active on the search engine; if so, they incur the fixed cost C. Each active firm located at χ then chooses a price P_χ for its product and an advertising strategy D_χ. The mass of active firms is denoted by h. Finally, consumers decide whether to use the search engine. If they do so, they incur search costs s, type in the keyword of the most preferred product ω, and start a sequential search among firms $d(\chi, \omega) \leq D_\chi$. The search engine draws firms in the respective range with equal probability.

What is the perfect Bayesian equilibrium with free entry of firms for this game? Once a consumer has decided to use the search engine and has entered the keyword ω, she obtains a search result showing the link to a firm in the support $[\omega - D^*; \omega + D^*]$. Suppose that all firms charge an equilibrium price of P^*. Then, the expected utility that a consumer gets from this search is

$$\int_{\omega - D^*}^{\omega + D^*} \frac{v(\theta, d(\chi, \omega), P^*)}{2D^*} d\chi = \int_0^{D^*} \frac{v(\theta, x, P^*)}{D^*} dx.$$

The consumer's optimal search behavior is a cutoff rule. That is, the consumer will buy the product of a firm χ if the distance $d(\omega, \chi)$ is lower than or equal to a reservation distance, denoted by R. If a consumer decides not to buy the product, she can improve her utility only by finding a firm that is located closer to her most preferred product because all firms charge the equilibrium price P^*. Therefore, for R^* to be an equilibrium reservation distance, the consumer must be indifferent between buying the product and continue searching; that is,

$$\int_0^{R^*} \frac{v(u, x, P^*) - v(u, R^*, P^*)}{D^*} dx = \int_0^{R^*} \frac{c(R^*) - c(x)}{D^*} dx = s.$$

The left-hand side is the expected gain from continuing to search, and the right-hand side represents the search costs. By totally differentiating this expression, one can show that R^* increases with s and D^*.

To determine the firms' optimal targeting strategy, note that a consumer will never come back to a firm if she does not buy from this firm immediately. This is because the consumer's stopping rule is stationary, and she will keep on searching as long as her match is at (weakly) lower distance than her reservation distance. This implies that the conditional purchase probability of a consumer after clicking on a firm's link is either 0 or 1. Because the firm has to pay only for consumers who click on the link, the optimal targeting strategy is simple and equal to $R^* = D^*$. Therefore, in equilibrium, consumers will not search more than once. This allows us to deduce the consumers' participation decisions regarding whether or not to use the search engine. The cutoff reservation value, such that a consumer is indifferent between using the search engine or not, is given by $\theta - P^* - s - E[c(d)|d \leq R^*] = 0$.

We now turn to a firm's optimal pricing decision. If a firm charges price P different from the candidate equilibrium price P^*, it will optimally also change its targeting strategy. In particular, it will target consumers located at a distance smaller than the new reservation distance $R(P, P^*, D^*)$, taking into account that all other firms follow the candidate equilibrium strategy P^* and D^*. Given this new strategy, the firm faces a mass of $2R(P, P^*, D^*)h^*$ competitors in equilibrium. This is because every consumer within distance $R(P, P^*, D^*)$ is targeted by exactly this mass of firms. Since all consumers buy without searching a second time, the firm's profit function per consumer is

$$\pi(P, P^*, p) = (P - p)\frac{R(P, P^*, D^*)}{R(P^*, P^*, D^*)h^*}.$$

The equilibrium price P^* is given by the first-order condition of this expression with respect to P. In equilibrium, the mass of participating consumers is given by $1 - F(\theta^*)$. Therefore, a firm's expected profit is $(1 - F(\theta^*))\pi(P, P^*, p)$. Since all firms charge the same price in equilibrium, the free-entry condition determines the mass of entering firms. Explicitly accounting for the dependence of P^*, θ^*, and h^* on p, we can write the free-entry condition as

$$(P^*(p) - p)\frac{1 - F(\theta^*(p))}{h^*(p)} = C.$$

Finally, we turn to the profit of the search engine. Since every consumer searches only once, the profit of the search engine is given by $\pi^{SE}(p) = p(1 - F(\theta^*(p)))$. This profit function shows the tradeoff faced by the search engine. Everything else being equal, the search engine obtains a higher revenue when increasing p. However, such an increase in the per-click fee leads to a higher price on the product market. Since consumers anticipate this, fewer of them will use the search engine. Maximizing $\pi^{SE}(p)$, we obtain that the optimal per-click fee is implicitly given by $p^* = \frac{1 - F(\theta^*(p^*))}{f(\theta^*(p^*))}$. It is evident that the search engine sets a positive p^*. Instead, the socially optimal fee equals zero. Hence, the equilibrium implies a distortion, as consumer participation is too low and product prices are too high.

Within de Cornière's (2013) model, we can now analyze the effects of targeting. Suppose that targeting is not possible. In the model, this corresponds to the case in which $D = 1/2$ for all products. The optimal reservation distance for consumers, R^*, is then implicitly given by $\int_0^{R^*} \frac{c(R^*) - c(x)}{1/2} dx = s$. Therefore, consumers may search more than once, and targeting reduces the expected number of clicks. Since the reservation distance is increasing in D, the expected mismatch costs are also lower with targeting. As a consequence, targeting reduces the search frictions.

Targeting has more subtle effects on the price of the final good. First, targeting changes the pool of firms from which consumers sample. In particular, with targeting, this pool is composed of firms that are expected to be a better match for consumers. This implies that the continuation value of searching is higher for consumers, inducing a downward pressure on prices. By contrast, without targeting, a firm cannot adjust its advertising strategy D along with its equilibrium price P. The per-click-price is therefore considered a fixed cost and is not passed through into the final good price.[60] As a consequence, the overall effect is ambiguous, and de Cornière (2013) shows that targeting can lead to a welfare loss.

Another important question regards the incentive of the search engine to choose the most relevant ads after a consumer has entered a keyword. To this end, suppose that the search engine can choose the value of accuracy of its search results by choosing D itself. So, the search engine has two choices, D and p. De Cornière (2013) shows that, in this case, the search engine can extract the whole profit from firms with the per-click fee. Consequently, the search engine chooses D in order to maximize firms' profits. The optimal matching accuracy for the search engine is, then, $D^{SE} \geq D^*$. The intuition behind the result is as follows. If the search engine sets $D < D^*$, the distance is strictly smaller than the consumers' reservation distance. Then, a price increase in the final good market does not lead to reduced demand. This implies that firms have an incentive to increase the price up to the reservation price of the marginal consumer, leading to a negative utility of the marginal consumer (remember that the search costs are sunk). As a consequence, consumers will not participate. Therefore, a high level of matching accuracy lowers product market competition, which dissuades consumers from using the search engine. Instead, when $D > D^*$, some consumers search more than once. This leads to lower firm prices and ensures higher consumer participation. Therefore, the search engine may find it optimal to set $D^{SE} \geq D^*$ but never $D^{SE} < D^*$. Therefore, the search engine does not have an incentive to choose a more accurate matching than advertising firms themselves.

To sum up, de Cornière (2013) demonstrates that keyword advertising induces better targeting by advertisers and thereby reduces the search frictions of consumers. However, it also changes product market competition. Because advertisers pay per click, they face higher marginal costs, which can lead to higher final consumer prices. In addition, a search engine may not want to offer the highest level of matching accuracy because this leads to a small number of results, reduces product market competition, and makes the search engine less attractive for consumers.

In the empirical literature, keyword advertising and targeting technologies on the Internet have also attracted considerable attention. For example, to determine the effectiveness of keyword advertising, Ghose and Yang (2009) use a panel data set of several hundred keywords from a nationwide retailer that advertises on Google. They find that click-through and conversion rates fall in the keyword rank. However, this is not

---

[60] Dellarocas (2012) provides an in-depth analysis of the implications of pay-per-click pricing on final consumer prices. He shows that performance-based advertising, such as pay-per-click pricing, leads to double marginalization. As a result, consumer prices are higher than with per-impression pricing.

necessarily true for profitability. In particular, keywords in middle positions are often more profitable than those at the very top of a search engine's results page. Interestingly, Ghose and Yang (2009) find that the effect of retailer-specific information in a keyword is very different from brand-specific information. Whereas retailer-specific information leads to an increase in conversion rates of up to 50.6%, brand-specific information leads to a decrease of 44.2%. Similar patterns are observed for CTRs. It could be of interest to extend the model outlined above (or related frameworks) to allow for many search results with different ranks to explain this empirical evidence.

Other studies also analyze the influence of the position (or rank) on click-through and conversion rates and provide an analysis distinguishing between different advertising effectiveness measures. For example, Agarwal et al. (2011) also find a positive effect on the CTR but demonstrate that the conversion rate is often higher for middle-ranked positions. Rutz and Trusov (2011) provide a model and an empirical analysis of the relation between CTRs and conversion rates, whereas Rutz and Bucklin (2011) demonstrate positive spillovers between generic and sponsored search. That is, a generic search often generates a subsequent sponsored search.

In a recent study, Blake et al. (2015) also measure the effectiveness of keyword advertising, explicitly distinguishing between brand and non-brand keywords. When a user types in a brand such as "Macys" or "eBay" as a query in a search engine, it is very likely that the user is already familiar with the brand. In response to the user's query, the search engine displays paid ads at the top of the search results, and the brand pays the PCP given that the user clicks on this query. However, the user would have found the brand's site almost surely through organic search. Blake et al. (2015) test this with data from eBay. They halted advertising for eBay-brand-related queries on the search engines Yahoo! and MSN for some time and found that 99.5% of traffic from the paid link was immediately captured by traffic from the organic link. Hence, substitution between paid and unpaid traffic for eBay is almost complete.[61] Is this also true for non-brand keywords? To answer this question, Blake et al. (2015) conducted another natural experiment by stopping eBay advertising via paid links in designated areas for 60 days. In addition, they segmented consumer groups into those who are frequent eBay visitors and those who are not. They found that paid links did not have a statistically significant effect on the first group since users of this group are already familiar with eBay. However, there was a significant increase in newly registered users and purchases in the second group due to exposure of paid links. This supports the informative view of advertising.

Several empirical studies focus on how targeted advertising interacts with other forms of advertising. Goldfarb and Tucker (2011b) conduct a large-scale field experiment exposing individuals to two different forms of online advertisements. The first is a

---

[61] A natural explanation is that eBay is a well-known brand and is therefore highly listed in the organic search results.

contextually targeted ad, such as a banner ad for a new computer displayed on a site devoted to computing and technology. The other is a highly visible ad, which users might consider obtrusive. For example, an ad is considered obtrusive if the ad is part of an in-stream audio or video, if it is a pop-up window, or if it automatically (non-user initiated) plays audio or video, among other characteristics. Goldfarb and Tucker (2011b) find that the effect of targeted ads *alone* (without obtrusiveness) and the effect of obtrusiveness *alone* (without targeting) have a positive influence on the effectiveness of advertising. However, both strategies *in combination* nullify this effect and are ineffective. An explanation for this can be that consumers perceive themselves to be manipulated, which reduces their purchase intentions. In particular, when exposed to targeted ads that are obtrusive, consumers may have privacy concerns. Goldfarb and Tucker (2011b) find evidence that supports this view.

More generally, advertising across different types of media and consumer online behavior are connected. Joo et al. (2014) study how advertising in an offline medium (television) affects consumers' online searches and thus search engine advertising. They consider TV advertisements of financial services and analyze how these commercials affect consumer search behavior. They find a significantly positive effect. For example, a few hours after being exposed to a TV ad for a particular brand, searchers have a stronger tendency to enter branded keywords instead of generic keywords.[62]

Overall, this suggests that, while online and offline advertising are substitutes, offline advertising stimulates online product search. Further research, both theoretical and empirical, could be fruitful to establish a solid pattern that links the influences of advertising in one medium to consumer behavior in another.

10.6. MEDIA PLATFORMS MATCHING ADVERTISING TO USERS

Internet media facilitate the targeting of ads to specific consumers. Traditional media provide tailored offers such that consumers self-select into particular programming and content. Advertisers then benefit from the correlation of consumer tastes with media content and with advertised products. Clearly, such tailoring strategies are also available on the Internet and were analyzed in the previous section. A novel feature of advertising on the Internet is the wealth of personal data available to data providers, which allows the matching of advertising to consumer tastes on media platforms irrespective of the media content that is consumed.[63] While this wealth of data raises serious privacy and data protection issues (not analyzed in this chapter), it also affects the way media platforms

---

[62] Rutz and Bucklin (2012) find a similar result for online advertising and online search.
[63] We are not claiming that the tailoring of advertising is a completely new phenomenon. For instance, advertisers may use personal information when sending out coupons by mail.

operate.[64] In addition, since consumers mostly visit multiple sites, excessive advertising beyond what consumers can digest also arises on the Internet.

10.6.1 Tracking and Personalized Offers

The Internet has opened new ways to track consumers by placing cookies. Cookies are small pieces of data sent from a website, which track the user's activities. To the extent that previous user behavior allows inferences on users' current tastes, it becomes possible to, at least partly, avoid wasteful impressions. Google explicitly writes in its information to users: "We use cookies to make advertising more engaging to users and more valuable to publishers and advertisers." Google then provides a more detailed explanation on the use of cookies: "Some common applications of cookies are to select advertising based on what's relevant to a user; to improve reporting of campaign performance; and to avoid showing ads the user has already seen." While perfect public tracking would, in particular, allow websites to best match advertising to users, in many markets media platforms may not share tracking information. Thus, tracking is often imperfect.

Tracking may allow for the segmentation of consumers according to some broad categories without fully personalizing the targeting of ads. This segmenting of the consumer pool may be based on past purchases (Malthouse and Elsner, 2006).[65] This information helps to increase the likelihood that the advertiser's product and the consumer's taste match.

Targeting can be based on personal characteristics. Some of the theoretical models presented below are based on this idea. Advertising has been shown to be more effective when it is targeted to particular consumers using consumer browsing behavior (Chen et al., 2009) or using inferred or observed demographics as consumer characteristics (Joshi et al., 2011).[66] Thus, the empirical literature indicates that tracking can increase ad effectiveness. A more challenging question is to uncover the impact of tracking on industry outcomes.

Beyond the collection of information from cookies, the matching of advertising to users may rely on information provided by database marketing companies. Marwick (2014) provides some information on the second largest company in the industry, Acxiom. According to Marwick (2014), Acxiom has 23,000 computer servers and processes more than 50 trillion data transactions per year, keeping records on hundreds of million US residents. Data include 200 million mobile profiles, information gathered from publicly available records (such as home valuations and vehicle ownership), information about online behavior (1.1 billion browser cookies, information on browser advertising, and other information), as well as data from customer surveys and offline

---

[64] Privacy issues are discussed in Chapter 11 of the Handbook.

[65] Other empirical work segments consumers according to their cognitive style (Hauser et al., 2009).

[66] This empirical work combines tailoring and tracking, as it combines consumer characteristics with content matching.

buying behavior. On average, for each US resident, Acxiom keeps about 1500 pieces of data. Thus, Acxiom has a wealth of information that it can sell to interested parties, in particular with the aim to better match advertising or services to user tastes.

While on traditional ad-financed media, the user pays with her attention, on Internet media, the user pays not only with her attention, but also with her personal data. Thus, websites including Internet media may make revenues even if they neither charge users nor carry any advertising. They can accomplish this by opening a third source of revenues—selling user information.

A number of theoretical efforts help in understanding the forces at play when media platforms track users or rely on third-party information in their effort to best match advertising to users. The model presented at the end of this subsection explicitly includes the sale of user data for the purpose of targeting.

A media platform may provide tracking information about consumers to advertisers. Doing so allows advertisers to bid for ads conditional on the information they receive. When advertising space is scarce, advertisers operating in such an environment internalize that in case of tracking their bids will only be successful if they provide better matches to consumers than other advertisers; absent tracking advertisers offer similar expected match quality. As a consequence, advertisers set higher retail prices with tracking information than without. While tracking improves average match quality, leading to higher retail prices and thus larger industry profits, it also reduces the share of industry profits that can be extracted by the platform, as advertisers set prices prior to learning consumer types.[67] Thus, it is not obvious whether the platform benefits from tracking.

de Cornière and De Nijs (2014) formalize this tradeoff and investigate the platform's incentives to install a tracking technology. Here, through a second-price auction, a monopoly media platform sells a single advertising slot to n advertisers.[68] This slot gives exclusive access to the consumer. Thus, sellers act as monopolists in the product market. The timing of the model is as follows: First, the platform decides whether to install a tracking technology. Second, advertisers simultaneously set the product price p_i, $i = 1, \ldots, n$. Third, the consumer type is revealed to advertisers under tracking; it remains unknown otherwise. Fourth, advertisers simultaneously place bids for the advertising slot conditional on the information they received. The consumer is matched to the winning advertiser.

---

[67] If prices were set conditional on consumer types and thus advertisers customize retail prices, they would extract a larger fraction of consumer surplus. However, this would drive up bids. Advertisers would be worse off since the difference between valuation of the winning bid and the valuation of the second highest bidder (and thus the price in the auction) shrinks when advertisers can customize the retail price compared to the setting where they cannot.

[68] Selling a single slot is perhaps the simplest setting and avoids the need to consider alternative multi-unit auctions. Suppose that advertisers are potential competitors in the market place. Then, it is optimal to sell a single slot if monopoly profits exceed industry profits with two or more firms.

A consumer is of type $(\theta_1,\ldots,\theta_n)$, where θ_i is i.i.d. across products and distributed according to F with density function f on $\left[\bar{\theta},\bar{\bar{\theta}}\right]$. Type θ_i for product i gives rise to a conditional demand function $D(p_i;\theta_i)$. A higher type is assumed to be associated with larger demand for the respective product (e.g., a larger probability to buy the product); i.e., $D(p_i;\theta_i) > D(p_i;\theta_i')$ if and only if $\theta_i > \theta_i'$. The profit of an advertiser selling to a consumer is $\pi_i(p_i,\theta_i) = (p_i - c)D(p_i;\theta_i)$. Absent tracking, if an advertiser's bid is successful, its expected profit gross of the advertising cost is $\int_{\bar{\theta}}^{\bar{\bar{\theta}}} \pi_i(p_i,\theta_i)f(\theta_i)\mathrm{d}\theta_i$. The profit-maximizing product price p^{NT} solves

$$\int_{\bar{\theta}}^{\bar{\bar{\theta}}} \frac{\partial \pi_i(p_i,\theta_i)}{\partial p_i} f(\theta_i)\mathrm{d}\theta_i = 0$$

in p_i. Since advertisers are homogeneous at the bidding stage, the media platform can extract the full expected industry profit $\int_{\bar{\theta}}^{\bar{\bar{\theta}}} \pi_i(p^{\mathrm{NT}},\theta_i)f(\theta_i)\mathrm{d}\theta_i$.

With tracking, the profit-maximizing product price p^{T} solves

$$\int_{\bar{\theta}}^{\bar{\bar{\theta}}} \frac{\partial \pi_i(p_i,\theta_i)}{\partial p_i} F^{n-1}(\theta_i)f(\theta_i)\mathrm{d}\theta_i = 0$$

in p_i, since advertiser i wins the auction if and only if θ_i is larger than θ_j, $j \neq i$, which occurs with probability $F^{n-1}(\theta_i)$. Compared to the case without tracking, this extra term captures that the firm with the largest θ_i wins the auction. As a consequence, it will set a higher price at the pricing stage than without tracking, $p^{\mathrm{T}} > p^{\mathrm{NT}}$. The price under tracking is increasing in the number of advertisers. Consequently, tracking results in a better match between advertiser and consumer and increases industry profits. With tracking, advertisers obtain a positive information rent and thus a strictly positive share of industry profits.

When deciding whether to install the tracking technology, the media platform faces the tradeoff between increasing efficiency (and industry profits) and rent extraction; such a tradeoff also obtains in Ganuza (2004).[69] As the number of advertisers turns to infinity, the product price p^{T} turns to the monopoly price of a firm facing a consumer with type $\bar{\bar{\theta}}$ and thus the information rent of advertisers disappears. Hence, for a number of advertisers sufficiently large, the media platform installs the tracking technology and shares the consumer information with advertisers.

Suppose now that the platform sells multiple advertising slots and advertisers offer independent products to consumers. Advertising slots are sold through a uniform price auction such that all advertisers with the highest bids pay the price equal to the highest bid among losing advertisers. Then, the equilibrium product price is shown to be decreasing in the number of advertising slots. In addition to the standard price–quantity tradeoff, an

---

[69] The objective function of the platform is to maximize its profit given user participation.

increase in the number of advertising slots renders winning a slot in the auction less informative about the expected elasticity of demand. When the number of slots is sufficiently large, de Cornière and De Nijs (2014) show that the platform chooses not to install the tracking technology since the losing bidder who determines the ad price in the auction tends to receive a rather bad signal with tracking.

Johnson (2013) also explores the effects of the tracking technology on advertiser profits and consumer surplus. While he does not include media platforms in his model, his analysis is useful in obtaining insights about the role of tracking when consumers can block advertising.

In his model, advertising creates an opportunity for advertisers and consumers to form a match. There is a mass 1 of advertisers and a mass 1 of consumers. For each advertiser–consumer pair, the probability of such a match is ϕ, which is distributed i.i.d. across all pairs according to some distribution function F with positive density of f on $[0,1]$. A match generates a surplus Λ for the advertiser and $1 - \Lambda$ for the consumer. Advertisers offer totally differentiated products.

The advertiser learns about the match probability with probability ψ and does not learn otherwise. In this model, improved tracking corresponds to a larger value of ψ. Thus, the probability of a match is $\psi\phi + (1 - \psi)E\phi$ if the consumer sees the ad.

Advertisers incur a cost of $\kappa > 0$ for sending an ad. Consumers have the possibility of blocking an ad with probability ς. Hence, an advertiser decides to advertise to a consumer with signal ϕ if

$$\kappa \le (1 - \varsigma)\Lambda[\psi\phi + (1 - \psi)E[\phi]].$$

A firm that sends an ad to consumers with signal ϕ will send an ad to all consumers with larger signals. If h is the mass of ads sent by an advertiser, we have $\phi(h) = F^{-1}(1 - h)$ as the signal of the marginal consumer. An advertiser's profit is, then,

$$-\kappa h + (1 - \varsigma)\Lambda\left[\psi\int_{\phi(h)}^{1} x\,\mathrm{d}F(x) + (1 - \psi)hE[\phi]\right].$$

All consumers are exposed to the same number of ads if they decide not to block them. Each ad they receive generates a nuisance γ from being exposed to it. However, advertising leads to consumption, which enters the consumer's utility as well. Thus, the expected utility from receiving h ads is

$$v = -\gamma h + (1 - \Lambda)\left[\psi\int_{\phi(h)}^{1} x\,\mathrm{d}F(x) + (1 - \psi)hE[\phi]\right].$$

If consumers block ads, they receive an outside utility u_0, which is distributed according to G, a continuously differentiable distribution function with support $(-\infty, 0]$. Taking h as given, each consumer compares her expected utility from receiving ads to the outside utility of blocking. Hence, the fraction of blocking consumers is $\varsigma = 1 - G(v)$. Consider the game in which, simultaneously, consumers decide whether to block and advertisers decide how many ads to send. A pair (ς^*, h^*) constitutes an equilibrium of this game. In this model, the cost–benefit ratios for advertisers and consumers, κ/Λ and $\phi/(1-\Lambda)$, play a decisive role. They reflect the cost of an ad relative to the benefit of a successful match.

Johnson (2013) shows that the second-best advertising level (when consumers are free to block advertising) is smaller than the equilibrium level h^* if and only if the cost–benefit ratio on the consumer side is larger than the cost–benefit ratio on the advertiser side. In equilibrium, advertisers are indifferent about whether to place the marginal ad. Since the marginal probability of trade is the same for advertisers and consumers, intuitively there is socially insufficient advertising if consumers place a higher value on ads than advertisers. If the reverse holds, advertisers post too many ads.[70]

Improved tracking—i.e., an increase in ψ—keeping blocking decisions unchanged, leads to more advertising if the surplus derived from the marginal ad exceeds the surplus derived from the unconditional average ad. If advertisers increase advertising due to improved tracking, this must mean that they gain more from the marginal ad than from the unconditional average ad. This must continue to hold if consumers adjust their blocking decision. Johnson (2013) shows that improved tracking increases advertiser profits in equilibrium, even though this may imply more blocking. Whether consumers gain or lose from improved tracking is ambiguous.[71]

Depending on the information available to advertisers, when there are multiple platforms, advertisers may waste impressions by hitting the same consumer more than once even if tracking is perfect on each platform. If, however, platforms share cookie information—a practice called cookie matching—advertisers can avoid such multiple exposures.

Athey et al. (2014) consider a market with two platforms that perfectly track consumers on their own platform (i.e., a consumer gets an ad at most once on this platform), but may not observe the exposure of consumers to advertising on the other platform.[72] They investigate the impact of this lack of cookie matching on market outcomes and

---

[70] The results of van Zandt (2004) and Anderson and de Palma (2009) can also be interpreted as showing the possibility of socially excessive advertising. In their models, socially excessive advertising may arise because lower-value ads crowd out higher-value ads, an issue we return to in Section 10.6.2. In contrast, in Johnson (2013), a larger ad level encourages consumers to block ads.

[71] If advertisers have to pay a media website to place ads (an issue not considered by Johnson, 2013), the website can manage the ad level of advertisers. Suppose that the media website charges a price per ad. This price enters the advertiser's profit function as part of its cost κ. A welfare-maximizing single media website (which cannot directly control blocking) will then implement the second-best optimal advertising level. A profit-maximizing, monopolistic ad-financed media website will also internalize the effect of ad levels on blocking. However, it will typically not implement the second best. The effect of the tracking technology on total and consumer surplus in such a media market has yet to be explored.

[72] Ghosh et al. (2012) provide a related analysis, which also shows that in some cases platforms prefer to share cookie information, whereas in others they do not.

media platforms' profits. In their model, as, e.g., in Ambrus et al. (2015), some consumers exclusively consume media content of one platform, while the others consume both (see Section 10.4.1). Thus, there are exclusive consumers and overlapping consumers.

Similar to previous models, media platforms provide access to consumers. To focus on advertisers' behavior, suppose first that media platforms do not make any decision (i.e., ad levels are fixed and exogenous) and that ad prices clear the market for ads. Consider a continuum of advertisers who are heterogeneous with respect to the profit per consumer they derive when successfully contacting a consumer. Their behavior determines the demand for advertising. The advertiser value per consumer is distributed between 0 and some upper bound. Advertisers with a high value per consumer have a stronger incentive to contact consumers than advertisers with lower value. If there were no overlapping consumers (and perfect tracking on each platform), there would exist a marginal advertiser such that every advertiser with a lower value per consumer would not advertise, whereas all advertisers above this threshold would deliver each impression to a distinct consumer. Thus, no impression would be wasted and advertising would be delivered efficiently.

Demand for advertising depends on the tracking technology. If tracking is perfect on each platform but there is no cookie matching, multi-homing advertisers waste some impressions as they sometimes show the same ad to switchers twice. This waste, together with advertiser heterogeneity, implies sorting of advertisers: low-type advertisers single-home (and miss some consumers), while high-type advertisers (who have a higher opportunity cost of not informing consumers) multi-home.

This establishes the main insight. With perfect tracking across platforms, the number of impressions would map one-to-one into the number of consumers reached by an advertiser. On the contrary, with the above imperfect tracking, some overlapping consumers will see the same ad twice and so their attention is wasted. By increasing the number of overlapping consumers waste becomes more prevalent under imperfect tracking and the value of the advertising inventory is further degraded.

The analysis can be extended to allow for the platforms simultaneous choosing advertising inventory. In the presence of overlapping consumers, platforms become essentially Cournot competitors. Athey et al. (2014) show that, in equilibrium, an increase in the fraction of overlapping consumers leads to higher advertising inventories and, in turn, lower equilibrium advertising prices.[73]

Taylor (2013b) provides a different perspective on the role of tracking. In his model, media platforms choose content quality, taking into account that it increases the likelihood that a consumer does not switch to another platform. The incentive to invest in content quality is affected by the tracking technology available to the platforms.

---

[73] Due to the heterogeneity of advertisers, the analysis is rather intricate and best-response functions are non-monotone.

Taylor's (2013b) model has a number of features different from those of the three previous models. First, a key ingredient is product market competition among advertisers;[74] second, consumers are uninformed about content quality before visiting a website and therefore access media platforms at random. Thus, Taylor (2013b) focuses on how content quality affects consumer behavior *after* consumers have clicked on the media website. Key to his results is the interaction between product market competition among advertisers and the consumer decision of whether to switch to another media platform (endogenous multi-homing).

In Taylor's (2013b) model, two ad-financed media websites provide content to a large number of consumers of measure D. Consumers enjoy media consumption but incur a cost c for visiting a website. The two media platforms choose content quality $q_i \in [0, 1]$ and incur cost $k(q_i)$.[75] Here, content quality measures the probability that a consumer is satisfied with the content and hence does not need to move to the other website for this topic. Content quality is a search good; thus, consumers cannot assess content quality before actually visiting the website. Consumers visit websites sequentially. If a consumer is satisfied by the content at the first website, she does not visit the second. If she is not satisfied, she visits the second website if the expected quality is larger than c. Consumers recall ads and make consumption choices after their media consumption.

Websites will, nevertheless, choose positive quality so as to retain the consumer's attention. Why? Websites bundle advertising to content and sell ads to advertisers.[76] More specifically, the website places an ad together with the content offer. Each consumer has a particular consumption interest (e.g., interest in a particular product category), and an advertiser matches this interest if it offers a product in this category. The surplus generated by a successful match between advertiser and consumer is normalized to 1. Advertisers are assumed to be Bertrand competitors if a consumer happens to see an ad from two advertisers within the same category. As it wants to raise revenues from selling ads, a website will carry only one ad of a given product category. Each website extracts the full advertiser profit.

The tracking technology determines the probability of a successful match; it allows the website to identify the product category of interest with probability ϕ and delivers any of the other categories with the remaining probability. If a consumer visits both

---

[74] Most theoretical papers on media economics postulate that advertisers have monopoly power over consumers in the product market. As discussed in Section 10.4.1, an exception is Gal-Or and Dukes (2003). In their model, as well as in Taylor's (2013b) model, intense product market competition creates incentives for media platforms and advertisers to sign exclusivity contracts of the form that the media platform agrees not to carry ads from competing advertisers.

[75] The cost function satisfies the appropriate properties so as to ensure an interior solution characterized by a first-order condition.

[76] In contrast to consumers, advertisers can assess a platform's quality because they need to be reassured that the platform makes retention efforts.

websites, she is exposed to the advertising on the other website. For simplicity, suppose that this other website draws on a different set of advertisers and therefore that a consumer will never see the same ad twice. If the consumer sees another ad in the product category of interest, she can choose between the two offers and will choose the offer at the lower price.

As long as some, but not all, consumers visit both websites (i.e., in any interior solution), there are consumers who observe one successful match and others who observe two. Thus, advertisers randomize over price. Each advertiser's equilibrium profit is equal to its monopoly price 1 × the likelihood that it provides the only match. Here, content quality helps, as it increases the probability that consumers do not visit multiple websites and thus prevents multiple exposures of advertising.

As Taylor (2013b) shows, equilibrium content quality can be calculated by equating marginal benefit from quality investment with marginal costs. This yields

$$q^* = (k')^{-1}\left(\frac{\phi^2 D}{2}\right).$$

The intuition is as follows: Since consumers do not observe quality, they visit platforms at random. Therefore, each platform gets $D/2$ first visits. The benefit of retaining a consumer is the security profit of that consumer, which is measured by ϕ.[77] Better tracking (i.e., an increase in ϕ) is valuable even in a monopoly context, as it increases the probability of a match between advertiser and consumer. Everything else being equal, this increases the incentive to invest in content quality. The tracking technology matters also for product market competition since better tracking makes it more likely that a consumer who visits both websites encounters two matches. Hence, better tracking makes product market competition more intense. In this case, the website would extract lower rents from advertisers. To reduce the probability of multiple exposures to ads within the same product category, a website has to increase its content quality. Due to this competition effect, websites may actually overinvest in content quality compared to the welfare-maximizing solution. More specifically, the result arises because of externalities between websites: If a website invests in content quality, it does not internalize that its rival's opportunity to provide impressions to consumers via ads gets lower. This is detrimental for welfare because it eliminates trade between some pairs of consumers and advertisers. This effect is particularly pronounced if ϕ is large because then many of the foregone impressions would have resulted in a match. As Taylor (2013b) illustrates, websites

[77] In the model, a consumer is retained (i) if she is satisfied with the content of the platform, and (ii) if she is not satisfied with the content on both platforms and the second platform could not identify her product category of interest. Therefore, the profit function of a website is $(D/2)\phi(q_i + ((1-q_i) + (1-q_{-i}))(1-\phi))$. Taking the derivative with respect to q_i and using platform symmetry yields q^*.

may actually suffer from improved tracking, as they are compelled to invest (excessively) in content quality.

Tracking is made feasible by data providers that handle large amounts of data that they obtain from placing cookies. Bergemann and Bonatti (2015) explore the interaction between data providers and advertisers. Advertisers face consumers with heterogeneous match value $v \in V$. Through cookies, they obtain precise information on consumers' value. This allows advertisers to segment the consumer side into two groups: a target group about which it collects detailed information and to which it makes personalized advertising offers; and an anonymous outsider group in which all consumers receive the same level of advertising as everybody else in this group.

If an advertiser were fully informed, he would reach a consumer with probability ϕ and then extract the full surplus v of the match between his product and the consumer. Thus, he would make revenue $v\phi$. To reach consumers with probability ϕ, he has to place $a(\phi)$ ads on the publisher's platform, which is assumed to charge p per ad. Hence, a fully informed advertiser makes profit $v\phi - pa(\phi)$. The advertiser's problem is that he knows only about some prior distribution of v and thus may not be able to appropriate the full surplus.

To better extract surplus, the advertiser may acquire data about the individual consumer. Such data provide a signal about the consumer's match value. This is where cookies come into play. A cookie, bought at a price P_c for a subset of types $W \subset V$, allows the advertiser to identify a consumer v. Hence, for all $v \in W$, the demand for advertising space is $v = pa'(\phi^*(v))$, where $\phi^*(v)$ is the full information demand for advertising space. For all $v \notin W$, the advertiser updates beliefs and acquires ad space according to $E[v|v \notin W] = pa'(\bar{\phi})$. Clearly, $\bar{\phi} = \phi^*(E[v|v \notin W])$. Figure 10.9 illustrates the market environment.

A fully informed advertiser makes profit $v\phi^*(v) - pa(\phi^*(v))$, which is convex in v. By contrast, absent any information, the advertiser's profit would be $v\phi^*(E[v]) - pa(\phi^*(E[v]))$, which is linear in v. An uninformed advertiser advertises too much to low-value consumers and too little to high-value consumers. Thus, the advertiser has an incentive to buy cookies.

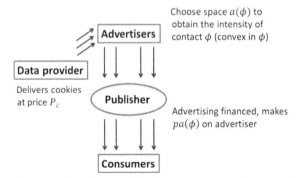

Figure 10.9 Internet advertising based on cookies in Bergemann and Bonatti (2015).

Bergemann and Bonatti (2015) characterize the demand for cookies for a given price P_c. An advertiser may buy from a single interval that includes either the lowest-value or the highest-value consumer. Alternatively, he may want to buy from two intervals, one of which includes the lowest-value consumer and the other the highest-value consumer. Bergemann and Bonatti (2015) then determine the optimal pricing by the data provider. The data provider may limit the amount of data being bought in equilibrium, as the data provider maximizes its profits. Hence, consumers benefit if the data provider enjoys some market power because, absent market power of the data provider, advertisers would become fully informed about the match value.

To put Bergemann and Bonatti (2015) into broader perspective, we note that the publisher may be vertically integrated with the data provider. In this case, the publisher has three potential sources of revenues: First, the publisher can charge consumers directly for its content services. Second, the publisher can charge advertisers for offering advertising space (to the extent that consumers dislike advertising, this constitutes an indirect charge to consumers). These two revenue sources are well established in media economics. Third, Bergemann and Bonatti (2015) formalize that the publisher may also offer advertisers data services for which it can charge a fee. As this allows advertisers to better extract surplus from consumers, providing this information constitutes another indirect charge to consumers.

Tracking allows advertisers to use a sophisticated targeting strategy. While the above models provide relevant insights into the role of the tracking technology, they are not embedded in a dynamic environment. In particular, consumers may search within a product category on a particular website but do not close their session with a purchase. Possible reasons are that they are still in doubt or that they decide that the offer is dominated by the outside option, which may include the possibility of searching again in the future. Due to tracking, advertisers become aware of the identity of such consumers. They may therefore "redouble" their efforts and retarget these consumers via advertising on this website or specific offerings on another website when consumers are visiting a website that is affiliated with the ad network selling ads to advertisers. For instance, Facebook has introduced retargeted ads in its users' newsfeed. With dynamic retargeting, the ad network identifies people with the help of the individual cookie profile and recalls the exact product a consumer has looked at before. With this information, it targets the consumer by displaying the same or a related product offered by the firm visited before. This is in contrast to generic retargeting, which uses cookie information only to select the firm of which an ad is shown (see Lambrecht and Tucker, 2013). It has been claimed that dynamic retargeting is four times more effective than generic retargeting and six times more effective than generic advertising using banner ads (Criteo, 2010).

Lambrecht and Tucker (2013) provide a detailed assessment of the effectiveness of dynamic retargeting, based on a field experiment with data from a travel website that sells hotel accommodations and vacation packages. In the field experiment, consumers were randomly assigned generic and dynamic retargeted ads when they visited an external website affiliated with the ad network. The generic ad showed a generic brand ad for the travel website, while the dynamic retargeted ad showed the hotel the consumer had looked at before, plus a few similar offerings. Perhaps surprisingly, the authors find that, on average, dynamic retargeting is not more effective, where effectiveness is measured by the probability that the consumer makes a purchase on the travel website within a specified time interval.

A possible explanation for the failure of dynamic retargeting vis-à-vis generic retargeting is that consumers may have had only a loose idea of what they were looking for (as argued by Lambrecht and Tucker, 2013). Thus, a generic ad may be more effective since consumers may have figured out that the specific offer they previously looked at was actually not what they wanted. However, such behavior seems less likely if consumers dedicate quite some effort on their search and make further inquiries. In this case, it appears likely that consumers have well-specified ideas of what they liked and may be inclined to revisit their previous searches. Lambrecht and Tucker (2013) try to proxy this by identifying consumers who used a review site. The empirical result supports the view that dynamic retargeting is more effective for those consumers. These findings suggest a rather complex effect of targeting on purchase intent. It suggests that simple and universal messages of how (re)targeting will affect market structure may be too much to expect.

10.6.2 Advertising Congestion and Limited Attention

Advertisers post ads to leave an impression on consumers and to make a profit by selling a product or service or by being able to sell at a higher price. To achieve this, advertisers have to overcome several hurdles. First, consumers must not block advertising; second, consumers have to remember the ad (remember the advertised product, product features, or the ad experience as a complement) when making a purchase decision; and third, advertisers must be able to make money from such a consumer. We touched upon the first hurdle in Section 10.6.1 in the context of targeting (Johnson, 2013). The third hurdle arises, for example, with competing advertisers in a Bertrand world. If a consumer receives two competing ads, the ad is essentially a wasted impression for the advertiser (Taylor, 2013b). The second issue is one of limited attention, which we did not elaborate on in the context of advertising. Advertising congestion can be seen as a mismatch between advertisers and consumers, since high-value advertisers may not capture consumers' attention and thus are not matched, whereas some lower-value advertisers do manage to gain the consumer's attention.

Anderson and de Palma (2009) formalize information congestion, postulating that consumer attention spans are limited (for a formal presentation of the model in a different context, see Section 10.3.2). Under "open access" to attention (for example, through billboards or bulk mail), attention is a common property resource to which all consumers have access. This common property resource tends to be excessively exploited, resulting in congestion in equilibrium. By contrast, a monopoly gatekeeper prices out congestion.

Anderson and Peitz (2014a) show how this approach can be integrated into a model of competing media platforms. Here, we illustrate their setting, closely following Anderson et al. (2012). To see how advertising congestion changes the nature of media competition, consider, first, the situation with a fixed amount of time spent by a representative user on each of the n media platforms. Website quality maps into usage time. The idea here is that consumers surf the web, spend more time on higher-quality websites and less on lower-quality ones. Advertisers are supposed to offer totally differentiated products. Thus, advertisers are monopolists vis-à-vis consumers. Suppose, furthermore, that advertisers extract the full expected surplus from consumers.

Consumers access pages of the different websites in random order. If they visit more pages of a website, they will be exposed to more ads from that website. Websites are assumed to benefit from industry-wide perfect tracking. If the value of the marginal advertiser is larger than the expected value of a repeated impression of a given ad (which holds if congestion is not too severe), all consumers will see an ad only once. Ads will be placed randomly. Even though advertising does not affect media consumption, the website will not post an unlimited number of ads. This is so because it cannot discriminate between different types of advertisers and thus has to lower the ad price as it takes in more advertisers.

Each media website decides how many ads to place at an initial stage since this is mostly a question of how to design the website or how to structure the bundle of content and advertising. Denote by σ_i the amount of time spent on website $i = 1, \ldots, n$, and by σ_0 the time spent not using the Internet (the outside option), and normalize the total time available to 1. If website i shows a_i ads and a consumer spends all her time on this site, the consumer's total exposure is a_i. To make a match between an advertiser and any given consumer, this consumer must be exposed to the corresponding ad and she must recall the ad. Each consumer will see $\Gamma = \sum_{i=1}^{n} a_i \sigma_i$ ads in total. However, if the (fixed) attention span φ of a consumer is less than this number—i.e., $\varphi < \Gamma$—the consumer will not remember some of the ads. Hence, for these ads no match is formed. Advertisers are ranked according to the willingness-to-pay to contact potential consumers. Hence, the a-th advertiser is willing to pay $p(a)$ to attract the attention of a consumer. With congestion, the willingness-to-pay of the a-th advertiser reduces to $p(a)\varphi/\Gamma$. With a_i ads on platform i, the ad price conditional on making an impression must be equal to the willingness-to-pay of the marginal advertiser—i.e., $p(a_i)\varphi/\Gamma$. Since the ad makes an impression with probability σ_i, each ad generates revenue $\sigma_i p(a_i)\varphi/\Gamma$. Thus, website i maximizes its profit as the product of number of ads and revenue per ad,

$$\sigma_i a_i \frac{p(a_i)\varphi}{\Gamma} = A(a_i)\frac{\sigma_i\varphi}{\Gamma},$$

with respect to the ad space a_i, where $A(a_i)$ is the revenue per ad per viewer. Strategic interaction between websites arises because of advertising congestion and the fact that consumers have a limited attention span for all ads combined across different websites. Thus, each website has access to the common property resource, which is the attention span of each consumer. Because of the free-rider problem, advertising in a market with strictly more than one website may result in congestion. In the monopoly case, the result of Anderson and de Palma (2009) applies, and the monopoly website always sets its ad level such that congestion does not arise. If the attention span is sufficiently large (i.e., $\varphi \geq \Gamma$), each website i chooses a_i so as to maximize revenue per ad per viewer—i.e., a_i^* solves $A'(a_i) = 0$ and all websites choose the same ad level. With congestion, when consumers spend the same amount of time on each website, the first-order condition of profit maximization becomes

$$A'(a)\frac{\varphi}{\Gamma} - A(a)\frac{\varphi}{\Gamma^2}\sigma = 0$$

after using symmetry—i.e., $\sigma = \sigma_i$ and $a = a_i$. This implicitly defines the equilibrium advertising level a^*. Since total advertising is $\Gamma = n\sigma a$, the equilibrium ad level is given by the solution to

$$\frac{aA'(a)}{A(a)} = \frac{1}{n}.$$

If $p(a)$ is log-concave, the left-hand side is decreasing in a. This implies that a larger number of websites leads to an increase in the advertising level of each website and thus to more severe congestion.[78] The intuition is that with more alternative websites around, each website internalizes to a smaller extent the negative effect that an increase in its ad level has on the resulting advertising price. In an asymmetric market, Anderson and Peitz (2014a) show that the larger website chooses a lower ad level a_i. This is intuitive, as a larger platform internalizes the congestion externality to a larger extent since more infra-marginal ad slots are affected by the price decrease resulting from a larger ad volume.[79]

The general lesson that emerges from the ad congestion model is that congestion generates interdependence among websites due to price effects on the advertiser side. To the extent that consumers consult a large number of ad-financed websites, the analysis suggests that congestion issues may be important drivers of competition between websites.

---

[78] A merger between two websites is beneficial because it leads to less congestion. For a detailed discussion of the merger effects in media markets and the regulatory environment, see Chapter 6 in this volume.

[79] Anderson and Peitz (2014a) extend their analysis to include advertising as a nuisance. This makes the advertising market two-sided, as consumers now care about the number of ads carried on each platform. Then, the higher-quality website still features a lower ad level. This is the opposite finding one would get if the consumers' attention span was unlimited.

10.7. CONCLUSION

In this chapter, we surveyed the literature on media economics as it applies to the Internet. A lot of progress has been made in understanding how media companies react to the challenges brought about by the Internet and how they adjust their business models or invent new ones. The theoretical and empirical studies show the potential for market failures on the Internet (e.g., on search engines or via targeting) and therefore inform firms and regulators. Naturally, our survey is restricted to recent developments, without any claim of completeness. However, due to technological progress, new revenue opportunities for websites are likely to arise soon. They are likely to provide new possibilities for innovative business models and create new regulatory and competition policy issues.

We want to point out a number of current phenomena that are not well understood and call for further research. First, we outlined at several points in this chapter that the Internet affects the diversity of content. Although content of very different topics and expertise is easily accessible, the Internet is prone to information overload, and so users need to select the content. As a consequence of this selection process, users may browse websites that are pre-selected on the basis of most-read websites. Therefore, an interesting question is whether the Internet broadens or stifles diversity. Second, an important question is whether the Internet is more inclusive than traditional media. For example, the data in Section 10.2 showed that the Internet is more popular among young people than among older ones. In addition, in more-developed countries, the percentage of Internet usage tends to be higher than in less-developed ones. This implies that the number of recipients of news differs between age groups and regions. This may lead to some individuals or regions lagging behind, which may have adverse effects on economic growth.[80] For example, poorer and rural users tend to have slower connections and thus less opportunity to articulate their opinions. Third, we focused on the content generated by professional websites with the intent of making profits. However, as outlined in Section 10.4.3, these websites increasingly compete with individuals, such as bloggers or Facebook friends, for the scarce attention of users. The activities of these individuals are not (necessarily) driven by monetary incentives, but, for example, by social concerns such as attention received from their followers or friends. An interesting question is how interaction and competition between "amateurs" and "professionals" play out. In particular, the presence of amateurs may change the business models of for-profit websites.

Finally, we note that many of the theories we presented focused on a particular problem of Internet media. Due to the complexity and the many layers of the problems, there is no unifying framework. However, many of the issues we discussed interact with each other. For example, the user behavior of switching more or switching less between

---

[80] For example, Czernich et al. (2011), using a panel data set from OECD countries, find that a 10% increase in broadband penetration rates leads to an increase in *per-capita* economic growth of around 1–1.5%.

websites affects the emergence and profitability of news aggregators. Similarly, the possibility of tracking users in a better or worse way has profound consequences on advertisers' willingness-to-pay and therefore on the profitability of Internet media platforms and search engines. Removing or refraining from net neutrality restrictions may change the advertisers' reservation prices for different content, with consequences for tailoring. While some of these interactions have been addressed in the literature, there remain many potentially interesting links to be explored in further research.

ACKNOWLEDGMENTS

We thank Simon Anderson, Alessandro Bonatti, Emilio Calvano, Alexandre de Cornière, Greg Taylor, Tim Thomes, Joel Waldfogel, and Ken Wilbur for helpful comments.

REFERENCES

Agarwal, A., Hosonagar, K., Smith, M.D., 2011. Location, location, location: an analysis of profitability of position in online advertising markets. J. Mark. Res. 48, 1057–1073.

Ambrus, A., Calvano, E., Reisinger, M., 2015. Either-or-both competition: a two-sided theory of advertising with overlapping viewerships. Am. Econ. J. Microecon. (forthcoming).

Ambrus, A., Reisinger, M., 2006. Exclusive Versus Overlapping Viewers in Media Markets. Unpublished Manuscript.

Anderson, C., 2006. The Long Tail. Hyperion, New York, NY.

Anderson, S.P., Coate, S., 2005. Market provision of broadcasting: a welfare analysis. Rev. Econ. Stud. 72, 947–972.

Anderson, S.P., De Palma, A., 2009. Information congestion. RAND J. Econ. 40, 688–709.

Anderson, S.P., Foros, Ø., Kind, H., 2010. Hotelling Competition with Multi-Purchasing. CESifo Working Paper 3096.

Anderson, S.P., Foros, Ø., Kind, H., 2014. Competition for Advertisers and for Viewers in Media Markets. Unpublished Manuscript.

Anderson, S.P., Foros, Ø., Kind, H.J., Peitz, M., 2012. Media market concentration, advertising levels, and ad prices. Int. J. Ind. Organ. 30, 321–325.

Anderson, S.P., Neven, D.J., 1989. Market efficiency with combinable products. Eur. Econ. Rev. 33, 707–719.

Anderson, S.P., Peitz, M., 2014a. Advertising Congestion in Media Markets. Unpublished Manuscript.

Anderson, S.P., Peitz, M., 2014b. Media See-saws: Winners and Losers on Media Platforms. Unpublished Manuscript.

Armstrong, M., 2006. Competition in two-sided markets. RAND J. Econ. 37, 668–691.

Athey, S., Calvano, E., Gans, J., 2014. The Impact of the Internet on Advertising Markets for News Media. Unpublished Manuscript.

Athey, S., Ellison, G., 2011. Position auctions with consumer search. Q. J. Econ. 126, 1213–1270.

Athey, S., Gans, J., 2010. The impact of targeting technology on advertising markets and media competition. Am. Econ. Rev. Pap. Proc. 100, 608–613.

Bagwell, K., 2007. The economic analysis of advertising. In: Armstrong, M., Porter, R. (Eds.), Handbook of Industrial Organization, vol. 3. North Holland, Amsterdam.

Banerjee, A., Chandrasekhar, A.G., Duflo, E., Jackson, M.O., 2014. Gossip: Identifying Central Individuals in a Social Network. Unpublished Manuscript.

Becker, G., Murphy, K.M., 1993. A simple theory of advertising as a good or bad. Q. J. Econ. 108, 942–964.

Belleflamme, P., Peitz, M., 2010. Industrial Organization: Markets and Strategies. Cambridge University Press, Cambridge.

Belleflamme, P., Peitz, M., 2014. Price Information in Two-Sided Markets. Unpublished Manuscript.

Bergemann, D., Bonatti, A., 2011. Targeting in advertising markets: implications for offline versus online media. RAND J. Econ. 42, 417–443.

Bergemann, D., Bonatti, A., 2015. Selling cookies. Am. Econ. J. Microecon. 7, 259–294.

Blake, T., Nosko, C., Tadelis, S., 2015. Consumer heterogeneity and paid search effectiveness: a large scale field experiment. Econometrica 83, 155–174.

Börgers, T., Cox, I., Pesendorfer, M., Petricek, V., 2013. Equilibrium bids in sponsored search auctions: theory and evidence. Am. Econ. J. Microecon. 5, 163–187.

Bourreau, M., Kourandi, F., Valletti, T., 2014. Net neutrality with competing Internet platforms. J. Ind. Econ. 63, 30–73.

Burguet, R., Caminal, R., Ellman, M., 2014. In Google We Trust? Unpublished Manuscript.

Butters, G.R., 1977. Equilibrium distributions of sales and advertising prices. Rev. Econ. Stud. 44, 465–491.

Cai, H., Chen, Y., Fang, H., 2009. Observational learning: evidence from a randomized natural field experiment. Am. Econ. Rev. 99, 864–882.

Calvano, E., Jullien, B., 2012. Issues in on-line advertising and competition policy: a two-sided market perspective. In: Harrington, J.E., Katsoulacos, Y. (Eds.), Recent Advances in the Analysis of Competition Policy and Regulation. Edward Elgar Publishing, Cheltenham.

Chen, Y., He, C., 2011. Paid placement: advertising and search on the Internet. Econ. J. 121, F309–F328.

Chen, J., Staellert, J., 2014. An economic analysis of online advertising using behavioral targeting. MIS Q. 38, 429–449.

Chen, Y., Narasimhan, C., Zhang, Z.J., 2001. Individual marketing with imperfect targetability. Mark. Sci. 20, 23–41.

Chen, Y., Pavlov, D., Canny, J., 2009. Large-scale behavioral targeting. In: Proceedings of the 15th ACM SIGKDD International Conference on Knowledge Discovery and Data Mining. ACM, New York, NY, pp. 209–218.

Chen, Y., Wang, Q., Xie, J., 2011. Online social interactions: a natural experiment on word of mouth versus observational learning. J. Mark. Res. 48, 238–254.

Choi, J.P., Jeon, D.S., Kim, B.C., 2013. Asymmetric Neutrality Regulation and Innovation at the Edges: Fixed vs. Mobile Networks. NET Institute Working Paper 13-24.

Choi, J.P., Kim, B.C., 2010. Net neutrality and investment incentives. RAND J. Econ. 41, 446–471.

Criteo, 2010. Targeting & Retargeting Interview with Criteo. Report, August 26, available at: http://behavioraltargeting.biz (accessed October 16, 2014).

Czernich, N., Falck, O., Kretschmer, T., Wössmann, L., 2011. Broadband infrastructure and economic growth. Econ. J. 121, 505–532.

d'Aspremont, C., Gabszewicz, J.J., Thisse, J.-F., 1979. On Hotelling's 'stability in competition'. Econometrica 47, 1145–1150.

de Cornière, A., 2013. Search Advertising. Unpublished Manuscript.

de Cornière, A., De Nijs, R., 2014. Online advertising and privacy. RAND J. Econ. (forthcoming).

de Cornière, A., Taylor, G., 2014. Integration and search engine bias. RAND J. Econ. 45, 576–597.

Dellarocas, C., 2012. Double marginalization in performance-based advertising: implications and solutions. Manag. Sci. 58, 1178–1195.

Dellarocas, C., Rand, W., Katona, Z., 2013. Media, aggregators and the link economy: strategic link formation in content networks. Manag. Sci. 59, 2360–2379.

Dukes, A., Gal-Or, E., 2003. Negotiations and exclusivity contracts for advertising. Mark. Sci. 22, 222–245.

Economides, N., Hermalin, B.E., 2012. The economics of network neutrality. RAND J. Econ. 43, 602–629.

Edelman, B., Lai, Z., 2015. Design of Search Engine Services: Channel Interdependence in Search Engine Results. Unpublished Manuscript.

Edelman, B., Ostrovsky, M., Schwarz, M., 2007. Internet advertising and the generalized second-price auction: selling billions of dollars' worth of keywords. Am. Econ. Rev. 97, 242–259.

Eliaz, K., Spiegler, R., 2011. A simple model of search engine pricing. Econ. J. 121, F329–F339.

Esteban, L., Gil, A., Hernandez, J., 2001. Informative advertising and optimal targeting in a monopoly. J. Ind. Econ. 49, 161–180.

Evans, D.S., 2008. The economics of the online advertising industry. Rev. Netw. Econ. 7, 359–391.

Evans, D.S., 2009. The online advertising industry: economics, evolution, and privacy. J. Econ. Perspect. 23, 37–60.

Gabszewicz, J.J., Laussel, D., Sonnac, N., 2004. Programming and advertising competition in the broadcasting industry. J. Econ. Manag. Strategy 13, 657–669.

Galeotti, A., Moraga-Gonzalez, J.L., 2008. Segmentation, advertising, and prices. Int. J. Ind. Organ. 26, 1106–1119.

Gal-Or, E., Dukes, A., 2003. Minimum differentiation in commercial media markets. J. Econ. Manag. Strategy 12, 291–325.

Gal-Or, E., Gal-Or, M., 2005. Customized advertising via a common media distributor. Mark. Sci. 24, 241–253.

Ganuza, J.-J., 2004. Ignorance promotes competition: an auction model of endogenous private valuations. RAND J. Econ. 35, 583–598.

Gentzkow, M., Shapiro, J.M., Sinkinson, M., 2014. Competition and ideological diversity: historical evidence from US newspapers. Am. Econ. Rev. 104, 3073–3114.

Ghose, A., Yang, S., 2009. An empirical analysis of search engine advertising: sponsored search in electronic markets. Manag. Sci. 55, 1605–1622.

Ghosh, A., Mahdian, M., McAfee, R.P., Vassilvitskii, S., 2012. To match or not to match: economics of cookie matching in online advertising. In: Proceedings of the 13th ACM Conference on Electronic Commerce (EC'12).

Goldfarb, A., 2014. What is different about online advertising? Rev. Ind. Organ. 44, 115–129.

Goldfarb, A., Tucker, C., 2011a. Search engine advertising: channel substitution when pricing ads to context. Manag. Sci. 57, 458–470.

Goldfarb, A., Tucker, C., 2011b. Online display advertising: targeting and obtrusiveness. Mark. Sci. 30, 389–404.

Hagiu, A., Halaburda, H., 2014. Information and two-sided platform profits. Int. J. Ind. Organ. 34, 25–35.

Hauser, J.R., Urban, G.L., Liberali, G., Braun, M., 2009. Website morphing. Mark. Sci. 28, 202–223.

Hoernig, S., Valletti, T.M., 2007. Mixing goods with two-part tariffs. Eur. Econ. Rev. 51, 1733–1750.

Hotelling, H., 1929. Stability in competition. Econ. J. 39, 41–57.

Hurkens, S., López, Á.L., 2014. Mobile termination, network externalities and consumer expectations. Econ. J. 124, 1005–1039.

IAB, 2009. IAB Social Advertising Best Practices. Interactive Advertising Bureau. Available at: http://www.iab.net/socialads (accessed September 9, 2015).

Iyer, G., Soberman, D., Villas-Boas, J.M., 2005. The targeting of advertising. Mark. Sci. 24, 461–476.

Jackson, M.O., 2010. Social and Economic Networks. Princeton University Press, Princeton, NJ.

Jackson, M.O., Wolinsky, A., 1996. A strategic model of social and economic networks. J. Econ. Theory 71, 44–74.

Jeon, D.-S., Nasr, E.N., 2013. News Aggregators and Competition Among Newspapers on the Internet. Unpublished Manuscript.

Johnson, G.A., Lewis, R.A., Reiley, D.H., 2014. Location, Location, Location: Repetition and Proximity Increase Advertising Effectiveness. Unpublished Manuscript.

Johnson, J.P., 2013. Targeted advertising and advertising avoidance. RAND J. Econ. 44, 128–144.

Johnson, J.P., Myatt, D.P., 2006. On the simple economics of advertising, marketing, and product design. Am. Econ. Rev. 96, 756–784.

Joo, M., Wilbur, K.C., Cowgill, B., Zhu, Y., 2014. Television advertising and online search. Manag. Sci. 60, 56–73.

Joshi, A., Bagherjeiran, A., Ratnaparkhi, A., 2011. User demographic and behavioral targeting for content match advertising. In: 5th International Workshop on Data Mining and Audience Intelligence for Advertising (ADKDD 2011). San Diego, CA.

Katona, Z., Knee, J., Sarvary, M., 2013. Agenda Chasing and Contests Among News Providers. Unpublished Manuscript.

Katona, Z., Sarvary, M., 2008. Network formation and the structure of the commercial World Wide Web. Mark. Sci. 27, 764–778.

Katz, M.L., Shapiro, C., 1985. Network externalities, competition, and compatibility. Am. Econ. Rev. 75, 424–440.

Katz, M.L., Shapiro, C., 1994. Systems competition and network effects. J. Econ. Perspect. 8, 93–115.

Kaye, B.K., Medoff, N.J., 2000. Just a Click Away: Advertising on the Internet. Allyn and Bacon, Boston, MA.

Kempe, D., Mahdian, M., 2008. A cascade model for advertising in sponsored search. In: Proceedings of the 4th International Workshop on Internet and Network Economics (WINE).

Krämer, J., Wiewiorra, L., 2012. Network neutrality and congestion sensitive content providers: implications for content variety, broadband investment, and regulation. Inf. Syst. Res. 23, 1303–1321.

Krämer, J., Wiewiorra, L., Weinhardt, C., 2013. Net neutrality: a progress report. Telecommun. Policy 37, 794–813.

Lambrecht, A., Tucker, C., 2013. When does retargeting work? Information specificity in online advertising. J. Mark. Res. 50, 561–5767.

Levin, J., Milgrom, P., 2010. Online advertising: heterogeneity and conflation in market design. Am. Econ. Rev. Pap. Proc. 100, 603–607.

Lewis, R.A., Nguyen, D., 2014. A Samsung Ad for the iPad? Display Advertising's Spillovers to Search. Unpublished Manuscript.

Lewis, R.A., Reiley, D.H., 2014. Online ads and online sales: measuring the effects of retail advertising via a controlled experiment on Yahoo!. Quant. Mark. Econ. 12, 235–266.

Liaukonyte, J., Teixeira, T., Wilbur, K.C., 2015. Television advertising and online shopping. Mark. Sci. 34, 311–330.

Malthouse, E., Elsner, R., 2006. Customisation with cross-basis sub-segmentation. J. Database Mark. Cust. Strategy Manag. 14, 40–50.

Marwick, A.E., 2014. How your data are deeply mined. In: New York Review of Books. January 9, 2014. Available at: http://www.nybooks.com/articles/archives/2014/jan/09/how-your-data-are-being-deeply-mined/ (accessed September 9, 2015).

Milgrom, P., Roberts, J., 1986. Price and advertising signals of product quality. J. Polit. Econ. 94, 796–821.

Nelson, P., 1974. Advertising as information. J. Polit. Econ. 82, 729–754.

OECD, 2014. Connected Televisions: Convergence and Emerging Business Models. OECD Digital Economy Papers, No. 231. OECD Publishing, Paris.

Oestreicher-Singer, G., Sundararajan, A., 2012. The visible hand? Demand effects of recommendation networks in electronic markets. Manag. Sci. 58, 1963–1981.

Pan, S., Yang, H., 2015. Targeted Advertising on Competing Platforms. Unpublished Manuscript.

Peitz, M., Schuett, F., 2015. Net Neutrality and the Inflation of Traffic. TILEC Discussion Paper 2015-006.

Peitz, M., Valletti, T.M., 2008. Content and advertising in the media: pay-tv versus free-to-air. Int. J. Ind. Organ. 26, 949–965.

Pew Research Center, 2013a. State of the News Media. Report. Available at http://stateofthemedia.org/ (accessed March 6, 2014).

Pew Research Center, 2013b. Social Media Update. Report. December 30, 2013. Available at: http://www.pewinternet.org/2013/12/30/social-media-update-2013/ (accessed September 9, 2015).

Pew Research Center, 2013c. News Use Across Social Media Platforms. Report. November 14, 2013. Available at: http://www.journalism.org/2013/11/14/news-use-across-social-media-platforms/ (accessed September 9, 2015).

Pew Research Center, 2013d. Photo and Video Sharing Grow Online. Report. October 28, 2013. Available at: http://www.pewinternet.org/2013/10/28/photo-and-video-sharing-grow-online/ (accessed September 9, 2015).

Pew Research Center, 2013e. Civic Engagement in the Digital Age. Report. April 25, 2013. Available at: http://www.pewinternet.org/2013/04/25/civic-engagement-in-the-digital-age/ (accessed September 9, 2015).

PwC, 2013. IAB Internet Advertising Revenue Report, 2012 Full Year Results. Report. April 2013.

Rochet, J.-C., Tirole, J., 2003. Platform competition in two-sided markets. J. Eur. Econ. Assoc. 1, 990–1029.

Roy, S., 2000. Strategic segmentation of a market. Int. J. Ind. Organ. 18, 1279–1290.

Rutt, J., 2011. Aggregators and the News Industry: Charging for Access to Content. NET Institute Working Paper 11-19.

Rutt, J., 2012. Targeted Advertising and Media Market Competition. Unpublished Manuscript.

Rutz, O.J., Bucklin, R., 2011. From generic to branded: a model of spillover dynamics in paid search advertising. J. Mark. Res. 48, 87–102.

Rutz, O.J., Bucklin, R., 2012. Does banner advertising affect browsing for brands? Clickstream choice model says yes, for some. Quant. Mark. Econ. 10, 231–257.

Rutz, O.J., Trusov, M., 2011. Zooming in on paid search ads—a consumer-level model calibrated on aggregated data. Mark. Sci. 30, 789–800.

Sahni, N., 2015. Advertising Spillovers: Field-Experiment Evidence and Implications for Returns from Advertising. Stanford University Graduate School of Business Research Paper No. 14-15.

Salaverría, R., 2005. An immature medium: strengths and weaknesses of online newspapers on September 11. Gazette 67, 69–86.

Sandvine, 2014. Global Internet Phenomena Report. 2H 2013. Available at: https://www.sandvine.com/downloads/general/global-internet-phenomena/2013/2h-2013-global-internet-phenomena-report.pdf (accessed September 9, 2015).

Seamans, R., Zhu, F., 2014. Responses to entry in multi-sided markets: the impact of craigslist on local newspapers. Manag. Sci. 60, 476–493.

Sun, M., Zhu, F., 2013. Ad revenue and content commercialization: evidence from blogs. Manag. Sci. 59, 2314–2331.

Tarantino, E., 2013. A simple model of vertical search engines foreclosure. Telecommun. Policy 37, 1–12.

Taylor, G., 2013a. Search quality and revenue cannibalisation by competing search engines. J. Econ. Manag. Strategy 22, 445–467.

Taylor, G., 2013b. Attention Retention: Targeted Advertising and the Ex Post Role of Media Content. Unpublished Manuscript.

Tucker, C., 2012. Social Advertising. Unpublished Manuscript.

Tucker, C., Zhang, J., 2011. How does popularity information affect choices: a field experiment. Manag. Sci. 57, 828–842.

van Zandt, T., 2004. Information overload in a network of targeted communication. RAND J. Econ. 35, 542–560.

Varian, H., 1980. A model of sales. Am. Econ. Rev. 70, 651–659.

Varian, H., 2007. Positioning auctions. Int. J. Ind. Organ. 25, 1163–1178.

White, A., 2013. Search engines: left side quality versus right side profits. Int. J. Ind. Organ. 31, 690–701.

Wilbur, K.C., Zhu, Y., 2009. Click fraud. Mark. Sci. 28, 293–308.

Xu, L., Chen, J., Winston, A., 2010. Oligopolistic pricing with online search. J. Manag. Inf. Syst. 27, 111–141.

Xu, L., Chen, J., Winston, A., 2011. Price competition and endogenous valuation in search advertising. J. Mark. Res. 48, 566–586.

Xu, L., Chen, J., Winston, A., 2012. Effects of the presence of organic listing in search advertising. Inf. Syst. Res. 23, 1284–1302.

Zhang, J., 2010. The sound of silence: observational learning in the U.S. kidney market. Mark. Sci. 29, 315–335.

INDEX

Note: Page numbers followed by *f* indicate figures and *t* indicate tables.